The Concentration Camp Brothel

World War II: The Global, Human, and Ethical Dimension

G. Kurt Piehler, *series editor*

The Concentration Camp Brothel

Forced Sexual Labor Under Nazi Rule

Robert Sommer
Translated by **Dominic Bonfiglio**
Foreword by **Annette F. Timm**

Fordham University Press | New York 2025

Fordham University Press also publishes its books in a variety of electronic formats. Some content that appears in print may not be available in electronic books.

Visit us online at www.fordhampress.com.

For EU safety / GPSR concerns: Mare Nostrum Group B.V., Mauritskade 21D, 1091 GC Amsterdam, The Netherlands, gpsr@mare-nostrum.co.uk

Library of Congress Cataloging-in-Publication Data available online at https://catalog.loc.gov.

Printed in the United States of America
27 26 25   5 4 3 2 1
First edition

Contents

Tables

Foreword

Annette F. Timm

For decades, scholars of the Holocaust have shied away from addressing the role of sexual violence in the Holocaust. The inevitable result has been the production of taboos and processes of silencing. How could anyone be surprised about this? Any serious scholar setting out to investigate the topic was immediately confronted not only with gender bias and moral squeamishness but also an avalanche of culturally produced sexual mythologies that were all the more enduring because they rested on rumor while confirming both political and gender ideologies.

A 1945 poem written in Hebrew by Yitzhak Sadeh under the pen name Y. Noded is a case in point. Sadeh was commander of the Palmach and later the chief of the general staff for the Haganah, both precursors to the Israel Defense Forces. His poem, entitled "My Sister on the Beach," presents the story of a fictional Jewish soldier's encounter with a "wild-haired" woman dressed in tatters who had just disembarked from a boat carrying illegal immigrants to Palestine. He immediately recognizes her as a Holocaust survivor and notices that "her flesh is branded: 'For Officers Only.'" Although the narrator is sympathetic, welcomes the woman "home," and tells her that he will do "everything" for her, the poet gives her no voice. Deeply identifying with her plight on the surface, the soldier does not ask but simply assumes that the woman performed sexual acts in order to survive. She remains a mute symbol of victimization in striking contrast to the agency of the soldier as he deploys her history of degradation to proclaim the values of a future Jewish state.[1] Given the prominence of the author and the fact that this poem was republished many times, we can assume that it either represented or helped foster (likely both) a dismissive and demeaning attitude toward female survivors. Sadeh's expression of empathy could not counter the religious and social prejudices against selling or living off the proceeds of sex. In her 1997 memoir, the Czech-Israeli journalist and translator Ruth Bondy, who survived Theresienstadt, Auschwitz-Birkenau, and Bergen-Belsen, describes the question often posed to her after she immigrated to Israel in 1948: "How did you live through it? What did you have to do to survive?

There was a glint of suspicion in their eyes: a kapo? A prostitute?"[2] That these questioners could only imagine survival in these deeply gendered terms—with the men serving as overseers over other prisoners and the women as whores—helps explain why Holocaust survivors quickly stopped speaking about interprisoner exploitation or about the most graphic aspects of their suffering.

The tendency to assume that female survivors had engaged in survival sex was particularly common in Israel,[3] but it was given international currency in literary and popular representations in the postwar period. Sadeh's branding imagery was repeated on the covers of one of the most successful Holocaust books of the postwar period: the 1953 novel *Beit habubot* (*House of Dolls*), by the Auschwitz survivor Yehiel De-Nur, writing in Hebrew under the penname Ka-Tzetnik (a moniker he claimed was common in Auschwitz and was derived from the German abbreviation for *Konzentrationslager*, or concentration camp). Although De-Nur sought to represent the authentic experiences of all Holocaust victims, and although like Sadeh, he intended *House of Dolls* to foster empathy for the sexual exploitation of Jewish women, his readership was influenced by the tendency to depict sexual violence as voyeuristic titillation in the popular culture of the 1960s and 1970s. Many of the English editions of *House of Dolls*, which sold over ten million copies by 1980, were adorned with an exploitative image of a woman baring her chest to reveal the tattooed word *Feld-Hure*—field whore, or a woman who served the sexual needs of the German military. This survivor/whore trope took flight after the media sensation of De-Nur's 1961 testimony against Adolf Eichmann—the first time that the true identity of the famous author Ka-Tzetnik was revealed. Both in Israel and many other countries, purveyors of smut turned De-Nur's well-meaning (though historically flawed) account of Jewish women's service in the "Joy Division" brothel of Auschwitz into pornography, both in trashy pulp fiction and Nazisploitation movies and in supposedly more respectable literature and film. A book that was written with the fierce intention of testifying to the suffering of Jewish women ironically helped inspire even more historically inaccurate and exploitative depictions of sexual exploitation in the Holocaust, which, collectively, frightened serious scholars away from the subject.

There is much to say about the social, political, and international dynamics of this phenomenon, and we now have a wealth of scholarship examining Holocaust representation, the sexualization of Nazi evil, and the gendered nature of persecution and survival. But for the purposes of introducing this book it suffices to say that the survivor/whore trope propagated in Sadeh's poem and De-Nur's novel helped ensure that the subject of sexual violence and exploitation in the Holocaust remained virtually unexplored for several decades after World War II. When Robert Sommer first published his Humboldt University dissertation (*Das KZ-Bordell: Sexuelle Zwangsarbeit in nationalsozialistischen Konzentrationslagern*, Schöningh) in 2009, he could rely on only very few previous studies of how women, girls, young men, and boys had been forced to perform sexual acts in order to survive the Holocaust. As is also clear in the translation you have before you, Sommer is very generous to pioneering scholars like Christa Paul and Claudia Schoppmann, who specifically wrote about female sexual persecution, and to Jerzy St. Giza and Wiesław Morasiewicz, who examined male sexuality in the Holocaust. But he still achieves something that these scholars did not: a meticulous, statistically convincing, and all-encompassing examination of forced sexual labor in the camps. No Holocaust scholar who has written about this subject since the publication of *Das KZ-Bordell* has failed to rely on its authoritative empirical research. It was only this book that definitively laid to rest the claims—popularized by Sadeh and De-Nur but circulated also through maliciously whispered rumor—that Jewish women had worked in concentration camp brothels. Having amassed an impressive and unimpeachable statistical accounting of all of the available evidence, Sommer has provided not only a convincing historical narrative but a treasure trove of data for future researchers.

Without summarizing the arguments of this book, let me briefly state what makes them so important. It is first of all noteworthy that Sommer has been able to determine the precise number of women who worked in camp brothels and has specific data for at least 80 percent of individual cases. These are impressive statistics, and they make it possible for Sommer to make definitive claims about the selection, experience, and treatment of these women. He demonstrates that the buildings looked quite different in each camp, that the organization meant to reward exemplary prisoners for their labor was not known as the "Joy Division"—a name that sprung from De-Nur's imagination—and that the small improvements in living conditions that the inhabitants enjoyed served only to ensure their survival and further deployment in ways that the architects of the Holocaust believed would serve military goals. In the twisted logic of Heinrich Himmler and other architects of the camp system, the women needed to be fed enough to keep their breasts so that other prisoners would see access to their bodies as a reward. Their clients were primarily other prisoners, rather than SS men, and at least within the camps, sexual exploitation followed Nazi guidelines on racial segregation. That a percentage of the women had been sex workers before the war tells us only that the Nazis were looking for workers they believed would be most suitable for the job. It does not disprove the forced nature of this work or the suffering it caused.

Sommer's attention to detail means that we are also informed about SS voyeurism, sexual torture, and tolerance of pedophilic and otherwise exploitative sexual relationships between kapos and younger male prisoners. Indeed, it is one of the great contributions of this book that Sommer does not separate male from female sexual exploitation, presenting them instead as part of the same sexual system of the camps: a subordination of all human sexual impulses to the purposes of labor productivity. That this logic was not only inhumane but unhinged from reality is demonstrated in the passages of the book that detail the very small percentage of prisoners who ever visited a brothel and the incredibly low labor productivity of the camps. In some cases, camp commanders ordered starving prisoners straight from hard physical labor to the brothel, believing that sex would somehow revive their exhausted bodies so that they could work harder the next day. Because Sommer covers all aspects of the phenomenon, we also learn that even men who voluntarily visited a brothel often found the sexual act either unimportant or secondary to another purpose. Several testimonies tell of men who simply sought a few minutes of genuine human contact and kept their pants on; others saw intercourse as a last human act before death—either as the first or the last time that they would have nonviolent physical contact with another human being. That some networks of resistors, particularly in camps with organized communists, bribed men not to have sex when the door to the brothel bedroom was closed is an indication that the women were viewed as victims by at least some of their fellow prisoners. This book exudes empathy for all those who suffered in these camps, carefully describing categories of relative privilege while making it unmistakably clear that the margin of difference between those at the top and those at the bottom of the camp hierarchy was only a matter of a few extra degrees of likelihood that survival might be possible.

Sommer is not, of course, the only commentator to have insisted on exploring the humanity of all the participants in the system of control that governed the camps. Many survivors—foremost among them Primo Levi—have argued that the "gray zones" of life in the camp were not antithetical to mechanisms of control but integral to the function of what De-Nur called "the other planet"—that universe of moral confusion and physical disorientation that survivors found so difficult to explain to anyone who had not experienced it. The fact that prisoners exploited other prisoners was as central to the operation of this other planet as the seemingly paradoxical reality that precious moments of human connection could be forged within physical encounters that were orchestrated to produce value only for the needs of the racial state. In highlighting these troubling moral realities, Sommer does more than achieve that cliché of all scholarly writing—filling a "gap" in the research by adding the story of a previously ignored group; he provides evidence that is central to our understanding of how Nazi racial persecution operated. This is a book that must be read by all scholars of the Holocaust because in the process of demythologizing the role of sex in the system of persecution, Sommer underlines key mechanisms of the Nazi system of power as a whole. Building on previous histories of sexuality in this period, he demonstrates that there was no unanimity about sexual matters in the Third Reich, and he provides evidence that in this sphere, as in almost every aspect of Nazi policy, an emphasis on economic "productivity" intertwined with racial logic to produce a system of unparalleled inhumanity.

I would like to highlight one aspect of Sommer's argument that may strike readers as counterintuitive or even heretical. Both in popular depictions and in scholarly writing that fails to take sexuality seriously as a legitimate object of historical investigation, sexual depravity often serves as a metaphor for Nazi evil. When otherwise serious authors only hint at sexual violence, they imply that it either cannot be explained historically or that directly addressing it threatens academic decorum or objectivity. The book you are about to read demonstrates with aplomb exactly how such attitudes have damaged our historical understanding. Allowing sex to remain taboo risks depicting those who deployed it for racial purposes as evil geniuses; it implicitly grants Heinrich Himmler and his followers expertise in human psychology and economic management that they did not possess. That neither the postwar public nor historians were willing to tackle this subject for so long made it particularly attractive to those seeking powerful metaphors for simplistic stories about the Holocaust. It is only through the kind of careful empirical study that you are about to read that we can take apart the pernicious effects of mentioning sex only in hushed tones or as jarring anecdotes whose ultimate function is only to titillate even when the intention is to demonstrate the authenticity of the account. Because it turns out that Himmler's ideas were not just inhumane and racist; they were also deeply irrational. This was a man, Sommer reminds us, who ordered subordinates to produce alcohol from the exhaust air of SS bakeries and who believed in the continuing relevance of carrier pigeons for modern communications. There was no economic genius in accepting only fifty-pfennig pieces in the brothels, creating a black market for that one coin that worked against the reward system. And there was no political genius in using sexual rewards to extract labor from walking skeletons. Although the clients of the brothels belonged to a relatively privileged class in the camps, the logic of thinking that sexual release could create superhuman levels of output is the same logic that made camp guards think that the discipline of hours-long roll calls and calisthenics would encourage the starving to perform useful work. The results were torturous, and the ideas were simply crazy. Let us finally get beyond the fantasies of Nazi omniscience and omnipotence that have only clouded our understanding of how they managed to achieve so many of their goals. This will mean revealing Himmler as the small-minded, prudish, and vastly overconfident man that he actually was rather than depicting him as the puppet master of brainwashed sex fiends.

I hope that this book will also leave readers with the impression that what happened behind the walls of the brothels was no more or less depraved than anything we have already learned about the concentration camp system. While it is critical to note that there was nothing voluntary about the labor performed in the brothels that this book describes, Sommer convincingly demonstrates that what took place there was not unlike the perfunctory acts common in brothels outside of the camps, with the important exception that the women worked under threat of murder and starvation. It is clear that some SS guards broke the rules to visit and abuse these women, but the most extreme acts of sexual depravity occurred outside the walls of the concentration camps, in the killing fields of Eastern Europe. It is only with this book, first in German and now in English, that this fact can be definitively demonstrated. It is also important to note that had we researched the history of the brothels sooner, we would have been able to gather more testimony from survivors and their protectors, further revealing the various gray zones of the camp experience. The evidence presented in this book demonstrates that some brothel clients helped the women create new lives even after the war by adamantly refusing to reveal their identity. This act of empathy for the "choiceless choices" (in Lawrence Langer's famous phrase) that these women also faced should inspire us.[4] Hearing their stories should also produce outrage at the way stories of sexual violence in this period were exploited for political purposes in the postwar world. The fact that we have looked away from this aspect of the Holocaust for so long says much more about the power of our own sexual taboos than it does about the core evil of the Holocaust, which was always racism. This book encourages us to approach the subject of the experience of forced sex with humanity rather than self-righteousness or moral indignation. By searching for every available trace of the authentic voices of those who either worked in or visited camp brothels, Sommer refuses to emulate the gesture of the

SS guards who voyeuristically looked through the peepholes. Instead of metaphors that equate loveless sex with evil or that credit the guards and their political bosses with having otherworldly insights or organizational skills, Sommer concentrates on the extremely human motivations of sex workers and their clients. He thus thoroughly revises popular misconceptions while avoiding the trap of righteous demythologization. Now finally available in English, this book points the way forward for a more nuanced scholarly, literary, and cultural approach to these subjects.

Preface

I visited Auschwitz for the first time in 2000 as part of a group of students on a week-long trip to learn about the former concentration camp. Five Auschwitz survivors accompanied us, acting as guides and recounting personal experiences of their time there. As we stood at the gate with the notorious wrought-iron sign *Arbeit Macht Frei*, the former Polish prisoner Stanisław Hantz explained that a camp brothel was located on the second floor of Block 24, directly behind the entrance. My immediate thought was that this must be where the Nazis housed one of their "joy divisions," the units of Jewish women forced to have sex with SS guards described in Yehiel De-Nur's novella *House of Dolls*. But, as Hantz then made clear to us, the brothel in Auschwitz was for *prisoners*. SS men were strictly forbidden entry. Why would the Nazis have a brothel for prisoners in a concentration camp? I wondered. Was this the only one? Who were the women who worked there? Who were the men who visited them? Those questions started me on an investigation that would occupy the next ten years of my life.

Sexual violence has been a weapon of war since time immemorial. World War II was no different. Many Jewish women were raped in Eastern Europe during the campaigns of mass murder perpetrated by the Nazis and their allies. There is also evidence that the Nazis used rape as form of sexual violence in ghettos and extermination camps. Forced sexual labor in concentration camps was a special case yet also an integral part of the history of the Holocaust. What made it unique, I would learn, is that forced sex in the camps was the most strictly controlled form of sexual violence during the war. The prisoner brothels were off-limits not only to the SS but also to Jews in general. This was another of the myths propagated by Yehiel De-Nur's *House of Dolls* that I would have to do away with. Ironically, it was Nazi ideology that kept Jewish women safe from this form of sexual violence, as race laws outlawed sexual relations between Jews and non-Jews. Nevertheless, the prisoner brothels were part of the concentration camp system, one of the main tools for the genocide of the Jews. Moreover, as I would later find out, several camp brothels with Polish sex workers existed specifically for Ukrainian SS men who had been deployed in the Belzec, Sobibor, and Treblinka extermination camps. The history of the camp brothels was, therefore, another chapter in what Dagmar Herzog calls the "invasion and control and destruction of human beings" that made up "sexuality in the Third Reich."

Why wasn't this common knowledge in 2000, when I first visited Auschwitz? Through my research, I learned that discussion of the camp brothels had been taboo for many years. At first, it seems many had a hard time believing in the existence of the brothels. Why would the Nazis be concerned about the sexual needs of people whom they were letting starve to death? Later, the subject did not fit into the postwar politics of memory endorsed by either of the two Germanys. A third factor was the status of the women forced to work in the brothels. In 1945, the governments of the Allies required that those persecuted by the Nazis on "racial, political, and religious" grounds receive compensation. This policy would fundamentally shape who was seen as a victim in the postwar Germanys. But its definition of victim neglected other persecuted groups, in particular Sinti and Roma, homosexuals, "criminals," and "antisocials." It was into this last category that many forced sex workers had been unjustly thrown. This meant that after the war they had no right to compensation and often faced stigmatization. Not only did postwar societies not want to hear their stories; they did not allow the victims to tell them.

This book is the result of research comprising more than seventy archives. Many documents—completed with proverbial German meticulousness—survived the war, including prisoner cards, transfer lists, and reports from various medical facilities, including the Hygiene Institute of the Waffen SS in Rajsko near Auschwitz. I also drew on interviews from concentration camp memorials and Holocaust research institutes and personally interviewed thirty concentration camp survivors, some of whom had visited the brothels themselves. Unfortunately, it was not possible for me to interview any of the former forced sex workers, though I did rely on several first-person interviews conducted by researchers in the 1990s. On the basis of the extensive material I collected, I was able to identify the origins and prison records of 88 percent of the women in the brothels for prisoners. This makes the group of forced sex workers one of the best-researched groups of victims of sexual violence in World War II.

I examine the subject matter from multiple perspectives: the perpetrators who created the brothel system, the women who were sexually enslaved in it, and the men it benefited. In addition, I consider the sexuality of prisoners and the strategies that forced sex workers adopted to cope and survive. I also inquire into the motives of the men who visited the camp brothels and how other prisoners regarded the practice.

This study closes one of the last major gaps in Holocaust research. One of the aims in closing that gap has been to tell the story of the women in the camp brothels. For decades they have been excluded from the histories of the camps. The book serves to remember the victims of the camp brothels in order that they posthumously receive the recognition they deserve. For it is only when we stop talking about the dead that we consign them to oblivion.

The Concentration Camp Brothel

Introduction: Myths and Taboos

In his 1946 memoir, Erich Roßmann, a former socialist member of the Reichstag incarcerated in Sachsenhausen for his political beliefs, recounts the shocked reaction of a friend on hearing that a brothel for prisoners had opened in the camp: "August Christ, with whom I discussed the matter, said in horror: 'Believe me, dear Roßmann, when we tell our friends and relatives on the outside, they won't believe it, and yet it is shameless reality.' I could only agree with him."[1] The brothel was one of ten that Heinrich Himmler ordered established between 1942 and 1945. In addition to Sachsenhausen, brothels were built in Mauthausen, Gusen, Flossenbürg, Buchenwald, the Auschwitz main camp, Auschwitz-Monowitz, Dachau, Neuengamme, and Mittelbau-Dora. Euphemistically called "special buildings" by the SS, the brothels were conceived as an incentive to make the prisoners work harder.

Today, eighty years after the downfall of the Nazi regime, the idea of prisoner brothels in Nazi concentration camps may seem as jarring as it once did to Erich Roßmann and his friend. Their existence stands at odds with the images passed down to us by eyewitnesses portraying concentration camps as places of horror: shaven heads, emaciated bodies, piles of corpses, gas chambers, crematoria.[2] Yet in the immediate postwar years, a number of former prisoners talked openly about the brothels. In the first systematic account of the Nazi concentration camp system, the 1946 *Der SS-Staat* (translated three years later as *The Theory and Practice of Hell*), the German historian and concentration camp survivor Eugen Kogon devotes a section to the camp brothel in Buchenwald.[3] Former prisoners at the Dachau, Sachsenhausen, and Neuengamme camps also report on brothels in their memoirs.[4] All note their astonishment, provide descriptions of the brothels, and record the existence of corruption and prisoner-led boycotts. For the most part, they portray the women who worked in the brothels as victims lured with false promises. The lone exception is Kogon, who opined that nearly all the women "were resigned to their fate with rather little restraint."[5]

The initial openness about the brothels grew out of the need to convey the suffering and horror of the concentration camps to the postwar public. This need can also be seen in other survivor accounts portraying aspects of camp life like sexuality and sexual violence.[6] But, as the historian Christl Wickert observes, the initial candor gave way to a period of growing silence as prejudices against former sex workers began to emerge.[7] The stigmatization of forced sexual labor and the reluctance to talk about the camp brothels were largely the result of the political situation in the two postwar German states.

In the 1950s, West Germany underwent a period of defensiveness and denial during which discussions of Nazi crimes remained largely absent from public discourse.[8] It was not until the end of the decade that the tide began to turn as committed intellectuals and, later, the students of the 1968 movement openly confronted the legacy of the Third Reich. The highly politicized environment demanded clear and unambiguous language: Coming to terms with Germany's past came with demands that victims be recognized and perpetrators punished. The problem was that the postwar government sought to suppress the original purpose of the camps by demolishing some buildings and repurposing others, as was the case at Dachau and Flossenbürg. Only a few of the most symbolically loaded structures—such as crematoria—were left standing. In the 1960s, the museum in Dachau presented a potted history of the camp through what Harold Marcuse describes as a "simplistic reconstruction and preservation of selected details."[9] A topic as complex as a camp brothel had no place in that history.[10] In this way, the buildings that once housed the camp brothels disappeared from the topography of memorial sites.[11]

In contrast to West Germany, the memory of Nazi crimes in East Germany took center stage. The country's founding myth was the victory of German antifascists and Red Army soldiers over Hitler's dictatorship. The Buchenwald concentration camp had a central place in this story on account of the Buchenwald Resistance, a group of prisoners with a strong communist presence that sought to undermine administrators and take control in the camp's final days.[12] After the war, the East German state instrumentalized the camp for its own political purposes by touting the group's heroic feats and papering over other aspects of the camp's history. An open discussion of camp brothels would have complicated efforts to portray the suffering of inmates and did not fit into a perfect story of victimhood and resistance, particularly because some of the leading party cadres had visited the brothels themselves.[13] Hence, the topic was declared taboo and deemed unworthy of remembering. In Buchenwald and elsewhere, the camp brothel was dismantled.[14]

Although the foundations of the camp brothel had been preserved at the Buchenwald memorial, they were not identified as such for visitors. The memorial's administrators had issued internal instructions not to point out "this unusual establishment in a fascist concentration camp."[15] In 1977, Walter Bartelt, a former Buchenwald prisoner and the then–vice president of the Buchenwald-Dora International Committee, explained the decision to the editor of the leading journal of history in the GDR: "We avoid writing or speaking about the special building because we believe that it is of no public interest to dwell on it."[16] Nevertheless, East German historians did study the topic of the camp brothel insofar as it supported the country's official historical narrative. For instance, the Mittelbau-Dora concentration camp, where slave laborers manufactured missiles in underground facilities, was seen to exemplify the nexus of capitalism, imperialism, and National Socialism. As several GDR-era historians observed, the construction of camp brothels to increase production underscored the inhumanity of those forces.[17]

Another reason for the relative silence about the camp brothels was the dearth of testimony from the women who had worked in them. Several factors contributed to the situation. One was that many former sex workers were ashamed to talk about their experiences and reluctant to revisit traumatic events.[18] The shame they felt was reinforced by harassment and stigmatization after the war.[19] A number of former prisoners, such as Eugen Kogon, the Spanish Buchenwald survivor Jorge Semprun, and several French survivors, spoke about the brothel workers in disparaging terms.[20] Another factor was that the women did not count as victims of National Socialism. Most German sex workers in the camps wore the black triangle, which designated them as "antisocial" in the Nazi system of prisoner identification. Under the restitution laws passed in West Germany, "antisocials" were denied any form of compensation or social rehabilitation. In East Germany, the group shared a similar fate. "Antisocials" were excluded from the victims of fascism in 1946 and remained so until the country's dissolution in 1990.[21] In addition, in 1968 East Germany made "antisociality" a criminal offense.[22] It wasn't until the 1990s that a few former brothel workers successfully sued for recognition, thanks to the initiative of various nongovernmental organizations, such as the Projektgruppe für die vergessenen Opfer des NS-Regimes in Hamburg, and the tireless work of Christa Paul, Reinhild Kassing, and other victim advocates. Nevertheless, the vast majority of former sex workers did not receive compensation for their time in concentration camps, and none tried to apply for compensation for the sexual exploitation they experienced in the camp brothels.[23]

In the early 1990s, historians began to turn their attention to brothels in Nazi concentration camps.[24] Their work was mainly focused on the female victims of sexual exploitation and was closely linked to political goals, especially social rehabilitation and financial compensation for "forgotten victims." Christa Paul's *Zwangsprostitution* (1994) was the first monograph on forced sexual labor in the Third Reich, and it has been frequently cited by historians and other scholars.[25] In the following years, a series of smaller volumes and articles appeared discussing the topic.[26] In addition to the history of camp brothels and forced sexual labor, researchers explored the postwar taboos surrounding the subject matter and how it compared with other forms of sexual violence in times of war.[27]

Since 2004, studies of concentration camp brothels have placed more emphasis on the significance of womanhood and gender-based violence in Nazism. Of particular note here is *Sexualisierte Gewalt*, a 2004 work by the Austrian sociologists Helga Amesberger, Katrin Auer, and Brigitte Halbmayr. It was the first study to explicitly address sexual violence against women in concentration camps, and it deals in part with the sexual exploitation of women in camp brothels.[28] One year later, the Viennese group Die Aussteller published a revised version of an exhibition catalogue on forced sexual labor, which discussed the topic in the context of Nazi racial ideology and women's politics.[29]

The subject has since attracted increasing amounts of historical interest in Germany. Today, all camp memorial sites that once housed brothels either explicitly address or mention forced sexual labor. However, the subject still remained on the margins of concentration camp research in Germany, as is clearly demonstrated by the scant attention that camp brothels receive in *Der Ort des Terrors* (2005–2009), a nine-volume encyclopedia series on the history of concentration camps.[30] The primary reason for the neglect was that quite a few historians understood the camp brothels to be insignificant to the survival of most prisoners and thus to the history of the concentration camps. The situation began to change in the 2010s, when works such as Nikolaus Wachsmann's groundbreaking 2015 study *KL: A History of the Nazi Concentration Camps* included the topic of the brothels in the history of the camps.[31] Another notable work is Joanna Ostrowska's 2018 book on forced sexual labor in Poland during the Nazi era, a topic that to this day remains taboo in that country.[32]

The importance of Christa Paul's book cannot be overstated for the scholarly discussion of forced sexual labor under Nazism. However, since it was published, some of its central claims have had to be revised on the basis of newly discovered sources. In one case, for instance, an interviewee stated that she was placed in a brothel for SS men at Buchenwald.[33] For many years, this served as the main evidence among German scholars for the existence of camp brothels for Nazis. But a subsequent evaluation of records from the Hamburg social welfare department showed that at that time the woman was not in Buchenwald but was incapacitated in a Hamburg welfare institution.[34]

Media interest in concentration camp brothels emerged soon after the publication of Paul's work. In 1995, the German public television broadcaster ARD featured a documentary on forced sexual labor in the Third Reich titled *Das große Schweigen* (The great silence).[35] In 2003, the television news magazine *Frontal 21* ran a show about "SS pimps."[36] Laurence Reese's BBC documentary on Auschwitz from 2005 contained a segment on the camp's brothels.[37] Media interest intensified after an exhibition on forced sex work in Nazi camps opened in the former brothel at the Mauthausen Memorial in 2006 and ran again at the Ravensbrück Memorial the following year.[38]

Interest in the connection between sexual violence and fascism did not first arise in the mid-aughts, however. It has been a source of enduring fascination since the 1950s. Unfortunately, much of what it has produced presents a distorted view of reality. The most prominent example is the 1953 novella *House of Dolls*, written by the Auschwitz survivor Yehiel De-Nur under the pen name Ka-Tzetnik 135633. It is about Jewish women put to work in "joy divisions" providing sexual services to Nazi soldiers, and De-Nur claimed it was based on his sister's diary.[39] The cover of many of the UK and US editions depict a woman baring her chest to reveal the tattoo of the word *Feld-Hure* (field whore) along with her Auschwitz serial number.[40] Similarly sensationalist images can be found on the covers and posters of so-called Nazisploitation, a genre featuring lurid and often pornographic stories of Nazi sex crimes. The *Stalag* comic books, which were popular in Israel in the 1950s and early 1960s, routinely featured tales of female Nazi officers sexually abusing male prisoners.[41] In the late 1960s and 1970s, films such as *Ilsa, She Wolf of the SS* combined soft-core sex, camp violence, and iconic Holocaust imagery.[42] Some directors attempted more artistically demanding portrayals of sexuality and fascism—Pier Paolo Pasolini in *Salò, or the 120 Days of Sodom* or Liliana Cavani in *Night Porter*[43]—but they too remained in the sensationalist vein of De-Nur and removed the subject of the camp brothel from its historical reality.[44] Such works only further cemented graphic images of Nazi sadism and sexual violence in the public imagination. Moreover, many helped fuel the myth that the brothels were places where Jewish women were routinely raped by the SS. The truth is that the Nazis committed sexual violence against Jewish women, but, for reasons I'll get to later, it did not happen in the camp brothels. Finally, when the camp brothels finally received more serious attention, some scholars and journalists added to the problem by seriously overestimating the number of women forced into prostitution and claiming that most brothel workers were subsequently murdered.[45] The exhibitions on forced sexual labor in the Mauthausen and Ravensbrück memorials in 2006 and 2007 triggered much exaggerated reporting, especially in the British press.[46]

Research Questions, Methods, and Sources

This book is a comprehensive study of camp brothels from two contrasting yet complementary perspectives. The first is to see the camp brothel as belonging to what David Rousset in 1945 called the concentration camp universe, that "world set apart, utterly segregated . . . with its own peculiar fatality."[47] This model, followed by Eugen Kogon, Wolfgang Sofsky, Giorgio Agamben, and many others, regards the Nazi concentration camp as an isolated cosmos with its own structures, rules, and logics.[48] The second perspective understands the concentration camp within the social environment and legal system of Nazi Germany.[49] In linking these perspectives, I help the reader grasp the complexity of the camp brothel as both an institution in the concentration camp system and a product of the mechanisms of regulation and control in the Third Reich.

The book examines four central questions: What were the intentions of the SS in establishing the camp brothels? How were the brothels organized? What were their effects on prisoners? And who were the women forced into sex labor? In answering these questions, I take two basic approaches. One is positivistic and inductive and presents the history of the camp brothels. This constitutes the first part of my book and comprises Chapters 1 through 3. The other approach is systematic and interdisciplinary and makes up Chapters 4 through 9. Here I explore aspects such as spatial organization, power, violence, sanitation, sexuality, psychology, and social science. In doing so, I bring together emphases from various disciplines to form an overall picture of the camp brothels and their significance for victims, perpetrators, and those who otherwise benefited.

In Chapters 1 and 2, I outline the history and legal treatment of prostitution in the Third Reich and trace the development of the Nazi concentration camp system. I also consider the economic efforts of the SS and Heinrich Himmler's ideas for increasing the output of forced labor and the subsequent introduction of quota-based bonus system. In Chapter 3, I consider the various strategies employed by the SS to recruit women for brothel work.

In the second part of the book, I turn to the specifics of brothel life. In Chapter 4, I discuss the space of the brothels in the topography of the concentration camp and examine how their location and construction served the power structures of camp administrators. I also discuss the organization of the brothels and the people who used them. I show how the SS mobilized an elaborate bureaucracy and a distinctive organization of space and time to enforce camp rules for disease prevention, sanitation, and racial hygiene. In Chapter 5, I address social relationships, the role of sexuality, and the coping strategies of forced sex workers. In Chapter 6, I discuss the women forced to work in the brothels—who they were, the daily itineraries they followed, their relationships with other prisoners, and their lives after they were released—before turning in the next chapter to the brothel visitors. In addition to the conditions for brothel use, the numbers of clients, and their motivations, I also shed light on a largely neglected topic in the literature on concentration camps and the Holocaust: male sexuality. I show how different notions of sexuality and masculinity collided during brothel visits to create a unique matrix of power and virility. In Chapter 8, I consider prisoners' views of the camp brothels and the women who worked there and describe examples of resistance to forced sexual labor. The book concludes with a summary discussing the general significance of the brothels within the concentration camp system and Nazi biopolitics more generally.[50]

Camp brothels make up only a small chapter in the history of Nazi concentration camps. Though ten concentration camps opened brothels between mid-1942 and May 1945, some closed after only a few months. The limited number of brothels that were established and the relatively narrow band of time that they were open allowed me to focus my research as I combed through the archival records.[51] Among the documents I consulted were files from the SS leadership, such as decrees from Heinrich Himmler, as well as documents from central institutions that superintended the concentration camp system: the Concentration Camps Inspectorate (IKL) and the SS Main Economic and Administrative Office (WVHA). The central authority responsible for the business enterprises and supply systems of the SS, the WVHA left behind records that proved particularly important for identifying the women who worked in the camp brothels. However, far more files for my study came from the local administrations of the concentration camps in which brothels were located. The camp SS officers were meticulous in recording every conceivable organizational process that occurred under their command, though the number of documents that survived varied greatly from camp to camp. For instance, the quantity of extant files from the Buchenwald concentration camp is enormous, while in Neuengamme, the SS succeeded in destroying almost everything. I considered relevant any documents that related directly to the camp brothels, such as job sheets from the Buchenwald brothel and the visitor logs from Mauthausen's Block 3. I also reviewed detailed medical notes from the venereal exams of Auschwitz brothel workers, which indicate the duration of the women's deployment in a brothel, the provisions they received, their abortion records, and their medical history.[52] I consulted outside records from judicial and health authorities for information about their criminal records. Finally, I took into account files from the postwar period tracking the subsequent fate of the sex workers. These included, for instance, applications for financial compensation and records from the occupation authorities, the West German judiciary, and the East German state security service.

A central tool of my work is the database of information on women from brothels that I began compiling when I started my research and expanded over the course of my work.[53] In many cases, it was possible to identify names and dates and places of birth, which allowed me to search for additional information in state, regional, and municipal archives across Europe. This database includes at least 80 percent of the women who worked in the camp brothels. (This includes both the ten concentration camps that had brothels for prisoners and at least three concentration camps that had brothels for Ukrainian SS guards.) The database contains information about the number of forced sex workers; their nationality, age, and marital status; the duration of their imprisonment in the camps and the period they worked in the camp brothels; and their lives after imprisonment. In view of the sensitive subject matter, I have entrusted the database to the Archives of the Ravensbrück Memorial in Germany, where it can be accessed by researchers on request.

Another crucial source of material for this book is eyewitness accounts, which provide insight into the reality of forced sex work, the function of camp brothels, and the role of sexuality in concentration camps. The ones I draw on come from published memoirs, eyewitness accounts of former prisoners collected in connection with the documentation of Nazi crimes, interviews conducted by me, and statements of eyewitnesses in court and in proceedings regarding disciplinary measures and compensation.

The quantity of published memoirs containing eyewitness accounts of camp life is immense. But while of great importance for the history of concentration camps, memoirs can be difficult to deploy as evidence given their literary treatment of the subject matter and their mixing of fact and fiction.[54] Unpublished accounts of concentration camp survivors recorded in the early postwar years are another invaluable type of source. These testimonies are richly detailed and often address aspects of camp life that were later deemed taboo, such as issues surrounding sexuality. The subjects of sexual exploitation and camp brothels rarely appear in these accounts, however.[55] The researchers who carried out the interviews wanted to document Nazi mass murder and thus focused their questions on that topic. Furthermore, reports about camp brothels are rarely found in the collections of Holocaust research centers because Jewish prisoners were generally excluded from visiting brothels.[56] Likewise, the eyewitness interviews conducted by the staff of concentration camp memorials devote scant attention to camp brothels. It was only in the 1980s that researchers began posing direct questions about sexuality, sexual violence, and camp brothels.[57] In the 1990s, four former forced sex workers were interviewed.[58]

In researching the history of camp brothels, I interviewed a total of thirty former inmates who had been detained at a camp that either had a brothel or enlisted women for sex work.[59] The interviews focused on four topics: brothels and recruitment, the bonus system, the psychology of survival, and the significance of sexuality. I created a special list of questions based on information regarding the arrest records of each individual. What the interviewees knew about the brothels varied greatly from person to person. Four had heard little to nothing about camp brothels; nine had known about them through secondary sources. Thirteen had had brief contact with a brothel. Four admitted to visiting one. The selection of interviewees in no way represents a cross-section of camp society. By the time my interviews began, many of the surviving prisoners had already died, and I was unable to locate and interview any former sex workers from the camp brothels. One individual denied ever having worked in a camp brothel, though years earlier, in a report about her detention in Auschwitz, she stated that she had.[60]

The use of oral history is of particular importance for understanding the history of the concentration camps. This applies first of all to the reconstruction of the history of specific concentration camps from which few documents have survived but also to aspects of camp life that cannot be deduced from files, such as everyday life and experiences. Just as oral history can illuminate such areas, it also has its limitations. "Memories," writes the historian Lutz Niethammer, "are not objective reflections of past reality or perception."[61] The testimonies of former prisoners are their subjective perceptions, and, in part because of memory lapses and the amount of time that has passed, often contain elements that are invented or simply false. Not infrequently, their statements rely on speculation because of the lack of information available in the camps, forcing them to fill in the gaps based on rumors or on other camp experiences.[62]

In my work, these problems are compounded by the highly taboo nature of the subject matter, especially among those who had visited the camp brothels. In particular, discrepancies between the sense of one's sexual self and one's actual sexual experiences can lead to conscious or unconscious adjustments to memory.[63] Worries about one's own guilt and the traumatizing experiences of the concentration camp can promote self-censorship. The former prisoners interviewed for this study understood their visit to the camp brothel as a marginal event in the totality of their concentration camp experience. Some spoke about salient aspects of the brothel visit, while others did not mention important details or made them up. Nevertheless, their narratives showed an unexpected openness, which I believe can be explained primarily because they regarded themselves as victims rather than as perpetrators.[64]

A much smaller portion of the sources I have drawn on consists of the testimonies of individuals involved in disciplinary and legal proceedings. This stems from the fact that sexual exploitation or violence was never the main subject of criminal prosecution—except in the disciplinary measures carried out by the East German Communist Party. Some former SS men have made statements about the camp brothels, but they often sought to downplay their importance or justify their establishment.[65] Only three former brothel workers are known to have made statements in West German court proceedings against SS perpetrators and in investigations against the SS. Of the three, only one has spoken about her time in the camp brothel.[66]

It is common practice in oral history to use surviving documents to verify or falsify statements. The large quantity of Nazi documents I evaluated and the database I created made it possible to reconstruct periods, determine the precise numbers of victims, and provide information about the victims' lives and the persecution they experienced. But firsthand testimonies can also shed light on social relationships and sexuality, which could hardly be gleaned from records alone. Accordingly, my use of oral testimonies and administrative documents is equal parts comparative and complementary.

Terminology, Pseudonyms

The authors of the first studies on camp brothels spoke of forced prostitution, but the term soon came under by fire by critics, who pointed out that describing women incarcerated in times of war as "prostitutes" leads to their stigmatization, as in the notorious case of the "comfort women" held by the Imperial Japanese Army.[67] Some researchers and activists instead advocated the use of the term *sexual slavery*, the term adopted by the United Nations.[68] In 2004, Helga Amesberger, Katrin Auer, and Brigitte Halbmayr coined the word *Sex-Zwangsarbeit*, which has since become increasingly common in German-language scholarship.[69] The term, which can be translated as "forced sexual labor," is preferable to "sexual slavery" because it ties the camp brothels to the Nazi system of forced labor and broadens its coercive character, which ranges from the mechanisms of recruitment to the organization of the workers. It also makes plain that the women who performed sex work in camp brothels should receive recognition as victims of Nazism and be included in Germany's culture of remembrance.[70] I thus use *forced sexual labor* throughout this book to describe the particular form of sexual exploitation that occurred in the camp brothels. Sometimes I use "forced sex work" for variety, and when referring to the women who served in the brothels, I prefer "forced sex workers" simply because it is less ungainly than "forced sex laborers," not because I wish to suggest an affinity to the "sex-positive" sense of sex work in the sex workers' rights movement.[71]

Brigitte Halbmayr has argued that the coercive nature of the sex work in the camp brothels lay in the inability of the women to barter sex for money, earn a profit, or engage in courtship.[72] As will become apparent in this book, this understanding of forced sex labor's coercive nature is both inadequate and misleading. I favor Norbert Campagna's model, which defines three parameters for coercion in prostitution: first, the freedom to choose to engage in prostitution; second, the freedom to choose practices and clients; third, the freedom to stop engaging in prostitution.[73] At the camp brothels, women lacked freedom in all three areas. When it comes to unregulated prostitution in prison camps and informal brothels, I refrain from using the specific term "forced sexual labor."[74] Instead, I think of such practices as a more general form of sexual exploitation.

The camp brothels in which the women were sexually exploited went by various names. The official designation by the SS was *Sonderbau*, or "special building." *Sonderkommando*, or "special detail," referred to the work performed there.[75] The term *Sonderbaracke* was also common in some camps to describe where the brothels were housed.[76] The use of the German prefix *sonder-* was a popular method used by the Nazis to disguise the true nature of a building or activity. For the most part, *sonder-* was a euphemism for death. *Sonderbehandlung* meant murder, and the Jewish prisoners who worked in the crematoria of Auschwitz-Birkenau belonged to the

Sonderkommando.[77] The use of *sonder-* for camp brothels and sex labor sometimes led to confusion. For instance, in the arrivals register for the Flossenbürg concentration camp, the women who would be working in the *Sonderbau* were designated "S.B." But since the abbreviation could also mean *Sonderbehandlung*, or extermination, "Sonderbau" was later added for clarification.[78] And when Auschwitz administrators were planning the construction of a camp brothel, they were careful to call it the Häftlings-Sonderbaracke B—the "B" stood for *Bordell*, or brothel—so as to make clear that its occupants were not slated for extermination.[79] Such confusion was a real possibility: The Auschwitz planners had put the brothel behind the camp lockup, where executions occurred routinely. The ambiguity of *sonder-* has occasionally tripped up scholars, too. In one case, historians studying Mauthausen erroneously interpreted a reference to the construction of a "special building" to mean that camp administrators were installing a gas chamber.[80]

Brothels for the Ukrainian guards were also referred to by the SS as "special buildings."[81] In camps with brothels for Ukrainian guards and brothels for prisoners, the latter were called "prisoners' special buildings" to avoid confusion.[82] Heinrich Himmler himself used the term *Lagerbordell* (camp brothel), which originally referred to brothels for foreign workers in forced labor camps.[83] Among prisoners, *Puff* (whorehouse), *Puffkommando* (whore unit), and *Nuttenbaracke* (hooker barracks) were common.[84] These terms, though vulgar, were not meant pejoratively. Rather, they were characteristic of *Lagerszpracha*, the mix of languages spoken by non-German speakers in the camps that often incorporated terms used by the SS.[85] In recent years, the term *prisoners' brothel* has established itself in historical scholarship. However, the word might be mistaken for a brothel in which female prisoners served SS men instead of other prisoners.[86] In the English translation, I mainly use the term "camp brothel" or a closely related variant. Occasionally, I also use the Nazi euphemism "special building."

Finally, a word about the pseudonyms I use when talking about former sex workers. Scholars have a special responsibility to protect the privacy of victims whose testimonies figure in their research. While none of the women who worked in the camp brothels are likely still to be alive today, the stigmatization surrounding forced sexual labor remains, so in the interests of their families and friends, I have pseudonymized the names of all persons whose cases involve sensitive information.[87] The pseudonyms I created retain the initial letters of individuals' real first and last names, however. When pseudonyms are used in previous published studies, I adopt the already established alias. For the sake of uniformity, individuals whose names were concealed in another work using a different nomenclature will receive a pseudonym in keeping with the others I have chosen (e.g., "Margarete W." becomes "Magdalena Walter" and "Frau X" becomes "Laura Büttig"). In the footnotes and statistical tables, I use initials instead of pseudonyms. A list of the pseudonyms that appear in this book can be found in the Appendix.

1 Prostitution in Nazi Germany

Adolf Hitler called for the elimination of prostitution in *Mein Kampf*, but the Nazis understood that enforcing such a demand was completely unrealistic. Prostitution policy in the Third Reich did not consist of outlawing prostitution and taking resolute action against those who participated in it. It was complex and far from coherent, and it grew out of various local strategies and compromises between ideological demands and real-life problems. At first, the Nazis limited themselves to banning prostitution in public spaces, but with the outbreak of war, the regime sought to gain centralized control over all forms of prostitution. A comprehensive system of state-controlled brothels emerged across Germany and its occupied territories covering all strata of society: civilians, members of the military, and forced laborers. As we will later see, the regulations introduced by the Nazis would ultimately apply even to the brothels for concentration camp prisoners, which is why it is important that I consider them in more detail here.[1]

History

Before the foundation of the German Empire in 1871, cities and municipalities were responsible for regulating prostitution in the German states. Though the rules differed from place to place, their main objective was to prevent the spread of venereal disease and protect public morality. Brothels were seen as an effective way of keeping prostitutes segregated from the population at large, and as a result local police usually tolerated the existence of "pleasure houses."[2] Once the German Empire was established, the legal provisions governing prostitution were standardized across the nation-state. The new regulations required that all prostitutes register with the police as *Kontroldirnen*. Anyone who didn't was arrested and charged with "clandestine" prostitution. Vice squads decided which women were prostitutes and thus required registration. They also had the power to define women as prostitutes simply for failing to comply with conventional social mores. (To be expunged from the police registry, women had to prove that they had a permanent job or were married.) Prostitutes had to find accommodation in a brothel within three days of registration and be checked for venereal disease twice a week by police doctors. The penal code forbade pandering (persuading individuals to work as prostitutes) and permitted pimping (receiving the proceeds from prostitutes) only in the case of brothel keepers.

Starting in the late 1870s, brothels came under increasing pressure. For one, more and more women were working as unregistered prostitutes, directly competing with brothels and decentralizing prostitution.[3] For another, the abolitionist campaigns to eliminate prostitution were gaining steam, and brothels were the most obvious targets. The closure of brothels forced the women who had worked in them onto the streets, marking the end of the imperial policy that sought to keep prostitutes out of the public eye. Given the housing shortage that prevailed in many places, prostitutes rented rooms with families and plied their wares openly. State institutions, welfare authorities, and business owners condemned such conditions as a "barbarization of morals."[4] Joseph Goebbels saw public prostitution as a reason to denounce the moral depravity of the Weimar Republic: "The joyless alley. Harlots stand at the doors and lure passers-by. Half-naked. What a terrible indictment! The body business! I want to cry! . . . This is the bourgeois state! Everything, everything is only rutting and business."[5]

Over the course of the 1920s, the number of prostitutes on the streets increased significantly. This was the result of a number of factors: economic hardship, the rejection of existing norms, an increased demand for sexual services, and the willingness of businessmen, bank employees, and other high-income clients to pay for them.[6] As municipal authorities worked to address the conditions that resulted from the closure of the brothels,[7] the national government enacted a law that would determine the regulation of prostitution in Germany for the next three decades: the Law for Combating Venereal Disease. The basic aim of the law, which came into effect on October 1, 1927, and was largely drafted by the German Society for Combating Venereal Disease, was to ensure that people with sexually transmitted diseases received medical treatment and to protect healthy people from infection through prophylaxis and education.[8] It was directed not only at prostitutes but all people who practiced "häufig wechselnden Geschlechtsverkehr," that is, who had sex with frequently changing partners.[9] The law sought to work against prostitution by making it a matter of health policy instead of a vice to be suppressed by the police.[10] It largely decriminalized prostitution except in the vicinity of schools, churches, and homes where children between the ages of three and eighteen lived. The common legal term "commercial fornication" was replaced with "soliciting or offering to engage in fornication," and prostitutes were liable to prosecution only if they behaved in a "manner contrary to custom and decency." But the new definition meant that women and men who did not work as professional prostitutes could also be prosecuted for the same behavior. Whereas before the vice squad kept "lists of harlots," the health authorities now kept lists of persons known to be promiscuous. For instance, the Hamburg health department created a card index recording all registered prostitutes and incidences of venereal disease. The agency's president ordered all registered prostitutes to undergo weekly examinations. If women did not comply, force could be used to compel them. After the Nazis seized power, the Hamburg health department was instrumental in the arrest and imprisonment of young women who failed to follow the regulations.[11] As I discuss in Chapter 6, this is how some of the women who were later forced to perform sex in the camp brothels ended up in concentration camps.

The legislators who passed the Law for Combating Venereal Disease were not persuaded by the arguments of health authorities and police departments, who wanted to reintroduce state-controlled brothels.[12] The nationwide relocation of the prostitution trade to the outdoors resulted in a rise of complaints in cities and large towns about the "deterioration of the streets." Moreover, the law's wording was vague about enforcement, and police had no clear instructions for intervention. Calls for tougher policing grew stronger throughout the empire, and various state institutions openly discussed making changes to the law.[13]

Prostitution Policy

A few months after the National Socialists came to power, an editorial by the new Reich Commissioner of the German Society for Combating Venereal Disease, Professor Bodo Spiethoff, appeared in the *Mitteilungen der Deutschen Gesellschaft zur Bekämpfung von Geschlechtskrankheiten*. In it, Spiethoff wrote that the fight against venereal disease must be carried out in accordance with the "ethos" of the Nazi state. The society had to consider not only hygienic but also "important national and ethical concerns."[14] The editorial was followed by a long excerpt from *Mein Kampf*, in which Hitler explicitly discusses the fight against venereal disease and the regulation of prostitution: "The struggle against syphilis and the prostitution which prepares the way for it is one of the most gigantic tasks of humanity, gigantic because we are facing, not the solution of a single question, but the elimination of a large number of evils which bring about this plague as a resultant manifestation. For in this case the sickening of the body is only the consequence of a sickening of the moral, social, and racial instincts."[15] According to Hitler, the Weimar government had failed to implement "thoroughgoing reforms" to clamp down on syphilis and prostitution; instead it "tinkered with the disease and left the causes untouched."[16] The "weakness" of Weimar's response was "a visible sign of a people's decay" and a forfeiture of their "right to live in this world of struggle."[17] For Hitler, the key to fighting venereal disease lay in addressing the root causes of prostitution. Though "a disgrace to humanity," prostitution "cannot be eliminated by moral lectures, pious intentions, etc." Rather, "its limitation and final abolition presuppose the elimination of innumerable preconditions. The first is and remains the creation of an opportunity for early marriage as compatible with human nature—particularly for the man, as the woman in any case is only the passive part."[18]

For all the pathos of his tirade against prostitution, Hitler's solution was far from effective. The only "precondition" he identifies is the male sex drive and its need for channeling. And the only solution he offers is early marriage. He denies that women have their own independent sexuality and instead reduces their sexual function to satisfying men. Apart from cementing patriarchal structures and demanding radical solutions for the "final abolition" of prostitution, Hitler's words are devoid of content. It was a vacuity that would come to epitomize the Nazi approach to prostitution until the war.

On May 16, 1933, Germany's Nazi-controlled government amended Section 361 of the country's penal code. The revised law restricted prostitutes' freedom of movement and gave police officers greater discretionary powers, thereby reversing the de facto impunity previously afforded to prostitution.[19] Three months later, Nazi legislators amended Section 11 of the criminal code to prohibit prostitution in communities with fewer than twenty thousand inhabitants. Women rounded up for peddling sex were to be reported to public health offices and subject to medical examinations.[20] The penal code gave local police departments the authority to take forceful action against prostitutes for "conspicuous exposure in public" and encouraged them to put those caught in workhouses.[21] Police departments seeking more punitive measures could invoke the Decree of the Reich President for the Protection of People and State, passed the previous February after the Reichstag fire.[22] Under the sweeping powers it granted to the state, police frequently conducted raids on prostitutes and their pimps.[23]

The Ministry of the Interior nevertheless stopped short of introducing an all-out ban on prostitution. The state understood that prostitution would never disappear completely. The point was to "suppress it . . . in such a way as to avoid harassing the public and endangering young people."[24] However, the relative restraint on the part of the Reich government did not prevent cities from acting on their own. In 1933, Hamburg forbade open prostitution and, in the "interest of the general public and public health," confined prostitutes to police-controlled streets.[25] Despite the insistence of Interior Minister Wilhelm Frick, who pointed out the existing ban on restricting prostitutes to certain areas, Hamburg and other cities that followed its lead refused to comply.[26] At the same time, municipal health officials tightened requirements for medical examinations. Prostitutes in Hamburg were required to appear at the city health office twice a week to be examined for sexually transmitted diseases. Women picked up during raids and patrols were immediately turned over to the health department's venereal disease clinic. In 1935, Hamburg reintroduced a prostitute registry and took control over all aspects of prostitutes' lives. The police prohibited them from being in certain parts of the city, and officials could stop and search them any time, whether at home or on the street. Violations of the rules came with harsh punishments.[27] The city made particular use of Section 327 of the penal code, which stated that a prison sentence could be imposed on anyone who violated state measures to prevent contagious diseases. Introduced in 1871 but until then never used for the purposes of curtailing prostitution, Section 327 allowed the city's venereal disease clinic to notify police when prostitutes failed to undergo required examinations. Violations usually brought prison sentences of up to four weeks for first-time offenders and up to two years for repeat offenders.[28] Under an ordinance on preventative measures to fight criminality, passed on December 14, 1937, prostitutes could be committed to reformatories, workhouses, or concentration camps after three violations.[29]

The beginning of the war marked a sea change in Germany's prostitution policy. On September 9, 1939, Reinhard Heydrich, at the behest of the Reich Ministry of the Interior, published a decree establishing total state control over prostitution. In other words, the system already in place in Hamburg was extended to all of Germany.[30] Heydrich, the chief of the Reich Security Main Office, explained that the decree ordered all prostitutes to register with the police and receive medical supervision from the health authorities. Its goal was to counteract rising levels of venereal disease, which led to an "impairment of military strength." The decree provided "an effective defense" against "prostitution's dangers to the Wehrmacht and the civilian population, especially in terms of health." It completely prohibited prostitutes from soliciting sex on the streets and permitted "commercial fornication" only in "special houses." If such houses were not available, the police had to provide them. Police and health authorities had to supervise brothels for "safety and health," and brothels had to follow "racial principles" by allowing "non-German prostitutes" in port cities and barring Jewish women from prostitution.[31] Prostitutes were allowed to solicit clients only in certain spaces and were not allowed to loiter outside the premises at night or in certain public places during the day. It forbade relationships between prostitutes and pimps as well as the production and use of sadomasochistic devices. Prostitutes were obliged to report changes of residence, to appear punctually for regular medical checkups, and to use "protective measures" for sex. The state's control of prostitution went one step further in May 1941, when Heydrich instructed German criminal police offices to provide a detailed list of existing brothels along with their "racial" and military function and information on the number and nationality of their prostitutes.[32] He also ordered all prostitution to be confined to brothels or closed brothel streets.

A key aspect of Nazi racist ideology was the separation of Germans and non-Germans.[33] But the war posed an obstacle to this policy given the severe shortage of labor in German production. The Nazi leadership attempted to compensate by using foreign workers. By August 1944, there were 7.8 million foreign civilian workers in Germany, most under forced labor conditions.[34] In many cities, foreign workers were now a common sight, and contact with Germans was inevitable. In Hamburg, the *Ausländerpromenade* in the Wandsbek woods became a popular meeting place for foreign workers and German women. Such liaisons violated Nazi racial ideology; if caught, foreign workers faced the death penalty, and German women could be publicly shamed or sent to concentration camps. The state published tables showing which foreign workers were allowed to have sex with German women.[35] The policy extended to smaller ethnic groups and was often inconsistent, changing with the political situation. Lithuanian men, for example, were not permitted to have sexual relations with German women, while starting in November 1943, Estonians and Latvians were.[36] Generally, enforcement was laxer when it came to Dutch and Flemish men. Relations between German women and French, Spanish, Hungarian, Romanian, and Yugoslavian men were not explicitly forbidden, but they were considered undesirable. Both the Nazi regime and the welfare authorities also demanded that German women be given proper educations about the dangers of sex with foreign men. To the chagrin of those who devised these measures, foreigners and Germans continued to engage in sexual relations.[37]

Heinrich Himmler personally took on the problem and found a solution in the establishment of brothels for foreign workers: "They can have brothels. They can have them in masses. I have nothing against that. But they will have nothing to do with our German people."[38] On January 17, 1940, Himmler ordered the construction of the first such brothel for foreign workers, the "Villa Nova" in Linz.[39] Hitler liked the idea, and on December 1940, he ordered the establishment of brothels for foreign workers because of the alleged danger the latter posed "to German blood."[40] At the end of January 1941, Heydrich sent letters to criminal police headquarters across Germany calling for the accelerated construction of brothels for foreign workers outside closed towns and near labor camps. The brothel for foreign workers in the city of Linz was to serve as the prototype. Only foreign prostitutes or "gypsies" in the occupied territories were to be "recruited" to work in the brothels, and they had to correspond as closely as possible to the ethnicity of the local foreign workers.[41] In October 1941, the regulations were made more specific. One prostitute was to be recruited for every three hundred to five hundred foreigners. Poles and Frenchwomen were the preferred candidates because it was easier for them to transfer money home. German, Dutch, Norwegian, and Italian women were forbidden. The principle was to match "nationality with nationality." The price for a brothel visit was between three and five Reichsmarks.[42]

The German Labor Front (DAF) took on the task of planning a nationwide brothel system for foreign workers and founded a company especially for the purpose of its construction and financing. All cities with significant numbers of foreign workers were required to provide demographic statistics for men and women. Then purely actuarial calculations were made as to which locations were suitable for the establishment of brothels.[43] But the nationwide plan often encountered resistance from local authorities and businesses.[44] For example, the mayor of the town of Hennigsdorf, just outside Berlin, complained about plans to establish a brothel in his town: "You cannot expect me to happily agree to the planned establishment of a brothel in Hennigsdorf. What I need are schools, a train station, children's homes, especially apartments and more apartments. . . . If pleasure houses are built for the many foreign workers here, I doubt very much whether our fellow citizens will understand."[45]

Racial mixing in prostitution was also a concern of the Wehrmacht, Germany's armed forces from 1935 to 1945. The Wehrmacht had run brothels for soldiers almost since its founding, following a centuries-old military tradition.[46] But until the territorial expansions during the first years of the war, the Wehrmacht-controlled brothels lay outside the German Reich in areas such Romania and Spain.[47] Within Germany, members of the Wehrmacht were permitted to visit brothels provided they operated under the auspices of the state health authorities; soliciting street prostitutes was strongly discouraged.[48] As the Wehrmacht took control of Europe, it worked together with mayors and other local authorities to set up military brothels in Germany's newly occupied territories; in France, the Wehrmacht commandeered urban brothels throughout the country. The brothel system in occupied Europe was a cornerstone in the Wehrmacht's efforts to control interactions with local populations and to monitor and direct the sexual activity of its soldiers. The aim was not only to prevent the spread of venereal disease but also to keep soldiers from revealing military secrets or of developing sympathies for foreigners.[49]

The Wehrmacht created military bordellos in most of the territories that Germany occupied: the Baltic States, Belgium, Greece, Croatia, Norway, Poland, Romania, and the Soviet Union.[50] Local commandants were responsible for setting up the brothels, and German medical officers or the local doctors in their charge were responsible for medical supervision. The Wehrmacht set the prices, and locals were generally banned from entering. Prophylaxis stations were set up next to the brothels, and signs reminded visitors to use a condom. Soldiers had to memorize the number of the prostitute they visited—every woman received a "control number"—and afterward had to submit to a checkup and receive treatment to prevent sexually transmitted diseases. The Wehrmacht also worked with local police to combat open prostitution in the streets and squares.[51]

In the Wehrmacht-controlled brothels, the Office of the High Command (OKW) introduced stricter measures than the rules specified in the decree of September 9, 1939. Specifically, doctors had to record the type and frequency of medical examinations for the women. Moreover, Jewish women were prohibited from working at the brothels, and German soldiers were forbidden from visiting brothels outside the control of the Wehrmacht in which local women worked. However, there is evidence that this prohibition was not always enforced in Germany's occupied territories, particularly in Africa.

SS Brothels

Heinrich Himmler was not only the commander of the SS in the Reich; he asserted control over the sex lives of its members. In his view, the male sex drive was a natural impulse that had to be placed in the service of Nazi population policy: He proclaimed in 1931 that SS members must receive his personal approval before marrying.[52] He refused to accept the "false modesty" associated with the "remnants of a particular Christian ethos."[53] For example, in 1939, despite considerable resistance from institutions in the NS regime, he issued the *Kinderzeugungsbefehl*, an edict that ordered SS men to produce more children by taking second wives.[54] In contrast to Hitler,

Himmler did not view prostitution as a "disgrace to humanity." Rather, it was a lesser evil that could be regulated by the state and used to achieve other objectives. In 1937, Himmler declared in a secret speech that prostitution could be used in the fight against homosexuality: "In this area [prostitution] we will be generous, because we cannot on the one hand try to prevent our youth drifting into homosexuality, and on the other hand bar every way out of this. That would be insane. After all, every opportunity that I close off to meet girls in the big cities—even if it involves money—brings a large contingent to the other side."[55] Himmler's belief in the need to channel male sexuality is particularly evident in his emphasis on state-regulated prostitution. The fight against homosexuality, for Himmler a "symptom of dying peoples," was the primary goal.[56] Homosexuality did not produce children and disturbed the "balance between the sexes."[57] Its cause was the lack of opportunities to satisfy the sex drive. He took a particularly harsh stance against homosexuality in the SS and police. Beginning in November 1941, any member of these institutions caught having homosexual relations was sentenced to death.[58]

After the war broke out, the SS leadership in Eastern Europe encountered problems similar to those faced by the Wehrmacht's High Command. Both the fear of venereal disease and the enforcement of racial ideology were central issues in the control of SS men's sexuality. Himmler forbade members of the police and the SS "any sexual contact with women and girls of other races."[59] However, SS men, like members of the Wehrmacht, did not always adhere to the rule. Particularly in Poland, there were cases of SS men having sexual relations with local women, which prompted Himmler in July 1941 to remind them explicitly of the prohibition on "sexual intercourse with Poles." Any SS man who disobeyed the order could be sent to a concentration camp. Despite this proscription, some SS men asked Himmler for permission to marry Polish women.[60]

In early June 1942, on receiving word of another sexual relationship between an SS man and a Polish woman, Himmler conceded that the situation in the General Government of Warsaw was difficult "in terms of sex" and stated that he had nothing in general against SS men having sex with "virtuous" German prostitutes who lived in brothels or who worked under state supervision.[61] A few weeks later, Himmler received a report from a military surgeon by the name of Dr. Rübel stating that approximately 90 percent of all SS and Wehrmacht men stationed in Warsaw had contracted venereal disease. According to the surgeon's report, infection had occurred almost exclusively from sexual intercourse with German prostitutes.[62] He thus suggested that the women be housed in brothels and examined weekly.[63]

Himmler agreed to this proposal. He would have the Higher SS and Police Leader East immediately establish brothels with German women in Warsaw. This would ensure "a healthy meeting with girls . . . without the risk of producing children, of men becoming ill, and of forging social bonds with the Polish *Volk*."[64] The Reichs-SS physician Ernst-Robert Grawitz initiated a detailed investigation of conditions in Warsaw and found that the incidence of venereal disease among the three thousand SS men stationed there was only 1.4 percent, which was below the peacetime rate of 2 percent.[65] Himmler determined that Rübel's allegations were untrue and asked the head of the Race and Settlement Main Office, SS-Obergruppenführer Hofmann, to investigate.[66] After this finding, it is unlikely that German prostitutes were placed in brothels, as Himmler originally demanded.

In another case, SS-Obergruppenführer Josef Dietrich reported to Himmler in January 1943 that seven thousand men in the SS division "Leibstandarte Adolf Hitler" stationed in France had venereal disease.[67] "Humanly speaking, the behavior of the men is very understandable," Himmler responded. "The troops who returned from the East were sexually starved."[68] Once more he believed he could solve the problem by establishing SS-controlled brothels. He ordered brothels to be created at all Waffen-SS locations and the provision of adequate medical supervision for SS troops. He ordered that the police help create a "system of medical control for women and girls,"[69] as the Wehrmacht had already done. Additionally, he wanted to make sure, through "strict orders and education," that SS men only associate with prostitutes who worked in brothels and possessed health cards.[70] As in Poland, Himmler demanded a detailed investigation of the case. Within a few days, the SS Health Department in Berlin produced a list of all cases of gonorrhea in the SS in France. According to this list, the Leibstandarte had only 244 cases, not seven thousand. At 1.23 percent, this was within the range of "customary percentages in the army."[71]

Nevertheless, it seems that Himmler was resolved to solve a problem that his own SS health officials said did not exist. In March 1943, the chief of the SS and police in France, Carl Oberg,[72] reported to Himmler that "everything necessary . . . has been set in motion" to get venereal disease under control and that strict orders had been issued to SS men.[73] The specifics of these orders are not known. It is likely that SS men were required to confine their sexual activity to "medically supervised women and girls" in brothels controlled by the Wehrmacht.[74] There is no evidence that special brothels were ever established for the SS, however.

And what of the SS men stationed in concentration camps? Ever since the publication of Christa Paul's 1994 book *Zwangsprostitution*, which presented an interview with a woman who claimed to have worked in a Buchenwald brothel for SS men, many historians have assumed that the SS also maintained bordellos for camp guards.[75] This assumption seemed to be supported by subsequently published survivor reports claiming that women in Ravensbrück had been selected for such brothels.[76] But these claims turned out to be unreliable, and all other evidence points generally to the absence of camp brothels for SS men—with some notable exceptions. For SS troops stationed at the camps, SS leaders generally relied on existing urban brothels, which were under medical supervision and were operated in accordance with the principles of Nazi racial ideology.

I want to illustrate by considering the Buchenwald complex. Buchenwald was built between 1937 and 1939 as an "SS city" on the outskirts of Weimar. It consisted of a prisoner camp, an industrial plant, SS barracks, and adjoining residential areas. The architecture of the residential buildings reflected the hierarchy among their occupants. High-ranking officers lived in detached villas; officers, in detached single-family and multifamily homes; the rank and file, in barracks.[77] SS men were generally forbidden to engage in sex in the barracks and could face disciplinary sanctions if they did. This may not have been as difficult as it might appear: Many of the men belonged to the Waffen-SS and were being trained for deployment to the front, so sex is not likely to have been at the forefront of their minds.[78] Those seeking entertainment could take a bus to Weimar via a route regularly servicing the camp. According to the psychologist and former Buchenwald inmate Ernst Federn, the SS troops "suffered greatly from their isolation and the lack of normal love relationships,"[79] and they had little success with the women of Weimar.[80] However, they had the opportunity to visit Rosmariengasse, the city's brothel street. Although there are no concrete records of visits by SS men, Wehrmacht soldiers stationed in Weimar were often seen there.[81] The same is true for the SS men stationed in Neuengamme, who were permitted to travel to Hamburg. Herbertstrasse, one of Hamburg's brothel streets, was frequented by hordes of young soldiers.[82] As for KZ Sachsenhausen, guards usually went to Berlin for entertainment. In Mauthausen, the SS men probably went to the state-controlled brothels in Linz.[83] SS men stationed in Dachau probably traveled to Munich.

The situation for the SS in Auschwitz was different. The town of Auschwitz (Oświęcim) was small and lacked any brothels. However, IG Farben had established a brothel for the Polish and French workers who were building the synthetic rubber plant in the nearby village of Monowitz.[84] Although it was meant for foreign workers only, some SS men disobeyed the regulation and engaged in "forbidden association" with the brothel workers. Rudolf

Höß, the commandant of Auschwitz, was forced to remind the camp SS several times of the prohibition. An order dated February 11, 1942, stated: "Effective immediately, all members of the SS are forbidden to enter the Polish pleasure house on Schloßstr. 4 in Auschwitz. Any violators will be severely punished."[85] Despite additional reminders and threats—anyone caught even in the vicinity of the brothel would be immediately arrested—some SS men continued to disregard the order.[86]

In September 1942, the head of the SS Main Economic and Administrative Office (WVHA), Oswald Pohl, demanded "the immediate establishment of a brothel for SS members in Auschwitz."[87] But it was not until 1944 that the foreign workers' brothel was expanded to include a section for Germans.[88] Arthur Liebehenschel, who succeeded Höß as camp commandant,[89] issued an order stating that starting on May 12, 1944, the brothel would be open to members of the Waffen-SS and the Wehrmacht stationed at Auschwitz from 6:00 p.m. to 11:00 p.m. on Mondays and Fridays, for five Reichsmarks per visit. During these times, the brothel was to be closed to civilians. The SS camp physician would assign a doctor or medical assistant for the medical supervision of the SS. In addition, the commandant pointed out that visiting this brothel would minimize the risk of contracting venereal disease and warned the garrison to refrain from any other form of "extramarital sexual intercourse."[90] The women who worked in the camp brothel were German prostitutes under the supervision of the security police in Katowice and the health department in Auschwitz.[91]

There is one other case in which existing camp brothels may have been converted for SS men: the brothel for forced laborers at Obersalzberg. After failing to yield a profit, the chief of the Nazi Party Chancellery, Martin Bormann, proposed in January 1943 that "the rooms of the brothel could be divided, one half with foreign women for foreign workers and the other with German women for the SS men stationed there, in order to spare them the trip to the brothel in Salzburg."[92] But it is unknown whether the plan was ever implemented.

Nevertheless, the SS did set up its own brothels for SS guards in and around the concentration camps. However, these were intended not for Germans but for Ukrainians. These guards were recruited by the SS primarily from Soviet prisoners-of-war camps in the Lublin district and trained at the SS training camp in Trawniki. The SS used the Ukrainian men for particularly brutal tasks, such as the "fight against partisans" and for guard duty at extermination and forced labor camps.[93] Although they were members of the SS, they, like other foreign workers, were not allowed to associate with German women or to visit German brothels, hence the decision of the SS leadership to set up separate brothels for them.

In Buchenwald, a brothel for Ukrainian guards existed for a time in the commandant's headquarters. At least two Polish women from the Ravensbrück camp performed forced sexual labor there.[94] One was sent back to Ravensbrück in March 1944 for being "useless."[95] There was also a brothel for Ukrainian SS men in Flossenbürg. A December 1943 memo issued by the Office Group D indicates that such brothels existed elsewhere, too.[96] The memo was addressed to all camps with brothels for Ukrainian guards, and its recipients included Mauthausen, Auschwitz, and Dachau in addition to Flossenbürg and Buchenwald.[97] Evidence suggests that Dachau lacked a separate brothel for foreign guards, however.[98] In Auschwitz, non-German SS men probably visited the local brothel for foreign workers. Another site with significant numbers of Ukrainian guards was the Sachsenhausen concentration camp. Though there are no records documenting a brothel for Ukrainians, one witness has testified to its existence. In Stutthof, a brothel for Ukrainian guards was established in Easter 1944.[99]

The memo from Office Group D provides explicit instructions regarding the establishment and organization of brothels. It states that men were to pay two Reichsmarks "for intercourse with the Polish brothel girls." Fifty percent of the fee was to go to the "brothel girls," while the other half was to be deposited in a special account. Money cards from two prostitutes in Buchenwald show that the SS regularly credited money to their camp accounts.[100] Each of these brothels was said to have two small, well-appointed rooms.[101]

Job sheets from prostitutes in Buchenwald show the dimension of forced sex work in the camp's brothel for Ukrainian guards. In the first ten days after the camp was opened, a total of seventy-three guards visited the brothel, with between four and thirteen men visiting each night. Each of the women had to see between two and eight men per day.[102] Eight of the women from camp brothels for Ukrainian guards are known by name. The total number is estimated to be twenty-four.[103] At least one of these women survived the war.[104] All of the identified women were Polish. Six had been sent to a concentration camp as "antisocials." Two were political prisoners. The average age of these women was twenty-one-and-a-half.[105]

A brothel for non-German SS units also existed in the Waffen-SS training camp in Heidelager, located in Puskow, Poland. (The brothel bore the euphemistic name Waldkaffee, "forest coffee.")[106] In addition to surviving floor plans, a report from a former Romanian SS man described the bordello.[107]

An examination list from the SS Hygienic Institute of the Waffen-SS in Rajsko, near Auschwitz, names five Polish women who worked in the brothel.[108] They were probably picked up by the SS during a raid and taken to Puskow. Evidence of the fate of these women is provided by statements of locals who brought the Polish women food and helped three of them escape to Krakow.[109]

While Hitler was calling prostitution a "disgrace" to be abolished, Heinrich Himmler was figuring out ways to put it under state control. Over the course of the 1930s and early 1940s, Nazis took over civilian brothels and established brothels for the military and foreign workers under the supervision of the police and health authorities. As I have shown in this chapter, one reason for the state's intervention was entirely ideological: racial segregation. The body of the *Volk* was to be kept pure in Germany and its occupied territories. Even in the realm of prostitution, Germans were not to mix with "lower races."[110] When the influx of foreign workers into the arms industry increased sexual contact between German women and non-German men, in violation of the tenets of Nazi race ideology, officials decided to channel the sexual urges of foreign workers into brothels staffed by foreign prostitutes. (That foreign men provided the only possibility of heterosexual contact for many German women concerned Nazi leadership preciously little.) Likewise, the decree of September 9, 1939, also served racial segregation by keeping German soldiers stationed in Europe from having sex with the wrong people.

On a more general level, Nazi prostitution policies were about shaping the behavior of the population. Besides racial segregation, the use of state-controlled brothels was a way to prevent the perceived spread of venereal disease in soldiers whose health was crucial for the war effort. Moreover, the introduction of a military brothel system was meant to satiate the hunger of "sexually starved" soldiers returning from the Eastern Front and reward them for their sacrifices, all while keeping them fit to serve again.

As we will see in the chapters to come, these three elements of Nazi prostitution policy—racial segregation, medical control, and reward—will play critical roles in the camp brothels for prisoners. In this regard, the material in this chapter provides a backdrop for understanding how the Nazis arrived at the decision that so startled Erich Roßmann. But before addressing the camp brothels head on, one additional detour is needed.

2 Concentration Camps and Forced Labor

To understand how brothels came to be introduced in Nazi concentration camps, we first need to understand the history of the camp system, its organization, and the role that prisoner labor came to play in the German war economy. By the end of this chapter, it will be clear that of these three aspects it was the last that would prove most decisive in the decision to establish brothels for camp prisoners. For at root, the brothels were a response to a stark dilemma: how to increase the output of forced labor—desperately needed for the war effort—without having the resources to keep prisoners healthy and well nourished. As we will see, the measures that camp officials devised to resolve that dilemma would fail again and again—no less so than in the case of the camp brothels.

The Establishment of a Concentration Camp System

The Nazi concentration camp system stretched across Europe in a complex network of twenty-four main camps and about one thousand subcamps.[1] Over the course of the Nazi dictatorship, the system underwent numerous transformations. The function of the camps changed, and the living conditions varied both among camps and across their individual stages of development. The history of the Nazi concentration camps can be divided into five phases.[2]

The first phase began immediately after the Nazis seized power and lasted until early summer 1936. During this period, makeshift camps were established throughout the German Reich in disused factories, meeting rooms, inns, cellars, and riding halls. The organizations in control of the camps differed from facility to facility—it could be the police, the SA, or the SS—and many closed after only a few weeks or months. The early camps were places of brutal violence. The beatings and torture that occurred in them were meant to deter further resistance from the population at large. In 1933, around eighty thousand people were placed in the camps.[3]

The legal basis for the camps and the unchecked terror they unleashed on the population was created the day after the Reichstag fire. On February

28, 1933, Paul von Hindenburg, at Hitler's urging, issued the Decree of the Reich President for the Protection of People and State, which suspended the civil liberties guaranteed by the Weimar Constitution. It permitted the Gestapo, the SA, and the SS to take suspects into "protective custody" (*Schutzhaft*) without a court order. One month later, the regime declared a state of emergency under the Enabling Act of 1933 and sent large numbers of communist functionaries and members of parliament to concentration camps. The wave of arrests was followed by a period of political consolidation during which many were set free. By August 1934, only about 1,200 prisoners remained in concentration camps. But the early camps had served an important purpose: They contributed to the atmosphere of menace that helped the Nazis maintain their hold on power and secured the reputation of the camps as places to be feared by all.[4]

An exception among the early camps was Dachau. Unlike the other camps during the first years of the Nazi regime, which were characterized by short-term detainment and haphazard violence, Dachau was conceived from the start for permanent, well-ordered internment. It was initiated by Heinrich Himmler, the commander of the Schutzstaffel and head of all concentration camp staff. He appointed SS Oberführer Theodor Eicke to run the camp in a way that could serve as a model for future camps throughout the Reich.[5] In 1934, Himmler, who by then oversaw the Gestapo and all German police outside Prussia, named Eicke chief of the Concentration Camps Inspectorate. The choice of Eicke was a clever move on the part of Himmler, for it placed the camps solely within the purview of the SS, outside the reach of the Ministry of the Interior and the Ministry of Justice. Under what would later be known as the "Dachau model," the small, improvised concentration camps were closed in favor of large, strictly regimented facilities with standardized rules governing prisoner behavior, punishment, and identification. By the spring of 1935, the restructuring was complete, and the Concentration Camps Inspectorate now oversaw Dachau, Lichtenburg, Esterwegen, Sachsenburg, Moringen, Bad Sulza, and Berlin's Columbia-Haus.[6]

The second phase of Nazi concentration camps began in the summer of 1936 with the opening of Sachsenhausen, the system's first modern camp. Based on the Dachau model,[7] it housed prisoners not in old industrial halls or abandoned buildings but in symmetrically arranged wooden barrack huts. It consisted of a prisoners' camp, a commandant's office, camp workshops, barracks for the SS guards (by then renamed the Totenkopfverbände), a guard training area, and residences for SS commanders. In 1938, the office of the Concentration Camps Inspectorate was established in the immediate vicinity of the camp, making Sachsenhausen the administrative hub of the camp system in addition to its largest facility. As at Dachau, prisoners had to follow a uniform system of rules and identification and were subject to draconian punishments for even minor offenses.[8]

The construction of Sachsenhausen was made possible by Hitler's decisions to organize SS camp guards into a military unit and to authorize the financing of the concentration camps with public funds. As a result, the SS could begin expanding and building a number of large camps following the new organizational model. In 1937, the SS demolished Dachau's old munitions factory, which housed prisoners, and built wooden barrack huts in its place. That same year, the SS established Buchenwald. In 1938, it erected the Flossenbürg camp outside Weiden and the Mauthausen camp near the Austrian city of Linz. In May 1939, the women's concentration camp in Lichtenburg was dissolved, and a larger women's camp, Ravensbrück, was established not far from the town of Fürstenberg. The locations of several of the new camps make plain their growing economic importance: Buchenwald, Flossenbürg, and Mauthausen were all next to quarries. The prisoners in the large camps consisted less of political opponents, as in the early years, than of "antisocials," "career criminals," "the work-shy," Jehovah's Witnesses, and homosexuals.[9] After the November pogroms in 1938, 26,000 Jews were sent to the camps. A large number of them were released on the condition that they immediately leave the German Reich and transfer their property to the state. At the end of 1938, approximately 12,000 prisoners were in Nazi concentration camps. About 70 percent of them were classified as antisocial.[10]

The outbreak of war, in 1939, marked the start of the third phase of the concentration camp system. During this phase, the system underwent a tremendous expansion. The number of prisoners increased rapidly, and by March 1942 had reached eighty thousand individuals. Space became scarce—most camps were designed for only five thousand prisoners—and the SS built six more concentration camps in border regions. In May 1940, the Auschwitz concentration camp was established east of Katowice. It was initially designed to hold ten thousand prisoners and later developed into the largest facility in the camp system. In the same year, Neuengamme, a subcamp of Sachsenhausen, was made an independent concentration camp. One year later, Groß-Rosen near Liegnitz and Natzweiler in Alsace followed suit. In 1942, the civilian prison camp Stutthof near Danzig was brought under the control of the Concentration Camps Inspectorate and made a state concentration camp. During this time, the demographic composition of the prisoner populations underwent significant changes. As German troops advanced into other countries, the SS began to send increasing numbers of foreign enemies to the camps. Most were Poles or Soviets, but they also included French, Czechs, Yugoslavs, Dutch, Belgians, and Norwegians. By early summer 1940, German prisoners made up only between 5 and 10 percent of prisoners in the camps.[11]

It was also during this time that prisoners faced deteriorating conditions in the camps. The mortality rate rose in Dachau from 4 percent in 1938 to 36 percent in 1942; in Buchenwald, from 10 percent in 1938 to 19 percent in 1942; and in Mauthausen, from 24 percent in 1939 to 76 percent in 1940.[12] It was also during this time that the concentration camps became places of execution and extermination. At Buchenwald, a horse stable was repurposed for shooting Russian prisoners of war; at Sachsenhausen, the SS shot them at a killing site known as "Station Z." In 1941, Soviet prisoners of war at Auschwitz were gassed for the first time. The SS dispatched others less directly through *gezielte Verelendung*, the "deliberate infliction of misery."[13]

In 1941, the Nazi's launched Operation Reinhard, whose purpose was the systematic murder of Jews in the Government General territory of German-occupied Poland. Odilo Globočnik, in direct contact with Hitler and Himmler, organized the mass murder of about two million Polish Jews in the gas chambers of Bełżec, Sobibór, and Treblinka, which lay outside the official SS-controlled system.[14] In 1943, after the guards finished their gruesome task and the extermination camps were dismantled, another camp, this one under the authority of the Concentration Camps Inspectorate, became the central site of Nazi mass murder and the Final Solution: Auschwitz. In early 1942, the SS began murdering Hungarian Jews in the gas chambers of Auschwitz-Birkenau. It wasn't long before Nazis were sending Jews, Sinti, and Roma from all over Europe to their deaths at the camp.[15]

Despite the campaigns of extermination, the number of prisoners increased. In April 1943, 203,000 people were held in concentration camps; by August 1944, the number had risen to more than half a million; by the end of the war, it was as high as seven hundred thousand. The proportion of Germans in the concentration camps fell below 10 percent.[16] The soaring numbers of inmates characterized the fourth phase of the concentration camps. It was driven by the growing importance of prisoner labor as the German economy geared up for total war. In spring 1942, Albert Speer took over as Minister of Armaments, and Fritz Sauckel became General Plenipotentiary for Labor Deployment.[17] The SS Main Economic and Administrative Office (WVHA) was established to organize and manage the economic projects of the SS.[18] Its head, Oswald Pohl, had been exploiting prisoner labor for SS enterprises since 1936.[19] The WVHA had the task of directing prisoner labor for the arms industry while ensuring that the prisoners remained under the control of the SS. The incorporation of the concentration camps into the war economy opened the sphere of influence of the SS among institutions and industries benefiting from forced labor. Beginning in 1943, the SS established subcamps near arms factories and private companies. The satellite camps changed the topography of the camp system. Instead of keeping prisoners locked up in a permanent camp, they were once again distributed among various temporary facilities. In most cases, the total number of prisoners in the subcamps exceeded that in the main camps.[20] In 1944, a new type of concentration camp emerged: the subterranean factory camp. Tens of thousands of prisoners had to dig underground caverns for relocating the production of V2 rockets and fighter planes. The average life expectancy in the subterranean factories was extremely low.[21]

The final phase of the camp system began in 1944, as the Allies began to push German forces back on both fronts. In July, the Red Army liberated thousands of prisoners from the Majdanek concentration camp near Lublin. Soon after, the SS began to evacuate Auschwitz. The goal was to ensure that no prisoner would be found alive by the Allies. The evacuation of the camps near the front caused deaths to skyrocket. Many prisoners were too weak to leave the camps. Those who were unable to march were left to die in the infirmaries. The prisoners who were able to make the trip eventually wound up at camps inside Germany. But these were soon overcrowded and short of supplies, making them veritable death camps. In the last weeks of the war, the SS closed the large concentration camps in Germany and drove the prisoners to destinations unknown. Prisoners at Flossenbürg and Dachau camps were told they were being taken to a fictitious Alpine fortress; prisoners from Sachsenhausen and Neuengamme were marched toward the North Sea. In most cases, there was no place to go; the goal was to let the exhausted prisoners starve to death. It is hard to know today the true death toll from the final months and weeks of the war. It is likely that between one-third and one-half of the seven hundred thousand people still imprisoned in January 1945 died. The exact number of all people murdered or left to die in the camps is unknown. It is assumed that, including the Jews murdered in the gas chambers of Auschwitz-Birkenau, between 1.9 and 2 million people died in the camps.[22]

"The society of the concentration camp," Wolfgang Sofsky writes, "was a system of glaring differences and extreme inequality."[23] One of the key mechanisms in that regime of discrimination was the identification system first used in Dachau and later introduced in all the Nazi concentration camps.

Colored triangles marked prisoners as belonging to distinct groups: Red triangles were for political prisoners; black triangles, for antisocials; green triangles, for criminals; pink triangles, for homosexuals; purple triangles, for Jehovah's Witnesses; and blue triangles, for foreign forced laborers and emigrants.[24] Jewish prisoners had to wear a yellow triangle underneath the other triangle at an offset, creating the appearance of a six-pointed star.

The groups had different positions in the camp hierarchy, and these had a direct effect on living conditions, which could mean the difference between life and death.[25] Following Nazi racial ideology, German and Austrian prisoners (referred to as *Reichsdeutsche*) were at the top of the hierarchy, while Soviet prisoners of war and Jews were at the bottom.[26] The triangles of non-German prisoners bore a letter indicating their ethnicity or home country. Among the non-Germans, standing in the camp system was based on the status afforded by Nazi Germany to the prisoner's ethnicity or country. In this way, the SS could segregate prisoners based on origins, creating a microcosm of the social hierarchy that Nazis sought to create in all the territories under their control.[27]

The groups in the camp formed roughly three strata. The lowest stratum was the largest. There, prisoners were constantly being exterminated, and the mortality rate was extremely high. At the very bottom, on the threshold of death, were the *Muselmänner*, prisoners who were nothing more than skin and bones.[28] The middle stratum consisted of prisoners with some degree of social capital, capable of bartering for resources and leveraging their experiences for survival.[29] At the top of the pyramid was a small percentage of prisoners who made up what Sofsky calls the "camp aristocracy." Most were ethnic Germans holding important key positions in the prisoner administration.[30] They benefited from privileges that prisoners in the other strata could only dream of.[31] While most other prisoners starved, they received sufficient rations or even food from the SS kitchen. They did not sleep on cots but in single beds, they owned shoes instead of clogs, and they organized sports competitions and music and theater performances. Some of them were even allowed a night out.[32] During the day, they fulfilled high functionary roles; in the evening, they ate extensively, drank, played cards, and had sex with younger prisoners. Despite having so many privileges, they consciously sought to distinguish themselves from the other prisoners through their manner and appearance and openly flaunted their chumminess with the SS. They wore pressed and tailored coats, walked in shiny polished boots, and even owned watches. Their rich diet became outwardly visible: The fatter a prisoner, the greater his status.[33] When they beat other prisoners, they did it to excess to demonstrate their physical strength, their power, and their membership in an elite.

This perfidious combination of power and privilege enjoyed by the prisoner functionaries had a price, however: If they fell out of favor with the SS, they could be punished with death or stripped of their protection by the guards, exposing them to the vigilante justice of the other prisoners. For all their influence, the prisoner functionaries had to obey SS officers unconditionally and commit violence at their behest.[34] Nevertheless, the power that prisoners in functionary roles could wield proved hard to resist. Early on, fierce competitions broke out among prisoners for the coveted positions. The struggle among the prisoners served the interests of the SS, who had an easier time controlling an inmate population that lacked solidarity.[35]

The system of prisoner functionaries, which had already been effectively used in the Soviet Gulag, was a way to handle the growing population of prisoners. By delegating work to prisoner functionaries, the SS could, with small teams of staff, superintend large numbers of inmates. The prisoner-run administration mirrored the organizational structure of the SS. At the top were the camp elder and his deputies. Below them were the block elders, who supervised the prisoners. The kapos commanded the work detachments. Other important functions were held by prisoners in the clerk room and the labor action office.[36] Some of the prisoners who worked in areas critical for routine operations, such as the kitchen, the laundry, the warehouses, the workshops, and the prisoner infirmary, had considerable influence as well in view of the shortage of food, clothing, and medicine in the camps.[37]

In filling the administrative positions, the SS followed criteria that were racial and political but also pragmatic. Many tasks in the camp administration were usually performed by German prisoners both because they were at the top of the racial hierarchy and because German was the administrative language. Performing administrative work also required bureaucratic skills and organizational talent, and the SS often recruited for those tasks German political prisoners, many of whom had experience working in offices. By contrast, the SS assigned particularly undesirable work details—i.e., those involving hard physical labor such as quarries and mines where life expectancy was very low[38]—to individuals at the bottom of the prison hierarchy. These "low-skilled" inmates could be replaced at any time and were of little value to the SS. In the 1940s, as the SS came to depend on skilled labor for its economic projects, the Nazis stopped using low-level prisoners for work details.[39]

The Economic Importance of Camp Labor

A central aspect in the history of the concentration camps is the seeming tension between the economic importance of camp labor and the mass torture and murder that happened in the camps. In the postwar trials, the Allies adopted the term "extermination through labor," but this did not resolve the matter once and for all. Experts continue to debate which variable was preponderant in the calculation of the Nazis.[40]

In March 1933, the SS began to build a concentration camp and an extensive SS base in an abandoned gunpowder and ammunition factory in Dachau. Unlike the concentration camps that Hermann Göring ordered to be built in Emsland, which belonged to the Prussian state, Dachau was under the control of the SS, though it was located on state property. The SS used prisoners to erect the camp buildings and produce equipment and clothing.[41] This marked the start of a new strategy that the SS would pursue until the end of the war: the exploitation of prison labor to supply and fund its operations. Indeed, prison labor was imperative for the realization of the camp system planned by the Nazis. In the years that followed, Dachau became the central supplier of building materials for the camps.[42] Moreover, Reichsführer-SS Himmler was able to put into practice at Dachau what would later happen on a larger scale: deploying state funds for the expansion and maintenance of concentration camps while allowing the SS to keep all the profits.

From 1933 to 1939, SS founded several economic enterprises in Dachau mostly connected to the implementation of plans envisioned by Heinrich Himmler.[43] Three served the exploitation of camp prisoners under commercial law. The first was the Deutsche Ausrüstungswerke GmbH (German Equipment Works Ltd.), which was founded in 1939. By 1943, the company had an annual revenue of 23.3 million Reichsmarks. Employing up to 18,000 prisoners, it supplied the SS with furniture and fixtures. The second was Texled Ltd., which specialized in textiles and leather and had its main plant in Ravensbrück.[44] The third was the Deutsche Lebensmittel GmbH (German Foods Ltd.), which established bakeries and meat processing plants in Dachau, Oranienburg, Auschwitz, and elsewhere. These companies were meant to be a reliable source of supplies for the SS in wartime in addition to a lucrative business model. The status of the companies as private legal entities allowed the SS to benefit from forced labor while using state funds to finance the ventures.[45] That is to say, the SS essentially earned "profits" from state funds it did not have to repay.[46] It was a win-win for the SS: The forced labor enabled self-sufficiency, and self-sufficiency kept state institutions at bay. In addition, the funds generated by the camp system were particularly useful for bailing the SS out of the financial straits in which it frequently found itself.[47]

In addition to meeting the needs of the SS, prison labor would become crucial for Hitler's megalomaniac construction projects. The enormous architectural projects of Nazis—the rally grounds in Nuremberg, the plans for the expansion of the Führer cities, which included remaking Berlin into a world capital known as Germania—exceeded the capacities of the German construction industry in terms of both building materials and labor. Bottlenecks first formed in 1937, soon after construction began on Deutsches Stadion in Nuremberg, which was designed to be the largest sports stadium in the world.[48] Hitler, Himmler, and Speer met and resolved that the SS should use concentration camp prisoners as slave labor for the construction of buildings and the manufacture of building materials.[49] The decision benefited Himmler in particular: It lent him Hitler's support for the creation of a concentration camp system and kept the camps outside the influence of other Nazi ministries.[50] In addition, the SS could sell materials such as bricks and granite for the autobahn and other large building projects and use the proceeds to fund the camps.[51] An important vehicle for this strategy was the Deutsche Erd- und Steinwerke GmbH (German Earth and Stone Works), or DEST, which was founded in 1938 to procure building materials and organize forced labor.[52]

One of the first projects of DEST was the establishment of the Buchenwald concentration camp along with a quarry and brickworks run on penal labor. The initial plans for Buchenwald go back to a 1936 meeting between the inspector of concentration camps, Eicke, and the Reich governor and gauleiter of Thuringia, Fritz Sauckel. Eicke did not believe that the state would agree to cover the costs of a concentration camp and therefore tried to convince Sauckel of the economic advantages of a camp for Thuringia. In particular, he reminded Sauckel that the city of Weimar would need low-cost building materials if it was to complete the Gauforum planned for the city, a massive structure in the neoclassical style of Nazi representative architecture. This was all the convincing that Sauckel needed. He agreed to support the establishment of the Buchenwald concentration camp not far from the city.[53]

DEST was also involved in several new operations for granite extraction that the SS began to set up in 1938. The SS had leased a quarry in the Upper Palatinate village of Flossenbürg and established a concentration camp there in May. In Austria, it surveyed potential sites outside the city of Linz, took over quarries and a stone processing plant in Gusen, commandeered an open pit near the village of Mauthausen, and built a number of camps between the two villages. No sooner had the first prisoners from Dachau been transferred to the new camps than the SS put them to work mining granite. Over the following years, the SS expanded the production facilities and the adjoining camps. The total expenditures for the construction were considerable. For example, the cost of building the Mauthausen-Gusen camp complex was 5.3 million Reichsmarks. However, the investment proved to be worthwhile: Large orders for materials to be used in the construction of the Deutsches Stadion in Nuremberg and the Soldatenhalle in Berlin made the Mauthausen-Gusen facilities some the most profitable of DEST.[54]

In addition to granite, the SS needed bricks and clinker. Probably at Albert Speer's suggestion, a brick plant was built in Oranienburg near Berlin with a planned capacity of 150 million bricks per year, which would have made it the world's largest. The profitability of the project seemed assured because Albert Speer, in his capacity as the General Building Inspector for the Reich Capital (GBI), wanted to purchase 120 million bricks per year over ten years, guaranteeing the purchase of 80 percent of production before the plant was even built. The construction of the brick works was to be carried out by prisoners from the nearby Sachsenhausen camp. However, the clay used for the bricks was of such poor quality that the project was a fiasco. In 1940, the facility produced just 3.1 million bricks, well short of the target of 150 million.[55] By contrast, the brick plant that DEST built in the Neuengamme district of Hamburg—meant to fill orders from Hitler's monumental projects at the port of Hamburg—proved profitable. The work in the new factory and a nearby recommissioned plant was carried out by prisoners from camps in the Neuengamme district.[56]

DEST also opened quarries in Groß-Rosen near the Silesian town of Liegnitz and in the village of Natzweiler in the Vosges mountains of eastern France (which contained the red granite that Speer required for the Deutsches Stadion). But the quarries barely made a profit. Compared with the facilities in Flossenbürg and Mauthausen-Gusen, production was low, and the adjoining concentration camps were small. The camps did not become large complexes until 1943, when granite mining was abandoned for arms production.[57]

A third major area of SS economic activity involved the "Germanization" of Nazi-occupied territories in the East. On October 7, 1939, Hitler named Himmler Reich commissioner for the consolidation of German nationhood. In this capacity, Himmler pushed through a megalomaniacal project that had been a fundamental part of the Nazi worldview since the 1920s: the Generalplan Ost.[58] It was meant to displace thirty-one million people in the occupied eastern territories in order to make room for ethnic Germans.[59] According to Himmler's plans, the SS was to provide the necessary resources for the settlement in the east.[60] Leading the effort was Hans Kammler, the head of Office Group C, which was responsible for all SS building maintenance and construction projects. Kammler would soon rise to become one of the most influential leaders of the Nazi state.[61] His job was to ensure the professional operation of SS construction enterprises. He was responsible for the establishment of regional construction services in eastern occupied territories and for the erection of extermination centers in the east.[62]

In December 1941, as the Wehrmacht advanced unchecked to the west and east—the previous month German troops had reached the outskirts of Moscow—Oswald Pohl issued a five-year "peacetime building program." It earmarked seven billion Reichsmarks for the construction of major police and SS buildings in the Reich and of SS housing and supply services in the occupied territories. It set aside an additional six billion Reichsmarks for police and SS bases and concentration camps "in the new eastern region." The construction volume was so enormous that it required DEST to prioritize building over production. Faced with a looming mountain of debt totaling 100 billion Reichsmarks, the Nazi state wanted to keep construction costs to a minimum. Himmler instructed Pohl to train prisoners as specialists so that they could perform highly skilled work.[63] To those ends, Kammler proposed in February 1942 the creation of "SS construction brigades" consisting of concentration camp prisoners and prisoners of war. Furthermore, he called for central building material depots and central equipment parks to be established across the eastern occupied territories. The change in the course of the war prevented the Nazis from realizing the plan, however.[64]

In early 1942, the Allies began major bombing raids on German cities. Himmler toured the Reich, considered the damage, and abruptly shifted the focus of prisoner labor to the repair of cities. He ordered that camp workshops begin the production of windows and door frames within ten days. The brick factory in Neuengamme was now to produce tiles for damaged roofs. In addition, prisoners assigned to the SS construction brigades were now to be used for repair work in the cities. The first repair brigade was established in October 1942.[65]

The repurposing of Neuengamme's manufacturing lines from bricks for large construction sites to roof tiles for damaged buildings marked a turning point in the economic objectives of concentration camp labor. On September 15, 1942, Speer, who had recently been appointed Reich Minister of Armaments and War Production, met with Himmler, Pohl, and Kammler to discuss three cardinal issues: the extermination of European Jews, the repair of bombed cities, and the ramping up of arms production. Speer approved 13.7 million Reichsmarks for the creation of three hundred barrack huts in Auschwitz for an additional 132,000 inmates. He and the others agreed to accept Himmler's proposal that camp prisoners be put to work in the manufacture of window and door frames for bomb-damaged buildings. Finally, they reached a consensus regarding the large-scale use of inmate labor for the arms industry.[66]

Once the SS began to convert its prisoner-powered enterprises for wartime production, the supply of building materials for architectural projects in the Reich and construction in the occupied eastern territories was no longer a priority. The focus now lay on arms manufacturing and repairing bomb damage.[67] In a secret October 1943 speech to the Reichleiters and gauleiters in Posen, Himmler stressed the importance of propping up Germany's wartime economy: "The establishment of concentration camps, so condemned in peacetime by circles outside the Party, plays a very large role. . . . I believe . . . that if these 50,000 to 60,000 political and criminal felons . . . were not in the concentration camps, then . . . we would have a hard time. But as it is, they are in the concentration camps together with 150,000 others, including a small number of Jews and a large number of Poles and Russians and other rabble. They are now performing about fifteen million working hours a month for comrade Speer's essential tasks."[68]

The realignment in production changed the basic organization of the concentration camps. The main camps became centers surrounded by networks of satellite camps established near plants in the arms industry. The number of prisoners in the satellite camps significantly exceeded that of the main camps. The latter became processing hubs where new prisoners were sent, registered, and quarantined before being distributed to the satellite camps.[69] In 1944, speaking before an assembly of Wehrmacht generals in Sonthofen, Himmler proudly noted the contributions that camp prisoners had made to the war effort:

> In the concentration camps today . . . forty million armament hours are performed each month. In the concentration camps, one-third of the German fighter planes are fabricated by the prisoners, most of whom—that is nine-tenths—are non-German inmates and criminals. Today, one-third of the German rifle barrels are manufactured by them, with one German foreman for every ninety prisoners. [The prisoners] manufacture innumerable other things, from the finest optical instruments to ammunition to huge quantities of grenade launchers and 3.7[cm] Flak guns. In addition, large underground factories have been built from the labor of these camps.[70]

Himmler did not mention the agony of the inmates who built the underground tunnels. As a rule, they survived only a few weeks under the burden of extreme physical exertion, poor rations, and inadequate sanitation. Nor did he tell the generals that many of the weapons the prisoners produced were defective.[71]

From the point that the Nazis took power in 1933, Himmler worked to expand the influence of the SS in the Nazi state.[72] Himmler's central strategy for doing so was to build new organizations in areas where state institutions already existed.[73] The Gestapo and concentration camps limited the reach of the judiciary; the Waffen-SS was an alternative combat branch to the Wehrmacht; the Sicherheitsdienst (SD) competed against the state's other intelligence-gathering services. Himmler also set up institutions for science, culture, and settlement policy to rival those controlled by the Nazi ideologue Alfred Rosenberg and Minister of Food and Agriculture Richard Darré. SS organizations also existed in the areas of population policy, social policy, foreign policy, educational policy, and, of course, economic policy.[74]

As we have seen, the economic operations of the SS were intended to provide building materials for large-scale architectural projects and to ensure the economic independence of the SS. Himmler planned to supply building materials and interior furnishings for settlement projects in the east and drive the expansion of SS facilities and concentration camps.[75] The profits generated from the operations would go to fill the chronically empty coffers of the SS and further buttress its efforts to become self-sufficient.

Some of Himmler's economic projects provided a public utility and were thus presented as "a service to the German national community."[76] Others were experimental in nature or downright bizarre. For example, Himmler pushed for research into the production of fuel from fir roots and for the use of exhaust air from SS bakeries to produce alcohol. He made the chief of telecommunications in charge of carrier pigeons in addition to radio technology.[77] These decisions, the German historian Hermann Kaienburg writes, reveal that "while Himmler was a skilled in power politics, he lacked experience and judgment when it came to technology and economics." Himmler's efforts to compensate produced mixed results: "He obtained his knowledge by reading and from hearsay but was often unable to find his bearings amid the abundance of information. His designs thus seem in part extraordinarily well thought-out and purposeful and in part irrationally fanciful and nonsensical."[78] As we will see, this aspect of Himmler's personality will prove particularly crucial in understanding the decision to establish brothels in the camps.

Labor Productivity

Forced laborers from concentration camps formed the backbone of the SS economy. Without the unfettered exploitation of camp inmates, the SS could not have built its economic empire. Before 1938, camp commandants had significant leeway in how they deployed the prisoners; most set the inmates to work constructing and expanding the camps. Then, starting in 1938, the WVHA deployed prisoners and built new camps in locations that met specific economic objectives. The new economic role played by concentration camp labor caused conflicts between the WVHA and the Concentration Camps Inspectorate. On November 11, 1938, regulations were passed giving the camp administration sole responsibility for the prisoners. If factory or plant managers required forced labor or had issues with prisoners, they had to speak to the camp commandant.[79] The new rules did not eliminate the conflicts, however. Operators often complained about the quality of prisoner labor. Many of the forced workers from the camps were hungry, exhausted, and mistreated, so their output was minimal, and prisoner turnover was high. Another problem was the lack of manpower and prolonged production stoppages, mostly on account of camp rules. Prisoners were not permitted to leave the camp in darkness or fog or during outbreaks of contagious disease. The result was a constant back and forth between the camps and the production facilities regarding the deployment of camp labor. The squabbles ended in 1942, when the inspectorate was incorporated into the WVHA, subordinating the concentration camps to the economic interests of the SS. Commandants were now obligated to deploy camp laborers in accordance with the principles of economic efficiency.[80] But this did not resolve a much larger problem: the shortage of skilled workers in SS factories and the low productivity of prisoners in general.[81]

Since opening the Dachau camp, the SS had deployed skilled concentration camp prisoners in its workshops. The positions were coveted among the prisoners because the workshops provided shelter from the weather. Moreover, the longer they worked in the workshops, the more familiar they became with the production process and the harder it was for the SS to replace them, which meant better treatment: The SS could ill afford to beat its most valuable workers. At first, the number of prisoners with manual skills was small; the vast majority possessed no specialty skills and continued to be subject to brutal treatment. But once the SS started using prisoners in factories, more and more inmates underwent specialty training—and then those prisoners became difficult to replace, too. If the SS continued in this fashion, it would risk swelling the number of privileged prisoners and upending a camp hierarchy that relied on repression. DEST thus decided to use concentration camp prisoners exclusively for unskilled labor and deploy civilians for skilled work. Prisoners performed heavy labor in the quarries and in the transport of materials and were subject to regular beatings from their supervisors. The workshops were reserved only for skilled stonemasons.[82]

In 1941, the SS reintroduced prisoners into skilled positions in an effort to save money. At first, only ethnic Germans were allowed to perform skilled jobs. Only later were foreigners—Czech craftsmen, Polish engineers, Dutch students—allowed to do the work. Starting in September 1940, DEST began systematically training prisoners to become skilled stonemasonry workers. The training was held in Flossenbürg and Mauthausen, and the trainees received special incentives including separate accommodations, extra rations and tobacco allowances, and permission to write and receive additional correspondence. In the second half of 1941, the training was accelerated amid orders to increase the production of cut stone. Expecting imminent victory, Himmler ordered the training of at least ten thousand bricklayers and five thousand stonemasons for construction projects in the eastern occupied territories. The trainees were to be singled out from the "indifferent masses"[83] and given additional rations and better clothing to increase their efficiency. In the following years, more and more workers received specialist training. At the DEST plant in Neuengamme, for example, the commercial office was under the direction of concentration camp prisoners. The SS promised the prisoners that they would be released if they performed well and, astonishingly, made good on their promise.[84]

Regardless of how many workers they trained, the SS still faced another hurdle: low productivity. The problem had already become severe as the SS began to ramp up production. For example, the productivity of a prisoner at the construction site of the brick works in Sachsenhausen was only 20 to 25 percent that of a civilian laborer. In the DEST quarries, prisoner productivity was only 10 to 20 percent that of a civilian. In highly mechanized SS operations, such as Texled, output was only slightly below that of a civilian worker.[85]

Low output was also a problem in Kammler's SS construction brigades. He planned to assign 175,000 prisoners to the units. The enormous number—the camps did not even hold that many prisoners at that time—resulted from a calculation of prisoner productivity. He assumed that the output of a prisoner would amount to 50 percent of a German worker.[86] Himmler agreed with Kammler's decision to create construction brigades but criticized his calculation:

> I am not satisfied with the simple calculation that prisoners are assigned only 50 percent of the labor power relative to skilled German workers. Simply taking twice the number is too simple and convenient. You have to go about it in the right way. In practice, the imprisoned unskilled worker must at least perform better than the free unskilled worker. It is not clear why the imprisoned skilled worker should not perform the same as the skilled worker living in freedom. Here is the greatest reserve of labor power. The means of extracting that potential has been entrusted by the Concentration Camps Inspectorate to the head of the Main Economic and Administrative Office.[87]

High productivity, Himmler explained, was especially needed if the Nazis were to succeed in "Germanizing" the eastern occupied territories.

Initial Efforts to Increase Labor Output

In 1941, IG Farben decided to build a new plant in Auschwitz for the production of synthetic rubber.[88] In addition to its proximity to the coal mines in Katowice, its sufficient water supply, and good connections to rail lines and highways, the advantage of the Auschwitz site was the ability to use concentration camp prisoners in the construction of the plant and then in production.[89] Heinrich Himmler, who initially saw Auschwitz as a "model project" for eastern settlement, was also interested in the construction of a large industrial complex at Auschwitz.[90] IG Farben and the SS agreed that the SS would receive three Reichsmarks per day per person for unskilled labor and four a day for skilled. This seemed to be a profitable deal for both sides, but the use of prisoners quickly proved problematic.[91]

At a meeting between Auschwitz's commandant Rudolf Höß and representatives of IG Farben on March 27, 1941, prisoner output was set at 75 percent that of a normal worker.[92] This figure would turn out to be pure fiction. IG employees estimated the output of prisoners to be 50 percent less than free workers because of their poor physical conditions and lack of manual skills, while factory directors put it at 30 to 40 percent.[93] A weekly report from IG Farben in Auschwitz in December 1941 states that the output of Polish forced laborers and concentration camp prisoners "still leaves much to be desired." "Based on our experience so far," it concludes, "only brute force has been effective with these people.[94]

The commandant of Auschwitz approved the use of brute force, but it was ultimately ineffective because the root causes lay in poor rations, disease, and the several-kilometer march from Auschwitz to Monowitz that the prisoners undertook each day.[95] In the following months, low productivity remained the subject of discussions between the SS and IG Farben.[96] At the end of 1941, IG Farben urged the SS to accommodate the concentration camp prisoners on the grounds of IG Auschwitz, at the Buna plant.[97] The WVHA agreed, and Oswald Pohl, who visited Auschwitz on September 22, 1942, personally advocated the speedy construction of a subcamp near the plant. The IG converted a labor camp known as "Camp IV" into a concentration camp for 4,500 prisoners. On October 28, 1942, the SS opened the Monowitz camp.[98]

The relocation of the prisoners to Monowitz failed to increase the prisoners' productivity, however. IG Farben began to consider a quota system for the prisoners in the spring of 1942. It already had experience with such systems; many plants had departments responsible for implementing quotas and bonuses. In this, it followed DEST, which started paying bonuses to hard-working prisoners probably as early as 1940. The total value of the bonuses paid out in 1941 was very low, which was probably attributable to the fact that only a few received such premiums in the first place.[99]

Walter Dürrfeld, the construction manager of the IG Farben plant in Auschwitz and its later director, commissioned the mechanical engineer Karl Häseler to devise a bonus system for concentration camp prisoners.[100] The system worked out by Häseler calculated the time allotted for work according to a standard model and compared it with the actual time required. Bonus vouchers were to be issued daily, with stamps indicating the type of reward. A soup spoon meant an extra portion of hot food; a bread stamp meant extra bread. A sun containing a number indicated days of early release.[101]

At a meeting with SS commanders at Auschwitz, Dürrfeld presented the proposed system. Commandant Höß considered it "quite feasible."[102] People at the meeting jokingly referred to it as the "FFF system." The letters probably stood for *Fressen, Freizeit,* and *Freiheit,* "food," "free time," and "freedom."[103] The bonus system that IG Farben and the SS devised for Auschwitz was introduced in 1942. The SS began to issue bonus vouchers that same year.[104] The individual IG Farben factories and workshops paid out cash bonuses in the form of vouchers based on assessments by factory foremen and engineers. The vouchers could be redeemed in the camp canteen.[105] Some prisoners were trained to calculate the bonuses. They first made a preliminary calculation and worked out time targets for determining the premium amounts. By mid-December 1944, there were about thirty prisoner "calculators," covering a total of almost five hundred prisoners in the areas of assembly and construction.[106]

The IG wanted to introduce a credit system that had previously been tried with English prisoners of war. For every ten hours they worked, unskilled laborers received three Reichsmarks' worth of vouchers, while skilled craftsmen received four Reichsmarks' worth.[107] Initially, IG planned to grant prisoners time off for the credits they earned, which increasing numbers of civilian workers requested.[108] The prisoners rejected this form of bonus, however, since they would always be employed in some way or another by the SS in the Monowitz camp even if they had time off from the factory.[109] IG Farben also considered paying prisoners who had been employed in an IG plant for more than half a year a premium of fifty Reichspfennigs per day. This amount was to be increased by the same amount for each additional half year. But given the high mortality rates of the prisoners, the proposal was completely absurd, and it was rejected by the WVHA's Office Group D.[110] Another proposal by IG Farben was to promise prisoners they could be released from the camp for doing good work. It, too, went unrealized.[111] Starting in 1942, the SS replaced the Polish prisoners working in Monowitz with Jews. With the establishment of the Final Solution, there could no longer be any question of releasing Jewish prisoners.[112] Besides, hiring out its prisoners was too profitable for the SS to forgo such a valuable source of revenue.

A "Natural" Incentive for Higher Output

In his letter to Pohl from March 23, 1942, Himmler proposed a new idea for "extracting the potential" from unskilled prisoners, "the greatest reserve of labor power." Fortunately, a solution for increasing productivity and helping the Nazis "Germanize" the east was at the ready: "I consider it necessary that women in brothels be supplied in the freest form to industrious prisoners." Coupled with "some small wage for meeting quotas," the brothels would increase work output "enormously."[113] In a letter written to Pohl the following year, Himmler conceded that his call for the introduction of brothels was not "exceptionally elegant." But he noted that it was "natural, and if I have this naturalness as a driving force for higher performance, I find that we are obliged to exploit this incentive."[114] He believed, in other words, that the sexual exploitation of women could be a powerful incentive for male prisoners.

This was the not the first time that Himmler had opted for this "natural" solution. As I discussed in the previous chapter, Himmler seems to have been convinced that sex could solve a great many problems. It could keep men from engaging in homosexual behavior, prevent foreign workers from having sex with German women, and satisfy "sexually starved" troops returning from the east. Because the male sex drive was natural, there was nothing shameful about using prostitution to channel male desires—whether to fight homosexuality or motivate prisoners to work harder.

Nor were the letters to Pohl the first evidence indicating Himmler's intent to create brothels for prisoners. We know that not long after visiting the DEST quarries outside Linz in the spring of 1941, Himmler must have devised the idea of introducing a prisoner brothel at Mauthausen.[115] For by October of that year, Himmler had ordered its construction; operation began in June 1942.[116] It is possible that Mauthausen was the first concentration camp to have a brothel given its proximity to Linz. Recall that Linz is where Himmler had ordered the construction of the "Villa Nova," the first of many brothels built especially for foreign workers in Nazi Germany in the hope that the ready availability of sex would keep them from engaging in sexual relations with German women. Perhaps it was Himmler's success with "Villa Nova"—Hitler and Heydrich immediately embraced the idea—that inspired him to try the same thing with the workers imprisoned in the concentration camps. Himmler, in other words, might have thought he was on a roll. Whatever his thinking, the letter to Pohl from March 23, 1942, makes plain that even before the Mauthausen brothel had opened Himmler had decided that prisoner brothels would play a much larger role in the camp system.[117] Indeed, by the end of 1942, the SS had established two more camp brothels, one at nearby Gusen and the other in Flossenbürg.

The SS persisted with these efforts the following year. A passage from the IG Farben weekly report from June 1–7, 1943, reads: "The discussions that had already taken place with the commandant of the concentration camp about introducing a kind of quota system for the purpose of increasing the work of the prisoners continued. It was agreed that the prisoners would receive certain benefits in the form of food allowances, the promise of freedom, or visits to women's barracks if they achieved certain goals."[118] In the testimony of former IG managers and employees at the 1947 IG Farben trial, no reference is made to the establishment of brothels for concentration camp prisoners. But the subject of bonuses was discussed at length in the cross-examinations.[119] Dürrfeld testified that he was "aware that there was a brothel in the Monowitz prisoner camp," but he stated that there was never any mention of granting a visit to a brothel as a bonus for good work.[120] It is possible that IG Farben was more interested in a system of bonuses than in creating structures to redeem them. At any rate, in the late summer of 1943, the SS established brothels at Monowitz and at the Auschwitz main camp.

Over the next year and a half, the SS would go on to establish brothels in five more camps: Buchenwald, Dachau, Neuengamme, Sachsenhausen, and Mittelbau-Dora, the last of which opened sometime in the first quarter of 1945. Starting in May 1943, all existing and future camp brothels became folded into a larger system designed to increase labor productivity. As we will see, Himmler and other SS officials believed that brothel visits would serve as a particularly motivating incentive afforded to only the hardest working prisoners. The reality, as we will also see, was quite different in execution and outcome.

The Bonus System

Himmler visited the Buchenwald concentration camp in the spring of 1943 to inspect rifle production.[121] He complained to Pohl about the problems he observed. First, he expressed his incomprehension at Weimar's resistance to the construction of a railroad line to the Buchenwald camp. He also criticized Thuringia's resistance to maintaining the camp after the war and the difficulties in setting up a plant for carbine production. He urged Pohl to use "the lash of our words" to push for the creation of arms factories in the concentration camps.[122] He seemed particularly annoyed that there was still no camp brothel in Buchenwald.[123] The Reichsführer-SS asked Pohl to "devote himself more intensively to the whole question of a quota system" and proposed the introduction of a three-tier bonus program.[124] At the first tier, workers would receive cigarettes and "similar extras." At the second tier, they were to earn a small amount of money per day, ten to twenty Reichspfennigs. The amount could be increased to thirty to forty Reichspfennigs a day if the worker performed well. Workers who reached the third tier could visit "the camp brothel once or twice a week."[125] He demanded that a man be found to "develop a bonus system for the camps that was ingenious, almost artful."[126] It is possible that he was thinking of Hans Kammler, who had already endeared himself to Himmler with his ideas for the SS construction brigades. The Reichsführer-SS was in a hurry to implement the bonus program. He wanted the new system in place by May 1, 1943, at the latest.[127]

What Himmler had in mind took its inspiration from the Gulag, a vast system of labor camps in which millions of prisoners had contributed significantly to the infrastructure and the industrialization of the Soviet Union.[128] Himmler writes: "It must be possible for us Germans to muster the same intelligence as the Russians, who, through their wage and food system, have driven an inherently sluggish Russian people to attain the most unbelievable achievements and invent here a veritable perpetuum mobile."[129] Himmler also speaks elsewhere of using a quota system based on the Soviet model. While discussing the construction of camps in Eastern

Europe, he mentioned forcing women and children from "gang populations" to do "useful work" such as weaving baskets and making their rations dependent on output. "Prisoners who complete their daily work quotas must, in accordance with the Russian quota and Stakhanovite system, receive adequate food."[130] There was one area, however, where the Gulag did not serve as a model: the provision of brothels for prisoners. Soviet officials seem never to have considered it necessary to offer sex as a "natural" incentive for greater output. Besides prostitution being illegal in the USSR, this is probably because the Gulag quota system worked well enough as it was.

On May 15, 1943, the WVHA issued the regulation "Dienstvorschrift für die Gewährung von Vergünstigungen an Häftlinge," establishing a mandatory system of bonuses in Nazi concentration camps. The preface to the regulation clearly shows that SS officials had reevaluated prisoner labor and production. The task of the concentration camps was no longer solely to "incarcerate persons who were hostile to people and state and whose behavior endangered the existence and security of people and state."[131] Instead, it was also to include "meaningful work toward the victory of the Greater German Reich through the use of prisoners in production facilities crucial for the war effort."[132] The productivity of the prisoners was generally good, but the "scope and urgency of the work . . . requires *the utmost output from every prisoner*."[133] Productivity was to be increased through "leadership and education" and "bonuses" for prisoners.[134] The regulation justified the bonuses as a means to help the war effort, though it did not mention that bonuses had already been paid for some time at DEST plants and at Auschwitz. Moreover, the assertion that prisoner productivity was generally good grossly mischaracterized the actual output. Indeed, the true purpose of the bonus system may have been to *conceal* the low levels of productivity in the concentration camps so that Himmler could resist the influence of Albert Speer and the Ministry of Armaments.

The new bonus system was to have five rewards as opposed to the three proposed by Himmler in March. The first benefit, *Hafterleichterung*, eased certain hardships imposed on prisoners. Prisoners could send or receive four instead of two letters or postcards per month. Additionally, ethnic Germans could receive a "short, military" haircut.[135] The second benefit afforded extra rations to skilled laborers, physical laborers, and high-performing workers. The regulation portrayed itself as magnanimous yet stern. For the "best workers" and "to spur them on to further achievement," the additional rations "could not be high enough."[136] But if the output of prisoners who received extra rations fell "below the previous level," rations would be reduced until they achieved the same output.[137]

The third type of benefit consisted of vouchers that had monetary value in the camps.[138] The SS sought to reward prisoners "who distinguished themselves through good performance, diligence, and particular interest."[139] The amount of the reward was to be based on the value of the extra work. It ranged from fifty Reichspfennigs to as much as ten Reichsmarks per week for cases of exceptional output. For prisoners working in teams, bonuses were based on collective output. Prisoners working in camp services (tailoring, shoemaking, repair workshops, kitchen details) were also to receive bonuses "in the case of exceptional performance."[140] Prisoners could use the vouchers to buy cigarettes, utensils, food, or a visit to the brothel. The bonus could also be credited to the prisoner's camp savings account. The vouchers were the camp currency and the only way to pay for items in the canteen. The bonuses were funded by the companies for which the prisoners worked. For prisoners who worked in camp services, the vouchers were to be funded by the Reich.[141] Before the introduction of the bonus regulation, prisoners had the option of having money sent to their camp account.[142] The new regulation froze existing funds in the prisoners' accounts; the only money that could be withdrawn came from the output bonuses.[143] "In this way," the regulation explains, "even prisoners who have had savings at the concentration camp since their arrival or from remittances will have to work harder to cover their personal needs in the camp."[144]

The desire to motivate output was particularly pronounced in the case of the fourth benefit identified in the bonus regulation: the ability to buy cigarettes and tobacco in the canteen. Prisoners who failed to meet the work quotas were not permitted to purchase these products even if they had previously earned vouchers for hard work.

The fifth bonus was the possibility of visiting the camp brothel. Unlike the others, it was a "special reward" reserved only for the "top-ranking prisoners."[145] "The prisoners . . . must submit a brief request via the camp director to the camp commandant, who is to examine it at once and make a decision."[146] The camp commandant was authorized to grant permission to visit the brothel a maximum of once a week.[147] The prisoner had to pay a fee of two Reichsmarks in vouchers for each visit. The SS may have based its fee on typical market prices: A visit to a Wehrmacht brothel in occupied Western Europe cost between two and three Reichsmarks; a visit to a foreign worker brothel cost between three and five Reichsmarks.[148] But the SS valued the worth of forced sexual labor much less than other goods in the concentration camp: The admission fee to the camp brothel was less than the three Reichsmarks it cost to buy twenty cigarettes in the canteen.[149] Moreover, of the two Reichsmarks the prisoner paid, forty-five Reichspfennigs were to go to the "inmate of the brothel" and five Reichfpennigs were to go to "the supervising female prisoner." The remaining 1.50 Reichsmarks was to be deposited and reported semiannually to the head of Working Group D.[150] It is still not clear today what this money was used for. Most assume that it served to enrich the SS.[151] It is more likely that the amount was made up of the estimated maintenance costs of the brothel (including food for the forced sex workers) and what was needed to pay off the costs of the brothel's construction. According to the construction application for the Auschwitz main camp, a sixteen-room camp brothel was calculated to cost thirty thousand Reichsmarks.[152] This amount was supposed to be amortized through revenue. In Buchenwald, for example, brothel revenues from July 11, 1943 (the day the brothel opened) to December 31, 1943, totaled 18,960 Reichsmarks, with 14,097 Reichsmarks going to the SS.[153] Revenues within the first months of brothel operation, therefore, covered a large part of the construction costs. This may be one of the reasons why, in February 1944, the SS decided to forgo its cut from the brothel's revenues—the brothel had already paid for itself.

Barely three months after the bonus regulation was issued, Obersturmbannführer Gerhard Maurer,[154] the head of the WVHA's Office DII (Labor Deployment of Prisoners), informed concentration camp commanders that the Reich Accounting Office had now also approved funds for bonuses.[155] In October of the same year, Oswald Pohl sent a secret letter to each of the nineteen camp commandants describing arms production in the concentration camps as "a factor of decisive importance for the war."[156] It was imperative, he stated, that the prisoner labor force be expanded. It was now the task of the SS leadership to enforce the "maintenance of the health and efficiency of the prisoners." Prisoners had to "contribute . . . to the achievement of a great victory by the German people."[157] As part of the effort to increase work productivity, Pohl called for a reduction of sick leave to a maximum of 10 percent of the workforce.[158] To this end, Pohl proposed a catalogue of improvements for the improvement of prisoner health. Provisions were to be made for "proper and adequate" food and clothing, for "the exploitation of all natural health products," for "the avoidance of all exertion not directly necessary for work," and for "productivity bonuses."[159] Precise guidelines were established for everything from prisoner diets to workplace lighting. The SS even offered prisoners prizes for "practical heat-protective clothing" ideas and for suggestions on how to improve the workplace.[160] But the proposed improvements were utterly absurd given the supply shortages, overcrowding, disease, and exhaustion that constituted camp life. Here, Himmler's grotesque solutions went hand in hand with a completely distorted perception of the living conditions in the camps. In times of chronic malnutrition, the SS wanted to improve the quality of the food; in times of acute material shortages, the SS wanted the huts to be heated; in times when the strain of standing for hours during roll call could be life threatening, the SS thought warm-up exercises were a good idea. But SS leaders were convinced these strategies would work, and they cited the productivity increases achieved by the Soviet system as proof. The rewards they offered prisoners for improvement suggestions were similar to the methods used by the Stakhanovite movement.

In his letter, Pohl characterizes the bonus regulation as "another essential means of increasing the output of prisoners."[161] It was crucial that camp commanders "continuously and conscientiously" exhaust the possibilities of this regulation. He requested that detailed progress reports and suggestions for improvement be submitted by January 15, 1944.[162] The bonus regulation was implemented with varying degrees of intensity in the concentration camps. At Neuengamme, bonuses were paid to prisoners beginning in the fall of 1943.[163] It seems that bonuses were distributed by the SS at Auschwitz but not at other concentration camps, such as Buchenwald.[164]

In 1943, IG Farben had already noticed that bonuses were failing to increase the labor output of Auschwitz prisoners. It demanded that the SS implement special measures such as the swift punishment of "labor evasion." Punishment was to be systematic and orderly. The IG did not want prisoners to be handled with kid gloves; nor did it want SS officers to abuse their authority. But disciplinary measures were needed all the same if the plant wanted to achieve rapid output increases.[165]

Less than a month after the deadline for feedback and suggestions, Pohl issued an "addendum with six supplementary points."[166] Sick prisoners were permitted to use the bonuses credited to their accounts to "meet their personal needs." New prisoners would have a chance during the three-week quarantine to access up to thirty Reichsmarks of the money they brought with them. In addition, prisoners who performed well were to be given the opportunity to visit the camp cinema.[167] Rewards for suggested improvements were included in the bonus regulations. Regarding visits to brothels, the decree stated that the fee for a visit to the "Sonderbau" would be reduced from two Reichsmarks to one. Ninety Reichspfennigs would go to the forced sex worker and 10 percent would go to the "supervising" prisoner. The SS would officially forgo its cut of the brothel earnings.[168]

The minor changes provided by the addendum could not improve the system. First, the camps lacked the basic supplies on which the changes depended. Since the war, almost all the items stocked by the camp canteens were unusable, or they were inedible for the prisoners in their weakened states. With so little for prisoners to buy, the bonus vouchers failed to have an incentive effect.[169] Another problem was that not enough prisoners were receiving bonuses. Heinrich Schwarz, the commander of Auschwitz III in Monowitz, stated in April 1944 that "the amount of bonus money issued by the firms is still too small in relation to the total number of prisoners employed."[170] Schwarz ordered the heads of the subcamps to contact factory directors and make sure that more vouchers were issued.[171] Prisoners also complained about the lack of bonuses.[172] It is likely that some factory operators were reluctant to buy bonus vouchers from the SS and sought to maximize their profits instead. But the main reason for the low number of bonus vouchers was most likely that the industry understood the scheme's ineffectiveness.[173] The SS insisted on the system, however, so they signed an agreement with the companies guaranteeing the distribution of bonus vouchers.[174] It had little effect, however. Prisoner output at the Flossenbürg quarries was just 12 percent that of civilians in 1941, the same year that DEST began distributing bonuses in Flossenbürg. By 1943, the productivity of prisoners had increased, but it was still only 17.4 percent that of regular workers.[175]

Against this backdrop, the meeting of representatives from various chemical plants in Katowice, Silesia, on December 11, 1944, was bitterly ironic. The participants noted that the bonus system had not shown the expected results and concluded that there was a direct correlation between prisoner diet and productivity. But the finding did not lead to improved treatment of the prisoners. Instead, the plants decided to redistribute the rations: The most productive prisoners were to receive more at the expense of the weaker ones. Their plan could not be put into practice, however: A few weeks later, the Red Army liberated Silesia.[176]

Alongside industry representatives, some concentration camp commanders also seemed to doubt the bonus regulation. While in Auschwitz the system was officially introduced on June 1, 1943, it did not arrive in Mauthausen until early January 1944. In Groß-Rosen, it did not come until March 1944.[177] The introduction of camp brothels was also delayed. In Dachau, Neuengamme, and Sachsenhausen, the brothels opened between

April and August 1944.[178] Although organizational problems and material shortages played a role, lack of confidence in the system and the effect of camp brothels seem to have been the primary reasons. The former camp physician of Sachsenhausen, Dr. Baumkötter, testified that the construction of the camp brothel occurred only after repeated reminders from the camp commandant, who was acting on Himmler's orders.[179] For the next few months, no more brothels were established in the larger concentration camps.[180]

But the WVHA continued to believe that the bonus system was working and even wanted to expand it. In 1944, it devised a plan that would give all prisoners a low wage.[181] It also relied on the bonus system in projects to relocate arms production underground after Allied bombing raids increased.[182] One of the thirty projects planned was the plant for the production of V2 rockets in Kohnstein, near Nordhausen. The Mittelbau-Dora camp located there was the last independent concentration camp to be established in the Third Reich and the center of a massive weapons manufacturing complex in the southern Harz region.[183] In February 1944, the SS began issuing bonuses that Mittelbau-Dora prisoners could use to buy food and other items in the camp canteen. Almost all the operations in the camp, comprising some thirty companies, issued vouchers.[184] Most of the bonuses went to the higher-skill inmates in the production units, on whom the SS depended. Only a very small number were given to the prisoners in the construction details, who were disposable.[185]

The production of V2 rockets fell far short of expectations, however. Under pressure to improve labor output at Mittelbau-Dora, the head of the Hygiene Institute of the Waffen SS, Joachim Mrugowsky, called for special measures to increase productivity, ranging from the distribution of cigarettes as bonuses to the introduction of recreational activities (such as cinema, live entertainment, and ball games).[186] In July 1944, Mrugowsky presented an extensive catalogue of improvements to working hours and rations.[187] The rocket engineer and V2 designer Wernher von Braun also demanded an increased "readiness for action" from the prisoners.[188]

A few months before the evacuation of Dora, the SS set up a brothel for prisoners.[189] The staff that supervised the Mittelbau complex came up with the idea of applying the camp brothel model to other SS enterprises, such as underground arms production. This led to plans to build a brothel at the Ebensee subcamp in Mauthausen, but they were never realized.[190] The staff frequently discussed the use of a bonus system, and at underground work sites they introduced a modified version called the "Russian method" that relied on the provision of extra food rations.[191]

Assessing the Bonus System

What influence did the bonus regulation have on living conditions in the camps? Let's consider the bonuses one by one, beginning with extra correspondence privileges. It's true that letters could lend prisoners strength as "treasures from the other half of the globe."[192] But they could also bring bad news, putting considerable strain on prisoners' already unstable mental states. Prisoners often had to wait weeks for a reply. "This terrible war of nerves represented one of the most demoralizing hazards of camp life," Eugen Kogon recalls. The SS exploited the prisoners' uncertainty by spreading lies about the fidelity of spouses and the well-being of children.[193] Moreover, it was difficult for the majority of prisoners to write letters because they had to be written in German, and the content of the letters was censored. Under these circumstances, it is highly doubtful that more correspondence would have produced a marked improvement in prisoners' living conditions or morale.[194]

The value of haircuts was equally dubious. To be clear, the privilege of having a haircut was less about the *cut* than about the *hair*. Among the masses of camp prisoners with shaven heads, hair conferred status in the camp hierarchy. It also provided a reminder of one's humanity and a boost of confidence.[195] But the prisoners who stood to benefit the most from hair were the ones who, like the prisoner functionaries, could afford to stand out. Normal prisoners did everything they could *not* to attract notice. Like letter writing, hair was a luxury in conditions where basic needs were not being met.

By contrast, extra rations could have truly improved a prisoner's situation—if only the system had worked as planned. In reality, kapos and the prisoner functionaries could arbitrarily withhold extra rations from prisoners who had earned them. And, more critically, food was scarce during the war; only in a few cases is there any evidence that extra rations were handed out. For instance, at the end of June 1944, IG Farben began distributing "Buna soup."[196] Named after the Buna Werke factory in Monowitz, the soup was a thin gruel consisting of a few potatoes and turnips, hardly enough to make a noticeable improvement to prisoners' diets.[197]

As for the bonus vouchers, distribution was often arbitrary and depended on the social position of the prisoner and the favor of the foreman. As a rule, prisoners in high-ranking positions received the most.[198] The bonuses tended not to reward hard workers; rather, they reinforced the prison hierarchy and promoted corruption. In addition, since war had broken out, the camp canteens had scarcely any food that was edible, never mind nourishing.[199] The reality of camp life was far removed from the improved diets called for in the bonus regulation. As the Buchenwald survivor Eugen Kogon writes: "The great majority of the prisoners were in a state of malnutrition and exhaustion. Newcomers usually lost up to fifty pounds in weight in the first two or three months. Many weighed less than 110 pounds. There was a marked shortage of vitamins, which greatly contributed to the spread of disease and epidemics."[200]

As I noted, the bonus regulation froze existing prisoner savings accounts, cutting off access to the money they had already received and barring them from future outside transfers. In other words, the regulation tied the prisoner's fate to bonuses. If a prisoner did not have vouchers because his work detail received only a few or because he did not have a good relationship with his foreman, his living conditions would deteriorate. All that prisoners could hope for was to get their hands on cigarettes, which could be traded for useful objects and food often unavailable in the camp canteen. Other privileges, such as visits to the cinema, could have a positive effect on a prisoner's morale, but they did not satisfy the basic needs of most prisoners. In order to survive, prisoners had to find enough food to fuel the energy they expended through labor. And they had to be able to protect themselves from violence and death at the hands of the SS and their helpers. The bonus regulation utterly failed to meet prisoners' existential needs. The perks it provided were scarcely a drop in the bucket.

And, finally, what of the camp brothels? Did they fulfill their intended purpose? The answer is no. On the contrary: They epitomized all the ways that the bonus system was out of touch with reality and bore the hallmarks of economic dilettantism. Like the other perks, the brothels were in no way tailored to the needs of most prisoners. At best they reached only the skilled workers and prisoner functionaries on whom the SS depended to run the camps. As I will discuss later, for the vast majority of prisoners, the camps lacked the conditions necessary to sustain a sense of one's own sexuality, let alone sexual desire. If prisoners did not have enough food to meet the desired labor output, how would sex, which requires expending even more energy, help them work harder? Ultimately, the brothels, like the bonus system, rewarded those whose work maintained the Nazis' hold on power. And by improving the lives of only a privileged few, they further fragmented the inmate population.

Why was Himmler so certain that the brothels could play a key role in boosting the output of forced laborers? No doubt part of the answer lies in Himmler's strange ideas about "natural" incentives and the power of sex to motivate men. But another part has to do with the daunting nature of Nazi Germany's labor requirements: The enormous construction projects envisioned by Himmler and Speer, the megalomaniac scope of the settlement plans in the east, and the urgent need for more arms production required armies of workers. Without the labor reservoir provided by the concentration camps, executing these projects would have been inconceivable. But even the hundreds of thousands of forced laborers at the disposal of the Nazis were not enough given the productivity levels of a weak and starving workforce. The bonus system Himmler introduced to increase output took its inspiration from the Soviet Gulag. But unlike the Gulag, which tied food rations to work output, the camp system lacked the resources to give prisoners proper nourishment, let alone bonus rations for exceeding quotas. It is possible, therefore, that the brothels were the product of wishful thinking: What was not provided by adequate diets and sanitary conditions could be achieved through sex's ability to inspire superhuman feats of will in men. This was obviously a wild fantasy. Industrial representatives and camp commandants were right to doubt the effectiveness of the brothels and other bonuses. But even had they embraced the system immediately, it would have made little difference. The system was simply incapable of handling the labor challenges faced by Nazi Germany.

3 Recruitment

The brothels may not have been effective in boosting labor output, but they did have an effect on camp prisoners—first and foremost, the women who served as forced sex workers. And the effect on these women took hold long before they set foot in a camp brothel. For once the Nazis had decided to establish brothels in concentration camps, they had to find women to work in them.

The recruitment process began in 1942 and continued through 1945 as new camp brothels were added and women in existing brothels needed replacing. The Ravensbrück concentration camp, which was for women, served as the primary site for the recruitment, selection, and preparation of forced sex workers; Auschwitz-Birkenau was added to the mix one year later. In 1944, the SS decentralized the process, recruiting women in subcamps and from evacuation transports or transferring them from one camp brothel to another. In the final months of war, as the Nazis began to disband the concentration camp system, they moved the main recruitment and collection point for camp brothel workers from Ravensbrück to Bergen-Belsen.

This chapter examines the various stages of the recruitment process in detail. I consider the sites of recruitment, the kind of women who were targeted, and the inducements that the Nazis offered. I am particularly interested in the circumstances of the women who became forced sex workers. What were their living conditions? How were they approached? What were their previous occupations? And what measures did the Nazis use to coerce the women into "volunteering"?

Ravensbrück

In May 1939, the SS established Ravensbrück near Fürstenberg, a popular recreational area fifty miles north of Berlin. It was the only camp exclusively for women until Auschwitz-Birkenau opened in July 1942. Ravensbrück's original structure resembled Dachau: two rows of barrack huts with an administration building at the head. In 1941, Ravensbrück was expanded to include a men's camp. During the six years of its existence, some 132,000 women were deported to Ravensbrück, about 28,000 of whom perished.[1] The Ravensbrück main camp served as a massive hub for selecting female forced laborers and distributing them throughout the Reich. Beginning in the summer of 1942, the main camp also became the camp system's central recruitment site for forced sex workers.[2]

The first forced sex workers were recruited for brothels in Mauthausen and Gusen in mid-1942. A few months later, the SS also selected women for the pseudomedical experiments at Dachau conducted by Dr. Sigmund Rascher, a close friend of Himmler's.[3] The experiments were designed to determine how best to revive pilots who had crashed in icy water. Soviet prisoners of war were immersed in ice water until they lost consciousness and then revived with a variety of methods. One set of experiments used "animal heat," a euphemism for sexual intercourse.[4] In mid-October 1942, four antisocials were transferred from Ravensbrück to Dachau to have sex with the unconscious test subjects. But Rascher refused to use them. The doctor had requested "gypsy" women, but the women sent to Dachau were ethnic Germans. One, the twenty-two-year-old Ursula Krause, had "impeccable Nordic racial characteristics," blonde hair, blue eyes, a "corresponding head shape," and a slim physique.[5] The use of German women in experiments with Soviet "subhumans" went counter to Rascher's racist ideology and would have constituted "forbidden contact" under Nazi laws. The women were returned to Ravensbrück in January 1943.[6]

Initially, the SS attempted to recruit women for the brothels on a voluntary basis, a common way to enlist prisoners for certain work details. The SS usually requested that block elders select "volunteers" but provided little information about the work, apart from promises of improved living standards. The SS deliberately requested prisoners from work details whose living conditions were particularly bad, such as penal companies, where desperation was so great that prisoners would jump at the chance for something better. If sufficient numbers did not volunteer, the SS selected the prisoners themselves.[7]

When putting together the first brothel work units, the SS looked for *Sittendiren,* former prostitutes imprisoned for repeated violations of health code regulations.[8] It was also important that the women were deemed no longer useful in Nazi efforts to increase the birth rate. Himmler set the recruitment profile for women in the camp brothels: "The only strumpets eligible for selection are those in whom it can be assumed that they can no longer be persuaded to live an orderly life based on their previous lives and attitudes, about whom we, on strict inspection, need never to reproach ourselves for corrupting a human being who could still be saved for the

German people."[9] Initially, at least, the SS followed Himmler's criteria, as corroborated by the former camp physician at Ravensbrück, Dr. Gerhard Schiedlausky.[10] Schiedlausky was tasked with reviewing the personnel files of the recruited women and determining whether the women had previously worked as prostitutes.[11] The reason for selecting former prostitutes was obvious: The SS had no experience as "pimps" or in organizing camp brothels. Moreover, they probably believed that former prostitutes would provide less resistance and that visitors would come more willingly if they knew that the women had volunteered for the work.[12]

Firsthand accounts from the camp suggest that the women recruited for the brothels were far from "volunteers," however. "Prostitutes were told to report to a brothel—they said brothel, not whorehouse, so noble," the former nurse Antonia Bruha remembers.[13] Living conditions were particularly difficult; the block was heavily overcrowded, and a large proportion of the women had to sleep on the floor. In her fictionalized biography *The Blessed Abyss*, the Ravensbrück survivor Nanda Herbermann, who in 1942 was assigned to the "whore block" as a block elder overseeing prostitutes of various ages, reports how the SS "requisitioned" ten women from her block for a brothel in Mauthausen.[14] When the SS wasn't coercing the women overtly, they told deliberate lies instead. In 1947, Schiedlausky testified that "the first women who came to Mauthausen had been promised that they would be released after half a year working as prostitutes."[15] This kind of promise was not unusual. The SS knew that prisoners longed for nothing more than to escape the hell of the camps.[16] The period of half a year seemed credible and was short enough that survival seemed possible.[17] On hearing about the promises, Himmler became incensed. "I found out that some madman in the women's camp . . . told the female prisoners that anyone who volunteered for the brothels would be released after six months. . . . Such women," he clarified to Pohl, "may then only be released from the camp if, based on their age, they do not pose a threat to youth, to public health . . . and to public order and safety."[18] The SS at Ravensbrück did not follow Himmler's admonitions, but it was of no consequence: No woman working in a camp brothel is known to have been released after six months.[19] Not that there was a legal basis for release, anyway. It was not the camp director or the "political department" that had the authority to release prisoners but the police station that had committed a person to the camp under the Decree on Preventive Measures by the Police to Combat Crime.[20] Word quickly spread among female prisoners that the promise of release was a lie.[21]

By mid-1943, the SS had built brothels in Buchenwald, Flossenbürg, Dachau, Neuengamme, and Sachsenhausen and thus needed more women, which forced it to cast a wider net.[22] Accordingly, the SS began recruiting German women from among all the antisocials, criminals, and *Bettpolitische* (women who had engaged in forbidden love affairs with foreigners).[23] Antonia Bruha describes how the SS used a "noblewoman from Carinthia" to recruit women from among their ranks, again with the promise of release after six months. Only a few came forward.[24] A more effective factor in recruitment was the inhumane living conditions at the camp, where death seemed certain.[25] In a letter to Himmler, Rascher describes what he heard about one woman's motivation for working in the brothels: "In response to my objection that it was a tremendous disgrace to volunteer as a brothel girl, I was told: 'Half a year in a brothel is better than half a year in concentration camp.' I then heard a list of the strangest conditions from Camp R. The conditions described were confirmed for the most part by the three other brothel girls and the guard who had come with them from Ravensbrück."[26] Herbermann describes how she tried and failed to dissuade a sick young woman from volunteering for the brothel in Mauthausen:

> I have yet to tell of you, beautiful, little Frieda! Many a night I sat on your cot while you convulsed from your severe attacks. I am still happy today about the fact that you always said to me: "You are my mother! I never had a mother besides you!" Yes, Frieda, you told me of your whole fate in life. Through tragic life circumstances you had landed in a bordello all too early, and begged me to help you so that you would be ready for a later life. I did what I could. You knew it. Wasn't it nice, when we prayed the Lord's Prayer together deep in the night? And you begged: "Say the prayer again!" You in particular could have begun a different life someday in freedom, you had a good foundation for that. But you disappointed me and volunteered yourself for the bordello in the Mauthausen Concentration Camp for Men, where the delivery of ten female inmates had been requested. I applied all my powers of persuasion with you, reminded you of your resolved good intentions, of your poor condition. Yes, I warned you that you would never survive it, and I was right. You never came back from Mauthausen.[27]

Parts of this passage are confirmed in other prisoner reports and SS files, in which Frieda is described as a Burgenland "gypsy" admitted to Ravensbrück in 1940 and classified as an "antisocial German." She was recruited for the camp brothel and remained in Mauthausen until its liberation. Although Herbermann later figured that Frieda died in the camps given her frailty, she was still alive in April 1945 and probably survived.[28]

Testimonies from other former prisoners provide some insight into why women decided to work in the brothels. Antonia Bruha reports of a young woman who had been committed to the concentration camp for "forbidden intercourse" and told that her widowed mother was poor and ill. A release after six months meant that she would be able to help her mother.[29] An older woman who volunteered for the "madam" at the camp brothel in Neuengamme is reported to have worked in a police unit responsible for maintaining order while transports were arriving at Ravensbrück.[30] The older woman indicated later that she was doing well in the unit but was afraid that the SS would murder her because she had fought on the side of the Republicans in the Spanish Civil War.[31] There were other women who came to the brothels from relatively good positions. For example, a woman from the Buchenwald brothel was previously an elder in Block 8 at Ravensbrück.[32] A forced sex worker from Sachsenhausen was in charge of barracks duty in her block before being transferred to the camp brothel.[33] Other women who worked in the brothels at the Auschwitz main camp, Flossenbürg, and Sachsenhausen had been imprisoned in the Kaiserwald camp, where the majority of the women were of Jewish origin and where German "antisocial" and "criminal" prisoners worked as supervisors. It can be assumed that the sex workers had performed such functions in Kaiserwald.[34] This may seem at odds with the SS practice of recruiting women from difficult work details. One possible explanation would be that the women had fallen out of favor with the SS for some reason—possibly because they had not performed their work with sufficient rigor or had helped other prisoners—and tried to escape from Ravensbrück by signing up for the brothel. Alternatively, they may have been placed in a penal company and were recruited for the camp brothels from there.[35]

As they sought to meet the demand for women in the brothels, the SS introduced more coercive methods in addition to casting a wider net for volunteer recruitment. The Spanish resistance fighter Lola Casadell, who came to Ravensbrück in 1944, describes how one morning her block elder shouted, "Those who want to go to a brothel should come by my room." "I warn you," the elder added, "if there are no volunteers, we will take you by force."[36] Magdalena Walter was in the Ravensbrück camp lockup when she was selected for the Buchenwald camp brothel in 1943.[37] "And one day . . . we were told not to go to roll call. Of course, we looked at each other stupidly. The work detail had left. After half an hour we were told to step out of the camp lockup. Little old me was there, too."[38] The camp commandant of Ravensbrück, the head female guard, a camp commander unknown to her, and other SS leaders stood in front of the women.[39] "They looked at each of us individually, and picked us out. This one and this one and this number had to step forward. . . . The others had to go back to the camp lockup."[40] It seems that the commanders of the camp in which the brothel was located helped select the women.[41]

The SS also openly selected women on the roll-call square. The Polish survivor Henryka Obidzinska, who was imprisoned in Ravensbrück for about six months in 1943, reports that she twice witnessed SS guards and officers walking past prisoners during a normal roll call and selecting women. Polish women were among them.[42] The practice continued in the following years.[43] In early 1945, Linda Bachmann was selected from the roll-call square for the Mittelbau-Dora camp brothel, one of the last women to be selected for a camp brothel.[44] She recounts that the SS simply called her number at the evening roll call: "And then my name was called and we were told to go to the . . . they didn't say brothel, but the special work detail. We were supposed to go to the camp command . . . and to report to the office of the special work detail. And once we were in the office, we had to wait. Yes . . . why should we go there? We weren't told, we didn't get any answer at all, mind you. And then we were sent to the infirmary."[45]

The SS also recruited women directly from the housing blocks. The manner of the selection could be utterly humiliating. The Ravensbrück survivor Irma Ostermann reports that the camp doctor Dr. Sonntag, together with the camp commandant Max Kögel, used "abusive and insulting language" to gather brothel workers from among "antisocial" women.[46] In the process, they also asked the women a wide variety of questions about their abilities.[47] It seems that the women had already been preselected for brothel work without their knowledge. Anni Kramer says: "I came to Mauthausen from Ravensbrück and did not know at all what to expect and where I was going. What should I have done? If I refused, I would have faced the gas chamber or the quarry. I had no choice."[48]

The women selected for the brothel were subjected to inspection. Magdalena Walter recounts how she and the other women had to go to the infirmary and undress in a room. Then the "whole squadron," consisting of the camp doctor, the commandants of Ravensbrück and Buchenwald, and other SS leaders, entered the room and examined them.[49] The camp doctor at Ravensbrück, Gerhard Schiedlausky, commented on Magdalena Walter's poor physical condition: "Do you want to take the skeleton with you, too?"[50] To which the Buchenwald commandant replied: "She's well-built, we'll feed her again."[51] Linda Bachmann remembers how she was taken to the infirmary, where swabs were taken from the women.[52] During the procedure, the SS treated her "roughly . . . and inhumanely."[53] She and the other women were brought to the camp commandant's office, where they had to strip naked and undergo examination by the SS men as if they were "meat being inspected."[54] Such procedures were not limited to Ravensbrück. The Mauthausen camp clerk Hans Maršálek reports that during the selection for the camp brothel, the commander had a bamboo stick he used to "examine" the naked women.[55]

Linda Bachmann recalled that she was not told what would happen to her. The SS had said that she and the other women would be sent to a "special detail" without stating the true nature of the work. "We didn't know where we were going. 'Special detail' could mean many things."[56] Weeks later, after she and the women arrived at Mittelbau-Dora, she asked about the work detail, but she was only told: "Shut up, you'll see."[57] It was only the camp elder who clued her in about the work.[58] Magdalena Walter tells a similar story. She and the others were "only told that we were being sent to a special detail. We were not promised anything. They didn't talk to us . . . at all. For them, we were just air . . . mere objects."[59]

The infirmary at Ravensbrück played a central role in organizing the brothels. It was the site of the women's recruitment and selection, and the women also underwent medical examinations and physical preparation for forced sex work there. The former infirmary nurse Antonia Bruha reports that women could sign up for a camp brothel at the infirmary. She mentions a particular case in which a young woman believed—falsely—that she'd be released after six months of brothel work. Bruha dismissed the woman and told her to tell the others that no more women would be recruited for the camp brothels. The SS head nurse learned of Bruha's actions and reported them to the SS physician Percival Treite.[60]

The women recruited for the brothel were presented in the infirmary to the SS, who then selected from the recruits. Bruha recalls that women who were deemed too old or ugly by the SS were sent back to the camp.[61] Laura Büttig reports: "On March 14, 1944, we were ordered to the infirmary. Before that, we had to bathe. The camp directors were there and picked out the girls. Lütkemeyer was the one who picked us. He picked six out of eighty girls. . . . We were naked. My friend . . . was actually too old, so she was to become a block elder. The girls were not supposed to be older than twenty-five."[62]

Bruha also reports that SS men "tried out" the women selected in the infirmary.[63] It is unclear whether this was merely a mortifying inspection or actual rape, as Halbmayr interprets it.[64] Former forced sex workers talked about the humiliation during the selection process, but none mentioned rape by SS men. Hans Maršálek believes that the SS refrained from open sexual violence.[65]

As the SS wanted to restore the health of the women scarred by concentration camp imprisonment, the selected women were kept isolated from the rest of the camp in the infirmary and "nursed back to health." Linda Bachmann reports that she and the other women selected for the brothel in Dora-Mittelbau no longer had to stand for roll call.[66] The women received antiseptic baths, calcium injections, sunlamp treatments for disease, and better food.[67] In addition, the women were screened for venereal disease. Women found to be positive served as test subjects for experimental drugs.[68]

Survivor memoirs have led researchers to assume for some years that both the Wehrmacht and the SS selected women for their own brothels in Ravensbrück.[69] A statement of Antonia Bruha, together with similar ones from other firsthand accounts, has played a central role in this view: "And then they divided them up. The most beautiful, and I know this exactly, the most beautiful were sent to the SS brothels. . . . The less beautiful ones went to the soldier brothels, and the worst to the concentration camps."[70] Another survivor of Ravensbrück recounts:

> The block elder entered with an announcement, but before everyone grasped what it was about, the questions were drowned in shouts, screams, jeers, and laughter from the French women.—Does one dare offer political prisoners the option of signing up for a brothel?!!! The block elder wanted to reassure them that they would not have anything to do with civilians. They would only be available for the "Wehrmacht." It took five minutes before the noise died down, and then voices half-choked with laughter called out five names. The block elder paused, and called to mind who they were: five seventy-year-olds. She turned around and walked out.[71]

The Spanish woman Antonia Frexedes reports how she and others had to line up in front of a barrack hut after the quarantine. The camp commandant then announced that he was looking for women of a certain age group for a soldiers' brothel in Berlin. The women began to cry, she remembers; only a young French woman of Polish descent came forward. Frexedes recalled a woman who returned to Ravensbrück after a brief stay at a Wehrmacht brothel: "Fourteen days later we saw her again in the camp. But what a state! Full of pimples and pustules, she was puffy and didn't speak anymore. They took her to the infirmary to 'never be seen again.'"[72]

There are no other references in surviving Wehrmacht documents regarding the use of women at Ravensbrück for Wehrmacht brothels.[73] It is known that in occupied France the Wehrmacht imprisoned prostitutes who sought to evade state control and then recruited them for brothels. But these camps were not under the control of the SS,[74] and a French police report on a brothel for Wehrmacht officers in La Rochelle, France, indicates that the use of female prisoners was not common: "The women are selected from among the freelance prostitutes registered by the vice squad. The selection is made by the German medical service."[75]

Because the aforementioned accounts resemble descriptions of SS brothels by women who returned to Ravensbrück and by other sources, it is likely that they are actually referring to SS brothels and that the source mistook SS leaders for Wehrmacht officers or that "Wehrmacht" was a translation error.[76] In her autobiographical novel *Das Höllentor* (The gates of Hell), Anja Lundholm describes how a block elder named Wanda sought out Polish women for SS brothels in the "tent," a makeshift lodging at Ravensbrück where the sanitary conditions were catastrophically poor.[77]

Magdalena Walter, a former forced sex worker at Buchenwald, explicitly stated that she was admitted to the infirmary in Ravensbrück with angina before being selected for brothel work. The kapo of the prisoners' infirmary, who was also a friend of hers, told her that women were being assembled for an SS brothel: "I asked, what do you do with them? She said, I am not allowed to tell you. I say, are they going to the other camp . . . ? No, they are going to Berlin, here and there. And she told me." That's when she learned that they were intended for the Bulgarian SS. But the kapo warned her: "Don't tell anyone, or it'll be your turn and mine."[78] It is evident that the kapo was referring to brothels for Ukrainian SS men, which may have been located in Sachsenhausen, a district of Oranienburg near Berlin.

In her novel, Anja Lundholm mentions women brought back to Ravensbrück from SS brothels—probably for Ukrainian guards. She cites a friend who said that "four physically and mentally ruined women who had been in an SS brothel were sent back to the camp, used up and unable to work."[79] However, there is no reference in SS records to the women described by Lundholm. But as I have shown, the records do show the existence of brothels for Ukrainian guards and document the names of the women who worked there.[80] In one case, a woman returned to Ravensbrück "useless" from a brothel for Ukrainian guards. A telegram from the Buchenwald camp commandant describes the state of a twenty-year-old Polish forced sex worker from Lodz: "Re: Telephone consultation with site physician in

Weimar on March 28, 1944. It is requested that B . . . , who is unusable in the Ukrainian special building due to illness, be replaced."[81]

In a list of prisoners at the Ravensbrück concentration camp dated March 11, 1944, the note "Returned from Flossenbürg" appears next to the names of three Polish women.[82] Since only women who worked in the "special building" were imprisoned in Flossenbürg at that time, it is almost certain that they were forced sex workers.[83] Two of the women had contracted venereal disease, probably from working at a brothel for Ukrainian guards. The third woman may have been a forced sex worker in the prisoners' brothel.[84] Another list of arrivals at Ravensbrück, dated February 15, 1944, shows the names of two women with the remark "Returned from Mauthausen."[85] As in Flossenbürg, there were no women in Mauthausen at this time except for the forced sex workers, so it is very likely that the women worked in a "special" detail, possibly in the Gusen brothel for the Ukrainian SS.[86]

Lundholm writes that the stories of Thea, who was deported to an SS brothel, "spread in all details, like everything else that concerns us, with lightning speed."[87] This statement, as well as the recollections of other firsthand accounts from female prisoners, shows that many prisoners in the Ravensbrück main camp knew about brothel recruitment. What information did Ravensbrück women have, and from what sources? As I have already shown, the SS rarely disclosed information to prisoners. Instead, female prisoners relied on the knowledge of other prisoners (such as Antonia Bruha), women involved in the selection process (Nanda Herbermann), former forced sex workers, and the women who came into contact with them (Anja Lundholm and, again, Antonia Bruha).

Ravensbrück inmates learned little about the women who went to work in the brothels, as few forced sex workers returned to the camp.[88] And those who did usually remained in the prisoner camp for only a short time before being transported to an external unit or released from detention.[89] Any forced sex worker who became pregnant would have been brought to Ravensbrück for an abortion, but very few did.[90] The SS returned one woman to Ravensbrück probably because she had been punished for violating camp rules.[91] In one case, the SS returned a forced sex worker from Sachsenhausen to the women's concentration camp as "unsuitable." Another was returned because of illness, and still another presumably because of venereal disease.[92] The women had probably worked at brothels for Ukrainian guards. Given the lack of firsthand accounts, knowledge about the brothels was fragmentary; the women had to supplement the little they knew with rumors and conjecture. Antonia Bruha provides an example when accounting for why so few women returned from the brothels: "I cannot verify that; perhaps they were in a brothel somewhere, with the SS or with the SA, and that they were later disposed of. But please, I say this with reservation, do you understand? It is only speculation, because so few of the seriously ill came back."[93]

Stories told by several women who returned to Ravensbrück from Ukrainian brothels with sexual diseases most likely spread at the camp, establishing the idea that the conditions in the brothels were horrible places of sexual disease in which women became "used up" or were murdered. This gruesome picture and the widespread fear of being assigned to a brothel had a direct impact on the Nazi's recruitment methods. Instead of compelling women to "volunteer," they increasingly used more draconian measures and focused on women in areas where living conditions were particularly poor, such as the tent or the lockup.[94] Magdalena Walter recounts her fear of being taken to a brothel: "What are they going to do with us? Are they going to gas us, or are we going to another camp? I knew from the infirmary kapo that there were brothels with women prisoners, including in Berlin, for the Yugoslav SS. And when these women became depleted . . . they were shot, and then a new prisoner transport came. I knew that."[95]

No statements by women who worked in SS brothels have survived.[96] Antonia Bruha reports that a woman from an SS brothel told her that the conditions were atrocious and that she had to have sex with fifty men a day: "Fifty a day, fifty a day. I am an old whore, but fifty a day, no human being can stand that. Fifty a day."[97] According to Bruha, this woman died soon after from her injuries.[98] Records from the Buchenwald brothel suggest that such accounts were largely exaggerated. The actual numbers were far lower in both brothels for prisoners and brothels for Ukrainian guards. Other recollections seem more realistic, such as that of Irma Ostermann: "According to the report of a returned woman, these victims were placed at the free erotic disposal of the male prisoners in Mauthausen under female and male SS guards for one hour, during which she had to change men six times."[99]

Auschwitz-Birkenau

The "women's department" of the Auschwitz concentration camp was established in the spring of 1942. Created as a satellite camp of Ravensbrück, it was initially located in a part of the Auschwitz main camp, fenced off with barbed wire. The first train of women arrived at Auschwitz on March 26, 1942, consisting of one thousand German women from Ravensbrück, the majority of whom were classified as "criminal" and "antisocial." They were to set up a women's camp and, in some cases, fill administrative positions.

The first train was followed by 999 Slovakian Jewish women. About four months later, the women's department was relocated to Birkenau, where the SS had built a prisoner of war camp from the bricks of residential buildings demolished in the surrounding area. After the majority of the Soviet prisoners of war died of malnutrition and exhaustion, the SS quartered the women there. Starting in July 20, 1942, the Auschwitz main camp assumed the administration of the women's department, which on March 20, 1943, was officially classified as the "women's camp." The sanitary conditions were atrocious, and hunger was rampant. Many women had to perform excavation work for the expansion of the Auschwitz camp. By the end of the war, 131,560 women had passed through Birkenau.[100]

The women's camp was the central site where forced sex workers were selected for the camp brothels in the Auschwitz main camp and in Auschwitz-Monowitz. The reason may have been pragmatic: Why take women from Ravensbrück, when a large number of women were imprisoned on site? In addition, one thousand German female prisoners had recently arrived in Auschwitz, who fit the mold for the camp brothels.[101] Nine women later became forced sex workers in the camp brothels.[102] The SS's primary recruitment method at Auschwitz-Birkenau was to find volunteers. Hermann Langbein writes that the head guard, Maria Mandel, "took care to have women assigned to this duty on a voluntary basis."[103] Here, too, the SS sought women who had already been prostitutes before their imprisonment.[104]

There are several known accounts of Auschwitz survivors describing recruitment for the camp brothels. In her autobiography *Smoke Over Birkenau,* the Italian writer and Holocaust survivor Liana Millu tells the story of a Dutch girl who volunteered for the brothel in the main camp after the *blockowa* asked the women in the block if they wanted to work in the "Auschwitz *Puffkommando.*"[105] In other blocks, however, the prisoner functionaries did not specify the type of work. Sonia Landau, in her survivor's account, written under the name Krystyna Zywulska, reports: "The kapo entered the barracks, the same one who had participated in the selection. Together with a guard, they walked from cot to cot, whispering to each other. We had already become very restless. Such a visit certainly did not bode well. The camp kapo asked loudly: 'Who wants to go to Auschwitz, to the city, to the men's camp? There is easy work there, civilian clothes and good food.' At this she smiled slyly and mischievously. 'Any volunteers?'"[106] The women were suspicious but found the terms enticing.[107] Zofia Bator, a Polish woman, reports that she spoke with a former forced sex worker who told her that the SS doctor had tried to dissuade her from reporting for the brothel, explaining that she might not be able to have children later. She responded that "she did not care what came later; now she wanted to eat."[108] For Millu, volunteering for the brothels reflected a special will to survive, one that demanded abandoning whatever remained of one's own dignity and sexual sovereignty. In her novel, the Dutch girl Lotti speaks of her reasons for volunteering:

> Well, I refused to be consumed and vanish like a cloud. I wanted to return to my house. I'm eighteen years old—I don't want to die. I know, no one wants to die, you'll tell me. But maybe I don't want to more than the others. Maybe that's the difference. Because I can feel how disgustingly wrong it is that I should have to die because I couldn't steal soup or I had no cigarettes to trade for bread, while other people who weren't as good as me, who might have committed crimes or led wicked lives, would somehow manage to survive. Oh sure, they'd still be here enjoying life, loving, singing, back home with their families. And where would I be? . . . Everyone in the lager goes around picking up leftovers from the garbage. They suck bones other people spit out—and I'm supposed to refuse life because it's offered on a dirty plate?[109]

Franz Hössler, the camp director, or *Schutzhaftlagerführer*, personally selected women for the brothels.[110] Langbein writes: "Hössler had young girls line up who were forced to work hard under the open sky, sleep in crowded quarters without facilities for washing and changing their underwear, and live in constant fear of floggings. He announced that anyone who volunteered as a *fille de joie* would be given her own room, clean clothes, sufficient food and cigarettes, and the opportunity to bathe every day."[111] It is easy to imagine how appealing such promises must have been to women in Birkenau, where no such luxuries existed. Moreover, Hössler also "intimated that occupants of the brothel might be released 'on good behavior.'"[112] The prospect of being released must have been very enticing to the women. One Auschwitz forced sex worker explained her decision to volunteer because "winter is coming and I work in the fields!"[113] She knew she would not survive another of these severe winters, especially in a work detail with no protection from rain, snow, and freezing cold.

One woman whom Hössler recruited—on the promise of release after six months of work—was the young Polish woman Izabela Michalek.[114] She was forced to perform sex from the day the main camp brothel opened until September 1944.[115] After Auschwitz was evacuated, she was sent to Bergen-Belsen. When the camp was liberated, Michalek encountered Hössler, who had been arrested by the Allies and put in prison there. She hurled insults and rotten food at him for not keeping his promise of releasing her.[116] In his interrogation, Hössler stressed that the women working in the camp brothels were volunteers—while failing to mention the false promises he had made to them.[117]

The women recruited by the SS were sent to the Auschwitz-Birkenau infirmary to receive cervical swabs and blood samples to test for syphilis.[118] Some women learned about the true nature of the work only here. Bator describes one woman's account: "An SS man, a doctor, saw her. . . . While examining her, he asked: Do you know where you are going? She said: No, I don't. They told me it was light work, where there was a lot of bread."[119] The SS doctors Fritz Klein and Josef Mengele selected some of the women for the camp brothels, just as they selected prisoners "unfit for work" for the gas chambers.[120] After the war, Klein told his interrogators that "it was one of my jobs to select girls for the work. . . . About fifteen were presented to me and I selected from them the ten best in my opinion."[121]

Following the medical examinations, the SS brought the women to the Political Department, where its head, Maximilian Grabner, made a further selection.[122] According to Dounia Ourisson-Wasserstrom, a member of the department, SS Rottenführer Pery Broad, discovered the remark "prostitute" in one woman's file and exclaimed, "In our camp, every prisoner can pursue his profession! Isn't this a model camp?"[123] The women were now sent to Block 10 of the main camp for quarantine. Previously, the gynecologist Carl Clauberg had conducted sterilization experiments on Greek Jewish women in that block, though his work was suspended while the forced sex laborers were housed there.[124]

Surviving *Begleitzettel* from the SS Hygiene Institute in Rajsko—record slips accompanying the examinations of Auschwitz forced sex workers—provide detailed information about the frequency of brothel selections. According to these records, examinations of women selected for the Auschwitz main camp and Monowitz camp brothels began on September 18, 1943.[125] On October 4, the SS transferred some of the women to the camp brothel in Block 24a of the main camp.[126] The SS transferred other women to the camp brothel in Monowitz starting on November 15.[127] In November–December 1943, March–April 1944, and June 1944, the SS selected more women for the camp brothel in the main camp.[128] On January 10, 1945, a few days before the evacuation of Auschwitz, the SS handed over a final group of twelve women for the camp brothel. These women had arrived in Auschwitz in late November 1944 and had probably been selected in Ravensbrück for brothels in the main camp and in Monowitz. Five of them later had to perform forced sex work in the Mittelbau-Dora camp together with other women.[129]

Based on the notes accompanying the examinations, almost 10 percent of the women had been in Birkenau for up to one month before being recruited to a brothel. About half had been there for up to half a year, and another 15 percent for up to a year. Around one-quarter had been in Auschwitz for more than a year; two women had been there for twenty-five months.[130]

There is only one known mention of women in Birkenau being selected for soldier or SS brothels. As described earlier, the women who worked in the part of the Auschwitz brothel that was accessible to SS men and Wehrmacht members were *Sittendiren* under police control, not concentration camp inmates.[131] But according to the Auschwitz survivor Simha Naor, who worked in the infirmary at Auschwitz-Birkenau, a German "criminal" named Hete who had tested positive for venereal disease said that she had worked at the officers' brothel.[132] There's good reason not to take this statement at face value, however. Not only is it the only reference to such a case; there is no evidence pointing to the existence of such a facility in Auschwitz. More to the point, even if such a brothel existed, women like Hete —ethnic Germans classified as "criminals"—were used for prisoner brothels, not officer brothels. Indeed, records from the Rajsko institute show that two women among the forced sex workers at Auschwitz bore the first name Hedwig, and one wore the green criminal's triangle. In addition, the institute's files contain the names of two patients with venereal disease, one of whom was named Helene.[133] "Hete" may have been Hedwig or Helene, or both.

Based on available testimony, it appears that fear of being selected for brothel duty was particularly great among Polish women, especially when attractive women were selected for unspecified work. Agnes Havas reports that she was selected with other women for a new work detail and taken to a new block whose elder wore an elegant nightgown. The women realized they were in a brothel and became afraid.[134] Irena Wiśniewska recounts that she worked in a relatively good detail in Auschwitz, but one day she found out that she would be sent away in a prisoner transport. Before departure, she and a friend met Hössler on the camp road. She summoned up all her courage and told him that they would rather stay in Auschwitz. The camp director then wrote down their numbers. Irena later learned that he was recruiting women for the camp brothel and that she would probably end up there. The help of a female friend who worked in the Political Department prevented this.[135]

Zofia Bator gives a detailed account of a selection where she feared being assigned to a brothel. At the end of 1944, she and around one hundred other women were selected from a group of a thousand female prisoners in the

Birkenau women's camp: "We didn't know at all what the Germans were judging us by, because during roll call a guard went around together with an SS man, and they tapped us on the forehead with a pencil. That must have been in November 1944. I, too, was tapped on the forehead with the pencil. I had to step out of line, and we waited and thought about what the selectors were acting on."[136] The women were taken to the "sauna"—the name given to the place where the prisoners were stripped, shaved, and tattooed—and had to take a shower. A group of SS men made the women line up naked in front of them. Bator remembers: "They were not allowed to make any shameful remarks. We had to turn around, raise our hands so the SS men could look at our bodies. . . . They were looking for ulcerations. Anyone with even the slightest ulcer or pimple was put aside. In this way, they picked fifty of us."[137] The women were taken to a separate block and locked up. The women speculated along the way about the work detail they'd be transferred to:

> We began to consider where, what for, and what intention they had to do with us. . . . Most of them were Polish, but there were also some Russians and a few Ukrainians. They were all young girls with beautiful complexions. Beautiful in the sense that they were clean, without any skin rashes or ulcers, fresh, healthy girls—given what was possible in the camp. Together with Irka we came to the conclusion that they were preparing a particularly large camp bordello. True, they had never done this before, they had never forced women to go, they went themselves, some happily, to eat lighter bread. But we could expect the worst.[138]

Later, the women were again deloused and transferred to a very clean block. There were sinks, a real bathroom, and beds with blankets and pillows. For the first time since their arrival at Auschwitz, the women were able to wash properly. Blood and stool tests were performed on them. After a period of quarantine, the SS led the women out of the camp. All indications were that the women had been selected for a brothel. But instead, they were taken to the SS kitchen, where the most beautiful ones were selected as waitresses to serve SS men and camp leaders. The rest of them, including Zofia Bator, had to perform unskilled labor.[139]

The End of the War

On September 1, 1944, the SS transferred authority over the women's satellite camps—including the brothels and other work details—from Ravensbrück to nearby men's camps and assigned the female prisoners new prisoner numbers. The restructuring ended Ravensbrück's role as the central recruitment and transit point for forced sex workers in the German Reich.[140] Increasingly, the SS recruited women from subcamps and other locations such as less important camp brothels. It also swapped out women in some brothels for women from others. For example, in mid-1944, forced sex workers were exchanged between Dachau and Gusen, Gusen and Mauthausen, and Auschwitz and Monowitz.[141]

The decentralization of the work details posed a particular challenge for the SS. One of the ways in which the SS met this challenge was the introduction of Hollerith punch cards in the summer of 1944 to organize forced labor. Developed in the mid-1880s by the German-American engineer Herman Hollerith, the punch cards were part of a WVHA plan to create a central registry for all prisoners.[142] To date, historians have found 148,247 prisoner cards numerically coded for the Hollerith system in German and Polish archives. They contain personal data (date of birth, marital status, number of children, sex), data on nationality and imprisonment (reason for imprisonment, nationality, the concentration camp to which the prisoner was admitted), assigned work detail, and occupation before imprisonment.[143] Index cards prepared for Hollerith machines have survived from thirty-one brothel workers.[144] The field indicating the type of forced labor contains the description "brothel woman" or "for special purposes."[145] The code for forced sexual labor was 998, the same number that city administrations used for "registered prostitute."[146] It is unclear whether the SS ever used punch cards to identify eligible women for the brothels, though the coded material they contained—previous occupation, work detail, reason for imprisonment, origin, age—would have simplified the process. At any rate, internal conflicts, lack of personnel, and, ultimately, the collapse of the concentration camp system at the end of 1944 undermined Nazi efforts to implement a comprehensive registry.[147]

In November 1944, the SS began to recruit women in Ravensbrück for Auschwitz brothels. At the end of the month, the SS selected fifteen German women,[148] and twelve arrived at the brothel of the Auschwitz main camp on January 10, 1945; the other three probably ended up in the Monowitz brothels. Three women from this transport, along with seven others, arrived at Mittelbau-Dora in February 1945, the first forced sex workers at the camp.[149] It may seem surprising that the SS did not recruit women from the Birkenau women's camp for the brothels in the main camp and in Monowitz, as had been the custom. The reason was probably that by this time the evacuations of women from Birkenau were already well underway, making it difficult to find women who met SS criteria.

The dissolution of the Ravensbrück women's concentration camp began in February 1945. When Sachsenhausen needed new forced sex workers after sending four women back to Ravensbrück in January, it recruited them from its own women's satellite camps in Auer and Velten.[150] One of the women whom the SS recruited for forced sexual labor from a woman's satellite camp happened to be an inmate who had previously worked as a forced sex worker in Monowitz.[151] How would they have found her without some form of registry system?

The SS often had to improvise, recruiting women from incoming transports from Mauthausen and other camps. The French woman Georgette W. reports that the SS tried to recruit women for a brothel from an evacuation transport while they were in the showers.[152]

In the final months of the war, the central organization of forced sex work was transferred to the Bergen-Belsen camp. The camp complex had been the main camp for all non-Jewish prisoners since August 1944.[153] The "examiners" selecting female prisoners for forced labor were now to come directly to Bergen-Belsen instead of visiting each of the other camps. The camp retained the function as a forced labor distribution center through February 1945. At that time, the camp had become the final stop for evacuation transports arriving from Eastern Europe.[154] Bergen-Belsen also became an assembly point for forced sex workers destined for camp brothels, especially the one established in Mittelbau-Dora.

In February 1945, a transport of 502 Jewish women arrived at the Bergen-Belsen women's camp. The transport included ten "Aryan" women who had previously been forced to perform sex in the camp brothels at Auschwitz and Monowitz. These women were brought to the Mittelbau-Dora brothel a few weeks later. It is likely that the SS wanted to quarantine the women in Bergen-Belsen because the arrival of evacuation transports had increased the risk of disease. It is also possible that the brothel in Dora had not yet been completed.[155]

A few weeks later, Bergen-Belsen became a transit camp for forced sex workers who had been selected in Ravensbrück. Linda Bachmann first came to Bergen-Belsen with other women whom the SS had forcibly recruited in Ravensbrück for the camp brothel. She remembers the conditions there with horror: "And then we arrived in Bergen-Belsen, where I saw the Bergen-Belsen camp. The conditions there were appalling. Ravensbrück was still . . . you know, for toilets, at least where we were, they had pits with beams over them. When people had to go, or had to go at night, they had to do it over a beam. It was disgusting. Anyone who happened to slip would topple over and disappear."[156]

Linda Bachmann and other selected women were placed in an isolated area of the Bergen-Belsen camp. She remained there for about two weeks. One morning, the SS called her name. Together with the other women, she was transported to Mittelbau-Dora.[157]

Another source reports that Bergen-Belsen was the site of recruitment for the Mittelbau-Dora brothel. The German Ilse Stephan was transported from Ravensbrück to Bergen-Belsen in February 1945 and housed in the large women's camp there. After a week, the SS ordered all the German women to stand outside their huts. The SS selected twenty women from the group, including Ilse Stephan. They were taken to the camp office, where an SS woman told the prisoners, "Do you know where you are going? You're going to the whorehouse, you old whores."[158] On hearing that, Ilse Stephan began to cry. She later said that the transport for the brothel left the Bergen-Belsen camp without her and was hit by a bomb in the Nordhausen train station.[159] Her statement is not credible, however. Nordhausen was not bombed by the Allies until early April 1945, and by that time two transports of forced sex workers had already reached Mittelbau-Dora. Furthermore, there is no indication that brothels were planned for other camps at this time. The SS woman may have wanted to demoralize or humiliate prisoners by claiming that they were destined for brothels.

4 Space and Organization

In the previous two chapters, I reconstructed the strange (and frankly illogical) thinking that led Nazi leaders to introduce brothels for prisoners and explained the process for recruiting forced sex laborers from the camps. This chapter delves into the nature of the brothels that awaited the new recruits. The first part considers the physical structure of the brothels. Where were they located inside the concentration camps? How were the brothel buildings designed? What did they look like inside? What sorts of interactions did their spatial configurations permit? In the second part, I turn to their administration. What regulations governed their operation? Who enforced them, and how were violations punished? How was time organized for the sex workers and their visitors? What sort of medical supervision was in place? As will become clear over the course of this chapter, the answers to the first set of questions converge on the answers to the second, for the space and organization of the camp brothels were in lockstep. Both reflected the desire of the SS to exert total control over sex workers and prisoners alike.

The Brothel Within the Topography of the Camps

"The concentration camp," Wolfgang Sofsky observes, was "a system of rigorous surveillance, a receptacle for violence."[1] The camps were designed by the SS to eliminate the prisoners' spaces for living and acting. Inmates were crammed together, reduced to an undifferentiated mass in a cosmos sealed off from normal life; their activities were subject to strict regulations and confined to specific zones designed to control them.[2] In the topography of the model concentration camp, each space was assigned a different function. There were separate places for work, for sleep, for isolation, for torture, and for murder. Most camps possessed a rectangular ground plan and a uniform arrangement of structures, optimizing prisoner surveillance and enabling quick expansion whenever more space was needed.[3] Internally, the camp was divided into functional blocks so that the SS could exercise precise control over prisoners' lives.[4] Open, unregulated spaces did not exist.

In the "condensed and segmented mass" of camp life, room to move was a privilege.[5] Only block elders, clerks, and other privileged prisoners had their own sleeping quarters. All the other inmates were assigned to communal bunks.[6]

Flossenbürg exemplified the spatial organization of Nazi concentration camps. A vertical axis divided the camp into areas for the SS and for prisoners. A road forming a horizontal axis and connecting the two sections ran from the commandant's office through the gate of the prisoner camp to the camp quarantine. Above the horizontal axis on the prisoner side were the prisoner barrack huts, which were surrounded by barbed wire. Directly across the vertical axis on the other side was housing for SS and camp staff. Below the horizontal axis were the "functional" buildings: the laundry, the infirmary, the lockup on the prisoner side; and the SS administration, the SS infirmary, and the block leader quarters on the other. The roll-call square formed the center of the prisoners' camp. The crematorium, in the camps that had one, was located outside the areas where prisoners lived and worked.[7]

In the topography of the concentration camps, the camp brothel was a poor fit. It was, as its euphemistic designation conveyed, "special." It belonged neither with the functional buildings responsible for daily operations nor with the barrack huts where the prisoners were housed, much less with the areas reserved for murder. It was meant for leisure, but no such space was provided for in the camp. When the first brothels were established in Mauthausen and Gusen, the SS put them at the entrance to the prisoners' camp, next to the roll-call area. In Mauthausen, the brothel was placed in a converted section of Block 1, while in Gusen it was set up in a newly constructed stone building next to the *Jourhaus*. The reason for the prominent location in each camp was to remind prisoners of the bonus that awaited them if they exceeded their quotas. Each brothel was close to its respective camp's roll-call squares because that is where the prisoners had to stand several times a day, sometimes for hours on end. The brothels were also near the barrack huts of the prisoner functionaries, who were more likely than other prisoners to be granted access. In Gusen, the building that housed the camp brothel also housed a brothel for Ukrainian SS guards. The proximity to the camp gate spared the guards from having to walk through the prisoners' camp to reach the brothel.[8]

But the prominent location of the first camp brothels did not meet the approval of Oswald Pohl, the WVHA head. A letter from Arthur Liebehenschel, the director of Office Group D who would go on to become the commandant of Auschwitz, stated that Pohl had "noticed during an inspection of completed special buildings that they were not particularly well-situated."[9] Pohl had ordered "that when erecting further 'special buildings,' care should be taken to ensure that they are somewhat out of the way in accordance with their intended purpose and cannot be gawked at by all kinds of people."[10] It seems that locating brothels at the camp entrance contradicted Pohl's idea of a well-ordered camp. Anything that could cause a stir was to be removed from view, especially in the model camps like Sachsenhausen, which was still receiving visits from civilians well after the war started.[11] As a rule, the SS took great care to ensure that the camps were tidy and clean. The curbs in the Auschwitz main camp were whitewashed every day, and Birkenau had flower beds.[12] The mountains of emaciated corpses that many today associate with concentration camps did not appear until the camps' final phase, after they had become overcrowded and when prisoners were dying and being murdered on a mass scale. "Piles of skeletons were the unplanned remains of the murder machine," Sofsky writes.[13] Earlier in the war, while things were still proceeding according to plan, the killing, the permanent violence, and the poor prisoner conditions were barely visible to outsiders.[14]

For Himmler, Pohl's "somewhat out of the way" did not go far enough. Himmler wanted them relocated to the periphery of the camp and kept secret. His November 1943 order reads: "During camp tours, brothels and crematoria are not to be shown. Nor may these facilities be discussed with tour participants. This requires the express permission of the Reichsführer-SS."[15] The order affected brothels in Sachsenhausen, Dachau, Neuengamme, and the Auschwitz main camp. In Flossenbürg, the SS had already learned from the experiences of Mauthausen and Gusen and built the brothel behind the camp lockup. In Buchenwald, the brothel was located next to a cinema near the infirmary in an isolated part of the camp. In Sachsenhausen, it was located at the outer corner of the camp triangle, in an isolated part of the infirmary near the heavily guarded border strip.[16] In Dachau, the SS built the barrack huts at the rear of the camp, next to an herb garden and a breeding facility for Angora rabbits.[17] The spatial marginalization of the camp brothel reached its zenith in Neuengamme, where the building was located *outside* the prisoner camp.[18] In Buchenwald, the brothel was surrounded by a six-and-a-half-foot-high wooden enclosure; those in other camps had simple wire mesh fences, some with mats woven into them for privacy.[19] For brothel buildings that lacked a fence, such as those in Flossenbürg or Auschwitz, an SS man stood guard at the entrance.[20]

As can be gathered from Himmler's order, the camp's peripheries were where the SS placed its other "special" facilities—those reserved for death and killing.[21] In Sachsenhausen, the SS built the camp brothel over the morgue cellar. In Dachau and Neuengamme, the brothel building was near the crematoria.[22] The "special building" in Flossenbürg was situated between the "death strip," the camp yard where executions were carried out, and the camp for dying prisoners.[23] But the idea to put camp brothels at the peripheries did not originally stem from Himmler or Pohl. In 1941, the chief of the security police decided to locate brothels for foreign workers close to labor camps outside towns.[24] This, in turn, followed a practice in Germany going back to 1933, when some cities started initiatives to prevent "conspicuous prostitution in public."[25] An important example of the efforts to suppress prostitution from public view was the introduction of brothel streets, as discussed in Chapter 1. Hamburg's Herbertstraße, which is still a brothel street today, featured privacy screens at both ends of the street—much like those later used in the some of the camps.[26] But the general idea of confining brothels to the peripheries of society has existed at least since the Renaissance, when brothels were often located either near or outside city walls.[27] It is perhaps no surprise that the German concentration camp, which scholars have likened to a "closed city," replicated the peripheralization of brothels that has long accompanied urban prostitution.[28]

Not all concentration camps had brothels located out of sight, however. In the Auschwitz main camp, the brothel did not go up behind the camp lockup, as originally planned. Rather, probably on account of material shortages and pressure from Himmler or Pohl to speed up construction, it was built directly next to the camp gate.[29] In Monowitz, the brothel was located at the front of the camp among the functional buildings between the kitchen, the workshop, and the garden.[30] The last brothel in the concentration camp system—the one established in Mittelbau-Dora toward the end of the war—was also built in the entrance area, directly on the roll-call square. At the time, the camp system was already in the process of being dissolved, and pragmatic considerations prevailed. The location kept the brothel near the camp's "official culture" (library, camp cinema) while improving surveillance. And as at Gusen, Mauthausen, Buchenwald, and Auschwitz, it made a key element of the bonus system highly visible during roll call, which the Nazis hoped would encourage prisoners to work harder.

The buildings that housed the brothels were extensions of the rigorous surveillance practiced in the camps. The first designs for camp brothels go back to January 17, 1940, when Himmler ordered the construction of a brothel for Czech foreign workers in the city of Linz.[31] It was to be the first of many brothels in or near forced labor camps in the years to come. The first of its kind, the brothel known as the "Villa Nova" was a solid structure shaped like an L. It was built in the immediate vicinity of Labor Camp 49 of the Reichswerke Hermann Göring. The building housed fifteen brothel rooms and was surrounded by a garden. The building had a waiting room measuring 650 square feet, a room for a doctor and police officer, and, in the smaller wing of the building, a bar.[32] The Villa Nova was intended to serve as a prototype for foreign laborer brothels, but the surviving plans from other brothels show major differences in terms of construction, size, and building materials. At Johann-Justus-Weg 2 in Oldenburg, for example, the "dragonfly" brothel was a spartan wooden structure ninety feet long with only five brothel rooms.[33]

The first concentration camp brothel was set up in Mauthausen near Linz two years after the construction of the Villa Nova. Part of an existing building, the brothel had a clearly defined spatial organization: A central corridor divided rooms for sex from the bedrooms and administrative quarters. The structure lacked the waiting area common in other brothels. Instead, the SS assigned the male prisoners to specific women and had them wait directly outside the brothel rooms.[34] It is likely that the SS drew on their experience with brothels for foreign workers when setting up the concentration camp brothels. But there were few similarities between the Villa Nova and the Mauthausen camp brothel apart from the arrangement of the brothel rooms. The latter had no waiting room, contained both living and working quarters, and lacked a space for relaxation. What is more, the longitudinal corridor did not just connect the entrance and the brothel rooms. It was first and foremost a space for surveillance and control. In its layout, the camp brothel was more like a camp lockup than a brothel, with peepholes on the doors and metal bars over the windows.

Other camp brothels resembled camp lockups as well. For example, Gusen's brothel, with its massive construction and impassable windows, looked like a prison from the outside.[35] In fact, after ceasing operations toward the end of the war, the brothel was converted into a prison.[36] The similarity to camp lockups is particularly evident in the floor plans of the brothel in the Auschwitz main camp, whose size and layout are almost identical to the camp's *Bunker*. The SS evidently used the plans of the camp lockup when converting the communal sleeping areas in the elite block. Other striking similarities were the peepholes set in the doors, which allowed the SS to monitor what was happening within each chamber, as well as the barred entrance areas.[37]

Before the construction of the brothel in Gusen had been completed, SS commanders at Flossenbürg decided to build their own. The planning and realization phase lasted almost a year. Given organizational difficulties, the designs were revised several times. Each draft reflected the efforts of the SS to integrate the brothel building, its organizational structures, and its procedures into the space of the concentration camp. The first draft was presented to the commandant by construction supervisors on July 18, 1942. The "special prisoners' building" (Figures 7 and 8) was to be erected behind the camp lockup. The plan provided for foundation walls made of quarry stone and interior walls built of solid brick. Inside, there was to be a doctor's room, a waiting room, a room for the guards, ten small rooms, a bathroom, a washroom, a lavatory, a broom closet, a communal bedroom, and a common room. The bathroom designs were comfortable by camp standards: three bathtubs, three bidets, and an electric water heater for hot water. Room heaters were to be installed to heat the common rooms. For construction planning, the management drew on experiences from Mauthausen. The total cost was estimated at 48,000 Reichsmarks.[38] In order to build the brothel, over six hundred feet of the camp's perimeter fencing had to be moved back some sixteen feet.[39]

Externally, the plans featured large windows, a high-pitched roof, and a planned terrace, which made the structure look more like a brothel for foreign workers than a camp lockup. The same goes for the interior design, with its waiting room, separate women's bathroom, and spacious common room. But the plan also divided the interior up into individual spheres—for men, for women, and for sex. This was in keeping with the two basic principles of spatial planning in the camps: the strict separation of the sexes and the equal division of the camp space into housing, camp services, and forced labor.[40] The line of demarcation ran along the longitudinal axis of the central corridor. On one of the long sides were two entrance doors, one for men and one for women. The men's entrance area initially contained the cashier's room—labeled as the "broom closet" on the plan—and the doctor's room. Opposite these rooms was a waiting room for male visitors. Ten brothel rooms were located in the middle of the building, arranged to the left and right of the central corridor. This was the only area in the camp in which men were permitted to have contact with women. At the other end of the building were the women's living quarters, which had a common room opening onto a terrace and a group bedroom. The central corridor and the clear divisions of space maximized control. A doctor performed medical exams, and a female supervisor handled the financial matters. An SS guard in the corridor kept watch over the entrance area, the rooms, and the women's quarters—an example of the rigorous control that the SS sought to exercise over the brothels.[41]

A few days after the Flossenbürg plans were submitted, the head of WVHA Office Group C, Hans Kammler, issued a building order for the construction of the brothel. However, the project was not included in the plans of the General Plenipotentiary for the Regulation of the Construction Industry—a post held by Albert Speer. As a result, no bricks or other rationed building materials had been allocated to the brothel. The only option was to build it as a wooden barrack hut, which required reworking the original design. The planning office of the SS Reich South building inspectorate prepared the new drawings.[42]

Construction on the foundations began in Flossenbürg in August 1942.[43] But work stopped at the end of October 1942 after the WVHA refused to give its approval.[44] One month later, the WVHA issued an order for a new design. It rejected the room layout and required that the builders simplify the structure and save costs and materials. The cuts came at the expense of the comfort of the building's future occupants. The heating system in the first draft was jettisoned, and the bathroom was given a concrete floor instead of tiles. The lavatory was merged with the bathroom, and the washbasins in the brothel rooms were nixed. The new plan retained the functional separation, however. The entrance for the men was in the front, allowing guards to monitor the visitors along the central corridor. In addition, there was now a room in the women's quarters for a female brothel supervisor.[45]

In January 1943, the SS Reich South in Dachau delivered to Flossenbürg building materials for a Wehoba type C military hospital unit.[46] The structure was larger than the planned brothel, and the surplus materials were to be used elsewhere in the camp.[47] By March, construction was in full swing, with up to 280 prisoners working each day on the site. The costs for the building totaled 75,000 Reichsmarks, which were to be paid from Reich funds.[48] On July 1, 1943, the construction was completed and the building was assigned the number 18.[49]

But the newly erected building was not to be the final version of the brothel. Two weeks after completion, the construction management in Dachau received a new WVHA construction order and made available another 12,000 Reichsmarks.[50] The main change was the addition of two brothel rooms, more spacious than the others. These were located in the area previously reserved for the common room. The function of the two rooms is not indicated in the plan, but the new design makes clear that the two rooms were meant for Ukrainian SS men. A separate entrance opened onto a short corridor leading to three rooms. On the one side was a "waiting room." On the other were the two larger brothel rooms. At the end of the hall was another door separating the brothel rooms from the women's quarters. The floor plan was likely based on the design of the brothel in Gusen, which seems to have also had a separate area for Ukrainian SS guards.[51] The room layout of the "combination brothel" in Flossenbürg clearly demarcated the different spheres of the brothel hierarchy. In the camp pecking order, the Ukrainian guards were far below the German guards, closer in status to prisoner functionaries. Yet they were also afforded far more comfort than any of the prisoners. The Ukrainian SS men had larger brothel rooms and could choose the woman they wanted while mingling with the sex workers in the waiting room. Male prisoners, by contrast, were denied any such opportunity: The SS chose the women for them.

It is possible that the brothel in Flossenbürg served as a model for other camp bordellos servicing Ukrainian SS guards. In December 1943, the head of Office Group D, Richard Glücks, issued a memo ordering "that the two rooms for the prostitutes be particularly well-appointed."[52] The brothel in Gusen was one influence on Flossenbürg, but it was certainly not the only one. By the time Flossenbürg was in planning, the SS had already designed several multipurpose brothels. In Auschwitz, for instance, the SS expanded a brothel for foreign workers to include members of the Wehrmacht and SS. A similar plan existed for the foreign worker brothel in Berchtesgaden.[53] The final redesign of the brothel in Flossenbürg was completed on July 15, 1943.[54]

The Wehoba military hospital unit erected in Flossenbürg, with its ample width of forty feet, was ideal for an arrangement of brothel rooms on both sides of a central corridor. Thanks to its modular construction, the length of the building could vary according to the number of forced sex workers. For instance, the Flossenbürg brothel had twelve brothel rooms—ten for prisoners, two for Ukrainian guards—and was 120 feet long. By contrast, the Wehoba unit planned for the "special prisoner building B" in Auschwitz was to have sixteen brothel rooms and span more than 120 feet (Figures 9 and 10), with the women assigned to double rooms instead of a single communal bedroom.[55] The common room for the women was moved to the entrance area. Next to it was a men's toilet.[56] There was no separate living area for the women, and the plans lacked a waiting room—the men had to line up outside. The brothel also lacked a doctor's room; medical exams were probably held in the nearby infirmary, as in Sachsenhausen and Mittelbau-Dora, where the men were examined before visiting the camp brothel.[57]

The "special prisoner building B" was never realized, however. Instead, as discussed earlier, the brothel was put in Block 24a, which had previously been reserved for elite prisoners. The same goes for the planned Wehoba unit for the Monowitz brothel. Aerial photographs and camp plans show a narrow building, which suggests that it was an RAD barrack hut mainly used in forced labor camps.[58] This type of barrack hut was the most common form of housing in the Monowitz camp, but of all the camp brothels it was the only one to consist of an RAD unit. Its smaller overall width—around twenty-five feet—changed the layout of the rooms. A survivor's sketch shows that the rooms were only on one side, and no separate bedrooms existed for the women. The forced sex workers had to spend the night in the brothel rooms.[59]

Starting in 1944, the Wehoba barrack huts became the standard building for camp housing. Although no plans have survived for the camp brothels in Buchenwald, Dachau, and Neuengamme, surviving photographs confirm the use of Wehoba huts.[60] The main advantage of these units, apart from the division of space and the surveillance possibilities they offered, lay in their adaptability, which suited the pragmatic approach of the SS and the varying conditions of the camps. In Sachsenhausen, for example, the SS built the barrack hut for the brothel next to the pathology building, where it shared not only its water and electricity lines but also the ceiling of the basement morgue, which provided part of the foundation.[61] The building was intended for only ten women. At a length of some eighty feet, it was considerably shorter than the version set up in Buchenwald. The entrance was on the side of the building, which precluded the ideal layout. Instead, the SS adopted the Mauthausen floor plan, with rooms located on one side of the central corridor and the women's sleeping quarters on the other. The guard rooms were located at the entrance. The bathroom was set up on the side facing the pathology department adjacent to the dissection room. In contrast to Buchenwald, the SS in Sachsenhausen locked the women in communal bedrooms at night.[62]

The brothel in Mittelbau-Dora was most likely established in an existing barrack hut, but no records have survived regarding its layout. The only documentary evidence is a film shot by the US Army after the liberation showing the building from the outside. It suggests that the barrack hut was also a Wehoba.[63]

The ten camp brothels probably shared the same basic furnishings. Many of the furnishings for the concentration camps were produced by the Deutsche Ausrüstungswerke (DAW) in Dachau, which also made furniture for SS barracks.[64] In Buchenwald, standard-issue furniture came from the stocks of the SS or prisoner camps; everything else was made to order.[65] The pictures on the walls mostly came from the camp library.[66]

In late 1943, the Buchenwald commandant Hermann Pister commissioned the photographic documentation of various facilities in the concentration camp as part of a comprehensive camp inventory. Prisoners from the photo department took the pictures. The photos were collected in an album titled *Buchenwald at the End of 1943*. In addition to photos of the commandant's office, the kitchen, the storage areas holding prisoner effects, and the laundry, the album contains seven photos of the "special building" pasted onto a separate page (Figures 19 to 24).[67] One photo shows the women's common room with a long wooden table and chairs. On the table are ashtrays and several vases filled with flowers (Figure 22). Against the wall is a wooden sideboard with more bouquets. A radio rests on the shelf above. The flowers lend the room a sense of everyday domesticity, suggesting a conscious effort to draw attention away from the fact that the women who lived here were forced sex workers. Another photo shows a brothel room with a single bed that occupies most of the space (Figure 24). The bed linen is folded with military precision. Despite the houseplants by the window and the two pictures on the wall, the room leaves a dreary impression.[68] The rooms in other camp brothels were similarly furnished. A former forced sex worker from the Mittelbau-Dora concentration camp recounts the interior: "Beds, tables, chairs. That was all there was. Washing facilities, toilet, that was it. So, not with any comfort."[69]

Another photo shows a room with two beds (Figure 23), each with a nightstand covered by a tablecloth. On the nightstand rest bouquets of flowers and photos of families. Are these actual family members of the women, or are the photos props to make the rooms look familiar and welcoming? One photo shows a table with chairs and a print of a German shepherd on the wall. The photo is jarring—it seems like a cruel joke given the brothel's function and location. Like the other rooms, this one seems staged to downplay the forced sex provided by the brothel.

Nevertheless, the women saw the clean, comfortable rooms as improvements to the mass sleeping quarters they knew from Ravensbrück and Birkenau.[70] Magdalena Walter recalled her first impression of the brothel in Buchenwald: "The barrack hut was different from the others because it was more humanly furnished. With benches and chairs and tables, and windows. Friendlier."[71] Objects that were not originally part of the inventory seem to have found their way into the brothel through illegal bartering or gifts. Jenny Spritzer wrote that after four weeks, the brothel in the Auschwitz main camp resembled the "most beautiful boudoir."[72] The statement may be exaggerated, but it seems that the SS did indeed tolerate private furnishings. "Carpets, pillows, eiderdowns, linen, pictures, etc. were fished up from the window at night on a long rope."[73] The prisoners who visited brothel rooms perceived them as particularly beautiful. The former Auschwitz inmate Piecha testified: "Everything was very elegant, with pastel colors."[74]

Administration

The pleasantly domestic interiors at Buchenwald should not mislead us about the true nature of the camp brothels, however. They were heavily bureaucratized, highly regulated, and under tight surveillance. The system of strict rules governing the brothels began with their admission criteria. The former block leader of the Buchenwald camp brothel, Max Beulig, said: "German, Polish, Czech and French prisoners of all categories could register with their block leader to visit the brothel. Jews and Russians were forbidden to visit."[75] Different foreign prisoners were permitted entry depending on the camp: Norwegians in Sachsenhausen, Dutch in Buchenwald, Belgians in Flossenbürg, and Ukrainians in Auschwitz and Monowitz.[76] In Mauthausen, only ethnic German, Austrians, and Poles could initially visit the camp brothel; Czechs and Spaniards were permitted only later.[77] In Neuengamme, the camp brothel was reserved for Germans.[78] The differences between the camps resulted from the different ethnic compositions of the camp and contradictory taxonomies of the prisoners.[79] Romek Dubitzki wondered why Poles were admitted to the brothel in the main camp at Auschwitz while Czechs were not.[80] In Flossenbürg, a Black man was admitted to the brothel because he was French.[81]

The SS enforced ethnic segregation in the camp brothels in keeping with laws on prostitution in the Third Reich.[82] According to its central tenet, each nation had to keep to itself. A German prisoner would never be allowed to visit a Slavic prostitute. Conversely, no Slavic prisoner could see a German prostitute. In practice, however, little distinction was made among non-German ethnic groups.[83]

At Mauthausen, applications usually had to be submitted to the brothel office.[84] Before the introduction of the bonus system, prisoners had to pay with the money that had been taken from them upon arrest and kept in an internal camp account or with money sent to them. This was common practice in other early camp brothels, such as Buchenwald and Flossenbürg.[85] In Mauthausen, fifty-pfennig pieces were the only accepted form of payment, which led to the emergence of a veritable black market in the coins.[86]

The Mauthausen system was adopted and modified as other brothels were introduced.[87] The commandant of Buchenwald, Hermann Pister, traveled to Mauthausen to inspect the operation there before opening the brothel in his own camp. He decided to make some improvements.[88] For example, Pister insisted that inmates desiring a visit to the brothel report to the block elder, who would then pass on the name to the office. There the name was written down on a slip of paper and sent to the camp's Rapportführer, who checked the name and stamped the slip of those he approved.[89] Prisoners cleared for a brothel visit had to undergo a checkup by the camp doctor.[90] Albert von Dijk describes the process:

> We went to the block elder, whom I knew, and I said: "I'd like to go to the special building."—"Pay two marks in cash." . . . in the evening or the next evening, or maybe the third evening, you were at the evening roll call . . . your name was taken from the . . . 7646—"Yes." "To the bathroom and bring a clean towel." Then you went to the bathroom, got clean underwear and, if the prisoner's uniform was no longer clean, a new prisoner's uniform, new shoes, i.e. wooden shoes.[91]

After being called, prisoners had to march to the camp brothel in single file. The Belgian Flossenbürg survivor Charles Dekeyser recalls that in Flossenbürg, after the evening roll call, the camp director Karl Fritzsch had approved prisoners line up in rows of two and then march to the brothel barracks. There they had to wait outside the door until the SS allowed them to enter.[92] In the corridor of the brothel in Mauthausen, the block leader sat at a table and checked the brothel tickets, prisoner numbers, and nationality of the prisoners.[93] In Neuengamme, the men were ordered to the office once the list of brothel visitors had been compiled. From there, the SS leader on duty marched the men into the brothel. He locked the brothel door behind him so that no one else could enter and no one could leave.[94]

At the medical examinations, prisoners had to drop their trousers. A Spanish visitor to the brothel at Mauthausen concentration camp reported that the block leader shouted, "Show your hog's fennel!"[95] The prisoner was then given an injection. Charles Dekeyser, talking about Flossenbürg, reported: "When you entered, you had to pull down your pants. Penis out. Then one of the two helpers took out a tube and put some ointment on you . . . what was it for? I assume it was for incidents, illnesses, or something like that. Then I got a number. The number of the room where you're supposed to go to."[96] A survivor of Auschwitz noted that everyone had to undergo this examination. Each prisoner had to show an orderly his genitals and try to pass urine—internal bleeding would be seen as a sign of a sexually transmitted disease. The orderly also asked whether the prisoner had already had syphilis. If he answered yes, he was forbidden to visit the brothel.[97] In the camp brothels that did not have a doctor's room, such examinations were carried out in the infirmary. Roßmann reports that a prisoner at Sachsenhausen had to be examined by a doctor before being admitted to the brothel in order to obtain a clean bill of health.[98] As the concentration camp system broke down, however, medical examinations became increasingly lax. Another Auschwitz inmate, for example, said that the examinations were merely a general inspection of the genitals and that no checkup occurred even after brothel visits.[99] Another inmate reported that at the end of 1943 he received neither ointment nor an injection when he visited a camp brothel.[100]

After the examination, men typically had to wait in the corridor until the SS assigned them to a woman.[101] Charles Dekeyser describes this situation at Flossenbürg: "We stood in front of the door. There was a kapo who . . . entered [the doctor's room], and then exited and stopped the others. And then . . . the Rapportführer walked around, stayed alert, and kept an eye on everything."[102] In camp brothels introduced later, such as Sachsenhausen or Neuengamme, there were special waiting rooms for the men.[103] A former forced sex worker from Neuengamme recalled: "When the men came back from the commode, they went to the common room. . . . We also called this room the contact room. There were tables and chairs in this room. . . . No SS man was allowed to enter."[104] However, the function of the room was not to establish actual contact between the men and the women, as would be the case in a conventional brothel. It merely served as a place for the men to wait before being assigned a room.[105]

Strict rules governed prisoner behavior in the brothel rooms. The SS determined the length and type of sexual acts that could be performed. In Auschwitz, the SS initially gave the men ten to fifteen minutes. Later, it was extended to twenty minutes.[106] In Buchenwald, visitors had twenty minutes.[107] In Mauthausen, the men were only allowed to stay in the brothel rooms for twelve minutes. Brothel-goers in Sachsenhausen had ten minutes.[108] In Monowitz and Mittelbau-Dora, they had fifteen.[109] Men were permitted to have sex only in the missionary position.[110] Shoes had to be removed. There was no uniform practice for instructing prisoners about these rules, however. Sometimes the SS neglected to inform the prisoners.[111] The situation was similar for the forced sex workers. "We hardly received any instructions," Laura Büttig remembered. "We were only told roughly how it would take place."[112]

SS guards monitored the activities in the brothel rooms by periodically looking through glass peepholes installed in the brothel doors.[113] If a prisoner did not finish within the prescribed time, he might be pulled out of the room by the ankle and his clothes thrown out after him.[114] The brothel operated like an assembly line under constant time pressure. Charles Dekeyser describes how he was sent directly from the medical exam to the brothel room, his trousers still around his ankles.[115] Embarrassed by the situation, he talked to the woman for about ten minutes until the SS man showed up. "My Rapportführer came in and beat me: 'Out!' My pants were down, although I didn't have anything anywhere. I pulled my pants up and ran out. Then he gave me another kick and a punch."[116] This was not an isolated case. A former prisoner in Dachau reported that the SS man shouted, "The man must get out!" after he exceeded the designated time.[117] In some concentration camps, such as the Auschwitz main camp and Mittelbau-Dora, the SS used bells for managing the prisoners' time.[118] They rang the bell at the beginning of the session, after the allotted quarter of an hour had passed, and five minutes later to signal the start of the next session.[119]

Though the official purpose of the peepholes was to keep an eye on what was happening in the brothel rooms, SS men and women used them for their voyeuristic amusement. The former block elder of the infirmary in Monowitz, Hermann Leonhardt, recalled that SS men had a grand time and made dirty remarks.[120] An unknown survivor from Dachau stated, "The SS leaders or female leaders often watched the people engage in coitus and knocked on the door with their boots if they took too long."[121] In Sachsenhausen, the camp director August Kolb often amused himself in the brothel, as did his colleague in Mauthausen, Georg Bachmayer, who was often drunk, to boot.[122] Eleonore Hodys, the alleged "lover" of Rudolf Höß, reported that she met a woman from the Auschwitz infirmary who told her that SS-Unterscharführer Friedrich Stiwitz liked to watch her having sex in the brothel.[123] Linda Bachmann said that SS men in Mittelbau-Dora "grinned maliciously" through the peepholes.[124] The SS justified the practice with the argument that it was to protect the women from violent inmates.[125]

In some camps the SS showed more restraint when it came to these voyeuristic practices. For instance, in Neuengamme, the camp commandant had grown up in the same town as a woman in the brothel and didn't want to tarnish his reputation at home. As Laura Büttig recalls, the Neuengamme SS rarely looked through the peepholes.[126] And while the SS humiliated the male prisoners for their own amusement, they were prohibited from sexually harassing the women,[127] and it seems that for the most part they adhered to this rule.[128] Moreover, the SS men were forbidden to enter the brothel rooms or the women's common room.[129] In some concentration camps, such as Flossenbürg, the inmates were sent straight back to the prisoner block after their visit.[130] In others, such as Auschwitz, inmates were given an injection in the doctor's room after having sex.[131] In Neuengamme, the inmates had to wait for the brothel to close and left the building as a group.[132]

The location of the brothel in the topography of the concentration camp and the organization of its interior make plain the total control that the SS sought to exercise over its visitors and the women who worked there. The brothel was sealed off from the rest of the camp, with access tightly monitored. All activities in the brothel were planned and regimented. Outside its short opening hours, the doors were bolted and an SS guard put on duty to make sure no one entered.[133] At night, women in the Auschwitz main camp were locked in a bedroom.[134] SS commanders, guards, and supervisors ensured that order was maintained. During opening hours, an SS man, typically the block leader, was present in the brothel to monitor operations.[135]

In the first camp brothels, female SS helpers served as brothel supervisors.[136] Starting in November 1943, these women were to be replaced, as Glücks decreed in a letter to the commandants of Auschwitz I and II, by "experienced female prisoners . . . who had already run brothels."[137] These women, alternately referred to as "madams," "prisoner supervisors," or "cashiers," were recruited in Ravensbrück or in the Birkenau women's camp.[138] They were mainly to be used for cashiering and accounting. Apparently, the SS needed skilled personnel to run the camp brothels and seem to have had bad experiences with female SS. Kogon writes that the two SS supervisors in the brothel in Buchenwald behaved like "battle-axes."[139] In Buchenwald, the forced sex workers did the accounting themselves until madams were deployed.[140] The records for medical examinations in the Auschwitz camp brothel also list a woman whose name was preceded by "M.," which probably stood for *Mutter*, short for *Puffmutter*, or madam.[141] The "cashiers" received five pfennigs per man to their camp account.[142] The accounting of the camp brothel's income was usually monitored by the block leader, who in turn was controlled by the Rapportführer.[143] In Neuengamme, the Rapportführer Wilhelm Dreimann took over the accounting of the brothel's income.[144]

A total of ten cashiers can be identified by name. Almost all of them were German citizens; at least six of them were imprisoned as "antisocials." In Dachau, only one of the "madams" was Ukrainian, and she probably worked at the brothel for Ukrainian guards in Gusen.[145] Mittelbau-Dora was the exception: There, the SS occasionally employed a Jehovah's Witness and a Jewish woman to handle the accounting. The SS probably believed that this would counteract corruption. In Sachsenhausen, an SS supervisor was also deployed alongside the "cashiers."[146]

As a rule, the SS did not tolerate attempts to challenge its authority. In the case of the brothels, this included any effort to establish personal relationships with women, which could range from sexual barter to emotional connections.[147] The relationships could take place both during the brothel's operation and outside its opening hours. Stephan Szymanski talks about his efforts to visit Izabela Michalek, a woman in the Auschwitz camp brothel with whom he had a personal relationship. He understood how the SS assigned rooms and took a position in line so that he would be assigned to Izabela's room. The SS guard in charge guessed what he was up to and assigned Szymanski to another room.[148] In order to prevent such personal contacts or agreements between male and female prisoners, the SS ordered the women to other rooms or swapped them out with women from other camp brothels.[149] The SS also tried to stop prisoners from courting women's favor with gifts. In Dachau, concerns about prisoners' developing relationships with the women led to a raid of the brothel followed by interrogations and punishments.[150] Max Beulig reported on a case from Buchenwald: "The German girl E. . . . had accepted a golden ring and a golden bracelet as a gift from a German prisoner (a career criminal). This was discovered by the prisoner Hauptmann, who was in charge of investigating criminal matters. The girl was punished by the camp leadership with six days of detention. The girl spent these six days in a brothel room that was used as a broom closet."[151] After serving her sentence, the woman returned to the camp brothel and resumed forced sex work.[152]

The SS also punished prisoners for unauthorized visits to brothels. Stephan Szymanski reports that he entered the brothel at the Auschwitz main camp one night without being noticed. A fight broke out among the women, and the SS raided the brothel. Szymanski managed to hide in the lavatory and remained undetected during the search, but the SS caught a Russian prisoner who had also entered the brothel without permission. The SS men beat the Russian and shortly afterward transferred him to Mauthausen with the note "Return undesirable!"—equivalent to a death sentence.[153] The deportation was not an isolated case. The camp elder of Monowitz was also caught during a nighttime visit to the brothel and transferred to the Fürstengrube satellite camp in 1944.[154]

Other punishments included bans on brothel visits, scorn, violence, and imprisonment. Beulig stated that he punished prisoners himself:

> Once a German prisoner climbed over the plank wall at night and visited a German woman. A German political prisoner named Hauptmann, who carried out investigations at the behest of the Rapportführer, discovered [the violation] when visiting the brothel the next day and arrested a prisoner in Block 19. I gave the detainee, who tried to hit me during the interrogation, two blows to the head with a pair of steel handcuffs. He did not fall unconscious and did not bleed. The prisoner was placed in the lockup, and the German woman's hair was cut off. Both punishments were ordered by the camp leadership.[155]

The visitor log for the brothels in Mauthausen and other camps contain the names of banned prisoners. One prisoner was barred entry for three months for swapping identities with another inmate.[156] The camp prisoner-police also intervened when inmates tried to visit the brothel at night. Kogon reports an incident in Buchenwald: "One night, drunken 'greens' climbed into the special building and threatened the women. The camp police were then called and surrounded the barrack hut. A wild brawl ensued. In the end, the camp guards managed to clean up the brothel."[157]

Nevertheless, the SS ideal of total control often collided with the reality of corruption. The ability to see a particular woman often depended on a favor from the SS guard on duty. Beulig admitted that though the men in Buchenwald were assigned to women in the office, he himself changed this "whenever possible based on the wishes of the prisoners."[158] Some SS men made a business out of it. Moniek Levi writes that in Monowitz, Oberscharführer Stolp issued kapos "admission tickets" to the brothel in return for currency from murdered prisoners.[159] Laura Büttig reports that the SS guards in Neuengamme "were all on the take," accepting cigarettes and other bribes from the prisoners.[160] The SS also refrained from punishing privileged prisoners for unauthorized visits to brothels. Stephan Szymanski reported that a kapo caught him in the Auschwitz brothel without permission and reported it to the SS. The camp director Hössler personally intervened and made the report disappear. Szymanski was under Hössler's protection as a kapo in the fire department—a "model" work detail.[161]

Another crucial factor in the organization of camp brothels was medical supervision. It was so important, in fact, that the brothels were subordinate to the prisoner infirmaries,[162] with the camp doctor directly responsible for the women's health.[163] The infirmary kapos often took over the supervision of the brothels.[164] In Buchenwald, a Czech prisoner who was a physician administered injections to the inmates before they visited the brothel. He also examined the women every morning.[165] In Neuengamme, the task was assigned to a prisoner who was a gynecologist by training.[166]

It is reported that at Monowitz SS leaders (usually Camp Director Schöttl or his deputy), a German medical orderly, a prisoner-doctor, and a prisoner-medical orderly were present to supervise the brothel visits on the three afternoons a week it was open.[167] The prisoner-physicians Stefan Bodziaezek and Henryk Rutkowksi, accompanied by an SS orderly, were responsible for examining the prisoners. Their task was to examine the visitors "in a special room—both before coitus . . . to detect possible venereal diseases, and after coitus . . . to carry out precautionary interventions."[168] The latter involved injecting a colloidal silver solution or applying a mercury ointment.[169]

The brothel women were regularly checked for venereal disease. In Auschwitz, the examinations took place twice a week and were carried out by a prisoner-doctor.[170] The former prisoner Karel Minc reports that Stefan Busziaszek, who was also the camp elder at Monowitz, summoned him for the first examination. The women were taken to the inmate infirmary and told to sit in the gynecological chair. The examinations were carried out by orderlies and doctors, but the camp elder was always present.[171] The block elder of the infirmary was responsible for the woman's health.[172]

The regularity of venereal examinations is evidenced in particular by the *Begleitzettel* that have survived for the entire period that the Auschwitz main camp brothel was in operation and from the end of 1943 to mid-1944 for the Monowitz brothel. According to these records—the *Begleitzettel* were slips of paper that tracked each woman's medical history—samples were regularly sent to the Hygiene Institute of the Waffen-SS in Rajsko to test for sexually transmitted diseases. Pap smears were used to detect gonorrhea. Syphilis tests required blood samples. Later, the SS established a department for dermatological and venereal disease in Monowitz, which performed the tests on site.[173] Similar documents have not survived for other concentration camps. It is known, however, that the Hygiene Institute of the Waffen-SS in Berlin examined blood samples from Sachsenhausen camp prisoners for venereal disease, which suggests that it also processed blood samples and cervical smears from the women who worked in the camp brothel.[174] Based on various eyewitness statements and medical records, cases of sexually transmitted disease in the camp brothels seem to have been extremely rare. The former block leader in Buchenwald stated that not a single case was detected in the camp.[175] In Auschwitz, medical records contain only two positive tests for gonorrhea during the entire sixteen months of the brothel's existence. One of the women was returned to

Birkenau after testing positive.[176] Her fate remains unknown. The other woman was infected only a few days before evacuation, when the SS was no longer interested in combating venereal disease. Her fate is likewise uncertain.[177] One female forced sex worker from Neuengamme was probably returned to Ravensbrück after testing positive for a sexually transmitted disease.[178] Given the paucity of documented cases, the widely held belief among prisoners that women who contracted sexually transmitted diseases in concentration camps were subject to medical experiments is likely false. If women with venereal disease were forced to undergo experimental procedures, it couldn't have been a frequent occurrence.

However, it does seem that female forced sex workers in the brothels for Ukrainian guards had a higher rate of infection than their counterparts in the prisoner brothels. Although only one woman is known to have contracted a disease, the comparatively frequent return of women from Ukrainian brothels to Ravensbrück and the high frequency of gonorrhea and syphilis among the Ukrainian SS suggest that infections were common.[179] At any rate, medical supervision seems to have become laxer for both men and women during the final months of the war. Linda Bachmann recalls that she was never once in the infirmary during her entire stay in the Mittelbau-Dora camp brothel. Inmate nurses or doctors performed no exams during the time the brothel was in operation.[180]

Given the infrequency of disease, why did the SS carry out venereal examinations so regularly? The motivation sprang less from concern for women's health than from a fear of epidemics in the camp. In July 1943, a report was filed against two inmates who tried to gain entry to the brothel with forged brothel tickets. The report emphasizes the seriousness of the offence: "Since such acts circumvent the medical examination and render it invalid . . . the danger that may arise for the camp should not be underestimated."[181] The case sheets of women in Ravensbrück also suggest that the SS regarded venereal disease as an epidemic risk. The sheets contain three main questions: "Sterilization requested? Sexually transmitted disease? Tuberculosis?"[182]

At first glance, it may appear ludicrous that the SS expended energy and resources to combat venereal disease while thousands of prisoners were struggling for survival in miserable conditions. Three main factors can account for the SS insistence on sexual hygiene. The first was ideological: gonorrhea, syphilis, and other sexually transmitted diseases were, in the Nazi worldview, not only medical conditions. They were social evils. In an article on prostitution and venereal disease from 1933, Hitler called them a "terrible poisoning of the body of the people" and "the result of a disease of the moral, social, and racial instincts.[183] As the Nazi elite, the SS led the fight against venereal disease, which Hitler regarded as a "task of the nation."[184]

The second factor was pragmatic: Ideological preoccupations notwithstanding, venereal disease did indeed pose a real threat.[185] The SS hygiene institutes were particularly important in the fight against venereal disease within the ranks of the armed SS as well as in camps, detention facilities, and the society at large.[186] In 1941, the SS Hygiene Institute in Berlin carried out over two hundred thousand blood tests on SS men and produced test serums with prisoners of "mixed blood" from Ravensbrück and Sachsenhausen. It monitored the water supply of the concentration camps and organized the fight against epidemic diseases, typhus in particular. The lab at the Hygiene Institute in Rajsko tested not only SS men and their secretaries[187] but also prisoners, employees of IG Farben, women from the Auschwitz municipal hospital, soldiers, and women from the SS brothel at the Heidelager military complex.[188]

The Nazi fight against venereal disease continued efforts going back to the 1920s to control epidemics of infectious disease and introduce hygiene protocol at repatriation and internment camps.[189] For this reason, the Nazis became sensitive early on to matters of camp hygiene. In 1935, Hans Pfeiffer, the hygienist and camp doctor of the Papenburg camp, stressed in his dissertation that because of the size of the prison camps, maintaining hygiene was key.[190] The structure of the camp, the furnishings of the accommodation blocks, the cleanliness of the kitchens, the quality of the food, the water supply, the clothing, the toilets, hygiene at work, and disease prevention were special matters of concern. In this, SS hygienists drew on the experience of earlier German health officials combating camp epidemics.[191]

But Nazi health officials were less concerned with the welfare of the prisoners than they were with the outbreak of infectious disease among the SS men and the civilian population.[192] Moreover, Nazi hygiene efforts contained a racial component that went beyond public health concerns. The German eugenicist Friedrich Erhard Haag, in a work on camp hygiene, wrote: "The national unity of the German people requires the clear separation of non-nationals. The use of foreign workers in our farming and urban families while supplying them with food and accommodation in individual households is dubious for reasons of national policy. Only the establishment of special small labor camps can bring about the desired separation."[193] In legitimizing ethnic segregation, he buttressed his racial arguments with health considerations: "Constant monitoring is essential. To protect the civilian population, regular examinations are necessary, especially for tuberculosis and for venereal and skin diseases."[194]

The third factor that contributed to SS diligence in monitoring venereal disease was legal. For one, the SS was accountable to local health authorities and had to record and report every case of infectious disease—among its own ranks and among the inmates.[195] For another, the rigorous monitoring of venereal disease in the camp brothels followed the legal protocols in other state-controlled brothels in the Third Reich. These required that prostitutes be examined for venereal disease twice a week by the local health authorities.[196] The rules also applied to brothels under the control of the Wehrmacht.[197] Since concentration camps were state institutions and did not exist in a legal vacuum, it is plausible that they too were subject to laws regarding hygiene, disease control, and prostitution.

5 Sexuality in the Camps

The history of modern prisons—those, in the words of French architect Louis Pierre Baltard, "complete and austere institutions"[1]—is the history of the subjugation of the human body. And a central element of that subjugation is the control of sexuality.[2] In the previous chapter, we saw how the space and organization of the brothels served to exercise total control over forced sex workers and prisoners seeking sex, from who was permitted entry and which sexual practices were permissible to mandatory medical examinations and treatment. But the total power that the SS exerted over the prisoners extended to their sexual lives outside the brothels as well. For this reason, it's worth considering sexuality more generally in the camps. What did sexuality mean in an environment where most prisoners were simply struggling to survive? What forms could it take under the austere conditions of the concentration camp?

The Control of Sexuality

The first element in the Nazi control of prisoner sexuality in the camps was the separation of the sexes. Before the early 1940s, the relatively small number of women in the camp system were segregated from the men and kept at a special camp in Lichtenburg. Later they were placed in Ravensbrück or in the women's camp at Auschwitz-Birkenau. As the concentration camp system became a powerful hub of weapons manufacturing, the SS moved women to camps in the vicinity of those reserved for men. At Auschwitz-Birkenau, Bergen-Belsen, and Ravensbrück, men's and women's camps existed side by side. The first two also had several mixed camps, but these were exceptions in the camp system.[3] The Nazis' decision to keep the sexes mostly separate was based on experiences in Soviet penal camps, where by the mid-1930s the problems of mixed-sex incarceration had become abundantly clear. In July 1936, the director of the Karlag prison complex complained about the collapse of discipline in the camps after various camp authorities had tolerated the open cohabitation of male and female inmates.[4] In his view, "sexual profligacy" and prostitution undermined camp discipline and led to theft, infidelity, and other "negative phenomena." In response, officials banned sexual relations and introduced punishments for violations. Moreover, they eliminated cohabitation, penalized sexual assault, and prohibited men from entering the women's block.[5]

At Nazi concentration camps, the rules did not explicitly prohibit sexual relations between men and women.[6] The reason for this may have been that the SS assumed that the separation of the sexes would lead to sexual abstinence. Furthermore, homosexuality between men was punishable in the Third Reich, so there was no need to include the prohibition in the camp regulations. The one camp that explicitly banned sexual activity was Ravensbrück. Though female homosexuality was not a crime in the Third Reich outside of Austria, Ravensbrück outlawed all forms of sexual relations between women.[7] Specifically, "whoever approaches other prisoners with lespian [*sic*] intent, whoever engages in lespian [*sic*] smut or fails to report such smut" was to be punished.[8] Like Gulag officials, the SS understood sexual activity as a form of disobedience that violated their claim to absolute authority. As a rule, sex was punished with beatings. For instance, regulations at the Natzweiler concentration camp prescribed ten blows for a "love affair with a woman," just as many as for the theft of food and parcels. The maximum penalty for "sexual intercourse with a woman" was twenty-five blows, the same as for an "escape attempt in connection with a burglary" or for the theft of gold or silver. The same applied to "masturbation with prisoners."[9] Statements by former inmates confirm the imposition of punishments for sexual activity.[10]

The Realities of Camp Life

In contrast to other types of prison camps, Nazi concentration camps required that prisoners make a radical break with the values and moral concepts of the outside world. The human psyche had to focus all its attention on mere survival. In 1947, the Austrian psychologist Viktor Frankl presented a study of the psychopathology of concentration camp life.[11] Drawing on his own experiences as a prisoner in Nazi concentration camps as well as on those of other inmates, Frankl developed a three-phase model to classify the typical "psychological reactions to camp life."[12] The first phase took place after prisoners arrived at the camp; the second phase began after they had grown used to camp life; the third stage came after they were freed.[13] I will concentrate on the first two phases as they are the most relevant for my study.

The most prominent feature of the first phase was shock. It began with the incarceration and culminated in a break with one's entire life up to that point. The induction process was particularly unsettling: Group showers, fumigation, and the shaving of prisoners' heads were the first acts of dehumanization. They were attacks on sexuality and intimacy aimed at the destruction of the individual.[14] Linda Bachmann observes that the women in her transport were treated like cattle. "The personal effects, everything was gone. We had nothing whatsoever. And then I saw others whose hair they [the prison guards] had cut off."[15] What had once been citizens were now masses of naked bodies crammed together.[16]

The second phase consisted of psychological adaptation to the horrors of camp life.[17] This involved habituation to fear, violence, and death and the onset of apathy in the prisoner's mind.[18] Suffering, illness, dying, and death were integral parts of a prisoner's daily struggle for survival. Hunger superseded all other needs. The urge to eat thrust itself into the center of existence.[19] It was typical for prisoners to experience a certain "gastric onanism" in place of masturbation, imagining all sorts of mouthwatering delicacies to pacify the pangs of hunger that accompanied their every waking hour. Self-preservation filled their entire horizon of awareness. Anything that did not serve this need became irrelevant.[20]

A critical skill that prisoners quickly learned was how to blend in with the other inmates. Remaining inconspicuous was one of the fundamental rules of survival because the consequences of attracting the attention of the SS or the kapos could be fatal. But the constant effort to avoid being singled out left them feeling "the radical worthlessness of individual human life."[21] They lost the sense that they were human agents and instead regarded themselves as entirely at the mercy of fate. The apathy rendered prisoners unable to take initiative, even as the camp often demanded split-second decisions determining life and death. Instead, they withdrew from their horrifying surroundings and sought refuge in the inner "realm of mental freedom."[22] Some contemplated intellectual or spiritual ideas; others escaped into feelings of love for a person far away.[23]

As the prisoners were still habituating themselves to the camp environment, their bodies began to break down. The rapid shock of the dehumanization of the mind eventually gave way to the inexorable decimation of the body. Amid this physical decline, prisoners' secondary sex characteristics became barometers of health. For example, in Auschwitz, full breasts were considered a mark of physical strength. Simha Naor writes:

> You know, the most important thing here is that the breasts remain good. Everything else is of no importance. . . . When the Germans look at you, they look first at the bosom . . . not because they are interested . . . [but because]

> as long as the bosom is good, your glands are still working, and the person counts as a work animal. Those whose breasts are wrinkled are selected for execution first.[24]

With each passing day, the physical capital of prisoners underwent a steady decline. First the body depleted its fat reserves. Next to go was the subcutaneous cell tissue. After that, the body consumed its own protein until muscles became severely atrophied.[25] Oszkár Betlen observed people who had become completely emaciated after only a few months of imprisonment at the Monowitz camp: "I saw for the first time what 'emaciated to the bone' means in reality. The people had no buttocks at all; their skeletal legs protruded directly from their skeletal backbones."[26] The Auschwitz survivor Dracjan Fijalkowski describes a group of female concentration camp inmates she observed in the washroom: "Naked, hairless skeletons huddled in a heap looked at us with dull, completely expressionless eyes, and only dried flaps of skin hanging from their chests testified that these were once women who were full of life."[27]

The disappearance of secondary sex characteristics led prisoners to stop seeing themselves as sexual beings.[28] For women, the changes felt particularly noticeable. As a Jewish survivor of Auschwitz recalls: "I don't know, I can't define it, but I know I didn't feel like I was a woman. During the early days, when I still looked strong, I was so skinny that I had no bosom at all. Interestingly, though, I also had no wrinkles and no loose skin. Everything was completely smooth. It was strange. I can't define it for you, I can't tell you the difference, or how the feeling that one is a woman or that one is sexless expresses itself. But I noticed it. There was a difference."[29] Men also noted women's genderless appearance. The Polish Sachsenhausen survivor Aleksander Kulisiewicz, describing the arrival of one thousand women at the camp, observes with cruel candor how his initial joy soon faded once he realized that they resembled the male prisoners. He searched for signs of femininity but could not find them: "The gaze seeks the calves. The gaze seeks and seeks. It finds crooked, unflattering heels. The legs? Ugh! So skinny. Warped like . . . those of a cab horse. The hips are like a long-forgotten violin that has lost its magic."[30] It is no surprise, therefore, that in camps like Auschwitz corpulence was seen as an expression not only of wealth but also of beauty.[31] Men, too, perceived the loss of their sexuality, though their accounts are far fewer in number.[32] This may stem from differing practices between men and women with regard to memory and narrative or from strong feelings of shame associated with the loss of masculinity.[33]

Despite their physical deterioration, some prisoners did what they could to improve their looks. A well-groomed appearance was a symbolic act against dehumanization and desexualization, and women in particular worked to maintain their outward appearance when possible.[34] At stake was not just a boost to one's morale; a healthy-looking exterior increased a prisoner's chances of avoiding selection.

The Meaning of Sexuality in the Camps

Despite the hardships of camp existence and the efforts of officials to eliminate sex, sexuality nevertheless persisted in Nazi concentration camps. This accords with studies in the early 1930s showing that humans remain sexual beings during imprisonment.[35] Still, the amount of sex inmates had and the experience of their sexuality varied widely. Some survivors speak of sexual desires disappearing completely. "The only thought was to stay on one's feet," Willi Frohwein, an inmate at Auschwitz, recalls. "Women made an impression only insofar as we knew what they were going through in Block 10.[36] They were more the object of sorrow and pity than . . . sex was on none of our minds."[37] Primo Levi also talks of sexual abstinence, but he makes clear that it was not a burden. Benedikt Kautsky estimates that for 90 percent of the men in the concentration camps the "sexual problem" found in detention centers and other types of camps did not exist.[38] The sociologist Anna Pawełczyńska writes that sex did not count among the basic needs of the prisoners at Auschwitz.[39]

Other accounts emphasize the importance of sexuality for inmates. The former Auschwitz prisoner Tadeusz Borowski reports that male inmates were obsessed with women. According to his account, young male prisoners fought to get into a work detail in the women's camp at Auschwitz-Birkenau. Some men were "downright sick."[40] Prisoners from other concentration camps have made similar statements. "Sexuality played an insane role," was how Ernst Federn, an inmate at Buchenwald, put it.[41] A former Dachau prisoner reports that despite the malnutrition, he missed sexual activity: "Many had sexual dreams at night or engaged in masturbation. I also had the silent desire to visit the camp brothel. However, the circumstances surrounding such a visit prevented me."[42]

Not long after war ended, doctors and psychologists took up the matter of sexuality in concentration camps. The psychoanalyst Paul Friedman, in a lecture at the annual meeting of the American Psychiatric Association in May 1948, examined the sexual lives of camp prisoners.[43] Starting in the late

1950s, various studies looked at the significance of sexuality in Auschwitz. In 1959, the Psychiatric Clinic of the Medical Academy in Krakow, under the direction of Professor Eugeniusz Brzezicki, conducted a study of seventy-seven former Auschwitz prisoners (sixty men and seventeen women). Of those interviewed, forty-four stated that they had completely lost their sexual drive in Auschwitz (57 percent). Only fourteen of those examined confirmed an existing sex drive (18 percent). Three of the survivors stated that they had masturbated in the camp. According to their own statements, they did so only when not afflicted by extreme hunger. Four men reported having had sexual intercourse in the camp, two of them for the first time and both in the camp brothel. With the exception of the female menstrual cycle, the study did not consider sex-specific topics.[44]

In the early 1970s, Polish physicians again addressed the issue of sexuality in concentration camps, this time in connection with "concentration camp syndrome," a posttraumatic stress disorder experienced by former prisoners.[45] The most significant study came from the Wroclaw sexologists Jerzy St. Giza and Wiesław Morasiewicz, who examined male sexuality using Frankl's three-phase model.[46] During the shock phase, which could last from two to six months,[47] the sex drive shut down. Erotic dreams, spontaneous erections, and sexual themes in conversations and thoughts remained absent as the entire psyche focused on survival. In the second phase, prisoners recovered somewhat from the initial shock. Fifty percent of the men involved in the study reported engaging in sexual activity.[48] The most widespread activity was masturbation. The inmates who masturbated the most in percentage terms did so only once every two to three months. They indicated that the urge to masturbate was less about satisfying sexual needs than about dispelling deep-seated anxiety. For young men, sexual activity was also a way to feel alive.[49]

In 1971, Giza and Morasiewicz studied the long-term effects of concentration camp imprisonment on a group of twenty female survivors, addressing some aspects of sexuality covered by the 1959 Brzezicki study.[50] One hardly surprising result was that stress and hunger had a decisive influence on women's bodily functions. Reports from female survivors indicate that the menstrual cycle often ceased soon after arrival at the camp, sometimes as early as the initial arrest.[51] Giza and Morasiewicz suspected that, in addition to shock and hunger, the administration of pharmaceutical substances also increased the number of menstrual irregularities.[52] At any rate, concentration camp life inflicted permanent damage on the reproductive systems of many women: The fertility rate of women who survived the camps was 50 percent lower than that of women in the average population.[53] In all likelihood, the breakdown of reproductive capacity was one reason why women later talked in such detail about feeling that they had lost their femininity in the camps.

The study by Giza and Morasiewicz found that the effect of the concentration camps on the sexual lives of women shared similarities with what men experienced. The stress of the camps eliminated sexual thoughts in most of the study's female subjects immediately after arrival in the camp. Women's sexual needs vanished amid the naked struggle for survival and worries about the well-being of loved ones—parents, husbands, children—left behind. Erotic dreams and nocturnal orgasms were exceedingly rare.[54] Forty-five percent of the women studied said that they masturbated in the camp, but only infrequently.[55] The motivation for masturbation in women, as with men, arose less from sexual urges than from neuroses and anxiety, the fear of infertility in particular.[56]

The studies mentioned here draw on only a small number of former prisoners and hence do not address the immense differences between inmates from different cultural and religious backgrounds and from various positions within the prison hierarchy. Nevertheless, they are of particular importance for understanding the function and expression of sexuality in concentration camps. As I later discuss, they also provide a crucial reference point when considering the coping strategies of forced sex workers and the motives of males for visiting camp brothels.

Sexual Relations in the Camps

Poor living conditions, constant outbreaks of violence, and gender segregation led to the emergence of specific forms of sexuality in the concentration camps. Let us begin with heterosexual relations, which outside the brothels were exceedingly rare. They occurred only where contact with prisoners of the opposite sex was possible, as in the mixed subcamps at Bergen-Belsen and Auschwitz-Birkenau. They were also conceivable in places where prisoners came across civilians, for example, at certain places of work. But relationships of this kind were reserved almost exclusively for privileged prisoners.[57] For the majority of prisoners, the idea of women in a men's camp was unthinkable. Accordingly, the few instances when women were housed in relatively close proximity to men created a sensation. The former prisoner Wieslaw Kielar describes the excitement caused by the establishment of the women's camp at Auschwitz-Birkenau: "After the temporary fence separating the prisoner-of-war camp from our own camp had been demolished, a high concrete wall was erected, partitioning off one-third of the whole camp. Rumor had it that this partitioned-off section was to house female prisoners.

Women in a men's camp! It was simply unbelievable."[58] Despite the short distance to the women's camp, however, many men in Auschwitz had no way of interacting with women. "Contact with the opposite sex was unimaginable at Auschwitz," Samuel Pisar writes. "Every day separate columns of marching men and women would cross each other. In the circumstances, only one thought prevailed: 'For us it's horrendous, but what must it be like for them?' That was how men and women 'met' at Auschwitz."[59]

It was different for prisoners of the upper echelons of prisoner society, especially prisoner functionaries.[60] It was common knowledge that kapos in the Auschwitz main camp attempted to establish contact and have sexual intercourse with the women in Block 10.[61] Stephan Szymanski recalls that at the time when the women's camp was still a separate part of the main camp, some kapos and block elders called out to the women from the second floor of their barrack huts, gesticulating wildly.[62] Unlike the majority of prisoners, who were exhausted, they were able to maintain a sex life in the camps. Paul Thygesen, a physician and survivor of Neuengamme, reports that privileged prisoners performed less physically demanding work and received larger portions of food, which translated into a surplus of strength and a rekindling of sexual desire.[63] To have a heterosexual sex life, male prisoners also had to have the ability to move between the various subcamps so as to come into contact with women.[64] The number of prisoners meeting both criteria was extremely small and was limited almost exclusively to the group of prisoner functionaries whose work details allowed for a certain degree of movement between camps.[65]

Sexual activity between men and women could take the form of a love affair, a transactional relationship, sexual exploitation, or rape.[66] The boundaries were often fluid.[67] Ella Lingens writes that young women who were able to get enough to eat had sexual relationships with young male prisoners.[68] These were not necessarily love relationships; often, people entered them for pragmatic reasons. The Auschwitz survivor Mali Fritz speaks of *kochanas*, female "loved ones" who received help from male prisoners.[69] In Auschwitz and other camps where contact between men and women occurred, such relationships were common, and an important survival strategy for the women who engaged in them.[70] By and large, however, these relationships were on option only for attractive women whose secondary sex characteristics were visible and who were not overly scarred by imprisonment. "Whoever was pretty and young had it easy; that was one of the camp principles," Elisabeth Szegö says. "Having a kochani was very important. Then you had it good. An unprecedented trade in luxuries was happening in Kanada [the warehouses in Auschwitz-Birkenau containing the personal effects of murdered prisoners]. For example, some girls wore new stockings every day, and just threw away the old ones. They got literally everything from their sweetheart."[71] Male prisoners who entered the Birkenau women's camp looking well groomed were highly sought after. Through them, women could barter for food and other necessities and thus increase their chances of survival. Kielar reports that women longed for the help and protection of male prisoners because it gave them "the strength to survive under conditions which animals would not stand."[72] Some male prisoners bragged to other inmates about their "conquests."[73]

During the war, sexual barter and informal prostitution were commonplace at other types of camps as well. For example, Meinhard Stark writes that female prisoners in the gulags prostituted themselves during work and received in return perks, clothing, food, and better jobs. Many women considered such exchanges to be completely normal.[74] The historian Anna Hájková found that such transactional relationships were widespread in the Theresienstadt ghetto, even during the worst periods of hunger.[75] The Italian Birkenau survivor Liana Millu, in her account of such relationships, cautions against passing moral judgment:

> If someone gave you three cigarettes, you could buy an extra ration of bread. It was possible to live three or four days longer, the time the provisions lasted. The math always worked out. Only I wouldn't call it prostitution. It was a means that helped one stay alive. That's what I would call it. You say selling the body. I mean, it wasn't a sale. It was something that I think is much more normal and natural than when a young girl today prostitutes herself in an everyday situation to get money for a pretty dress. By contrast, if you make your body available because you know it will keep you alive, then that is a simple means of survival.[76]

At Auschwitz-Birkenau, the SS housed women selected for murder in the unfinished "Mexiko" section of the camp when the gas chambers were full. The women there lived miserably, without sufficient clothing, food, and water. As Kielar reports, the trade in sexual services was one of the few ways for women who still had feminine features to obtain food and water.[77] The situation was similar in the Birkenau "Gypsy" camp.[78] Though the people housed there did not have to work, were allowed to keep their hair, and lived in family quarters, they received scarcely any rations from the SS. Instead, they bartered for food with valuables and sexual favors. According to various reports, kapos and SS leaders frequently amused themselves in the Gypsy camp, where they drank and engaged in debauchery. The young women in the camp fed entire families by providing sex. "What did innocence mean here?" asks Kielar. "It was better that they lost it than that they starved. Young girls maintained entire families, and not only that, they even got back the gold and jewelry that had been previously sold by their fathers for the low price of a few bowls of turnip greens and were now returned to them as gifts from their protectors."[79]

Not only did the catastrophic living conditions force women to make their "bodies available."[80] Prisoners in positions of power threatened to kill them if they didn't perform sexual acts on command. In his Auschwitz memoir, *Of Blood and Hope*, Samuel Pisar mentions that the compost heap at Auschwitz-Birkenau was a spot for dragooning women into sex. The men who pushed the garbage carts to the heap were privileged kapos. The women who carted in refuse from their camp had been selected for their looks by female supervisors in on the arrangement. Pisar, whose job was to compost the garbage and mix it with human ashes for fertilizer, watched as women were taken against their will to a nearby house. There he "witnessed some of the orgies, being charged with keeping the participants supplied with water." "After the first moment of panic, the instinct for survival made the young women overcome their revulsion and even pretend to enjoy the privilege of submission to our obsessed little gods: because if not pleased, gods can punish. A girl whose embrace proved unsatisfactory would have a black mark against her, the kapos warned, and would be beaten or executed on her return to camp."[81] But, as Pisar notes, sometimes such abuse was "touched by a hint of tenderness and beauty." In one episode he witnessed, a kapo who had been "violent and cruel" suddenly planted "a tender kiss on a girl's lips" and sank "helplessly and quietly away from her arms." "Such sights," Pisar muses, "contributed, perhaps, to my emotional development, leaving me with a sense that nothing that lives is quite beyond the reach of Eros, and that even among the most wicked or the most damaged, some wisp of human feeling can be found."[82]

These examples of informal prostitution and sexual coercion arose from the specific situation in Birkenau, the close proximity of male and female sectors, and the particularly poor living conditions in the women's camp. The situations in the temporary Mexiko and Gypsy camps were unique in the concentration camp system. A few similar cases existed at other concentration camps, but these were often made possible by the increased mixing of women's and men's work details toward the end of the war amid the general deterioration of living conditions.[83]

Same-sex sexual behavior was far more common than heterosexual relations in the concentration camps given the strict separation of the sexes; indeed, it was often the only possible way to have a sex life.[84] This form of sexuality, known as situational homosexuality, often emerges in all-male prisons and internment camps, and it was the most common way of meeting sexual needs in the Nazi camps.[85] Generally, such relationships took place between two heterosexual prisoners who simulated a heterosexual relationship by assuming male and female roles. The former Buchenwald prisoner and psychologist Ernst Federn says that it was usually easy to recognize which prisoners were engaging in situational homosexuality. Men would exclusively seek out girlish-looking boys and adolescents.[86] Female prisoners took sexual partners to whom they gave male roles and names.[87]

Situational same-sex relationships in concentration camps took various forms. Some were emotional in nature. Others were pragmatic. Often, however, these relationships were exploitative or coerced. The most widespread were relationships with *Pipel,* often underage youths who served male and female kapos and performed sexual favors.[88] Langbein calls them a "customary remedy for sexual distress."[89]

A detailed account of *Pipel* relationships comes from the former camp elder of Sachsenhausen, Harry Naujoks, who was transferred to the Flossenbürg concentration camp in 1943.[90] In October 1945, Naujoks wrote a report on conditions in Flossenbürg that describes the practice in detail.[91] He writes that it behooved a prisoner functionary to have a *Lustknabe,* or "boy toy." Most were young Russians or Poles. Hermann G., a "criminal" who served as elder of the barrack huts for new prisoners, chose the prettiest boy from each transport. He gave him a special bed, fed him food and small treats, and let him stay in the huts during the day so that he would not have to work. After a few days seeing the others return physically exhausted and starving, the boy began to understand what could become of him if he lost the elder's protection. At that point, Hermann G. usually took him to his bed. A boy who refused was forced to do hard physical labor in the quarry the next day. After that, he was ready for anything. According to Naujoks, almost every block elder or foreman had such a *Pipel.*[92]

A negative undertone runs through former prisoners' accounts of the youths involved in *Pipel* relationships. They contend that the adolescents acted voluntarily and accuse them of exploiting their proximity to the camp elite. The Holocaust survivor Hans Adler describes a fat, rosy-cheeked fourteen-year-old boy in the Auschwitz-Birkenau camp whose job was to run errands for the block elder: "He does not even come up to the shoulders of most inmates but is a strong lout who can do whatever he likes, an aggressive, cantankerous creature. His slaps in the face are well aimed; he is permitted to flog the strongest men, and they cannot defend themselves because the young rascal is under the protection of the block elder, who might kill anyone his darling complains about."[93] Of course, this account and others like it forget that the boys and girls who served as *Pipel* were in sexually exploitative relationships with higher-ranking prisoners and were powerless to defy them.[94]

Very few *Pipel* who survived the concentration camp have spoken about the sexual exploitation they experienced.[95] One exception is the Polish Jew Keith Random,[96] who was deported to Flossenbürg in 1943 when he was seventeen. He concealed that he was Jewish and was classified as Polish. One day, the elder from Block 17, a man named Willy who was notorious for his violent treatment of the inmates, called Random to him. Willy had chosen Random after going with the other block elders to pick a new "bedman" at Block 19, where the youths were housed, and he offered the teen the neighboring cot. One evening Willy ordered the boy to undress and get into his bed. He raped the boy, who was sexually inexperienced in every way, resulting in great physical pain. But eventually the block elder began to treat Random better, rewarding him with extra rations of bread or soup, and the pain became tolerable for the boy. A few weeks later, Willy gave Random to another block elder, Max, who was less brutal. The boy understood that sexual submission could ensure his survival and did everything to remain in the elder's favor.[97]

As in the exploitative relationships between men and women, violence and pragmatism were intertwined in many same-sex relationships. Sexually exploited prisoners understood the sexual violence that they experienced purely in terms of physical pain, which lines up with a psychology focused solely on survival; their bodies had lost any sexual connotation. The physical pain of sexual violence and exploitation was small compared with the pain of hunger and the fear of death. Indeed, submitting to sexual exploitation was one of the few survival strategies for boys. Langbein mentions a young man named Thomas Geve, who "was told by an acquaintance of the same age that his kapo was exploiting him sexually." "What else could have protected me from hard labor, hunger, and disease?" the acquaintance was said to have asked.[98]

Relatively little has been reported about *Pipel* relationships between female functionaries and younger girls. This may be explained by the general underrepresentation of female firsthand accounts. But the studies by Giza and Morasiewicz and, more recently, the work of Claudia Schoppmann have shown that such relationships were not unusual in women's camps, where they appear to have been the most common form of living out one's sexuality. For example, six women interviewed in Giza and Morasiewicz's 1971 study

(30 percent of the sample) report having had a lesbian relationship while imprisoned. Each of the women stated that they had been coerced into sexual acts by female prisoner functionaries. The coercion consisted of strong psychological pressure and was often reinforced with gifts such as food or clothing. As for male *Pipel*, these sexually exploitative relationships were a basic means for survival.[99]

The SS was aware of the violations of the prohibition on sex and of the existence of situational homosexuality. Indeed, the former commandant of Auschwitz, Rudolf Höß, pays great attention to this topic in his memoirs.[100] There he notes that homosexuals were already a "problem" when he was a block leader in Dachau. There, same-sex activity was reported even after placing known perpetrators in separate blocks. Höß believed that isolation was a solution and proposed that all known homosexuals be kept alone in the same hut.[101] The men were also to be kept under "strict watch" to prevent intercourse.[102] These measures, in combination with particularly hard labor, such as pushing "heavy rollers used to level the camp streets," ensured that "the epidemic was at once stopped from spreading."[103]

In Sachsenhausen, homosexuals were generally locked in a separate hut. They, too, were assigned to a back-breaking work detail: the brickworks. The hard work, Höß writes, was intended to lead some prisoners to renounce their homosexuality and to exhaust the rest. In 1944, Heinrich Himmler had some homosexuals at Ravensbrück undergo "renunciation tests" for "homosexuals whose recovery was still in doubt."[104] They were to be "set to work in company with whores, and their behavior carefully observed." Then "the whores were ordered to approach the homosexuals inconspicuously and attempt to excite them sexually."[105] If the male prisoner responded to the women, he was considered "improved" and was next subjected to a second test in which men offered them intercourse. If he did not respond to the offer, he was released back into the men's block.[106] Prisoners caught by the SS engaging in homosexual activities were castrated.[107] Under certain circumstances, the discovery of a homosexual relationship could mean the death of one or both individuals.[108]

In Flossenbürg and Auschwitz, special attempts were made to prevent the sexual exploitation of boys and adolescent males by keeping them in their own huts, which protected them from nighttime assaults and forced prostitution.[109] In Ravensbrück, by contrast, the SS tried to prevent homosexual acts by imposing draconian punishments, up to and including execution. Even holding hands was enough to get women prisoners accused of engaging in lesbian sex.[110]

Various survivor accounts link the establishment of camp brothels to the SS's crackdown on homosexuality, and several contend that the latter was either the primary or secondary cause of the former.[111] But neither surviving SS files nor testimonies of former SS officers provide evidence for that connection. As I showed in Chapter 2, the available evidence suggests that camp brothels were established as part of a bonus system to increase labor output.[112] Furthermore, the introduction of camp brothels had no influence on the number of homosexual acts that took place.[113]

I have stressed from the outset of this book that, contrary to the portrayals of Yehiel De-Nur and the authors of Nazi sexploitation literature, SS guards did not brutally rape Jewish women in the camp brothels. Jewish women weren't recruited as forced sex workers, and SS guards weren't permitted to have sex with those who were. Nevertheless, sexual relations between prisoners and SS men did occur in the camps. Indeed, quite a few accounts testify to the existence of such relationships in Auschwitz.[114] Hermann Langbein writes: "Anyone who knows how little attention members of the SS paid to prohibitions will not be surprised to learn that despite all those strict prohibitions many of them started sexual relationships with prisoners. It is understandable that this gave rise to numerous rumors in the camp, but some of these relationships can be documented."[115] Rudolf Höß describes the relationship of a female guard at Auschwitz with a "criminal" kapo,[116] and other SS officers told of similar relationships. The former prisoner Wiesław Kielar details a sexual relationship between Oberscharführer Schillinger and a female kapo named Anni.[117] Two relationships in particular achieved a level of notoriety and appear repeatedly in survivors' accounts. One was the liaison between the first Rapportführer of Auschwitz, the SS Scharführer Gerhard Palitzsch, who was known for his cruelty, and a female prisoner from the Gypsy camp.[118] The other relationship is that between the camp commandant Rudolf Höß and Eleonore Hodys, a Viennese woman who worked as an aide in Höß's villa. But though the latter affair is well documented in the detailed testimony of Hodys, its credibility has been disputed.[119]

Accounts of sexual relations between SS men and prisoners at other concentration camps are extremely rare.[120] In this regard, Auschwitz appears to represent a special case. Langbein attributes these sexual relations to the "atmosphere of the extermination camp,"[121] in which corruption, alcoholism, madness, and rule violations were rampant. What is striking about the heterosexual relationships reported between prisoners and the SS is that the female inmates were often members of the prisoner elite and hence stood closer to the SS in the camp hierarchy.[122] Still, these relationships, like those between prisoners, were mostly transactional, driven by the will to survive.

Little is currently known about the rape of women, especially Jewish women, by SS men. This topic remains woefully understudied, and the question of its frequency is controversial among researchers.[123] Some survivors, especially from Auschwitz, do mention cases of sexual violence.[124] Nevertheless, rape seems to have been relatively rare.[125] By contrast, statements exist testifying to the SS's having raped women before their murder in the Bełżec, Sobibór, and Treblinka camps, where the "atmosphere of the extermination camp" prevailed in extreme form.[126]

This chapter makes plain what many might have guessed: Only a small minority of concentration camp prisoners had anything approaching a sex life. The destruction of individuality that prisoners encountered on entering the camps was followed by a rapid loss of sexual identity. Most women ceased to menstruate and soon lost their secondary sex characteristics from brutal work and permanent malnutrition. The bodies of men and women deteriorated until, in the end, they were nothing more than skin and bones. The sex drive disappeared as hunger came to dominate consciousness. The destruction of the body was meant to bring with it the extermination of sexuality. As Langbein observes, the mere thought of sex occurred only "in the thin stratum of well-nourished prisoners," that is, prisoner functionaries or inmates with the means to barter for food.[127]

But what this chapter also has shown, more surprisingly, is that within this stratum, expressions of sexuality were not uncommon. Kieler mentions that some female kapos resumed menstruation[128] and that women working in the sick bay in Birkenau never missed an opportunity to approach male prisoners.[129] Some were downright profligate in their pursuit of sex. The camp elder of the Kaiserwald concentration camp, near Riga, was known to maintain a veritable "harem."[130] An active sexuality in the camps was a sign of status and power in addition to physical health. Likewise, those who possessed a sexualized body had capital that could be exchanged for food and protection. While these exchanges were transactional, they were not free of coercion. They were a response to the poor living conditions in the camp and sometimes to direct death threats from other prisoners. Moreover, the exchange could also be accompanied by violence and exploitation. Coercion no doubt played a role in the kapos and block elders who used their power to sexually exploit children and adolescents. The victims of sexual violence experienced it as a necessary evil and the price for life. The former

Pipel Keith Random recalls thinking, "If this is the price of life, let it be."[131] Or as the Belgian Flossenbürg survivor Charles Dekeyser writes: "It saved many a young boy's life. You can stand above it however you like. . . . If your life or death depends only on some sexual act, you would rather go along with it and live. And that is the rule for every person who wants to live."[132] The rules for survival in the concentration camp demanded that prisoners abandon their moral values and their sense of disgust. Only those who adapted had any chance of making it out alive.

Yet despite everything—the strict control, the harsh conditions, the violence that could erupt at any moment—the preservation of a sexual identity could sometimes also be an act of self-assertion against the life-destroying machinery of the camps. Liana Millu describes how women found solace in feminine behavior and drew strength from the preservation of their femininity.[133] The attempt to reclaim a female identity also meant reactivating one's sexuality. As the studies by Giza and Morasiewicz show, masturbation was motivated less by the desire to satisfy one's sexual needs than by the desire to reaffirm one's own physical existence and combat anxiety.[134] In this regard, the act of returning to sexuality, of resexualizing oneself, could be a form of resistance that challenged the SS's claim to absolute power.

As we will see in the next chapter, the sex workers in the camp brothels belonged to the thin stratum of prisoners with sex lives. The coerced nature of that work ensured that sexuality for them was rarely a form of affirmation, though the "privilege" of having a sexuality would nevertheless prove crucial for their survival.

6 The Lives of Forced Sex Workers

One day in July 1943, at half past three in the morning, the feared Ravensbrück guard Dorothea Binz threw open the door of the cell holding Magdalena Walter and several other women and, baton in hand, shouted, "Out! Out! Out!" Binz lined up the women in the corridor and took them to the commandant's office. Two other female guards appeared, gave each of the inmates a piece of bread and some liver sausage, and marched them a little over a mile to the Fürstenberg train station, where a train was waiting.[1] The women disembarked in Berlin for a connection. One guard threatened to shoot the women if they tried to escape. In the new train, they were told nothing about their ultimate destination. The train finally halted in Weimar. Their carriage was decoupled from the others, and the train pulled away. The women had no idea what would happen to them.[2]

In her later statements, Magdalena Walter revealed very little about what was going through her mind that morning—only the fear that she was being taken to a brothel for SS men, a rumor that she had heard about at Ravensbrück. The other women in the transport were confused, and they all felt a strong sense of disorientation.[3]

At the Weimar train station, an SS man herded the women out of the train car and toward a truck. An officer yelled, "Tarp aside, flap down . . . everyone on!" and they quickly boarded.[4] Through a plastic window in the tarp the women watched as the truck drove into a men's camp and stopped in front of barrack huts surrounded by a wooden fence. The huts looked like nothing Magdalena Walter knew in Ravensbrück; only later would she find out that it was Buchenwald. The women were taken to a waiting room, where they finally learned what was to become of them: "We were told that we would now be in a prisoners' brothel. We would have it good, and we would eat and drink well. And if we complied, that is, if we behaved properly, nothing would happen to us."[5] Then the women were assigned rooms. Magdalena Walter was placed in room number 13.[6]

The women remained in quarantine for about a week.[7] On July 11, 1943, the camp brothel at Buchenwald was opened. Magdalena Walter remembers that she resisted when the first prisoner came to her: "I indicated to him with a pair of scissors that I would stab him to death if he touched me."[8] She kept silent about the rest, though the schedule for that day reveals appointments with six men.[9]

Daily Routines

For all the uncertainty and apprehension that accompanied Magdalena Walter's arrival at Buchenwald, it quickly became apparent that camp life followed a monotonous routine, characterized by fixed wake-up times, mealtimes, and working hours. In 1947, Max Beulig, a former block leader at the Buchenwald camp brothel, soberly described daily life: "I woke them up at seven o'clock. The women washed and cleaned their rooms. From eight to nine, a female prisoner, who also worked as a prostitute in the brothel, supervised their early morning exercises. . . . From nine to twelve the women were allowed to attend to their personal affairs—washing, ironing, repairing stockings, etc."[10] The women had breakfast in their rooms between seven and eight o'clock and lunch at 11:30 in the lounge.[11] The afternoon schedule was as follows: "From 12 to 2 o'clock the women had to stay in their rooms for a siesta. After that, the women sewed for the clothing department. The work usually did not take the whole afternoon. When the women were done, they could do whatever they wanted, such as play ball games, and, in nice weather, sunbathe on the small lawn that surrounded the brothel."[12]

The daily routine at brothels in other concentration camps seems to have been organized similarly, with some differences.[13] At Auschwitz, the women also had to pick herbs and nettle plants; in Neuengamme they had to repair stockings for guards.[14] Magdalena Walter's memory of the daily routine largely accorded with that of Beulig.[15] More noteworthy are the differences in emphasis. Beulig's description downplays the difficulties of brothel life, while Magdalena Walter highlights the hours of emptiness and waiting that preceded the sex work in the evening.[16]

The women were allowed to take walks beyond the brothel grounds only rarely and only under the supervision of the SS, and they were kept completely isolated from the other inmates. The Polish Buchenwald survivor Adolf Górski remembers that the men were only permitted to make eye contact with the women and that the walks took place only after the male prisoners were already in the blocks. The women always stayed together.[17] The walks do not seem to have offered any escape from the monotony of camp life. Magdalena Walter describes the days in Buchenwald as follows: "One day was like the other. There was no Christmas party, there was no Easter party. . . . Sunday was just as much a working day as a weekday."[18]

The living conditions of the women in the Buchenwald brothel were better than in other camp brothels. In Mauthausen, the women were kept locked up in the brothel building, whose windows were outfitted with iron bars. The women were not allowed to leave the brothel rooms during opening hours and had to sleep there at night. Curtains in front of the windows gave the impression of a private sphere, but their real function was to prevent others from looking in.[19]

Whether in Buchenwald or elsewhere, the women's general isolation meant that they knew little of the goings-on at the camp. This is clearly illustrated by the example of Linda Bachmann. After being transferred to Mittelbau-Dora, she learned next to nothing about the camp. She was familiar only with the office and the roll-call square, which she could see from the brothel's windows. She knew nothing about the camp's underground facilities for rocket production. She merely thought that the camp had a quarry.[20]

From Mondays to Saturdays, the transition from the women's daily routine to their sex work began in the early evening. Beulig put it decorously: "At five o'clock, the women prepared for the evening's work, washed, bathed, and changed clothes."[21] Magdalena Walter calls this time the "two cursed hours."[22] On Sundays, things were different. Prisoners had to work only in the mornings, so the camp brothel was open longer and the women had more visitors, though interest ebbed over time.[23] The opening hours were not fixed. As a rule, the brothel was open "until all the men were finished."[24] The sex work proceeded as if on an assembly line. Magdalena Walter describes the process:

> For two hours every evening, we had to let the men mount us. They came in, went to the doctor's room, got an injection, went to [their assigned] room number [i.e., sex worker] . . . and did the deed. In, up, down, out, back again. Then they got another injection . . . and had to leave. We had a bathroom with toilets, so there was no lack of cleanliness. And then the next one came. On and on. And they didn't have more than a quarter of an hour.[25]

The number of men that the women had to serve per shift varied greatly. In Neuengamme, Laura Büttig explains, each woman had to punch "six cards" per evening.[26] Linda Bachmann says that women in the Dora brothel typically had seven to eight men and sometimes as many as ten. She herself did not have that many because the camp elder protected her. She assumed that the numbers were fixed.[27]

Based on brothel records, it is possible to determine how many men the SS assigned to each woman at Buchenwald. In the first month of the brothel's operation, each woman had to have sex with between three and fifteen men per day. In the months that followed, the number averaged nine per day. By March 1945, the maximum number of men had dropped to six.[28] The documents also show that the SS assigned more prisoners to some women than to others. For example, one Polish woman was forced to serve far more men than the German women. Some records provide shocking evidence of the dimension of forced sex work. By the end of the brothel's first nine months, the women had had sex with between 666 and 1,381 men each.[29]

Living Conditions

In terms of sanitary conditions and nutrition, women in the camp brothels were better off than most other concentration camp inmates. In some camps, the women received double food rations or even the same rations as the SS. Beulig says that each morning they received half a liter of coffee substitute, a pound of brown bread, and about two-thirds of an ounce of butter or margarine. At noon, the women were brought boiled potatoes; on most days, a piece of meat; and fresh vegetables and fruit, including cabbage and on occasion apples, pears, and lettuce. Three times a week, soup was served in the evening. On other days, they received "cold rations" such as sausage, butter, and margarine.[30] Linda Bachmann corroborates Beulig's account. "We received good food there. What do I mean by good? It was at least better than the food at Ravensbrück."[31] Laura Büttig provides a similar report for Neuengamme.[32]

The women in the camp brothels usually dressed in civilian attire. "The women wore a colored blouse, which was their personal property," Beulig recalls. "All women, except those who did not work, also wore a short white linen skirt which they had received from the camp clothing department. The women also wore lingerie."[33] Some women received clothing from male prisoners.[34] There was no general dress code for the camp brothels; clothing varied depending on what the women owned and what the camp had available.[35] The sex workers were allowed to let their hair grow to a certain length.[36] At Buchenwald, the SS initially assigned the brothel a barber. Later, the women had to cut their own hair.[37]

Survivor accounts make repeated mention of the earnings of the sex workers. For example, the former Ravensbrück inmate Elisabeth Lynhard notes that ten women returned to Ravensbrück after a three-month stay in a brothel having earned between 75 and 500 Reichsmarks.[38] Himmler himself issued a directive stipulating that women were to receive money for sex work in the camp brothel. He wrote that the women can "save the money they earn for old age."[39] Beulig reports that some women were paid 1,500 to 2,000 marks on leaving the brothel.[40]

Job sheets from the Buchenwald camp provide more detailed information about sex worker earnings. For instance, of the approximately 25,600 Reichsmarks that the brothel earned from July 1943 to April 1944, its sixteen sex workers received 7,010 Reichsmarks, with an average income ranging from 360 to 703 Reichsmarks.[41] It is unclear, however, how much of this income, if any, actually reached the women. Initially, the women were able to use the money to buy food in the camp canteen.[42] The money was also sent to women transferred to Ravensbrück. The Buchenwald sex worker Antonia Michaelis, who was transported to Ravensbrück in December 1944, is a case in point.[43] The Buchenwald administration credited money to her camp account in Ravensbrück totaling 65.30 Reichsmarks. A few weeks later, however, the money was returned to Buchenwald on account of its being undeliverable.[44] The SS then sent a money order to the woman's place of residence. The SS deducted the postage from the transferred amount.[45]

Withdrawal and remittance slips show that the SS allowed women in the Buchenwald brothel to send relatives between 100 and 200 Reichsmarks of the money credited to their camp accounts.[46] This practice was an exception among the Nazi concentration camps. Normally, money was only ever sent *to* a concentration camp, not *from* it.[47] Laura Büttig, who was held at the Neuengamme camp brothel, says that the money "was credited to the girls" but that they "never saw any money."[48] According to Linda Bachmann, the situation at Mittelbau-Dora was the same.[49] But neither woman was released until the end of the war, which may be why they were never paid.[50]

Menstruation, Pregnancy, Disease

For most of the women sent to concentration camps, menstruation ceased at the moment of their arrival.[51] The cycles of women who held better positions in the camps resumed later, however.[52] In the Neuengamme brothel, forced sex workers were required to stay in the infirmary during menstruation. But according to Laura Büttig, it was rare for a woman to get her period.[53] In Buchenwald, menstruating sex workers were marked "sick" on the job sheets. Almost all the women who performed sex work in the brothel from July 1943 to April 1944 were recorded as "sick" for several days at regular intervals, which almost certainly indicated the resumption of their menstrual cycles. This surely had to do with the better supply of food, better sanitary conditions, the absence of hard labor, and the absence of physical violence from the SS or the guards.[54] At any rate, the onset of menstruation meant a break from sex.

The women in the camp brothel did not have access to sufficient birth control. "There was nothing," Linda Bachmann explains. The women "had to look after themselves . . . they could douche afterwards."[55] The SS man Max Beulig corroborated the account.[56] In Neuengamme, the women had to go to the prisoners' doctor every time they had sex to rinse their vaginas with lactic acid.[57] Magdalena Walter notes that after sexual intercourse the women in Buchenwald "had to go immediately to the toilet, rinse, rinse, and rinse again."[58] The use of condoms, though common in military brothels, was unknown in the concentration camps.[59]

Sex without effective contraception inevitably meant that some women became pregnant, as firsthand accounts from various camps report. Stephan Szymanski testified that Izabela Michalek, who worked in the brothel at Auschwitz's main camp, met this fate.[60] And Max Beulig stated that during his time as block leader of the camp brothel, two women became pregnant and were then forced to have an abortion. Both women were three months pregnant when the abortion was performed in the infirmary. They remained there for three weeks, and then returned to the brothel and were forced to perform sex work again two weeks later.[61] The abortion was requested from the chief of Camp Health and Hygiene (D III) of the SS Main Economic and Administrative Office in Berlin. Under National Socialist law, abortions were prohibited and could be performed only with special permission.[62]

At Mauthausen, an entry in the camp's logbook of surgical procedures dated November 7, 1944, lists the name of a German sex worker with the remark "abortus post curettage."[63] The logbook does not note any other abortions performed on sex workers. Because the surgery log covers the entire period of the brothel's existence, this was likely the only such procedure performed on a woman in the Mauthausen brothel.[64] In Neuengamme, a total of two sex workers became pregnant; for both women, the abortion was performed in Ravensbrück.[65] In Dora, Linda Bachmann recalls, no woman became pregnant, though the brothel was in operation for only several months.[66]

Why did relatively few sex workers become pregnant, despite having access only to douching, an ineffective birth control method? First, a large number of the German women working in the camp brothels had already been forcibly sterilized by the Nazis for antisocial behavior.[67] Furthermore, the conditions in some concentration camps, such as Auschwitz, had a direct impact on the reproductive ability of women and led to infertility in some cases.[68] Generally, the SS seemed indifferent to the issue of contraception and pregnancy in the camp brothels and regarded pregnancy as an occupational hazard, so to speak.

The logbook of surgical procedures at Mauthausen contains evidence of diseases contracted from sex work. In one case, camp doctors removed a woman's fallopian tubes, which had become obstructed by serous secretions, a potential aftereffect of chlamydia or gonorrhea. In another, they removed abnormal tissue from the uterus caused by inflammation.[69] Sex workers were also treated for other illnesses at Mauthausen, such as benign soft tissue tumors or warts.[70] In Beulig's telling, illness at Buchenwald was rare,[71] but the job sheets of the brothel list some women as sick for months.[72] Magdalena Walter says that she was given "heart water" after being forced to give blood in Ravensbrück.[73] According to her recollections, this spared her from sex work for four weeks.[74] There is also evidence of sickness among women at the camp brothel in Auschwitz.[75]

Coping Strategies

Kogon's statement that the camp sex workers "were resigned to their fate with rather little restraint" was largely responsible for the stigmatization of forced sex workers in discussions of Nazi concentration camps in postwar Germany.[76] In reality, the resignation that they showed was possible only because they employed a diversity of coping strategies. In their interviews with Christa Paul and Reinhild Kassing, Linda Bachmann and Magdalena Walter explicitly addressed this issue. Both accepted the fate forced on them and submitted almost lethargically to the monotony of the work. Submission, like mistrust, was a special feature in the psychological constitution of concentration camp inmates. Here is Magdalena Walter's account:

> You become numb. Life simply doesn't matter anymore because they have ruined everything for you as a human being. It started the moment they took me away from the estate. . . . By the time I arrived in Rostock [where she was held in custody] and was moved to Ravensbrück, the numbness had already set in. I became apathetic. How can I put this? You have this sense that nothing can shock you anymore. It was the same when I had three weeks of strict detention. . . . After Commandant [Max] Kögel said ten times, "You going to steal again, you communist pig?" it didn't bother me a bit. It couldn't have provoked me less. They could have done anything they wanted with you. We knew we were at their mercy. You couldn't resist, so what the hell. We just said to ourselves, the sooner the better. That's how far along we were. It wasn't just me.[77]

The dehumanizing machinery of the SS psychologically destroyed and demoralized the women. In the eyes of the SS, they were nothing, "just a number."[78] The women surrendered to the sex work just as the other prisoners did to their work details. Paradoxically, though, the apathy that the women felt also served as a coping strategy. Linda Bachmann explains that even the knowledge that she would be sent to the brothel would not have triggered a modicum of resistance. "And besides," she added, "I don't think any of us would have put up a fight."[79] After the brutalities of the concentration camp, the brothel seemed like an improvement:

> We told ourselves that it was better than being at Ravensbrück or Bergen-Belsen. What were we supposed to do? Put up a resistance? We had already done so much. Internally, of course, it was a shock. But that's understandable, isn't it? You know, the whole thing had already left us so numb. . . . In Ravensbrück, when you woke up early, you were lying next to a dead person. . . . And when you told the barrack elder, "There's a dead one lying here," he'd say, "Yes, throw her down." And, you know, it was every man for himself. I didn't think I'd survive. Everything had already left me so numb. I had all but accepted that my life was over.[80]

When interpreting this statement, one must keep in mind that Linda Bachmann's interviews took place forty-five years after her imprisonment. Memory can be selective, and it can repress some aspects and play down others.[81] Of course, many concentration camp prisoners already had to put aside the mental and physical pain they experienced and seize every opportunity to improve their living conditions. Linda Bachmann formulates it this way: "It didn't matter to us. The main thing, I have to say honestly, was that we had escaped the hell of Bergen-Belsen and Ravensbrück. You can imagine it for yourself only when you are there. Then, afterwards, you are already so diminished and you say to yourself, no matter what, the main thing is that you survive, that you survive in the first place."[82] This meant tolerating demeaning situations and pushing through psychological pain. Once, while she was having sex with a prisoner, she noticed an SS man watching through the peephole and grinning maliciously. She had learned to ignore such humiliation: "But, you know, by then you were already numb. I thought, drop dead, you ass."[83]

In the face of the SS's total power over them and their own mental deterioration, the women had no choice but to endure the forced sex with a mixture of apathy and detachment.[84] Putting up with boundary violations and sexual exploitation was a means of survival. In a cruel way, their behavior demonstrated the success of the SS's efforts to deprive prisoners of their moral sense and dignity.

Dissociation is evident in the choice of words Magdalena Walter uses to describe her experience of sexual exploitation. She says that the women let the male prisoners "slide over them"[85] or that the prisoners could spend "a quarter of an hour plugging away."[86] In these descriptions, she seems absent, as though talking about a stranger. To my mind, this suggests an effort to repress the experience, whether consciously or unconsciously. It is understandable that Magdalena Walter sees the sexual exploitation in Buchenwald as the lesser evil when measured against her experiences in Ravensbrück, where she received beatings with a bullwhip and other daily hardships on the road construction crew.[87] Like Linda Bachmann, Magdalena Walter relativizes forced sexual labor by putting it in the larger framework of the concentration camp experience.

Their accounts belie Kogon's claim that the women were resigned to their fate with rather little restraint. Rather, in focusing on survival, the women endured the forced sexual labor and repressed its mental and physical pain. Like the *Pipel* who were raped and sexually exploited in the camps, they dissociated themselves from the psychological damage, reduced it to physical pain, and put it in relation to other experiences. In a sense, those affected by sexual exploitation regarded it as the price of survival. The food or protection they received in return was a bulwark against the death with which they were directly or indirectly confronted, whether it came from specific individuals or was caused by the conditions of the camp in general. In the cruel logic of camp life, brothel workers understood that resistance could mean being sent back to Ravensbrück or Auschwitz-Birkenau, forfeiting better food and sanitary conditions. The coping strategies they employed—repression, dissociation, apathy— belonged to the psychology of survival in the camps.[88]

Social Relations

Another strategy for coping with forced sexual labor was the forging of personal relationships. They offered opportunities that were otherwise impossible in the brothels. They could ensure survival, provide food and protection, and reduce the number of men the women had to serve. Magdalena Walter believed that two political prisoners saved her life: "Arthur, a nurse in the euthanasia block, where all experiments on people were carried out, and Heinz, from Eckernförde, a member of the camp fire department who had his own dog." From these two she "received many benefits." "They gave money to other prisoners to serve as alibis so that I could fill the quota." All the women, she added, "had to fill the quota every evening, and a record was kept."[89] She describes how she met one of them. He approached and said that "he worked there and there . . . and that he could be very helpful." Immediately, she understood that "there was a chance that little by little he could get her stuff."[90] Magdalena Walter remained in contact with both of them through secret messages smuggled out of the brothel by a man who worked in the boiler room. They brought her food and information about the camp and offered her protection from other prisoners.[91] In return, the two expected sexual services. Magdalena Walter agreed to the arrangement, and the two prisoners took turns visiting her.[92]

At first, Magdalena Walter did not know how the men bribed the other prisoners. Only later did she learn what the two were doing. "When we could talk for longer . . . he told me the details. Some wanted to; others did not. A few they bribed with things other than money—until they said, okay then, give me the two marks and I'll scram."[93] To be sure, it was impossible to keep all the men away. There were those who said, "I want to experience pleasure, I want to have fun." For those men, Magdalena explained, "You couldn't say no." "But," she added, "that's what the others, the ones who got bought off, were for. They put a bandage over the peephole and didn't touch you."[94]

Linda Bachmann tells a similar story. "I was fortunate because of the camp senior."[95] He approached her and said he would bribe the other prisoners to forgo sex with her. Bachmann agreed to the arrangement, but she hardly had a choice in the matter. The camp senior was the highest-ranking prisoner functionary in the camp.[96] Defying him would have brought severe penalties. The sex workers were at the mercy of the camp's hierarchical power structures, so even these transactional relationships were coercive. Neither Linda Bachmann nor Magdalena Walter was free in this regard. They were promised only food and protection, which they paid for with sexual services. For Linda Bachmann, this was nothing out of the ordinary. "Well of course he came to me. It was only natural."[97] This shows how difficult it is to assess these relationships from today's perspective. In the violent world of the concentration camp, where nearly all necessities were scarce, nothing was free. Assistance had a price. As a rule, it required something in return. Surviving in the brothel meant following the rules of the black-market barter economy that prevailed in the camps.

Despite their involuntary nature, these transactional relationships were of great importance for improving a person's conditions and were widespread among the sex workers. "Everyone tried to snatch a kapo who had privileges," Linda Bachmann recounted. "That was normal in the situation."[98] Some of the women developed relationships with multiple prisoners.[99] In Mauthausen, the camp senior was known to have a relationship with one of the women, whom he wooed with gifts such as clothing, food, treats, and alcohol.[100] Zofia Bator reported about a woman in Auschwitz's Block 24a. "She too had her 'favorites' who would bring her wonderful things, first and foremost food, for in the camp that had the greatest value. There were sausages, chocolate, make-up, hosiery."[101] In Flossenbürg, a prisoner who worked in the building that housed the SS officers nicked some wine and gave it to his lover.[102] Arno Lieske, the *Kalfaktor*, or trusty, of the guard at the Buchenwald dental station, gave the women gold fillings.[103] In some cases, packages addressed to prisoners were stolen and the contents given to the sex workers.[104]

The relationships did not preclude emotional attachment. Linda Bachmann describes her friendship with the camp elder: "He liked me, I made friends with him right away. They [the brothel workers] were happy to meet someone who was good to them."[105] Some sex workers developed personal relationships with male prisoners, occasionally with strong emotional ties. One case is the relationship between Stephan Szymanski, a twenty-year-old Auschwitz inmate, and a sex worker in Auschwitz's main camp. Instances are also known from Neuengamme and Mauthausen in which relationships between women from the brothel and prisoners from the camp continued after the war and even resulted in marriage.[106]

But close emotional relationships like these were rare. As a rule, camp inmates mistrusted one another and avoided conversation unless they had been friends before arriving in the camps. Revealing personal information to strangers was risky, for it could get back to the SS or their underlings.[107] According to Magdalena Walter, the relationships between the women in the Buchenwald brothel were not unlike those between prisoners in Ravensbrück. It was "quite normal" for each woman to keep to herself.[108] In the monotony of the brothel, the women "passed the time aimlessly" and "said little."[109] They were suspicious of the other sex workers and felt unable to speak candidly: "Don't ask me what specific individuals thought . . . I don't know. Who trusted anyone?"[110]

Magdalena did learn a little about the women in the brothel, however. In her interviews, she mentions two women by name who had tried to escape Ravensbrück but were caught by the SS.[111] She also spoke about her roommate, Anna Harder, who had told her that she had been arrested for passing on leaflets dropped by Allied planes.[112] In reality, as court records show, Anna Harder had worked as a prostitute in Hamburg and, after receiving multiple prison sentences for failing to comply with the city's strict health codes, was put in Ravensbrück for "antisocial behavior."[113] The fact that Anna lied to Magdalena about why she was imprisoned is evidence of the general mistrust in the brothel and the women's fear of being stigmatized for sex work. At any rate, Magdalena's account of her relationships with the other sex workers tallies with what Linda Bachmann experienced at Mittelbau-Dora. Linda told her interviewers that she had superficial relations with all the women at the brothel save for one.[114] That woman, whom Linda considered a friend, told her that she had been imprisoned by the Nazis for making a joke about Hitler while she was at the hairdresser's.[115]

There was a specific reason for the mutual suspicion among the sex workers besides the general mistrust that prevailed in the concentration camps. As I discussed previously, almost all the women cultivated transactional relationships with male prisoners in which they exchanged sexual services for protection or food. The SS severely punished these relationships because they undermined their total control over the prisoners' lives. Accordingly, the women sought to keep their quid pro quo arrangements under wraps. Once, Anna Harder, in the hope of gaining special favors, divulged to an SS guard that the camp commandant's barber had procured meat for the women. When the other women found out, they became furious and punished Anna by wrapping sticky flypaper around her body and genitals.[116] "Squealing and snitching," Magdalena explains, "was the meanest thing you could do to your comrades in suffering."[117]

The incident with Anna Harder shows the ambiguity of the women's relations with the SS. Though the SS were adversaries and tormenters, their position at the top of the camp hierarchy meant that they could procure perks for women to whom they were favorably inclined. But the nature of their encounters with the women was fundamentally different from that of the prisoners. First and foremost, the SS were forbidden to approach the women or to have sexual relations with them, and most seem to have complied.[118] Linda Bachmann reports that the SS kept their distance and left interactions with the women to the prisoner functionaries. "They neither shouted nor did anything else to get their hands dirty. They had the camp elders do everything. They just stood there and grinned."[119] "They didn't care about us at all," was how she summed it up. "For them, we were air and dirt."[120] Her personal testimony contains no mention of sexual harassment on the part of the SS.[121]

Some SS did break the rules, however. In Sachsenhausen and Monowitz, SS officers amused themselves by observing prisoners having sex.[122] The former inmate Carl Cärtig stated that high-ranking SS men at Buchenwald would enter the camp brothel at night and take part in "veritable orgies."[123] At Mauthausen, Georg Bachmayer, the head of the so-called protective custody camp, liked to visit the brothel while drunk. The prisoners of the camp did not know what he was up to, but they did hear the gunfire when he'd shoot at the lamps in the brothel, as he sometimes did. Only a few prisoners were privy to the activities of SS officers in the brothel. One of those prisoners was Mauthausen's infirmary kapo. According to Hans Maršálek, it was for this reason that the camp lockup supervisor Josef Niedermayer strangled to death the kapo the day he was released from the camp.[124]

Judging by the evidence, it seems that the behavior of SS men toward the women varied greatly. Magdalena Walter mentions multiple SS men who treated her decently. One man named Schobert talked with her and even discussed his private life. Another gave her cigarettes, coffee, a double mattress, and novels when she was locked up for two weeks in the "bunker."[125] Then there were the ones who were "a little different." According to Magdalena, Hermann Hofschulte was the "biggest bastard" among them.[126] At Neuengamme, the SS officers Wilhelm Dreimann and Anton Thumann were alleged to have beaten the women who worked in the brothel.[127] Laura Büttig recalls that Dreimann told her, "If I knew my daughter was going to be like you . . . I would beat her to death."[128] By contrast, the Neuengamme commandant Max Pauly, concerned about his reputation in his hometown, personally worked to improve the living situation of the sex workers. He "behaved very well" toward the women.[129] He even allowed a Dutch accordion player to come to the camp brothel on Sunday afternoons and play jazz for the women.[130]

After the war, some forced sex workers testified in court that the SS men with whom they had contact behaved properly and treated them with decency. For instance, Angelika Leuchter, who came from the same town as Commandant Max Pauly, stated in an affidavit that Unterscharführer Heinrich Klockmann, who frequently stopped by the camp brothel, had "always been very friendly" to the women.[131] "He even gave me cigarettes when there was a high penalty for giving things to prisoners," she continued. "We were always happy when Klockmann came to us. As a prisoner at that time, I can only say good things about Klockmann."[132]

At Mauthausen, Rapportführer Josef Riegler is known to have led the sex workers in walks around the camp and to have locked arms with at least one of them.[133] Maršálek noted that when Mauthausen's leaders organized boxing or theater events for prisoners on Sundays, the sex workers were brought out of the camp brothel to keep the SS men company.[134] Stephan Szymanski reports that Franz Hössler, the director of the Birkenau women's camp, had expressed interest in a sex worker but did not act on it. The woman in question, Izabela Michalek, believed that it was on account of Hössler's intervention that she was able to leave the brothel and obtain a job as an auxiliary kapo in the camp extension. According to Michalek, it was also Hössler who ensured her survival after she was transferred to

Bergen-Belsen, where he was later deputy camp commander and where food rations were in short supply.[135] When the British army was only twelve miles away from the camp, Hössler suggested that they escape together. She refused because she was afraid that he would rape and shoot her.[136]

Of course, the women in the camp brothels were still prisoners and, like the other inmates, were subject to punishment for falling out of line. Women who broke the rules governing sex work or who established personal relationships with male prisoners faced harsh disciplinary measures. Beulig described that in one such case a woman's hair was cut off.[137] Magdalena Walter, for her part, served three stints in the camp lockup.[138] Once she was caught sending a secret message. Her hair was shaved off, and she was placed in the "bunker."[139] The second time, the SS put her behind bars for attacking Anna Harder after she snitched on the other women. The third time was for trying to take her own life. The attempt came six months before the end of the war, after one of the men she had an arrangement with received a Christmas package from his mother and showed her the enclosed letter. Magdalena became forlorn. Her father was a Nazi, and she knew she wouldn't receive any letters or packages from her family. So she decided to slit her wrists. "I didn't want to do it anymore, I was fed up, I wanted to end it all,"[140] she says. An SS guard found her and immediately took her to the infirmary. When she recovered, she was placed in the camp prison for two weeks.[141]

Sex Worker Statistics

Based on documents from the various camps, I was able to compile a database of the nationalities and arrest records of the forced sex workers.[142] I identified 183 women who worked in camp brothels.[143] Of the 174 women known by name, 168 were in brothels for prisoners and eight in brothels for Ukrainian guards. Two of the sex workers from a Ukrainian brothel had previously been in a brothel for prisoners.[144] During the existence of the brothels, a total of 214 women labored as sex workers; of them, 190 worked in the brothels for prisoners. Another eleven women identifiable by name worked as "cashiers" (SS jargon for "madams").

Of the forced sex workers known by name, 114 were *Reichsdeutsche*, people born in the German Reich.[145] Eighty-eight women (over 85 percent of the total) had been sent to a concentration camp for "antisocial" behavior. Three of the women were classified as "gypsies." Only nine wore the red triangle marking them as "political" prisoners, and only four wore the green triangle for "criminals."[146] Two women were initially given the black triangle when they entered the camp but were later assigned the red triangle. Ultimately, they had to wear the black triangle again.[147] Three German political prisoners were sent to Ravensbrück for "intercourse with Poles." Three women were listed as Poles in some records and as Germans in others.[148] For eleven women, the reason for imprisonment is no longer known.[149]

Forty-six sex workers were Polish. Eight of the Poles were used by the SS in brothels for Ukrainian guards. Twenty-six Polish women were classified as political prisoners (two worked at a brothel for Ukrainian guards) and ten as antisocial prisoners (six at a brothel for Ukrainian guards). In ten cases, the reason for imprisonment is unknown. One of the women was sent to a concentration camp for having had contact with a German, which was forbidden. Six Soviet women were categorized as Russians, but based on their birthplace or name, they were from Ukraine, Belarus, and central Russia.[150] Each wore the red triangle. In the case of four other women, their nationality cannot be precisely determined, though the names suggest Ukrainian or Polish origin. One "political" prisoner was from the Netherlands. There is no serious evidence that any of the women were Jews. A WVHA index lists one of the women as Jewish, but three other surviving documents show that she was imprisoned for antisocial behavior and that her nationality was German. One woman at the Mittelbau-Dora brothel was Jewish, but she was employed as a "cashier" and not for sex work.[151] The nationality of the women in the brothels varied from camp to camp. While in Neuengamme Reich Germans made up all the brothel workers, in Auschwitz they accounted for only 60 percent of the commando.[152] The SS probably based the composition of the brothels on the nationalities of the male prisoners and the prisoner functionaries.

The average age of the sex workers identifiable by name was twenty-five at the time of their transfer to a camp brothel and twenty-two for women from brothels for Ukrainian guards. The average age of women who were used as "cashiers" was forty-one.[153] The length of stay in one or more camp brothels varied greatly. In Auschwitz, one of the women spent only two days in the brothel, whereas in Mauthausen several women worked in the brothel for the entire period of their imprisonment, which amounted to thirty-four months.[154] The average stay was ten months.[155] At least thirty-two women worked in more than one camp brothel. At least eleven women were released from concentration camps before the end of the war. All but one of those released early worked at the Buchenwald brothel.[156]

Survival and Status

Some firsthand accounts claim that the chances of survival for women in the camp brothels were low and that they were taken to Ravensbrück for extermination when they were "finished."[157] But as I have shown, the reality was different: The chances of survival for women in camp brothels were extraordinarily high. For Buchenwald, it can be stated with a high degree of certainty that there were no deaths in the brothels.[158] There is no evidence of brothel deaths in other concentration camps, either.[159] The only reference to a concrete death was the rumor circulating at Sachsenhausen that a nineteen-year-old Polish student from the camp brothel had been executed after becoming pregnant. But as I noted earlier, that rumor was debunked by another sex worker at the camp.[160] There is evidence that some women who survived the camp brothel died in another concentration camp before liberation. Three Polish women who had worked at a brothel in Auschwitz likely died in Ravensbrück or at one of its subcamps after Auschwitz was evacuated.[161] In another case, a German sex worker at the camp brothel in Monowitz died in a subcamp of Flossenbürg at the end of 1944.[162] A former inmate at Flossenbürg mentioned that a twenty-sex-year-old waitress from Potsdam did not survive the war. But he appears to have meant Elenora Franke, who did indeed survive and went on to live in the United States, before returning to Germany.

Another aspect of the lives of forced sex workers was their prisoner category—"criminal," "antisocial," "political," etc.—which, nominally at least, indicated the reason for their imprisonment. In her study on prostitution in prisons, the historian Christa Schikorra has argued that the forced sex workers who entered the camps as political prisoners were designated as "antisocial" when they began work in the brothels, which placed them at a lower rung in the camp hierarchy. Her claim is based on the discovery of a handwritten note in the records from Ravensbrück reclassifying a Polish woman who had returned to the camp after performing sex work at the Mauthausen brothel. But this was most likely a clerical error that occurred during the hectic intake rather than a deliberate attempt to stigmatize the sex workers.[163]

In a few cases, the reasons recorded for the imprisonment of women who later worked as sex workers were contradictory or unclear, but they can be traced back to clerical errors.[164] In three cases, for example, the reason for imprisonment was unclear because the record keeper altered their nationalities.[165] At Dachau, two women received the black triangle when they entered Ravensbrück but the red triangle when they were sent to Dachau—a de facto advancement in the prisoner hierarchy. How this came about could not be determined. When they were transferred back to Ravensbrück in January 1945, they again had to wear the black triangle.[166] Accordingly, it is generally not possible to establish a direct link between a change in a woman's reason for imprisonment and a change in her position in the camp hierarchy on account of working in a camp brothel.

Information about the effect of women's work in a brothel on their position in the camp hierarchy is limited. It is clear that in some cases their status improved. The sex workers in Mauthausen and Gusen were employed as "prisoner supervisors" after the camp brothels were closed.[167] At Auschwitz, sex workers also moved on to better work details after leaving the brothel. As previously mentioned, Izabela Michalek became a kapo's assistant in the extension adjacent to the main Auschwitz camp.[168] Zofia Bator talks about a woman from the Auschwitz camp brothel whom she later met in the women's camp. "After a few days of rest, [the woman] said that she could still work 'there' today. [She had worked there] for at least nine months. She did not know why 'they' had dismissed her, although she had begged them to. After some time, I met her in the camp. She was carrying kettles and was a room elder—by camp standards, this was an excellent assignment."[169]

Women who stopped working at the Auschwitz camp brothel remained in the Auschwitz complex, and a number of them received better work details. The situation was different after the camp was evacuated, however. Some women were transferred to other camp brothels. The rest were transferred to other camps, where the women likely found unfamiliar work structures and poorer living conditions, as evidenced by the number who later died or probably died. Some of the women from the camp brothel in Dachau were transported to Ravensbrück. During the journey, a few managed to escape. Seven of the other women were taken to the Dachau women's subcamp in Munich (Agfa Kamerawerk München), where living conditions were comparatively good.[170] Two women from Buchenwald who were forced to work in a brothel for Ukrainian guards were later sent to a subcamp. There are a few cases in which women held a high-status position before being sent to the camp brothel and then resumed the position after leaving sex work. Minna Möller was a cleaner instructor before her transfer to the Sachsenhausen brothel and joined the camp police after her return to Ravensbrück.[171]

These cases show that the women's living conditions after leaving camp brothels varied significantly, and it is impossible to say that their lot improved or worsened in general. Nevertheless, sex work did have an indirect influence on their chances of survival after leaving a brothel. For one thing, their health was often better than that of women in physically challenging work details. They were more likely to survive periods of malnourishment and to pull through during the evacuations and death marches. Moreover, the transactional relationships they forged in brothels increased their social capital, which could prove useful later provided they remained in proximity to male prisoners, as was the case in Auschwitz. The men in the transactional relationships could leverage their privilege to obtain extra food for the women and place them in better work details.[172] Some of the men who were with the SS also offered protection, as the example of Izabela Michalek shows.[173] However, for sex workers transferred to other camps, the social capital they accumulated did little to increase their chances of survival.

There were two other factors that may have helped ensure a better position in the camp hierarchy: nationality and reason for imprisonment. For example, the SS at Gusen and other camps often recruited ethnic German women classified as antisocials or criminals as camp guards.[174] Most of the sex workers had been previously designated "antisocials." Some were labeled "criminals."[175]

As stressed several times before, there is no evidence that the SS released women after six months in a camp brothel, promises notwithstanding. At Buchenwald, forced sexual labor may have affected the length of time the women were held in a concentration camp, however. In late 1944 and early 1945, eight women were released from the concentration camp after over fifteen months of sex work. Many of the women had been able to transfer relatives the money credited to their accounts for sex work. In an ironic twist, the police departments that had arrested the women may have regarded their sex work as "earned income," absolving them of their "antisociality" and effecting their release.[176]

Criminal Records

The files I analyzed indicate that most of the forced sex workers were of German origin and that almost 70 percent—and over 85 percent of the Germans—had been arrested for "antisocial" behavior. Nearly 30 percent of the women had been placed in concentration camps as political prisoners, while 3 percent were designated as "criminals."[177] Initially, the SS recruited women for the brothels who had been or who were assumed to be prostitutes before arriving in the concentration camps. This was particularly true for the women who worked in the first camp brothels, those of Mauthausen and Gusen.[178] They had been arrested as part of the criminalization of sex work outside the surveillance apparatus of the health authorities. According to Section 327 of the Nazi criminal code, a woman who worked as a prostitute was liable to prosecution if she did not have herself examined for venereal disease twice a week at the public health office. Decrees on "preventive crime control" gave the criminal police the legal means to put women in a concentration camp after being convicted three times of a crime.[179] In other cases, the women had violated Nazi race laws. Some German women had had sexual relations with Polish men. Several Polish women had been charged with having intercourse with a German.[180] The German Elisabeth Stein was sent to a concentration camp multiple times because of a sexual relationship she had had with a Polish civilian.[181] In August 1942, she was placed in Ravensbrück for having had sex with foreigners at a brothel. Her camp records contain the remark "repeat offender."[182] Some women were sent to concentration camps for other sexual offenses such as "sleeping with someone despite having gonorrhea."[183] These examples all suggest that the SS regarded women with histories of sexual crimes as eligible for sex work. As I pointed out in an earlier chapter, the SS was looking for "skilled workers" and appeared to believe that women found guilty of certain crimes would be specially qualified to work in the brothels.

The women categorized as "antisocial" had records that appear to have no bearing on their recruitment for sex work. The offenses they had been charged with include theft, embezzlement, fraud, and document forgery.[184] Others had been arrested for violating the terms of their employment or for failing to complete the mandatory labor service instituted by the Nazi regime.[185]

It is more difficult to reconstruct the criminal records of foreign sex workers. A Polish woman at the Flossenbürg brothel was arrested in Lodz in November 1942 for violating her employment contract and later placed in a concentration camp, where she was made to wear the red triangle.[186] She may have been classified as a political prisoner because she tried to escape from a forced labor detail. A Polish woman from the Buchenwald camp brothel was sent to a concentration camp by the Stettin police in 1942 for "labor sabotage" after being previously convicted for "refusing to work." The SS labeled her a political prisoner. Had she been a German citizen, however, they would have designated her an "antisocial." A sex worker from the brothel for Ukrainian guards in Buchenwald was placed in a concentration camp for stealing ration cards.[187]

Some of the women's arrests may be attributable to the work their husbands performed. For example, one Ukrainian woman from the Mittelbau-Dora brothel was married to a Red Army officer. A Dutch forced sex worker was married to a Dutch policeman. Several forced sex workers from the Soviet Union and Poland were put in concentration camps as civilian workers and given the red triangle.[188] A Polish woman who performed forced labor at the Breslau municipal waterworks was accused of sabotage and sent to Auschwitz without trial.[189] Another Polish woman was sent to

Auschwitz by the Munich police for theft, even though it had been her first criminal offense. Since she was a foreigner, she had to wear the red triangle.[190] Polish women who were sent to concentration camps as "antisocials" are likely to have been charged with offenses similar to those committed by German women who wore the same stigmatizing identification badge.

Life After Forced Sexual Labor

On April 13, 1945, a few days before being liberated by US soldiers, the former Dachau prisoner Nico Rost recorded a story he had heard from the library's kapo: "[He] told me that one of the Polish women from the camp brothel wanted to borrow a copy of Dante's *Inferno.* 'Preferably an edition with lots of pictures,' she had said. She believed that the book was an exact description of hell. She feared that she'd end up there one day and wanted to know what was awaiting her!"[191]

For many forced sex workers, liberation from the concentration camps did not mean the end of persecution and stigmatization. Women who had been sexually exploited in the camp brothels—but who had survived for this very reason—were not readily regarded as victims of the concentration camps and were sometimes even accused of complicity. After the US military authorities took over Buchenwald, all prisoners had to answer questions about their personal details, reason for arrest, positions held in the camp, and membership in the Nazi Party or any affiliated organization. In the case of two former sex workers, the soldier in charge of the questioning entered "prostitution" under "positions held during confinement," indicating that the women had volunteered for the assignment. Later the soldier added "forced by the SS" next to the answer. The two women, along with another sex worker and a "cashier" from the brothel, were not released until June 20, 1945, seventy days after the liberation of Buchenwald.[192] Evidently, the US military administration in Buchenwald was unsure whether they were victims or hangers-on of the regime.

Most of the former forced sex workers kept quiet about their time in a camp brothel. Anni Kramer, who came from a large working-class family in Danzig, was sent to Ravensbrück for trying to sabotage a munitions factory and later recruited for the Mauthausen camp brothel. After the war, she never discussed the sex work with her relatives: "I never talked about it. Only some of my family knows what happened to me. For instance, I never told my mother what happened. My children don't know anything either. They are my stepchildren. I couldn't have children of my own."[193]

The former sex workers remained silent about their past for various reasons. Magdalena Walter told her interviewers that after the war, one of the men with whom she had a transactional relationship in Buchenwald sought her out in the restaurant where she worked because he wanted to buy her boat. But afterward the man refused any more contact with her. Later, she asked another former prisoner to find him, but he said that the man she described did not exist.[194] It seems that her former "friend" had no interest in maintaining contact with a woman who had once been a sex worker. [195] This may have been another reason why Magdalena Walter was so careful about whom she told. "When I knew what sort of person I was talking to, and where it was appropriate, I would mention it. And where it was not appropriate, I would not."[196] She did not note her detention in Buchenwald when applying for compensation under the German restitution laws.[197] Nor did she, in later life, mention it to doctors when the epileptic seizures she suffered from grew worse.

Linda Bachmann's life after the war is a sad reminder of the perils of talking openly about the past. After the liberation, she returned to her native city of Halle. She fell in love with a Russian officer, but the Soviet military administration had forbidden relationships between Russian soldiers and German women, and once theirs was discovered the officer was imprisoned, and Linda Bachmann fled to the West. She eventually met a man nineteen years her senior, and they married. One day she told him about her past, but instead of giving her sympathy he began beating her regularly while calling her a "concentration camp pig" and saying that he would have killed her "had he been a guard." She explained the situation in an interview: "Well, we had been together for so long, and sometimes he could be so reasonable that I thought he would change." But he never did. "Until he died, I had to listen to that all the time."[198] After the death of her husband, in 1969, Linda Bachmann "had had it."[199] It was some time before she took a girlfriend into her confidence. Much later, when Linda Bachmann was receiving assisted care, a social worker recommended that she apply for compensation.[200] After everything she had been through, Linda didn't want anything to do with the authorities. But the social worker got her the application and persuaded her to fill it out. If she had not done so, her story would not be known today. "And that's really who I am," Linda said, before adding, "otherwise, I would have remained silent."[201]

Another example of concealment comes from a Dutch woman who performed sex work at the Mittelbau-Dora brothel. After the war, her name appeared on the lists of Dutch prisoners detained in the Vught concentration camp. On one, the names Ravensbrück and Bergen-Belsen, two other concentration camps in which she was confined, were added next to her name. However, the list does not indicate that she was later transferred to

Mittelbau-Dora, presumably because she was too ashamed to mention it to authorities.[202] Another case was recounted by the Polish Auschwitz survivor Stanisław Hantz. In 1942, he met a young woman in Auschwitz-Birkenau whom he knew from his hometown. By that point, she was already emaciated and exhausted. A little later, the woman volunteered for the brothel in Block 24a of the Auschwitz main camp, where he saw her once at the window. After the war, he encountered her by chance one day. She looked frightened. Hantz promised that he'd keep quiet about her time in the brothel. She was afraid that if it came out she'd be stigmatized and lose her right to compensation. He never revealed her identity. In my interview with him in 2003, he insisted that she had already died.[203] Tomasz Jablonski describes a similar example. In a displaced persons camp near Flensburg, he met a woman with whom he had had sex in an Auschwitz brothel. The woman told him, "Just so you know, I am engaged to a Polish captain." He promised her, "What happened in Auschwitz will remain between us and completely confidential."[204]

Some survivors did try to be open about their past, at least initially. Izabela Michalek was well known in a Warsaw club for former Auschwitz detainees and regularly attended the club's meetings in the first years after the war. It was common knowledge that she had been a forced sex worker in Auschwitz. However, after a certain period of time she stopped going. Stephan Szymanski suggests that this was because women from camp brothels were being stigmatized.[205] A woman held in Monowitz told her story to the archives of the Auschwitz State Museum and included that she had worked at the camp's brothel. She later married, and her husband demanded that the archive surrender the testimony to him, and the staff complied. To this day, it remains the only known account of a Polish forced sex worker from Auschwitz. When I asked the woman for an interview, she denied ever having worked at a camp brothel.

Elenora Franke, a former forced sex worker at Flossenbürg, was known within the camp community, as was her work in the brothel. Jack Terry, who knew her from the concentration camp and corresponded with her after the war, met her in 1995 at a survivors' meeting in Flossenbürg. According to Terry, she was not worried about being recognized as a former sex worker and did not feel stigmatized.[206] This might have been because at the time Flossenbürg was a forgotten camp, largely ignored in the public culture of remembrance, which kept its survivors out of the public eye.[207] But Elenora Franke also saw herself as a victim of sexual exploitation under the Nazi regime. In an application for reparations submitted in 1966, she explicitly mentioned her time in the camp brothel.[208] Her lawyer stressed the coercive nature of the sex work and identified it as a central reason for the "damage to her body and health" that had reduced her earning capacity by over 25 percent.[209] However, Elenora Franke's application was rejected on the grounds that the statute of limitations had expired on April 1, 1958. She was also denied a claim for immediate assistance because she had not been a German citizen at the time of her imprisonment in the camp. Her father was a Pole while her mother was German, rendering her "stateless."[210]

7 Brothel Visitors

My examination of the camp brothels has so far focused on the physical spaces they occupied, the rules governing their operation, and the lives of the women who worked in them. For the remaining two chapters, I turn my attention to the men held in the ten concentration camps with brothels for prisoners. What do we know about the inmates who visited the brothels? How were the brothels perceived by the prisoner population at large? What was their significance—personal, moral, political, and otherwise—for the prisoners? As I discussed in Chapter 5, very few of those detained in the camps could afford a sex life, which is to say, only a small fraction of prisoners possessed much of a sex drive, let alone the energy and will to visit a brothel. Even so, the brothels had an impact beyond their walls, one that would have consequences for some prisoners long after they left the camps.

The motives of those who did visit the camps were both social and personal. For regular visitors, frequenting the camp brothel had social significance: It demonstrated sexual strength and membership in the camp elite. By contrast, some of the younger prisoners were virgins when they were imprisoned and saw the camp brothel as an opportunity to have their first sexual experience—perhaps the last they'd have. Older prisoners who felt death was near wanted to have sex one last time. Yet coitus was not necessarily the aim of those who visited the brothels. Many were physically unable to have sex. All they wanted was to talk or feel closeness. The brothel women were perceived as sources of comfort by the prisoners and even by some of the SS men.

For the SS, the brothel was a reward—and a way to spell out relations of power. The SS allowed selected prisoners to have sex, elevating their standing, but it also underlined their position in the camp hierarchy. The highest-ranking prisoner had to christen the camp brothel, while the vast majority never got near its doors. The SS presented itself as the master not only of life and death but also of sex. It decided between those who were permitted to experience male virility and the power it symbolized and those who were not, whether because they were barred from the brothels or because physical exhaustion left them unable to perform.

Prerequisites for Entry

Prisoners who wanted to visit a camp brothel faced significant hurdles. To start, only non-Jewish prisoners were generally allowed in brothels. Some camp brothels were more permissive, especially during the final years, though Jews and Russians were barred without exception.[1]

Race alone was not enough to gain entry. Prisoners had to possess a bonus voucher, and acquiring one almost necessarily meant belonging to the class of privileged prisoners or knowing prisoners who received the vouchers or who were responsible for distributing them.[2] Of course, the bonus system dovetailed with the racial criteria: The class of privileged prisoners consisted almost entirely of ethnic Germans who were citizens of Germany or Austria. By contrast, the vast majority of the rest had no access to the vouchers, if they heard of them at all.[3] And the relatively few with the right race and connections had to be healthy enough to have sex, which was by no means a given. The miserable conditions in the camps—the hard labor, the inadequate rations, the poor nutrition— diminished the sex drives of prisoners. The addition physical exertion of sex would have brought half-starved prisoners closer to death.[4] Most brothel visitors came, therefore, from the upper echelons of prisoner society assigned to light work details, in particular the kitchen, the hairdresser, the infirmary, the butcher, and the crematoria.[5] It also included prisoners who had important functionary positions in the camp.[6]

A final hurdle that prisoners needed to clear was their conscience. Many political prisoners refused to visit the brothels on the strength of their convictions. According to various sources, brothel visitors consisted mostly of antisocials and criminals. The visitor log for the Block 3 brothel in Mauthausen contains the names of the prisoners admitted to the brothel for the first six months of the brothel's operation starting in June 1942.[7] The names are listed together with their concentration camp number, date of birth, reason for imprisonment, nationality, and number of visits. A total of ninety prisoners are listed between August and December 1942. Of these, fifty-seven actually visited the brothel.[8] With the exception of one Polish prisoner, all were German citizens of the Reich. Of these, over 60 percent were classified as criminals, 23 percent as antisocials, and 12 percent as politicals.[9]

The "criminals" and "antisocials" who visited the brothel were often accused of depravity by other inmates.[10] However, the reasons for the dominance of "blacks" and "greens" among the Mauthausen brothel clientele may have had more to do with their elevated status than with morality. When Mauthausen opened, the SS picked inmates from these groups to fill all the important functional positions in the camp. Hence, they were over-represented among the prisoner elite, the ones most able to afford a visit physically and financially.[11] The situation was similar in other camps where blacks and greens held leading functionary positions.[12] Near the end of the war, the SS permitted some Polish, Czech, and Spanish prisoners at Mauthausen to visit the brothel after they took functionary positions.[13]

The situation was different in the "red" camps such as Buchenwald and Dachau, where "politicals"—mostly German resistance fighters, socialists, and communists—occupied functionary positions. Although the Buchenwald survivor Herbert Weidlich wrote that the visitors to the camp brothel "consisted mostly of German criminals and antisocials,"[14] this was not necessarily the case. Magdalena Walter noted that she saw men from other groups.[15] And records from the Communist Party of Germany show that among brothel visitors were "red" kapos and some leading figures of the communist resistance.[16] This shows that the inmate category was less decisive for brothel attendance than class membership.

Visitor Statistics

Several survivors have estimated the number of people who visited the brothel. According to Heinz Heger, one hundred prisoners went to the camp brothel in Flossenbürg on the first day. The number increased in the days that followed.[17] On December 31, 1942, 3,515 prisoners were registered in Flossenbürg, which meant that brothel visitors made up about 2.8 percent of all inmates.[18] For the brothel in the Auschwitz main camp, Stanisław Hantz puts the number of daily visitors at between one hundred and two hundred, or between 0.33 and 0.66 of the thirty thousand inmates registered at the time.[19] In the case of Buchenwald, Herbert Weidlich stated that at the beginning daily visitors reached as many 450 to 500 (3.5–3.9 percent of the total prison population) but that the number later fell to 180 to 200 (1.2–1.3 percent).[20]

Accounting records from the Buchenwald camp brothel provide relatively precise information about the number of brothel visitors from its opening on July 11, 1943, to April 1, 1944.[21] In the first month, in which the brothel was open for twenty-one days, the records logged 2,018 visits. This meant an average of ninety-six visitors per day, equivalent to 0.76 percent of the prisoners in the main camp. The highest total number of daily visitors was 150, recorded on Sunday, July 18.[22] The number of visitors quickly fell in the following weeks, however. The 1,800 visits recorded in August dropped to 1,525 a month later. In the period from September 1943 to April 1944, between forty-three and fifty-nine inmates visited the brothel each day.[23] In March 1945, no more than 413 visits to the brothel can be documented, an average of twenty-four per day. This was only 0.07 percent of the 36,000 inmates who populated the camp at the time.[24] Of course, the number of visits to the brothel is not the same as the total number of visitors; some prisoners visited the brothel more than once. Max Beulig remembers his experience in the Buchenwald brothel: "I mostly saw the same ones, usually once or twice a week. The rule was that an inmate was allowed to visit the brothel only once a week, but Wolf often issued permits for a second time."[25] In terms of concrete numbers, the visitor log for the Block 3 brothel in Mauthausen indicates that fifty-seven inmates visited the brothel 519 times over the August–December 1942 period, with each man averaging 9.1 visits.[26] In Buchenwald, the job sheets show 7,468 visits from August to December 1943.[27] If the average number of visits was the same as in Mauthausen, then some 820 inmates visited the Buchenwald camp brothel during this period.[28]

As Weidlich notes and as the analysis of the brothel accounting records bear out, the number of visitors to the Buchenwald camp brothel declined in the months following its opening. Weidlich attributes the declining interest primarily to moral condemnation from political prisoners.[29] Other factors surely played a role, however. First and foremost among these were the ever-worsening living conditions amid a rapidly growing inmate population owing to the arrival of prisoners evacuated from camps in the east.[30] It stands to reason that as the daily struggle for survival grew harder, prisoners had fewer resources to muster. The former Buchenwald inmate Fred Löwenberg remembers that the SS responded to the dwindling interest with exhortations over the camp loudspeaker. On one Sunday afternoon in early 1944 came the announcement, "Go to the brothel, you pigs!"[31] Despite their efforts, Löwenberg notes, the SS were unable to arouse more interest from the inmates.[32]

We can see, then, that the total number of brothel visitors is hard to estimate given the differences between the camps, the declining living conditions, and the spottiness of the records. The most complete information available comes from Buchenwald, where from July 1943 to March 1945 somewhere between 0.07 and 0.76 percent of the main camp inmates visited the brothel each day. A total of 13,773 visits were recorded for this period. Assuming that the number of visits per individual was the same as in Mauthausen would yield a figure of 1,500 discrete visitors.[33] No reliable figures are available from other concentration camps, but the estimates from various inmates suggest that the number of brothel visitors was negligible in relation to the total number of prisoners.

Motives for Visiting the Camp Brothels

The visitor log for the Mauthausen brothel provides information not only on the number of visitors and the number of visits but also on the frequency at which individuals entered the brothel. From the records, three groups of visitors can be identified during the five-month period. Of the fifty-seven individuals mentioned in the visitor log, nineteen visited at least twice a month.[34] These were the regulars. One of them frequented the brothel as many as forty-three times, which amounts to once or twice a week.[35] Twenty-five prisoners were sporadic visitors, going to the brothel between two and nine times. Thirteen visitors used the brothel only once. Obviously, the groups accounted for different proportions of the total number of visits: Regular brothel-goers made up 33.3 percent of individual brothel visitors but more than 75.5 percent of visits; sporadic visitors made up 44 percent of discrete visitors and 22 percent of visits; one-time visitors, who made up 22.8 percent of individual visitors, accounted for only 2.5 percent of the total number of visits.[36]

The Flossenbürg survivor Heinz Heger recalls that brothel visitors came from very different classes of prisoner: "Looking at these prisoners laughing and happy as they marched to the 'broads,' one noticed not only men still full of vigor—these were mostly kapos and foremen—but also miserable figures, emaciated and starved human wrecks, moving between life and death and looking as if they could collapse dead at any moment, yet who also still wanted to have their 'fun' with the 'broads.'"[37] Why did these "miserable figures" go to the brothel? Wasn't sex at odds with their survival? I will examine the individual motives in more detail in what follows.[38]

Consider, first, the regular brothel visitors responsible for most of the visits. Files from the Mauthausen concentration camp show that many occupied elite positions in the camp system: kapos, block clerks, block elders, camp firemen.[39] The same goes for camp brothels at other camps. Various reports by survivors repeatedly name high-ranking prisoners as regular brothel visitors. These include camp elders at Auschwitz, Monowitz, Flossenbürg, Sachsenhausen, Buchenwald, Mittelbau-Dora, and Mauthausen.[40] For instance, a block elder from Monowitz named Emil is said to have been a "particular lover of the brothel."[41] Indeed so great was his love that he also visited the brothel outside at night. (He was caught and subsequently transferred to the Fürstengrube satellite camp in 1944.)[42] Similar reports exist for kapos especially fond of the camp brothel.[43] In addition to kapos, regular visitors at the Buchenwald camp brothel included an orderly and a camp elder.[44]

Prisoners from the camp elite led vastly different lives from those of other inmates. They lavishly consumed the camp's scarce resources and indulged in behaviors that other prisoners would have regarded as downright extravagant.[45] That included sex. Unburdened by hard labor and starvation rations, their sex drives remained intact and demanded satisfaction, either in the brothels or in abusive sexual relationships with *Pipel*. But sex not only met physical needs. It signaled one's position in the camp hierarchy and provided a mark of distinction vis-à-vis other prisoners.[46] Eugen Kogon describes the behavior of the camp elite in *The Theory and Practice of Hell*: "Among the thousands of pitiful wraiths forever hovering on the borderline between life and death, there were still plenty of these braggarts, provocatively regaling their fellows with tales of their prowess the previous night. There were others too who drained their last physical reserves at the brothel. Nor was the place scorned by the SS officers, who could often be found there at advanced hours of the night."[47]

Other examples make plain the connection between power, extravagance, and the camp brothels. Dachau prisoners reported that the kapo Wilhelm Scholz became commander of the camp police after denouncing another prisoner. He "gorged himself and strutted into the camp brothel in a suit specially cut to fit his waist."[48] The highfalutin lifestyle of Ernst Busse, the kapo of the Buchenwald inmate infirmary, earned him the name "Pasha" among the prisoners. He was known to have visited the brothel several times.[49] Near the end of the war, the camp SS at Mauthausen filled functionary positions with Spanish prisoners. Previously, they had been forbidden from visiting the brothel. After joining the upper class, they were allowed this privilege.[50] Paul Tillard reports that some German kapos and other prominent figures resisted the change on the grounds that Spaniards shouldn't have sex with German women. They urged the forced sex workers to refuse the Spaniards.[51] Although racist stereotypes dominated the attitudes of the German kapos, the incident illustrates that visiting a brothel signaled membership in the camp upper class.

Most of the individuals who went to the brothels were sporadic visitors and one-timers. In contrast to the members of the camp elite, who were seeking to reaffirm status, their motives were more personal and often about death. Young prisoners who feared the end was near wanted to have a sexual experience with a woman at least once before they died. The former Dutch prisoner Joris Brouwer, who worked as a translator in the political department at Auschwitz, reported on his visit to the camp brothel: "A Dutch comrade worked in the SS butcher's shop and he had these tickets. He said that I hadn't been with a woman yet and that I should go once. So I went to a really fat prostitute, Anni from Hamburg."[52]

Langbein reports that a young Austrian who had been sent to a concentration camp for opposition to the Nazi regime had never had a sexual relationship with a woman before his arrest and experienced his "first great love" in the brothel.[53] Herbert Weidlich writes of young comrades among the inmates in Buchenwald "who had never known the physical love of a woman" and worried they would not survive the camp to find out.[54] Albert van Dijk, imprisoned in Buchenwald, was another to have his first sexual experience in the camp brothel.[55] In Lesniak's survey of former Auschwitz inmates, two survivors stated that they had visited the camp brothel in Auschwitz and that neither had had sex with a woman before.[56] Even sexually experienced prisoners wanted to have sex one last time before they died.[57] Romek Dubitzki reports that an older man who had never married told him he'd do anything for an entry pass.[58]

A different motivation can be found in a young Czech man who had been arrested by the National Socialists for his work in the communist resistance and sent to the Mauthausen concentration camp at the age of eighteen. He was able to survive thanks to a kapo who offered protection in return for sex. When the brothel in Mauthausen opened, however, he saw it as a chance to find out whether he was capable of having sex with a woman. As he explained to fellow inmates, the forced homosexual relationship with the kapo had been his only sexual experience. He ended up visiting the brothel, but only once. The reproaches from comrades in the communist resistance for sleeping with a sex worker were nevertheless cutting and followed him for decades.[59]

Some prisoners went to the brothel in search of companionship. In the camps, talking openly about personal matters was nearly impossible given the ubiquity of informers. Being with a woman in a room with the door closed at least had the semblance of privacy. Many inmates, especially political prisoners, hadn't seen a woman since being arrested after the Nazis seized power in 1933.[60] Linda Bachmann, the former forced sex worker from Mittelbau-Dora, observes: "The [men] had been locked up for years and were glad when they had a human encounter or people they could talk to. It didn't always come to sexual intercourse. Sometimes just conversation. Nobody knew. They were just happy to have a conversation with another human."[61]

Of course, many men were physically unable to have sex. Hunger, terror, and hard labor left them with erectile dysfunction.[62] One prisoner reported that fear of impotence was a reason to avoid the brothel.[63] Jakub Piecha describes his first and only brothel visit: "It was impossible to carry out a sexual relationship. . . . So we sat together on the edge of the bed and for fifteen minutes at turns talked or said nothing. We didn't have sex. Then the doorbell rang. I said goodbye to her after ten minutes. That was my adventure with the 'brothel.'"[64] Of course, it didn't help that the brothel was hardly a place for erotic encounters, what with its strict timetable, voyeuristic SS guards, and sexual exploitation.[65] Here is how Heinz Heger describes the situation: "What joyful relief was expected of me, what feeling of pleasure was I supposed to get, when the emaciated prostitute, lying in bed, lifted her legs and shouted, 'Go on, go on!' so that she could be done with something that was as embarrassing for her as it was for me, and when I knew for a fact that one of the SS commanders was watching me through the peephole?"[66]

Erich, a gay former prisoner from the Flossenbürg camp, explained in an interview that he decided one day to visit the camp brothel. Though he didn't state a clear reason for visiting, he may have wanted to signal to other prisoners that he was straight in view of the poor treatment homosexuals received in the camp.[67] At the brothel he got to know Else, who came from Potsdam and had been a waitress. She was a lesbian, and they became friends. He arranged to meet her several times. She was the only person he had made friends with during his ten years in the concentration camp.[68]

Like Erich, many inmates regarded the women as sources of comfort.[69] Magdalena Walter talks about an inmate who worked in the Buchenwald typhus ward who told her about a murder campaign by the SS in which medical orderlies were involved: "Then A . . . D . . . comes and says, imagine that tonight again many people perish, I don't know how many. I said, what are you doing with them? —Yes, he said, I'm not doing it. The other prisoners, they have to do it. —I said, it's a dirty business! —Yes, he said, and the worst thing is that the Jews still have their teeth broken out and any gold they have is taken away! And everything for these pigs, he says, for the SS people!"[70] The confession required a great deal of trust, which wouldn't have been possible without a personal relationship between the inmate and the forced sex worker. Some prisoners who visited the brothels feared that there were listening devices in the rooms. Jakub Piecha said that he was afraid to have a serious conversation with the women. "I suspected that they were spies, simple as that. So I tried not to talk to her about anything. Nothing concrete."[71] Magdalena Walter later denied that forced sex workers were used as spies by the SS.[72]

Some inmates reported building a personal relationship or falling in love with a forced sex worker. The Dutch Buchenwald survivor Albert van Dijk was in a cleaning detail that one day had to work in the camp brothel. "And that's where I had my first sexual adventure! Well, I already knew her, a young woman named Frieda. And Frieda was only four or five years older than me. For me as an eighteen-year-old . . . an adult woman!"[73] According to his own account, Frieda asked if she could smoke a cigarette while he was cleaning and then blew the smoke into his mouth. He remembers the incident as his "first sexual adventure."[74] He had his mother send him money and visited Frieda in the brothel several times.[75] In an interview, he describes the relationship in great detail. It is an intense sexual experience in stark contrast to the hunger, illness, torture, and near death of camp life.[76]

There is a story from the Auschwitz main camp about a love affair between the Polish inmate Stephan Szymanski and the Polish forced sex worker Izabela Michalek.[77] The twenty-one-year-old Polish woman had been in the Birkenau women's camp for a year when Hössler, the camp director, recruited her for the brothel in September 1943.[78] Szymanski had been sent to Auschwitz as a teenager and was able to survive there because he was promoted to kapo of the prisoner camp fire department.[79] He once visited the camp brothel and was assigned to Izabela Michalek's room. He was sexually inexperienced and found their encounter disturbing. Nevertheless, he wanted to see the young woman again and went to see her at least eight times during the brothel's normal hours of operation.[80] He also visited her outside the brothel and arranged with prisoners from the kitchen detachment to bring food on the weekends. If the SS man on duty recognized him, he would bribe him.[81] At night, he climbed through an open window to the second floor of Block 24a, where the brothel was located. He had a key to the women's sleeping quarters made for him by a prisoner friend.[82] The trysts came with considerable risk and could have resulted in punishment or even death.[83]

There is evidence that the relationship was mutual. Izabela Michalek gave him several gifts and signaled to him through the window when he was near.[84] The relationship continued after Izabela Michalek was released from the brothel in September 1944.[85] During the evacuation of Auschwitz she was transported to Bergen-Belsen, where she lived to see the end of the war. Szymanski, who remained in constant contact with her, visited Bergen-Belsen a few weeks after liberation.[86] Later, she returned to Poland; he immigrated to England and then to Canada. They met again in Poland many years after the war.[87]

As emerges from the interview with Stephan Szymanski, the emotional bond with the young woman was of great psychological importance despite the danger it posed. It gave life in Auschwitz a certain meaning and provided a mental escape from the cruel realities of the camp. Szymanski adopted behaviors that were diametrically opposed to the typical survival strategies in the camp. He embraced emotions that other prisoners repressed. He even allowed other prisoners to see his feelings, which violated the basic tenets of camp survival: secrecy and self-control.[88] His openness eroded his defense mechanisms, which freed his emotions further still. "With the return of emotions," he recounts, "I fell deeper and deeper in love."[89] Long-forgotten feelings, such as jealousy, resurfaced.[90]

The love between Stephan Szymanski and Izabela Michalek is not an isolated case; emotional relationships between forced sex workers and inmates in concentration camps were not uncommon.[91] As Maršálek notes, some of the men "hanging in the arms of the women during sexual intercourse were . . . really in love."[92] As in the case of Stephan Szymanski, there were also scenes of jealousy. Maršálek remembers that sometimes two or three men were in love with the same woman, leading to arguments.[93]

The visitors to the camp brothels included men compelled against their will. Charles Dekeyser remembers making a deal with a block elder in Flossenbürg who wanted to go to the brothel but had no money. Dekeyser would report to the brothel after roll call and swap places with the block elder on the way. In return, the elder promised him a fifth loaf of bread. The plan worked only once, however. The second time the men tried it, the Rapportführer accompanying the inmates to the brothel personally made sure that Dekeyser entered the brothel. Under the circumstances, though, he didn't feel like having sex. He merely talked to the woman.[94]

The Monowitz survivor Jan Stolecki remembers that at the opening of the brothel, Vinzenz Schöttl, the camp director, personally selected the first ten brothel visitors and had them line up outside the building.[95] The former prisoner Mieczysław Zając recalls that Schöttl wanted to reward an inmate who worked as a skilled worker at IG Farben by taking him to the brothel. The man was an older political prisoner with no desire to visit the brothel, yet he discovered that the reward was an order he could not refuse.[96] Eugen Kogon writes that the SS forced Erich Reschke, the camp elder and a communist, to be the first to visit the Buchenwald camp brothel after it opened.[97] It was the duty of the highest-ranking prisoner functionary to christen the brothel. Selecting prisoners for the brothel's opening day was common in other camps.[98] Stanisław Hantz reports that Josef Schillinger, the Rapportführer in the Auschwitz-Birkenau men's camp, had all the prisoners line up one day in 1944 because he had noticed that a block elder was paying regular visits to a woman in the Birkenau women's camp. He summoned the kapos and sent them to the camp brothel. It turned out that the "privilege" was part of a collective punishment: On their return, the prisoners were made to do physical activity by alternately lying down and standing up. They returned to Birkenau completely exhausted.[99]

Another example is described by Jean Michel, a former French prisoner at Mittelbau-Dora. One evening, a fellow inmate named Delaroche and the other men in his work detail were returning to the camp after a night shift in the underground V2 production facilities. An SS man stopped the prisoners and ordered them to the brothel:

> The men were stupefied. There they were marching in ranks towards the barrack which had been transformed into a house of ill-repute. The poor fellows were drunk with fatigue and only wanted to sleep after twelve hours of work. The first line was put one in front of each door and commanded to drop their trousers. The doors were still closed. The girls must have been inside. The second order was given: "Enter!" They went in, trousers lowered, feeling as much like making love as an ailing octogenarian. Delaroche found himself face to face with a woman who was waiting. He was worried and blushing with confusion. How could he manage it? The "little Frenchies" were about to fail to live up to their reputation. That is how legends are destroyed![100]

Heinz Heger writes that the SS in Flossenbürg forced homosexuals to visit the brothel in the belief that sex with women would "cure" their condition.[101] Although the camp SS at Sachsenhausen tested prisoners to make sure they had given up homosexuality, no reports exist of gay prisoners being forced to visit brothels at other camps.[102] According to the former Buchenwald inmate Fred Löwenberg, gays in the camp were not forced to visit brothels.[103] Starting in June 1944, the Danish physician Dr. Carl Værnet did conduct a series of experiments on gay inmates, implanting them with artificial glands supposed to induce heterosexuality, but none is known to have been made to visit the brothel.[104] It is possible that the forced visits in the Flossenbürg camp brothel described by Heger were a special case, perhaps the result of a sadistic whim on the part of the camp commandant Max Koegel.

8 Perception and Resistance

Of the multiple factors that shaped prisoner perceptions of the camp brothels, one stands out: whether an inmate had knowledge of them to begin with. In some camps, the "special buildings" lay on the peripheries, out of view for most. In other cases, prisoners were housed in the camp where the brothel was located only for a few days before being transferred to satellite camps and hence knew next to nothing about the sex workers. Prisoners who had been imprisoned for long periods tended to know about the brothels because they were familiar with the camp and its structures. The brothels elicited jocular talk about sex but also triggered serious debates about morality.[1] Because so few prisoners had the opportunity to obtain more detailed information about the interior of the brothels and the women confined there, we have a limited number of reports specifically describing forced sex workers, and the reports that do exist tend to emphasize how different the women in the camp brothel lived compared with the abysmal conditions of ordinary prisoners.

Prisoners' Views of the Brothels

The Austrian psychologist and former Buchenwald prisoner Ernst Federn recalls the "immense excitement" caused by the arrival of the brothel workers in the camps.[2] It heralded an experience that the inmates had hitherto considered impossible: contact with women. As the horizon of what was conceivable in the camps broadened, prisoners began to think and talk about sex, much as they might have done in their normal lives. Jokes, which were "rarely heard before," began "flourishing" after the brothel in Dachau opened, Edgar Kupfer-Koberwitz observed.[3] The presence of the brothels aroused great curiosity. The former block leader of the Buchenwald camp brothel, Max Beulig, mentioned that two to three times a week he'd catch prisoners peeking through the wooden fence that surrounded the building. He punished them by slapping them on the side of the head or beating them with a baton.[4] As the Norwegian Odd Nansen noted about the Sachsenhausen camp brothel, however, the fascination did not last. It wasn't long before the subject of the brothel stopped eliciting much discussion, let alone "crude jokes."[5]

Despite the sensation caused by the arrival of the women, many prisoners never learned of the camp brothels. Knowledge of the brothels depended on various factors. The first was the visibility of the brothel building. As I discussed in Chapter 4, camp brothels could be in one of two areas, depending on the camp: near the roll-call square or on the camp periphery. Recall, for instance, that the camp brothel in Flossenbürg was behind the lockup in an area to which prisoners were not normally given access. According to Charles Dekeyser, most prisoners knew something was going on but did not know what.[6] The prisoners in subcamps working for remote labor detachments near the end of the war were entirely in the dark, as the "special buildings" were in the main camps, except in the cases of Gusen and Monowitz. New prisoners stayed in the main camps only long enough to complete a period of quarantine. The isolation and general lack of knowledge about the layout of the camps meant that the prisoners learned little about the brothels.[7] Of course, many who never saw the brothel buildings learned of their existence secondhand. Word of mouth was an important and common source of information, especially for regular prisoners who had no knowledge of the camp's organization.[8] Unsurprisingly, the information conveyed was not always reliable. "The wildest rumors circulated," Federn writes, "often fueled by youthful fantasies about raped and abused girls."[9]

Another factor that determined what prisoners knew was interest. The vast majority were preoccupied with the daily struggle to stay alive. As Dekeyser writes, "The masses long only for one thing: grub, grub, grub."[10] The Italian prisoner Vernanzio Gibillini remembers being housed in the quarantine hut in Flossenbürg, which was located near the camp brothel. Everyone knew about the brothel, but all the prisoners in the quarantine talked about was survival. Every day he saw *Muselmänner* stagger by, emaciated, exhausted, and close to death. The overwhelming horror of camp life left prisoners indifferent to the brothels.[11] Similar stories exist from Buchenwald, Neuengamme, Sachsenhausen, and other camps.[12] But the indifference, though a product of the camps' miserable conditions, was also a blessing: One of the basic rules in the camp was to see as little as possible and make yourself invisible to the SS.[13] It was dangerous for prisoners to know too much.

In camps like Monowitz, where the brothels were in a central location, many prisoners knew of their existence.[14] The Jewish survivor Gerd Maschkowski said: "You couldn't miss it. It was in the middle of the camp. And the women came out too."[15] In the Auschwitz main camp, it was common knowledge that Block 24a contained a brothel.[16] In Mittelbau-Dora, the brothel stood on a hillside directly above the roll-call area. The Ukrainian survivor Vasili Lykianov describes the view from below: "And there at the roll-call square, you could see the ladies. They were sunbathing. . . . There were rumors that there was probably a brothel in the barrack hut."[17] As in camps where the brothel remained unseen, most prisoners had neither the strength nor the will to think about what was going on in the brothel. Consider the testimony of the former prisoner Willi Frohwein depicting a typical day in Mittelbau-Dora:

> You marched into the tunnel in the morning. Yes, you didn't get anything to eat. The bread in the morning was always in the evening. That wretched sauce was the only thing. And then we were in the tunnel for twelve hours. Then you came out of the tunnel and in the evening, after roll call, nothing interested you anymore. You might have sat in front of the block for a while. As I said, you exchanged recipes, talked a bit. And then you were happy when you got to the cot, because you were so exhausted, so wiped out, that you just couldn't go on any longer.[18]

In the Auschwitz main camp, prisoners had learned to fear the block housing the brothel, for it was there that a dreaded Rapportführer named Oswald Kaduk frequently made the rounds. Frohwein, who was imprisoned in Auschwitz as well as in Mittelbau-Dora, recalls that he was once ordered to the camp gate near Block 24a. There he came across Kaduk, who was, as often the case, staggeringly drunk. Willi Frohwein couldn't help but grin. When Kaduk saw this, he struck Frohwein so hard that he fell to the ground, knocking out two teeth. "You automatically forget that there's a brothel there," he said in an interview.[19]

Reports from survivors of the Monowitz concentration camp indicate that despite the central location of the brothel, few prisoners met forced sex workers. The building was isolated by a fence, and an SS man guarded the entrance.[20] During the day, the women could leave only to go for walks around the camp or to collect herbs, and an SS guard accompanied them wherever they went.[21] Most prisoners in Monowitz labored in workshops or on the construction sites of the Buna factory and hence never saw the women.[22] Fredi Diament, a nineteen-year-old Polish Jew, could move around the camp fairly freely because he was the trusty of the camp elder Paul Kozwary. He approached the brothel a few times. He remembers that he once saw the women swimming in a pond whose water was used to put out fires.[23] Tadeusz Borowski depicted the sex workers he observed in the

Auschwitz main camp: "The women in the windows are very affectionate and alluring, but inaccessible, like goldfish in an aquarium."[24]

Mario Raimondi, a prisoner in Flossenbürg, was placed in the lockup after a friend tried to escape and was caught. From the window of his cell, he could see the women in the brothel next door. At one point, one of the women gestured with her hand as if to ask why he was in prison. That was the extent of their communication.[25] Other prisoners encountered the women because of their work. Jack Terry, then only a boy, worked in the laundry at Flossenbürg and regularly brought fresh clothes and sheets to a woman in the brothel named Elenora Franke, who in return gave him a piece of bread whenever the SS man on duty was not looking.[26] Romek Dubitzki was deployed by the SS as a locksmith in Auschwitz's Block 24a and had to lock the women in the sleeping quarters after the brothel closed. As he was usually accompanied by an SS guard, however, opportunities for speaking with the women were fleetingly rare.[27] Even prisoners who met the women through their work, such as the Mauthausen camp clerk Hans Maršálek, knew little to nothing about them.[28]

A longer conversation between a sex worker and a camp inmate could take place only if both were alone in a room for a longer period. The most extensive conversation with a woman from the brothel was recorded by the Polish Auschwitz survivor Zofia Bator: "One day I observed a young girl with coiffed hair. Her eyes and eyebrows were painted with henna and she was wearing a beautiful blue shirt with black lace. Draped over her arm was a sky-blue robe. On her feet were high-heel clogs. She walked through the block with a certain careless to and fro and the block elder walked in front of her and led her to the bed. It was a phenomenon for us. A painted woman? Surely she came from freedom!"[29] Zofia Bator asked the young woman where she came from. She replied, "From the brothel!" She said that the SS had recruited her, and she talked about life in the "special building."[30] In her autobiography, the Auschwitz survivor Liana Millu describes the brothel detachment in detail. One day, while her work group was delivering blankets to the main camp, a bomb siren sounded. In the hectic rush for cover, the SS locked the women in the stairwell of Block 24a. A forced sex worker wearing a blue dress invited them into the brothel. The women were led to a well-appointed room, the sight of which astonished the Birkenau women.[31] One of the women in the room was "strikingly beautiful and dressed in a flashy, somewhat careless way." The other "was fair, with strong features and a wary, stubborn expression."[32] Millu reports that the Birkenau women were timid and at first remained standing at the doorway. But the sex workers offered food, "two huge rolls smelling of bacon and caraway seeds" along with "split pea soup with potatoes." After their "utter disbelief" passed, the Birkenau women started to eat. "Each separate taste bud tingled with rapture, in a frenzy of pleasure at those fantastic, forgotten sensations."[33]

The perception of the camp brothel as *another world* within the concentration camp is common in statements of other former prisoners, especially those in women's camps.[34] Ella Lingens vividly contrasts two women she met in the Auschwitz-Birkenau infirmary. One was a "young Polish fighter . . . who stayed here voluntarily so as not to sell out her national honor."[35] The other was a prostitute with "bored eyes, a frozen smile, and a painted face . . . who had been brought to us from the camp brothel with gonorrhea and who hoped to return soon to her place of work, a single room with a comfortable couch and next to a room with hot showers."[36] But Lingens refrains from judging and presents the choice to work in the brothel as "a chance to survive."[37] A charcoal drawing by the Italian Lodovico Barbiano di Belgiojoso illustrates the choice in stark terms. The left-hand side of the drawing shows a forced sex worker standing with a kapo at the entrance to the Gusen camp brothel; on the right is a dead prisoner at the edge of the roll-call square.[38] A less existential but equally vivid fault line separating the brothel workers from the rest of the camp was appearance. Prisoners often emphasized the femininity of the sex workers and the clothing they wore. Both Bator and Millu describe women from the camp brothel as pretty.[39] Gerd Maschkowski, who once saw the brothel women walking outside the Monowitz camp brothel, remembers them as "beautiful."[40]

Critical Opinions

Many statements of former prisoners about the forced sex workers contain value judgments, ranging from harsh criticism to open defense of the women's decision to work in the brothels. Recall Kogon's disparaging remark cited in the Introduction that the women in the Buchenwald camp brothel "were resigned to their fate with rather little restraint."[41] Jorge Semprún published the names of the women from the Buchenwald brothel in his autobiography *What a Beautiful Sunday* and talked about them in a disrespectful manner.[42] Heinz Heger, who was gay, explained that he could understand the block elders and kapos who maintained relationships with *Pipel* rather than go to the camp brothel: "I couldn't blame them, because the Russian and Polish boys, although I had never been intimate with any of them, also seemed cleaner to me and more human than the worn and puffy 'girls' from the brothel."[43] A former prisoner from Auschwitz put it more starkly: "I am overcome by immediate disgust when I have to look at these ladies. And I don't know what I would do if I had to spend twenty-five minutes with one of them."[44] Negative evaluations can also be found in reports by former female "political" prisoners. For example, in a book based on her experiences as a prisoner in Auschwitz-Birkenau, Krystina Zywulska describes a scene where women shout at a girl who was about to report for the brothel: "A Polish woman, what a disgrace, shame on you!"[45]

By contrast, Kupfer-Koberwitz emphasizes the courage and mental fortitude that women showed during an interrogation at Dachau. He heard secondhand that in the wake of a brothel raid the women had been taken to the camp director. One was said to have worn "provocative beachwear."[46] When an SS man criticized her, she is said to have scolded him: "Are you telling me how I should dress? If you don't like it, I'll strip naked, then I'll go naked. What do you want from me?"[47] Kupfer-Koberwitz continues: "The other women also gave him a tongue lashing. They had been well dressed, they ranted and raved, none of them had been afraid. It is also said that the women had not betrayed any of the prisoners, despite being questioned by the camp director. They certainly have much professional honor. Who knows whether the 'stronger sex' will not be weaker and betray the 'weaker sex.' When women are brave, they are usually braver than average men."[48] Other survivors attest to the generosity that the women showed toward other prisoners, such as giving away bread.[49] The women from the Neuengamme brothel gave food to Jewish children evacuated from Auschwitz and housed in a separate part of the brothel building.[50] Naftali Fürst, who arrived at Buchenwald while still a boy, recalls that shortly before the end of the war he was placed in the camp brothel after a stay in the infirmary: "I still fondly remember how one of the nurses—most likely a whore—held me close and calmed me down. On the whole, the treatment I received here was excellent. The food was wonderful. I was even given chocolate and cake. From one moment to the next, I had gone from hell to heaven."[51]

In her memoirs, Liana Millu explains her decision to become a sex worker. "Everyone in the lager goes around picking up leftovers from the garbage," a young woman from the brothel says. "They suck bones other people spit out—and I'm supposed to refuse life because it's offered on a dirty plate?"[52] Other former prisoners, such as Stephan Szymanski, explicitly argue that former sex workers should have the right to political rehabilitation and compensation. In his opinion, the accusations of collaboration leveled against forced sex workers, Polish women in particular, were completely absurd.[53] Even the former camp elder of Mittelbau-Dora called the camp brothel a "great shame."[54]

Resistance to Camp Brothels

As I discussed in previous chapters, prisoners did not merely form opinions about the brothels; those most critical of them organized various forms of resistance. The intensity of the resistance varied from camp to camp and depended on the composition of the camp society. The most decisive factor was whether the camp elite consisted mostly of political prisoners ("reds") or mostly of prisoners deemed "criminal" or "asocial" ("greens" or "blacks"). In Auschwitz and Monowitz, prisoner functionaries mostly belonged to the latter groups, and no collective calls to boycott the camp brothel emerged from their ranks. The same goes for Mauthausen, Gusen, Flossenbürg, Sachsenhausen, and Mittelbau-Dora, where "criminal" and "asocial" prisoners held the most important positions at the time the camp brothels opened. Nor did any significant resistance come from Polish political prisoners, who occupied important leadership positions in Auschwitz and other camps but lacked political coherence.[55]

By contrast, resistance to brothels was significant in the "red" camps, especially in Dachau. A collective of authors consisting of former Dachau prisoners wrote: "The moral attitude of the prisoners in this matter was astounding even for the greatest optimist."[56] Long before the brothel opened, the prisoners issued a slogan: "We must eat what the SS puts in front of us, but we will only love those who really want us."[57] The majority of the "old reds" joined the call for a boycott because they believed that visiting the brothel was a scandal and an act of complicity. This resistance was supported by social democrats, communists, and imprisoned trade unionists. Clergymen opposed the brothels as a "branch of hell."[58] On the day the brothel opened, political prisoners from multiple countries formed a gauntlet on the camp road and made fun of the brothel visitors.[59] Rudolf Kalmar writes: "On the opening day, the political prisoners protested against a few criminals and antisocials who had broken the boycott . . . incurring the wrath of the Rapportführer on duty, who performed his work in the waiting room, approving, booking, collecting tickets, and assigning men with zeal."[60] The camp leaders intervened and threatened punishment for everyone if all the prisoners did not appear at roll call during the brothel's opening hours. They told the boycotting prisoners that further resistance would lead to retribution.[61] But this did not seem to have deterred many political prisoners from joining the call. The former Dachau prisoner Otto Oertel wrote: "For us as political prisoners, the strict prohibition was: none of us are going [to the camp brothel]. With a few exceptions, we have so far stuck to this decision."[62] The resistance of the Dachau prisoners may have contributed to the brothel's being closed down at the end of 1944 after only eight months of operation.[63]

Other smaller acts of resistance took place across a variety of concentration camps, regardless of their elite's composition. The Italian Auschwitz survivor Teo Ducci reported that a German prisoner wanted to enter the brothel in the main camp at Auschwitz but was prevented from doing so by a group of people booing him at the entrance.[64] In Neuengamme, the prisoners put on a variety show to ridicule the camp brothel before its opening. The highlight came from the artist Teddy Ahrens, who sang a song he had written himself: "I am the female boss of the brothel, now line up and prepare to mount."[65] Politically minded prisoners in Neuengamme also discussed forms of assistance for the sex workers, who faced a "double burden" in the brothels.[66] They encouraged others to visit the brothel not to "use the women" but "to bring humanity."[67] In Flossenbürg and other camps, resistance by political prisoners was limited to moral condemnation of brothel visitors from their own ranks.[68]

Resistance also took the form of helping sex workers directly. David Pike, in his study *Spaniards in the Holocaust*, mentions the case of Salvador Ginestrà, who donated blood to a sick Sinteza in the Mauthausen brothel and saved her life.[69] Magdalena Walter says that she received a typhoid vaccination from a nurse she knew in Buchenwald after the outbreak of an epidemic.[70] She also refers to the assistance she received from camp communists, including the time two "politicals" bribed inmates not to have sex with her. She notes, however, that political prisoners helped "only a small percentage" because "they couldn't get to the other prisoners." "If they could have," she says, "they would have done so."[71] Other political inmates from Buchenwald supported the women with food.[72]

The Buchenwald Communists

In Buchenwald, German political prisoners—consisting mainly of communists alongside some socialists and social democrats—held important positions in the camp administration from April 1939 to the fall of 1941 and again starting in 1943. This made it possible to establish a resistance infrastructure that worked better than in other camps and actively improved prisoners' living conditions. But the organized and disciplined actions of red prisoner functionaries also aided the operation of the concentration camp, which conflicted with their political aims. The reds served as rescuers and helpers but also as accomplices in SS crimes—up to and including murder.[73]

The Buchenwald reds saw their actions in the camp as subordinate to a higher goal: the fight against National Socialism and collective preparation for a postwar Germany. For them, existence in the camp meant resistance. Job number one was to endure the camp's hardships and oppose their planned extermination. Military self-discipline and principled action lay the foundation of that resistance. To foster both, the communists drew up ten commandments for camp prisoners. The seventh addressed sexuality: "Keep yourselves fit, do not go crazy, do not go to the whorehouse, keep yourselves clean."[74] Fred Löwenberg, who came to the Buchenwald camp as a young inmate, describes how the communists taught him the principles of self-discipline:

> For us younger ones, education for correct physical behavior . . . was very important for us—including sexual behavior. From the very beginning, we were taught by our elders: "*Meide Salzwasser, Stange, sonst lebst du nicht lange.*" [Roughly: if you want to live long, avoid salt water and schlong.] *Salzwasser* ["salt water"] accumulates when you're hungry, leading to water retention. *Stange* ["erect penis"] was the name for masturbation. . . . It wasn't adhered to. But it was this kind of education, this kind of experience passed on again and again by older prisoners. . . . Or that we had to wash ourselves in cold water every day. The whole body and so on. It was all about keeping physically fit. And we were, me and my comrades anyway.[75]

Physical hygiene, like celibacy, was thought to strengthen individual resilience and increase the chances of survival.[76]

The emphasis on sexual abstinence grew out of concerns that sex could undermine the resistance movement. For one, the jealousy and emotional ties of intimate sexual relationships could harm solidarity and distract prisoners from the political struggle.[77] For another, prisoners caught engaging in homosexual acts, informal prostitution, and other prohibited sexual behaviors faced arrest or death, which could jeopardize the efforts of the resistance. Some political prisoners cracked down on inmates' sexual activities. A former Dachau prisoner noted: "Homosexuality was prevented by the terror of the prisoners themselves."[78] In this respect, the Dachau and Buchenwald men's camps were not unique; on the contrary, the principle of abstinence was also widespread among female political prisoners. Margarete Buber-Neumann describes how passionate friendships developed between political prisoners at Ravensbrück that nevertheless remained platonic—in contrast to the sexual relationships between the antisocials and criminals. There is no talk of homosexuality among inmates in Ravensbrück's political block. Schoppmann attributes this to a puritanism on the left, and she points out that homosexual relationships also occurred between female political prisoners.[79] Federn also observes that red principles did not always accord with reality. "The communists covered it up by denying sexuality: A communist has no sexuality! A communist does not masturbate! And of course he has no homosexual contacts either."[80] "We know that there were of course homosexual relationships," Fred Löwenberg said in an interview. "I myself once had to defend myself against an attempt by a good friend of mine. And I have to say . . . that the prisoners were consistently against it."[81]

When it came to the brothels, additional factors impelled sexual abstinence. The prevailing view in Marxist thinking was that women ought not to be seen as commodities, and most communists disavowed prostitution in general.[82] More crucially, however, was the fear that the SS would use the sex workers to destroy the resistance. The construction of the *Sonderbau* in Buchenwald was accompanied by discussions among German political prisoners about what the SS intended to achieve with the brothel. The inmates were not convinced by the reason provided by the SS: increasing labor output. After much speculation, the communist party leadership eventually settled on the theory that the brothel was a means to discover underground organizations, humiliate prisoners, and pit them against one another.[83] One of their communications reads: "We are of the opinion that a communist should not lower himself to the special building!"[84] In the minds of the communists, the brothel was enemy territory. Statements made by the former Buchenwald inmate Herbert Weidlich exemplify this way of thinking: "For security reasons, the anti-fascist resistance organization could not be indifferent" to who visited the brothel and "what kind of lifestyle the women of the 'special building' led before their imprisonment."[85] The communists tended to see the sex workers themselves as victims because they insisted that they had never worked as prostitutes before the camps and that they had been recruited with false promises.[86] Weidlich writes: "It must not have been difficult for these women to choose this 'work' in order to escape the punishing living conditions of the Ravensbrück women's camp."[87]

But Buchenwald's communist leaders did not issue a call for a boycott, which their comrades in Dachau had done.[88] Rather, a "silent agreement"[89] emerged: The communists would exert influence on brothel visitors from their own ranks via "political and moral means."[90] For instance, the party leadership had a plant guarding the gate on the way to the brothel; his job was to dissuade communist prisoners from visiting. Political block elders also tried to coerce prisoners into abstinence, and antifascist resistance members in the infirmary kept tabs on inmates tested for venereal disease, a prerequisite for brothel entry.[91]

The "political and moral" pressure applied by the communists in Buchenwald is evident in a pamphlet of poetry titled "Kampf gegen das Häftlings-Bordell" ("Fight against the prisoners' brothel"), written by an unidentified inmate likely while still imprisoned in Buchenwald.[92] One poem ". . . Und Deine Mutter, Deine Braut?" (". . . And your mother, your bride?") accuses men who frequent the brothel of lacking gratitude for the support of their mothers, wives, and girlfriends:

Where the road to the valley stretches,
Lies behind wire fencing and planks,
A whorehouse for camp needs
When it comes to spring thoughts.
Once again, a parcel from mother,
And next, she wrote, I'll send money,
So that my boy can buy something
And maintain his health.
Motherly love, that's what she sends
Everything she scrimped and saved,
And her grief for her boy
Which she kept deep in her heart.
And with the gifts: a painful letter,
From the girl to whom he swore fidelity;
Who had not lost her love for the sunny boy
In spite of parting and woe.
Touched, the boy unwraps the glory
That a mother . . . forsook,
Pockets the pension bank bills with a grin
For which a mother toiled.
Reads the brave letter with moist eyes
Of the girl and praises her loyalty . . .
Then he wantonly casts the sacrifice
Before shameless whorehouse swine.
That, caring mother, is your boy.
That, girl, is the reward for your love:
Nothing of character and masculine pride,
A servant only of carnal instincts.[93]

The poem, which rhymes in the original, addresses the double standards of male prisoners who visit the brothel and exploit the generosity of their loved ones. The author contrasts the self-sacrificing women helping the antifascist resistance fighter with the "shameless brothel swines" who seduce the man into betraying his values and his family.[94] The women forced to work in the brothel are depicted as seductive accomplices. We don't hear about their suffering, their confinement in the brothels, and the false promises that brought them there. "We are too good to share bread with whores," the author writes in another poem.[95] Evidently, some communists regarded the sex workers as antisocial and sexually deviant, even though in the main the party considered them to be victims of sexual exploitation. Weidlich himself, despite his understanding for the women who decided to work in the brothel, seems to share this prejudice when describing their post-camp lives: "During the stormy transformation in the life of the liberated camp, these women went into hiding in Weimar and the surrounding area. Some continued their acquaintance with former prisoners. As far as I know, the women who remained in the territory of the GDR were resocialized into society."[96]

Although the communist leadership in Buchenwald was aware that visiting the brothel posed a problem for the internal discipline of the resistance movement, it considered expulsion from the party to be excessively harsh. Ernst Busse, one of the three leaders of the German communists in Buchenwald, stated in 1946: "If we wanted to exclude all of them, there wouldn't be many left."[97] Albert van Dijk stated that the resistance movement had him transferred to the physically grueling Mittelbau-Dora camp for frequently visiting the brothel. This was a common means of eliminating opponents and collaborators in Buchenwald.[98] Whether it was also commonly used to dispose of communists who visited brothels remains doubtful, as there is no evidence to back up van Dijk's story, and, at any rate, his is the only such incident reported.[99]

Since the war, clear evidence has emerged of brothel visits among the Buchenwald communists.[100] Many of them had gone a decade without seeing a woman, and many came from the pool of prisoner functionaries, which is to say, they lived under better conditions than other inmates and hence were more likely to have surplus energy for sex. At the end of April 1945, a party control commission was set up to assess candidates' suitability for political office in the "New Germany." While conducting background checks, the commission identified seven comrades who had visited camp brothels and issued them sharp reprimands for their behavior.[101]

9 The Camp Brothel: An Outpost of Nazi Biopolitics

Nazi concentration camp brothels were a historically unique form of bureaucratized sexual exploitation. They were the only places in the camps where women officially performed forced sexual labor and the only places built for the "pleasure" of male prisoners. The brothels were conceived as part of a system of incentives to increase the abysmally low output of the malnourished inmates. They combined the basic features of the quota systems tested in the Soviet Gulag with Himmler's absurd notion that giving male prisoners access to women so that they could satisfy their "natural" sex drives would increase productivity. The system was predicated on the idea that the sexual exploitation of female sex workers would drive men to push themselves to the limits of what was physically possible. It combined aspects of state-controlled prostitution in Nazi Germany with the techniques of subjugation and exploitation employed in the concentration camps.

The SS sought to exercise total control over the camp brothels. Although the SS set up the first brothels at central locations in the camps, they later moved them to the peripheries, close to areas reserved for death and killing. The interiors of the military huts in which most brothels were located can be traced back to the nineteenth-century panopticon: the central corridor, from which the SS could quickly reach every room in the brothel; the uniform arrangement of the rooms to either side of the corridor; and peepholes in every door.[1]

When recruiting women for the camp brothels, the SS targeted female inmates who had worked as prostitutes or who were suspected of having done so. Most had repeatedly run afoul of Nazi Germany's restrictive prostitution policies and had been placed in a camp as punishment. The SS also recruited "antisocial" prisoners and those who had been sent to a concentration camp for having intercourse with foreigners. Officials exploited the stigma attached to these women to imply that they were promiscuous and legitimize their placement in the brothels. In addition to German women, the SS found women from Poland, the USSR, and the Netherlands for non-German brothel visitors. Contrary to the stories in De-Nur's *House of Dolls* and Nazi sexploitation literature, none were Jewish. The SS selected Polish women for Ukrainian SS guards, who as Slavs were considered subhuman and forbidden to have contact with German women. Some of the Ukrainians sexually abused the Polish women in the brothels reserved for them, but, again, not a single one was a Jew.

The SS initially drew the women for the brothels from Ravensbrück. Later, officials included the Auschwitz-Birkenau women's camp and smaller subcamps. They approached women assigned to hard labor details and promised them release from imprisonment after six months of service. Accordingly, the decision to join the brothel was by no means voluntary, as the alternative was to remain in miserable conditions and face likely death. Toward the end of the war, the SS selected women for forced sexual labor without telling them beforehand. For them, women were merely matériel to be used as needed.

The same camp doctors and SS leaders who selected prisoners for murder examined women for the brothels. Although the SS men humiliated the women in the process, it is highly unlikely that any rapes occurred. For although the SS possessed absolute power over the women, they still faced imprisonment for violating rules, and despite everything, respect for the rules prevailed at concentration camps in Germany—in contrast to the extermination camps in Eastern Europe.

The SS claimed total control over the sexuality of prisoners. Camp guards and administrators decided who was allowed to have a sex life and who was not. In the case of the women selected for the camp brothels, the SS carried out forced resexualization. They nursed them back to health in the Ravensbrück infirmary or in the Auschwitz block for medical experiments in order to restore their femininity for the sole purpose of sexual exploitation. Once the women were assigned to a brothel, the SS controlled the space, time, and nature of the encounters. They kept the women isolated and permitted contact with men only in predetermined rooms and at predetermined times. Private contact between women and men was forbidden.

Camp guards permitted brothel workers to have sex only in the missionary position, required that they receive regular medical checkups, and determined whom they were to have sex with. Female and male prisoners were objects in a space constructed and superintended by the SS. In it, the authority of the SS was the unchallenged power; they alone decided who could have a sex life and the form it must take. The *Sonderbau* was not a "place of tolerance," as Foucault described brothels in *The History of Sexuality*, but a perfidious combination of sexual exploitation and complicity.[2] Moreover, the camp brothels operated on a rigid gender model. Masculinity followed the Nazi dogma of male virility: dominant, hegemonic, exploitative, and in need of channeling. By contrast, female sexuality was passive, subordinate, something that men had the patriarchal right to access. For German women in good standing, the purpose of female bodies was to provide more "Aryan" offspring. For German women not in good standing, along with the other women in the camps, female bodies were for increasing output, either directly as laborers or indirectly as sex workers.

The administration of the camp brothels followed that of prostitution in Nazi Germany generally. Since September 1939, all prostitution had been under the control of the police and the state health authorities. In the concentration camps, the brothels were run by the SS, which was controlled by Himmler, who in turn had complete authority over the police force. And just as registered prostitutes in German cities had to appear for regular checkups at the health authorities, forced sex workers had to receive regular venereal exams. The checks were performed not only to prevent the spread of sexually transmitted disease but also to stop "racial decay." Another common denominator shared by brothels inside and outside the camps was the principle of ethnic segregation: Only like races were allowed to meet, while Jewish women and, by extension, Jewish men, were kept out.

Forced sexual labor in the camps was similar to state-controlled prostitution in Nazi Germany in other ways as well. For example, the SS set the price of a brothel visit based on typical market prices. When it came to the number of forced sex workers for each camp brothel, the SS seems to have used the DAF's ratio for foreign worker brothels: one woman for every three hundred to five hundred men. Other aspects of the organization, such as medical examinations before and after sex, are reminiscent of the compulsory hygiene regimen for soldiers after visiting Wehrmacht brothels. Involving doctors in the selection of women for brothels was also a Wehrmacht practice.[3] As with other work deployments in the camp, the labor statistics department meticulously recorded information regarding personnel, revenue, and visitors. The details of the forced sex workers were recorded in the central WVHA registry.

The link between the inner world of the concentration camp and society at large was not specific to the camp brothel. Toward the end of the war, concentration camps became embedded in the existing infrastructure of nearby villages. German prisoners were covered by social insurance, and the SS paid their monthly contributions.[4] The SS were also required to issue reports to local health authorities.[5] Even if concentration camp brothels were not set up explicitly to enforce Nazi biopolitics, they nevertheless became an integral part of it.

In the concentration camp, individual expressions of sexuality violated a regime that aimed at the total control of all social relationships and were therefore subject to draconian punishment. The dehumanization that new arrivals experienced was accompanied by the destruction of their sexual selves. For the vast majority, the sex drive played no role in the daily struggle for survival. Only those belonging to the upper echelons of prisoner society could afford to have sex lives.

The most common form of sex life in the camps was situational homosexuality, in which heterosexual men entered into relationships with adolescent boys or forced them to provide sexual services. Heterosexual contact was possible only in camps where the men and women were kept in close proximity, such as Auschwitz-Birkenau and Bergen-Belsen. But even there, most women had lost their secondary sex characteristics. Those who still had a feminine body possessed a special resource that greatly aided their survival, even if sexual barter for food and protection was often exploitative and violent.

Submission to sexual exploitation was both a form of violence and a survival strategy. The paradox can clearly be seen in the fate of the forced sex workers. In terms of food, sanitary conditions, and work, the conditions in the brothels were many times better than in most of the women's camps. For many, forced sexual labor was a lesser evil compared with the constant physical violence, starvation, and death they had faced elsewhere in the camps. The claims that many women died in the brothels or returned sexually ill or pregnant are not supported by the evidence.[6] On the contrary, it is highly likely that the women survived the brothels, and the vast majority survived imprisonment in the camps. This is attributable not only to the better living conditions in the brothels but also to the opportunities the forced sex workers had to accumulate social capital by forging relationships with better-off prisoners.

The establishment of the camp brothels marked a turning point in the sexual policy of the SS: It made sex among prisoners legal for the first time. Of course, sex was a privilege reserved for elite non-Jews and was bureaucratically administered and rigorously monitored by the SS. No space existed in the brothels where women and men could mingle, indicate preferences, and negotiate prices. Still, the control sought by the SS was, in practice, less than totalizing. Prisoners found ways to make contact with forced sex workers outside the brothels. In doing so, they created spaces of quasi autonomy where women could also benefit.

The motives of brothel visitors varied. Only a very small number were regulars. For them, visiting the brothels was about demonstrating their sexual potency and membership in the upper echelons of the prison population. Most visitors turned up at the brothels sporadically or only once. They were seeking an emotional relationship, proximity to a woman, their first sexual experience, or their last. Far from satisfying the red-blooded notions of male virility imagined by the SS, many visitors just wanted some form of human contact. Of course, being exposed to sexual situations may also have served to rekindle their sense of individual sexual identity. But any sex prisoners had with the brothel workers would have made them complicit in the sexual exploitation of women. This underlines the perfidious nature of the brothel system, which further victimized women while making perpetrators out of the men.

The total number of forced sex workers was low—some 190 women in the brothels for prisoners and twenty-four in the brothels for Ukrainian guards. The same goes for the visitors, who made up less than 1 percent of the camp population. Given the hundreds of thousands of prisoners held in the camp system, it is fair to ask whether the brothels had much significance. Likewise, one might wonder whether the SS could have regarded such a relatively small operation as a success.

But the numbers do not paint a complete picture of the brothels' significance. The visitors, though few in proportion to the total number of prisoners, were often prisoner functionaries who were of particular value because they managed the daily functioning of the camps. Accordingly, the brothels were one of the institutions for maintaining camp order, and in this sense they might be considered a partial success. When it came to increasing labor output, however, they were counterproductive and did more to promote corruption than incentivize prisoners to exceed their quotas. An improvement in living conditions and an end to daily violence could have led to an increase in labor productivity—but the SS seemed uninterested in such benevolent changes.

The camp brothels emerged in response to Hitler's megalomaniacal construction projects. These include the rally grounds in Nuremberg and the planned city of Germania, both inconceivable without enormous amounts of cheap labor and materials. The same goes for the General Plan East, which aimed to resettle ethnic Germans in Poland and parts of the Soviet Union after local populations had been murdered or forcibly relocated. The SS also relied on prisoner labor in the underground factories of

Mittelbau-Dora for the production of V2 rockets meant to terrify the populations of London and Antwerp and avert defeat. Himmler believed that the camp brothels would play a key role in ramping up labor output for all of these projects.

Though the camp brothels were not directly connected to SS extermination policy, they belonged to structures that facilitated its reign of terror. The bonus system was meant to overcome the basic contradiction between work and survival and maximize the exploitation of prisoners. The most prominent example is Auschwitz, where the establishment of camp brothels coincided with the beginning of the murder of Hungarian Jews in the gas chambers of Birkenau. While male prisoner functionaries visited the brothels, the SS gassed thousands of Jews every day.

This study has shown that the recruitment of women for the brothels took place under false promises, coercion, or both. The brothels functioned as forced labor details in which women were subject to total surveillance and control. The women operated as if on an assembly line, and they had no control over the men they had sex with or the kind of sex they had. Furthermore, they had no option to transfer to other work details if they wished. Despite better living conditions in the camp brothel, it would be unfair to claim that the women were collaborating with the SS. In the concentration camp, prisoners had to submit completely if they were to have any chance of survival. Bruno Bettelheim put it as follows: "What I am doing here, or what is happening to me, does not count at all; here everything is permissible as long and insofar as it contributes to helping me to survive in the camp."[7] The decision to work at the brothels and endure sexual exploitation was a survival strategy. Those able to summon this strength deserve recognition. In an interview, the Polish Holocaust survivor Stanisław Hantz, talking about a young Polish woman recruited for the Auschwitz brothel, said, "She did well, because she survived!"[8] Her survival itself was a form of resistance against the death machinery of the concentration camp.

In early 2016, the Auschwitz survivor Ruth Klüger addressed the German Bundestag on International Holocaust Remembrance Day. She called forced sex workers forgotten victims of the Holocaust. It was the first time that brothel workers had received mention on such a national stage, and it had a significant impact on German politics. Four years later, the German parliament passed a motion to "recognize those persecuted by the National Socialists as 'antisocials' and 'career criminals.'" This was tantamount to a social rehabilitation of 70 percent of the forced sex workers in the brothels, making them eligible for compensatory payments. This decision came far too late, of course: By 2020, even the youngest survivor would have been approaching one hundred years of age. Furthermore, the new law applied only to German victims. It ignored the Polish, Soviet, and one Dutch woman who made up the other 30 percent of the forced sex workers. Nevertheless, Klüger's speech and the new legislation ensured that their names would be included in the remembrance of Nazi crimes and the Holocaust. For the sake of these victims, we must acknowledge the "shameless reality" that Erich Roßmann thought no one outside the camps would believe. The aim of this book has been to help make sure that we do.

108 121
Konzentrationslager Floßenbürg
PRÄMIENSCHEIN
Nennwert: RM 1.–
1452

Figure 1: Bonus voucher, Flossenbürg (source: AGF)

Prämienschein über RM 1.–
Häftlingsgeldverwaltung
KL. Auschwitz
Auschwitz, den
SS-Obersturmführer

Figure 2: Bonus voucher, Auschwitz (source: APMO)

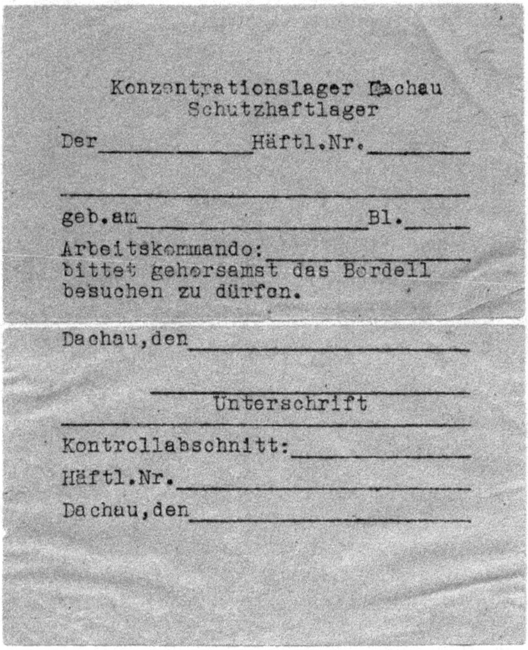

Konzentrationslager Dachau
Schutzhaftlager
Der ____________ Häftl.Nr. ________
____
geb.am ________________ Bl. ______
Arbeitskommando: ______________
bittet gehorsamst das Bordell
besuchen zu dürfen.
Dachau,den ______________________
____
Unterschrift
____
Kontrollabschnitt: ______________
Häftl.Nr. ______________________
Dachau,den ______________________

Figure 3: Request for brothel visit, Dachau (source: AGD)

Figure 4: Heinrich Himmler inspects Mauthausen, 1941 (photo: SS; source: AMM)

Figure 5: The "special building" in the Gusen subcamp before 1945 (photo: SS; source: Museu d'Història de Catalunya, Barcelona/Amical de Mauthausen)

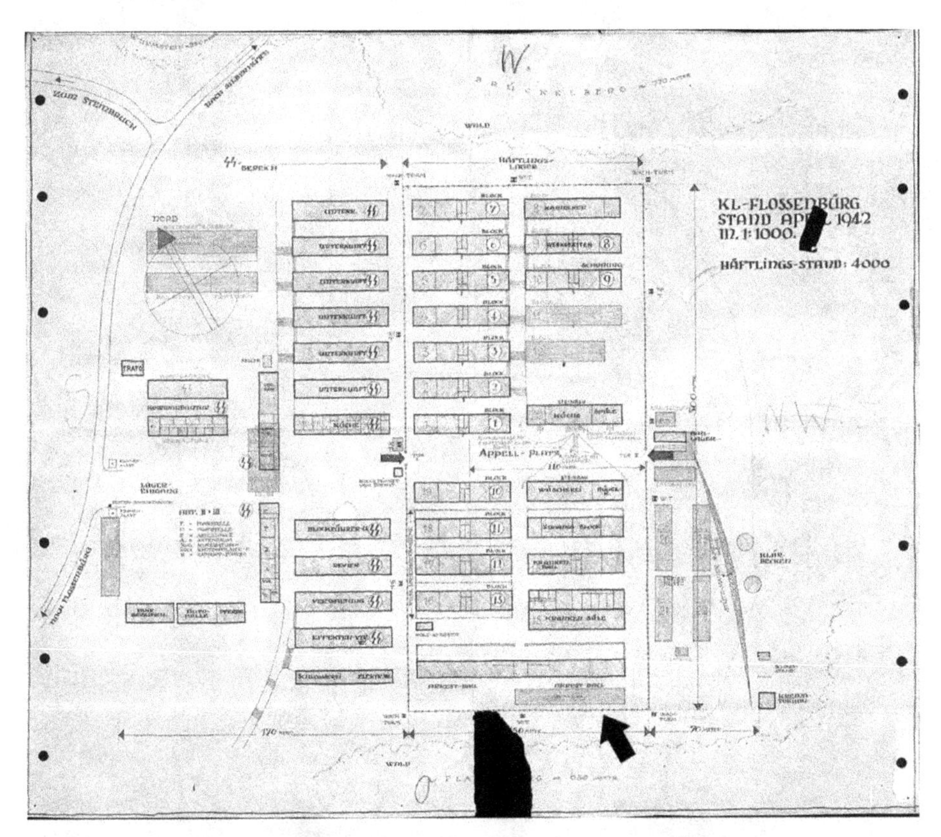

Figure 6: Flossenbürg site plan, prepared by the SS (source: AGF)

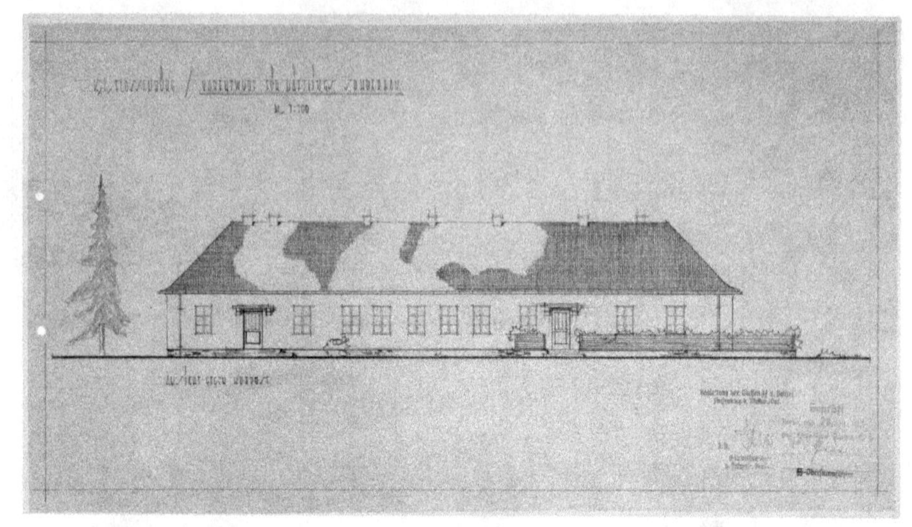

Figure 7: Side view; draft of a prisoner brothel for Flossenbürg, July 1942 (source: BArch, NS 4 Fl/283)

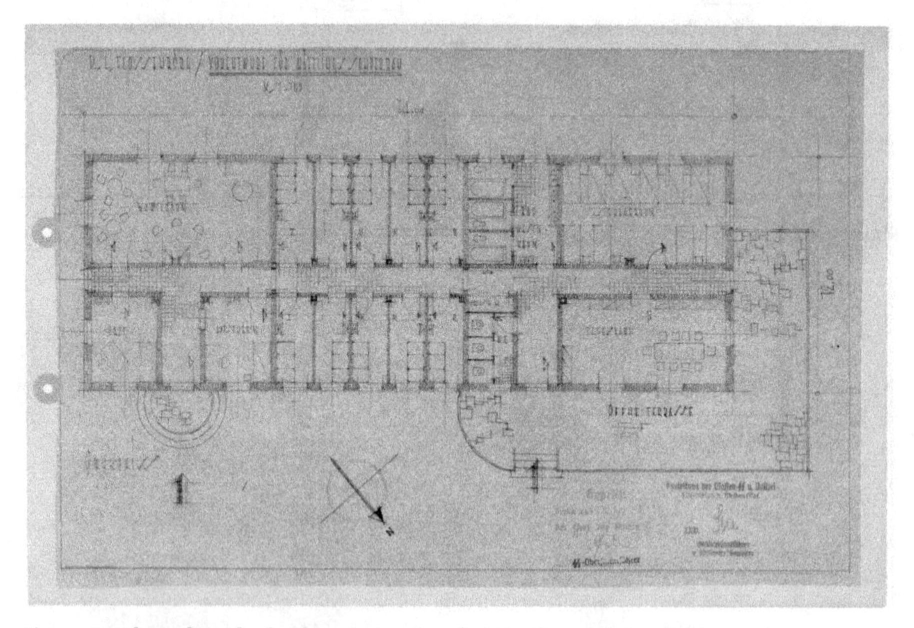

Figure 8: Floorplan; draft of a prisoner brothel for Flossenbürg, July 1942 (source: BArch, NS 4 Fl/283)

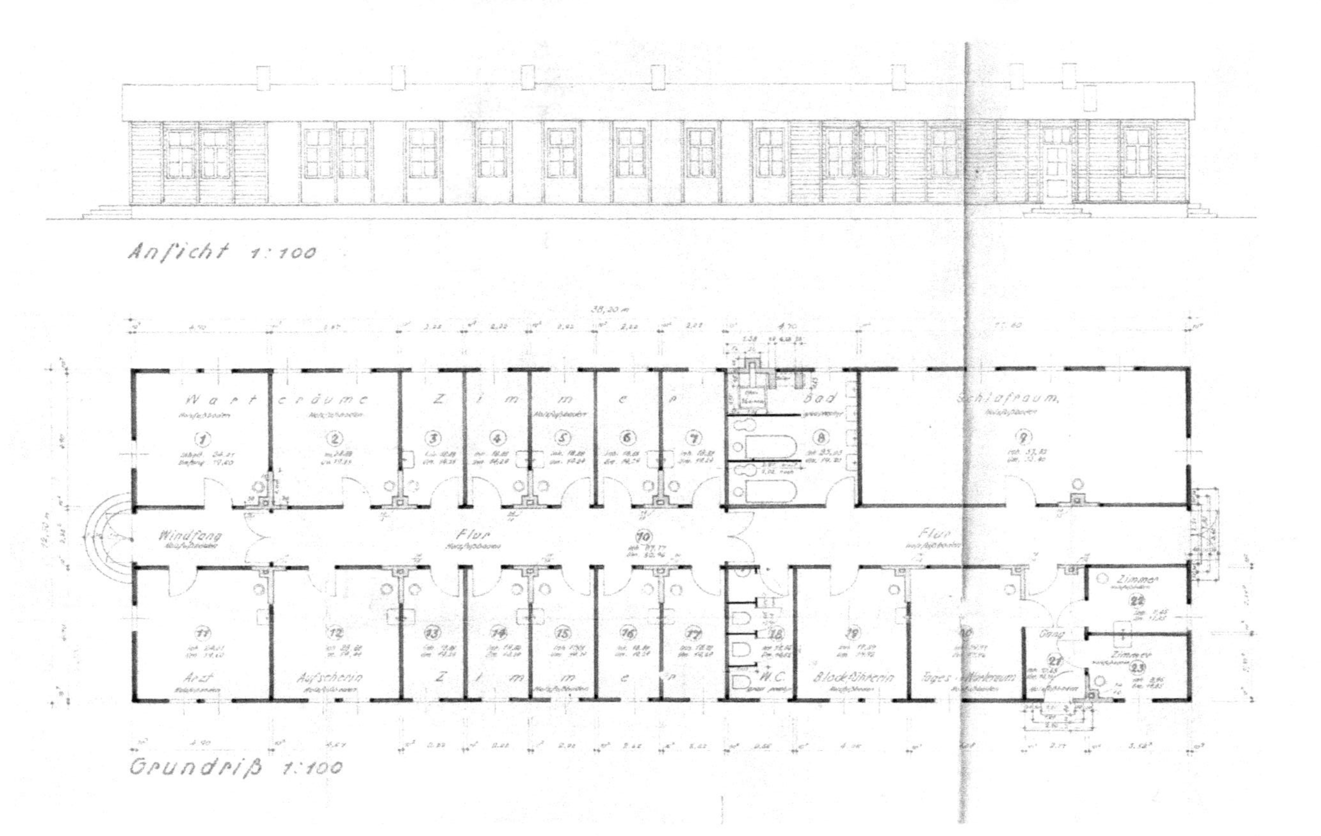

Figure 9: As-built plan of the Flossenbürg camp brothel, March 1944 (section) (source: BArch, NS 4 Fl/285)

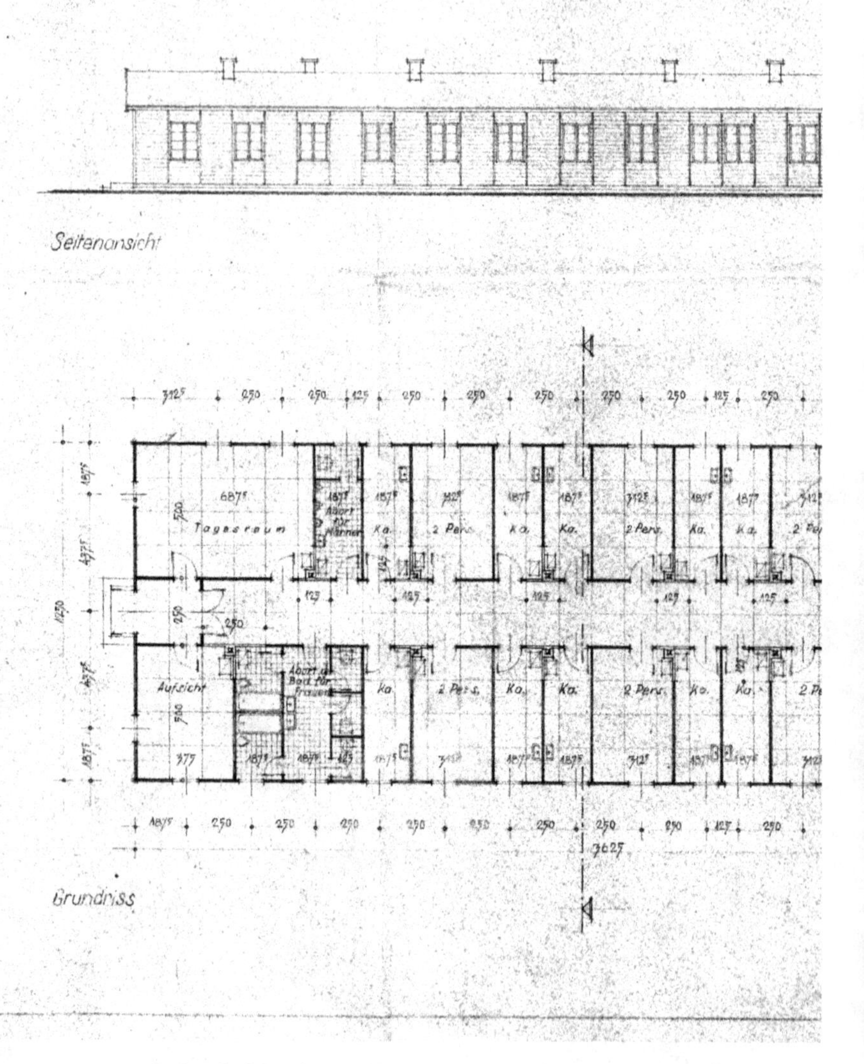

Figure 10: Drawing of a brothel for the Auschwitz main camp (source: APMO)

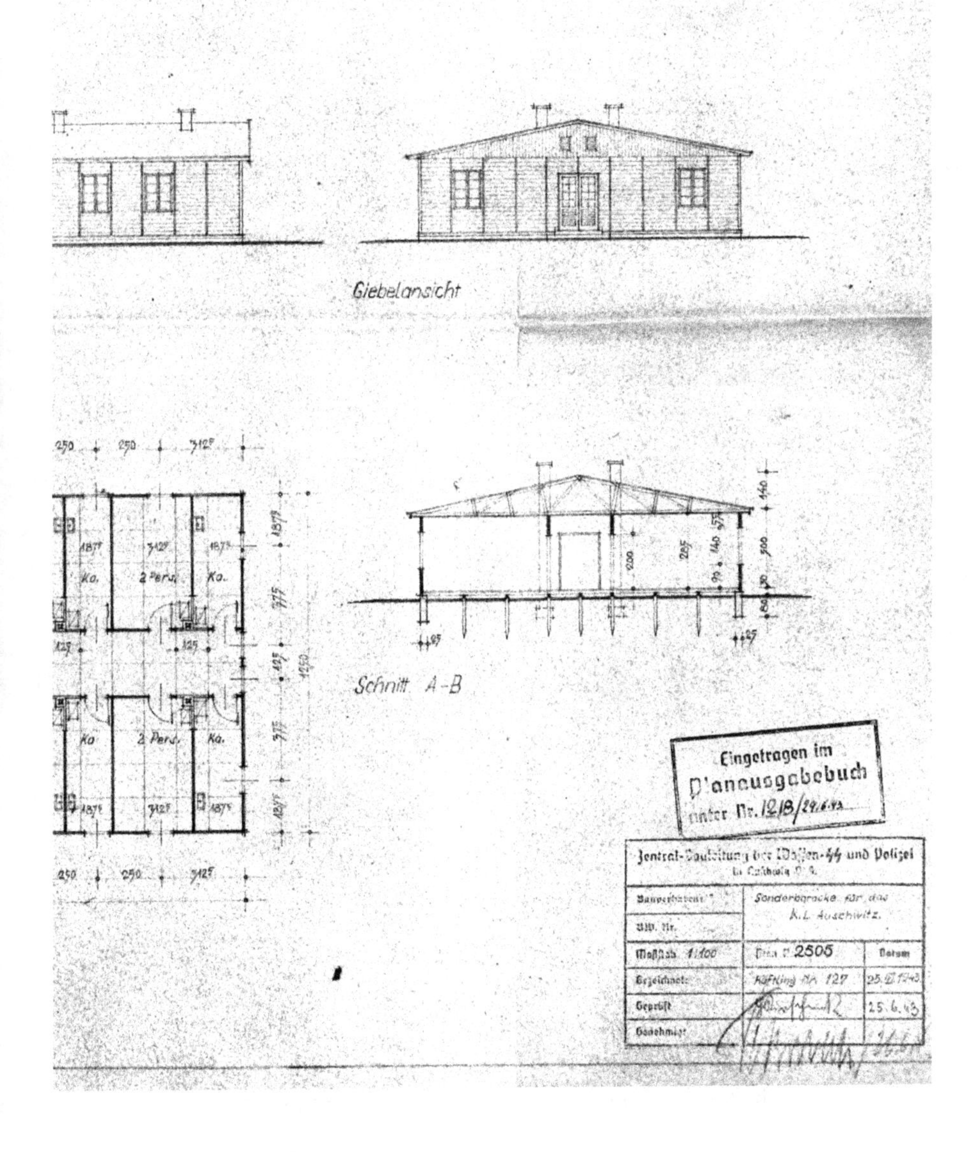
Giebelansicht
Schnitt A-B
Ka.
2 Pers.
Eingetragen im
Planausgabebuch
unter Nr. 1218/29.6.43
Zentral-Bauleitung der Waffen-SS und Polizei
Sonderbaracke für das
K.L. Auschwitz.
Maßstab 1:100
2505
Häftling Nr. 127
25.6.43

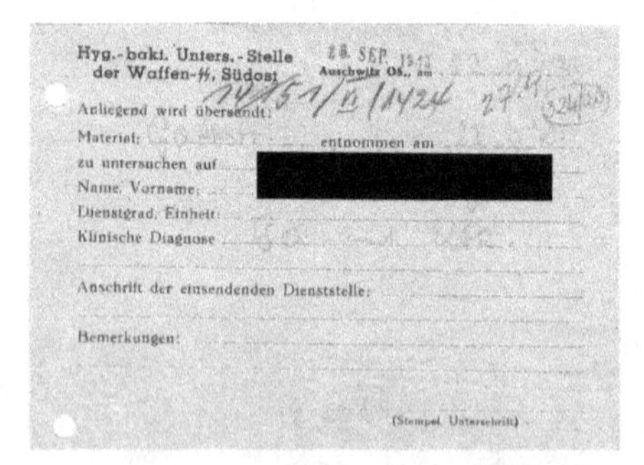

Hyg.-bakt. Unters.-Stelle der Waffen-SS, Südost
Auschwitz OS., am 28. SEP 1943

Anliegend wird übersandt: 24151/B/1424

Material: entnommen am

zu untersuchen auf

Name, Vorname:

Dienstgrad, Einheit:

Klinische Diagnose

Anschrift der einsendenden Dienststelle:

Bemerkungen:

(Stempel, Unterschrift)

Figure 11: Record (*Begleitzettel*) of a gonorrhea test for a woman who was recruited in Birkenau for a camp brothel, dated September 22, 1943 (source: APMO)

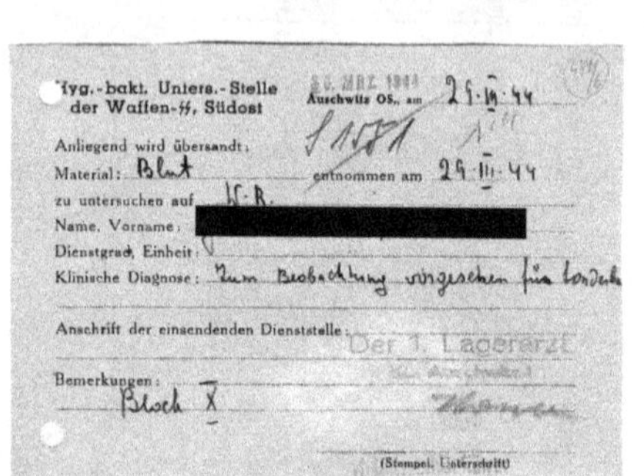

Hyg.-bakt. Unters.-Stelle der Waffen-SS, Südost
Auschwitz OS., am 29.III.44

Anliegend wird übersandt: 11571

Material: Blut entnommen am 29.III.44

zu untersuchen auf W.R.

Name, Vorname:

Dienstgrad, Einheit:

Klinische Diagnose: Zum Beobachtung vorgesehen für Sonderb...

Anschrift der einsendenden Dienststelle: Der 1. Lagerarzt

Bemerkungen: Block X

(Stempel, Unterschrift)

Figure 12: Record (*Begleitzettel*) of a blood sample to test for syphilis, dated March 29,1944 (source: APMO)

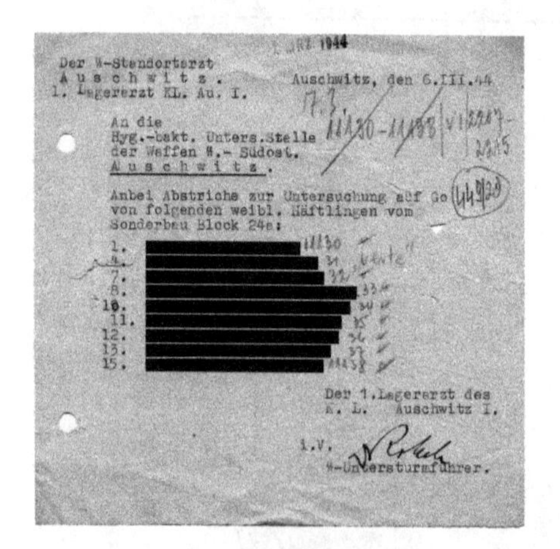

Der SS-Standortarzt Auschwitz.
1. Lagerarzt KL. Au. I.

Auschwitz, den 6.III.44

An die
Hyg.-bakt. Unters.Stelle
der Waffen SS.- Südost.
Auschwitz.

Anbei Abstriche zur Untersuchung auf Go von folgenden weibl. Häftlingen vom Sonderbau Block 24a:

1.
4.
7.
8.
10.
11.
12.
13.
15.

Der 1.Lagerarzt des K. L. Auschwitz I.

i.V.

SS-Untersturmführer.

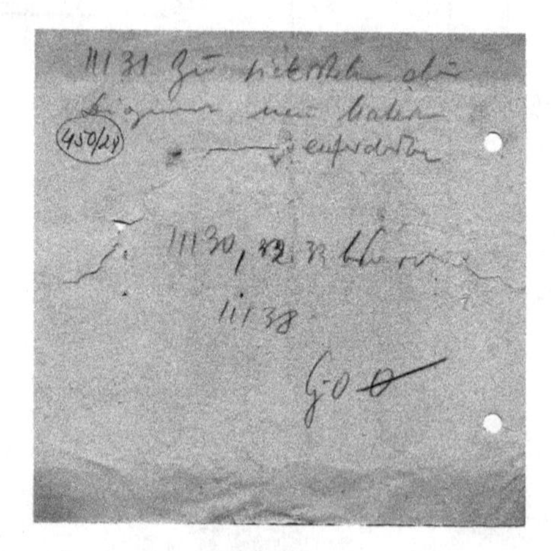

Figures 13 and 14: Records (*Begleitzettel*) of gonorrhea tests for women from the brothel in Block 24a at the Auschwitz main camp, dated March 6, 1944 (source: APMO)

Häftlingskarte

Einlieferungsstelle	Einlieferungsdatum (Tag / Monat / Jahr)	Häftlingsart	Geburts- (Tag / Monat / Jahr)	Geschlecht	Familienstand	Kinder (m / w)
Kripo	21 / 3. / 42	Asozial	21	männlich 1 ☐ weiblich 2 ☒	ledig 1 ☐ verheiratet 2 ☐ verwitwet 3 ☐ geschieden 4 ☐	

Staatsangehörigkeit	Hauptberuf	1. Nebenberuf	2. Nebenberuf	3. Nebenberuf
R. D. R.	Bürogehilfin			

Wehrdienstverhältnis	T.-Grad	Anzahl Vorstrafen	Gefängnis Monate	Zuchthaus Monate	Eingeliefert in KL
		4			Ravensbrück

Zugangsart	Überstellung an KL	Häftlings-Nr.	eingesetzt als	Abgangs- (Art / Tag / Mon / Jahr)	Holl. Verm. (Zu / Ab)
	Ravensbrück	9898	Bordellfrau		
	Fürstenberg/Meckl.				

Bemerkungen:

Kontrollvermerk: ausgestellt / verschlüsselt / Lochk. geprüft

Figure 15: Prisoner card from the WVHA registry for a former forced sex worker at Mauthausen (source: BArch D-H, NS 3/1577)

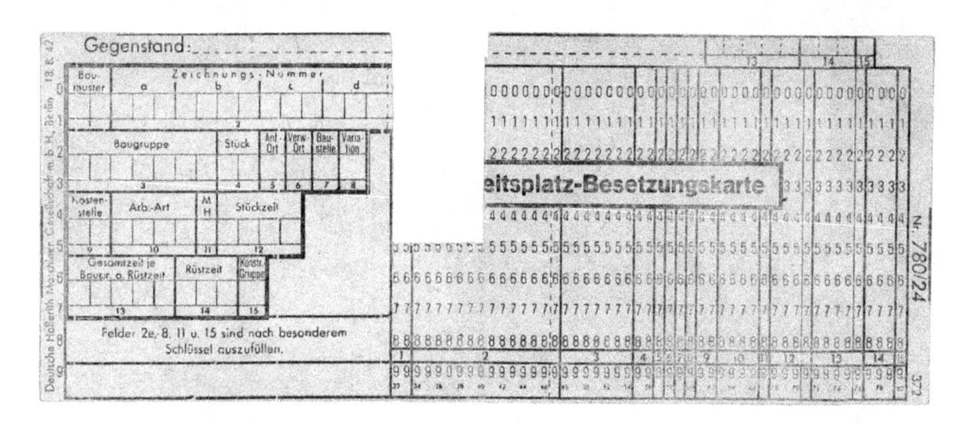

Gegenstand:

Bau-muster	Zeichnungs-Nummer a	b	c	d

Baugruppe	Stück	Anf.-Ort	Verw.-Ort	Bau-stelle	Varia-tion

Kosten-stelle	Arb.-Art	M H	Stückzeit

Gesamtzeit je Bausr. o. Rüstzeit	Rüstzeit	Kostr. Gruppe

Felder 2e, 8, 11 u. 15 sind nach besonderem Schlüssel auszufüllen.

Deutsche Hollerith Maschinen Gesellschaft m. b. H., Berlin 18. 8. 42

...eitsplatz-Besetzungskarte

Nr. 780/24

Figure 16: Workplace staffing card reconstructed from record fragments of the Deutsche Hollerith-Maschinen Gesellschaft mbH (source: ITS/KLD/Buchenwald/Arbeitskarten [R])

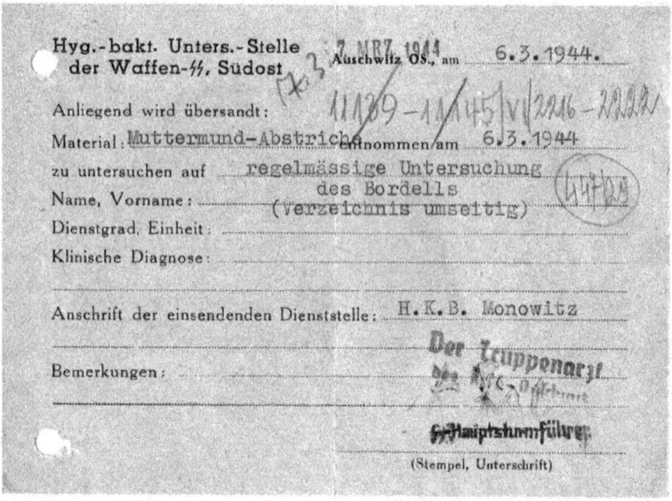

Hyg.-bakt. Unters.-Stelle
der Waffen-SS, Südost

7. MRZ. 1944
Auschwitz OS., am 6.3.1944.

Anliegend wird übersandt: 11139–11145 | V | 2216–2222

Material: Muttermund-Abstriche entnommen am 6.3.1944

zu untersuchen auf regelmässige Untersuchung des Bordells

Name, Vorname: (Verzeichnis umseitig)

Dienstgrad, Einheit:

Klinische Diagnose:

Anschrift der einsendenden Dienststelle: H.K.B. Monowitz

Bemerkungen:

Der Truppenarzt
SS-Hauptsturmführer

(Stempel, Unterschrift)

Figure 17: Record (*Begleitzettel*) of cervical smears performed on women from the Monowitz brothel as part of regular screenings (source: APMO)

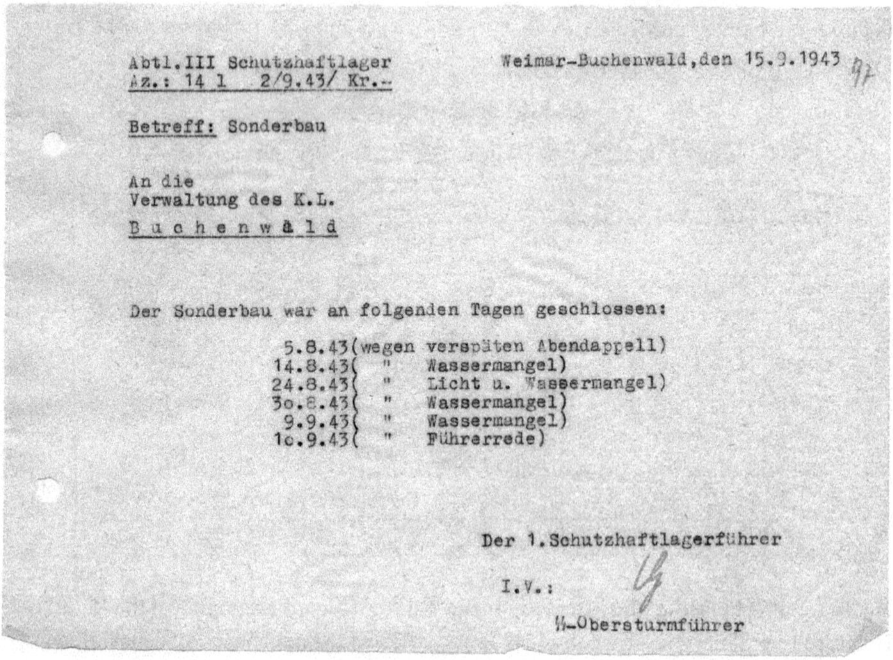

Abtl.III Schutzhaftlager
Az.: 14 1 2/9.43/ Kr.-

Weimar-Buchenwald,den 15.9.1943

Betreff: Sonderbau

An die
Verwaltung des K.L.
B u c h e n w a l d

Der Sonderbau war an folgenden Tagen geschlossen:

5.8.43 (wegen verspäten Abendappell)
14.8.43 (" Wassermangel)
24.8.43 (" Licht u. Wassermangel)
3o.8.43 (" Wassermangel)
9.9.43 (" Wassermangel)
1o.9.43 (" Führerrede)

Der 1.Schutzhaftlagerführer

I.V.:

SS-Obersturmführer

Figure 18: Report from the first camp director of Buchenwald indicating the days that the brothel was closed and the reasons why (source ThHStA, NS 4 Bu/41)

Figure 19: The Buchenwald camp brothel; this and the following photos are from "Buchenwald at the end of 1943," an album prepared by the SS (photo: SS; source: Musée de la Résistance et la Déportation, Besançon)

Figure 20: Doctor's room at the Buchenwald camp brothel, end of 1943 (photo: SS; source: Musée de la Résistance et la Déportation, Besançon)

Figure 21: Main hallway at the Buchenwald brothel, end of 1943 (photo: SS; source: Musée de la Résistance et la Déportation, Besançon)

Figure 22: Common room at the Buchenwald brothel, end of 1943 (photo: SS; source: Musée de la Résistance et la Déportation, Besançon)

Figure 23: Bedroom with two beds for women at the Buchenwald brothel, end of 1943 (photo: SS; source: Musée de la Résistance et la Déportation, Besançon)

Figure 24: Brothel room at the Buchenwald brothel, end of 1943 (photo: SS; source: Musée de la Résistance et la Déportation, Besançon)

Figure 25: Prisoners in Buchenwald; the building behind the fence is the brothel, or "Le Pouf." Illegal photo taken by the French Buchenwald prisoner Georges Angéli, June 1944 (source: AGB)

Figure 26: Film still showing officers of the U.S. Army as they visit the liberated Mittelbau-Dora camp on April 11, 1945; in the background is the former camp brothel (source: NARA, AGMD)

Figure 27: Block 170a (left) of Dachau after liberation in April of 1945; the block housed the camp brothel until the end of 1944. Photo taken by the survivor Václav Balon (source: AGD)

Figure 28: The "special building" in Neuengamme, 1945 (origins unknown; source: AGN)

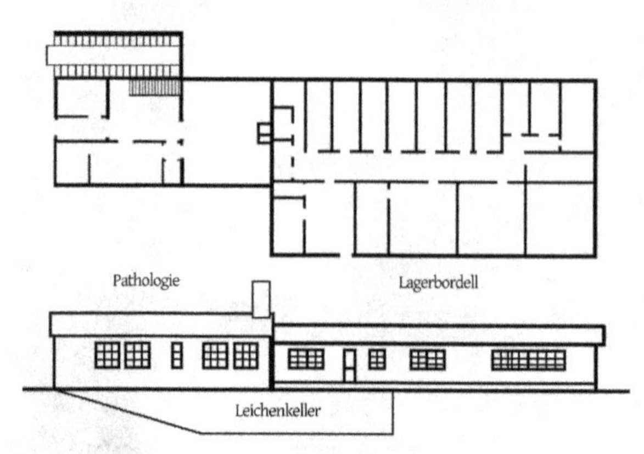

Figure 29: Floorplan of the camp brothel in Sachsenhausen, built alongside the pathology building and partly over the morgue (illustration by Robert Sommer based on the site plan of the Soviet special camp)

Figure 30: Door of a brothel room in the brothel of the Auschwitz main camp; today the room is used by the archive of the state museum (photo: Robert Sommer, 2005)

Figure 31: Block 24a of the Auschwitz main camp; the camp brothel was located on the second floor (photo: R. Sommer, 2005)

Acknowledgments

This book is an abridged and revised version of *Das KZ-Bordell,* which first appeared in 2009. I'm very grateful to all those who made the English-language edition possible, especially Fred Nachbaur of Fordham University Press, Dagmar Herzog, Annette F. Timm, and Pascale R. Bos. My deepest thanks go to Dominic Bonfiglio, whose contribution was much more than just the translation.

I would like to thank all those who have supported this project over the past twenty-five years, especially the directors and staff of the concentration camp memorial sites in Germany, Austria, and Poland. These include Insa Eschebach (Mahn- und Gedenkstätte Ravensbrück); Jens-Christian Wagner, Brita Heinrichs, and Regine Heubaum (KZ-Gedenkstätte Mittelbau-Dora); Sabine and Harry Stein (Gedenkstätte Buchenwald); Piotr Setkiewicz and Wojciech Płosa (Muzeum Auschwitz-Birkenau); Albert Knoll (KZ-Gedenkstätte Dachau); Günter Morsch, Monika Knop, and Monika Liebscher (Gedenkstätte und Museum Sachsenhausen); Cordula Hundertmark (Mahn- und Gedenkstätte Ravensbrück); Bärbel Schindler-Saefkow (Arbeitsgemeinschaft Gedenkbuch Ravensbrück); Susanne Leverenz, Karin Heddinga, and Christian Römmer (KZ-Gedenkstätte Neuengamme); Jörg Skriebeleit, Ulrich Fritz, Klaus Heidler, and Johannes Ibel (KZ-Gedenkstätte Flossenbürg); Robert Vorberg, Andreas Baumgartner, Barbara Wagner, and Christian Dürr (KZ-Gedenkstätte Mauthausen); Michlean Amir (United States Holocaust Memorial Museum); Bernd Horstmann (Gedenkstätte Bergen-Belsen); and Axel Braisz and Irmtrud Wojak (International Tracing Service in Bad Arolsen).

For their assistance I would like to thank the staff of the state archives, especially Reiner Eiselt from the Stasi Records Agency (BStU), and the teams at the Hauptstaatsarchiv Weimar; the state and regional archives in Bremen, Hamburg, Baden-Württemberg, Brandenburg, and Bavaria; and Yale University's Fortunoff Video Archive for Holocaust Testimonies.

I would also like to pay tribute to the memory of the concentration camp survivors who granted me interviews for this book, especially Stanisław

Hantz, Gianfranco Mariconti, and Vernanzio Gibillini. My special thanks go to their relatives, especially Walter and Yolanda, with whom I have a deep friendship.

My thanks go to the researchers and institutions who provided me with interview materials, including Robert Kuwalek (State Museum at Majdanek), the Institut für Konfliktforschung (Vienna), Linde Apel (Werkstatt der Erinnerung Hamburg), and Beate Hugk (Project Group for the Forgotten Victims of the Nazi Regime). I would also like to thank Christa Paul for the many years of collaboration, enriching discussions, help examining files, and access to interviews. For their feedback and ideas, I owe special thanks to my friends and colleagues, in particular Brigitte Halbmayr, Na'ama Shik, Regina Mühlhäuser, Joanna Ostrowska, Alexander Korb, Alexa Stiller, Christa Schikorra, Christl Wickert, Andrea Genest, Jürgen Lemke, and Anna Hájková. I would also like to thank Karin, Florian, Tina, and Tommie from Bildungswerk Stanislaw-Hantz e.V. for many years of cooperation.

Finally, I would like to thank my family, my parents, my daughter, and my wife, Helin, who were always there when I needed them, as well as Tania, Stefan, and Hagen for their mental support, and the many other colleagues, researchers, friends, and helpers who encouraged me along the way.

Berlin
May 1, 2024

Appendix: Brief Histories and Sex Worker Statistics by Camp

This appendix provides an overview of the ten prisoner brothels in Nazi concentration camps, arranged in the chronological order that they were established. Each section contains the history of the camp, the history of its prisoner brothel, the background and makeup of the women recruited to work there, and tables summarizing basic facts and figures. A concluding table presents statistics for all forced sex workers at Nazi concentration camps.

Mauthausen and Gusen

Mauthausen concentration camp

A few days after the Nazis annexed Austria, on March 12, 1938, Himmler decided to build a concentration camp at quarries near Linz. On a hill above Mauthausen on the Danube, a group of three hundred career criminals, or *Berufsverbrecher*, from Dachau was enlisted for the job. In the following years, thousands of Poles, Republican Spaniards, Soviet prisoners of war, Jews, and ten thousand inmates from German prisons were transferred to Mauthausen. The camp was a "category three" camp, the harshest level in the camp classification system. The average lifespan in Mauthausen was short: In 1943, prisoners working in the quarry survived no longer than six months.[1]

The arrival of large evacuation transports led to serious overcrowding and deteriorating living conditions as the prison population swelled to 84,000 prisoners by the end of 1944. In early May 1945, the SS fled the camp and put the Vienna fire police in charge of guarding the prisoners. US Army soldiers disarmed the police on May 5. From August 1938 to the beginning of 1945, 205,000 people passed through Mauthausen. About 105,000 people died there.[2]

Mauthausen camp brothel

The camp brothel in Mauthausen was the first in the concentration camp system and the one that remained open the longest. On May 31, 1941,

Heinrich Himmler visited Mauthausen and Gusen to inspect the quarries and granite production.[3] On October 8, 1941, he ordered the construction of a brothel in Mauthausen. The furnishings for the brothel were to be supplied by the workshops of the Deutsche Ausrüstungswerke (DAW) in Dachau.[4] In early 1942, the SS set up the brothel in Barrack Hut 1, located near the camp gate.[5] In the process, the left side of the barrack was divided lengthwise by a central corridor approximately seventy feet long. On the right side, ten brothel rooms were established, each measuring five by ten feet. On the left side, six rooms measuring nine by ten feet were partitioned off, which were intended for bathing and showering facilities or were used as sleeping quarters. The door to the brothel faced the camp entrance. In the entrance area was the doctor's room and an administration room. The brothel rooms each had a barred window. The furnishings consisted of a bed, a table, an armchair, and a sink. However, the rooms were hardly larger than the bed itself. Slits were built into the doors so that guards could look inside.[6] In June 1942, the SS at Ravensbrück recruited ten women for the brothel,[7] which began operating began on June 11, 1942.[8]

In the beginning, only German and Austrian prisoners who lived in the functionary blocks were allowed to visit the brothel. Later, the SS also allowed Czechs and Spaniards to visit the brothel.[9] In order to visit the brothel, the prisoner needed a brothel ticket, also known as a *Sprungkarte*.[10] To receive one, prisoners had to submit an application to be approved by the camp director, Georg Bachmayer, or the Rapportführer, Josef Riegler.[11]

The SS were not allowed to visit the camp brothel, though Bachmayer liked to come while drunk and shoot at lamps.[12] It is also known that Rapportführer Riegler led the forced sex workers around the camp and usually locked arms with at least one of the women.[13]

In spring 1945, the SS closed the camp brothel in Mauthausen after female prisoners began to arrive in large numbers. The forced sex workers were given uniform-like clothing and were made block leaders for the other female prisoners.[14] The reason for the decision was probably that the SS preferred to use German "antisocials" and "criminals" in leadership positions.[15] Later, in early April 1945, the brothel rooms were used to host "honorary prisoners." After the SS abandoned the Mauthausen concentration camp, the brothel was one of the buildings on which the prisoners unleashed their destructive rage.[16]

Gusen concentration camp

Gusen opened in May 1940, the first of several subcamps that would be built near Mauthausen. At the end of 1939, DEST had pushed to establish a separate prisoner camp at a granite quarry three miles away from the main camp. Gusen later became a site for the war economy. In the spring of 1944, construction began on caverns for underground production.[17] Evacuation transports from Eastern Europe began reaching Gusen in early 1945. In February, the SS registered approximately 26,000 prisoners in Gusen. Many of them were murdered or transferred to the main camp, Mauthausen. On May 5, 1945, US Army troops liberated the camp.[18]

Gusen camp brothel

Himmler ordered the construction of the camp brothel in Gusen during his visit to the Mauthausen camp complex on May 31, 1941. In contrast to Mauthausen, Gusen did not have a barrack hut available for a brothel. In the fall of 1942, the SS had a brothel made of solid masonry built at the southern camp wall, between the main entrance and Block 1.[19] On October 12, 1942, the construction management handed over the building to the camp administration.[20] The brothel probably went into operation the same month.

The brothel in Gusen differed from the one in Mauthausen. It was solid and larger, and it had two entrances instead of one. Although no blueprints have survived, other evidence besides the dual entrances points to a two-part design: one brothel for prisoners and the other for the Ukrainian guards stationed at Gusen.[21]

At the end of April 1945, the SS appointed the forced sex workers in Gusen as "prisoner supervisors"—like those in the Mauthausen brothel.[22] Three hundred Ukrainian guards who had refused to follow the orders of the SS were locked up in the brothel building, whose solid construction and barred windows made it a perfect prison.[23]

Forced sex workers

From June 1942 until their closing, the brothels in Mauthausen and Gusen each had a staff of ten forced sex workers.[24] The size of the camp population was certainly a factor. An April 30, 1942, the Mauthausen main camp had approximately 5,500 inmates, which amounts to one forced sex laborer for every 550 male prisoners. The SS probably followed the RSHA guidelines for the establishment of brothels near forced labor camps, which recommended one prostitute for every three hundred to five hundred foreign workers.[25]

The forced sex workers were the first women in Mauthausen.[26] The majority of the male prisoners knew little about them. The women left the brothel only for supervised walks between Blocks 1 and 2 in the mornings and afternoons, when most of the prisoners in the camp were working in the nearby factories.[27] In Gusen, they were released only to do "sports" behind the building or when they underwent medical examinations in the infirmary.[28]

Most of the forced sex workers in Mauthausen and Gusen can be identified based on surviving prisoner records.[29] Between 1942 and 1945, Mauthausen and Gusen had twenty-seven forced sex workers. Two more probably worked in the brothel for the Ukrainian guards in Gusen. Two of the forced sex workers were used in both the brothel for prisoners in Mauthausen and the brothel for Ukrainian guards in Gusen.[30]

In September 1944, the register of new arrivals at Mauthausen contained the names of twenty women assigned to the two camp brothels.[31] But the number does not represent a de facto transfer, only a pro forma one. That month, all Ravensbrück satellite camps for women passed into the command of the nearest men's camp in their vicinity. Nine women who had previously been in Mauthausen or Gusen had already been transferred by the SS to other camps. Among them were five women who were moved from the Gusen brothel to the Dachau brothel in July 1944 and exchanged for women who had previously been in the Dachau brothel.[32]

In February 1944, the SS brought two Polish women back from Mauthausen to Ravensbrück. Since there were no women other than forced sex workers in Mauthausen at that time, it is almost certain that those women were from the camp brothel.[33] The same applies to a German prisoner whose name is found in the camp's logbook of surgical procedures in February 1943. By July, she was no longer in Mauthausen.[34] Another woman came to Mauthausen in the summer of 1944 from Dachau, where she had most likely been in the camp brothel.[35] Three female SS guards from Ravensbrück who were assigned to serve in the Mauthausen brothel can also be identified.[36] They were later replaced by female prisoners. Evidence of who these women were can be found in the logbook of surgical procedures from July 1944, which includes a prisoner named "Ema," described as a "Puffmutter."[37] Another woman from Ukraine can be identified. She was transported from Dachau to Mauthausen in August 1944 and was possibly employed as a cashier in the Ukrainian brothel in Gusen.[38]

Of the twenty-nine known forced sex workers in the brothels at Mauthausen and Gusen, twenty-two were Germans. Of them, three were political prisoners,[39] and nineteen were "antisocials." Among those women was a "gypsy" from Burgenland, along Austria's eastern border.[40] Two of the women wore the red triangle only after being transferred to the Dachau camp.[41] The six other women were Polish; four were classified as "antisocials" and two as political prisoners. According to various sources, another woman was either Polish or German and classified as a "recidivist," which suggests that she had been sent to a concentration camp for the second time.[42] More than half of the women had worked in the Dachau or Mittelbau-Dora brothels in addition to the Mauthausen or Gusen facilities.[43]

It is certain that the twenty women assigned Mauthausen prisoner numbers remained in the brothels until their closure in April 1945.[44] It is very likely that most of these women had already been in Mauthausen or Gusen since the brothels opened. Based on an entry in the logbook of surgical procedures, one of the women had been at Mauthausen since at least October 1943.[45] The total number of forced sex workers in the prisoner brothels at Mauthausen and Gusen was probably thirty-five. Around eight women worked in the brothel for Ukrainian guards.[46]

The women in the prisoner brothels were between the ages of nineteen and twenty-eight.[47] One woman from the brothel for the Ukrainian guards was younger, but she probably did not have to have sex until she turned seventeen or eighteen.[48] Eighty-six percent of the women were unmarried. One woman was divorced, and two (or 10 percent) were married. All but two of the women were childless. It is likely that many of the women had already been forcibly sterilized for being "antisocial." Proof of sterilization exists in the case of one woman.[49]

According to SS records, at least five were prostitutes.[50] The other women had occupations unrelated to sex work. Nearly 20 percent of them were factory workers, and almost 30 percent were domestic workers or housewives. Other occupations appearing in prisoner records include farmhand, saleswoman, typist, office assistant, and artist.[51]

It is very likely that most of these women survived the Mauthausen and Gusen concentration camps.[52] One of the women from the Ukrainian brothel was freed from Bergen-Belsen; two of the forced sex workers transferred from Gusen to Dachau were freed from the Dachau camp and a Dachau subcamp. One woman who worked at the Mauthausen and Dachau camp brothels was able to escape from Ravensbrück on January 13, 1945.[53] According to the former camp scribe Hans Maršálek, another woman from the brothel, a Sinteza from Burgenland, also survived the war. He ran into her by accident in 1946 in Vienna.[54]

Table 1: Sex Worker Statistics for the Mauthausen and Gusen Prisoner Brothels

Woman[55]	*Brothel*	*Nationality/ prisoner category*[56]	*Age*[57]	*Discharge*	*Marital status*[58]	*Children*[59]	*Previous occupation*[60]
M.S.	Gu Ukr SS[61]	Polish, antisocial	16	–	–	–	–
C.P.	Gu Ukr SS	Polish, antisocial	21	liberated from B-B[62]	–	–	–
L.R.	Ma	Reich German, Sch[63]	26	–	–	–	–
C.K.	Gu, Da	Reich German, antisocial/Sch[64]	25	–	divorced	1	prostitute
L.S.	Gu, Da	Reich German, Sch	20	escaped[65]	–	–	–
B.R.	Gu, Da	Reich German/ Sch[66]	22	–	–	–	–
H.O.	Gu, Da	Reich German, Sch	19	liberated from Agfa[67]	–	–	–
E.R.	Gu, Da	Reich German, Polish, Sch[68]	19	liberated from Da	–	–	–
I.B.	Ma, Gu	Reich German, antisocial	22	liberated from Ma	single	0	domestic worker
H.B.	Ma	Reich German, antisocial	22	liberated from Ma	single	0	worker/ prostitute[69]
S.C.	Ma, Gu Ukr SS	Polish, antisocial	22	liberated from Ma	single	0	prostitute
S.D.	Ma	Reich German, antisocial	24	liberated from Ma[70]	single	3	laborer
C.D.	Ma	Polish, antisocial	23	liberated from Ma	single	0	salesperson
I.G.	Ma	Reich German, antisocial	27	liberated from Ma	single	0	domestic worker
I.H.	Ma	Reich German, antisocial	21	liberated from Ma	single	0	office aide
M.H.	Ma, Gu	Reich German, antisocial	22	liberated from Ma	single	0	laborer
K.K.	Ma	Reich German, antisocial	28	–	single	0	prostitute
C.O.	Ma, Gu Ukr SS	Polish, antisocial	23	–	single	0	prostitute

Woman[55]	*Brothel*	*Nationality/ prisoner category*[56]	*Age*[57]	*Discharge*	*Marital status*[58]	*Children*[59]	*Previous occupation*[60]
H.S.	Ma, Gu	Reich German, antisocial	21	liberated from Ma	single	0	domestic worker
A.S.	Ma	Reich German, antisocial	20	–	single	0	domestic worker
I.T.	Ma	Reich German, antisocial[71]	23	liberated from Ma	single	1	laborer
B.W.	Ma, Gu	Reich German, antisocial	24	liberated from Ma	married	0	domestic worker/ composer[72]
F.W.	Ma	Reich German, antisocial	20	liberated from Ma	single	0	artist
F.S.	Ma, Gu	Reich German, antisocial/"gypsy"	20	liberated from Ma	single	0	laborer
C.S.	Da, Gu	Reich German, antisocial[73]	22	liberated from Ma	married	0	housewife[74]
W.S.	Da, Gu	Reich German, antisocial[75]	20	liberated from Ma	single	0	salesperson
E.W.	Da, Gu	Reich German, antisocial[76]	24	liberated from Ma	single	0	agricultural worker
I.P.	Da, Gu	Polish, antisocial	20	liberated from Ma	single	0	shorthand typist
E.B.	Da, Gu	Reich German, antisocial	20	–	–	–	

Nationality, prisoner category	*Number*[77]	*Percentage*
Reich German, antisocial	16	55.2%
Reich German, political	3	10.3%
Reich German, antisocial ("Gypsy")	1	3.4%
Reich German, antisocial (later reclassified as political)[78]	2	6.9%
Reich German/Polish, political, recidivistic[79]	1	3.4%
Polish, antisocial	4	13.8%
Polish, political	2	6.9%
Total	29	

(continued)

Marriage status before concentration camp	*Number*[80]	*Percentage*
Single	18	85.7%
Married	2	9.5%
Divorced	1	4.8%
Total	21	

Forced sex workers in camp brothels[81]	*Number*	*Percentage*
Only Mauthausen	10	34.5%
Mauthausen and Gusen	5	17.2%
Mauthausen and brothel for Ukrainian SS in Gusen	2	6.9%
Gusen and Dachau	9	31.0%
Gusen, Dachau, and Mittelbau-Dora	1	3.5%
Only at brothel for Ukrainian SS in Gusen	2	6.9%
Total	29	

Table 2: Brothel Visitors to Block 3 of the Mauthausen Concentration Camp

Visitors	*Number*	*Percentage*	*Frequency of visits*[82]	*Number of visits*	*Percentage*
Regular[83]	4	7.0%	30–43	138	26.6%
	6	10.5%	20–29	134	25.8%
	9	15.8%	10–19	120	23.1%
Sporadic	25	43.9%	2–9	114	22.0%
One-time	13	22.8%	1	13	2.5%
Total	57		1–43	519	

Nationality, prisoner category[84]	*Number*	*Percentage*
German, antisocial[85]	13	23%
German, career criminal	36	63%
German, political	7	12%
Polish, political	1	2%
Total	57	

Flossenbürg

Concentration camp

In March 1938, the SS decided to establish a new concentration camp near a large granite deposit in Flossenbürg, a village in eastern Bavaria. Soon after, the first hundred prisoners from Dachau arrived in the newly built camp. By the end of 1938, the camp had 1,500 prisoners. Flossenbürg was the first DEST plant to begin operations, and it generated a modest profit. In this first phase, prisoners built the camp and performed heavy quarrying and processing in the DEST quarries. In 1942, arms manufacturing was relocated to Flossenbürg because it was less prone to bombing.[86]

The first prisoners of Flossenbürg were predominantly "career criminals," "preventive detainees," "antisocials," and "gypsies." In 1940, one thousand German political prisoners came to Flossenbürg, followed in 1941 by Czech and Polish prisoners and two thousand Soviet prisoners of war. Though German prisoners became a minority in the camp, the green-triangle-wearing "criminals" among them continued to occupy functionary positions until the end of the war, giving Flossenbürg the reputation as the "Green Camp."

In April 1945, the SS began to clear the camp and send the surviving prisoners on death marches. On April 16, the US Army entered nearby Weiden. The SS left the camp in a hurry but returned a day later to continue the evacuation. On April 23, 1945, the last prisoners remaining in the camp were freed.

Camp brothel

A preliminary design for the brothel was submitted to the Flossenbürg camp commandant on July 18, 1942. It was to be built at an isolated location behind the lockup.[87] Construction work began on August 28, but it was to take almost a year before it was completed owing to design changes and organizational problems. As in Gusen, the brothel in Flossenbürg was divided into two parts. One part consisted of ten brothel rooms for the prisoners; the other consisted of two larger rooms for the Ukrainian guards. The sections were separate, and each had their own entrance.[88] The brothel opened in the first half of July 1943.[89] On April 19, 1945, the SS put the brothel women together with about one thousand mostly sick prisoners and about thirty-five elite inmates on a train and sent them away.[90]

Forced sex workers

As in Mauthausen and Gusen, the prisoner brothel in Flossenbürg usually had ten women. Two more women were in the brothel for the Ukrainian SS guards.[91] There was also a madam who came from Dortmund.[92]

Two weeks after completion of the brothel, on July 1, 1943, a detachment of ten women appeared on the work schedule of the Flossenbürg camp.[93] Because the detachment was still under the official authority of Ravensbrück, Flossenbürg records make scant reference to them.[94] A list of incoming prisoners at Ravensbrück from March 1944 contains the names of three Polish women "back from Flossenbürg." Two of them were probably forced sex workers at the brothel for the Ukrainian guards. One was transferred to the Sachsenhausen camp brothel in October 1944.[95]

On September 1, 1944, the Ravensbrück camp formally placed the brothel women under the authority of Flossenbürg. A list of all the women at Flossenbürg and its subcamps shows that seventeen women were assigned to the brothel. The women were numbered 52447 to 52463 in the Flossenbürg prisoner register. Three days later, the SS brought five of the women back to Ravensbrück, probably in exchange for other women. On September 12, twelve women were in the "Sonderbau," ten in the brothel for prisoners and two in the brothel for the Ukrainian guards.[96]

From SS records, twenty-one of the women who worked at the Flossenbürg brothels can be documented by name. Four of them were most likely at the brothel for Ukrainian guards.[97] The majority of women in the brothel were Polish, which may be attributable to the higher overall percentage of Polish prisoners at Flossenbürg. Five Polish women were "antisocials"; seven were "politicals."[98] The records indicate that one of the Polish political prisoners had been committed for having a sexual relationship with a German and another for "breach of labor contract."[99] A third woman was classified as a "political" Russian, but judging by her name she was Ukrainian. Seven of the "antisocials" were Germans. The reason for their incarceration is known for certain only in one case: a "registered" prostitute who had been sent to Ravensbrück in August 1942 after being convicted several times for failing to appear at the Hamburg health office for mandatory venereal disease examinations.[100] It is probable that one of the German women came from Alsace-Lorraine.[101] The age of the women ranged from seventeen to thirty on the day the brothel opened.[102]

It can be assumed that the twelve women incarcerated in the Flossenbürg brothel in mid-September 1944 remained in the camp until the end of the war.[103] The number of women in the camp brothel (including the four women of the brothel for Ukrainian guards) probably totaled twenty-one.[104] No deaths of forced sex workers have been recorded in extant SS files.[105]

Table 3: Sex Worker Statistics for the Flossenbürg Prisoner Brothel

Nationality, prisoner category	*Number*	*Percentage*
Reich German, antisocial	7	33.3%
Reich German, antisocial; Polish, political	1	4.8 %
Polish, antisocial	5	23.8%
Polish, political	7	33.3%
Russian, political[106]	1	4.8 %
Total	21	

Age when the camp brothel opened[107]	*Number*	*Percentage*
17–20 years old	3	14.3%
21–23 years old	3	14.3%
24–26 years old	10	47.6%
27–30 years old	5	23.8%
Total	21	

Buchenwald

Concentration camp

Buchenwald was built in 1937 on a limestone massif near Weimar. The SS planned to excavate building materials from the nearby quarry for representative Nazi buildings on the Weimar's *Gauforum*, an area devoted to Nazi Party buildings. In October 1938, the number of inmates at Buchenwald exceeded ten thousand. By March 1944 it was over 42,000. As the war neared an end, Buchenwald became the final stop for evacuation transports. Overcrowding led to catastrophic conditions in the camp.[108]

Shortly before liberation, the SS tried to clear the camp, but organized resistance on the part of the prisoners prevented them. Nevertheless, 28,000 prisoners were sent on death marches, during which 12,000 prisoners died of exhaustion. On April 11, 1945, prisoners of the organized resistance captured the guard towers and pinned down more than one hundred SS men. Shortly after they liberated the camp, units of the 3rd US Army arrived at Buchenwald to find 21,000 prisoners still alive.[109] In total, some 56,000 of the prisoners sent to Buchenwald died.

Camp brothel

The establishment of the brothel in Buchenwald came from an order of Himmler's following his visit to the camp in early 1943.[110] The construction was given the highest priority.[111] The Buchenwald camp commandant Hermann Pister visited Mauthausen to understand the organization of the camp brothel there.[112] He decided to build the prisoners' brothel near the infirmary, while a brothel for Ukrainian SS guards would go up outside the camp.[113] Pister later went to Ravensbrück to select women personally.[114]

A few days after the completion of the brothel, two transports arrived from Ravensbrück, one on July 2, 1943, with eleven women, and another on July 4, with five women.[115] Regular brothel operations began on July 11.[116] On the first day, a Sunday, more than ninety prisoners visited the camp brothel. A week later there were up to 150 visitors. After two weeks, the number of daily visitors dropped.[117]

Visits to the brothel were permitted for German, Polish, Czech, French, and Dutch prisoners of all categories.[118] SS-Unterscharführer Max Beulig testified that in order to visit the brothel, a prisoner first had to report to his block elder; he, in turn, passed the report to the camp orderly office.[119] Each morning Beulig reported to the office the number of women fit for work.[120] In the brothel for Ukrainian SS men, two women had to see between two and eight men per evening.[121] In the evenings, Beulig checked the prisoners' entry tickets and supervised the accounting. Each evening, the money was handed over to the Rapportführer on duty.[122]

Officially, the brothel was also under the supervision of the physician Gerhard Schiedlausky, but he never personally examined the women. This was performed by a Czech prisoner, who also gave injections to the brothel visitors.[123] The brothel was open between the end of the evening roll call and 10 o'clock.[124] It was closed during late roll calls, when light and water were in short supply, when new prisoners arrived at the camp, during air raid alarms, and during the broadcast of the Führer's speeches.[125]

The brothel for Ukrainian guards may have closed at the end of 1944.[126] The prisoners' brothel in Buchenwald remained in operation until March 23, 1945.[127] The building was later used to house sick people from the nearby infirmary.[128]

Forced sex workers

Initially, sixteen women were at the brothel, but the SS released two women from the brothel and from camp detention in August and September 1943.[129]

In December, two cashiers were transferred to the camp brothel to replace the SS guards and handle the accounting.[130]

In February 1944, two Polish women were assigned to the brothel for Ukrainian SS guards.[131] Those women lived in the prisoner brothel building. Every morning at 9, the block leader Beulig brought them to the camp gate and handed them over to the SS-Sturmscharführer Partun. They had to work until 10 p.m. One of the "cashiers" also worked there.[132] In April 1944, one of the Polish forced sex workers was returned to Ravensbrück, probably after she contracted venereal disease.[133] She was then sent to the women's satellite camp HASAG-Meuselwitz in October 1944.[134] The second woman was also returned to Ravensbrück and transferred to Meuselwitz.[135]

In May 1944, another woman joined the brothel. By September, when the brothel was formally under the command of Buchenwald, there were seventeen forced sex workers—including the two women in the brothel for Ukrainian guards—and two "cashiers."[136] No other women were assigned to the brothel until the liberation of the camp in April 1945. In late 1944 and early 1945, a total of eight sex forced laborers were released from concentration camp detention.[137] On April 11, 1945, soldiers of the US Army liberated the nine remaining forced sex workers and a cashier from the Buchenwald brothel.[138] Six of the women had been in the brothel since it had opened twenty-one months earlier.[139]

The number of forced sex workers in the Buchenwald brothel for prisoners totaled nineteen. The women were between twenty-one and thirty years old. The two Polish women forced to work in the brothel for Ukrainian SS men were twenty and twenty-four. These women were probably exchanged by the SS; thus there were a total of four women in the SS brothel.[140] In addition, starting in December 1943, two German women in their forties worked as "cashiers," one in the brothel for prisoners and the other in the brothel for the Ukrainian SS. One had worked as a registered prostitute before being sent to the concentration camp.[141]

According to SS records, one of the forced sex workers had also been a prostitute before being sent to the concentration camp. The occupations of the other women were waitress, salesperson, train conductor, tailor, laborer, counter girl, and domestic worker.[142] Of them, fifteen were "antisocial" Germans. One was a "gypsy," and another was from Lorraine. Three women were Polish, of whom two wore the black triangle and the other a red triangle.[143] One woman is variously identified in the records as a German or Polish antisocial.[144] Another woman was convicted of illegal prostitution under Section 327 of the criminal code.[145]

After liberation, the remaining nine women initially remained at Buchenwald, which was now administered by the U.S. Army. The Office of Military Government of Germany assessed each individual prisoner before releasing them and required all remaining prisoners to fill out a questionnaire. The US staff received questionnaires from three forced sex workers and one cashier. After determining that they were victims of the Nazi regime, the Americans released them at the end of June 1945.[146]

Table 4: Sex Worker Statistics for the Buchenwald Prisoner Brothel

Nationality, prisoner category	Number[147]	Percentage
Reich German, antisocial	13	68.4%
Reich German, antisocial ("Gypsy")	1	5.3%
Reich German, antisocial (Lothringen)	1	5.3%
Polish, political	1	5.3%
Polish, antisocial	2	10.5%
Polish/Reich German, antisocial[148]	1	5.3%
Total	19	

Occupation[149]	*Number*[150]	*Percentage*
Waitress	2	10.5%
Salesperson	3	15.8%
Conductor	1	5.3%
Tailor	1	5.3%
Worker	3	15.8%
Counter girl	1	5.3%
Domestic worker	4	21.1%
Without preoccupation	3	15.8%
Unknown	1	5.3%
Total	19	

Age[151]	*Number*[152]	*Percentage*
20–23 years old	7	36.8%
24–26 years old	5	26.3%
27–29 years old	5	26.3%
30 years old	2	10.5%
Total	19	

Table 5: Time Forced Sex Workers Spent at the Buchenwald Prisoner Brothel[153]

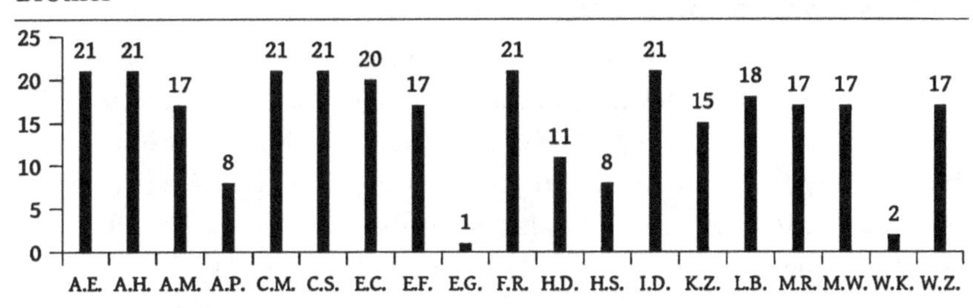

Table 6: Number of Daily Visitors to the Buchenwald Prisoner Brothel

Month	*Brothel visitors (daily)*[154]	*Brothel visitors (monthly)*	*Size of the main camp*[155]	*Brothel visitors (daily, percentage)*[156]
July 1943	96	2018	12711	0.76%
August 1943	69	1800	–	–
September 1943	59	1525	14983	0.39%
October 1943	52	1607	15989	0.33%
November 1943	43	1198	20073	0.21%
December 1943	46	1338	18706	0.25%
January 1944	51	1423	–	–
February 1944	45	1314	–	–
March 1944	50	1501	21498	0.23%
March 1945	24	413	36083	0.07%

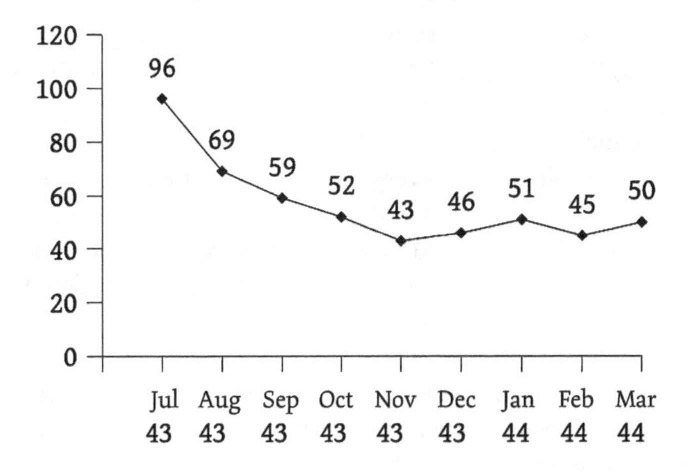

Auschwitz and Monowitz

The Auschwitz complex

Auschwitz was the largest of the Nazi concentration camps. It had originally been planned as a model agricultural and industrial zone for the occupied territories of Eastern Europe.[157] It was established in May 1940 and initially housed only Polish prisoners. In the years that followed, Auschwitz was expanded into a massive complex, with the main camp (Auschwitz I) serving as the administrative center. In September 1941, a labor camp for one hundred thousand prisoners of war was established in Birkenau, two miles away. The SS forced ten thousand Soviet POWs to build the brick barrack huts of the new Birkenau camp. Five months later, barely more than nine hundred of them were still alive. It quickly became a complex all on its own and consisted of several sectors: the women's camp, the men's camp, a men's quarantine camp, a family camp for Jews from Theresienstadt, a "Gypsy" camp, a men's prisoner infirmary, and the never-completed "Mexiko" transit camp, where Jewish women had to wait before being murdered.

In 1943, Auschwitz-Birkenau (or Auschwitz II) was expanded into an extermination camp. Crematoria II, III, IV, and V were built outside the prisoner camps and equipped with gas chambers. After the occupation of Hungary, Birkenau became the central site for the murder of five hundred thousand Hungarian Jews.[158]

The heart of the economic development in Auschwitz was a chemical plant for the synthetic production of rubber, built by IG Farben in nearby Monowice.[159] The IG Farben took a camp originally built for forced laborers and had it converted to house camp prisoners. At the end 1943 the Monowitz camp (also known as Auschwitz III) housed seven thousand prisoners. In July 1944, the camp population peaked at 11,000 males, most of whom were Jews.[160]

Approximately 75 percent of the prisoners worked in construction crews. The mortality rate was very high. Of the four thousand prisoners in the Buna camp at the end of 1942, only two thousand were still alive in February 1943. Although IG Farben pressed for better medical care, the SS instead selected prisoners who were unfit for work and murdered them in the Birkenau gas chambers. All told, some twenty to twenty-five thousand prisoners did not survive.[161]

Between January 17 and 23, 1945, the SS put approximately sixty thousand prisoners on death marches. On January 27, 1945, the Red Army reached Auschwitz, liberating first Monowitz, then the main camp and

Birkenau. More than one million people incarcerated in the Auschwitz complex had died. The majority had been murdered in the gas chambers of Birkenau.[162]

Camp brothel in the main Auschwitz camp

On April 20, 1943, the head of Office Group D, Richard Glücks, requested "the accelerated construction of a special building 'B' for prisoners" at Auschwitz I—which had been expressly demanded by Himmler.[163] A sketch from the head of Office C I (construction) dated April 30, 1943, was used as a model for the building. The sketch was almost identical to the one erected in Buchenwald.[164] The construction department also identified a particularly secluded location for the brothel, behind the camp's lockup in Block 11.[165] The estimated budget was 30,000 Reichsmarks.[166] Funds had been applied for, but they were not approved.[167]

The wooden building was never built. Instead, in the fall of 1943, the SS decided to put the brothel on the second floor of Block 24a, which was located just to the left of the entrance gate.[168] The SS converted the former sleeping quarters for the prisoner functionaries into single rooms. In subdividing the rooms, the SS apparently took their inspiration from Block 11, the camp lockup.[169]

As of October 4, 1943, there were twenty-one forced sex workers living in Block 24a. The brothel probably went into operation at the beginning of the month.[170] The SS selected the first prisoners allowed to visit the brothel.[171] The camp commandant Rudolf Höß, the Lagerführer Hans Aumeier, and the Rapportführer Gerhard Palitzsch appeared at the opening.[172]

The entrance to the camp brothel was blocked with a metal gate. An SS man stood guard at the entrance and locked it at closing time.[173] The role of the female guard was assumed by a German "madam."[174] Only non-Jewish prisoners—mostly Germans, Poles, and Ukrainians—were allowed to visit the brothel.[175] Slavic and German women were kept in separate rooms, and male prisoners were assigned to women based on their ethnicity and national origin.[176] The brothel was open to both prisoners of the main camp and of Birkenau. However, visits from Birkenau were rare.[177] The SS also allowed prisoners from the satellite camp Eintrachthütte to visit the brothel.[178] The SS themselves were forbidden to visit the brothel.[179]

Brothel visitors had to undergo a medical examination in the doctor's room in Block 24a.[180] The women were brought to the infirmary once a week for a medical examination. There, they took cervical swabs and blood samples and had them tested for gonorrhea and syphilis at the Waffen-SS Hygiene Institute in Rajsko.[181]

Men visiting the brothel were assigned to a room by the SS guard.[182] Some prisoners tried to court the women's favor with gifts, such as beauty-care products, jeweled feathers, brassieres, or even decorated silk lingerie and handwritten poems.[183] Those gifts were usually smuggled into the brothel at night, often pulled upstairs with a rope. Some prisoners even entered Block 24a at night.[184] To prevent that, the women were locked in a communal sleeping area.[185] Beginning in March 1944, the SS replaced the women several times with women from the brothel in Monowitz and with newly recruited women from Birkenau.[186]

The main camp brothel stayed open until several days before the start of the evacuation, on January 17, 1945.[187]

Forced sex workers in the main camp

When the brothel opened, sometime in the first week of October 1943, twenty-one women worked there.[188] The number of women initially recruited for the brothel was higher, but the SS had returned some "unsuitable" women to Birkenau, while they were still being quarantined in Block 10.[189] Once the brothel opened, the number of women who worked there fluctuated. On November 1, nineteen women worked at the brothel.[190] In the following months—for example, in November/December 1943 and in March/April and June 1944—the SS swapped out several forced sex workers. In March 1944, fifteen women were on duty there. In September, the number climbed to nineteen. In January 1945 it was eighteen.[191]

The length of the time the women spent in the brothel varied greatly. Three women from Block 24a (one of whom was also in the Monowitz brothel) were forced sex workers for fifteen months—the entire time of the brothel's existence.[192] About 10 percent of the women stayed in the brothel for more than a year, and half of the women stayed between four and twelve months. About 30 percent of the women stayed for one month or less. In one case, a woman lasted only two days.[193]

Thirty-seven women were German and at least seventeen were Polish. Five were described as Russians, but four of them were from Ukraine. In the case of four women, the name suggests a Slavic origin, but the nationality cannot be identified.[194] The name of one woman seems French; it is possible that she, like a woman in the Buchenwald brothel, came from Alsace-Lorraine.[195] There is no evidence of Jewish, Sinti, or Roma women in the Auschwitz brothels.[196] Nine Germans arrived with the first transport of women from Ravensbrück to Auschwitz.[197] Seven women were forced to perform sex labor in the Block 24a and Monowitz camp brothels.[198] At least seven forced sex workers from Auschwitz were taken to the Mittelbau-Dora camp brothel after the evacuation of Auschwitz; another woman was later assigned to the Sachsenhausen camp brothel.[199] There is no evidence that any women in Block 24a died.[200]

Nine days before the camp was to be evacuated, the SS replaced all the women in the main camp brothel with a new group of forced sex workers.[201] The reason for the decision is unknown, but the nine new women bore consecutive numbers, indicating that they had been brought from Ravensbrück to Auschwitz at the end of November 1944.[202] Three women did not appear on the *Begleitzettel* of January 10; they were probably placed in the camp brothel at Monowitz.[203]

When the SS evacuated Auschwitz, the women from the main camp brothel were returned to Birkenau and marched toward the town of Hindenburg, where they were crammed into railroad cars with Jewish women and transported to Bergen-Belsen.[204]

Camp brothel in Monowitz

In the late summer of 1943, the SS began construction of a brothel building in the Monowitz camp.[205] The building was built near the camp kitchen and surrounded by a wire fence. Lamps were installed on two pillars for lighting.[206] An SS man stood guard at the entrance.[207] The brothel probably opened at the end of October 1943.[208] The camp leader of Monowitz, Vinzenz Schöttl, personally selected ten prisoners to inaugurate the establishment.[209] The brothel in Monowitz consisted of eleven bedrooms and a common room supervised by a German "madam."[210] It was open three days a week and employed a shift system, with visits limited to fifteen minutes.[211] The brothel served the subcamps of Auschwitz as well, such as Janinagrube, Eintrachthütte, and Fürstengrube.[212] Only non-Jewish prisoners, a very small minority in Monowitz, were permitted to visit the brothel. Most were Germans filling functionary positions, and a few were Polish kapos.[213] The forced sex workers were regularly examined for venereal disease in the prisoner infirmary. The medical staff also examined the male prisoners and administered injections before and after visits.[214]

Forced sex workers in Monowitz

Records beginning on November 15, 1943, allow us to identify the first eight women who worked in the Monowitz brothel.[215] Their names can already be found a month earlier in the *Begleitzettel* for cervical smears from Block 10 in the main camp, where they were quarantined together with the women assigned to Block 24a.[216] A total of twelve forced sex workers at Monowitz can be identified by name. Four of them were Polish, six were German, one was from the Soviet Union, and the name of another woman suggests a Ukrainian origin. The SS also used seven women from the main camp. Another woman was assigned to the Sachsenhausen camp brothel several months later.[217] There is evidence that three more German women worked at the Monowitz camp brothel. They were transferred to the Mittelbau-Dora brothel after the evacuation of Auschwitz.[218]

Only scant information is available about the fate of the women after their stay in the brothel. One forced sex laborer from Monowitz died in November 1944 in Graslitz, a satellite camp of Flossenbürg.[219] When Auschwitz was evacuated, the women from the Monowitz brothel followed at the back of a column of prisoners marching toward Gleiwitz.[220] Sixty-seven of the forced sex workers in the two camp brothels at the Auschwitz complex can be identified by name, though the actual total number is higher, probably seventy. Thirty-nine of the women were of German origin. Most had been sent to the camp as "antisocials." Nineteen women were Polish, five were "Russian"—which included Belarusians and Ukrainians—and four from unknown Eastern European countries.[221]

Table 7: Sex Worker Statistics for the Auschwitz and Monowitz Prisoner Brothels

Nationality of forced sex workers[222]	*Number*			*Percentage*
	Monowitz	*Block 24a*	*All*	
Polish	4	17	19	28.4%
Reich German	6	37	39	58.2%
Russian[223]	1	5	5	7.5%
Eastern European[224]	1	4	4	6.0%
Total	12	63	67	

Time sex workers spent at the Block 24a brothel[225]	*Number*	*Percentage*
0–1 month	14	27.5%
2–3 months	7	13.7%
4–6 months	16	31.4%
7–12 months	9	17.6%
13–14 months	2	3.9%
15 months	3	5.9%
Total	51	

Forced sex workers at:	*Number*[226]	*Percentage*
Auschwitz and Monowitz	7	10.4%
Auschwitz and Dora[227]	7	10.4%
Monowitz and Sachsenhausen	1	1.5%
Auschwitz	48	71.6%
Monowitz	4	6.0%
Total	67	

Dachau

Dachau concentration camp

Dachau was the very first Nazi concentration camp, opened in 1933. The first prisoners were German political opponents—communists, social democrats, and trade unionists along with monarchists and conservative politicians—and later included people who rejected National Socialism because of their religious convictions. The German political prisoners became a slim minority as Germany went to war with its neighbors. By the time of its liberation, it housed prisoners from twenty-seven countries. In total, over two hundred thousand people were imprisoned in Dachau and its subcamps. More than 43,000 of them were murdered by the SS.[228]

Camp brothel

In the summer of 1943, the SS erected a building at the northeast end of the prisoners' camp.[229] The camp brothel was probably opened on April 18, 1944.[230] The forced sex workers had arrived in Dachau two days earlier.[231] Before the opening, political prisoners issued a call to boycott the brothel. When the brothel opened the political prisoners stood in line along the camp road and made fun of visitors.[232] That angered the Rapportführer on duty in the brothel, who threatened collective punishment. In its first weeks the brothel was sparsely visited.[233]

In the beginning, most of the prisoners who visited the brothels were Germans. Prisoners from satellite camps were allowed to come only on Sundays.[234] The brothel accounts indicate that seventy-six prisoners visited the brothel on October 24, 1944.[235] In June 1944, the SS conducted a search of the camp brothel and found money, alcohol, meat, silk underwear, and shoes from the camp cobbler's shop.[236] On July 1, the women were interrogated by the camp director. They showed notable courage and refused to betray the other prisoners.[237]

As a consequence, on July 17, 1944, five female forced sex workers were transferred to the Gusen camp brothel.[238] In return, five women from the Gusen brothel were assigned to the brothel in Dachau, along with a new cashier from Ravensbrück.[239] In addition, the camp elders were to take over the brothel duties previously performed by the camp runners. Staff members from the camp office were permitted to enter the brothel only with written permission.[240]

At the end of December 1944, eight months after its opening, the SS closed the camp brothel.[241] After the camp brothel was closed, the SS used the building to house "prisoners of honor."[242] After the US Army took over Dachau, the International Prisoners Committee (IPC) wanted to free up the former brothel for high-ranking Russian officers, but General Mikhailov refused the proposal.[243] The former brothel building was demolished before 1957.[244]

Forced sex workers

The first six women for the camp brothel were transferred to Dachau on April 16, 1944.[245] Five women were German; one was Polish.[246] Two weeks later, two more German forced sex workers from Ravensbrück arrived in Dachau.[247] On June 3, 1944, another transport with six women arrived at the camp brothel, three of whom were German, one Polish, and one Ukrainian, who most likely assumed the function of cashier.[248] A sixth woman from this transport is classified in various lists as German or Polish. The SS returned her to Ravensbrück at the beginning of August 1944, possibly because she was found unfit for the brothel.[249] In July 1944, the SS exchanged five women from the Dachau brothel command for forced sex workers from Gusen.[250] On August 8, one more German woman was transferred to the brothel, the last of the forced sex workers added to the unit. One German woman was released from the concentration camp on December 10, 1944.[251] On December 12, 1944, a total of twelve women were working in the brothel together with one German cashier.[252]

In total, nineteen women in the Dachau camp brothel can be identified by name. Two other women were cashiers. Fifteen women were German and two were Polish. Seven of the German women were "antisocials," five were "politicals," one was a convict in preventative detention. Two women wore the black triangle in Ravensbrück, the red triangle in Dachau, and the black triangle again when they returned to Ravensbrück.[253] The youngest woman was only seventeen when she entered the brothel commando; the oldest was thirty-five.[254]

The brothel closed at the end of December 1944.[255] The three German women who had previously worked in the camp brothel in Gusen were returned to Ravensbrück. They later attempted to escape, but only one woman succeeded.[256] One of the women was recruited for the Mittelbau-Dora brothel a few months after arriving at Ravensbrück, in March 1945, and was transferred to Dora by way of Bergen-Belsen.[257] The SS took seven women to the Dachau women's subcamp at Agfa Kamerawerk Munich. The two who remained in the main camp were set free by the US Army.[258]

Table 8: Sex Worker Statistics for the Dachau Prisoner Brothel

Nationality, prisoner category[259]	*Number*	*Percentage*
Reich German, antisocial[260]	7	36.8%
Reich German, political	5	26.3%
Reich German, political/antisocial	2	10.5%
Reich German, PSV[261]	1	5.3%
Reich German, political/Polish, political	2	10.5%
Polish, political	2	10.5%
Total	19	

Age[262]	*Number*	*Percentage*
< 20 years old	1	5.3%
20–24 years old	11	57.9%
25–29 years old	4	21.1%
30–35 years old	3	15.8%
Total	19	

Neuengamme

Neuengamme concentration camp, located southeast of Hamburg, was established in 1938 as a subcamp of Sachsenhausen.[263] In the spring of 1940, it became an independent camp, and by the end of the year, it housed 2,900 prisoners. In 1942, the SS redirected the camp labor to war manufacturing, and arms factories were established in the immediate vicinity. By September 1943, the main camp was bursting at the seams, forcing the majority of prisoners to be distributed among ninety newly built subcamps. The evacuation of Neuengamme began on April 19, 1945. Prisoners were marched toward the Bay of Neustadt and the Bay of Kiel. There, the SS loaded the prisoners onto two moored ships, the SS *Cap Arcona* and the SS *Thielbeck*. On May 3, the ships were destroyed when two hundred British fighter-bombers launched a massive air raid on nearby German vessels. Of the approximately ten thousand prisoners, only about four hundred survived. When the British Army arrived in Neuengamme a short time later, it was completely empty (the only one the Allies would find that way). Overall, 42,900 of the prisoners held in Neuengamme and its subcamps—about half their total population—perished.

Camp brothel

The planning for the brothel of Neuengamme started no later than Christmas 1943.[264] The brothel was erected just outside the camp, between the infirmary and the industrial yard. It was surrounded by barbed wire and located directly behind a guard tower. To make it accessible from the camp, a gate was added to the fence.[265] The brothel featured modern washbasins and bidets with hot water, comforts utterly unknown to prisoners in Neuengamme. Like the other camp brothels, the building contained brothel rooms, several sleeping areas, a 215-to-270-square-foot common room for the forced sex workers, and a room for a prisoner-doctor, who worked under the supervision of a medical orderly.[266] The brothel was opened on May 29, 1944. Initially, it was reserved exclusively for ethnic German citizens. The brothel was under the authority of the prisoner infirmary and SS-Rapportführer Wilhelm Dreimann.[267] He was responsible for compiling the list of visitors to the brothel and personally made sure that none of the prisoners stayed overnight.[268]

Forced sex workers

In April 1944, the first six women in Ravensbrück were selected for the Neuengamme brothel by the camp director Albert Lütkemeyer—five for forced sexual labor, another as the "cashier."[269] On April 19, they received their civilian clothes and left for Neuengamme late in the evening by train.[270] One of the women later became pregnant, and another was probably infected with venereal disease. The SS returned both to Ravensbrück.[271] The new Ravensbrück camp director Anton Thumann selected another six women, who were transferred to Neuengamme in September 1944.[272] Besides sex, the women had to perform other work such as entertaining guests in the SS Führerheim, gardening, and darning.[273]

Based on prisoner cards from the central index of the WVHA, it is possible to provide detailed information about the women in the Neuengamme brothel.[274] All the women in the brothel were citizens of the German Reich. But two came from occupied Poland and another from the former Czechoslovakia.[275] Nine women, one of them a "cashier," were "antisocials."[276] The other "cashier" and a forced sex laborer were registered as "political" prisoners. Both had been placed in concentration camps for intercourse with Polish men.[277] Among the "antisocials" was a "Gypsy."[278] One forced sex worker had been imprisoned in the Uckermark juvenile concentration camp for "deviant" girls and young women and then transferred to Ravensbrück when she reached the age of eighteen.[279] In the period before incarceration, one woman had worked as a seamstress, another as a waitress, and three as housemaids. Five had no given occupation. In two cases, the information in the prisoner records suggests that the women had worked as prostitutes and were convicted for violating health regulations.[280] One of the two cashiers had already been a registered prostitute with the health authorities. One woman was married and had one child. The others were unmarried.[281] The women's ages ranged from twenty-one to twenty-five. In total, ten forced sex workers and two cashiers were assigned to the Neuengamme camp.[282] One of the women in the first group of women selected for the brothel, Angelika Leuchter,[283] came from the same town as the Neuengamme commandant Max Pauly.[284] Perhaps out of concern for his reputation in his hometown, he made an effort to treat the women of the brothel well.[285] In contrast to Pauly, Dreimann and Thumann were known to beat the women.[286]

N.N. reports that the cashier was born in Strasbourg and spoke perfect French and German. She had worked as a nanny in Spain, joined the Republican faction during the Spanish Civil War, and was later arrested. At Ravensbrück, she was assigned to the camp police. Although she was able to ensure her survival thanks to her elevated position, she was afraid that the SS would murder her for being a "Red Spaniard." She signed up as a brothel cashier in the hopes of staying under the radar.[287] The women in the camp brothel were provided with food from the SS kitchen. According to the recollections of the former prisoner Dr. Henri Garrigoux, the women shared their food with other prisoners by passing bread and sausage under the brothel fence.[288]

In mid-April, the women were transferred from the camp brothel to the Drägerwerke subcamp in Hamburg-Wandsbek. Some ended up at the Eidelstedt satellite camp for women, where they were soon liberated by British soldiers. Others were taken by the SS to the women's satellite camp in Sasel and then transported to Denmark on Red Cross buses. These women thus escaped the tragic fate that befell many of the other prisoners at Neuengamme.[289]

Table 9: Sex Worker Statistics for the Neuengamme Prisoner Brothel

Nationality, prisoner category[290]	*Women*[291]	*Percentage*
Reich German, antisocial	7	70%
Reich German, antisocial ("Gypsy")	1	10%
Reich German, political	2	20%
Total	10	

Occupation[292]	*Women*	*Percentage*
Waitress	1	10%
Domestic worker[293]	3	30%
Seamstress	1	10%
Without occupation	5	50%
Total	10	

Age[294]	*Women*	*Percentage*
21 years old	3	30%
22 years old	1	10%
23 years old	3	30%
24 years old	2	20%
25 years old	1	10%
Total	10	

Sachsenhausen

Sachsenhausen concentration camp

In the summer of 1936, Sachsenhausen was established in the town of Oranienburg, just north of Berlin. By 1938, the main camp, originally designed for ten thousand prisoners, had already exceeded its capacity.[295] The same year the prisoners erected a building to house the Concentration Camps Inspectorate, making Oranienburg the administrative center of the camp system.[296] Sachsenhausen labor was meant to supply building materials for the massive construction projects in Berlin. The SS built the world's largest brickworks in the immediate vicinity of the camp. Prisoners also worked in factories of the war industry, such as the plant producing Heinkel bombers for the Luftwaffe. Between 1936 and 1945, more than two hundred thousand people were imprisoned in Sachsenhausen, thousands of whom died.[297]

Camp brothel

Work on a brothel began in the spring of 1944 and finished in July 1944.[298] The SS built the brothel in the southwestern corner of the camp's triangular layout, alongside a stone-walled pathology department, with the ceiling of an underground morgue providing part of its foundation.[299] The brothel's sanitary facilities were attached to those of the pathology department. The building was divided lengthwise into two parts by a six-and-a-half-foot wide corridor. On one side were ten brothel rooms.[300] On the other were two 250-square-feet bedrooms, a common room, a cashier's office, and an examination room.[301]

The camp brothel opened on August 8, 1944. On the first day, the camp elite were allowed to visit; on the second, *Reichdeutsche*; and on the third, Norwegians.[302] The brothel was open from evening roll call until evening curfew and on Sundays from 3 to 8 p.m. On Sunday afternoons, the prisoners from the satellite camps were allowed to visit the brothel.[303]

On April 17, 1945, the SS began to shut down the brothel. It transferred two women to the new women's quarters in the main camp. Two days later, the other eight women followed.[304] According to a former forced sex laborer named Karola Groß, however, the female inmates in the brothel were returned to Ravensbrück.[305]

At the end of the war, the Soviets took control of Sachsenhausen and converted the brothel building into a barracks for hospital personnel.[306]After the Soviets left, the camp became a much-needed source of building materials and firewood for locals. The remains of the former brothel building were removed probably in 1956.[307]

Forced sex workers

The first ten women were brought from the Ravensbrück concentration camp in August 1944.[308] In October 1944, the Ravensbrück commandant's office sent another three women to the camp brothel in Sachsenhausen to "replace sick or unsuitable prisoners."[309] It is possible that the "unsuitable" woman was a nineteen-year-old Polish virgin who had resisted having sex with brothel visitors. There were rumors that camp director August Kolb had her mauled to death by dogs, but that was never proven.[310] Karola Groß testified that no women from the brothel died.[311]

At the beginning of 1945, ten women worked in the brothel.[312] On January 22, four women were returned to Ravensbrück and replaced by two German and two Polish women from the Sachsenhausen subcamps of Auer and Velten.[313] One of the German women had previously worked in the Monowitz camp brothel.[314]

It is possible to identify the names of ten of the forced sex workers in Sachsenhausen, though there were probably seventeen women in total.[315] Of the identified women, half were German, and the other half were Polish. All the German women were antisocials; four of the Polish women were political prisoners, and one was "antisocial." The youngest woman was only seventeen; the oldest was twenty-eight. The length of stay in the brothel ranged from two to eight months.[316] One Polish forced sex laborer had previously been in the Flossenbürg camp brothel before March 1944. A German had been in the Monowitz camp brothel from November 1943 to June 1944.[317]

Two former forced sex workers made statements regarding their time in the brothel as part of postwar criminal investigations.[318] Karola Groß stressed that the brothel had been located above the basement morgue, which caused psychological stress.[319] Minna Möller was one of the first women in the camp brothel and was brought back to Ravensbrück in October 1944.[320] After the war, she was charged in East Germany with mistreating prisoners while serving with the Ravensbrück camp police and found guilty. According to the verdict, Minna Möller reported to the Sachsenhausen brothel in 1943, spent six months there, and then returned to Ravensbrück, where she was immediately assigned to the police.[321] She was imprisoned after the war by the Soviets and released in 1950.[322]

Table 10: Sex Worker Statistics for the Sachsenhausen Prisoner Brothel

Nationality, prisoner category[323]	*Women*[324]	*Percentage*
Reich German, antisocial	5	50%
Polish, political[325]	4	40%
Polish, antisocial	1	10%
Total	10	

Age[326]	*Women*[327]	*Percentage*
17–20 years old	1	10%
21–23 years old	4	40%
24–26 years old	4	40%
27–28 years old	1	10%
Total	10	

Time in camp brothel	*Women*[328]	*Percentage*
2 months	3	17.6%
3 months	6	35.3%
5 months	2	11.8%
6 months	1	5.9%
8 months	5	29.4%
Total	17	

Mittelbau-Dora

Mittelbau-Dora concentration camp

In August 1943, the SS decided to produce V1 and V2 missiles in tunnels beneath the anhydrite-rich Kohnstein massif in the southern Harz region. The SS established Mittelbau-Dora there as a subcamp of Buchenwald. In the following months, transports with prisoners arrived almost daily. By the end of 1943, Dora had grown to 10,500 prisoners. Living conditions were particularly harsh because prisoners had to sleep in the tunnels. Between October 1943 and March 1944, nearly 2,900 prisoners died; another three thousand were transferred to extermination camps. When weapons production began, in January 1944, the SS housed prisoners in the barracks of a new camp built just outside the underground plant. In the fall of 1944, Mittelbau-Dora was separated from Buchenwald and made into an independent complex of camps containing more than forty thousand prisoners in all.[329]

The SS began to evacuate Mittelbau-Dora on April 3, 1945. Many prisoners were loaded onto freight and cattle cars and transported to Bergen-Belsen, Sachsenhausen, and Ravensbrück. Others were forced to march on foot. The SS left behind several hundred sick and dying prisoners in the main camp. They were liberated by soldiers of the US Army on April 11, 1945.

Camp brothel

The first transport of forced sex workers arrived on February 18, 1945, and the brothel likely opened at the end of February.[330] The brothel was located on a hill north of the roll-call square.[331] The women in the camp brothel had to line up at the window for the morning roll call, providing an incentive for the prisoners below. When public executions were scheduled, the SS led the women out of the camp.[332]

As at Monowitz, there were day and night shifts in the brothel.[333] Prisoners from the work details usually came in the evenings. The kapos visited the brothels during the day.[334]

A few days before the camp was evacuated, the town of Nordhausen was the target of a nighttime bombardment. A revolt had broken out, and prisoners took the women to the men's barracks.[335] On April 5, 1945, the women were transported from the camp brothel in cattle cars to Bergen-Belsen.[336] The female SS guards accompanied the prisoners.[337] The train broke down en route, and almost all the forced sex workers escaped.[338]

Forced sex workers

On January 28, 1945, a transport with 512 women from Auschwitz arrived in Mittelbau-Dora. Five hundred and two women were Jewish. The other ten were for the camp brothel. Seven women had previously been forced sex workers in the Auschwitz brothel. The others were probably in the one at Monowitz. After a stop at the Bergen-Belsen concentration camp, the ten women arrived at Mittelbau-Dora.[339] Seven of them were German, two were Soviet citizens, and one was Polish.[340] According to statements from the last camp elder, Roland Drung, one of the Soviet women had been married to a Russian officer. She was captured by the Germans in Kharkov and deported to Auschwitz,[341] where she was forced into sex work.[342] They were assigned the numbers F1 to F10.[343]

At the end of March 1945, a transport arrived at Mittelbau-Dora with eleven women for the camp brothel. One of them was the cashier. Nine women were German citizens, and one was Dutch.[344] The Dutch woman was a political activist rounded up by the Nazis; she had been sent to the Scheveningen camp and later to the Vught concentration camp. In November 1944 she arrived in Ravensbrück.[345] The former prisoner physician Dr. H. L. Groeneveld, who had examined the women for sexually transmitted diseases, met her again after the war.[346] One of the German women had already worked in the Gusen and Dachau camp brothels.[347]

All twenty forced sex workers at Mittelbau-Dora are known by name. Sixteen of them were German, two were Soviet citizens, one was Polish, and one was Dutch.[348] Eight women were "antisocials" and two were "criminals." One of the women was a "political" and was brought to the concentration camp for having repeated sex with a Polish man.[349] Another had been imprisoned in a Uckermark youth camp before coming to Ravensbrück in January 1945.[350] The women's ages ranged from twenty-one to thirty-two.[351] The SS filled the cashier position with a female prisoner who was a Jehovah's Witness.[352] Later, a Jewish woman served as a cashier.[353]

Among the women on the second transport of forced sex workers to Mittelbau-Dora was Linda Bachmann. Selected by the SS in Ravensbrück, she arrived with other women to Mittelbau-Dora after a stay of several weeks in Bergen-Belsen.[354] Linda Bachmann learned that there were already women in the camp brothel, but she did not meet them; they were soon transported to another camp, probably Bergen-Belsen. At least two of them survived the war.[355]

When the SS evacuated the camp, the prisoners were sent to Bergen-Belsen in cattle cars. Most forced sex workers escaped. Linda Bachmann could not because she had pneumonia.[356] At a station en route to Bergen-Belsen, the SS forced Linda Bachmann and the other prisoners to continue on foot. Linda Bachmann was freed near Trebbin, south of Berlin.[357]

Table 11: Sex Worker Statistics for the Mittelbau-Dora Prisoner Brothel

Nationality[358]	*Women*[359]	*Percentage*
German	16	80%
Polish	1	5%
Russian (Belarusian/Ukrainian)	2	10%
Dutch	1	5%
Total	20	

Age[360]	*Women*[361]	*Percentage*
20–22 years old	6	30%
23–26 years old	7	35%
27–30 years old	4	20%
> 30 years old	2	10%
Unknown	1	5%
Total	20	

Table 12: Sex Worker Statistics for All Camp Brothels

Total number

Concentration camp	*Type of brothel*	*Number of sex workers identified by name*[362]	*Estimated total*
Mauthausen/Gusen	Brothel for prisoners	27	35
Gusen	Brothel for Ukrainian SS	4[363]	8
Flossenbürg	Brothel for prisoners	17	17
Flossenbürg	Brothel for Ukrainian SS	4	4
Buchenwald	Brothel for prisoners	19	19
Buchenwald	Brothel for Ukrainian SS	2	4
Auschwitz main camp	Brothel for prisoners	63	63
Auschwitz Monowitz	Brothel for prisoners	12	15
Auschwitz total (excluding duplicates)	Brothel for prisoners	67	70
Dachau	Brothel for prisoners	19	19
Neuengamme	Brothel for prisoners	10	10
Sachsenhausen	Brothel for prisoners	10	17
Sachsenhausen	Brothel for Ukrainian SS	0	4
Mittelbau-Dora	Brothel for prisoners	20	20
Stutthof	Brothel for Ukrainian SS	0	4
Total (excluding duplicates)	*Brothels for prisoners*	168	190
Total	*Brothels for Ukrainian SS*	8	24
Total number of forced sex workers in the concentration camp system (excluding duplicates)		174[364]	214

Age, nationality, prisoner category

Age on arrival in the camp brothel[365]	Number	Percentage
< 20 years old	10	6.8%
20–24 years old	70	47.6%
25–29 years old	45	30.6%
30–34 years old	18	12.2%
35–39 years old	2	1.4%
40-44 years old	1	0.7%
45-50 years old	1	0.7%
Total of those whose age is known	147	

Nationality[366]	*Number*	*Percentage*
German	114	65.5%
German/Polish[367]	3	1.7%
Polish	46	26.4%
Russian[368]	6	3.5%
Eastern European[369]	4	2.3%
Dutch	1	0.6%
Total	174	

Prisoner category[370]	*Number*	*Percentage*
Antisocial	98	65.8%
Political	44	29.5%
Criminal (SV, PSV, BV)	4	2.7%
Political/antisocial[371]	3	2.0%
Total of those whose category is known	149	

Prisoner categories for German forced sex workers[372]	*Number*[373]	*Percentage*
Antisocial	85	82.5%
Antisocial (Gypsy)	3	2.9%
Criminal[374]	4	3.9%
Political	9	8.7%
Antisocial/political	2	1.9%
Total of those whose category is known	103	

Prisoner categories for Polish forced sex workers[375]	*Number*[376]	*Percentage*
Political	26	72.2%
Antisocial	10	27.8%
Total of those whose category is known	36	

Notes

Foreword by Annette F. Timm

1. I am relying on the translation and analysis in Pascale Bos, "Sexual Violence in Ka-Tzetnik's *House of Dolls*," in *Holocaust History and the Readings of Ka-Tzetnik*, ed. Annette F. Timm (Bloomsbury Academic, 2017), 115–17.

2. Quoted and translated in Rivka Brot, "Julius Siegel: A Kapo in Four (Judicial) Acts," trans. Avner Greenberg, *Dapim: Studies on the Holocaust* 25: 74; from Ruth Bondy, *Shevarim Sheleimim* (Gevanim, 1997), 44. In other places, for example, the documentary *Stalags* [*Stalagim*] (Heymann Brothers Films, Yes Docu, New Israeli Foundation for Cinema & TV, Cinephil, 2007), Bondy discusses having her tattoo removed in a more general way, without referring to suspicions that she had prostituted herself.

3. See Na'ama Shik, "Sexual Abuse of Jewish Women in Auschwitz-Birkenau," in *Brutality and Desire: War and Sexuality in Europe's Twentieth Century*, ed. Dagmar Herzog (Palgrave Macmillan, 2009), 242; and Bos, "Sexual Violence in Ka-Tzetnik's *House of Dolls*," 117.

4. Lawrence L. Langer, *Versions of Survival: The Holocaust and the Human Spirit* (State University of New York Press, 1982), 72.

Introduction: Myths and Taboos

1. Erich Roßmann, *Ein Leben für Sozialismus und Demokratie* (Rainer Wunderlich, 1946), 175.

2. Cornelia Brink, *Ikonen der Vernichtung: Öffentlicher Gebrauch von Fotografien aus nationalsozialistischen Konzentrationslagern nach 1945* (Akademie Verlag, 1998), 9–22.

3. Eugen Kogon, *The Theory and Practice of Hell: The Classic Account of the Nazi Concentration Camps Used as a Basis for the Nuremberg Investigations*, trans. Heinz Norden (1950; Berkley Books, 1998).

4. See Dachauer Häftlinge, *Konzentrationslager Dachau* (Stern Verlag, 1945); Heinrich Christian Meier, *So war es: Das Leben im KZ Neuengamme* (Phönix-Verlag, 1948), Rudolf Kalmar, Zeit ohne Gnade (Schönbrunn-Verlag, 1946); Günther Bullerjahn, "Der Sonderbau im KZ-Sachsenhausen," in *KZ Sachsenhausen*, ed. Lucie Großer (Lucie Großer, 1948); and Odd Nansen, *Fra dag til dag* (Dreyers Forlag, 1946).

5. Kogon, *The Theory and Practice of Hell*, 135. Kogon's derogatory portrayal of the female forced sex workers in Buchenwald was a major factor in the stigmatization of women. For criticism of Kogon, see Brigitte Halbmayr, "Arbeitskommando 'Sonderbau'. Zur Bedeutung und Funktion von Bordellen im KZ," *Dachauer Hefte 21* (2005): 210.

6. Grete Salus describes aspects of female sexuality in detail for the Archives of the Wiener Library, London. In a later publication, however, these passages were deleted from the text. See the testimony of Grete Salus, Wiener Library, Section 2 (Eyewitness Accounts), Reel 53; and Grete Salus, *Niemand, nichts—ein Jude: Theresienstadt, Auschwitz, Oederan* (Verlag Darmstädter Blätter, 1958).

7. Christl Wickert, "Tabu Lagerbordell: Vom Umgang mit der Zwangsprostitution nach 1945," in *Gedächtnis und Geschlecht: Deutungsmuster in Darstellungen des nationalsozialistischen Genozids*, ed. Insa Eschebach, Sigrid Jacobeit, and Silke Wenk (Campus, 2002), 51.

8. Rudolf Morsey, *Die Bundesrepublik Deutschland: Entstehung und Entwicklung bis 1969* (Oldenbourg Wissenschaftsverlag, 1990), 186–89.

9. Harold Marcuse, "Die museale Darstellung des Holocaust an Orten ehemaliger Konzentrationslager in der Bundesrepublik," in *Erinnerung: Zur Gegenwart des Holocaust in Deutschland-West und Deutschland-Ost*, ed. Bernhard Moltmann et al. (Haag and Herchen, 1993), 89.

10. Edgar Wolfrum, "Die beiden Deutschland," in *Verbrechen erinnern: Die Auseinandersetzung mit Holocaust und Völkermord*, ed. Volkhard Knigge and Norbert Frei (C. H. Beck, 2002), 133–49. Norbert Frei, *1945 und wir. Das Dritte Reich im Bewußtsein der Deutschen* (Deutscher Taschenbuch Verlag, 2005), 23–62.

11. In Dachau, the former camp brothel was probably used as a canteen when the former concentration camp was a camp for displaced persons and refugees. It was demolished by 1957. See Harold Marcuse, *Legacies of Dachau: The Uses and Abuses of a Concentration Camp, 1933–2001* (Cambridge University Press, 2001), 165–66, and the site plan.

12. Hasko Zimmer, *Der Buchenwaldkonflikt: Zum Streit um Geschichte und Erinnerung im Kontext der deutschen Vereinigung* (Agenda-Verlag, 1999).

13. An internal paper issued by the Buchenwald National Memorial states that information about the camp brothel "in all its ambiguity would have to be very extensive and would run counter to the actual purpose of the tours" (Herbert Weidlich, "Der Sonderbau [Bordell] im ehemaligen Schutzhaftlager Buchenwald," unpublished manuscript, Berlin, 1978, Archiv der Gedenkstätte Buchenwald (AMGB), Sign. 56-8-4, p. 1).

14. In Sachsenhausen, the former camp brothel was demolished during the construction of a memorial. However, places of terror and death—such as the crematorium, the pathology department, and the cell block—were preserved and shown during guided tours. See Protokoll der Beiratssitzung zur Vorplanung der Gedenkstätte Sachsenhausen, 11, December 1956, Archiv der Gedenkstätte Sachsenhausen (AGS), NMG 11/5/3.

15. Weidlich, "Sonderbau," AMGB, Sign. 56-8-4, p. 1.

16. Bartelt to the editor of the *Zeitschrift für Geschichtswissenschaft* (ZfG), February 3, 1977, AMGB, Sig. 56-8-1.

17. Bartelt to the editor of the *Zeitschrift für Geschichtswissenschaft* (ZfG). On the concentration camp as "part of the system of oppression and exploitation," see Erhard Pachaly and Kurt Pelny, *KZ Mittelbau-Dora: Zum antifaschistischen Widerstandskampf im KZ Dora 1943 bis 1945* (Dietz Verlag 1990), 24–50; and Heinz Kühnrich, *Der KZ-Staat: Die faschistischen Konzentrationslager 1933–1945* (Dietz Verlag, 1980), 152. Erika Buchmann devoted an entire chapter to this topic in "Mädchenhändler in SS-Uniform," in *Die Frauen von Ravensbrück*, ed. Komitee der Antifaschistischen Widerstandskämpfer der DDR (Kongress-Verlag, 1961), 85–86.

18. See Helga Amesberger, Katrin Auer, and Brigitte Halbmayr, *Sexualisierte Gewalt: Weibliche Erfahrungen in NS-Konzentrationslagern* (Mandelbaum Verlag, 2004), 33–51.

19. See Christa Paul, "Frühe Weichenstellungen: Zum Ausschluss 'asozialer' Häftlinge von Ansprüchen auf besondere Unterstützungsleistungen und auf Entschädigung," in *Opfer als Akteure: Interventionen ehemaliger NS-Verfolgter in der Nachkriegszeit*, ed. Fritz Bauer Institut and Katharina Stengel (Campus Verlag, 2008), 67–86.

20. Particularly derogatory remarks by two French survivors can be found in the documentary *Das große Schweigen* (The great silence). See *Das große Schweigen*, dir. Maren Niemeyer and Caroline von der Tann, ARD, first broadcast on November 9, 1995.

21. See Sven Korzilius, *"Asoziale" und "Parasiten" im Recht der SBZ/DDR: Randgruppen im Sozialismus zwischen Repression und Ausgrenzung* (Böhlau, 2004), 52–60.

22. See Korzilius, *Randgruppen im Sozialismus*, 401–54. See also Insa Eschebach, "Das Stigma des Asozialen: Drei Urteile der DDR-Justiz gegen ehemalige Funktionshäftlinge des Frauenkonzentrationslagers Ravensbrück," in *Abgeleitete Macht: Funktionshäftlinge zwischen Widerstand und Kollaboration*, ed. KZ-Gedenkstätte Neuengamme, Beiträge zur Geschichte der nationalsozialistischen Verfolgung in Norddeutschland, no. 4 (Edition Temmen, 1998), 69–81.

23. Not a single former sex forced worker is known to have submitted an application to the Ravensbrück Memorial, a prerequisite for receiving compensatory benefits. See Sammlung Haftanfragen (HaftA), Mahn- und Gedenkstätte Ravensbrück, as of September 2010.

24. See Reinhild Kassing and Christa Paul, "Bordelle in deutschen Konzentrationslagern," *K(r)ampfader* 6 (1/1991): 26–31; and Christa Schulz, "Weibliche Häftlinge aus Ravensbrück in den Bordellen der Männerkonzentrationslager," in *Frauen in Konzentrationslagern: Bergen-Belsen. Ravensbrück*, ed. Claus Füllberg-Stolberg et al. (Edition Temmen, 1994), 135–46.

25. Christa Paul, *Zwangsprostitution: Staatlich errichtete Bordelle im Nationalsozialismus* (Edition Hentrich, 1994).

26. See Hans-Peter Klausch, "Das Lagerbordell von Flossenbürg," in *Beiträge zur Geschichte der Arbeiterbewegung* 4 (1992): 86–94; Andreas Baumgartner, *Die vergessenen Frauen von Mauthausen: Die weiblichen Häftlinge des Konzentrationslagers Mauthausen und ihre Geschichte* (Edition Mauthausen, 1997); Kerstin Engelhardt, "Frauen im Konzentrationslager Dachau," *Dachauer Hefte* 14 (1998): 218–44; Peter Heigl, "Zwangsprostitution im KZ-Lagerbordell Flossenbürg," *Geschichte Quer* 6 (1998): 44–45; Christa Schikorra, "Prostitution weiblicher Häftlinge als Zwangsarbeit: Zur Situation 'asozialer' Häftlinge im Frauen-KZ Ravensbrück," *Dachauer Hefte* 16 (2000); and Christa Schulz, *Kontinuitäten der Ausgrenzung: "Asoziale" Häftlinge im Frauen-Konzentrationslager Ravensbrück* (Metropol, 2001).

27. See Wickert, "Tabu Lagerbordell"; and Gabi Zipfel, "'Blood, sperm and tears': Sexuelle Gewalt in Kriegen," *Mittelweg 36*, Heft 15 (5/2001): 3–20.

28. The book includes interviews with Austrian women who had been deported to the Ravensbrück concentration camp. See Helga Amesberger and Brigitte Halbmayr, *Vom Leben und Überleben—Wege nach Ravensbrück: Das Frauenkonzentrationslager in der Erinnerung*, Band 2: *Lebensgeschichten* (Promedia 2001). More recent studies to tackle the subject of sexual violence in the Holocaust include Doris L. Bergen, "Sexual Violence in the Holocaust: Unique and Typical?," in *The Holocaust in International Perspective: Lessons and Legacies*, ed. Dagmar Herzog (Northwestern University Press, 2006), 7:180; Anna Hajkova, Elissa Mailaender, Doris Bergen, Patrick Farges, and Atina Grossmann, "Forum: Holocaust and History of Gender and Sexuality," *German History* 36, no. 1 (2018): 78–100; Steven T. Katz, "Thoughts on the Intersection of Rape and Rassenchande During the Holocaust," *Modern Judaism—A Journal of Jewish Ideas and Experience* 32, no. 3 (October 2012): 293–322; Katarzyna Person, "Sexual Violence During the Holocaust: The Case of Forced Prostitution in the Warsaw Ghetto," *Shofar* 33, no. 2 (Winter 2015): 103–21; Annette F. Timm, "The Challenges of Including Sexual Violence and Transgressive Love in Historical Writing on World War II and the Holocaust," *Journal of the History of Sexuality* 26, no. 3 (September 2017): 351–65; Doris L. Bergen, Sara E. Brown, Stephanie Corazza, Paula David, Henry Greenspan, and Sara R. Horowitz, "Buried Words: A Forum on Sexuality, Violence, and Holocaust Testimonies," *Holocaust Studies: A Journal of Culture and History* (2021), https://doi.org/10.1080/17504902.2021.1894018; and Marta Havryshko, "Listening to Women's Voices: Jewish Rape Survivors' Testimonies in Soviet War Crimes Trials," in *If This Is a Woman: Studies on Women and Gender in the Holocaust*, ed. Denisa Nešťáková, Katja Grosse-Sommer, Borbála Klacsmann, and Jakub Drábik (Academic Studies Press, 2021), 221–42, https://doi.org/10.2307/j.ctv26rrb42.

29. See Die Aussteller, ed., *Sex-Zwangsarbeit in NS-Konzentrationslagern. Katalog zur Ausstellung* (Die Aussteller—Verein zur Förderung von historischen

und kunsthistorischen Ausstellungen, 2005); and Baris Alakus, Katharina Kniefacz, and Robert Vorberg, eds., *Sex-Zwangsarbeit in nationalsozialistischen Konzentrationslagern* (Mandelbaum Verlag, 2007).

30. Florian Freund and Bertrand Perz, "Mauthausen-Stammlager," in *Der Ort des Terrors: Geschichte der nationalsozialistischen Konzentrationslager,* Band IV, *Buchenwald Sachsenhausen,* ed. Wolfgang Benz and Barbara Distel (C. H. Beck, 2005), 310; and Hermann Kaienburg, "Sachsenhausen-Stammlager," in Benz and Distel, *Ort III,* 38. The account on Flossenbürg is considerably longer and more appropriate. See Jörg Skriebeleit, "Flossenbürg-Stammlager," in *Der Ort des Terrors: Geschichte der nationalsozialistischen Konzentrationslager,* Band IV, *Flossenbürg, Mauthausen, Ravensbrück,* ed. Wolfgang Benz and Barbara Distel (C. H. Beck, 2006), 43–44.

31. See Nikolaus Wachsmann, *KL: A History of the Nazi Concentration Camps* (Abacus, 2015), 411–44.

32. See Joanna Ostrowska, Przemilczane, *Seksualna praca przymusowa w czasie II wojny światowej Okładka książki Przemilczane* (Marginesy, 2018).

33. A version of the interview is in Paul, *Zwangsprostitution,* 107–13.

34. See Christa Paul and Robert Sommer, "SS-Bordelle und Oral History: Problematische Quellen und die Existenz von Bordellen für die SS in Konzentrationslagern," in *BIOS* 19, (1/2006); and Pflegeamtsakte Frau D., Staatsarchiv Hamburg (StA-HH), Arbeits- und Sozialfürsorge, Sonderakten, Sig. 351–14.

35. See Niemeyer and von der Tann, *Das große Schweigen.*

36. *Die SS als Zuhälter: Zwangsprostitution im Dritten Reich,* dir. Eva Schmitz-Gümbel and Karsten Deventer (documentary, Frontal 21, ZDF), broadcast on October 28, 2003.

37. *Auschwitz: The Nazis and "The Final Solution,"* BBC, documentary, dir. Laurence Reese (2005).

38. Insa Eschebach and Katja Jedermann, "Sex-Zwangsarbeit in NS-Konzentrationslagern: Anmerkungen zu einer Werkstatt-Ausstellung der Gedenkstätte Ravensbrück," *Feministische Studien* 1 (May 2007): 122–28.

39. Ka-tzetnik 135633 [Yehiel De-Nur], *House of Dolls,* trans. Moshe Kohn (Frederick Mueller, 1955). The work is now understood to be fictional. See Annette F. Timm, "Testimony in Holocaust Historiography," in *Holocaust History and the Readings of Ka-Tzetnik,* ed. Annette F. Timm (Bloomsbury, 2018), 37–66.

40. The serial number deviates only slightly from De-Nur's own. See Annette F. Timm, "Introduction: The Dilemmas of Ka-tzetnik's International Fame," in *Holocaust History and the Readings of Ka-Tzetnik,* ed. Annette F. Timm (Bloomsbury, 2018), 1–12.

41. Isabel Kershner, "Israel's Unexpected Spinoff from a Holocaust Trial," *New York Times,* September 6, 2007. The cover art of the pulp novels known as "men's adventure magazines" (e.g., *Man's Epic, World of Man, Man's Story, Real Man, Men in Conflict*) can be seen as an American counterpart. In those, direct references to the history of Nazi concentration camps as well as Ka-tzetnik's

House of Dolls can be found. See "Stripped for the Swastika," *Man's Darling* (May 1965); "Himmler: The SS Brothel Plot to Destroy the Allies," *War Criminals* (April 1964); and "Brides of the Garotte for the Gestapo Monster," in *Man's Story* (February 1970). See also Steven Heller, "Sweat, Nazis, and SS Sex Slaves: A Social History," in *Men's Adventure Magazines in Postwar America*, ed. Max Allan Collins et al. (Taschen, 2004), 285–90.

42. Alongside *Ilsa, She Wolf of the SS*, some of the most prominent examples of Nazi sexploitation films come from Italy. See, for instance, *SS Experiment Camp* (1976) and *SS Camp 5* (1976), dir. Sergio Garrone; and *SS Girls* (1976), dir. Bruno Mattei. On the SS sexploitation genre, see Marcus Stiglegger, *Sadiconazista: Faschismus und Sexualität im Film* (Gardez! Verlag, 1999).

43. See Stiglegger, *Sadiconazista*, 106–31, 151–57.

44. On the pornographization of fascism, see Silke Wenk, "Rhetoriken der Pornografisierung: Rahmen des Blicks auf die NS-Verbrechen," in Eschebach, Jacobeit, and Wenk, *Gedächtnis und Geschlecht*, 290–91.

45. Peter Roos, "Gepäppelt und verbraucht: In Mauthausen ist die erste Ausstellung über Bordelle in den Konzentrationslagern zu sehen," *Die Zeit*, June 20, 2006.

46. For example, on January 24, 2007, the *Daily Mail* published an article titled "Horror of Nazi Sex Slaves Forced to Work in Camps." David Edwards reported exclusively in his article "Joy Divisions" on January 27, 2007, in the *Daily Mirror*: "In this ordinary looking room women were destroyed by the evil of the Nazis. Forced to work in Himmler's death-camp brothels, they were the tragic victims of them."

47. David Rousset, *A World Apart* [1945], trans. Yvonne Moyse and Roger Senhouse (Secker and Warburg, 1951), 12.

48. See Kogon, *The Theory and Practice of Hell*; Wolfgang Sofsky, *The Order of Terror: The Concentration Camp*, trans. William Templer (Princeton University Press, 1999); and Giorgio Agamben, *Homo Sacer: Sovereign Power and Bare Life*, trans. Daniel Heller-Roazen (Stanford University Press, 1998).

49. See, for instance, the historian Jens-Christian Wagner's study of Mittelbau-Dora in *Produktion des Todes: Das KZ Mittelbau-Dora* (Wallstein, 2001).

50. Following the model of biopower (*le biopouvoir*) introduced by Foucault, I define biopolitics as the totality of all political undertakings of state power aimed at the preservation and destruction of life. The main components of this policy are sexual and population policy. In this way I distinguish myself from Agamben's model of a sovereign power that administers "naked life" (*nuda vita*). See Agamben, *Homo Sacer*, 166–77; and Michel Foucault, *The History of Sexuality*, vol. 1: *An Introduction*, trans. Robert Hurley (Pantheon, 1978).

51. Raul Hilberg, *Sources of Holocaust Research: An Analysis* (Ivan R. Dee, 2001).

52. Another tranche of documents I examined included camp command orders (*Standortbefehle*), camp population reports (*Stärke- und Veränderungsmeldungen*), correspondence between commandant offices (*KZ-Kommandanturen*), labor statistics (*Arbeitsstatistik*), kitchen books (*Küchenbücher*), transfer lists, camp infirmary files, and logbooks of surgical procedures (*Operationsbücher*).

53. This database was created based on research in the archives of various concentration camp memorial sites in Germany, Austria, and Poland. It contains personal information from files that the SS created when administering the concentration camps. I expanded this data using prisoner databases in the Auschwitz-Birkenau State Museum and the metadatabase of the Ravensbrück Memorial, as well as documents from the United States Holocaust Memorial Archives, the US National Archives in Maryland, and the database of the concentration camp memorial Lichtenburg. After the public gained access to the archives of the International Tracing Service of the Red Cross (ITS) in Bad Arolsen in November 2007—one of the most important collections of data from victims of Nazi crimes—I supplemented and corroborated information I had previously collected on forced sex workers. The database contains the following information for every woman who worked in a camp brothel: camp brothel, name, nationality, reason for imprisonment, date and place of birth, date of entry into and exit from a camp brothel, length of stay in the brothel, prisoner serial number, the date of imprisonment and release, the police department responsible for putting the woman in the camp, marital status, date of sterilization, number of children, religion, professions, previous convictions, personal address, police identification, and, if applicable, history of persecution after the war. See Robert Sommer, Forced Sex Worker Database, last updated 11/2020, AMGR, MS_Sommer.

54. One example is the memoir by the Italian Auschwitz survivor Liana Millu. Primo Levi calls her book a significant "eyewitness account" (*testimonianza*) and vouches for its accuracy. She describes how she and her work detail sought shelter in the Auschwitz camp brothel during a bombing raid. She reports on forced sex workers at the Auschwitz main camp brothel and provides their names and nationalities. But a cross-check with the notes from the venereal exams for the Auschwitz brothels, which names all the women who worked in the Auschwitz main camp brothel, contradicts some of Millu's statements. See Primo Levi, "Prefazione," in Liana Millu, *Il Fumo di Birkenau* (Firenze: Giuntina, 2001), 7; Hygiene-Institut der Waffen-SS Rajsko, Archiwum Państwowe Muzeum Auschwitz-Birkenau w Oświęcimiu (APMO), Akta HI Rajsko.

55. The Wiener Library London, founded in 1933, conducted extensive interviews with Holocaust survivors in the 1950s and 1960s. See Wiener Library London, Section II (Eyewitness Accounts). On the history of the Wiener Library, see Ben Barkow, *Alfred Wiener and the Making of the Holocaust Library* (Vallentine Mitchell & Co, 1997).

56. See, for example, the Oral History collection of the United States Holocaust Memorial Museum in Washington and the Fortunoff Video Archive for Holocaust Testimonies at Yale University.

57. See the questionnaires from the Sachsenhausen Museum and Memorial for former prisoners passed out during the fiftieth anniversary of the liberation of the camp. Sexuality and sexualized violence were particularly discussed in the surveys for Austrian Ravensbrück survivors by the Vienna Institute for Conflict Research (IKF). These surveys form the basis for the Amesberger, Auer, and Halbmayr's *Sexualisierte Gewalt.*

58. See the testimony of M.W. (pseudonym Magdalena Walter) and L.B. (pseudonym Linda Bachmann) in Paul, *Zwangsprostitution,* 45–57; and Werkstatt der Erinnerung Hamburg (WdE), sig. 295 & sig. 294T; the testimony of Kramer in Niemeyer and von der Tann, *Schweigen*; and the testimony of Laura Büttig ("Frau X"), Archiv der Gedenkstätte Neuengamme, transcription, no archive signature.

59. The interviews were conducted in German, English, French, Italian, Polish, and Russian. Thirteen of the respondents had German citizenship or were of German-Jewish descent. Nine interviewees were born in Poland and three in Italy. A Swiss, a Ukrainian, a French, an Austrian, and a Belgian were also interviewed. The interviewees were predominantly men (twenty-four). One reason for that is that women represented a minority in the concentration camp cosmos. On January 1, 1945, 479,292 men and 156,294 women were imprisoned in the camp system. See the Zusammenstellung des WVHA vom January 1, 1945, in Hans Maršálek, *Die Geschichte des Konzentrationslagers Mauthausen: Dokumentation* (Mauthausen-Komitee Österreich, 1980), 130. The interviews are referred to in the text as "Interv. Sommer" followed by the date of the interview and the survivor's name.

60. She later retracted the statement at the insistence of her husband. See the testimony of Anna Taborska, letter from Sommer to APMO, June 5, 2005; and the response on July 5, 2005 (private collection of the author).

61. "Einleitung des Herausgebers," in *"Die Jahre weiß man nicht, wo man die heute hinsetzen soll": Faschismuserfahrungen im Ruhrgebiet,* ed. Lutz Niethammer (Verlag J. H. W. Dietz Nachf., 1983), 19.

62. See Niethammer, "Einleitung des Herausgebers," 19; Ulrike Jureit and Karin Orth, *Überlebensgeschichten: Gespräche mit Überlebenden des KZ-Neuengamme* (Dölling & Galitz Verlag, 1994), 175–211; "Einleitung," in *Verletzungen: Lebensgeschichtliche Verarbeitung von Kriegserfahrungen*, ed. Ulrike Jureit und Beate Meyer (Dölling & Galitz, 1994), 6–25; and Mark Roseman, "Surviving Memory: Truth and Inaccuracy in Holocaust Memory," *Journal of Holocaust Education* 8 (January 1999): 1–20.

63. Sabine Grenz, *(Un)heimliche Lust: Über den Konsum sexueller Dienstleistungen* (VS Verlag für Sozialwissenschaften, 2005); and Dieter Kleiber

and Doris Velten, *Prostitutionskunden: Eine Untersuchung über soziale und psychologische Charakteristika von Besuchern weiblicher Prostituierter in Zeiten von Aids* (Nomos-Verl.-Ges., 1994), 40–41.

64. See Edgar Kupfer-Koberwitz, *Dachauer Tagebücher: Die Aufzeichnungen des Häftlings 24814* (Kindler, 1997), 294. David W. Pike had a similar experience during his interviews with Spanish survivors. He noticed that they were relatively open about talking about their visits to the Mauthausen camp brothel. See email from Pike to Sommer, July 28, 2007, private collection of the author.

65. See Eidesstattl. Erklärung Schiedlausky, Institut für Zeitgeschichte München (IfZ), NO 2332 (Sachsenhausen); the testimony of Klein, APMO, Oświ/Klein/332 and the testimony of Franz Hössler, APMO, Oświ./Hössler/329 (beide Auschwitz); and the testimony of Max Beulig in front of the Military Government Court, April 24 1947, AUSHMM, RG-06.005.05M, Reel 1, US Army Cases not Tried (Buchenwald).

66. See the testimony of Frau G., HStA Düsseldorf, Akte Gerichte Rep. 338 Nr. 122. On the concealment of her stay in the brothel, see the testimony of H.N. in front of the LG Frankfurt, March 6, 1974, Bundesarchiv Ludwigsburg (BArch L), B. 162–9808; and the testimony of "Minna Möller," Bundesbeauftragte für die Unterlagen des Staatssicherheitsdienstes der ehemaligen Deutschen Demokratischen Republik (BStU), MfS—HA IX 11 AV 8/74 Bd. 37.

67. See Paul, *Zwangsprostitution*; Zipfel, *Sexuelle Gewalt*, 3–20; and Northeast Asian History Foundation, *The Truth of the Japanese Military "Comfort Women"* (Northeast Asian History Foundation, 2007), 15. On the legal definition of sexual violence in wars, see Fionnuala D. Ní Aoláin, "Rethinking the Concept of Harm and Legal Categorizations of Sexual Violence During War," in *Theoretical Inquiries in Law* 1, no. 2 (2000): 307–40.

68. See Christa Paul, "Prostitution, Krieg und sexuelle Sklaverei," in *Sexarbeit: Prostitution—Lebenswelten und Mythen*, ed Elisabeth von Dücker and Museum der Arbeit (Edition Temmen, 2005), 302–4.

69. See Amesberger, Auer, and Halbmayr, *Sexualisierte Gewalt*. For instances of how the term has spread, see Alakus, Kniefacz, and Vorberg, *Sex-Zwangsarbeit*; Brigitte Halbmayr: "Sexzwangsarbeit in NS-Konzentrationslagern," in *Frauen in Widerstand und Verfolgung. Jahrbuch 2005*, ed. Dokumentationsarchiv des österreichischen Widerstandes (Lit Verlag, 2005), 96–115; and Robert Sommer, "Die Häftlingsbordelle im KZ-Komplex Auschwitz-Birkenau. Sexzwangsarbeit im Spannungsfeld von NS-'Rassenpolitik' und der Bekämpfung von Geschlechtskrankheiten," in *Nationalsozialistische Lager: Neue Beiträge zur Geschichte der Verfolgungs- und Vernichtungspolitik und zur Theorie und Praxis von Gedenkstättenarbeit*, ed. Akim Jah, Christoph Kopke, Alexander Korb, and Alexa Stiller (Klemm & Oelschläger, 2006), 81–103.

70. Insa Eschebach, "Rede zur Ausstellungseröffnung 'Sex-Zwangsarbeit in NS-Konzentrationslagern,'" unpublished manuscript, January 14, 2007.

71. See Juno Mac and Molly Smith, *Revolting Prostitutes: The Fight for Sex Workers' Rights* (Verso, 2018); and Maya Czajka, "Huren in Bewegung," in von Dücker and Museum der Arbeit, *Sexarbeit*, 206–7.

72. See Halbmayr, "Arbeitskommando Sonderbau," 220–1; and Robert Sommer, "'Sonderbau' und Lagergesellschaft. Die Bedeutung von Bordellen in den KZ," in *Theresienstädter Studien und Dokumente 2006*, ed. Jaroslava Milotová, Michael Wögerbauer, and Anna Hájková (Sefer, 2007), 320.

73. See Norbert Campagna, *Prostitution: Eine philosophische Untersuchung* (Parerga Verlag, 2005), 176–77.

74. See Halbmayr, "Sexzwangsarbeit in NS-Konzentrationslagern," 100–2.

75. See Überstellung, "Sonderkommando" Buchenwald, September 30, 1944, AMGR, AGGB, no signature.

76. On Neuengamme, see the testimony of Damgaard, AGN, 207.

77. See Maršálek, *Mauthausen*, 209; Jan Południak, *Sonder: An Interview with Sonderkommando Member Henryk Mandelbaum* (Frap-Books, 2008); and Gideon Greif, *We Wept Without Tears: Testimonies of the Jewish Sonderkommando from Auschwitz* (Yale University Press, 2014).

78. See Zugangsbuch Flossenbürg, AUSHMM 1996.A.0342 Reel 4.

79. See Bauantrag zur Erstellung einer Häftlings-Sonderbaracke "B" BW 93 im K.L. Auschwitz, June 29, 1943, AUSHMM, RG-11.001M, Reel 23.

80. See Bertrand Perz, "Der Arbeitseinsatz im KZ Mauthausen," in *Die nationalsozialistischen Konzentrationslager: Entwicklung und Struktur*, ed. Ulrich Herbert, Karin Orth, and Christoph Dieckmann, 553.

81. Liste ukrainische Wachmannschaften "gesperrt für Sonderbau," BArch, NS 4 Fl/388.

82. Erläuterungsbericht zum Vorentwurf für die Erstellung eines "Häftlings-Sonderbaus," BArch, NS 4 Fl/183.

83. See geheimes Schreiben Himmler an Pohl, November 15, 1942, in Internationaler Militärgerichtshof Nürnberg, *Der Nürnberger Prozess gegen die Hauptkriegsverbrecher vom 14. November 1945–1. Oktober 1946. Urkunden und anderes Beweismaterial. Bd. 3–4* (Reichenbach Verlag, 1947), 349; and Errichtung eines Lagerbordells, Staatsarchiv Nürnberg (StAN), Rep. 501 Kriegsverbrecher-Prozesse VI G 4, Document NO. NI-2550.

84. For Gusen, see Ludovico Barbiano di Belgiojoso, *Notte, Nebbia–Racconto di Gusen* (Guanda, 1996). On Auschwitz, see the testimony of Ostermann, Interv. Sommer 2003-05-22 Ostermann, p. 1; Liana Millu, *Smoke Over Birkenau*, trans. Lynne Sharon Schwartz (Varda, 2001), 139; and the testimony of Bator, APMO, Oświ/68/Bator; testimony of Setina, AGN, 2.8./951.

85. See Danuta Wesołowska, *Wörter aus der Hölle: Die "Lagerszpracha" der Häftlinge von Auschwitz*, trans. Jochen August (Impuls, 1998), 37–84.

86. See Rosemarie Mieder and Gislinde Schwarz, "Alles für zwei Mark: Das Häftlingsbordell von Buchenwald," radio feature, MDR 2002, broadcast on RBB Kulturradio, April 22, 2018.

87. This includes forced sex workers, visitors to camp brothels, and survivors who have disclosed intimate information about themselves.

1. Prostitution in Nazi Germany

1. A comprehensive study of prostitution in the Third Reich has yet to be written. However, several studies exist on instances of it in specific locations. See Annette F. Timm, "Sex with a Purpose: Prostitution, Venereal Disease, and Militarized Masculinity in the Third Reich," in *Sexuality and German Fascism*, ed. Dagmar Herzog (Berghahn, 2002), 223–55; Julia Roos, "Backlash Against Prostitutes' Rights: Origins and Dynamics of Nazi Prostitution Policies," *Journal of the History of Sexuality* 11, nos. 1–2 (January/April 2002): 67–94; Michaela Freund-Widder, *Frauen unter Kontrolle: Prostitution und ihre staatliche Bekämpfung in Hamburg vom Ende des Kaiserreiches bis zu den Anfängen der Bundesrepublik.* (LIT, 2003); Gabi Zürn, "Prostitution in Hamburg im 'Dritten Reich' 1933–1945," MA thesis, Universität Hamburg, 1989; Sabine Haustein, "Weibliche Prostituierte und Prostitution in Leipzig in den Jahren 1933 bis 1945," in *Frauenforscherinnen stellen sich vor*, ed. Ilse Nagelschmidt (Leipziger Universitätsverlag, 1995), 130–51; and Sabine Haustein, "Zur Geschichte von Prostituierten in Leipzig in der NS-Zeit," in *Frauenalltag in Leipzig: Weibliche Lebenszusammenhänge im 19. und 20. Jahrhundert*, ed. Susanne Schötz (Böhlau, 1997), 237–70.

2. See Margret Lohner, "Die Prostitution und ihre Bedeutung in der venerologischen Sicht," PhD diss., Medizinische Fakultät der Technischen Universität München, 1991, 11–17. On the praxis of the regulation of prostitution between 1900 and 1914, see Dagmar Herzog, *Sexuality in Europe: A Twentieth-Century History* (Cambridge University Press, 2011), 10–15.

3. See Freund-Widder, *Frauen unter Kontrolle*, 27–31.

4. For Hamburg, see Freund-Widder, *Frauen unter Kontrolle*, 41–46.

5. Joseph Goebbels, diary entry April 30, 1926. Quoted in Freund-Widder, *Frauen unter Kontrolle*, 46.

6. See Freund-Widder, *Frauen unter Kontrolle*, 53–54.

7. See Freund-Widder, *Frauen unter Kontrolle*, 57–81.

8. The German Society for Combating Venereal Disease (DGBG) was founded in 1902 by the Social Democrat Alfred Blaschko. It was the most important institution in the fight against venereal disease in Germany. On the history of the DGBG, see Gabriele Brömmer, "Die Bedeutung Alfred Blaschkos bei der Bekämpfung von Geschlechtskrankheiten in Deutschland," PhD diss., Medizinische Fakultät der Humboldt-Universität zu Berlin, 1986, 57–62.

9. On the Law for Combating Venereal Disease, see Lohner, *Prostitution*, 30–54.

10. See Freund-Widder, *Frauen unter Kontrolle*, 81–88.

11. See Freund-Widder, *Frauen unter Kontrolle*, 81–88.

12. See letter of Nationalkomitees zur Bekämpfung des Mädchenhandels, December 17, 1927, Generallandesarchiv Karlsruhe (GLAK), Abt. 330 Zug. 1991/34/Nr. 136.

13. On nationwide discussions about changes to the law, see Mitteilungen der Deutschen Gesellschaft zur Bekämpfung der Geschlechtskrankheiten (MDGBG) 1927–1933; Freund-Widder, *Frauen unter Kontrolle*, 81–88, 97–101; and Wolfgang Ayaß, *"Asoziale" im Nationalsozialismus* (Klett-Cotta, 1995), 185–86.

14. Bodo Spiethoff, "Leitartikel," *MDGBG* 31, no. 5/6 (1933): 81.

15. Quoted in Spiethoff, "Leitartikel," following Adolf Hitler, *Mein Kampf*, trans. Ralph Mannheim (Houghton Mifflin, 1943), 255–56.

16. Hitler, *Mein Kampf*, trans. Mannheim, 256.

17. Hitler, *Mein Kampf*, trans. Mannheim, 257.

18. Hitler, *Mein Kampf*, trans. Mannheim, 251. On the history of the genesis and reception of *Mein Kampf*, see Othmar Plöckinger, *Geschichte eines Buches: Adolf Hitlers 'Mein Kampf' 1922–1945* (Oldenbourg Wissenschaftsverlag, 2006).

19. See Freund-Widder, *Frauen unter Kontrolle*, 112–15.

20. The legislation required that police and health departments work closely. See the letter of Minister of the Interior, August 19, 1933, GLAK, Abt. 330 Zug. 1991/34/Nr. 136.

21. Letter of Minister of the Interior, September 29, 1934, GLAK, Abt. 330 Zug. 1991/34/Nr. 136.

22. Letter of Minister of the Interior, August 19, 1933, and June, 16 1934, GLAK, Abt. 330 Zug. 1991/34/Nr. 136. The decree suspended the Weimar constitution and lay the legal groundwork for Nazi terror. See Dietmut Majer, *Grundlagen des nationalsozialistischen Rechtssystems: Führerprinzip, Sonderrecht, Einheitspartei* (Kohlhammer, 1987).

23. See report of Criminal Police Karlsruhe in the letter from Badisches Landeskriminalpolizeiamt to Minister of the Interior, August 7, 1934, GLAK, Abt. 330 Zug. 1991/34/Nr. 136. For Hamburg, see Freund-Widder, *Frauen unter Kontrolle*, 115–18.

24. Letter of Minister of the Interior, June 16, 1934, "betr. Bekämpfung des Dirnentums und der Zuhälterei," GLAK, Abt. 330 Zug. 1991/34/Nr. 136.

25. Letter of Criminal Police to Finanzverwaltung, November 7, 1934. Quoted in Freund-Widder, *Frauen unter Kontrolle*, 118. These were Herbertstraße, Kalkhof, and Winkelstraße.

26. See letter of Minister of the Interior, September 29, 1934, GLAK, Abt. 330 Zug. 1991/34/Nr. 136.

27. See Freund-Widder, *Frauen unter Kontrolle*, 126–31.

28. See Freund-Widder, *Frauen unter Kontrolle*, 126–31.

29. Through the Decree on Preventive Measures by the Police to Combat Crime (*Runderlass über vorbeugende Verbrechensbekämpfung durch die Polizei*), of December 14, 1937, people could be sent to a concentration camp without a court order and held there indefinitely. Those particularly affected by these

measures were people making their living from criminal activity (*Berufsverbrecher*), engaging in chronic "antisocial" behavior, "work-shy people" (*Arbeitsscheue*), homeless people, Sinti and Roma, prostitutes, and homosexuals. People who had been sentenced three times to a prison sentence of at least three months could be placed under "scheduled police surveillance." Anyone who had been sentenced three times to a prison sentence of at least six months could be transferred to "preventive police custody" (*polizeiliche Vorbeugehaft*). See Ayaß, *Asoziale*, 139–65; and Wolfgang Ayaß, ed., *"Gemeinschaftsfremde." Quellen zur Verfolgung von "Asozialen" 1933–1945* (Bundesarchiv, 1998), 94–97.

30. See Ayaß, *Gemeinschaftsfremde*; Freund-Widder, *Frauen unter Kontrolle*, 52–53. In other German states, such as Baden, prostitutes had been living in special houses since 1927 and were regularly examined by the health authorities. See letter from Staatliche Kriminalpolizei Karlsruhe to Reich Minister of the Interior, November 27, 1939, GLAK, Abt. 330 Zug. 1991/34/Nr. 136.

31. Confidential circular letter of Heydrich, September 9, 1939, GLAK, Abt. 330 Zug. 1991/34/Nr. 136. In Hamburg, the Gestapo had a brothel built on Valentinskamp with funds from the Jewish community. The Law for the Protection of German Blood and German Honor from 1935 forbade extramarital sex between Jews and Aryans. However, the brothel had to close because of a lack of demand. See Freund-Widder, *Frauen unter Kontrolle*, 176–77.

32. Circular letter of Heydrich, May 5, 1941, GLAK, Abt. 330 Zug. 1991/34/Nr. 136.

33. On the practice of ethnic segregation, see Dietmut Majer, *"Fremdvölkische" im Dritten Reich: Ein Beitrag zur nationalsozialistischen Rechtssetzung und Rechtspraxis in Verwaltung und Justiz unter besonderer Berücksichtigung der eingegliederten Ostgebiete und des Generalgouvernements* (Boldt, 1981).

34. For example, see Annette Schäfer, *Zwangsarbeiter und NS-Rassenpolitik: Russische und polnische Arbeitskräfte in Württemberg 1939–1945* (Kohlhammer, 2000), 131–59; Birthe Kundrus, "Forbidden Company: Romantic Relationships Between Germans and Foreigners, 1939 to 1945," *Journal of the History of Sexuality* 11 (2002): 201–22; Freund-Widder, *Frauen unter Kontrolle*, 170–71; and Ulrich Herbert, *Fremdarbeiter: Politik und Praxis des "Ausländer-Einsatzes" in der Kriegswirtschaft des Dritten Reiches* (J. H. W. Dietz Nachfolger, 1999), 74–81, 170–76.

35. See letter of Chef der Sicherheitspolizei and SD, June 2, 1944, AUSHMM, RG-14.002, Reel 9.

36. Himmler had personally decided that Estonians and Latvians should be exempt from the "GV ban." ("GV" stood for *Geschlechtsverkehr*, or sexual intercourse). However, this did not apply to Lithuanians. See letter from Himmler to Chef der Sicherheitspolizei and SD, September 8, 1943, BArch, NS 19/382.

37. See the statement made by Barths at the Ausländerarbeitskreis of the RSHA, in a memo of the Ausländerarbeitskreis RSHA, August 23, 1941, regarding

questions of brothels, BArch, R 16/162; and Richtlinien für die Überwachung fremdvölkischer Arbeitskräfte, Oktober 25, 1942, BArch, R 187/216. On dealing with "uninhibited women" ("*hemmunglose Frauen*"), see Freund-Widder, *Frauen unter Kontrolle*, 170–75.

38. Speech of Himmler in front of Oberabschnittsführer and Hauptamtschefs on June 9, 1942, in *Heinrich Himmler: Geheimreden 1933 bis 1945 und andere Ansprachen*, ed. Bradley F. Smith and Agnes F. Peterson (Propyläen, 1974), 159.

39. See the letter from the mayor of Linz to Zweigstelle Ostmark des Reichsarbeitsministers, March 18, 1940, Stadtarchiv Linz, Bestand Neubau Städte/Bauvorgang Tschechenbordell; and the circular letter of Martin Bormann, January 27, 1941, BArch, NS 6/334. On the history of "Villa Nova," see Hermann Rafetseder, "Der 'Ausländereinsatz' zur Zeit des NS-Regimes am Beispiel der Stadt Linz," in *Nationalsozialismus in Linz. Bd. 2*, ed. Fritz Mayrhofer and Walter Schuster (Archiv der Stadt Linz, 2001), 1163–67.

40. Circular letter of Bormann, December 7, 1940, GLAK, Abt. 330 Zug. 1991/34/Nr. 269.

41. Letter of Heydrich, January 16, 1941, GLAK, Abt. 330 Zug. 1991/34/Nr. 269.

42. See report issued by Friedrich Riese, October 11, 1941; and circular letter of RSHA, June 4, 1942, GLAK, Abt. 330 Zug. 1991/34/Nr. 269.

43. See letter of Heydrich, May 18, 1941, GLAK, Abt. 330 Zug. 1991/34/Nr. 269.

44. See circular letter of Bormann, April 16, 1941, BArch, NS 6/334. On the difficulties in building such facilities, see the planning of "B. Baracken," GLAK, Abt. 330 Zug. 1991/34/Nr. 269, 235.

45. Confidential letter from the mayor of Hennigsdorf to Landrat in Nauen, October 20, 1941, Brandenburgisches Landeshauptarchiv (BLHA), Rep.2A I Kom Nr. 1048.

46. See Joachim Nigmann, "Prostitution und Nachwuchs im Hinblick auf das Ehegesundheitsgesetz," inaugural dissertation, Ludwig-Maximilians-Universität, Munich, 1943, 32. Other German military organizations, such as the navy and the Waffen-SS, maintained brothels under their own control. See Franz Seidler, *Prostitution Homosexualität Selbstverstümmelung: Probleme der deutschen Sanitätsführung 1939–1945* (Kurt Vowinkel, 1977), 158; Frank Vossler, *Propaganda in die eigene Truppe: Die Truppenbetreuung in der Wehrmacht 1939–1945* (Ferdinand Schöningh, 2006), 355; and Paul, *Zwangsprostitution*, 103.

47. Extensive writings on prostitution and the military can be found in the *Zeitschrift für Bekämpfung der Geschlechtskrankheiten* 15 (1914), 16 (1915/16), and 19 (1919/20).

48. See Seidler, *Probleme der deutschen Sanitätsführung*, 145.

49. See Insa Meinen, *Wehrmacht und Prostitution während des Zweiten Weltkrieges in Frankreich* (Edition Temmen, 2002), 8–15; Vossler, *Propaganda in die eigene Truppe*, 347–89; Seidler, *Probleme der deutschen Sanitätsführung*, 135–87; and Regina Mühlhäuser, "Rasse, Blut und Männlichkeit: Politiken sexueller

Regulierung in den besetzten Gebieten der Sowjetunion (1941–1945)," *Feministische Studien 1* (2007): 55–69.

50. In Poland and the Soviet Union, Wehrmacht brothels existed in Ternopil, Lviv, Mogilev, Gomel, Lublin, Wrzesnia, Brody, Zamość, Drohobycz, Smolensk, Moshni, Yasnoziria, and Bezobrazia; in Latvia, there were brothels in Riga and Liepāja; in Lithuania, there was a brothel in Vilna; and in Romania there was a brothel in Tjestnanovna. See Wendy Jo Gertjejanssen, "Victims, Heroes, Survivors: Sexual Violence on the Eastern Front During World War II," PhD diss., University of Minnesota, 2004, 221–22, http://www.victimsheroessurvivors.info/VictimsHeroesSurvivors.pdf. For Norway, see Vossler, *Truppenbetreuung*, 353; and Meinen, *Wehrmacht*, 213.

51. See decree of OKW, January 27, 1943, BLHA, Rep 45 D Westhavelland 1.

52. See letter of Bormann, January 13, 1941, BArch, NS 6/334; and Robert-Jan van Pelt and Debórah Dwork, *Auschwitz von 1270 bis heute* (Büchergilde Gutenberg, 1999), 84.

53. Letter from Himmler to Krüger et al., June 30, 1942, BArch, NS 19/1913.

54. See order for the SS and police, October 28, 1939, BArch, Film 1576.

55. Speech of Himmler to Gruppenführer, February 18, 1937, in Himmler, *Geheimreden*, 98.

56. Speech of Himmler, 90.

57. Speech of Himmler, 93–95.

58. See circular letter including the purity (*Reinhaltung*) decree of the SS and police, March 7, 1942, AUSHMM RG-48.004M Reel 02.

59. Letter of Himmler betr. Geschlechtsverkehr mit Polinnen, July 3, 1941, BArch, NS 19/1913. Several SS leaders also seemed to tolerate sexual relations between SS men and Poles. See the note by Rübel in the letter from Himmler to Krüger et al., July 17, 1942, BArch, NS 19/2491.

60. See letter of Dr. Grohmann regarding whether R [. . .] M [. . .] was eligible for marriage, April 8, 1942, BArch, NS 48/24.

61. Letter from Himmler to Krüger et al., June 30, 1942, BArch, NS 19/1913.

62. It is probable that they were not prostitutes registered with health authorities.

63. See the note by Rübel in the letter from Himmler to Krüger, July 17, 1942, BArch, NS 19/2491.

64. Note of Rübel.

65. See Grawitz's report regarding the note by Rübel, July 25, 1942, BArch, NS 19/2491.

66. See the letter from Himmler to Hofmann, July 28, 1942, BArch, NS 19/2491.

67. See the letter from Himmler to Oberg, January 5, 1943. On correcting the number to 7,000, see the letter of the head of the SS-Sanitätsamtes, January 18, 1943, both BArch, NS 19/264.

68. Letter from Himmler to Oberg, January 5, 1943, BArch, NS 19/264.

69. Letter from Himmler to Oberg.

70. Letter from Himmler to Oberg.

71. Letter from SS-Führungshauptamt to Himmler, January 18, 1943, BArch, NS 19/264.

72. The notoriously brutal Obergruppenführer and general of the police Carl Albrecht Oberg was known as the "Butcher of Paris." See Ruth Bettina Birn, *Die höheren SS- und Polizeiführer: Himmlers Vertreter im Reich und in den besetzten Gebieten* (Droste Verlag, 1986), 252–56.

73. Letter from Oberg to Himmler, March 3, 1943, BArch, NS 19/264.

74. Letter from Himmler to Oberg, January 5, 1943, BArch, NS 19/264.

75. See Paul, *Zwangsprostitution*, 107–16; and Auer, Amesberger, and Halbmayr, *Sexualisierte Gewalt*, 39–141.

76. See Anja Lundholm, *Das Höllentor: Bericht einer Überlebenden* (Rowohlt, 1988), 42–43; the testimony of Lynhard, AMGR, Bd.17/55, 10; and the testimony of Anthonia Bruha, in Karin Berger and Elisabeth Holzinger, eds., *"Ich geb Dir einen Mantel, dass Du ihn noch in Freiheit tragen kannst": Widerstehen im KZ, Österreichische Frauen erzählen* (Promedia, 1987), 49.

77. See Karina Loos, "Planen und Bauen im Nationalsozialismus: Ein Überblick zu Weimar," in *Klassikerstadt und Nationalsozialismus: Kultur und Politik in Weimar 1933–1945*, ed. Justus Ulbricht (Glaux, 2002), 136–37.

78. This can be shown by the very euphemistic memories of Herbert Brunnegger, who finished his Waffen-SS training in Sachsenhausen and Flossenbürg.

79. Ernst Federn, "Versuch einer Psychologie des Terrors (1946/1989)," in *Ernst Federn—Versuche zur Psychologie des Terrors*, ed. Roland Kaufbold (Psychosozial, 1998), 57.

80. See Ernst Federn, "Eros hinter Stacheldraht. Interview-Auszug," in *Stimmen aus Buchenwald: Ein Lesebuch*, ed. Holm Kirsten und Ulf Kirsten (Wallenstein, 2002), 70.

81. Karl-Heinz B., who was with a military patrol in Weimar on the day of the assassination attempt on Hitler, writes that Rosmariengasse was "swarming" with soldiers. See Walter Kempowski, "'Das Wichtigste: Unser Führer lebt.' Der 20. Juli 1944—Echo eines Attentats. Ein Zeitbild aus Tagebüchern, Briefen und Erinnerungen," *Die Zeit, Dossier*, July 8, 2004.

82. See Freund-Widder, *Frauen unter Kontrolle*, 156.

83. The former camp clerk (*Lagerschreiber*) at the Mauthausen concentration camp, Hans Maršálek, testified: "There was supposedly an SS brothel in Linz, yes, that's where the SS people supposedly went" (testimony of Maršálek, IKF, Marsalek Video-Int. 2, 14–19). See also Amesberger, Auer, and Halbmayr, *Sexualisierte Gewalt*, 137.

84. See site map of camp II Buchenwald, AUSHMM, RG-11.001M Reel 71.

85. Standortbefehl Nr. 7/42, in Norbert Frei et al., eds., *Standort- und Kommandanturbefehle des Konzentrationslagers Auschwitz 1940–1945: Darstellungen und Quellen zur Geschichte von Auschwitz* (De Gruyter, 2000), 1:106.

86. See Standortbefehle, December 22, 1943, and January 28, 1944, in Frei et al., *Standort- und Kommandanturbefehle*, 385, 399.

87. Memo of meeting from September 23, 1942, AUSHMM, RG-11.001M Reel 19.

88. This information is from Pietr Setkiewicz, April 28, 2003, Oświęcim, Poland.

89. Arthur Liebehenschel (1901–1948) began his concentration camp career as an adjutant in the Lichtenburg concentration camp and moved to the Concentration Camps Inspectorate (Inspektion der Konzentrationslager) IKL in Oranienburg in 1936. In 1942 he took over the DI office group that had been formed there in the newly founded WVHA. In 1943 Liebehenschel replaced Höß as camp commandant of Auschwitz. His tenure brought a "period of improvement in living conditions" for prisoners. He abolished the execution of prisoners caught while escaping. In May 1944, Liebehenschel was appointed commandant of the Majdanek concentration camp. After the war, the US Army captured Liebehenschel and extradited him to the People's Republic of Poland. He was put on trial in 1947, sentenced to death, and executed in 1948. See Danuta Czech, *Kalendarium der Ereignisse im Konzentrationslager Auschwitz-Birkenau 1939–1945* (Rowohlt, 1989), 1011–12.

90. Standortbefehl, May 8, 1944, in Frei et al., *Standort- und Kommandanturbefehle*, 145–46.

91. See letter to Staatliches Gesundheitsamt and Sicherheitspolizei Auschwitz, November 2, 1944; and letter to Kripo-Leitstelle Hamburg December 10, 1944, Stadtarchiv Oświęcim, Zespot Bürgermeister Segr. Ftezka 33.

92. Note of meeting (Aufzeichnung von der Unterredung), Chef der Häuser- und Barackenbau GmbH, Konitzky, with Kriminal-Obersekretär Ernstberger, January 12, 1943, Staatsarchiv München (StAM), Best. Polizeidirektion 8001.

93. See Sergei Kudryashov, "Ordinary Collaborators: The Case of the Travniki Guards," in Mark Erickson and Ljubica Erickson, eds., *Russia: War, Peace, and Diplomacy: Essays in Honour of John Erickson* (Weidenfeld & Nicolson, 2004), 226–39.

94. See Chapter 3, "Auschwitz Birkenau"; and the testimony of Max Beulig, AUSHMM, RG-06.005.05M Reel 1, 8. Longer passages of Beulig's testimony are quoted in Gertjejanssen, *Victims, Heroes, Survivors*, 234–51; David A. Hackett, *The Buchenwald Report* (Westview, 1995); and Herbert Weidlich, "Der Sonderbau (Bordell) im ehemaligen Schutzhaftlager Buchenwald," unpublished manuscript, Berlin 1978, AMGB, 56-8-4, 7.

95. Telex, March 29, 1944, to Lagerkommandant of K.L. Ravensbrück, Thüringisches Hauptstaatsarchiv Weimar (ThHStA), KZ and Haftanstalten Buchenwald Nr.10, Bl. 587. See also Tripper und Lueskarteien, BArch, NS 4 Fl/388.

96. See letter, Head of Office Group D (Amtsgruppe D), December 15, 1943, BArch, NS 3/426.

97. See letter, Head of Office Group D; and Baumgartner, *Frauen von Mauthausen*, 98.

98. On Dachau, see letter from Albert Knoll to Robert Sommer, December 21, 2007.

99. See Chapter 2, "The Establishment of a Concentration Camp System."

100. See money cards (*Geldkarten*) of W.C. and B.M., ITS, KLD/Buchenwald, Envelope Nr. 16686 and 3293.

101. See letter from the Chef der Amtsgruppe D, December 15, 1943, BArch, NS 3/426.

102. See job sheets from "Sonderbau" Buchenwald February 26–March 6, 1944, BArch, NS 4 Bu/41.

103. For Buchenwald, the "political" Polish women W.C. and B.M. were known to be forced sex workers in the brothel for Ukrainian security guards. See job sheets from the Häftlingsbordell, BArch, NS 4 Bu/41; telex from March 29, 1944, ThHStA, KZ und Haftanstalten Buchenwald Nr.10 Bl. 587. C.P. and M.S., who were both "antisocial" female Polish prisoners, were most likely in the Ukrainian brothel in Gusen. See Ravensbrück Zugangsliste February 15, 1944, AMGR, AGGB, 01062702; and C.O. and S.C., ITS, KLD/Mauthausen, T/D No. 1948659 and 1033117; Schikorra, "Prostitution weiblicher Häftlinge," 21; and Bernhard Strebel, *Das KZ Ravensbrück: Geschichte eines Lagerkomplexes* (Schöningh, 2003), 209. It can be assumed that the "antisocial" Polish women M.Z. and I.C. had to serve in the brothel for Ukrainian SS men in Flossenbürg. See Ravensbrück Zugangsliste, March 11, 1944, AMGR, AGGB, 01069801. In total, eight women can be identified. Since all these women were eventually changed out and a brothel for Ukrainian guards also existed in Stutthof and probably in Sachsenhausen, the total number of forced sex workers was probably twenty-four.

104. See the list of names of liberated prisoners C.P. (or K.P.), Archiv der Gedenkstätte Bergen-Belsen (ABB), L162.

105. See Robert Sommer, Forced Sex Worker Database, last update 11/2020, AMGR, MS_Sommer.

106. Map Ausbildungslager Debica (1942), in Stanislaw Zabierowski, *Pustków. Hitlerowskie obozy wyniszczenia w służbie poligonu SS* (Krajowa Agencja Wydawnicza, 1981).

107. See Friedrich Bolaritsch, *Wege des Schicksals* (Elfriede Wild, 1998), 50–61.

108. There are six rooms mentioned on this list. It is therefore likely that at least six women had to serve at that brothel. See Sammelliste zur Einsendung von Material zur bakteriologischen Untersuchung vom Standortarzt des SS-TrÜb. Pl.-Heidelager, May 12, 1944, APMO, Akta HI Rajsko, 385/8.

109. The local researcher Mirek K. reported: "I know one based on a description from my aunt, who as child (she was about ten) carried food to the brothel (pears, apples, milk, cream, etc.). She told me that one day three girls came to their house who had run away from the brothel. They told her they were caught on the street in Krakow and sent to Pustkow. My grandmother organized their transportation to Krakow" (email from Mirek K., April 11, 2005, Privatsammlung Sommer).

110. The use of state-controlled prostitution for racial segregation has its roots in colonial sexual politics. See Philippa Levine, *Prostitution, Race, and Politics: Policing Venereal Disease in the British Empire* (Routledge, 2003), 177–98.

2. Concentration Camps and Forced Labor

1. Wolfgang Benz and Barbara Distel, "Vorwort," in *Der Ort des Terrors: Geschichte der nationalsozialistischen Konzentrationslager*, vol. 1, *Die Organisation des Terrors*, ed. Wolfgang Benz and Barbara Distel (C. H. Beck, 2005), 7–9.

2. On the periodization of the history of concentration camps, see Ulrich Herbert, Karin Orth, and Christoph Dieckmann, "Die nationalsozialistischen Konzentrationslager: Geschichte, Erinnerung, Forschung," in *Die nationalsozialistischen Konzentrationslager: Entwicklung und Struktur*, ed. Ulrich Herbert, Karin Orth, and Christoph Dieckmann (Wallenstein, 1998), 17–40; Falk Pingel, *Häftlinge unter SS-Herrschaft: Widerstand, Selbstbehauptung und Vernichtung im Konzentrationslager* (Hoffmann und Campe, 1978); Angelika Königseder, "Die Entwicklung des KZ-Systems," in Benz and Distel, *Ort I*, 30–42; and Wolfgang Sofsky, *The Order of Terror: The Concentration Camp*, trans. William Templer (Princeton University Press, 1999), 28–43.

3. See Herbert, Orth, and Dieckmann, *Konzentrationslager*, 24–26; and Sofsky, *The Order of Terror*, 28–29; Königseder, "Entwicklung des KZ-Systems," 30–31.

4. See Sofsky, *The Order of Terror*, 28–31; and Königseder, "Entwicklung des KZ-Systems," 31. For other important testimony, see Gerhart Seger, *Oranienburg: Erster authentischer Bericht eines aus dem Konzentrationslager Geflüchteten* (Verlagsanstalt Graphia, 1934).

5. Theodor Eicke (1892–1943) left secondary school in 1909 before graduating to become a professional soldier. After serving in the army he joined the police but he failed in all of his attempts to build a career. In 1928 he joined the NSDAP. He was initially a member of the SA; in 1930, he joined the SS. He was arrested for making explosive devices and fled to Italy. After being admitted to a mental institution, he was expelled from the SS in 1933. Through the aid of Dr. Werner Heyde, who would later become a doctor at the "Euthanasie"-Zentrale, Eicke was released from the institution and reintegrated into the SS. Himmler appointed Eicke commandant of the Dachau concentration camp because of his organizational talent and brutality. From May 1934 to November 1939, Eicke was the *Inspekteur der Konzentrationslager* (inspector of the concentration camps), and in 1939 he was appointed commander of the SS Death's Head Units. In 1943, Eicke was shot down in his plane by the Red Army. See Johannes Tuchel, *Die Inspektion der Konzentrationslager 1938–1945: Das System des Terrors* (Edition Hentrich, 1994), 32–33.

6. See Herbert, Orth, Dieckmann, "Konzentrationslager," 26; and Königseder, "Entwicklung des KZ-Systems," 32.

7. See letter of Himmler, February 8, 1937, BArch, R2/24006.

8. See Sofsky, *The Order of Terror*, 32.

9. "Antisocials" included vagrants, beggars, ruffians, prostitutes, those with venereal disease, homosexuals, alcoholics, psychopaths, traffic offenders, troublemakers, and Sinti and Roma. See Wolfgang Ayaß, *"Asoziale" im Nationalsozialismus* (Klett-Cotta, 1995), 138–65.

10. See Sofsky, *The Order of Terror*, 32–34, Königseder, "Entwicklung des KZ-Systems," 32–34; and Herbert, Orth, and Dieckmann, "Konzentrationslager," 28–29.

11. See Sofsky, *The Order of Terror*, 34–36; Herbert, Orth, and Dieckmann, "Konzentrationslager," 29; and Königseder, "Entwicklung des KZ-Systems," 34.

12. These numbers are according to Pingel, *Häftlinge unter SS-Herrschaft*, 81–82.

13. See Danuta Czech, "Entstehungsgeschichte des KL Auschwitz: Aufbau- und Ausbauperiode," in *Auschwitz: Nationalsozialistisches Konzentrationslager*, ed. Staatliches Museum Auschwitz-Birkenau (Staatliches Museum Auschwitz-Birkenau, 1997), 43–45; and Sofsky, *The Order of Terror*, 38.

14. Odilo Globočnik (1904–1945) was an Austrian Nazi who fought for the annexation of Austria and became gauleiter of Vienna. From 1941 he was the SS and police leader of the Lublin district and later, as head of "Aktion Reinhardt," the central figure in the murder of Jews in the General Government. He was later transferred to the Adriatic Coastal Operation Zone to fight partisans. See Siegfried Pucher, *". . . in der Bewegung führend tätig": Odilo Globočnik—Kämpfer für den "Anschluß," Vollstrecker des Holocaust* (Drava, 1997); and Gutman, *Encyclopedia*, 589–90. On extermination camps in Eastern Europe, see Arno Mayer, *Der Krieg als Kreuzzug: Das Deutsche Reich, Hitlers Wehrmacht und die Endlösung* (Rowohlt, 1989); Raul Hilberg, *The Destruction of the European Jews* (Holmes & Meier, 1985), 221–59; and Gitta Sereny, *Into That Darkness: An Examination of Conscience* (Knopf, 1995).

15. See Franciszek Piper, "Massenvernichtung von Juden in Gaskammern des KL Auschwitz," in Staatliches Museum Auschwitz-Birkenau, ed., *Auschwitz*, 254.

16. See Herbert, Orth, and Dieckmann, "Konzentrationslager," 30; and Königseder, "Entwicklung des KZ-Systems," 37–38.

17. Fritz Sauckel (1894–1946) was a member of the NSDAP since 1923. From 1927 he was NSDAP gauleiter, then prime minister and interior minister and from 1933 Reich governor of Thuringia. In 1942 he became General Plenipotentiary for Labor Deployment, making him into what the German historian Steffen Raßloff called "Hitler's slave owner." By recruiting millions of foreign forced laborers, he was supposed to make the "final victory" possible. In 1946 he was sentenced to death and executed for war crimes and crimes against humanity by the International Military Tribunal in Nuremberg. See Steffen Raßloff, *Fritz Sauckel: Hitlers "Muster-Gauleiter" und "Sklavenhalter"* (Landeszentrale für politische Bildung Thüringen, 2007).

18. On the history of the WVHA, see Jan Erik Schulte, *Zwangsarbeit und Vernichtung: Das Wirtschaftsimperium der SS. Oswald Pohl und das SS-Wirtschafts-Verwaltungshauptamt 1933–1945* (Schöningh, 2001).

19. Oswald Pohl (1892–1947) had been a professional soldier in the Reichsmarine since 1912 and rose to become chief paymaster. In 1922 he joined the NSDAP. In 1934 he became head of administration and Reich treasury administrator of the SS and in 1939 head of the Main Office for Administration and Economics and Main Office for Budget and Buildings (Hauptamt Haushalt und Bauten) in the Reich Ministry of the Interior. From 1942 he was head of the SS-WVHA. In May 1946 the British Army arrested him, and in 1947 he was sentenced to death in the follow-up proceedings to the Nuremberg Trials. After his appeal was rejected, he was executed by hanging in Landsberg in 1951. See Israel Gutman, ed., *The Encyclopedia of the Holocaust* (Macmillan, 1990), 3:1142–43.

20. See Sofsky, *The Order of Terror*, 41.

21. See Sofsky, *The Order of Terror*, 55–56; and Joachim Neander, *Das Konzentrationslager "Mittelbau" in der Endphase der national-sozialistischen Diktatur: Zur Geschichte des letzten im „Dritten Reich" gegründeten selbständigen Konzentrationslagers unter besonderer Berücksichtigung seiner Auflösungsphase* (Papierflieger, 1998), 85–166.

22. In addition, around two million Jews were murdered in Bełżec, Sobibór, and Treblinka. They are not included in the number of victims of the concentration camps because these camps lay outside the concentration camp system. See Karin Orth, *Die Konzentrationslager-SS: Sozialstrukturelle Analysen und biografische Studien einer nationalsozialistischen Führungselite* (Wallstein, 2001), 84–85; and Herbert, Orth, and Dieckmann, "Konzentrationslager," 31.

23. Sofsky, *The Order of Terror*, 117.

24. The group of "criminals" included both "career criminals" placed in preventive police custody, as well as "preventive detainees," who were in custody because of an agreement between Himmler and Justice Minister Otto Georg Thierack in August 1942. See Annette Eberle, "Häftlingskategorien und Kennzeichnungen," in Benz and Distel, *Ort I*, 103.

25. See Sofsky, *The Order of Terror*, 117–19; and Eberle, "Häftlingskategorien und Kennzeichnungen," 91–109.

26. See Sofsky, *The Order of Terror*, 118–20. There were exceptions in particular in Auschwitz and Monowitz, where the SS also used Jews as privileged prisoners. See Hermann Langbein, *People in Auschwitz*, trans. Harry Zohn (University of North Carolina Press, 2004), 169–77.

27. See Sofsky, *The Order of Terror*, 118–20; and Bruno Bettelheim, "Individual and Mass Behavior in Extreme Situations," *Journal of Abnormal and Social Psychology* 38, no. 4 (1943): 417–52.

28. On the *Muselmann*, see Langbein, *People in Auschwitz*, 89–105; and Sofsky, *The Order of Terror*, 199–205.

29. See Sofsky, *The Order of Terror*, 129.

30. See Sofsky, *The Order of Terror*, 128–29.

31. Himmler's speech to generals in Sonthofen, May 5, 1944, in Himmler, *Geheimreden*, 200.

32. See Sofsky, *The Order of Terror*, 145–52; and Lutz Niethammer, ed., *Der "gesäuberte" Antifaschismus: Die SED und die roten Kapos von Buchenwald* (Akademie Verlag, 1994), 257–330.

33. See Sofsky, *The Order of Terror*, 145–150; Harry Naujoks, *Mein Leben im KZ Sachsenhausen 1936–1942: Erinnerungen des ehemaligen Lagerältesten* (Dietz, 1989), 341; Langbein, *People in Auschwitz*, 143–68; and Wiesław Kielar, *Anus Mundi: 1500 Days in Auschwitz/Birkenau*, trans. Susanne Flatauer (Times Books, 1980), 279–90. Camp elder I of Mauthausen, Magnus Keller, weighed 110 kilograms. See Maršálek, *Geschichte des Konzentrationslagers Mauthausen*, 61.

34. This dilemma is clearly shown by the example of the prisoner camp police at Buchenwald concentration camp. This patrol benefited the SS and the resistance movement at the same time. It relieved the SS guards and guaranteed order in the camp. On the one hand, the resistance movement had a "legal" armed body. Enemies, informants, and traitors could be eliminated in this way. Resistance prisoners, on the other hand, were able to move freely around the camp at night under their protection. See Hackett, *Buchenwald-Report*, 294–96; Karin Orth, "Gab es eine Lagergesellschaft? 'Kriminelle' und politische Häftlinge im Konzentrationslager," in *Ausbeutung, Vernichtung, Öffentlichkeit: Neue Studien zur nationalsozialistischen Lagerpolitik*, ed. Norbert Frei, Sybille Steinbacher, and Bernd C. Wagner (K. G. Saur, 2000), 109; and Sofsky, *The Order of Terror*, 137–38.

35. See Sofsky, *The Order of Terror*, 136.

36. The inmates working in the *Schreibstube*, or camp office, recorded prisoner numbers, transfers, new arrivals, departures (deaths and releases), and block assignments. The prisoners at the *Arbeitsstatistik*, the labor statistics office, compiled the work histories of those transferred to the subcamps. See Sofsky, *The Order of Terror*, 133–34.

37. On the importance of social capital in concentration camps, see Sofsky, *The Order of Terror*, 126–27.

38. See Sofsky, *The Order of Terror*, 125.

39. See Rainer Fröbe, "KZ-Häftlinge als Reserve qualifizierter Arbeitskraft: Eine späte Entdeckung der deutschen Industrie und ihre Folgen," in Herbert, Orth, and Dieckmann, *Konzentrationslager*, 636–81.

40. The Hamburg historian Hermann Kaienburg has carefully considered the competing interests of the SS and the economic significance of the camp system. See Hermann Kaienburg, *Die Wirtschaft der SS* (Metropol, 2003), 1049–53.

41. See Kaienburg, *Die Wirtschaft der SS*, 123–29.

42. See Kaienburg, *Die Wirtschaft der SS*, 123–29.

43. See Kaienburg, *Die Wirtschaft der SS*, 139–250.

44. "Texled" stood for Gesellschaft für Textil- und Lederverwertung mbH. In 1944 it was renamed Deutsche Textil- und Bekleidungswerke GmbH (German Textile and Clothing Manufacturing, Ltd.).

45. See Kaienburg, *Die Wirtschaft der SS*, 857–59.

46. On the central importance of public funds for the SS, see Schulte, *Zwangsarbeit und Vernichtung*, 81–88.

47. See Kaienburg, *Die Wirtschaft der SS*, 978–88.

48. See Regine Kießling, Gisela Kraut, and Ulrich Wanitzek, "Großbauten des Staates und der Partei (München, Nürnberg, Berlin)," in *Kunst im 3. Reich. Dokumente der Unterwerfung*, ed. Georg Bussmann (Zweitausendeins, 1979), 124–26; and Hans-Ulrich Thamer, "Von der 'Ästhetisierung der Politik': Die Nürnberger Reichsparteitage der NSDAP," in *Faszination und Gewalt: Zur politischen Ästhetik des Nationalsozialismus*, ed. Bernd Ogan and Wolfgang Weiß (Tümmel Verlag, 1992), 95–105.

49. See Kaienburg, *Die Wirtschaft der SS*, 606; and Schulte, *Zwangsarbeit und Vernichtung*, 111–12.

50. See Schulte, *Zwangsarbeit und Vernichtung*, 123–25.

51. For an analysis of power relations, see Pingel, *Häftlinge unter SS-Herrschaft*, 64. For an economic perspective, see Kaienburg, *Die Wirtschaft der SS*, 606.

52. On the history of DEST, see Kaienburg, *Die Wirtschaft der SS*, 603–770.

53. On the construction of representative buildings in Weimar, see Christine Wolf, "Zentralpunkt nationalsozialistischen Lebens: Der Platz Adolf Hitlers in Weimar," in Ulbricht, *Klassikerstadt*, 157–67; and Loos, "Planen und Bauen," in Ulbricht, *Klassikerstadt*, 128–44. On the history of the quarry in Buchenwald, see Hackett, *Buchenwald-Report*, 219–21. See also Kaienburg, *Die Wirtschaft der SS*, 604–5.

54. See Kaienburg, *Die Wirtschaft der SS*, 607–10, 622–33.

55. See Kaienburg, *Die Wirtschaft der SS*, 648–72.

56. See Kaienburg, *Die Wirtschaft der SS*, 690–93.

57. See Kaienburg, *Die Wirtschaft der SS*, 618–22, 639–47, 695–727.

58. In his 1939 speech in Posen, Himmler stressed that he imagined 20 million Germans settling in Eastern Europe in fifty to eighty years. See Van Pelt and Dwork, *Auschwitz*, 87–92, 151.

59. The *Generalplan Ost* was developed in May 1942 by the Agricultural Faculty of the University of Berlin under the leadership of the geographer Konrad Meyer. See Van Pelt and Dwork, *Auschwitz*, 154–57; and Isabel Heinemann and Patrick Wagner, eds., *Wissenschaft—Planung—Vertreibung: Neuordnungskonzepte und Umsiedlungspolitik im 20. Jahrhundert* (Franz Steiner Verlag, 2006).

60. See Karola Fings, *Krieg, Gesellschaft und KZ: Himmlers SS-Baubrigaden* (Schöningh, 2005), 34–35.

61. Hans Kammler (1901–1945) was SS Obergruppenführer and general of the Waffen-SS. Kammler, an architect by profession, headed Amtsgruppe C (Bauwesen) of the WVHA and the Hauptamt Haushalt und Bauten (HAHB) from February 1941. In August 1943, Kammler became head of the expansion program for the underground production facilities for the V2 rocket. From March 1944 he

was responsible for the implementation of the large-scale underground construction work to produce the Messerschmitt Me 262, and in 1944 he created the largest underground factory for this purpose in St. Georgen/Gusen. Kammler probably committed suicide on May 9, 1945. His body was never found. See Fings, *SS-Baubrigaden*, 325.

62. See Fings, *SS-Baubrigaden*, 34–35.

63. See Fings, *SS-Baubrigaden*, 38–39.

64. See Fings, *SS-Baubrigaden*, 36–39.

65. See Fings, *SS-Baubrigaden*, 48–58.

66. See Fings, *SS-Baubrigaden*, 51–52.

67. See Fings, *SS-Baubrigaden*, 51–52.

68. Speech of Himmler to Reichsleiters and gauleiters in Posen, October 6, 1943, in Himmler, *Geheimreden*, 168.

69. Schulte, *Zwangsarbeit und Vernichtung*, 227–31. On the conversion to the defense industry, see Schulte, *Zwangsarbeit und Vernichtung*, 386–88; on the network of subcamps at Flossenbürg, see Kaienburg, *Wirtschaft der SS*, 618.

70. Speech of Himmler to generals in Sonthofen, June 21, 1944, in Himmler, *Geheimreden*, 199.

71. Every second V2 rocket manufactured in the Mittelbau-Dora concentration camp shattered upon reentry into the atmosphere. See Jens-Christian Wagner, *Produktion des Todes: Das KZ Mittelbau-Dora* (Wallstein, 2001), 203.

72. See Heinrich Fraenkel and Roger Manvell, *Himmler, Kleinbürger und Massenmörder* (Ullstein, 1965), 80–126. On the self-image of the SS, see Bernd Wegner, *Hitlers politische Soldaten: Die Waffen-SS 1933–1945. Leitbild, Struktur und Funktion einer nationalsozialistischen Elite* (Schöningh, 1990).

73. See Kaienburg, *Wirtschaft der SS*, 997.

74. See Kaienburg, *Wirtschaft der SS*, 997.

75. As Kaienburg points out, this tendency was not only widespread in the SS but almost representative of the Nazi state, whose economic policy was based on "national isolation." See Kaienburg, *Wirtschaft der SS*, 1006.

76. Kaienburg, *Wirtschaft der SS*, 1010. Kaienburg mentions, among other things, the use of SS construction brigades in clearing up bomb damage, the production of "German pepper" on the "plantation" in Dachau, and the extraction of vitamins from gladioli. The latter two also fall into the category of Himmler's "favorite projects" and show his inclination toward anthroposophy. See Kaienburg, *Wirtschaft der SS*, 1009–16.

77. See Kaienburg, *Wirtschaft der SS*, 1015–16.

78. Kaienburg, *Wirtschaft der SS*, 1016.

79. See Kaienburg, *Wirtschaft der SS*, 1017–19.

80. See *Allgemeine Dienstanweisung für die Schutzhaftlagerführer*, November 7, 1941. Quoted in Kaienburg, *Wirtschaft der SS*, 1056.

81. See Kaienburg, *Wirtschaft der SS*, 1054–58; and Hermann Kaienburg, "KZ-Haft und Wirtschaftsinteresse: Das Wirtschaftsverwaltungshauptamt der SS als Leitungszentrale der Konzentrationslager und der SS-Wirtschaft der SS," in *Konzentrationslager und deutsche Wirtschaft 1939–1945*, ed. Hermann Kaienburg (Leske + Budrich, 1996), 41–44.

82. See Kaienburg, *Wirtschaft der SS*, 1057–59.

83. Letter from Himmler to Pohl, December 5, 1941, BArch, NS 4 GR/6.

84. See Kaienburg, *Wirtschaft der SS*, 694, 1060–61.

85. See Kaienburg, *Wirtschaft der SS*, 672.

86. See Fings, *SS-Baubrigaden*, 40–41.

87. Letter from Himmler to Pohl, March 23, 1942, BArch, NS 19/2065. Kammler had also suggested to Himmler that he introduce "maneuver rations" for the prisoners in the construction brigades. Himmler rejected this and called for "rations similar to the rations of Roman soldiers or the rations of Egyptian slaves, which contain all the vitamins and are simple and cheap" (letter of Himmler to Pohl).

88. In preparation for the attack on the Soviet Union, the Reich Ministry of Economics had already invited the IG Farben managers Fritz ter Meer and Otto Ambros to a secret meeting in 1940. At this meeting they planned to increase the production of synthetic rubber to such an extent that Germany would become independent of raw material supplies. For this purpose, IG Farben's managers decided to build a new factory. See Joseph Borkin, *Die unheilige Allianz der IG Farben: Eine Interessengemeinschaft im Dritten Reich* (Campus Verlag, 1990), 108.

89. See Borkin, *Unheilige Allianz*, 108–9. See also Piotr Setkiewicz, "Häftlingsarbeit im KZ Auschwitz III-Monowitz: Die Frage nach der Wirtschaftlichkeit der Arbeit," in Herbert, Orth, and Diekmann, *Konzentrationslager*, 590.

90. See Van Pelt and Dwork, *Auschwitz*, 217–57.

91. See Borkin, *Unheilige Allianz*, 110–11.

92. Rudolf Höß (1900–1947) came from a strict Catholic family in Baden-Baden. At the age of fifteen he went into the First World War as a volunteer and achieved the rank of noncommissioned officer in 1917. In 1934 he joined the SS and began training for service in the Dachau concentration camp that same year. In 1938 he became adjutant in the Sachsenhausen concentration camp and in 1940 commandant of the Auschwitz concentration camp. At the end of 1943 he took over Department D1 in the WVHA, but at the end of June 1944 he was sent again to Auschwitz to oversee the murder of 430,000 Hungarian Jews in Birkenau. After the war he went into hiding under a false name; he was recognized and arrested in 1946. In 1947 the Supreme Court in Warsaw sentenced him to death. On April 16, 1947, he was executed on the site of the former Auschwitz I concentration camp. See Czech, *Kalendarium*, 1007; Gutman, *Encyclopedia*, 691–92.

93. See Eidesstattl, Erklärung Dipl.-Ing. Fritz Dion, StAN, Rep. 501 KV-Prozesse Fall 6 G 4, Due-784, 2–3; and Setkiewicz, "Häftlingsarbeit im KZ Auschwitz III-Monowitz," 588.

94. Wochenbericht No. 30 (Dec. 15– 21, 1941), APMO, D-Au III-Monowitz/4, 111–12.

95. See Wochenbericht No. 30 (Dec. 15– 21, 1941), 112; and Setkiewicz, "Häftlingsarbeit im KZ Auschwitz III-Monowitz," 584–605.

96. See Setkiewicz, "Häftlingsarbeit im KZ Auschwitz III-Monowitz," 589–93.

97. See Eidesstattl, Erklärung Dürrfeld, February 18, 1947, APMO, D-Au III-Monowitz/4, p.160. The name "Buna" refers to the process for producing synthetic rubber.

98. At the end of 1944, Auschwitz III was renamed "Monowitz Concentration Camp," and all Auschwitz subcamps were placed under it. See Bernd C. Wagner, *IG Auschwitz: Zwangsarbeit und Vernichtung von Häftlingen des Lagers Monowitz 1941–1945* (K. G. Saur, 2000), 96–97.

99. See Kaienburg, *Wirtschaft der SS*, 613.

100. See Eidesstattl, Erklärung Dipl.-Ingenieur Karl Haeseler, StAN, Rep. 501, KV-Prozesse Fall 6 G 4, Due-460.

101. See Eidesstattl, Erklärung Haeseler.

102. Aktennotiz Dürrfeld, meeting Mai 14, 1942, in Working Group of Former Prisoners of the Auschwitz Concentration Camp of the Committee of Anti-Fascist Resistance Fighters in the German Democratic Republic, ed., *IG-Farben-Auschwitz—Mass Murder: On the Guilt of IG-Farben from the Documents on the Auschwitz-Trial* (Halle: n.p., 1964), 18.

103. See Aktennotiz Dürrfeld.

104. The polish Auschwitz survivor Stanisław Hantz remembers that he received bonuses as early as 1942 while working as a carpenter during the construction of the "Sola Bridge," which was to connect the Auschwitz camp directly with the Monowitz plant. The bridge was built for IG Farben. According to Hantz, the command, which consisted of thirty prisoners, received a one-off payment of seven bonus vouchers. See Interview, Sommer 2003-02-01 Hantz, 00.08.00, AMGR, MS Som.

105. See Eidesstattl, Erklärung Haeseler, September 22, 1947, StAN, Rep. 501, KV-Prozesse Fall 6 G 4, Due-460.

106. See Eidesstattl, Erklärung Dipl.-Ing. Fritz Dion, StAN, Rep. 501, KV-Prozesse Fall 6 G 4, Due-784, p. 2–3; and Eidesstattl, Erklärung Albert von Lohm, StAN, Rep. 501, KV-Prozesse Fall 6 G 4, Due-48.

107. See Eidesstattl, Erklärung Ludwig Daub, StAN, Rep. 501, KV-Prozesse Fall 6 G 4, Due-1027.

108. See Eidesstattl, Erklärung Dipl.-Ingenieur Karl Haeseler, StAN, Rep. 501, KV-Prozesse Fall 6 G 4, Due-460.

109. See Eidesstattl, Erklärung Dipl.-Ing. Fritz Dion, StAN, Rep. 501, KV-Prozesse Fall 6 G 4, Due-784, 3.

110. See Eidesstattl, Erklärung Karl Sommer, StAN, Rep. 501, KV-Prozesse Fall 6 G 4, Due-427, 6. On the rejection of the proposal, see Eidesstattl, Erklärung of Gerhard Maurer, StAN, Rep. 501, KV-Prozesse Fall 6 G 4, Due-77, 2–3.

111. Many of the prisoners were Poles, who were generally classified as political prisoners in "protective custody." For these prisoners, the period of imprisonment lasted as long as the SS considered necessary. See the testimony of Häseler, StAN, Rep. 501 KV-Prozesse Fall 6 G 4, Due-460.

112 See Setkiewicz, "Häftlingsarbeit im KZ Auschwitz III-Monowitz," 597.

113. Letter from Himmler to Pohl, March 23, 1942, BArch, NS 19/2065.

114. Letter from Himmler to Pohl, March 5, 1943, IfZ, MA 304/0812. Printed in Helmut Heiber, ed., *Reichsführer! . . . Briefe an und von Himmler* (Deutsche Verlags-Anstalt, 1968), 194–96.

115. See Figure 4. Himmler's work diary contains the following entry for May 31, 1941: "10.00 a.m. journey to Mauthausen/inspection of Mauthausen by SS Group Leader Pohl/afterward: journey to Gmund." See Peter Witte et al., eds., *Der Dienstkalender Heinrich Himmlers 1941/1942* (Christians Verlag, 1999), 165.

116. See Maršálek, *Geschichte des Konzentrationslagers Mauthausen*, 117.

117. See the testimony of Haeseler, StAN, Rep. 501, KV-Prozesse Fall 6 G 4, Due-460.

118. See the discussion on June 3, 1942, in Wochenbericht Nr. 54 (June 1–7,1942), APMO, D-Au III-Monowitz/4, 117.

119. See Kreuzverhör Rudolf Doemming, StAN, Rep. 501, KV-Prozesse Fall 6 G 4, A 47, 14 287–14 288.

120. See Eidesstattl, Erklärung Dürrfeld, February 18, 1947, APMO, D-Au III-Monowitz/4, 160.

121. See letter from Himmler to Pohl, March 5, 1943, IfZ, MA 304/0812. Printed in Heiber, *Reichsführer*, 194–96.

122. Letter from Himmler to Pohl, March 5, 1943.

123. Letter from Himmler to Pohl, March 5, 1943.

124. Letter from Himmler to Pohl, March 5, 1943.

125. Letter from Himmler to Pohl, March 5, 1943.

126. Letter from Himmler to Pohl, March 5, 1943.

127. Letter from Himmler to Pohl, March 5, 1943.

128. Himmler's familiarity with the Soviet model is evident in his letter to Pohl of March 5, 1943. He calls it a "wage and food system," he follows Lenin in talking about a "sluggish Russian people," and he speaks of the "most incredible achievements" of the Soviet system, probably in reference to major construction projects such as the White Sea Canal. Moreover, in a letter to Kammler, Himmler borrowed a Soviet official's description of prisoners as "labor slaves" and suggested that prisoners in the construction brigades should be fed like Roman soldiers or Egyptian slaves. See letter of Himmler to Pohl, March 23, 1943, BArch, NS 19/2065. There is no doubt, in other words, that Himmler knew about the methods employed in the gulags. This is not surprising. The Soviet Union

publicly discussed the role of concentration camps in increasing labor productivity. For another, discipline and reeducation in forced labor camps were subjects of official publications. The most popular example was a volume edited by Maxim Gorki on the White Sea Canal. But most of all, it was the striking similarities regarding prisoner organization, prisoner self-administration, and camp slogans that showed the depth Himmler's familiarity with the Soviet system.

129. Letter from Himmler to Pohl, March 5, 1943, IfZ, MA 304/0812.

130. Letter from Himmler to Chief of RSHA et al., July 20, 1943. Quoted in Heiber, *Reichsführer*, 223.

131. Dienstvorschrift für die Gewährung von Vergünstigungen an Häftlinge, May 15, 1943, BArch, NS 3/426.

132. Dienstvorschrift für die Gewährung von Vergünstigungen an Häftlinge, May 15, 1943.

133. Dienstvorschrift für die Gewährung von Vergünstigungen an Häftlinge, May 15, 1943. Emphasis in original.

134. Dienstvorschrift für die Gewährung von Vergünstigungen an Häftlinge, May 15, 1943.

135. Dienstvorschrift für die Gewährung von Vergünstigungen an Häftlinge, May 15, 1943.

136. Dienstvorschrift für die Gewährung von Vergünstigungen an Häftlinge, May 15, 1943.

137. Worker performance was monitored by the commanders, the administrative heads, and the foremen of the blocks and work details. In the case of prisoners who were deployed in satellite camps in armaments factories, leaders of the respective labor camp were supposed to monitor the prisoners' performance and its improvement in "close contact with the company's operations manager" (Dienstvorschrift für die Gewährung von Vergünstigungen an Häftlinge, May 15, 1943).

138. See Figures 1 and 2.

139. Dienstvorschrift für die Gewährung von Vergünstigungen an Häftlinge, May 15, 1943.

140. The evaluation of prisoner output was to be made by the camp commander or the administrative head. See Dienstvorschrift für die Gewährung von Vergünstigungen an Häftlinge, May 15, 1943.

141. The companies that paid out bonuses (e.g., construction management and commercial and armaments firms) were supposed to buy the bonus vouchers in advance and issue them to the prisoners to be rewarded once a week. See Dienstvorschrift für die Gewährung von Vergünstigungen an Häftlinge, May 15, 1943.

142. The leaflet "Arbeitsvorgang der Häftlingskasse" from the Sachsenhausen concentration camp provides detailed information about the accounting of

prisoners' money from Sachsenhausen concentration camp, BLHA Rep 35 H Nr. 5, 6.

143. Dienstvorschrift für die Gewährung von Vergünstigungen an Häftlinge, May 15, 1943.

144. Dienstvorschrift für die Gewährung von Vergünstigungen an Häftlinge, May 15, 1943.

145. Dienstvorschrift für die Gewährung von Vergünstigungen an Häftlinge, May 15, 1943.

146. Prämien-Vorschrift. Emphasis in original.

147. See Prämien-Vorschrift.

148. See Seidler, *Sanitätsführung*, 146. However, for particularly well-equipped brothels the price could be increased to five Reichsmarks. On brothels for foreign workers, see circular letter of RSHA, June 4, 1942, GLAK, Abt. 330 Zug. 1991/34/Nr. 269.

149. See the testimony of Albin Luedtke, BArch D-H, ZM 1173 A. 1.

150. See Prämien-Vorschrift, BArch, NS 3/426.

151. See Günther Bullerjahn, "Der Sonderbau im KZ-Sachsenhausen," in *KZ Sachsenhausen*, ed. Lucie Großer (Lucie Großer, 1948), 34.

152. See Bauantrag Bauwerk 93, AUSHMM, RG-11.001M Reel 23.

153. This is the amount listed as "collected" on the statements. During this period, the brothel was closed for ten days. Two days are not recorded. These days were not included in the total. See Abrechnungsbögen KZ Buchenwald, BArch, NS 4 Bu/41.

154. Gerhard Maurer (1907–1953) had been a member of the NSDAP since December 1931 and joined the SS in August 1932. From 1939 he worked in the SS Main Office for Administration and Economics and headed the DAW. In March 1942, Maurer became head of the Office Group D II of the WHVA and acted as the central coordinator of the work of the concentration camp prisoners. In November 1943 he was promoted to deputy of the concentration camp inspector Richard Glücks. At the end of the war, he went into hiding with false documents. He was arrested in March 1947, extradited to Poland, sentenced to death in 1952, and executed in 1953. See Tuchel, *Inspektion der Konzentrationslager*, 18.

155. See letter from Maurer to the camp commandants et al., August 13, 1943, BArch, NS 3/426.

156. See letter from Pohl to the camp commandants, October 26, 1943, BArch, NS 3/386.

157. Letter from Pohl to the camp commandants, October 26, 1943.

158. This wasn't necessarily an improvement. A common way of decimating the number of sick people was to murder prisoners "unable to work" using lethal injections or Zyklon-B. For Monowitz, see Wagner, *IG Auschwitz*, 163–92.

159. Letter from Pohl to the camp commandants, October 26, 1943, BArch, NS 3/386.

160. Letter from Pohl to the camp commandants, October 26, 1943.

161. Letter from Pohl to the camp commandants, October 26, 1943.

162. See letter from Pohl to the camp commandants, October 26, 1943.

163. See the testimony of Albin Luedtke, BArch D-H, ZM 1173 A. 1.

164. In 1944, bonuses were distributed in Auschwitz-Birkenau to multiple work units. They included Birkenau prisoner of war camp construction, the clothing workshop, roofing felt unloading, storage facilities for prisoners' personal effects, the fire pond and laboratory in Rajsko, sewer cleaning, painting, SS hairdressing, composting, tower construction, construction office, and road construction. See Prämienscheine Auschwitz, AUSHMM, RG-04.065M Reel 8 und 9.

165. See Wochenbericht, October 18– 31, 1943, APMO, D-Au III-Monowitz/4, 127.

166. 1. Nachtrag zur Dienstvorschrift für die Gewährung von Vergünstigungen an Häftlinge, February 14, 1944, BArch, NS 3/427.

167. At the Buchenwald concentration camp, the cinema was right next to the brothel barracks. See map of Buchenwald, in Hackett, *Buchenwald-Report,* 16.

168. See 1. Nachtrag zur Dienstvorschrift für die Gewährung von Vergünstigungen an Häftlinge vom 14. Februar 1944, BArch, NS 3/427.

169. See Dachauer Häftlinge, *Dachau,* 24.

170. Heinrich Schwarz, order dated April 22, 1944, in Frei, Grotum, Parcer, Steinbacher, and Wagner, *Standort- und Kommandanturbefehle,* 439. SS-Hauptsturmführer Heinrich Schwarz (1906–1947) was camp commandant of Auschwitz III-Monowitz from November 1943 until the evacuation and then commandant of the Natzweiler concentration camp. A French military court sentenced him to death as a war criminal; the sentence was carried out in 1947. See Wagner, *IG Auschwitz,* 109–10; and Jadwiga Bezwinska et al., *KL Auschwitz in den Augen der SS* (Krajnowa Agencja Wydawnicza, 1981), 316.

171. Heinrich Schwarz, order dated April 22, 1944, in Frei, Grotum, Parcer, Steinbacher, and Wagner, *Standort- und Kommandanturbefehle,* 439.

172. See the testimony of Feuchtbaum, APMO, Ośw./Feuchtbaum/1981, 10.

173. See Setkiewicz, "Häftlingsarbeit im KZ Auschwitz III-Monowitz," 598.

174. See Franciszek Piper, *Arbeitseinsatz der Häftlinge aus dem KL Auschwitz* (Verlag Staatliches Museum in Oświęcim, 1995), appendix 22.

175. See Kaienburg, *Wirtschaft der SS,* 613.

176. See Setkiewicz, "Häftlingsarbeit im KZ Auschwitz III-Monowitz," 600.

177. See letter from Schwarz to Bauleitung, June 1, 1943, AUSHMM, RG-11.001M Reel 20 (Auschwitz); and letter of Kommandantur Groß-Rosen, March 18, 1944, AUSHMM, RG-04.006 M Reel 8; and Wolfgang Sanner, "Zwangsarbeitseinsatz der Häftlinge i. K.L. Mauthausen," BArch, NS 4 Ma/57.

178. The brothels opened in Dachau in April 1944, in Neuengamme on Pentecost 1944, and in Sachsenhausen in August 1944. For more, see the respective sections in the appendix.

179. Dr. med. Heinz Baumkötter (1912–2001) was a military doctor at the Mauthausen, Natzweiler, and Wewelsburg concentration camps. In 1942 he was initially assigned to Sachsenhausen as a troop doctor; he then took on the role of first camp doctor there from January 1943 until the "evacuation." In April 1945 he was taken prisoner by the British and was later handed over to the Soviet occupation troops, who accused him of crimes against humanity and large-scale criminal experiments and sentenced him to life imprisonment with forced labor. Baumkötter was a prisoner in the gulag in Vorkuta until January 1956 and was then extradited to the Federal Republic of Germany as a nonamnestied person. In 1962 the Münster regional court reopened proceedings against Baumkötter and sentenced him to eight years in prison. See Mildt and Rüter, *Justiz, Bd. 18*, 216–28; and Astrid Ley and Günter Morsch, *Medizin und Verbrechen: Das Krankenrevier des KZ Sachsenhausen 1936–1945* (Metropol, 2007), 188–90.

180. There is no evidence of the existence of camp brothels in other larger concentration camps such as Majdanek, Natzweiler, Groß-Rosen, and Stutthof. An SS telex has been handed down from Stutthof with the subject "Inmate brothel income," which states: "KL. Stutthof reports no reports of this. No report was made because no brothel had been set up here and the regulations did not state that a report was required" (Telex, January 21, 1944, ITS, Sachdok. Stutthof 5, 291).

181. See Schulte, *Zwangsarbeit und Vernichtung*, 382.

182. See Bertrand Perz, *Projekt Quarz: Steyr-Daimler-Puch und das Konzentrationslager Melk* (Verlag für Gesellschaftskritik, 1991), 148–50; and Schulte, *Zwangsarbeit und Vernichtung*, 406–15.

183. On the history of Dora concentration camp, see Wagner, *Produktion des Todes*.

184. See the testimony of W. Simon. Quoted in Jens-Christian Wagner, "Noch einmal: Arbeit und Vernichtung. Häftlingseinsatz im KL Mittelbau-Dora 1943–1945," in Frei, *Ausbeutung*, 19.

185. See Jens-Christian Wagner, "Noch einmal," 19; and Friedrich Kochheim, *Bilanz. Erlebnisse und Gedanken* (Westkreuz-Verlag, 2003), 74.

186. See Wagner, *Produktion des Todes*, 201–5. Prof. Dr. med. Joachim Mrugowsky (1905–1948) joined the SS in 1931 and became a full-time SS leader in 1935. On a part-time basis he taught "Human Heredity and Racial Hygiene" at the TH Hannover. In 1937 Himmler appointed Mrugowsky head of the Hygiene-Instituts der Verfügungstruppe der SS (Hygiene Institute of the SS Disposition Force). At the same time, he served as a doctor in the bodyguards who protected Adolf Hitler. He completed his habilitation at the University of Halle with a hygienic study of a mining village in the Mannsfelder Land and became a lecturer at Berlin University. From 1943 he was chief hygienist and Amtschef III at the Reichsarzt SS and police department. Mrugowsky took part in numerous medical experiments on concentration camp prisoners, faced charges at the Nuremberg Medical Trial in 1946, and was hanged in 1948 after being sentenced

to death. See Angelika Ebbinghaus and Klaus Dörner, eds., *Vernichten und Heilen. Der Nürnberger Ärzteprozeß und seine Folgen* (Aufbau Taschenbuch, 2001), 636.

187. See Aktenvermerk Telefonat Mrugowsky-Dring, June 26, 1944; and letter of Arbeitsdauer und Leistungsfähigkeit der Häftlinge, July 20, 1944, BArch, NS 48/26.

188. See letter from Wernher von Braun to Sawatzki, August 15, 1944. Quoted in Fröbe, "Reserve," 649.

189. See Robert Sommer, "Das Häftlingsbordell im Kontext der Wirtschaftsinteressen der SS: Das Beispiel Mittelbau-Dora," lecture, November 10, 2003, Nordhausen, print version, AGMD.

190. See Florian Freund, *"Arbeitslager Zement": Das Konzentrationslager Ebensee und die Raketenrüstung* (Verlag für Gesellschaftskritik, 1989), 170.

191. See Perz, *Projekt Quarz*, 331.

192. Karin Graf, *Zitronen aus Kanada: Das Leben mit Auschwitz des Stanisław Hantz. Bibliografische Erzählungen* (Verlag des Staatlichen Museums Auschwitz-Birkenau, n.d.), 77.

193. Eugen Kogon, *The Theory and Practice of Hell: The Classic Account of the Nazi Concentration Camps Used as a Basis for the Nuremberg Investigations*, trans. Heinz Norden (1950; Berkley Books, 1998), 130.

194. On the importance of letters in Mauthausen, see Hans Maršálek, "Das KZ Mauthausen (Stammlager) 1938–1945," in *Oberösterreichische Gedenkstätten für KZ-Opfer*, ed. Land Oberösterreich (Oberösterreichisches Landesarchiv, 2001), 55–56.

195. As I discuss in Chapter 5, the presence of hair was especially important for women's sense of their own sexuality. I have not been able to determine if the haircut privilege was afforded to female prisoners, however.

196. Eidesstattl, Erklärung Dipl.-Ing. Fritz Dion, StAN, Rep. 501KV-Prozesse Fall 6 G 4, Due-784.

197. See Setkiewicz, "Häftlingsarbeit im KZ Auschwitz III-Monowitz," 589.

198. This is evident in the bonus list of the Sachsenhausen subcamp Falkensee for the last week of January 1944. Various camp officials there received relatively high bonuses: the camp elder (3 RM) and the gardening foreman (2 RM). Inmates from the camp office, prisoner nurses, SS hairdressers, stokers, and messengers received far less (1 RM), while prisoners in the kitchen received only 0.50 RM. See Prämienliste Arbeitslager Falkensee, January 15–31, 1944, BLHA, Rep 35 H Nr. 5.

199. See, for instance, Eidesstattl, Erklärung Dipl.-Ing. Fritz Dion, StAN, Rep. 501,KV-Prozesse, Fall 6 G 4, Due-784, 3–4.

200. Kogon, *The Theory and Practice of Hell*, 117. On food in Mauthausen, see Maršálek, "Stammlager," 63–71. A letter from the Buchenwald site doctor Dr. Schiedlausky makes this clear. In an external detachment of the Buchenwald concentration camp, the prisoners were observed to be chronically hungry, "but this cannot be explained because the prisoners received heavy

labor rations" (Gerhard Schiedlausky, letter dated March 17, 1945, in Maršálek, "Stammlager," 140).

3. Recruitment

1. On the history of the Ravensbrück concentration camp, see Bernhard Stebel, *Das KZ Ravensbrück: Geschichte eines Lagerkomplexes* (Ferdinand Schöningh, 2003).

2. On the selection of females from Ravensbrück for brothels, see Sommer, *Sonderbau,* 63–90; Schulz, "Häftlinge," 138–46; Paul, *Zwangsprostitution,* 30–44; Schikorra, *Kontinuitäten,* 195–205; and Halbmayr, "Arbeitskommando," 222–24.

3. Sigmund Rascher (1909–1945) was a concentration camp doctor and friend of Himmler. He carried out various human experiments in the Dachau concentration camp, including "altitude experiments" in 1942, in which he used prisoners to investigate the effects of overpressure on the human organism. Before the end of the war, Rascher was arrested in connection with a case of child abduction and sent to a concentration camp. A few days before the end of the war, the SS executed him in Dachau by shooting him in the neck. See Wolfgang Benz, "Dr. med. Sigmund Rascher—Eine Karriere," *Dachauer Hefte* 4 (1988): 190–214.

4. Classified report (*Geheimbericht*) of Dr. Rascher, February 12, 1943, in Fred Mielke and Alexander Mitscherlich, *Das Diktat der Menschenverachtung: Der Nürnberger Ärzteprozess und seine Quellen* (Schneider, 1947), 44–45.

5. Memorandum of Dr. Rascher, November 5, 1942, AMGR, Bd. 26, 416.

6. See the memorandum of Dr. Rascher; and Engelhardt, *Frauen,* 222.

7. On the "freiwilligen Meldung," see Sommer, *Sonderbau,* 65–68.

8. See also Chapter 1, "Prostitution Policy."

9. Geheimes Schreiben from Himmler to Pohl, November 15, 1942, in Internationaler Militärgerichtshof Nürnberg, *Prozess,* 349.

10. Dr. Gerhard Oskar Schiedlausky (1905–1947) studied in Berlin and Innsbruck. He joined the NSDAP in 1931 and the General SS in 1939. In the same year, he was drafted into the Waffen-SS and worked as a doctor in various concentration camps from 1941 to 1945, including Mauthausen, Flossenbürg, Ravensbrück, Natzweiler, and Buchenwald. He was sentenced to death in the first Ravensbrück trial and executed in Hameln on May 3, 1947. See Silke Schäfer, "Zum Selbstverständnis von Frauen im Konzentrationslager: Das Lager Ravensbrück," PhD diss., Fakultät I Geisteswissenschaften Technische Universität Berlin, 2002, 141–42.

11. See the testimony of Schiedlausky, AMM, K 2/5, 4. The files only showed the criminal records; it was up to the Nazi authorities to classify women as prostitutes.

12. See Edgar Kupfer-Koberwitz, *Dachauer Tagebücher,* 293–94.

13. Testimony of Bruha, IKF, Rav-Int.20_3, 32.

14. Nanda Herbermann, *The Blessed Abyss*, Inmate #6582, in *Ravensbrück Concentration Camp for Women*, trans. Hester Baer (Wayne State University Press, 2000), 131. Buber-Neumann mentions that the SS selected twelve women for the Mauthausen camp brothel in Block 2. This was probably the block described by Herbermann. See Margarete Buber-Neumann, *Als Gefangene bei Stalin und Hitler: Eine Welt im Dunkel* (Ullstein TB, 2002), 228.

15. Statutory declaration (*Eidesstattl. Erklärung*) of Dr. Schiedlausky, March 4, 1947, IfZ, NO 2332, 4. See also the testimony of Ursula Krause about Rascher, in Nürnberger Dokumente, Doc. No. 323. Quoted in Mielke and Mitscherlich, *Diktat*, 44. See also the testimony of Antonia Bruha, in Berger and Holzinger, *Widerstehen im KZ*, 150. A few witnesses mention a different timeframe. Hilde Boy-Brand speaks of about two years. See the testimony of Hilde Boy-Brandt, AMGR, 15/17.

16. Bruha remembers that the SS also promised Roma women that they would be released after six months if they underwent sterilization. See the testimony of Bruha, in Amesberger and Halbmayr, *Wege nach Ravensbrück 2*, 39.

17. See the testimony of Bruha. Quoted in Amesberger, Auer, and Halbmayr, *Sexualisierte Gewalt*, 109.

18. Classified letter from Himmler to Pohl, November 15, 1942, in Internationaler Militärgerichtshof Nürnberg, *Prozess*, 350.

19. See, e.g., Flossenbürg, Interv. Sommer 2003-07-19, Terry, 6; and Hugo Walleitner, *Zebra: Ein Tatsachenbericht aus dem Konzentrationslager Flossenbürg* (self-published, 1947), 97. On Buchenwald, see Weidlich, AMGB, 56-8-4, 7; and Kogon, *The Theory and Practice of Hell*, 214; on Neuengamme, see the testimony from Büttig (Frau X), AGN, transcription, 19; on Dachau, see Kupfer-Koberwitz, *Dachauer Tagebücher*, 294; on Auschwitz, see Interv. Sommer 2005-01-28 S. pt. 1, 00.23.00. See also appendix, "Buchenwald"; and the testimony of Büttig (Frau X), AGN, transcription, 19.

20. "Grunderlass zur vorbeugenden Verbrechensbekämpfung," in Ayaß, *Gemeinschaftsfremde*, 94–98.

21. See the testimony of Henryka Obidzinska, Interv. Sommer 2002-03-16 Obidzinska, 1. Older prisoners had a keen sense for detecting such lies. See Mali Fritz, *Essig gegen den Durst: 565 Tage in Auschwitz-Birkenau* (Verlag für Gesellschaftskritik, 1986), 69–70; and Lundholm, *Höllentor*, 145.

22. Nanda Herbermann reported that the SS requested between eight and ten women for prisoner brothels approximately every three months. As Herbermann was only in Ravensbrück until March 1943, it is likely that she was referring to the selections for women from the brothel commandos in Buchenwald and Flossenbürg. See Herbermann, *The Blessed Abyss*, 131.

23. See Berger and Holzinger, *Widerstehen im KZ*, 150. In the case of M.W., a forced sex worker from Neuengamme, the SS noted on the list of new arrivals in Ravensbrück: "Verkehr mit Polen" (intercourse with Poles). See Zugangsliste May 5, 1944, AMGR, MF Nr. 135 Sygn. 66, 20–22.

24. Bruha did not provide any further details about the woman named. See the testimony of Bruha, IKF, Rav-Int.20_3, 33; and Berger and Holzinger, *Widerstehen im KZ*, 149.

25. Antonia Bruha even speaks of women coming forward "in droves for a brothel commando" (testimony of Bruha, IKF, Rav-Int.20_3, 32).

26. "Angeforderter Bericht über KL-Dirnen," November 5, 1942, in Mielke and Mitscherlich, *Diktat*, 44.

27. Herbermann, *The Blessed Abyss*, 131.

28. According to her prison records, Frieda came from Königsberg and was a laborer. First, she was forced to do sex work in the brothel in Mauthausen, and then in Gusen. On April 12, 1945, she was deployed in Gusen as a *Häftlingsaufseher*, or prisoner supervisor. See Zugangsliste Ravensbrück, September 28, 1940, AMGR, AGGB, 01012601. Herbermann's description of the "beautiful, little Frieda" corresponds to information provided in the prison records of F.S. indicating that she was just over five feet tall. See Zugangsliste Frauenlager Mauthausen (AMGR, AGGB, 030259) and Häftlings-Personal-Karte, NARA, Arolsen Bestand, Reel 7. The Spaniard Salvador Ginestrà describes her as "exceptionally beautiful" (David Wingate Pike, *Spaniards in the Holocaust: Mauthausen, the Horror on the Danube* [Johns Hopkins University Press, 2000], 335). Maršálek describes her as a "sehr hübsche Frau" (very pretty woman) (Maršálek, testimony, IKF, H. Marsalek Video-Int. 2, 15). She is the only woman named Frieda in the Mauthausen camp brothel we know of.

29. See the testimony of Bruha, IKF, Rav-Int.20_3, 33.

30. I don't consider *Puffmütter* (madams), *Kassiererinnen* (cashiers), *Häftlings-Aufseherinnen* (prisoner supervisors), or *aufsichtsführende Häftlinge* (supervising prisoners) to be forced sex workers, since their work lay outside sex.

31. See the testimony of N.N., AGN, 2.8./1391, p. 4–5; WVHA-Häftlingskartei (Ne 6305), BArch D-H, NS 3/1577.

32. This is C.S. See the testimony of the witness H.N. in the lawsuit against Hertha Ehlert before the Landgericht Frankfurt/Main, March 9, 1974, BArch Ludwigsburg, Sig. 162-9808.

33. See Urteil in Strafsache gegen M.M. wegen Verbrechen gegen die Menschlichkeit, May 3, 1952, BStU, MfS—HA IX/11AV 8/74, Bd. 37, 454–58.

34. See Zugangsliste of KZ Ravensbrück, June 12, 1944 (transport from Riga), AMGR, AGGB, 01097102.

35. There is evidence of punishments in Ravensbrück in the case of some female forced sex workers. A.E., a former forced sex worker in Buchenwald, reported to the US Army that in Ravensbrück she had received twenty-five lashes from a bullwhip and was locked inside a dark room for eight weeks. The reason for her punishment is not known. Magdalena Walter testified that Mrs. C.S. and another woman had escaped from Ravensbrück but were recaptured and punished by the SS. See Military Government of Germany, Fragebogen für

Insassen der Konzentrationslager, ITS, KLD/Buchenwald, envelope Nr. 4519; and the testimony of M.W. (1988), WdE, Sig. 295, 5–6.

36. Testimony of Casadell, in Neus Català, *"In Ravensbrück ging meine Jugend zu Ende": Vierzehn spanische Frauen berichten über ihre Deportation in deutsche Konzentrationslager*, trans. Dorothee von Keitz and Andreas Ruppert (Walter Frey, 1994), 91.

37. The name is a pseudonym. The camp lockup, referred to in German as a punishment block, was a kind of concentration camp within a concentration camp. It involved constant deprivation, hard labor, and daily abuse. For more on the punishment block, see Herbermann, *The Blessed Abyss*, 132.

38. Testimony of M.W., WdE, Sig. 295, 20.

39. This was the Buchenwald commandant Hermann Pister.

40. Testimony of M.W., WdE, Sig. 295, 20.

41. On Flossenbürg, see Walleitner, *Zebra*, 93–94. Laura Büttig, who worked in the Neuengamme camp brothel, describes a similar practice. See the testimony of Büttig (Frau X), AGN, transcription, 4.

42. Testimony of Henryka Obidzinska, Interv. Sommer 2002-03-16 Obidzinska, 00.08.00.

43. Testimony of Nada Verbic, AGN, NG 2.8., Bericht 1093, transcription, 5.

44. The name is a pseudonym.

45. Testimony of L.B., WdE, Sig. 294T, 9.

46. Testimony of Irma Ostermann, AMGR, 18/111.

47. See the testimony of Hilde Boy-Brandt, AMGR, 15/17.

48. Testimony of Kramer, in Niemeyer and von der Tann, *Schweigen*. The name "Anni Kramer" is a pseudonym.

49. Testimony of M.W., WdE, Sig. 295, 21.

50. Testimony of M.W.

51. Testimony of M.W.

52. See the testimony of L.B., WdE, Sig. 294T, 10.

53. Testimony of L.B.

54. Testimony of L.B.

55. Testimony of Maršálek, IKF, H. Marsalek: Video-Int. 2, 14–15.

56. Testimony of L.B., WdE, Sig. 294T, 10.

57. Testimony of L.B., 10–11.

58. See the testimony of L.B., 21.

59. Testimony of L.B., 27.

60. Bruha escaped punishment because the SS doctor Dr. Treite sympathized with her behavior and destroyed the punishment report. See the testimony of Bruha, IKF, Rav-Int.20_3, 34; Bruha, in Berger and Holzinger, *Widerstehen im KZ*, 150.

61. See the testimony of Bruha, IKF, Rav-Int.20_3, 33. Linda Bachmann reports matter-of-factly that in 1945 the SS took women "who still looked

somewhat like something. And who were young, above all" (testimony of L.B., WdE, Sig. 294T, 11).

62. Testimony of Büttig (Frau X), AGN, transcription, 4. The name "Laura Büttig" is a pseudonym.

63. Testimony of Bruha, IKF, Rav-Int.20_3, 33.

64. See Halbmayr, "Arbeitskommando," 222.

65. Testimony of Maršálek, IKF, H. Marsalek Video-Int. 2, 16.

66. See the testimony of L.B., WdE, Sig. 294T, 10.

67. See the remark from Mlada Tauferova, AMGR, 29/507, 2; and the testimony of Bruha, in Berger and Holzinger, *Widerstehen im KZ*, 149; Irma Trksak, in Holzinger, *Widerstehen im KZ*, 124.

68. See the testimony of Bruha, IKF, Rav-Int.20_3, 33. The medical experiments involved the testing of sulfonamides, which were regarded as a miracle cure for syphilis. For sulfonamide experiments, see the letter from Himmler to Grawitz dated November, 11 1942, BArch, NS 19/111.

69. See Seidler, *Probleme der deutschen Sanitätsführung*, 154; Schulz, "Häftlinge," 139; Paul, *Zwangsprostitution*, 106; Meinen, *Wehrmacht und Prostitution*, 214; and Amesberger, Auer, and Halbmayr, *Sexualisierte Gewalt*, 105.

70. Testimony of Bruha, IKF, Rav-Int.20_3, 33. This is similar to Berger and Holzinger, *Widerstehen im KZ*, 149.

71. Testimony of a Polish survivor. Quoted in Amesberger, Auer, and Halbmayr, *Sexualisierte Gewalt*, 119.

72. See the testimony of Antonia Frexedes, in Català, *Jugend zu Ende*, 101.

73. This applies to the archival collection RW 2 Chef OKW and RW 6 (Allgemeines Wehrmachtsamt) at the Bundesarchiv-Militärarchiv Freiburg. In the collection RH 12–23 (Army Medical Inspection), there are also records relating to prostitution in connection with the fight against venereal diseases. None suggest that female prisoners were selected for Wehrmacht brothels.

74. See Meinen, *Wehrmacht und Prostitution*, 131–92.

75. "Sûreté nationale de La Rochelle au commissaire central." Quoted in Meinen, *Wehrmacht und Prostitution*, 205.

76. See the testimony of Krystyna Razinska, AG, NG 2.8., Bericht 1584, transcription, 18–19; and the testimony of Obidzinska, Interv. Sommer 2002-03-16 Obidzinska, 00.08.00.

77. Lundholm, *Höllentor*, 124, 166–67.

78. Testimony of M.W. 1988, WdE, Sig. 295, 21. In another interview, she speaks of bordellos for the "Yugoslav SS."

79. Lundholm, *Höllentor*, 143.

80. In the period from February 26 to March 7, 1944, the names of the Polish women W.C. and B.M. appeared on job sheets from the "Sonderbau." It is clear that they were working in the brothel for Ukrainian guards in Buchenwald. See Abrechnungsbögen Häftlingsbordell, BArch, NS 4 Bu/41.

81. Fernschreiben vom KZ Buchenwald an den Lagerkommandanten des K.L. Ravensbrück, March 29, 1944, ThHStA, KZ und Haftanstalten Buchenwald Nr. 10, 587.

82. Zugangsliste Ravensbrück March 11, 1944, AMGR, AGGB, 01069801.

83. See also Strebel, *KZ Ravensbrück*, 209.

84. J.U. later had to work in the Sachsenhausen camp brothel. She had probably been a forced sex worker in the Flossenbürg camp brothel before that. See Schreiben betr. Häftlinge für den Sonderbau SH, October 5, 1944, AMGR, AGGB, 03017001; and Appendix, "Sachsenhausen."

85. Zugangsliste Ravensbrück, February 15, 1944, AGGB, 01062702. See also Schikorra, "Prostitution," 121; and Strebel, *KZ Ravensbrück*, 209.

86. It is likely that these women had become infected with gonorrhea or syphilis in the Ukrainian guard's brothel. The prevalence of these diseases among Ukrainian SS men is indicated by a surviving index card listing the men who were barred from visiting the brothel. See Tripper und Lueskarteien, BArch, NS 4 Fl/388.

87. Lundholm, *Höllentor*, 125.

88. See Antonia Bruha, IKF, Rav-Int.20_3, 37. It is estimated that thirty women returned to Ravensbrück from the camp brothels. Fewer than fifteen returned from the brothels for Ukrainian guards. See Robert Sommer, Forced Sex Worker Database, last updated 11/2020, AMGR, MS_Sommer.

89. On the length of the stay of the women from Ravensbrück in camp brothels, see Appendix, "Mauthausen and Gusen," "Flossenbürg," "Buchenwald," "Dachau," "Neuengamme," and "Sachsenhausen."

90. Hilde Boy-Brandt testified that she had once seen a woman come back pregnant. In that case, too, an abortion was carried out immediately. See the testimony of Hilde Boy-Brandt, AMGR, 15/17. It is possible that she was a woman from the Neuengamme brothel. See Christiansen, Lebenslauf, AGN, 2.8./1273, 95; and Appendix, "Neuengamme."

91. See the Meldung von C. T. wegen Zerschneidens eines Bettlakens zum Fertigen von Privatkleidung, February 14, 1944, BArch, NS 4 Fl/371. Since the woman's name can no longer be found on the transfer list of women for the "Sonderbau" from September 1944, it can be assumed that she was returned to Ravensbrück and put on a penal work detail. See Überstellliste, September 17, 1944, AMGR, AGGB, 02006901.

92. See the Schreiben betr. Häftlinge für den Sonderbau SH, October 5, 1944, AMGR, AGGB, 03017001.

93. Testimony of Bruha, IKF, Rav-Int.20_3, 36.

94. M.W. mentioned that the women for the SS brothels were also recruited in the punishment block. See the testimony of M.W., AGN, KZ-SyS. 1.4.4.2-267 W., 6.

95. Testimony of M.W., WdE, Sig. 294T, 21.

96. The exception is the false testimony of Ms. D discussed in Chapter 1.

97. Testimony of Bruha, IKF, Rav-Int.20_3, 35–36.

98. See the testimony of Bruha., 36.

99. Testimony of Irma Ostermann, AMGR, 18/111.

100. See Czech, *Kalendarium*, 5, 189; Strebel, *KZ Ravensbrück*, 340–55; Irena Strzelecka, "Die Frauenabteilung im Stammlager," in *Hefte von Auschwitz* 20 (1997); and Franciszek Piper, "Die Zahl der Opfer von Auschwitz," in *Auschwitz: Nationalsozialistisches Konzentrationslager*, ed. Staatliches Museum Auschwitz-Birkenau (Verlag Staatliches Museum Auschwitz-Birkenau, 1997), 284.

101. Most women in the transport were classified as "antisocial" or "criminal." See Strebel, *KZ Ravensbrück*, 347.

102. See Robert Sommer, Forced Sex Worker Database, last updated 11/2020, AMGR, MS_Sommer.

103. Langbein, *People in Auschwitz*, 406. Maria Mandel (1912–1947) worked as a guard at the Lichtenburg concentration camp from October 1938 to May 1939 and then at Ravensbrück until October 1942. She was then transferred to Auschwitz, where she rose to the position of head guard. The prisoners gave her the name Maria-der-Tod ("Maria Death"). In November 30, 1944, she became a supervisor at the Mühldorf concentration camp. She was captured in 1947 and later sentenced to death by a Polish court in Krakow and hanged. See Czech, *Kalendarium*, 1012.

104. See Jenny Spritzer, *Ich war 10 291: Tatsachenbericht einer Schreiberin der politischen Abteilung aus dem Konzentrationslager Auschwitz* (Verlag Darmstädter Blätter, 1980), 117.

105. Millu, *Smoke Over Birkenau*, 174. Neither the name nor nationality of the young woman could be verified by using documents from Auschwitz. It is most likely that the woman is fictional. See Robert Sommer, Forced Sex Worker Database, last updated 11/2020, AMGR, MS_Sommer.

106. Krystina Zywulska, *Wo vorher Birken waren: Überlebensbericht einer jungen Frau aus Auschwitz-Birkenau* (Verlag Darmstädter Blätter 1980), 58–59.

107. See Zywulska, *Wo vorher Birken waren*, 58–59.This was not an isolated case, as Zofia Bator's statement shows: "Once it was announced that they were looking for volunteers to do 'light work' and she signed up for 'light work' without knowing what that was" (testimony of Bator, APMO, Ośw/68/Bator, 28).

108. Testimony of Bator.

109. Millu, *Smoke Over Birkenau*, 171–72. There were also women for whom loyalty and virginity were irrefutable values and who would have preferred death to forced sex work in a brothel. See Liana Millu, *Die Brücken von Schwerin* (Fischer Taschenbuch, 2001), 54.

110. SS-Hauptsturmführer Franz Hössler (1906–1945) was a photographer by profession and began serving in the Dachau concentration camp in 1933. From September 1942 to May 1944, Hössler was the camp director of the Auschwitz-Birkenau women's camp. At his side stood the senior supervisor Maria Mandel. From the end of February 1945 to April 16, 1945, he held this position in the

Mittelbau-Dora concentration camp. Hössler took the last evacuation transport to Bergen-Belsen and became the deputy camp commander there. After the war, a British military court sentenced Hössler to death. He was executed on December 13, 1945. See Alexandra-Eileen Wenck, *Zwischen Menschenhandel und "Endlösung": Das Konzentrationslager Bergen-Belsen* (Schöningh Verlag, 2000), 359; and the testimony of Franz Hössler, APMO, Ośw./Hössler/329; and Bezwinska and Czech, *Augen der SS*, 306–7.

111. Langbein, *People in Auschwitz*, 406. A former prisoner in the camp fire brigade found out about the falseness of that promise from his friend, who had been working as an interpreter for Hössler. See the testimony of Dubitzki, Interv. Sommer 2004-04-06 D., pt. 2, 00.01.00.

112. Langbein, *People in Auschwitz*, 406.

113. Testimony of Dubitzki, Interv. Sommer 2004-04-06 D., pt. 1, 00.44.00.

114. The name is a pseudonym.

115. See, e.g., Begleitzettel, October 4, 1943, APMO, Akta HI Rajsko 391/20a.

116. See the testimony of I.M., in Szymanski, Interv. Sommer 2005-01-28 S., pt. 1, 00.23.00.

117. See the testimony of Franz Hössler, APMO, Ośw./Hössler/329, 152.

118. See Hans Bludau and Herta Burger, *Ausführung und Beurteilung serologischer Untersuchungsverfahren: Arbeitsanweisungen für Laboratorium und Klinik der Waffen-SS, Berlin, Heft 2.*, ed. Joachim Mrugowsky (Urban & Schwarzenberg, 1942).

119. Testimony of Bator, APMO, Ośw/68/Bator.

120. Fritz Klein worked as a doctor at the Auschwitz concentration camp and then in Neuengamme from December 1943 to December 1944. See the testimony of Klein, APMO, Ośw./Klein/332, 147. Josef Mengele (1911–1979) was the camp doctor at Auschwitz-Birkenau and notorious for his experiments on inmates. After the war he fled Germany, setting off a global manhunt. He was never caught. See Czech, *Kalendarium*, 1012–14.

121. Testimony of Klein, APMO, Ośw./Klein/332, 147.

122. See Spritzer, *Ich war 10291*, 117. The Political Department was located at the Auschwitz main camp in the immediate vicinity of Crematorium 1. Jenny Spritzer worked there as a secretary.

123. Spritzer, *Ich war 10291*, 117. Pery Broad (1921–1993) joined the Waffen-SS as a foreigner in 1941. After his time on guard duty in Auschwitz, he was transferred to the Political Department in June 1942, where he carried out interrogations together with Grabner. After the war he was arrested several times, charged, and sentenced to four years in prison in 1965. See Czech, *Kalendarium*, 1001.

124. See the testimony of Dr. Wolken, APMO, Ośw./Wolken/27; and Langbein, *People in Auschwitz*, 406–7. Carl Clauberg (1898–1957) was an associate professor of gynecology in Königsberg and an SS reserve group leader. Starting in 1943 he carried out experiments in Block 10 at the Auschwitz main camp in

search of a cheap and efficient method of sterilizing women. After the evacuation of Auschwitz, he continued his medical experiments in Ravensbrück. In 1948 he was sentenced to twenty-five years in prison in the Soviet Union but was released early in 1955. After his return to West Germany, he was arrested but died before the trial began. See Czech, *Kalendarium*, 1002.

125. See Image 17. The earliest verifiable study of women selected for a camp brothel squad is the individual examination of E.K. See Begleitzettel, September 18, 1943, APMO, Akta HI Rajsko 152/20. The first verifiable examination of twenty-one women occurred on September 27, 1943. See Begleitzettel, APMO, Akta HI Rajsko, 22/20. Brewda speaks of twenty-five women. See R. J. Minney, *I Shall Fear No Evil: The Story of Dr. Alina Brewda* (Kimber, 1966), 120.

126. See Begleitzettel, Block 24a, October 4, 1943, APMO, Akta HI Rajsko, 391/20a.

127. See Regelmäßige Untersuchung des Bordells in Monowitz, November 15, 1943, APMO, Akta HI Rajsko, 1201/23.

128. In November/December 1943 four women were selected for both Auschwitz brothels (Begleitzettel Block 10, December 23, 1943, APMO, Akta HI Rajsko, 231/26 and 562/24). In March/April 1944 six women were selected (Begleitzettel Block 10, March 9, 1944, APMO, Akta HI Rajsko, 821/30; and Begleitzettel Einzeluntersuchungen April 19, 1944, APMO, Akta HI Rajsko, 117/32b, 115/32b, 121/32b and 137/32b). In June 1944 thirteen women were again selected for brothel services (Begleitzettel [Wa.R. and Go tests] of Block 10, June 2, 1944, APMO, Akta HI Rajsko, 683/38 and 394/9).

129. See Begleitzettel Go/Wa.R.-Untersuchungen Block 24a, January 10, 1945, APMO, Akta HI Rajsko, 95/62; and Liste Zugänge Mittelbau-Dora from Bergen-Belsen February 18, 1945, AGMD, DMD-D1b, Bd.5, Bl. 113.

130. See Robert Sommer, Forced Sex Worker Database, last updated 11/2020, AMGR, MS_Sommer.

131. See Aufnahmebestätigung von vier Frauen, November 2, 1944, Stadtarchiv Oświęcim, Zespot Bürgermeister Segr. Ftezka 33.

132. See Simha Naor, *Krankengymnastin in Auschwitz: Aufzeichnungen des Häftlings Nr. 80574* (Herder, 1989), 86–88.

133. See Begleitzettel für venerologische Untersuchungen (Go) Block 24a August 28, 1944, APMO, Akta HI Rajsko, 70/46, 767/53, 74/61 and 189/62; and Robert Sommer, Forced Sex Worker Database, last updated 11/2020, AMGR, MS_Sommer.

134. See the testimony of Havas, APMO, Oświ./88/Havas, 88.

135. See the testimony of Wiśniewska, APMO, Oświ./Wiesniewska/1164, 100.

136. Testimony of Bator, APMO, Oświ/68/Bator, 133–82.

137. Testimony of Bator.

138. Testimony of Bator.

139. See the testimony of Bator. Prisoners from the kitchen detail were also regularly examined for infectious disease. See Begleitliste für Stuhl- und

Blutproben von Häftlingen des Küchenkommandos, APMO, Akta HI Rajsko, 63/26c.

140. See Strebel, *KZ Ravensbrück*, 459–502.

141. See Appendix, "Mauthausen and Gusen," "Dachau," and "Auschwitz and Monowitz," as well as Tables 1, 7, 8.

142. See Edwin Black, *IBM and the Holocaust: The Strategic Alliance Between Nazi Germany and America's Most Powerful Corporation* (Crown, 2001), 333–74. "Recorded by Hollerith" stamps can be found on prisoner personnel cards. See, e.g., Häftlings-Personal-Karte C.S., AUSHMM, 1996.A.0342 Reel 120. For more on the WVHA plan, see Johannes Ibel, *Vorläufige Dokumentation der bekannten Teile der WVHA-Häftlingskartei: 148.247 Häftlingskarten in deutschen und polnischen Archiven* (Unpublished report, Flossenbürg, 2004), AGF.

143. All information was coded numerically and entered in a box next to each term. If the referral office was the Gestapo, 01 was entered in the adjacent box. For the Kripo, the code was 02. For gender, 01 was male and 02 female. Job titles were coded with three-digit numbers. A factory worker was given the number 790; a sales clerk received the number 554. See WVHA-Kartei ("Hollerith-Vorkartei"), BArch, NS 3/1577.

144. Such cards have survived from all ten forced sex workers from Neuengamme. There are two different cards from one of the women (Ng 6306) and two "cashiers." There are also index cards from twenty women at the Mauthausen and Gusen camp brothels, as well as one at Dachau. See WVHA-Kartei ("Hollerith-Vorkartei"), BArch, NS 3/1577 and Figures 15 and 16.

145. The note "*für Sonderzwecke*" (for special purposes) was used exclusively for women from the Neuengamme brothel. In one case, the SS described the work there as "*Sonder-Arb. Prostit*" (*Sonder-Arbeit Prostitution*/special work prostitution). See WVHA-Kartei, BArch, NS 3/1577.

146. If the SS used the work detail "for special purposes," they coded it with the number 798. "Sonder-Arb. Prostit." received the code 899. See WVHA-Kartei ("Hollerith-Vorkartei"), BArch, NS 3/1577.

147. See Schulte, *Wirtschaftsimperium*, 384.

148. They were assigned the numbers 89251 to 89265. The exact day the transport arrived is unknown. It must have been in the last days of November 1944. On November 29, a girl was born in Birkenau; she was given the number 89325. See Czech, *Kalendarium*, 936.

149. These are the women with the numbers 89259, 89261, and 89264. The last number does not appear on the transfer list to Mittelbau-Dora. One finds instead the number 89254, which belonged to a forced sex worker from Block 24a. But this was most likely a typo. See Liste Zugänge Mittelbau-Dora aus Bergen-Belsen February 18, 1945, AGMD, DMD-D1b, Bd.5, Bl. 113; and Begleitzettel, January 10, 1945, APMO, Akta HI Rajsko, 95/62.

150. The two women from AL Velten were of Polish origin; the one from Auer was German. See Veränderungsmeldung, January 23, 1945, AGS, D1A 1/26.

151. See Veränderungsmeldung Sachsenhausen January 22, 1945, AUSHMM, RG-11001M Reel 85.

152. See the testimony of Georgette W. Quoted in Baumgartner, *Die vergessenen Frauen*, 170.

153. See the testimony of SS-Hauptsturmführer Karl Sommer. Quoted in Wenck, *Bergen-Belsen*, 343.

154. Wenck, *Bergen-Belsen*. See also Rolf Keller, ed., *Konzentrationslager Bergen-Belsen: Berichte und Dokumente* (Vandenhoeck und Ruprecht, 1995).

155. See Appendix, "Mittelbau-Dora."

156. Testimony of L.B., WdE, Sig. 294T, 11.

157. See the testimony of L.B. Bachmann stated that she was transferred to Bergen-Belsen in January 1945. However, it can be assumed that she didn't arrive there until February or possibly March 1945. Their transport reached the Mittelbau-Dora concentration camp at the end of March. For more, see Appendix, "Mittelbau-Dora."

158. Andreas Pflock, "'Bitteschön, und jetzt können Sie mich verhaften': Ilse Stephan," in Füllberg-Stolberg et al., *Frauen*, 294.

159. See Pflock, "Ilse Stephan," 294.

4. Space and Organization

1. Wolfgang Sofsky, *The Order of Terror: The Concentration Camp*, trans. William Templer (Princeton University Press, 1999), 47.

2. See Sofsky, *The Order of Terror*, 47–48.

3. See Ute Wrocklage, "Neuengamme," in Hoffmann, *Gedächtnis*, 185; and Sofsky, *The Order of Terror*, 50.

4. See Sofsky, *The Order of Terror*, 48.

5. See Sofsky, *The Order of Terror*, 52.

6. See Sofsky, *The Order of Terror*, 52–53.

7. See Figure 6.

8. In Buchenwald, the brothel for the Ukrainian guards was set up outside the prisoner camp. See Chapter 1, "SS Brothels."

9. Liebehenschel to commandants of KZ Sachsenhausen, Dachau, Neuengamme, and Auschwitz, June 15, 1943, BArch, NS 3/426.

10. Liebehenschel to commandants.

11. See Naujoks, *Leben*, 83–86.

12. See Staatliches Museum Auschwitz-Birkenau, eds., *Auschwitz: A History in Photographs* (Auschwitz-Birkenau State Museum, 1999), 63.

13. Wolfgang Sofsky, *Zeiten des Schreckens: Amok, Terror, Krieg* (S. Fischer, 2002), 223.

14. See Betlen, *Leben*, 528; and Sofsky, *The Order of Terror*, 53–54.

15. Letter from Glücks to commandants of KZ Dachau, Sachsenhausen, Buchenwald, et al. November 10, 1943, BArch, NS 3/426.

16. See Appendix, "Sachsenhausen."

17. See aerial photograph of the camp in Detlef Hoffmann, "Dachau," in *Das Gedächtnis der Dinge: KZ-Relikte und KZ-Denkmäler 1945–1995*, ed. Detlef Hoffmann (Campus, 1998), 41.

18. See KZ-Gedenkstätte Neuengamme, ed., *Zeitspuren: Die Ausstellungen. Dreisprachige Ausgabe: Deutsch—English—Français* (Edition Temmen, 2005), cover.

19. For Buchenwald, see Figure 25; and Weidlich, "Sonderbau," AMGB, Sig 31-494, 5. For Dachau, see Figure 27; and Kalmar, *Zeit*, 172.

20. See the testimony of Terry, Interv. Sommer 2003-07-19 Terry, 4.

21. As I discuss earlier in the book, the SS used the term *Sonder* ("special") as a general euphemism for killing (*Sonderbehandlung*), as well as for the camp brothel buildings (*Sonderbauten*). For more on the location of mass murder in the camps, see Sofsky, *The Order of Terror*, 53–54.

22. The stench of the nearby crematorium wafted into the brothel. See Kalmar, *Zeit*, 173–75.

23. See Figure 6. In Auschwitz, the construction of the brothel was planned between the camp prison and the death zone. See Appendix, "Auschwitz." In Neuengamme, the SS locked women slated for execution in the brothel because it was the only place for female prisoners in the main camp and was isolated from the rest of the site. See the testimony of Büttig (Frau X), AGN, transcription, 24–25.

24. See letter of chief of SIPO and SD, January 16, 1941, GLAK, Abt. 330 Zug. 1991/34/Nr. 269.

25. Erlass RMI, July 12, 1934. Quoted in Freund-Widder, *Kontrolle*, 118.

26. See Freund-Widder, *Kontrolle*, 118–26.

27. See Eduard Fuchs, *Illustrierte Sittengeschichte: Renaissance* (Albert Langen Verlag 1909), 418–19.

28. See, in particular, Stefanie Endlich, "Die äußere Gestalt des Terrors: Zu Städtebau und Architektur des Konzentrationslagers," in Benz/Distel, *Ort I*, 210–29. The comparison with urban spatial planning is by no means absurd. A former prisoner of Mittelbau-Dora described the concentration camps as "cities without women" (Kochheim, *Bilanz*, 71).

29. See Appendix, "Auschwitz."

30. This area contained the warehouses, workshops, administration barracks, and the kitchens. See Frankenthal, *Rückkehr*, 150–51. As I discuss in the Appendix, Monowitz was originally conceived as a camp for foreign workers, and IG Farben and the SS had to improvise when it came time to create a camp brothel—this explains the unique shape of its brothel building.

31. See Schreiben des Bürgermeisters von Linz an die Zweigstelle Ostmark des Reichsarbeitsministers, March 18, 1940 betr. u.a. Bau eines Tschechenbordells, SdtAL, Bestand Neubau Städte/Bauvorgang Tschechenbordell.

32. See floor plan and cross-sectional view of "Fr.-Haus," SdtAL, Bestand Neubau Städte/Bauvorgang Tschechenbordell. On the history of Villa Nova, see Rafetseder, *Ausländereinsatz*, 1163–67.

33. See Bauakte Johann-Justus-Weg 2, September 17, 1939 to February 19, 1947, Stadtarchiv Oldenburg, FD Bauordnung und Denkmalschutz, no signature.

34. See Bestandsskizze Baracke 1, AMM, no signature.

35. On the construction history of the camp prisons, see Andreas Ehresmann, "Der Zellenbau im Konzentrationslager Ravensbrück—Eine bautypologische Annäherung," in *Ravensbrück: Der Zellenbau. Geschichte und Gedenken. Begleitband zur Ausstellung*, ed. Insa Eschebach (Metropol, 2008), 50–73.

36. See Appendix and Figure 5.

37. See Chapter 4, "Administration."

38. See Erläuterungsbericht zum Vorentwurf für die Erstellung eines Häftlings-Sonderbaus im Konzentrationslager Flossenbürg/Opf., BArch, NS 4 Fl/183.

39. See Bestandsblatt Bauwerk Häftlings-Sonderbau, BArch, NS 4 Fl/185.

40. See Figures 7 and 8.

41. See Figure 8; and Sofsky, *The Order of Terror*, 47.

42. See Baubefehl 406, August 6, 1942 and Schreiben Bauinspektion der Waffen-SS und Polizei, September 14, 1942, BArch, NS 4 Fl/183.

43. Construction began in August 28, 1942, when forty prisoners were set to work laying the foundations. The SS charged the SS-WVHA 30 Reichspfennigs per prisoner per day. See Abrechnung Häftlingseinsatz für Bauwerk 17 (Sonderbau), BArch, NS 4 Fl/183.

44. See Aktenvermerk November 7, 1942, BArch, NS 4 Fl/183.

45. See Baubefehl Nr. 666, November 27, 1942, in Schreiben Bauinspektion der Waffen-SS und Polizei Reich-Süd, December 5, 1942; and Bauzeichnung, BArch, NS 4 Fl/183.

46. "Wehoba" stood for Weilheimer Holzbau-Hallen-Barackenbau, a Bavarian company that specialized in the manufacture of wooden structures.

47. See Letter, Bauverwaltung Dachau, January 18, 1943, BArch, NS 4 Fl/183. The raw stones for the foundations were ordered from DEST and delivered from the nearby quarry.

48. See Kostenberechnung für Häftlings-Sonderbau, February 12, 1943, BArch, NS 4 Fl/185.

49. See Vollzugsmeldung, March 25, 1944, BArch, NS 4 Fl/185.

50. See Baubefehl Nr. 1064, May 28, 1943, BArch, NS 4 Fl/185.

51. See Figures 5 and 9; and Bestandsplan des "Häftlings-Sonderbaus," BArch, NS 4 Fl/185.

52. Letter from Chef der Amtsgruppe D, December 15, 1943, BArch, NS 3/426. Richard Glücks (1889–1945) became a member of the NSDAP in 1930 and of the SS in 1932. At the end of July 1933, he took over the position of *Stabsführers des SS-Oberabschnitts* West, and in March 1936 he was appointed to be the *Stabsführer des Inspekteurs der Konzentrationslager*. From November 1939 until the end of the war he was *Inspekteur der Konzentrationslager*, and because the IKL had been incorporated into the WVHA, he was also "head of Office

Group D" (*Chef der Amtsgruppe D*). In May 1945 he evaded arrest in the Flensburg-Mürwik naval hospital by killing himself with cyanide. See Tuchel, *Inspektion der Konzentrationslager*, 58–61.

53. See Chapter 1, "SS Brothels."

54. See Bestandsblatt BW 18/1942, April 4, 1944, BArch, NS 4 Fl/185; and Figure 9.

55. On the plan, the bedrooms are labeled "2 Per[sonen].," and the brothel rooms are labeled "Ka." (i.e., "Cabinets"). See Figure 10.

56. See the testimony of M.W., WdE, Sig. 295, 23.

57. See Bordellschein, in Sommer, *Sonderbau*, 97; and Autorenkollektiv, "Sonderbau," 3. For Mittelbau-Dora, see the testimony of L.B., WdE, Sign. 294T, 29. The only exception is Neuengamme, whose brothel had a doctor's room. See the testimony of Büttig (Frau X), AGN, transcription, 17.

58. RAD barrack huts were designed for the Reich Labor Service—Reichsarbeitsdienst in German, abbreviated as RAD—but they were also used by the Wehrmacht, in industrial and highway construction, and in forced labor and concentration camps. The lateral arrangement of the corridor can also be found in the camp hospital barrack huts in Ravensbrück. See Reinhard Plewe and Jan Thomas Köhler, *Baugeschichte Frauen-Konzentrationslager Ravensbrück* (Edition Hentrich, 2000), 46–51.

59. See the drawing in the testimony of Makowski, APMO, Ośw./Makowski/1097, 7. On RAD barrack huts, see Plewe and Köhler, *Baugeschichte Frauen-Konzentrationslager Ravensbrück*, 46–51.

60. For Buchenwald, see Figures 19 and 25; for Neuengamme, see Figure 28; and photographs of "Sonderbaracke," AGN, 1981-493, 1993-180, 1996-47; for Dachau, see Figure 27.

61. See Bauplan der neuen Pathologie des KZ Sachsenhausen, BArch, NS3/377; and Lazarettplan des Krankenbaus, AGS, 49/59.

62. This is clearly reflected in the size of the rooms. See Figure 29. In Neuengamme, the women lived in four-bed rooms. See the testimony of Büttig (Frau X), AGN, transcription, 25.

63. See Figure 26. The film footage is from April 11, 1945. See Metro Det. H Camera Le Gault, Roll No. 1, AGMD, no signature. After liberation, several of the former brothel buildings were used as medical huts. In the Neuengamme internment camp, the former brothel was used for the sick, while the brothel in Sachsenhausen housed medical personnel. On the plan of the Neuengamme camp, the former brothel barrack is labeled "Inf. Barrack." See the map Internierungslager des ehemaligen KZ Neuengamme, in Wrocklage, "Neuengamme," 184; and the Lazarettplan des Krankenbaus Sachsenhausen (Bestandsaufnahme), AGS, 49/59.

64. For Gusen, see Tätigkeitsbericht 2, entry April 28, 1943, AMM, no signature.

65. See Weidlich, "Sonderbau," AMGB, Sig 31–494, 2.

66. See Kalmar, *Zeit*, 172.

67. Flowers decorated the rooms in other brothels as well. Laura Büttig said about Neuengamme: "The barracks were excellently furnished for that time—that is, during the war. Of course, it was more suitable for showing off than the camp. We also had clay vases—probably from the brickworks. In these vases were gladioli or dahlias . . . from the nursery" (testimony of Büttig [Frau X], AGN, transcription, 25). See AMGB, Bestand Buchenwald-Foto Nr. 1/67–73; and Bestand Besançon F1 4057-4063.

68. Beulig described the furnishings of the brothel rooms as follows: "This room was somewhat smaller than the bedroom. There was a chaise longue and a chair, also a rack with flowers and a washbasin with hot and cold running water, pictures, and flowers" (testimony of Beulig, AUSHMM, RG-06.005.05M Reel 1).

69. See the testimony of L.B., WdE, Sign. 294T, 29. Laura Büttig describes a brothel room in Neuengamme: "There was a lounge there [in the cabins] and there was a washbasin—first with cold water, later with warm water— and a stool. There was a peephole on the door" (testimony of Büttig [Mrs. X], AGN, transcription, 18). Piecha describes such a room in Auschwitz: "A bed, washbasin, chair, window, curtains, that was all" (Interv. Sommer 2003-05-05 P. II, 19). See similar testimony in Dubitzki, Interv. Sommer 2004-04-06 D., pt. 3, 00.30.00.

70. See Interv. Sommer 2005-01-28 S., pt. 1, 01.10.00 (Auschwitz); Kalmar, *Zeit*, 172 (Dachau).

71. Testimony of M.W, WdE, Sig. 295, 23.

72. Spritzer, *Tatsachenbericht*, 117.

73. See Spritzer, *Tatsachenbericht*.

74. Interv. Sommer 2003-05-05 P. II, 19.

75. Testimony of Beulig, AUSHMM, RG-06.005.05M Reel 1, 5.

76. See Nansen, *Tag*, 188 (Sachsenhausen); the testimony of Albert van Dijk, in Mieder and Schwarz, "Häftlingsbordell" (Buchenwald); Interv. Sommer 2003-07-19 Dekeyser (Belgiens); and the testimony of Petrykowski, APMO, Ośw./Petrykowski/1931, 138.

77. See Interv. Sommer 2005-02-15 Beck, 3 (Czech); and Pike, *Spaniards*, 335 (Spanish).

78. See the testimony of Büttig (Frau X), AGN, transcription, 18.

79. On the taxonomy, see Sofsky, *The Order of Terror*, 117–29.

80. See Interv. Sommer 2004-04-06 D., pt. 2, 00.26.00.

81. See Interv. Sommer 2003-07-19 Terry, 13.

82. See circular letter, RSHA June 4, 1942, GLAK, Abt. 330 Zug. 1991/34/Nr. 269.

83. Roßmann writes the following about Sachsenhausen: "Ten German and five Polish women were taken from a female concentration camp, the latter being reserved for Polish and Russian prisoners" (*Leben*, 176). Apparently Roßmann is referring to Ukrainian prisoners who were categorized as Russians

in the concentration camp. For the case of a Polish prisoner assigned by the SS to a Ukrainian woman, see Interv. Sommer 2005-01-28 S., pt. 1, 00.55.00.

84. See the testimony of Beck, Interv. Sommer 2005-02-15 Beck, 1.

85. Von Dijk states that he had his mother send him twenty-five Reichsmarks, which he spent in the camp brothel. See the testimony from van Dijk, in Mieder and Schwarz, "Häftlingsbordell," 14.

86. The possession of money was also forbidden in the camp. See the testimony of Gerhard Kanthack, AMM, V 3/20, 24. In Mauthausen, any money sent was converted into vouchers. See Interv. Sommer 2005-02-15 Beck, 2.

87. Jakob Boulanger and Michael Tschesno-Hell, *24073 Eine Ziffer über dem Herzen. Erlebnisbericht aus zwölf Jahren Haft* (Verlag des Ministeriums für Nationale Verteidigung, 1960), 118.

88. Pike, *Spaniards*, 73.

89. In other concentration camps, the SS organized the compilation of the lists themselves. In Neuengamme, this was done by Rapportführer Dreimann. See the testimony of Büttig (Frau X), AGN, transcription, 13. The following is reported about Flossenbürg: "The order of the prisoners in the 'Sonderbau' was determined on a list drawn up by the adjutant. Naturally, prisoners were not allowed to express their wishes regarding their figure, hair color, or even nationality. According to the list, inmate no. XX, for example, was given cabin no. 7" (Walleitner, *Zebra*, 96).

90. See the testimony of Beulig, AUSHMM, RG-06.005.05M, Reel 1, 5.

91. Testimony of van Dijk, in Mieder and Schwarz, *Häftlingsbordell*. In other concentration camps, too, the men had to wait several days to visit the brothel. Mr. J. speaks of about three days in Auschwitz. See the testimony of Herr J., Privatsammlung Paul, no signature, 3. It is also known from Neuengamme that prisoners had to bathe before visiting brothels. See the testimony of Büttig (Frau X), AGN, transcription, 13.

92. See Interv. Sommer 2003-07-19 Dekeyser, 4–5. In Monowitz, prisoners also had to wait outside the door.

93. See Pike, *Spaniards*, 72. In Buchenwald, an SS man sat in a special room and checked the list of names. See the testimony of Beulig, AUSHMM, RG-06.005.05M Reel 1, 5.

94. See the testimony of Büttig (Frau X), AGN, transcription, 13.

95. Pike, *Spaniards*, 72; and the testimony of Maršálek, IKF, H. Marsalek Video-Int. 2, 16.

96. Interv. Sommer 2003-07-19 Dekeyser, 4–5.

97. See the testimony of Szymanski, Interv. Sommer 2005-01-28 p., pt. 1, 00.42.00.

98. See Roßmann, *Leben*, 175.

99. See the testimony of Piecha, Interv. Sommer 2003-03-30 P. I, 5.

100. See the testimony of Szymanski, Interv. Sommer 2005-01-28 S., pt. 1, 00.43.00.

101. See the testimony of Piecha, Interv. Sommer 2003-05-05 P. II, 18; and Interv. Sommer 2003-07-19 Dekeyser, 8. In Mauthausen, which served as the prototype of the camp brothel, male prisoners were given a card with the number of the brothel room written on it after a visit to the doctor. See Pike, *Spaniards*, 72–73.

102. Testimony of Dekeyser, Interv. Sommer 2003-07-19 Dekeyser, 8.

103. See Engemann, AGS, R 34, 1 (Sachsenhausen); and the testimony of Büttig (Frau X), AGN, transcription, 13 (Neuengamme).

104. Engemann, AGS, R 34, 1 (Sachsenhausen); and the testimony of Büttig (Frau X), AGN, transcription, 13 (Neuengamme).

105. Laura Büttig stated the following: "The SS were not alone with the girls, nor were any prisoners. Except for the time in the so-called small rooms, in the cabins" (testimony of Büttig [Frau X], AGN, transcription, 11).

106. See Interv. Sommer 2003-03-30 P.I, 6; and Interv. Sommer 2004-04-06 D., pt. 1, 00.52.00f. and pt. 2, 00.06.00.; and Interv. Sommer 2005-01-28 S., pt. 1, 01.16.00.

107. See the testimony of Beulig, AUSHMM, RG-06.005.05M Reel 1, 6; and Kogon, *The Theory and Practice of Hell*, 135.

108. See Pike, *Spaniards*, 73; and Nansen, *Tag*, 188.

109. See the testimony of Niedojadło, APMO, Ośw./Niedojadło/997, 7; and the testimony of Fischer, AGMD, DMD-EB/HT-81, 5.

110. Szymanski recounted: "And they warned us that we had to make sex only the normal way. . . . We were not allowed to have French sex. . . . I think, maybe that was the kapo or maybe it was the *Pfleger* downstairs who was examining and telling us everything. Anyhow, we knew it" (Interv. Sommer 2005-01-28 S., pt. 1, 00.47.00). See also the testimony of Piotrowski, AGN, 839; the testimony of Büttig (Frau X), AGN, transcription, 18 (both Neuengamme); and the testimony Maršálek, IKF, H. Marsalek Video-Int. 2, 14–19 (Mauthausen).

111. See the testimony of Dekeyser, Interv. Sommer 2003-07-19 Dekeyser, 15 (Flossenbürg); and Dubitzki, Interv. Sommer 2004-04-06 D., pt. 2, 00.07.00 (Auschwitz).

112. Testimony of Büttig (Frau X), AGN, transcription, 11.

113. At the Mauthausen camp brothel, the doors had slits instead of peepholes.

114. See Pike, *Spaniards*, 73.

115. See Interv. Sommer 2003-07-19 Dekeyser, 6.

116. Interv. Sommer 2003-07-19 Dekeyser, 7.

117. Paul Matussek, *Die Konzentrationslagerhaft und ihre Folgen: Monographien aus dem Gesamtgebiete der Psychiatrie* (Springer Verlag, 1971), 29.

118. See the testimony of Dubitzki, Interv. Sommer 2004-04-06 D., pt. 2, 00.07.00 (Auschwitz); and the testimony of Fischer, AGMD, DMD-EB/HT-81, 5 (Mittelbau-Dora).

119. See the testimony of Dubitzki, Interv. Sommer 2004-04-06 D., pt. 2, 00.07.00 (Auschwitz); and the testimony of Fischer, AGMD, DMD-EB/HT-81, 5 (Mittelbau-Dora).

120. See the testimony of Leonhardt, APMO, Oświ./Leonhardt/1509, 3; and the Appendix, "Auschwitz and Monowitz."

121. Matussek, *Konzentrationslagerhaft*, 29.

122. See the respective sections in the Appendix.

123. See the testimony of Hodys, APMO, Oświ./Hodys/377, 10. Voyeurism was also reported at Flossenbürg. "At the instigation of the camp director, peepholes were built into the individual cabins to allow his lustful eyes to feast one hundred percent on the varied activities of the special building. Of course, there was no shortage of SS subjects who were happy to poke their noses into these peepholes" (Walleitner, *Zebra*, 96–97). [Translation my own.—Trans.]

124. See the testimony of L.B., WdE, Sign. 294T, 30.

125. See the testimony of Beulig, AUSHMM, RG-06.005.05M Reel 1, 6.

126. See the testimony of Büttig (Frau X), AGN, transcription, 13.

127. See the testimony of Beulig, AUSHMM, RG-06.005.05M Reel 1, 6 (Buchenwald); testimony of Szymanski, Interv. Sommer 2005-01-28 S., pt. 1, 00.58.00 (Auschwitz); Interv. Sommer 2004-06-15 Diament, 00.08.00 (Monowitz); Interv. Sommer 2005-02-15 Beck, 2 (Mauthausen); Interv. Sommer 2003-07-19 Terry, 4 (Flossenbürg); and Interv. Sommer 2004-02-05 Stenzel, pt. 2, 00.28.00 (Sachsenhausen).

128. When asked whether the SS ever sexually harassed her while at Mittelbau-Dora, Laura Bachmann replied: "No, they didn't. They didn't" (Testimony of L.B., WdE, Sig. 294T, 30). Magdalena Walter states that she too was never sexually harassed in Buchenwald. See the testimony of M.W, WdE, Sig. 295, 16.

129. See the testimony of Büttig (Frau X), AGN, transcription, 12.

130. See Interv. Sommer 2003-07-19 Dekeyser, 8.

131. See Interv. Sommer 2004-04-06 D., pt. 2, 00.41.00.

132. See the testimony of Büttig (Frau X), AGN, transcription, 18.

133. See interv. Sommer 2003-07-19 Terry, 4 (Flossenbürg); Interv. Sommer 2004-06-15 Diament, 00.11.00 (Monowitz); and Interv. Sommer 2003-03-30 P. 1, 5–6 (Auschwitz).

134. Romek Dubitzki reports that the SS gave him the task of locking the women in the sleeping quarters at night. However, he made a copy of the key so that his friend Stephan Szymanski could visit his "lover" at night. See Interv. Sommer 2004-04-06 D., pt. 1, 00.40.00.

135. For Monowitz, see Interv. Sommer 2004-06-15 Diament, 00.09.00.

136. See the testimony of M.W., WdE, Sig. 295, 9.

137. Letter of Glücks to the commandants of Auschwitz I and II et al., November 20, 1943, IFZ, Fa. 506-12.

138. Letter of Glücks.

139. Kogon, *The Theory and Practice of Hell*, 135. [The book's translator, Heinz Norden, renders *Flintenweiber* as "camp followers," but this does not convey the term's gendered and pejorative meaning. –Trans.] This contradicts the statement by Magdalena Walter. See the testimony of M.W., WdE, Sig. 295, 28.

140. This is shown by the job sheets. Starting in December 13, 1943, two women are listed who were employed as "Puffmütter" (i.e., "cashiers"). See Abrechnungsbögen, BArch, NS 4 Bu/41. Beulig testified that he sat in the day room with one of the two "cashiers" and checked the brothel slips of the male prisoners. The other woman was employed in the brothel for the Ukrainian guards. See the testimony of Beulig, AUSHMM, RG-06.005.05M Reel 1, 5–8.

141. Begleitzettel March 24, 1944, APMO, Akta HI Rajsko, 57/7a.

142. Abrechnungsbögen, "Sonderbau" Buchenwald, BArch, NS 4 Bu/41; and Prämien-Vorschrift, BArch, NS 3/426.

143. See the testimony of Beulig, AUSHMM, RG-06.005.05M Reel 1, 5.

144. Laura Büttig says: "He sat down with us in the day room. He also told us stories from his youth. . . . He always settled up afterward. The women had to hand in their cards—1 card equaled 1 RM. He then ticked them off very carefully according to his list" (testimony of Büttig (Frau X), AGN, transcription, 19).

145. These are the Germans E.T. and G.H. (both Neuengamme); M.G. and H.J. (both Buchenwald); G.O. (Auschwitz I); F.E. and L.S. (both Dachau, the latter was also at a brothel for Ukrainian guards in Gusen); and L.R. and B.G. (both Mittelbau-Dora). There is also a woman with the first name "Ema" in the Mauthausen logbook of surgical procedures. See Robert Sommer, Forced Sex Worker Database, last updated 11/2020, AMGR, MS_Sommer.

146. See Appendix, "Sachsenhausen."

147. For more examples of illegal visits, see the Appendix.

148. See Interv. Sommer 2005-01-28 S., pt.1, 00.43.00.

149. This can be seen in Auschwitz, Dachau, and Gusen. See their respective sections in the Appendix.

150. See the Buchenwald section in the Appendix.

151. Testimony of Beulig, AUSHMM, RG-06.005.05M Reel 1, 8.

152. See the testimony of Beulig, AUSHMM, RG-06.005.05M Reel 1, 8.

153. See Interv. Sommer 2005-01-28 S., pt. 1, 01.05.00f. The survivor Olszówka, who worked in the camp office in Mauthausen, remembers that a prisoner named Diestel was transferred to Mauthausen because he had broken into the brothel. See the testimony of Olszówka, APMO, Ośw./Olszówka 72, 139; and the testimony of Kanthak, AMM, V 3/20, 59.

154. See the Appendix sections on Auschwitz and Monowitz.

155. Testimony of Beulig, AUSHMM, RG-06.005.05M Reel 1, 7–8.

156. See O.W. and ("Rap. f. Nowak") (report for Nowak), Bordellbuch Block 3, AMM, K 2/1.

157. Kogon, *SS-Staat*, 215. [The passage is not included in the published English translation of *The Theory and Practice of Hell.* Translation my own.—Trans.]. See also Hackett, *Der Buchenwald-Report*, 272.

158. Testimony of Beulig, AUSHMM, RG-06.005.05M Reel 1, 5.

159. See the testimony of Moniek Levi, WL, Section II, Reel 53. On the black market for "admission tickets" to the brothel in the Auschwitz main camp, see Borowski, *Auschwitz*, 144.

160. Testimony of Büttig (Frau X), AGN, transcription, 12.

161. See Interv. Sommer 2005-01-28 S., pt. 1, 00.20.00f.

162. On Flossenbürg, see the testimony of Dekeyser, Interv. 2003-07-19 Dekeyser, 10.

163. In Sachsenhausen, Dr. Baumkötter was in charge of women's health (Interv. Sommer 2004-02-05 Stenzel, pt. 2, 00.31.00). In Buchenwald, it was Dr. Schiedlausky (testimony of Beulig, AUSHMM, RG-06.005.05M Reel 1, 7).

164. This role was assumed in Buchenwald by the kapo of the infirmary, Ernst Busse, and in Monowitz by the German block elder of the infirmary, Hermann Leonhardt. See the testimony of M.W., WdE, Sig. 295, 25; and the testimony of Leonhardt, APMO, Ośw./Leonhardt/1509, 2–3.

165. See the testimony of M.W. 1988, WdE, Sig. 295, 10; and the testimony of Beulig, AUSHMM, RG-06.005.05M Reel 1, 7.

166. See the testimony of Büttig (Frau X), AGN, transcription, 11.

167. The former prisoner-doctor Makowski was present at these examinations. See the testimony of Makowski, APMO, Ośw./Makowski/1097, 7; Makowski, "Organisation," 166; the testimony of Leonhardt, APMO, Ośw./Leonhardt/1509, 2–3; and Niedojadło, APMO, Ośw./Niedojadło/997, 7.

168. Makowski, "Organisation," 166.

169. See Makowski, "Organisation," 166.

170. See the testimony of Klein, APMO, Ośw./Klein/332, 147.

171. See the testimony of Minc, APMO, Ośw./Minc/1942, 167.

172. See the testimony of Makowski, APMO, Ośw./Makowski/1097, 7; and the testimony of Leonhardt, APMO, Ośw./Leonhardt/1509, 2–3.

173. On the establishment of a department for skin and venereal diseases, see Eugeiusz Niedojadło, "Der Lager-'Krankenbau' in Buna," in *Przegląd Lekarski. Anthologie*, vol. 2, part 2, ed. Internationales Auschwitz Komitee (International Auschwitz Committee, 1970), 51.

174. See Blut-, Stuhl- und Liquoruntersuchungen im Hygiene-Institut der Waffen-SS in Berlin von 1942, AUSHMM, RG-11.001M Reel 89.

175. See the testimony of Beulig, AUSHMM, RG-06.005.05M Reel 1, 7.

176. These women are A.Z. (Begleitzettel October 24, 1944, January 6 and 9, 1945, APMO, Akta HI Rajsko, 767/53, 74/61 and 189/62) and H.S. (Begleitzettel Block 24, August 28, 1944, APMO, Akta HI Rajsko, 70/46).

177. See the Begleitzettel für venerologische Untersuchungen Block 24, January 6 and 9, 1945, APMO, Akta HI Rajsko, 189/62 and 74/61.

178. Laura Büttig reports that there were no cases of venereal disease in Neuengamme. See the testimony of Büttig (Frau X), AGN, transcription, 29.

179. See Chapter 3, "Ravensbrück."

180. See the testimony of L.B., WdE, Sig. 294T, 28–29.

181. Meldung, July 21, 1943, BArch, NS 4 Bu/41.

182. Krankenblatt A.G., AMGR, AGGB, 040182. Several cases are known in which women were already infected with a sexually transmitted disease before their imprisonment in a concentration camp. For example, E.P., who was in the Sachsenhausen camp brothel from the beginning of 1945, was examined for gonorrhea in the Ravensbrück infirmary on August 21, 1944, and diagnosed as negative. She had already been diagnosed with gonorrhea on August 30, 1934. See Revierkarte E.P., ITS, KLD/Ravensbrück, Umschlag Nr. 4212. Other examples are H.R., E.B., and M.S., all of whom were at the Auschwitz camp brothel. See ITS, KLD/Ravensbrück Umschläge Nr. 4557, 5675 and 213.

183. Adolf Hitler, "Zum Kampf gegen Prostitution und Geschlechtskrankheiten," *MDGBG* 31, nos. 5/6 (1933): 74, 81.

184. Adolf Hitler, quoted in Spiethoff, "Vorwort," 73. Johannes Breger, a physician, also described the fight against sexually transmitted diseases as a "national task." See Johannes Breger, *Die Geschlechtskrankheiten und ihre Gefahren für das Volk* (R. v. Decker's Verlag and G. Schenk, 1937).

185. See Chapter 1, "SS Brothels."

186. For example, the Berlin Hygiene Institute of the Waffen-SS examined samples from prisons and forced labor camps. See the Archiv der Humboldt Universität zu Berlin (AHUB), Hygiene Institut Sig. 168, 170, 171, 189.

187. SS-Oberscharführer Wilhelm Boger, who worked in the Political Department of the Auschwitz concentration camp, was "urgently" examined for gonorrhea on April 18, 1944. See APMO, Akta HI Rajsko, 488/7. See also Begleitzettel Sekretärin des SS-Sturmbf. Pflaum, April 10, 1944, APMO, Akta HI Rajsko, 163/5.

188. See Begleitzettel, APMO, Akta HI Rajsko, 385/8, 397/12, 264/5a, 521/11.

189. See the archival collections of the Thuringian Ministry of the Interior to combat epidemics in prisoner-of-war and other camps, ThüHStA, MDI E, 649, 1456. For an example of camp hygiene protocol before the Nazi era, see the archival materials on camp hygiene and epidemic control, BArch, R 86 2402.

190. Papenburg was initially a concentration camp consisting of three camps. It was established in 1933 and is known today as the "Emsland camp." On the history of the Emsland camps, see Habbo Knoch, "Die Emslandlager 1933–1945," in *Benz and Distel, Ort II*, 533–70.

191. See, for instance, Hans Pfeiffer, "Über Lagerhygiene: Erfahrungen aus den Strafgefangenenlagern bei Papenburg-Ems," inaugural dissertation, University of Bonn, 1935.

192. Arbeitsbericht des Hygiene-Instituts der Waffen-SS Berlin, January 29, 1942, AHUB, Hygiene Institut Sig. 192. The significance of the fight against the

epidemic often remained hidden from the prisoners. For them, the examinations were simply humiliating. Romek Dubitzki reports on the case of a prisoner whose venereal disease led to his murder: "Kaduk would select Jews. He would sit in a chair, Jews would come up, being naked—this was with the transports. A really nice-looking boy came up. But when he looked at the genitals, he saw something called Spanish collar. He had never seen that before. There were various diseases, but he had never seen something like that. Kaduk shouted at him, and he had to go to the right. That was the end of him" (Interv. Sommer 2004-04-06 D., pt. 2, 00.42.00).

193. Friedrich Erhard Haag, *Lagerhygiene* (J. F. Lehmanns Verlag, 1943), 58.

194. Haag, *Lagerhygiene*, 58.

195. In 1937, Himmler required the SS to report incidents of contagious disease to the health authorities on a weekly basis. See Himmler, letter, über den Austausch der Wochennachweise übertragbarer Krankheiten, August 24, 1937, ThüHStA, MDI E Nr.1456. Records from the camp infirmary have survived from Buchenwald and Mittelbau-Dora listing the weekly cases of illness. As I already noted, however, syphilis and gonorrhea were extremely rare among inmates. See Infektionsmeldungen KZ Buchenwald including Außenlager Dora 1944/1945, BArch, NS 4 Bu/48. On Monowitz, see Niedojadło, "Krankenbau," 51.

196. See Freund-Widder, *Kontrolle*, 126–31.

197. See Erlass OKW, January 27, 1943 betr. Bekämpfung der Geschlechtskrankheiten, BLHA, Rep 45 D Westhavelland 1.

5. Sexuality in the Camps

1. Quoted in Michel Foucault, *Discipline and Punish: The Birth of the Prison*, trans. Alan Sheridan (Pantheon, 1977), 235.

2. See Foucault, *Discipline and Punish*, 231–40; and Pieter Spierenburg, "Four Centuries of Prison History: Punishment, Suffering, the Body, and Power," in *Institutions of Confinement: Hospitals, Asylums, and Prisons in Western Europe and North America, 1500–1950*, ed. Norbert Finzsch and Robert Jütte (Cambridge University Press, 1996), 17–96. On the history of prisons in Germany and the United States and the use of penal labor, see Norbert Finzsch, "Comparing Apples and Oranges? The History of Early Prisons in Germany and the United States, 1800–1860," in Finzsch and Jütte, *Institutions of Confinement*, 213–33.

3. In Auschwitz-Birkenau, in addition to the women's camp, there also existed the "gypsy camp" and the "Theresienstadt family camp." Most of the people incarcerated there were murdered in the gas chambers when the two camps were dissolved. See Michael Zimmermann, "Die nationalsozialistische Zigeunerverfolgung, das System der Konzentrationslager und das Zigeunerlager in Auschwitz-Birkenau," in Herbert, Orth, and Dieckmann, eds., *Konzentrationslager*, 887–910; and Miroslav Kárný, "Das Theresienstädter Familienlager (BIIb) in Birkenau: September 1943– Juli 1944," *Hefte von Auschwitz* 20 (1997): 133–237. The men's camp at Ravensbrück was established

in 1941 to provide male labor for the expansion of the Ravensbrück camp. About twenty thousand men were imprisoned there. See Strebel, *Ravensbrück*, 289–319.

4. The Karaganda Corrective Labor Camp (KARLag) was a Kazakh penal camp complex and part of the Soviet Gulag. See Wladislaw Hedeler, "Das Beispiel KARLag: Die Verwaltung eines Besserungsarbeitslagers," in *Stalinistischer Terror 1934–1941: Eine Forschungsbilanz*, ed. Wladislaw Hedeler (BasisDruck Verlag, 2002), 109–32.

5. See the circular issued by the head of KARLag to all camp divisions, July 5, 1936. Quoted in Stark, *Frauen*, 382–84. Interestingly, after the liberation of Dachau and the abolition of gender segregation, the risk of sexual coercion and sexual assault increased enormously. A few days after the liberation, the International Prisoners Committee decided to remove the remaining women from the camp area, as their safety could no longer be guaranteed. See the report of the eighth session of the IPC, May 9 and 17, 1945, BArch D-H, Dok/K 183/11.

6. See Lagerordnung des KZ Esterwegen, AUSHMM, RG-11.001M Reel 91; Blockordnung des KZ Natzweiler, BArch, Film 1576; and Disziplinar- und Strafordnung für das Gefangenenlager Dachau, in *Hefte von Auschwitz* 3 (1960): 35–37.

7. On the history of the persecution of homosexuals under National Socialism, see Günter Grau, ed., *Homosexualität in der NS-Zeit: Dokumente einer Diskriminierung und Verfolgung* (Fischer Taschenbuch, 1993); and Burkhard Jellonnek, *Homosexuelle unter dem Hakenkreuz: Die Verfolgung von Homosexuellen im Dritten Reich* (Schöningh Verlag, 1990).

8. Lagerordnung des FKL Ravensbrück, quoted in Claudia Schoppmann, *Nationalsozialistische Sexualpolitik und weibliche Homosexualität* (Centaurus Verlag & Media UG, 1997), 254.

9. See "P. Strafen" of KL Natzweiler, BArch, NS 4 Film 1575.

10. The Auschwitz survivor Jerzy Skotnicki recalled the following incident: "An SS man on duty at the sauna accused me of talking to women bathing in the sauna. Although I took exception and it was not true, the SS man told me that he had an order from Höß, who strictly forbade any contact between male and female prisoners, and so he punished me with twenty-five blows of the cane" (quoted in Staatliches Museum Auschwitz- Birkenau, ed., *Architektur des Verbrechens: Das Gebäude der "Zentralen Sauna" im Konzentrationslager Auschwitz II-Birkenau* [Verlag Staatliches Museum Auschwitz-Birkenau, 2001], 112). See also WL, Section II, Reel 53, testimony of Grete Salus, 45.

11. See Viktor E. Frankl, *Ein Psycholog erlebt das Konzentrationslager* (Verlag Jugend und Volk, 1947), 7–15.

12. Frankl, *Psycholog*, 15.

13. See Frankl, *Psycholog*, 15.

14. On the concept of dehumanization, see Na'ama Shik, "Weibliche Erfahrungen in Auschwitz-Birkenau," in Bock, *Geschlecht*, 105.

15. WdE, Sign. 294T, 8, testimony L.B.

16. The sight of unclothed people came as a tremendous shock for many, and in quite a few cases family members saw each other naked for the first time in their lives. See Staatliches Museum Auschwitz-Birkenau, *Architektur*, 153. Although women in particular experienced this as traumatizing, some men also regarded it as a humiliating intrusion into their private spheres. The Italian survivor Gianfranco Mariconti reports that the Italian general Cantaluppi faced his son naked in a shower in the sauna at Flossenbürg concentration camp. Out of shame, both closed their eyes. See Interv. Sommer 2004-05-12 Mariconti 2, 1. See also Janet Anschütz, Kerstin Meier, and Sanja Obajdin, "'. . . dieses leere Gefühl, und die Blicke der anderen . . .' Sexuelle Gewalt gegen Frauen," in *Frauen in Konzentrationslagern: Bergen-Belsen. Ravensbrück*, ed. Claus Füllberg-Stolberg et al. (Edition Temmen, 1994), 123–34; Staatliches Museum Auschwitz, *Architektur*, 99–172; and Jureit and Orth, *Überlebensgeschichten*, 185.

17. See, for example, Lucie Begov, *Mit meinen Augen: Botschaft einer Auschwitzüberlebenden* (Bleicher, 1983). A study by the Psychiatric Clinic of the Medical Academy in Krakow on the psychiatric problems of Auschwitz prisoners also addresses this acclimatization to the camps. Out of seventy-seven respondents (seventeen women and sixty men), thirty-five adapted in less than a month, thirteen in less than a year, and seventeen longer than a year. See Roman Lesniak et al., "Einige psychiatrische Probleme des KZ-Lagers Auschwitz im Lichte eigener Untersuchungen," *Przegląd Lekarski* 1 (1962): 42–46.

18. See Berger and Holzinger, *Mantel*, 104.

19. See Frankl, *Psycholog*, 32–44. Oszkár Betlen wrote: "And the people below me, around me, talked about the food. Food, food, and food again. . . ." Betlen, *Leben*, 34.

20. See Frankl, *Psycholog*, 43–47.

21. Frankl, *Psycholog*, 73.

22. Frankl, *Psycholog*, 51.

23. See Frankl, *Psycholog*, 53–71, 75–79.

24. Quoted in Anschütz, Meier, and Obajdin, *Gewalt*, 126. See a similar remark by Fania Fénelon quoted on the same page. The former prisoner functionary from Auschwitz, Wieslaw Kielar, describes how breasts marked social status in Auschwitz: the dying *Muselfrau* had sagging breasts, while the female kapo had plump ones. See Wieslaw Kielar, *Anus Mundi: 1500 Days in Auschwitz/Birkenau* (Times Books, 1980), 133, 147–48.

25. See Frankl, *Psycholog*, 43–44.

26. Betlen, *Leben*, 23.

27. Quoted in Anschütz, Meier and Obajdin, *Gewalt*, 126.

28. See Schäfer, "Selbstverständnis," 53.

29. Quoted in Anschütz, Meier and Obajdin, *Gewalt*, 127.

30. Aleksander Kulisiewicz, *Adresse Sachsenhausen: Literarische Momentaufnahmen aus dem KZ* (Bleicher Verlag 1997), 58–59.

31. See Langbein, *People in Auschwitz*, 404.

32. A former Italian Flossenbürg camp prisoner describes the loss of masculinity as manifested by sexual disinterest toward women as well as erectile dysfunction. See Interv. 2005-04-22 Raimondi, 2.

33. Matussek found that the content of men and women's accounts of concentration camp imprisonment differs. Whereas women reported on the restrictions to intimate life, men talked about political persecution. See Matussek, *Konzentrationslagerhaft*, 28. On the taboo of loss of masculinity and male victims of sexual violence, see Yvonne Peer, *Gewalt gegen Männer in heterosexuellen Beziehungen—Ein gesellschaftliches Tabu*. Diplomarbeit am Fachbereich Sozialwesen (University of Applied Sciences, 2001), 24, http://www.frauengewalt.fall.vn/Frauengewalt/Wissenschaft/2008-04-17_Yvonne_Peer_Diplomarbeit_Gewalt_gg_Maenner.pdf.

34. See Anschütz, Meier and Obajdin, *Gewalt*, 131–32.

35. See the pioneering study by Karl Plättner, *Eros im Zuchthaus: Sehnsuchtsschrei gequälter Menschen nach Liebe. Eine Beleuchtung der Geschlechtsnot der Gefangenen, bearbeitet auf der Grundlage von Eigenerlebnissen, Beobachtungen und Mitteilungen in achtjähriger Haft* (Verlag Paul Witte, 1931).

36. Block 10 was an isolated block in the main camp where Prof. Dr. Carl Clauberg conducted sterilization experiments on Greek Jewish women.

37. Interv. Sommer 2003-05-07 Frohwein, pt. 4, 00.25.58.

38. See Langbein, *People in Auschwitz*, 402.

39. See Anna Pawełczyńska, *Werte gegen Gewalt: Betrachtungen einer Soziologin über Auschwitz* (Verlag des Staatlichen Museums Auschwitz-Birkenau, 2001), 165. Grete Salus knew only two dominant feelings in the concentration camp: hunger and fear. See WL, Section II, Reel 53, 44.

40. See Borowski, *Auschwitz*, 146.

41. Federn, *Eros*, 69.

42. Matussek, *Konzentrationslagerhaft*, 29.

43. See Paul Friedman, "Aspekte einer Konzentrationslager-Psychologie," in *PSYCHE: Zeitschrift für Psychoanalyse und ihre Anwendung* 44, no. 2 (1990): 165–72.

44. See Lesniak, "Probleme," 42–52.

45. On the KZ-Syndrome, see Antoni Kępinski, "Das sogenannte KZ-Syndrom: Der Versuch einer Synthese," in *Die Auschwitz-Hefte: Texte der polnischen Zeitschrift "Przegląd Lekarski" über historische, psychische und medizinische Aspekte des Lebens und Sterbens in Auschwitz. Band II*, ed. Hamburger Institut für Sozialforschung, 7–14.

46. Between 1964 and 1967 and in 1971 and 1972, a survey on male sexuality was conducted with former inmates who had been sixteen to twenty years old at the time of their incarceration. The survey dealt with erotic dreams, spontaneous ejaculations, masturbation, and heterosexual and homosexual contacts. See Jerzy

St. Giza and Wiesław Morasiewicz, "Z zagadnień popędów w obozach koncentracyjnych. Przyczynek do analiz tzw. KZ-syndromu," in *Przegląd Lekarski* 1 (1973): 29–41.

47. See Giza and Morasiewicz, "Z zagadnień popędów," 31–32.

48. Of those men, seventeen were under twenty, and seven were between twenty-one and thirty. See Giza and Morasiewicz, "Z zagadnień popędów," 32–34.

49. See Giza and Morasiewicz, "Z zagadnień popędów," 29–41.

50. See Jerzy St. Giza and Wiesław Morasiewicz, "Poobozowe zaburzenia seksualne u kobiet jako elemet tzw. KZ-syndromu," *Przegląd Lekarski* 1 (1974): 68–75.

51. According to the study, 75 percent of the women had menstrual cycle disorders and 20 percent had no menstrual periods at all. The studies included analyses of female sexuality before, during, and after imprisonment and were conducted in 1966, 1967, and 1972, respectively. All the women studied had been incarcerated in a concentration camp between the ages of sixteen and twenty. According to the two gynecologists, this period is the most intense period in the psychosexual development of women. In most cases, the absence of menstruation resulted in noncyclical bleeding caused by psychogenic factors or by infections. In young, inexperienced women, these symptoms resulted in panic reactions, feelings of serious illness, anxiety, and concerns about having lost one's femininity. See Giza and Morasiewicz, "Poobozowe zaburzenia seksualne," 67–75.

52. See Giza and Morasiewicz, "Poobozowe zaburzenia seksualne," 73–75. The concentration camp survivor and physician Dr. Philip Arons takes a contrary position: "Hunger changed people psychologically as well as physically. . . . In the case of women, the unaccustomed hunger caused internal disturbances of the secretory glands, which caused the monthly periods to cease completely. It is erroneous to believe that something was added to the food to interrupt the period"(WL, Section II, Reel 55, testimony of P. Arons).

53. See W. Witusik and R. Witusik, "The Auschwitz Environment," in *It Did Not End in Forty-Five: Przegląd Lekarski. Anthology*, vol. 3, part 1, ed. International Auschwitz Committee (Warszawa, 1971), 139–46; and Zdziłsaw Maciej Maciejewski, "Wyniki badań ginekologicznych byłych więźniarek mieszkających w Koszalinie," in *Przegląd Lekarski* 1 (1975): 67–70.

54. See Giza and Morasiewicz, "Poobozowe zaburzenia seksualne," 73–74.

55. See Giza and Morasiewicz, "Poobozowe zaburzenia seksualne," 69–74.

56. See Giza and Morasiewicz, "Poobozowe zaburzenia seksualne," 73–74.

57. Only a few cases of heterosexual relations between prisoners and civilians have been reported. They were the exception and were often connected with special rights granted by the SS to privileged prisoners. For example, the kapo of the Buchenwald infirmary, Ernst Busse, was once visited by his wife, Anna. See Niethammer, *Antifaschismus*, 268. The deputy camp elder of the Ebensee subcamp in Mauthausen, Lorenz Dähler, was regularly allowed to visit a friend in the nearby village of Rindbach. See Freund, *Ebensee*, 170. Arthur

Lehmann describes that in the external command of Monowitz called Laurahütte the approximately fifty women and girls working there were among the "most desirable targets" of the prisoner functionaries. See WL, Section II, Reel 53, testimony of A. Lehmann.

58. Kielar, *Anus Mundi*, 81. See also Kulisiewicz, *Momentaufnahmen*, 58–59.

59. Samuel Pisar, *Of Blood and Hope* (Cassell, 1980), 76.

60. The bandmaster of the Auschwitz camp orchestra, together with some prisoner doctors, was caught having sex with women who had come from a satellite commando to the clinic in the main camp to have teeth pulled. The SS man who surprised the men hit their genitals with a club. See Tadeusz Borowski, *Here in Our Auschwitz and Other Stories*, trans. Madeline G. Levine (Yale University Press, 2021), 15.

61. See Borowski, *Here in Our Auschwitz.*

62. See Tanenbaum, *Prisoner*, 35.

63. See Thygesen, "Arzt," 97.

64. See Interv. Sommer 2003-04-30 Długoborski, 6–7.

65. Dubitzki reports that in his function as a camp fireman he could easily find an excuse to get into the women's camp. A friend of his maintained a relationship with a woman imprisoned there in this way. See Interv. Sommer 2004-04-06 D., pt. 2, 00.58.00.

66. One of the few surviving love stories is the one between Mala Zimetbaum and Edek Galinski. It was already known in Auschwitz. See Sara Nomberg-Przytyk, *Auschwitz: True Tales from a Grotesque Land*, trans. Roslyn Hirsch (University of North Carolina Press, 1985), 100–4.

67. Simha Naor recounts a conversation between two German women prisoners in Bergen-Belsen. One of them talked about a conversation with her lover: "Do you know that Franz was in a very bad mood the other day. Yesterday he asked me for the first time (I've known him for more than a year) if I loved him . . . funny question. He gets what he asks for and I have my bread" (Simha Naor, *Krankengymnastin in Auschwitz: Aufzeichnungen des Häftlings Nr. 80574* [Herder, 1989], 130).

68. See Langbein, *People in Auschwitz*, 404.

69. See Mali Fritz, *Essig gegen den Durst: 565 Tage in Auschwitz-Birkenau* (Verlag für Gesellschaftskritik, 1986), 108.

70. Langbein reports in the German original of *People in Auschwitz* that in the Clauberg block every woman had a "Kochany" (Langbein, *Menschen in Auschwitz*, 595).

71. WL, Section II, Reel 54, testimony of Elisabeth Szegö.

72. Kielar, *Anus Mundi*, 136. Kielar also describes female functional prisoners who approached him sexually (140–45) and sexual love relationships between different prisoners (131, 149). See also Kielar, *Fünf Jahre*, 317, 347–48; and Constanze Jaiser, "Repräsentation von Sexualität und Gewalt in Zeugnissen jüdischer und nichtjüdischer Überlebender" in Bock, *Geschlecht*, 126.

73. Kielar, *Anus Mundi*, 211.

74. Antonie Satzger wrote: "I took it for granted. They are people. I knew for sure they couldn't get caught. It was cat sex. I saw it myself" (quoted in Stark, *Frauen*, 169).

75. See Hájková, "Strukturen," 206; and Interv. Sommer 2004-03-19 2x Maschkowski, 2.

76. Quoted in Gudrun Jäger, "'Was für ein schönes Seidenhemd ich hatte!' Liana Millu über die 'Umwertung der Werte' in Auschwitz-Birkenau und die weibliche Lebenswelt im Konzentrationslager," in *Werkstatt Geschichte* 20 (1998): 100. See also a remark by Renata Laquer quoted in Anschütz, Meier, and Obajdin, *Gewalt*, 130.

77. See Kielar, *Anus Mundi*, 211–13.

78. The "gypsy" camp was a separate subcamp located in the Birkenau construction section BIIe. Approximately 22,600 Sinti and Roma were housed there starting in 1943. In early August 1944, the SS dissolved the camp to make room for the temporary housing of Jews from Hungary who were later to be murdered. The Sinti and Roma were taken to the Birkenau crematoria and gassed. In total, more than 19,300 people died during the seventeen-month existence of the camp. See Zimmermann, "Zigeunerlager," 887–910.

79. Kielar, *Fünf Jahre*, 255. This passage does not appear in the English translation of *Anus Mundi*.

80. See Kielar, *Anus Mundi*, 180–84; Kielar, *Fünf Jahre*, 252–56; Interv. Sommer 2005-01-28 S., pt. 1, 01.20.00, testimony of Szymanski; Interv. Sommer 2003-05-05 P. II, 21, testimony of Piecha; and Charles Liblau, *Die Kapos von Auschwitz* (Verlag des Staatlichen Museums Auschwitz-Birkenau, 1998), 110.

81. Pisar, *Of Blood and Hope*, 76.

82. Pisar, *Of Blood and Hope*, 76.

83. On sexual barter in Bergen-Belsen, see the testimony of Ruth Stein, WL Section II, Reel 55.

84. See Pawelczynska, *Werte*; Anchütz, Meier, and Obajdin, "Gewalt"; and Schoppmann, "Homosexualität." Giza and Morasiewicz write that none of the women interviewed in the camp had a heterosexual relationship but that 30 percent of the women had a lesbian relationship. With one exception, none of them had lesbian preferences before the concentration camp imprisonment. See Giza and Morasiewicz, "Zagadnień popędów" and "Poobozowe zaburzenia seksualne."

85. In 1913 Hans Blüher wrote: "Our emotional life and our sexual direction are indeed much more unstable than one can imagine . . . . An irrevocable heterosexual . . . does not know the capacities that sexual need creates and does not know the adaptability of the drive. And, as is known, the sexual drive is much more adaptable than the food drive" (Hans Blüher, *Studien zur Inversion und Perversion: Das uralte Phänomen der geschlechtlichen Inversion in natürlicher Sicht* [Franz Decker Verlag, 1965], 126). On situational homosexuality in POW

camps in World War I, see Edwin Erich Dwinger, *Die Armee hinter Stacheldraht: Das sibirische Tagebuch* (E. Diederichs Verlag, 1941), 155–56.

86. See Federn, "Psychologie," 57.

87. See Schoppmann, *Homosexualität*, 244–45; and Jaiser, "Repräsentation," 125. Buchmann writes: "Many of the inmates are lesbians, but only a few are lesbians by nature. Most of them don't know how to act out their sexual urges. . . . It happens that you have to wait at night in front of locked toilet doors until the various couples feel like releasing one of the small compartments" (quoted in Schoppmann, *Homosexualität*, 247).

88. Other names for "Pipel" were "Bubis" (Interv. Kuwalek 2003- 03-19-Gorski, 5), "Schwungs" (testimony of A.D., AGMD, DMD/EB/HN-6; Wesołowsk, *Wörter*, 108), and "Ponymeymänner" (Naujoks, *Leben*, 341). In women's camps, the female *Pipel* often gave themselves male first names. See Schoppmann, *Homosexualität*, 235.

89. Langbein, *People in Auschwitz*, 405.

90. See Naujoks, *Leben*, 338.

91. Part of this testimony is found in the memoirs he published after the war about his time as a camp elder in Sachsenhausen. See Naujoks, *Leben*, 341.

92. See BArch, BY5 V279/74, testimony of H. Naujoks, October 28, 1945.

93. Quoted in Langbein, *People in Auschwitz*, 405. At Majdanek, a *Pipel* called "Bubi" was known throughout the camp for the joy he took in beating up prisoners. Naujoks wrote: "The Ponymeyman could do whatever he wanted. . . . If he needed something, he simply took it away from another prisoner. Nobody dared to say anything for fear of the block elder. . . . The Ponymeyman was king in the block" (BArch, BY5 V279/74, testimony of H. Naujoks). The term "Ponymeyman" derives from the Russian verb понимать (Я понимаю = I understand). It literally means the "man who understands." See BArch, BY5 V279/74, testimony of H. Naujoks; Interv. Kuwalek 2003-03-19 Gorski, 5.

94. Maršálek is one of the few survivors to understand that relationships with *Pipel* were a form of sexual violence. See IKF, H. Marsalek Video-Int. 2, 25.

95. An exception is the account of the Israeli writer Roman Frister. In his published autobiography he describes how he was raped by a privileged prisoner named Arpad Basci. One night Basci gave him a piece of bread. While Frister ate it, Basci penetrated him. See Roman Frister, *The Cap: The Price of a Life* (Grove/Atlantic, 2001), 240–41.

96. The name is a pseudonym. His testimony was recorded in a video interview by the Fortunoff Video Archive of Holocaust Testimonies, Yale University Library in 1990. K.R. had already spoken about the concentration camp imprisonment in an interview for the archive of the Wiener Library in 1955, but in this interview, he did not mention having experienced sexual violence. See Fortunoff Video Archiv for Holocaust Testimonies, T-2367, testimony K.R., min 15:15–29:05 und WL Section II Reel 56.

97. See FVA, T-2367, testimony of K.R.

98. Quoted in Langbein, *People in Auschwitz*, 405.

99. Giza and Morasiewicz, "Poobozowe zaburzenia seksualne," 69–74.

100. Höß wrote about the women's camp of Birkenau with a homophobic tone: "Like homosexuality among the men, an epidemic of lesbianism was rampant in the women's camp" (Rudolf Hoess, *Commandant of Auschwitz*, trans. Constantino Fitz Gibbon [Popular Library], 1961), 148). See also Schoppmann, *Homosexualität*, 246.

101. Hoess, *Commandant of Auschwitz*, 94.

102. Hoess, *Commandant of Auschwitz*, 94.

103. Hoess, *Commandant of Auschwitz*, 94.

104. Hoess, *Commandant of Auschwitz*, 98.

105. Hoess, *Commandant of Auschwitz*, 98.

106. Hoess, *Commandant of Auschwitz*, 98. Höß writes extensively about homosexuals, including a "hustler" from Berlin and a "Romanian prince" who "had grown tired of women through his gluttonous existence." This passage was deleted from the edition edited by Martin Broszat but published in the English translation. See the handwritten part of the testimony, IfZ, F 13/2, 100–1; Höß, *Kommandant*, 80–81; and Hoess, *Commandant of Auschwitz*, 7, 94–95. Regarding the latter case, Himmler believed that this homosexual "would be cured in a short time by hard work and the hard life in the concentration camp."

107. Castrations seem to have been carried out particularly frequently in Auschwitz. See Tanenbaum, *Prisoner*, 34; Langbein, *People in Auschwitz*, 405; Interv. Sommer 2004-04-06 D. pt. 2, 01.00.00; Interv. Sommer 2005-01-28 S., pt. 1, 1.19.00 (all on Auschwitz-Stammlager); and Betlen, *Leben*, 77 (Auschwitz-Monowitz).

108. See Federn, "Psychologie," 57.

109. See Interv. Sommer 2006-08-31 Terry II; Interv. Sommer 2003-07-19 Terry, 8 (Flossenbürg); and Interv. Sommer 2003-05-01 Hantz, pt. 2, 00.09.00 (Auschwitz).

110. See Schoppmann, *Homosexualität*, 255–56.

111. Magdalena Walter also reports that the reason for the establishment of camp brothels was to combat homosexuality in concentration camps. See WdE, Sig. 295, testimony of M.W. 1988, 11; and AMGB, 56-8-4, testimony of Weidlich, 2. See also Meier, *Neuengamme*, 51; and Matussek, *Konzentrationslagerhaft*, 29 (on Dachau).

112. The only reference to it is in a statement from the camp commander of Mauthausen, Franz Ziereis, captured by the US Army, dated May 24, 1945. The English translation of his statement reads as follows: "In order to prevent the prisoners from having intercourse with each other a brothel was built!" (AUSHMM, RG-09.018-01, testimony of F. Ziereis). Ziereis's statement has been handed down in different versions, which differ greatly in content. Moreover, the records suggest that the former commander was in a confused state. See the testimony of F. Zeireis in AMM, P18-02-01 and BArch, NS 4 Ma/57.

113. Federn wrote: "When the brothel came, it very soon became apparent that from among the elite of the camp elders, many would rather have had a boy than a prostitute" ("Eros," 71). See also Federn, "Psychologie," 59; Meier, *Neuengamme*; and Heger, *Männer*, 141 (on Neuengamme).

114. For research on the subject, see Auer, Amesberger, and Halbmayr, *Sexualisierte Gewalt*, 143–58; Jaiser, "Repräsentation," 126–27; and Shik, "Erfahrungen," 110–11.

115. Langbein, *People in Auschwitz*, 408.

116. See Hoess, *Commandant of Auschwitz*, 148.

117. See Kielar, *Anus Mundi*, 140–45. The SS man Fritz Schramme (SS-Fahrbereitschaft) and the doctor of the women's camp, Franz von Bodmann, are alleged to have had sexual relations with women prisoners. See Langbein, *People in Auschwitz*, 408, 410.

118. See Langbein, *People in Auschwitz*, 409; and Interv. Sommer 2004-04-06 D., pt. 2. 00.09.00; Kielar, *Fünf Jahre*, 255.

119. The central source is Hodys's testimony at an SS court in 1944. It is very detailed, but some statements sound improbable. Langbein believes a former kapo from the women's camp, who describes the alleged liaison with Höß as an attempt to cover up a diamond smuggling operation. Ella Lingens, who met Hodys in the infirmary, also has doubts about the veracity of the testimony. See Manfred Deselaers, *"Und Sie hatten nie Gewissensbisse?" Die Biografie von Rudolf Höß, Kommandant von Auschwitz, und die Frage nach seiner Verantwortung vor Gott und den Menschen* (St. Benno Verlag, 1997), 194; Langbein, *People in Auschwitz*, 411–13; and APMO, Ośw./Hodys/377, transcript of the interrogation of Hodys.

120. One exception is the report of a contemporary witness from Ravensbrück about the Eberswalde subcamp there. The camp leader had a sexual relationship with a young Russian woman. When the relationship ended, he had her put out naked on the roll-call square and beaten to death. See Amesberger, Auer, and Halbmayr, *Sexualisierte Gewalt*, 144.

121. Langbein, *People in Auschwitz*, 404.

122. The applies to Eleonore Hodys as well as to the "lovers" of Palitzsch and Schillinger.

123. See Gisela Bock, "Einführung," in Bock, *Geschlecht*, 13. Two opposing positions that can be seen here are those of Na'ama Shik versus those of Rochelle G. Saidel and Sonja M. Hedgepeth. Shik assumes that sexual assaults by SS men at Auschwitz were extremely rare. Hedgepeth and Saidel emphasize that the absence of statements and descriptions about rapes does not mean that they did not occur. See Na'ama Shik, "Sexual Abuse of Jewish Women in Auschwitz-Birkenau," in *Brutality and Desire: War and Sexuality in Europe's Twentieth Century*, ed. Dagmar Herzog (Palgrave Macmillan, 2009), 221–47; and Sonja M. Hedgepeth and Rochelle G. Saidel, eds., *Sexual Violence Against Jewish Women during the Holocaust* (Brandeis University Press, 2010), 2.

124. A survivor named Weichselbaum recalled in her testimony: "I saw how SS men used some women and girls, also abnormally, which caused them great pain, but they were then immediately shot. Through a window I observed that SS men also took girls of twelve to thirteen years out alone, took advantage of them, these were also shot afterward" (WL, Section II, Reel 53, testimony of Weichselbaum). See also a passage from Ruth Elias quoted in Anschütz, Meier, and Obajdin, "Sexuelle Gewalt gegen Frauen," 30.

125. On this, I follow the findings of the Israeli historian Na'ama Shik, "Sexual Abuse," 221–47.

126. See Jankiel Wiernik, quoted in Alexander Donat, ed., *The Death Camp Treblinka: A Documentary* (Holocaust Library [distr. Schocken Books], 1979); and Vasily Grossmann, *Die Hölle von Treblinka* (Verlag für fremdsprachige Literatur, 1946), 42.

127. Langbein, *People in Auschwitz*, 403. See also Matussek, *Konzentrationslagerhaft*, 29.

128. See Kielar, *Fünf Jahre*, 167.

129. See Kielar, *Anus Mundi*, 131–34.

130. See Jeanette Wolff, *Mit Bibel und Bebel: Ein Gedenkbuch* (Verlag Neue Gesellschaft, 1980), 33.

131. FVA, T-2367, min 29.05, testimony of K. R.

132. Interv. Sommer 2003-07-19 Dekeyser, 6.

133. See Jäger, "Seidenhemd," 99.

134. See Giza and Morasiewicz, "Zagadnień popędów," 29–41.

6. The Lives of Forced Sex Workers

1. See the testimony of M.W. 1988, WdE, Sig. 295, 9–10. According to SS documents, the women were taken to Buchenwald in two transports. In the camp's service log, the following entry, dated July 2, 1943, is found under "special incidents": "6:00 pm: eleven female prisoners for brothel transferred from Ravensbrück camp." Two days later, another five women arrived at lunchtime. See Diensttagebuch Buchenwald, BArch D-H, Sig. A 4926.

2. See Diensttagebuch Buchenwald. Laura Büttig describes her transportation to Neuengamme in a similar way: "There was a female guard in uniform. We were also guarded by an SS man. We were given a cold ration of food. . . . The female supervisor sat with us on the train. They had darkened the windows by painting them blue. They had left only a small slit at the top. We drove and drove. Dawn was breaking. . . . We then arrived in Hamburg at the main station. The supervisor went to make a phone call. We were taken to the waiting room and sat there and waited. . . . After three quarters of an hour, a car arrived with three SS men . . . they picked us up and took us to Neuengamme" (testimony of Büttig (Frau X), AGN, transcription, 4–5.)

3. See the testimony of M.W., WdE, Sig. 295, 22. Linda Bachmann also recalls that the SS told them that they would be placed in a "special work detail," but she had no idea what that meant (testimony of L.B., WdE, Sig. 294T, 28).

4. Testimony of M.W. 1988, WdE, Sig. 295, 10.

5. Testimony of M.W., WdE, Sig. 295, 24.

6. See the testimony of M.W. 1988, WdE, Sig. 295, 10, 23.

7. See the testimony of M.W., WdE, Sig. 295, 24. The Buchenwald brothel job sheets show that it was only about a week. The women arrived in Buchenwald on July 2 or 4, 1943. The brothel began operating on July 11, 1943. See Abrechnungsbögen, BArch, NS 4 Bu/41.

8. See the testimony of M.W., WdE, Sig. 295, 15.

9. See Abrechnungsbögen, July 11, 1943, BArch, NS 4 Bu/41.

10. Testimony of Beulig, AUSHMM, RG-06.005.05M Reel 1, 3.

11. See the testimony of Beulig, 4.

12. Testimony of Beulig, 4.

13. See the testimony of Büttig (Frau X), AGN, transcription, 26.

14. See the testimony of König, Interv. Sommer 2004-02-05 König, 4 (Monowitz); and the testimony of Dubitzki, Interv. Sommer 2004-04-06 D., pt. 1, 00.54.00 (Auschwitz main camp). Laura Büttig reports: "When there was no work—mending socks. When there was no work at all for a long time, they [the SS] came up with the idea that we had to mend socks for the guards. . . . Socks, woolen socks. . . . There were at most four girls with us who could darn. I couldn't do it (testimony of Büttig [Frau X], AGN, transcription, 38).

15. See the testimony of M.W., WdE, Sig. 295, 28.

16. See the testimony of M.W.

17. See Interv. Kuwalek 2003-03-19 Gorski, 2. Maršálek reports on Mauthausen: "They were almost always locked up, sometimes, but I can't say how often they walked between huts 1 and 2, in the afternoon, when the mass of prisoners was working. Because there was no one there"(testimony of Maršálek, IKF, H. Marsalek Video-Int. 2, 16). On Buchenwald, see the testimony of Beulig, AUSHMM, RG-06.005.05M Reel 1, 4.

18. Testimony of M.W., WdE, Sig. 295, 29.

19. See Pike, *Spaniards*, 73.

20. See the testimony of L.B., WdE, Sign. 294T, 12, 27.

21. Testimony of Beulig, AUSHMM, RG-06.005.05M Reel 1, 4.

22. Testimony of M.W., WdE, Sig. 295, 24.

23. On Saturday, July 17, 1943, ninety-three prisoners visited the camp brothel; on the following Sunday there were 150. On December 18, 1943, there were forty-one; one day later there were fifty. On Saturday, January 29, 1944, fifty-eight men went to the brothel; on the following Sunday there were only forty-four. See Abrechnungsbögen July 1943–February 1944, BArch, NS 4 Bu/41.

24. Testimony of Beulig, AUSHMM, RG-06.005.05M Reel 1, 5.

25. Testimony of M.W., in Mieder und Schwarz, *Häftlingsbordell.*

26. Testimony of Büttig (Frau X), AGN, transcription, 11.

27. See the testimony of L.B., WdE, 22, 31. Magdalena Walter says that she had to "let eight men get on top of her" that evening (Mieder und Schwarz, *Häftlingsbordell*, 13). Based on the job sheets, she had to take up to ten men a day.

In the first three weeks, there were between three and ten men per evening. See Abrechnungsbögen "Sonderbau" July 1943, BArch, NS 4 Bu/41.

28. See Abrechnungsbögen "Sonderbau." By comparison, the two forced sex workers in the brothel for Ukrainian guards had to serve two to eight men every day. See Abrechnungsbögen "Sonderbau," February 26 to March 6, 1944, BArch, NS 4 Bu/41.

29. From July 11, 1943, to April 1, 1944, the German A.E. had to serve a total of 666 men; the Polish woman F.R. had sex with 1,381 men. See Abrechnungsbögen "Sonderbau," July 11, 1943 to April 1, 1944, BArch, NS 4 Bu/41. However, as I will explain later, quite a few of the men accounted for in the job sheets likely did not have sexual intercourse with the women.

30. See the testimony of Beulig, AUSHMM, RG-06.005.05M Reel 1, 4. The Buchenwald kitchen books include mentions of pork, beef, spinach and potatoes, paprika, and pudding powder. See Küchenbücher Buchenwald, BArch, NS 4 Bu/77, Fl/366 and 367; and the testimony of M.W., WdE, Sig. 295, 28.

31. Testimony of L.B., WdE, Sign. 294T, 25.

32. Laura Büttig reports: "We got . . . hot food from the SS canteen four to five times a week, sometimes in the evening, sometimes at lunch time . . . good food. . . . In addition, we got our normal food" (testimony of Büttig [Frau X], AGN, transcription, 20–21). Jenny Spritzer wrote about Auschwitz: "As far as food was concerned, the women had it much better. They were given soup specially prepared for them from the prisoners' kitchen" (Spritzer, *Tatsachenbericht*, 118).

33. Testimony of Beulig, AUSHMM, RG-06.005.05M Reel 1, 8. See also the testimony of M.W., WdE, Sig. 295, 29.

34. See the testimony of L.B., WdE, Sig. 294T, 14.

35. Linda Bachmann says about Dora: "Private clothes. . . . We got our private clothes from Ravensbrück. Which we wore when we came there" (testimony of L.B., WdE, Sig. 294T, 24).

36. See the testimony of M.W., WdE, Sig. 295, 29.

37. See the testimony of Beulig, AUSHMM, RG-06.005.05M Reel 1, 4.

38. See the testimony of Lynhard, AMGR, Bd. 17/55, 9.

39. Secret letter from Himmler to Pohl, November 15, 1942, in IMG, *Prozess*, vol. 3–4, 350.

40. See the testimony of Beulig, AUSHMM, RG-06.005.05M Reel 1, 5.

41. A.M. ("Antonia Michaelis") received 359.55 RM, and F.R. received 703.35 RM. The average earnings of the women during this period was 462 RM. See the Abrechnungsbögen "Sonderbau," June 1943 to April 1944, BArch, NS 4 Bu/41. In Dachau, the women were credited between RM 7.20 and RM 9 per day. See the Einzahlungsschein Bordell Dachau, October 26, 1944, AGD, 20.277.

42. This is supported by the fact that A.M. was credited with at least 361 RM, according to the brothel job sheets, but only 65.30 RM were sent to Ravensbrück when she left the brothel at the end of 1944. See Abrechnungsbögen "Sonderbau," June 1943 to April 1944; and Einzahlungsschein Nr. 56 (undated), BArch, NS 4 Bu/41.

43. The name is a pseudonym. See Frauenkarte A.M., ITS, KLD/Buchenwald, Umschlag Nr. 15661; and Einzahlungsschein, Beleg Nr. 37, January 25, 1945, BArch, NS 4 Bu/127.

44. See Einzahlungsschein, Beleg Nr. 37.

45. See Einlieferungsschein Restguthaben A.M., December 13, 1944, ITS, KLD/Buchenwald, Umschlag Nr. 15661.

46. A number of report slips bear witness to this. On one such slip, for example, L.B. asked the Buchenwald camp director "to send my impecunious father 150 RM from my account" (Rapport, January 14, 1944, ITS, KLD/Buchenwald, Umschlag Nr. 2863). Surviving prisoner money cards and payment slips document these transfers. See Rapport, January 14, 1944, ITS, KLD/Buchenwald, Umschlag Nr. 2863; and ITS, KLD/Buchenwald/Einzahlungsscheine Häftlingsverwaltung. See also the money transfers of forced sex worker from Buchenwald, ITS, KLD/Buchenwald, Umschläge Nr. 3092 (E.C.), 4519 (A.E.), 6819 (M.G.), 16222 (C.M.), 19265 (F.R.), 19352 (M.R.), 23140 (C.S.) 27238 (M.W.), 27724 (W.Z.), and 27977 (K.Z.).

47. The amounts varied greatly. While the SS only paid out RM 12.60 to M.W., the "madam" H.J. received a total of RM 1,710. See Auszahlungsscheine, January 10 and March 19, 1945, ITS, KLD/Buchenwald/Einzahlungsscheine der Häftlingsverwaltung.

48. Testimony of Büttig (Frau X), AGN, transcription, 19.

49. See the testimony of L.B., WdE, Sig. 294T, 31.

50. Magdalena Walter was released from Buchenwald in December 1944, but she also reports never receiving any money from the SS. See the testimony of M.W., WdE, Sig. 295, 9; Häftlingskarte, ITS, KLD/Buchenwald, Umschlag Nr. 27238; and letter to the Politische Abteilung, December 12, 1944, ITS, KLD/Buchenwald/Entlassungsbefehle.

51. See Chapter 5, "The Realities of Camp Life."

52. See Kielar, *Fünf Jahre Auschwitz*, 167. [The passage quoted is not in the English translation of *Anus Mundi*.—Trans.]

53. See the testimony of Büttig (Frau X), AGN, transcription, 17.

54. See Abrechnungsbögen, July 1943 to April 1944, BArch, NS 4 Bu/41.

55. Testimony of L.B., WdE, Sig. 294T, 22.

56. See the testimony of Beulig, AUSHMM, RG-06.005.05M Reel 1, 7.

57. Testimony of Laura Büttig (Frau X), AGN, transcription, 29.

58. Testimony of M.W., WdE, Sig. 295, 24.

59. See, for instance, the testimony of Büttig (Frau X), AGN, transcription, 29 (Neuengamme); and the testimony of L.B., WdE, Sig. 294T, 22 (Mittelbau-Dora).

60. See the testimony of Szymanski, Interv. Sommer 2005-01-28 S., pt. 1, 00.46.00 and pt. 2, 00.13.00f.

61. See the testimony of Beulig, AUSHMM, RG-06.005.05M Reel 1, 7. Between October 23 and December 18, 1943, Mrs. K.Z. was listed as "sick" or as a "cashier" and did not serve any men. The note "Revier" ("hospital") appears on

three different days (November 8, 11, and 18, 1943). These probably consisted of the two checkups and the abortion appointment. See Abrechnungsbögen, BArch, NS 4 Bu/41.

62. See letter from the Standortarzt der Waffen-SS Weimar, December 11, 1944, BArch, NS 4 Bu/41. Abortions were generally prohibited under the German criminal code. They were permitted only when the pregnant woman's life was in danger or where there was a "state of emergency." See Gisela Bock, *Zwangssterilisation im Nationalsozialismus: Studien zur Rassenpolitik und Frauenpolitik* (Westdeutscher Verlag, 1986), 141–68.

63. Operationsbuch Mauthausen, AMM, H 12/2, 278. See also Baumgartner, *Frauen von Mauthausen*, 101.

64. The entries begin on January 8, 1940 and end on February 12, 1945. See Operationsbuch, AMM, H 12/2.

65. See the testimony of Büttig (Frau X), AGN, transcription, 29; testimony of Christiansen, AGN, 1273, 95.

66. See the testimony of L.B., WdE, Sig. 294T, 22–23; and Bock, *Zwangssterilisation*, 299–409.

67. Files on sterilization procedures have survived for two women from the Flossenbürg camp brothel. In 1936, for example, the Bremen Genetic Health Court ordered the "infertilization" of E.F., who was still a minor at the time (Akte Erbgesundheitsgericht, Staatsarchiv Bremen [StA-B], 4,130/2-EG.XIII. Nr.127/1936 E.F.). The Genetic Health High Court in Jena also denied Mrs. W.L. the right to have children of her own on the grounds that she had "genetic criminal tendencies" (ThHStA Weimar, Thüringisches Landesamt für Rassewesen Nr. 5 982, 40–42).

68. On the destruction of female sexual and reproductive organs through concentration camp imprisonment, see Witusik/Witusik, "Auschwitz Environment," 139–46; and Maciejewski, "Wyniki badań ginekologicznych," 67–70.

69. On December 13, 1944, I.G. made the following entry: "Hydrosalpinx dx torquata (min 360°)" (congestion of a serous secretion in the fallopian tubes) and "Typhalatonica Salpingectomia" (removal of the fallopian tubes). I.H.'s uterus underwent curettage on October 2, 1944, after an inflammation ("Eudomentritis c. Laemirrlagia; Curettage"). See the Operationsbuch Mauthausen, AMM, H 12/2.

70. A soft tissue tumor in K.K. ("Ganglion dorsi man sin; Exturbatio. L.a.") on October 15 and November 13, 1944, and a wart in I.H. on July 13, 1944 ("Nodi hoemorrhidales ext. Fissura; Verruca labri maj. sin.; Exorlip Gond.; Ae Nare ani.") (Operationsbuch Mauthausen, AMM, H 12/2).

71. See the testimony of Beulig, AUSHMM, RG-06.005.05M Reel 1, 7.

72. For instance, L. B. was ill for more than forty days twice in the period before April 1944. K.Z. was ill for two months in a row. See Abrechnungsbögen 1943/44, BArch, NS 4 Bu/41.

73. According to her testimony, the SS took blood from prisoners, which weakened them even more. See the testimony of M.W., WdE, Sig. 295, 20. Such

practices have received little attention so far. However, it can be proven that the SS Hygiene Institute in Berlin produced test serums from the blood of prisoners in Ravensbrück and Sachsenhausen. See Arbeitsbericht des Hygiene-Instituts der Waffen-SS Berlin, January 29, 1942, AHUB, Hygiene Institut, Sig. 192. See also Chapter 5, "The Realities of Camp Life."

74. See the testimony M.W., November 15, 1988, WdE, Sig. 295, 11. However, the duration of the illness cannot be confirmed based on the job sheets. See Abrechnungsbögen, BArch, NS 4 Bu/41.

75. Mrs. Hodys testified that she met a certain H.G. in the infirmary in Auschwitz. The name of the woman mentioned by Hodys can be found on the accompanying notes for venereal examinations in the camp infirmary in Auschwitz. Hodys gives no information about the nature of the illness. She mentions another woman who may also have been in Block 24a. See Hodys, Vernehmungsprotokoll, APMO, Oświ./Hodys/377, 10.

76. Kogon, *The Theory and Practice of Hell*, 135.

77. Testimony of M.W., WdE, Sig. 295, 16.

78. Testimony of L.B., WdE, Sig. 294T, 31.

79. Testimony of L.B., 28.

80. Testimony of L.B., 21.

81. On selective perception and the construction of memory in the statements of former prisoners, see Jureit and Orth, *Überlebensgeschichten*, 182–94.

82. Testimony of L.B., WdE, Sig. 294T, 23.

83. Testimony of L.B., 30.

84. Linda Bachmann said: "We didn't even ask [what would happen to us]. We didn't give a shit" (testimony of L.B., 21).

85. Testimony of M.W., 1988, WdE, Sig. 295, 11.

86. Testimony of M.W., WdE, Sig. 295, 24.

87. See the testimony of M.W., 1988, WdE, Sig. 295, 15.

88. See Bruno Bettelheim, "Individual and Mass Behavior in Extreme Situations," *Journal of Abnormal and Social Psychology* 38 (1943): 417–52.

89. Testimony of M.W., in Mieder and Schwarz, *Häftlingsbordell.*

90. Testimony of M.W., WdE, Sig. 295, 16.

91. See the testimony of M.W., WdE, 26–29; and the testimony of M.W., 1988, WdE, Sig. 295, 11.

92. See the testimony of M.W., in Mieder and Schwarz, *Häftlingsbordell.*

93. Testimony of M.W., WdE, Sig. 295, 31.

94. Testimony of M.W., 26.

95. Testimony of L.B., WdE, Sig. 294T, 22.

96. See the testimony of L.B., 22–25.

97. Testimony of L.B., 25.

98. Testimony of L.B., 21.

99. Anni Kramer reports: "I even had something like a friendship with one man. He was also from Danzig, I didn't know him before. A little Pole was also a

friend of mine. His wife sent him an extra 50 Pfennigs for the brothel" (testimony of Kramer, in Niemeyer and von der Tann, *Schweigen*).

100. See the testimony of Kanthack, AMM, V 3/20, 24–25. On Auschwitz, see the testimony of Brandhuber, BJBS, without signature, 3; and the testimony Dubitzki, Interv. Sommer 2004-04-06 D., pt. 1, 01.05.00.

101. Testimony of Bator, APMO, Ośw./68/Bator.

102. See W. Vosseler, "Niederschrift zur Tätigkeit des S. im KZ Flossenbürg," January 12, 1946. Quoted in Klausch, *Widerstand*, 91.

103. The *Kalfaktor*, from the Latin for "heater," was a prisoner who provided assistance to the supervisor. See the statement of Franz Dobermann from October 13, 1946, while being investigated by the East German SED, in Niethammer, *Antifaschismus*, 294.

104. See Niethammer, *Antifaschismus*, 287.

105. Testimony of L.B., WdE, Sig. 294T, 13.

106. This was information provided by Christl Wickert, March 4, 2002. See also Otto Wahl (Lagergemeinschaft Mauthausen), in Paul, *Zwangsprostitution*, 60.

107. See the testimony of M.W., WdE, Sig. 295, 24; testimony of Mr. J., Interview Paul Herr J, 4.

108. See the testimony of M.W., WdE, Sig. 295, 17.

109. Testimony of M.W, 17.

110. Testimony of M.W, 17.

111. The names of the women were recorded in documents kept at the Buchenwald brothel. But it is possible that Magdalena mixed up the names. See the testimony M.W., 1988, WdE, Sig. 295, 5–6.

112. See the testimony of M.W., WdE, Sig. 295, 24.

113. StA-HH, JüngGefKart 242-1II Abl.13 and StA-HH, 242-1II GefVerwaltung II Abl. 2000/1 U-Haft-Kartei Frauen 1930–1952 and Einweisung in das KZ Ravensbrück, June 6, 1942, AMGR, AGGB, 01023101.

114. See the testimony of L.B., WdE, Sig. 294T, 31.

115. See the testimony of L.B., 21. Neither the name of the woman nor the reason for her arrest can be confirmed using the records that have survived from the Ravensbrück concentration camp. See Robert Sommer, Forced Sex Worker Database, last updated 11/2020, AMGR, MS Sommer.

116. Magdalena Walter testified: "She was once mean to the other women and we took revenge for that. . . . We took flypaper . . . wrapped it around her naked body from the back down to the front to the genitals. And it stuck like crazy. That was the punishment" (testimony of M.W., WdE, Sig. 295, 8–9).

117. Testimony of M.W., WdE, Sig. 295, 8.

118. See the testimony of M.W., WdE, Sig. 295, 28. Maršálek said: "I don't think so—possibly, I don't know. There was allegedly an SS brothel in Linz, yes, where the SS men allegedly went. . . . As far as I know, I don't think the SS members had sexual intercourse with the women" (testimony of Maršálek, IKF, Marsalek Video-Int. 2, 16).

119. Testimony of L.B., WdE, Sig., Sig. 294T, 21.

120. Testimony of L.B., 29.

121. See the testimony of L.B., 30.

122. See the respective sections in the Appendix.

123. Testimony of Maršálek, IKF, Marsalek Video-Int. 2, 16.

124. See Paul, *Zwangsprostitution*, 73.

125. Testimony of M.W., 1988, WdE, Sig. 295, 18.

126. Testimony of M.W., 1988, 28.

127. See "Neuengamme," in the Appendix.

128. Testimony of Büttig (Frau X), AGN, transcription, 19.

129. Testimony of N.N., AGN, 2.8./1391.

130. See the testimony of Büttig (Frau X), AGN, transcription, 23.

131. Leumundszeugnis A.L. in Spruchgerichtsakte von Heinrich Klockmann, BArch Koblenz, Z 42 III/102.

132. Leumundszeugnis A.L. Karola Groß, a former sex worker at Sachsenhausen, also gave positive testimony regarding the camp's SS officers. See Zeugenaussage K.G., HStAD, Akte Gerichte Rep. 388 Nr. 12, 188–89.

133. See the testimony of Kanthack, AMM, V 3/20, 25.

134. See the testimony of Maršálek, IKF, H. Marsaek Video-Int. 2, 16.

135. Szymanski said the following about Bergen-Belsen: "There were thousands of women dying in Bergen-Belsen. Women who survived Auschwitz, who had good jobs, worked in the kitchen, they went to Bergen-Belsen and they died in two weeks" (Interv. Sommer 2005-01-28 S., pt. 1, 01.03.00).

136. See Interv. Sommer 2005-01-28 S., pt. 1, 00.19.00.

137. See the testimony of Beulig, AUSHMM, RG-06.005.05M Reel 1, 7–8.

138. See the testimony of M.W., WdE, Sig. 295, 29–30. The imprisonment in the bunker is also documented by the job sheets. See Abrechnungsbögen, BArch, NS 4 Bu/41.

139. Testimony of M.W., 1988, WdE, Sig. 295, 13.

140. Testimony of M.W., WdE, Sig. 295, 30.

141. Fifty years later, she said the following about her suicide attempt: "Unfortunately, I wasn't able to carry it out. I got fourteen days in the bunker for doing it. I'm still alive today, but under what conditions!" (testimony of M.W.).

142. This chapter is based on the analysis of information from Sommer, Forced Sex Worker Database, AMGR, MS Sommer.

143. Nine forced sex workers cannot be identified by name, but their stay in a camp brothel can be proven by the prisoner number assigned to them. These are the women with the Neuengamme prisoner numbers 6583 and 6584 as well as the women with the Sachsenhausen women's numbers 500, 501, 502, 504, 505, 506, and 508. These women are not included in the analysis because little information about them has survived.

144. In the case of Buchenwald, two women can be identified as forced sex workers. In Flossenbürg and Gusen, two in each camp are very likely to have been forced sex workers.

145. This also included women from Austria. One woman came from Lorraine.

146. Two "criminal" women were "preventive detainees." Two others were "professional criminals" (BV).

147. The women, B.R. and C.K, were forced sex workers in Dachau. See the Dachau section in the Appendix. C.S., a forced sex worker at the Dachau and Gusen camp brothels, was classified as a "political" prisoner according to an ITS list compiled after the war. According to the prisoner and inmate cards issued by the SS, however, she had been registered as an "antisocial" in Ravensbrück. See WVHA-Häftlingskartei Barch D-H, NS 3/1577; and Liste Häftlinge Dachau ITS and Häftlings-Personal-Karte, AUSHMM 1996.A.0342 Reel 120.

148. Two women had both citizenships and were categorized as "political": E.R. in Dachau and Gusen (Zugangsliste Ravensbrück, June 5, 1942, AMGR, AGGB, 01023002—Polish/political, recidivist; Zahlungsbeleg Dachau brothel, December 12, 1944, AGD, Dok Ad 87/3—German Reich /political); and S.R. in Ravensbrück (Kartei ehemalige Häftlinge Ravensbrück, AMGR, AGGB, 020390). S.L. in Flossenbürg was an "antisocial German" (Nummernbuch Flossenbürg, AUSHMM, 1996.A.0342 Reel 4) and a "political Pole" (Zugangsbuch June 6, 1942, AMGR, AGGB, 01023101). See Sommer, Forced Sex Worker Database, AMGR, MS Sommer.

149. See Sommer, Forced Sex Worker Database, AMGR, MS Sommer.

150. These women's places of birth include Kharkov (Ukraine), Stalino (now Donetsk, Ukraine), Klintsy (central Russia), and Schlobin (Belarus). See Sommer, Forced Sex Worker Database, AMGR, MS Sommer.

151. B.G.'s name is mentioned together with the names of ten female forced sex workers from the Mittelbau-Dora concentration camp on a slip accompanying blood samples for a serological examination. See Appendix, "Mittelbau-Dora." On a prisoner card, E.S.'s reason for imprisonment is given as "protective custody, Jew." Her prisoner number and date of birth can be corroborated but not her date of admission (August 8, 1944) or her job description ("unskilled worker"). It can be assumed that the card index was compiled incorrectly. Another prisoner card exists for E.S. categorizing her as a "Reich German/antisocial." The Ravensbrück admission list and the list of women in the Dachau camp brothel classify her as "RD antisocial" as well. See WVHA-Häftlingskartei, BArch D-H, NS 3/1577; Zugangsliste July 9, 1943, AMGR, AGGB, 01025102; and Liste Frauen Lagerbordell Dachau, December 12, 1944, AGD, Dok Ad 87/3 (987). On the nationality of forced sex workers, see Appendix, Table 12.

152. In Neuengamme, only German men were allowed to visit the brothel, which explains why the SS only recruited women of German nationality. See the testimony of Büttig (Frau X), AGN, transcription, 11. By contrast, relatively few Germans and many Poles were imprisoned in Auschwitz.

153. I am using the average age at the time of entry to the first camp brothel. For a detailed breakdown of the age structure, see Appendix, Table 12; and Robert Sommer, Forced Sex Worker Database, AMGR, MS Sommer.

154. E. N. was in the camp brothel for two days; Frieda S. was there for thirty-four months. See Begleitzettel October 12,1943, APMO, Akta HI Rajsko 20b/534; and Zugangsbuch Mauthausen AMGR, AGGB, 030259.

155. The earliest verifiable stay in the brothel was used as the date of entry. In cases where this was not available, the opening date of the brothel was used. See Sommer, Forced Sex Worker Database, AMGR, MS Sommer.

156. These were E.C., E.G., M.W., E.F., M.R., W.Z., W.K., K.Z., A.M., and L.B. from Buchenwald as well as L.B. from Dachau. See Sommer, Forced Sex Worker Database, AMGR, MS Sommer.

157. Schikorra, *Prostitution*, 119.

158. This is explicitly stated by Beulig and is corroborated by the brothel job sheets. See BArch, NS 4 Bu and 41.

159. See Sommer, Forced Sex Worker Database, AMGR, MS Sommer.

160. See the testimony of K.G., HStAD, Akte Gerichte Rep. 388 Nr. 12, 118.

161. In all three cases, the name is very common, and records documenting the date of birth have not survived. However, the dates of death do not contradict the period spent in the camp brothel. M.K. died in Ravensbrück on April 6, 1945 (Nationale Mahn- and Gedenkstätte Ravensbrück and Projekt Gedenkbuch, *Gedenkbuch*, 342), K. (née R.) died in Ravensbrück on March 1, 1945 (Ravensbrück and Projekt Gedenkbuch, *Gedenkbuch*, 344), and S. died in Neubrandenburg on December 29, 1944 (Ravensbrück and Projekt Gedenkbuch, *Gedenkbuch*, 607).

162. H.P. died on November 4, 1944. See Ravensbrück and Projekt Gedenkbuch, *Gedenkbuch*, 490.

163. See Schikorra, *Prostitution*, 122. On the list of arrivals cited by Schikorra, almost all 264 Polish women on the transport that arrived that day were initially classified as "political" prisoners. Most foreigners were placed in this group. For several women, however, the reason for detention was indicated by a handwritten note indicating either that they were "asocial" or "career criminals." See Zugangsliste Ravensbrück, April 10, 1942, AMGR, AGGB, 01019907; Sommer, "Lagergesellschaft," 302.

164. Here are two examples: A woman from the Dachau camp brothel (Dachau number 91 138) is listed as Jewish on one prisoner card and as an "antisocial" German on another, almost identical card (WVHA-Kartei, BArch D-H, NS 3/1577). She is also listed as an "antisocial" German in the register of incoming prisoners at Ravensbrück (July 9, 1942) and on an ITS list (AMGR, AGBB, 01025102 and list ITS, AUSHMM 1996 A.0342 Reel 19). Magdalena Walter stated that the SS changed the triangle first from red to black and then blue (for "stateless") when she was sent to the concentration camp. See the testimony of M.W., 1988, WdE, Sig. 295, 15. The ITS stated the reasons for her detention as "protective custody," "antisocial," and "work-shy." See letter from ITS to Projektgruppe für die vergessenen Opfer des NS-Regimes in Hamburg e.V., May 9, 1989, Private Collection Sommer; and ITS, KLD/Buchenwald, Umschlag Nr. 27238.

165. These are the Dachau sex forced workers with the numbers 69845 and 80173 as well as the Flossenbürg survivor with the number 52. See Sommer, Forced Sex Worker Database, AMGR, MS Sommer.

166. See Zugangsliste Ravensbrück January 12, 1945, AMGR, AGGB, 01149401.

167. Baumgärtner writes that those women were forced to work as block leaders for the newly arrived Jewish women. See Baumgärtner, *Frauen*, 102. The prisoner cards of M.H., B.W., F.S., and C.S. indicate that the women worked as prisoner supervisors from April 12, 1945, onward. See Häftlings-Personal-Karte, AUSHMM, 1996. A.0342 Reel 120; NARA, Arolsen Documents, Mauthausen Reel 7 and 8.

168. See the testimony of Szymanski, Interv. Sommer 2005-01-28 S., pt. 1, 1.02.00.

169. Testimony of Bator, APMO, Ośw./68/Bator.

170. See Schalm, *München*, 396–98.

171. See the transfer of three women from Ravensbrück to Sachsenhausen in exchange for "sick or unsuitable prisoners," October 5, 1944, AMGR, AGGB, 03017001. After the war, Minna Möller was put on trial in the GDR for her work with the camp police and punished with imprisonment. The court considered it proven that she had mistreated prisoners. On the persecution of M.M. in the GDR, see BStU, MfS—HA IX/11 AV 8/74 Bd. 37, Part 1. While the historiography of the GDR celebrated the prisoners of the camp police in Buchenwald as communist resistance fighters, Minna Möller, who was classified as "antisocial," was charged with working for the camp police. See Eschebach, *Stigma*, 72.

172. See the testimony of Domke, in APMO, Ośw./Domke/1208, 7.

173. In his interview, Szymanski talks about the help Izabela Michalek received from Hössler: "Anyhow, after six months, when I . . . was out of this Puff, Hössler helped her. He sent her to the *Lagererweiterung* in Auschwitz and she got some job not as a kapo but as some *Unterkapo* in the tailor's shop, or something like that. And also, when she came to Bergen-Belsen. So Bergen-Belsen. Again Hössler helped her and he gave her *leichte Arbeit* [easy work]" (testimony of Szymanski, Interv. Sommer 2005-01-28 S., pt. 1, 00. 26.00).

174. This can be seen in the example of the Auschwitz women's camp, where the prisoner functionaries consisted of women from the first transport of one thousand prisoners from Ravensbrück. Most of them were German women assigned a black and green triangle. See Strebel, *Ravensbrück*, 346–47. Women from the same group of prisoners were also deployed as supervisors and in functional positions in the Riga concentration camp (Kaiserwald). See Maja Abramowitch, *To Forgive . . . but Not to Forget: Maja's Story* (Vallentine Mitchell, 2002), 62; Bernhard Press, *Judenmord in Lettland: 1941–1945* (Metropol Verlag, 1992), 124–37; and Jeanette Wolff, *Mit Bibel und Bebel* (Verlag Neue Gesellschaft, 1991), 35–36.

175. See Appendix, Table 1; and Sommer, Forced Sex Worker Database, AMGR, MS Sommer.

176. This would also be supported by the fact that all these women were German "antisocials." According to the Decree on Preventive Measures by the Police to Combat Crime, imprisonment of antisocials and criminals was to be reviewed at regular intervals. See Ayaß, *Gemeinschaftsfremde*, 97.

177. See Appendix, Table 12.

178. On Mauthausen and Gusen, see Appendix, Table 1.

179. See Chapter 1, "Prostitution Policy." For example, L.K. was imprisoned several times in Hamburg's Fuhlsbüttel women's prison in 1940, 1941, and 1942 for violating paragraph 327. She was transferred to Ravensbrück on August 29, 1942. It is possible that she had already been in another prison camp. See Haftkarteikarten L-K, StA-HH Jüngere Gefangenen Kartei 242-1II Abl.13; StA-HH 242-1II Gefangenen Verwaltung II Abl. 2000/1; and U-Haft Kartei Frauen 1930-1952. Similar instances of prosecution can be found for E.G. and A.H. (both Buchenwald; StA-HH 242-1II Abl. 13 JüGefKart), G.S. (Flossenbürg; BStU MfS SkS Blatt C 54732), I.S. (Auschwitz/Mittelbau-Dora; StA-HH 242-1II Gef-Verwaltung Abt. 13, jüngere Kartei Frauen), M.P. (Mittelbau-Dora; BStU, MfS SK 5 Blatt B 43886), C.K. (Dachau/Gusen; StA-HH Jüng GefKart 242-1II Abt. 13), and WVHA-Karte female prisoner Neuengamme 6 583 (Barch D-H, NS 3/1577).

180. S.(Z.)B. (Flossenbürg) was sent to Ravensbrück on August 2, 1944, because of "intercourse with a German" (*Verk. m. Deutschem*). See AMGR, AGGB, 01110401. The following German women were sent because of sexual intercourse with a Pole: M.W. (Neuengamme; Zugangsliste Ravensbrück, May 5, 1944, AUSHMM, RG-04.006 M Reel 22), E.S. (Mittelbau-Dora; AMGR, AGGB, 01014201), and L.B. (Dachau; Verfahrensakte L.B. HStAD, Sig. RW 58-5758).

181. Elisabeth Stein is a pseudonym.

182. Verfahrensakte gegen E.S. aus dem Jahr 1958, BStU, MfS D SK5 88342 and MfS D SK 5 86615; and Zugangsliste Ravensbrück, August 21, 1942, AMGR, AGGB, 01027502. The first imprisonment is on December 7, 1940, for "intercourse with a Pole" ("Verk. m. Polen"). AMGR, AGGB, 01014201.

183. In W.L.'s case, these offenses were added as reasons for sterilization. See Akte Sterilisationsverfahren gegen W.L., ThHtA, Th LA für Rassewesen, Nr. 5982, 40–41.

184. For theft, see H.S. and S.D. (Mauthausen/Gusen; Häftlings-Personal-Karte, AUSHMM 1996.A.0342 Reel 120); and F.W. and B.W. (Mauthausen/Gusen; NARA, Arolsen Documents, Mauthausen Reel 8). For embezzlement, see, for instance, I.G. (Mauthausen; Häftlings-Personal-Karte, AUSHMM 1996.A.0342 Reel 120) and B.W. (Mauthausen/Gusen; Häftlings-Personal-Karte, NARA, Arolsen Documents, Mauthausen Reel 8). For fraud, see, for instance, I.H. (Mauthausen; Häftlings-Personal-Karte, AUSHMM 1996.A.0342 Reel 120) and B.S. (Sachsenhausen; StA-HH 213-11 Staatsanwaltschaft Landgericht Strafsachen 6648/41). For document forgery, see I.H. (Mauthausen; Häftlings-Personal-Karte,

AUSHMM 1996.A.0342 Reel 120) and L.B. (Dachau; HStAD, Sig. RW 585758 Verfahrensakte).

185. See H.T. (Auschwitz; StA-HH 242-1 II Gefängnisverwaltung II Abl. 13, Jüngere Karte); I.H. and M.H. (Mauthausen; Häftlings-Personal-Karte, AUSHMM 1996.A.0342 Reel 120); and H.S. (Buchenwald; Häftlingsakte, NARA, Arolsen Documents, Buchenwald Reel 66). For the latter, see L.S. (Sachsenhausen; StA-HH 213-11 Staatsanwaltschaft Landgericht Strafsachen 6648/41).

186. J.P. (Flossenbürg; Gefängnisbuch Frauengefängnis Danziger Straße/ Archivum Państwowe w Łodzi [APL], Wigzienie dla Kobiet przy u.l. Gdanskiej, Sig. 2).

187. See Häftlings-Personal-Karte A.P. and B.M., ITS, KLD/Buchenwald, Umschlag Nr. 16686 as well as 18560.

188. For example, a forced sex worker from Auschwitz was categorized by the SS as an "RZA," or Russian civilian worker (Häftlings-Personal-Karte O.S., ITS, KLD/Flossenbürg, Umschlag Nr. 010159). Three Polish forced sex workers from Flossenbürg were civilian workers (S.P, J.P., and St.B., Häftlings-Personal-Karten, ITS, KLD/Flossenbürg, Umschläge Nr. 007545, 007982 and 000919).

189. See Antrag auf Haftnachweis, A.P., ITS, Ablage, T/D—1012870.

190. See Häftlings-Personal-Karte I.L., ITS, KLD/Buchenwald, Umschlag Nr. 14362.

191. Nico Rost, *Goethe in Dachau* (Ullstein TB, 2001), 277–78.

192. These were the forced sex workers C.S., A.E., and A.H., as well as the "cashier" M.G. See Military Government of Germany, questionnaire for concentration camp inmates, ITS, KLD/Buchenwald, Umschlag 23140, 4519, 8591, 6819. The uneven line spacing between "prostitution" and "forced by the SS" indicates that the sheet was fed into the typewriter a second time. For a copy of the questionnaire, see Robert Sommer, "Warum das Schweigen? Berichte von ehemaligen Häftlingen über Sex-Zwangsarbeit in nationalsozialistischen Konzentrationslagern," in *Krieg und Geschlecht: Sexuelle Gewalt im Krieg und Sex-Zwangsarbeit in NS-Konzentrationslagern*, ed. Insa Eschebach and Regina Mühlhäuser (Metropol, 2008), 148.

193. Testimony of Kramer, in Niemeyer and von der Tann, *Schweigen*. These children were her stepchildren, as she was unable to have children of her own after the war. She may have been forcibly sterilized before being sent to a concentration camp. There is no indication of an abortion or sterilization in the Mauthausen logbook of surgical procedures. See Operationsbuch Mauthausen, AMM, H 12/2.

194. See the testimony of M.W., WdE, Sig. 295, 18.

195. M.W. uses the term "friend."

196. Testimony of M.W.

197. See the testimony of M.W., 18–19. On February 25, 1966, her application for recognition and compensation per BEG §1 was rejected by the Hamburg District Court. The reason was that her prisoner category ("antisocial") excluded

her from receiving compensation. See email from Beate Hugk, Projektgruppe für die vergessenen Opfer des NS-Regimes e.V., January 22, 2007. Two other cases are known in which women applied for compensation but concealed their stay in a camp brothel. These were the Polish woman I.L. and the German woman H. von B. (both Auschwitz). ITS, Ablage/T/D–978130 and 809165.

198. Testimony of L.B., WdE, Sig. 294T, 19.

199. Testimony of L.B., 20.

200. See the testimony of L.B., 32.

201. Testimony of L.B., 31–32.

202. See list of female prisoners of Vught concentration camp, AMGR, AGGB, without signature.

203. See Interv. Sommer 2003-05-01 Hantz II, 1.

204. Testimony of Herr J., Privatsammlung Paul, without signature, 5.

205. See the testimony of Szymanski, Interv. Sommer 2005-01-28 S., pt. 2, 00.14.00.

206. See the testimony of Terry, Interv. Sommer 2003-07-19 Terry, 5.

207. See Jörg Skriebeleit, "KZ Gedenkstätte Flossenbürg: Retrospektiven und Ausblicke," *Gedenkstättenrundbrief* 83 (1998): 13–17; and Jörg Skriebeleit, "Neue Perspektiven für die KZ-Gedenkstätte Flossenbürg," in *Informationen für Mitglieder, Freunde und Förderer des Vereins "Gegen das Vergessen—für Demokratie" e.V.* (Flossenbürg, 1998), 47–50.

208. Her lawyer stated: "Ms . . . was imprisoned in the Ravensbrück and Flossenbürg camps from April 1942 to 1945 as prisoner no. . . . She was listed there as work-shy or antisocial but was actually imprisoned because of outspoken statements about the Nazi regime and its 'Führer.' As far as is known, she was sterilized and forced to perform services in the camp brothel" (Schreiben an des Landesamt für Wiedergutmachung Bremen, September 26, 1966, StA-B, 4,56 E 12004).

209. Her depression, nervous breakdowns, and mood disorders "can also be explained by the fact that the applicant was forced to work as a camp prostitute in the Ravensbrück and Flossenbürg camps" (Einschreiben an das Landesamt für Wiedergutmachung Bremen, August 31, 1967, StA-B, 4,56 E 12004).

210. See Bescheid des Landesamts für Wiedergutmachung Bremen, March 29, 1968, StA-B, 4,56 E 12004; and Akte Erbgesundheitsgericht, Staatsarchiv Bremen (StA-B), 4,130/2-EG.XIII. Nr.127/1936 E.F.

7. Brothel Visitors

1. See Chapter 5, "Administration."

2. Before the premium system was introduced in May 1943, prisoners had to pay with money from their camp account. See Chapter 5, "Administration."

3. Willi Frohwein said that he did not even know that a bonus system existed in Auschwitz, Monowitz, and Gross-Rosen. He had only heard of bonus vouchers in Mittelbau-Dora. See Interv. Sommer 2003-05-07 Frohwein, pt. 2, 00.25.55.

4. Testimony of Maršálek, IKF, H. Marsalek Video-Int. 2, 16.

5. In Auschwitz-Birkenau, Jewish prisoners had to work in the crematoria and gas chambers. They were murdered by the SS at regular intervals. Because of their origin, they were excluded from visiting brothels. In concentration camps where the crematoria were not primarily used as mass murder facilities, the SS employed non-Jewish prisoners who belonged to the privileged class and who were thus allowed to visit the camp brothel. See the testimony of K.G., HStAD, Akte Gerichte Rep. 388 Nr. 12, 118. See also Gideon Greif, *We Wept Without Tears: Testimonies of the Jewish Sonderkommando from Auschwitz* (Yale University Press, 2014); and Staatliches Museum Auschwitz-Birkenau, ed., *Inmitten des grauenvollen Verbrechens: Handschriften von Mitgliedern des Sonderkommandos* (Verlag Staatliches Museum Auschwitz-Birkenau, 1996).

6. Sofsky, *The Order of Terror*, 145–52; and the testimony of Maršálek, IKF, H. Marsalek Video-Int. 2, 16. In the Mauthausen concentration camp, the group of privileged prisoners was also composed of DEST-trained stonemasons, nearly all whom were Germans. See the testimony of Maršálek, IKF, H. Marsalek Video-Int. 2, 14.

7. See Bordellbuch Block 3, June 11 to December 31, 1942, AMM, K 2/1.

8. Since records for the months of June and July 1942 are incomplete, I consider August 1, 1942, to be the date on which visitors began using the brothel. In the early months, 128 prisoners were listed, ninety of whom visited the brothel. See Bordellbuch Block 3, AMM, K2/1.

9. See Appendix, Table 2.

10. The communist Vosseler is clear on this point. See Vosseler: Niederschrift zur Tätigkeit des S. im KZ Flossenbürg. Quoted in Klausch, *Widerstand*, 91. See also Weidlich, "Sonderbau," AMGB, 31–494, 4.

11. Figures from Mauthausen show that a disproportionate share of these groups came from the prisoner elite. As of February 23, 1945, the camp's 184 prisoner functionaries consisted of 114 German criminals and twenty German political prisoners. The other political prisoners were nineteen Czechs, eighteen Poles, eight Spaniards, and five Yugoslavians. See Maršálek, *Geschichte des Konzentrationslagers Mauthausen*, 58, 62.

12. For instance, Linda Bachmann, the former forced sex worker from Mittelbau-Dora, noted the many greens among the brothel visitors. See the testimony of L.B., WdE, Sig. 294T, 26. And a former prisoner from Flossenbürg, Hugo Walleitner, writes that "political prisoners did not use the special building at all on the first day and very rarely later (Walleitner, *Zebra*, 96). Vosseler mentions a few "political" prisoners who were brothel visitors. See Klausch, *Widerstand*, 91.

13. See the testimony of Maršálek, IKF, H. Marsalek Video-Int. 2, 14; and Pike, *Spaniards in the Holocaust*, 73.

14. Weidlich, "Sonderbau," AMGB, Sign. 56-8-4, 6.

15. See the testimony of M.W., WdE, Sig. 295, 26.

16. See Niethammer, *Antifaschismus*, 48, 279–80, 312; and Chapter 8, "The Buchenwald Communists."

17. See Heger, *Männer*, 139.

18. See Skriebeleit, "Flossenbürg–Stammlager," 40.

19. See the testimony of Hantz, Interv. Sommer 2003-02-01 Hantz, 00.22.00.

20. See Weidlich, "Sonderbau," AMGB, Sig 31–494, 6. For purposes of comparison, the number of prisoners in the Buchenwald main camp on July 1 (12,711 prisoners) and September 1, 1943 (14,983 prisoners) was used. See Stein, "Funktionswandel," 178, 188.

21. See Appendix, Table 6.

22. See Abrechnungsbögen "Sonderbau," July 11 to August 10, 1943, BArch, NS 4 Bu/41. During this period, the brothel was closed for one day because of a "lack of water." This day was not included in the calculation.

23. These are average monthly figures. In general, the number of visitors fluctuated between nine and seventy-six during this period. See Abrechnungsbögen "Sonderbau," August 1943, BArch, NS 4 Bu/41.

24. See Appendix, Table 6; and Abrechnungsbögen "Sonderbau," BArch, NS 4 Bu/41.

25. An inmate named Wolf who worked in the Buchenwald camp office compiled lists of brothel visitors. See the testimony of Beulig, AUSHMM, RG-06.005.05M, 5–6. One survivor's account of Dachau states that only a small circle of "regular customers" visited the brothel. See Dachauer Häftlinge, *Dachau*, 25.

26. See Appendix, Table 6.

27. See Appendix, Table 6; and Abrechnungsbögen "Sonderbau," August 1—December 31, 1943, BArch, NS 4 Bu/41.

28. On average, a prisoner visited the brothel 9.1 times. On the ratio of visits and male brothel visitors, see Appendix, Table 6.

29. See Weidlich, "Sonderbau," AMGB, Sig 31–494, 6.

30. On the increase in prisoner numbers, see Appendix, Table 6.

31. Interv. Sommer 2004-04-06 Löwenberg, 00.31.00.

32. In an interview, Löwenberg writes: "I think at the table where I was, in block 39, the so-called celebrity block, nobody reacted to it. The older people were used to it and it wasn't interesting for us young people. I didn't get any, I don't know, interested approval. . . . Sometimes we talked about intimate things with close comrades, but no, not an issue at all, not an issue at all" (Interv. Sommer 2004-04-06 Löwenberg, 00.32.00f).

33. The calculation is based on the assumption that the ratio of visits and visitors in Buchenwald is similar to that in Mauthausen. See Appendix, Table 6; Abrechnungsbögen "Sonderbau," BArch, NS 4 Bu/41; and Bordellbuch Block 3, AMM, K2/1.

34. A total of 128 prisoners are listed for the entire period of the visitor log (from the start of June to the end of December 1942). Of these, ninety (or 70 percent) visited the brothel. As the first two months have not been handed down

in full, only the analysis from August 1942 onward can be used in this context. See Bordellbuch Block 3, AMM, K2/1.

35. Four prisoners visited the brothel between thirty and forty-five times during this period. See Bordellbuch Block 3, AMM, K2/1.

36. For a detailed breakdown, see Appendix, Table 6.

37. Heger, *Männer*, 139.

38. Following Kleiber and Velten, I examine the social and individual motives of male prisoners. Kleiber and Velten divide the motives for visiting brothels into the categories of "social" and "sexual." I have defined the latter category more broadly. See Kleiber and Velten, *Prostitutionskunden*, 65–68.

39. O.W. (No. 2 111), who visited the brothel twenty-four times in six months, was a kapo in the disinfection unit. H.M. (No. 1 853) was a scribe (thirty-nine visits). P.G. (No. 1 030) was a kapo (forty-three visits). E.H. (No. 709) was a cook in the camp kitchen (twenty-eight visits). All data refer to the period from August 1 to December 31, 1942. See Häftlingszugangsbuch Mauthausen, AMM, Y 44; Aufstellung der Lagerschreibstube von Häftlingen, die zum Tragen einer Uhr berechtigt waren, AMM, L 7/2; and Häftlings-Personal-Karten, AMM, without signature.

40. In Auschwitz, this included a German "criminal" named Bruno, who was between fifty and sixty years old. See the testimony of Piecha, Interv. Sommer 2003-05-05 P. II, 2 (Auschwitz). On other camps, see Jack Terry and Alicia Nitecki, *Jakub's World: A Boy's Story of Loss and Survival in the Holocaust* (State University of New York Press, 2005), 70–71 (Flossenbürg); the testimony of Engemann, AGS R 34, 1 (Sachsenhausen); Niethammer, *Antifaschismus*, 310 (Buchenwald); the testimony of L.B., WdE, 22, 31 (Mittelbau-Dora); and the testimony of Kanthack, AMM, V 3/20, 24–25 (Mauthausen).

41. See the testimony of Posener, APMO, Ośw./36/Posener, 27; see also Heger, *Männer*, 141.

42. See the testimony of Stanisław Łapiński, APMO, Ośw./Łapiński/933, 5. A former Belgian prisoner of the Neuengamme concentration camp reports that block elders, foremen, kitchen kapos, and some privileged people were allowed to go to the brothel. See the testimony of van Ausloos, AGN, Sig. 33. Borowski names the camp elder, the camp kapo, doctors from the camp infirmary, and other kapos as brothel visitors in Auschwitz. See Borowski, *Auschwitz*, 143; and the testimony of Petrykowski, APMO, Ośw./Petrykowski/1931.

43. Heger describes the "gypsy kapo" with whom he had a sexual relationship as a regular brothel visitor. See Heger, *Männer*, 194. Pike speaks of a Spaniard who was the kapo of the cobbler's workshop in Mauthausen. See Pike, *Spaniards*, 335. Cantaluppi identifies a kapo who worked at the camp office. See Cantaluppi, *Flossenbürg*, 60.

44. In addition to the first camp elder (Erich Reschke) and the kapo of the infirmary (Ernst Busse), the kapo in the food warehouse (Heinz D.), the kapo of the SS-Führerheim and the SS canteen (Karl G.), and an orderly in the infirmary

(Helmut T.) were known to have visited the brothel. See Niethammer, *Antifaschismus*, 279–80, 312, 315, 493–519.

45. See Sofsky, *The Order of Terror*, 145.

46. See Sofsky, *The Order of Terror*, 169.

47. Kogon, *The Theory and Practice of Hell*, 136. Fredi Diament, a former prisoner of Monowitz, describes how he overheard prisoners in the elite block boasting about what they had done in the "Sonderbau." See the testimony of Diament, Interv. Sommer 2004-06-15 Diament, 00.13.00.

48. Dachauer Häftlinge, *Dachau*, 45. On the connection between food and prostitution in the world outside, see Grenz, *Lust*, 136.

49. Testimony of Gärtig, in Niethammer, *Antifaschismus*, 312. On Ernst Busse, see Chapter 8, n73.

50. Pike describes how the distribution of bonus vouchers, which were necessary for visiting brothels, was a sign of the "growing prestige of the Spaniards in the camp" (Pike, *Spaniards*, 73).

51. According to Tillard, this led to violence among the prisoners. The SS intervened and murdered the six Spaniards by hanging. Pike, however, argues that this story could also be a camp anecdote. See Pike, *Spaniards*, 73.

52. The name is a pseudonym. See the testimony of J. B., BJBS, without signature, 5.

53. Langbein, *People in Auschwitz*, 408. The extent to which truth and fiction are mixed here is unclear. This statement appears to be a rumor that exaggerates a fact that is essentially true.

54. Weidlich, AMGB, Sig 31–494, 5.

55. See the testimony of van Dijk, in Mieder and Schwarz, "Häftlingsbordell," 12–13.

56. See Lesniak, "Psychiatrische Probleme," 42–52.

57. Magdalena Walter reports about an older communist prisoner who visited her in the camp brothel: "And that he always said, this is the last, this is also the end of me here. I won't get to freedom, I'll die here" (testimony of M. W., WdE, Sig. 295, 26).

58. Romek Dubitzki stated: "There was an older driver in his team. The third mechanic. And he begged him to give him his ticket. He said, 'Please, I wash your shirt! I give you nice shirts, whatever you want! Please give me your ticket to the brothel!' He was an old bachelor" (Interv. Sommer 2004-04-06 D., pt. 1, 01.17.00).

59. See the testimony of Hájková, Interv. Sommer 2006-02-13 Hájková, 00.07.00. See also IKF, H. Marsalek Video-Int. 2, 16–17.

60. See Roßmann, *Sozialismus*, 177; the testimony of Piecha, Interv. Sommer 2003-03-30 P. I, 3; the testimony of Löwenberg, Interv. Sommer 2004-04-06 Löwenberg, 00.07.00; and Paul, *Zwangsprostitution*, 45, 76–77.

61. See the testimony of L.B., WdE, Sig. 294T, 30. The forced sex worker Elenora Franke told Heigl: "The prisoners just wanted to be hugged" (Heigl, *Zwangsprostitution*, 45). Matussek quotes a former prisoner from Dachau: "Many

went there to talk to a woman for once . . ." (Matussek, *Konzentrationslagerhaft*, 29). Theo Fischer (Dora) stated: "To the credit of most of the prisoners, it must be said that they did not make use of the right they had acquired, but regarded it as an interesting camp diversion to be able to talk to a woman undisturbed for once after a long time" (Mittelbau, AGMD, DMD-EB/HT-81, 5).

62. See the memory log of Paul about the conversation with E.F., Privatsammlung Paul. Kupfer-Koberwitz recounts a story he was told: "This shyness of the still foreign personality has such a strong inhibiting effect that the men are usually not capable at all.—He did tell me about one man who, while waiting in the corridor, was so stimulated by onanistic acts that all he had to do then was continue.—But what an animal he must be to approach the girl, excited by himself, and assault her straight away" (Kupfer-Koberwitz, *Tagebücher*, 315).

63. Mr. J. explained: "Nobody wanted to go in there, you see, because first: everyone had inhibitions, hadn't had anything to do with girls for a long time, so they didn't know what to do, what to ask, so let's say there weren't many people there" (testimony of Herr J., Privatsammlung Paul, without signature, 2).

64. Testimony of Piecha, Interv. Sommer 2003-03-30 P. I, 3.

65. One former Dachau prisoner confessed: "I also secretly wanted to go to the camp brothel. However, the circumstances surrounding such a visit prevented me from doing so. The SS leaders or female leaders often watched the people having sex and banged on the door with their boots if they took too long" (Matussek, *Konzentrationslagerhaft*, 29).

66. Heger, *Männer*, 140.

67. See Lemke, *Ganz normal anders*, 26–27.

68. See Lemke, *Ganz normal anders*, 27.

69. See Grenz, *(Un)heimliche Lust*, 62–66; and the testimony of M.W., 1988, WdE, Sig. 295, 27–28.

70. Testimony of M.W., 1988, WdE, Sig. 295, 14.

71. Testimony of Piecha, Interv. Sommer 2003-03-30 P. I, 3. Mr. J. also reported the fear of being spied on in the camp brothel. See the testimony of Herr J., Privatsammlung Paul, without signature, 2.

72. See the testimony of M.W., 1988, WdE, Sig. 295, 26.

73. Testimony of van Dijk, Mieder and Schwarz, "Häftlingsbordell," 10.

74. Mieder and Schwarz, "Häftlingsbordell."

75. Mieder and Schwarz, "Häftlingsbordell," 17. The name "Elfriede" can also be found on job sheets from the Buchenwald camp brothel. It can be assumed that this is the woman described. See Abrechnungsbögen, July and August 1943, BArch, NS 4 Bu/41.

76. "She had long hair, she looked well-groomed and cared for. And then everything else went by itself and I immediately got excited, I sat down on the bed with her, I asked her questions and everything happened quickly. But I still had to get to know love. But the fact that she was wearing silk stockings was so exciting for me and then the underwear is no longer like underwear today and

yet I can't describe exactly what she was wearing" (testimony of van Dijk, Mieder and Schwarz, "Häftlingsbordell," 13).

77. See Tanenbaum, *Prisoner 88*, 34–35. See also Interv. Sommer 2003-05-05 P. II, 20; and the testimony of Dubitzki, Interv. Sommer 2004-04-06 D., 4–5. The illustrator Władysław Siwek included this story in a watercolor depicting a column of prisoners marching out of the Auschwitz main camp. A forced sex worker can be seen waving to a prisoner from the window. The window corresponds to room 13, where Izabela Michalek was at the time. See Władysław Siwek, "Marching Out to Work" (1946), in Staatliches Museum Auschwitz-Birkenau, *Photographs*, 232.

78. She was sent to the Auschwitz concentration camp on October 9, 1942. See Czech, *Kalendarium*, 317. The accompanying documents from the Hygiene Institute in Rajsko show that she was transferred from Birkenau to quarantine in Block 10 at the end of September and was deployed in the camp brothel from October. See Begleitzettel für venerologische Untersuchungen, September 24, 1943 and October 4, 1943, APMO, Akta HI Rajsko, 418/20 and 391/20a; and the testimony of Szymanski, Interv. Sommer 2005-01-28 p., pt. 1, 00.11.00.

79. See the testimony of Szymanski, pt. 1, 00.01.00f; and the testimony of Dubitzki, Interv. Sommer 2004-04-06 D., 3–18.

80. He tried to stand in the right position in the line of waiting prisoners so that he would be assigned to room 13. See the testimony of Szymanski, Interv. Sommer 2005-01-28 S., pt. 1, 43.00f. and pt. 2, 00.30.00.

81. Testimony of Szymanski, pt. 1, 00.51.00.

82. According to his comrade Romek Dubitzki, this happened almost every day. See Interv. Sommer 2004-04-06 D., pt. 1, 01.05.00. Szymanski speaks of only ten visits at night. See the testimony of Szymanski, Interv. Sommer 2005-01-28 S., 00.51.00.

83. Once he was locked in the block during the day and had to climb out of a window. He was caught by the camp kapo, who reported the incident to the SS. The SS commander Engelschaar did not pass the report up the chain of command, because he needed Stephan Szymanski to serve as kapo in the camp fire department. See the testimony of Szymanski, Interv. Sommer 2005-01-28 S., pt. 1, 00.21.00–00.28.00, 00.50.00–00.52.00, 01.05.00–01.08.00.

84. During a medical examination at the camp infirmary, she secretly had a photo of herself taken. It was smuggled out of the camp and sent to Stephan Szymanski's relatives. See the testimony of Szymanski, pt.1, 00.30.00–00.36.00. For a copy of this picture, see Tanenbaum, *Prisoner 88*, 38. She also had a necklace with his engraved initials made for him in the camp's locksmith's shop. See interv. Sommer 2005-01-28 S., pt. 1, 00.36.00.

85. Her last stay in the camp brothel was September 12, 1944. See Begleitzettel Block 24, September 14, 1944, APMO, Akta HI Rajsko, 880/48. She then worked as an auxiliary kapo in the camp extension. Stephan Szymanski visited her there several times. See interv. Sommer 2005-01-28 S. pt. 1, 00.25.00.

86. After the fire department commando was transferred to Sachsenhausen in November 1944, the two kept in touch via letter. See the testimony of Szymanski, 00.29.00.

87. Testimony of Szymanski, pt. 2, 00.10.00–00.14.00 and pt. 2, 00.31.00.

88. In his testimony, Jakub Piecha says the following about the relationship: "He was very much in love with her . . . always stood in front of the block and looked to her window, and she stood at the window the whole time, room 13. And also looked at him, so there was eye contact" (testimony of Piecha, Interv. Sommer 2003-03-30 P. I, 5).

89. Tanenbaum, *Prisoner 88*, 39.

90. He is said to have told his comrade Romek Dubitzki: "If I see anyone with I. . . . I'll kill him!" (Testimony of Dubitzki, Interv. Sommer 2004-04-06 D., pt. 1, 01.17.00). Joris Brouwer also remembers seeing a very beautiful girl in the brothel and knowing that she was the lover of the fire chief. See the testimony of J.B., BJBS, without signature, 6.

91. On Neuengamme, see information from Christl Wickert, March 4, 2002; for Mauthausen, see the testimony of Otto Wahl, in Paul, *Zwangsprostitution*, 60.

92. Testimony of H. Maršálek, IKF, H. Marsalek Video-Int. 2, 15. Borowski writes: "Some Juliet has a steady suitor, and apart from assurances of eternal love, apart from promises of a better, happier life together after the camp, apart from arguments and reproaches, you also hear concrete conversations that mainly deal with soap, perfume, silk panties, and cigarettes" (Borowski, *Auschwitz*, 143).

93. See the testimony of H. Maršálek, IKF, H. Marsalek Video-Int. 2, 15–16; Christiansen, AGN, 1273, 96 (Neuengamme); and Federn, *Eros*, 71 (Buchenwald).

94. See the testimony of Dekeyser, Interv. Sommer 2003-07-19 Dekeyser, 2–7; and Thomas Muggenthaler, *"Ich lege mich hin und sterbe!": Ehemalige Häftlinge des KZ Flossenbürg berichten* (E. Vögel, 2005), 93–94.

95. See the testimony of Stolecki, APMO, Ośw./Stolecki/1703, 9.

96. See the testimony of Zając, APMO, Ośw./Zając/2045, 106. Christiansen reports something similar at Neuengamme. He was once ordered by an SS man by "official order" to visit the brothel. Christiansen replied that he was married and had a son and "would not think of cheating on my wife as I would expect my wife to do." The SS man then left him alone. See Christiansen, AGN, 1273, 95.

97. See Niethammer, *Antifaschismus*, 48–49. However, Reschke himself was later known in the camp to have regularly visited the brothel. See Niethammer, *Antifaschismus*, 310.

98. See the Neuengamme section in the Appendix.

99. See Interv. Sommer 2003-02-01 Hantz, pt. 1, 00.10.00.

100. Jean Michel, *Dora: The Nazi Concentration Camp Where Modern Space Technology Was Born and 30,000 Prisoners Died* (Holt Rinehart & Winston, 1980), 156–57.

101. Heger claims that the camp director ordered him to visit the brothel on three occasions, though the statement could not be verified. See Heger, *Männer*, 140.

102. See Chapter 5, "The Realities of Camp Life."

103. Löwenberg states that he was friends with a man known to be gay. See the testimony of Löwenberg, Interv. Sommer 2004-04-06 Löwenberg, 01.03.00.

104. See Hackett, Buchenwald-Report, 108; Wolfgang Röll, *Homosexuelle Häftlinge im Konzentrationslager Buchenwald* (Nationale Mahn- und Gedenkstätte 1991), 35–43; and Hans Davidsen-Nielsen, *Carl Vaernet: Der dänische SS-Arzt im KZ Buchenwald* (Edition Regenbogen, 2004).

8. Perception and Resistance

1. See Kupfer-Koberwitz, *Tagebücher*, 294.

2. Federn, "Versuch einer Psychologie des Terrors," 59. The former Auschwitz inmate Przybyła reported that "masses of inmates" gathered and looked longingly at the women when they were taken to the infirmary for examinations. See the testimony of Przybyła, APMO, Ośw./Przybyła/2287, 18–19. On Monowitz, see the testimony of Szpunar, APMO, Ośw./Szpunar/1935, 13.

3. Kupfer-Koberwitz, *Tagebücher*, 293. Kupfer-Koberwitz mentions the brothel several times and offers some related anecdotes. The discrepancy between sexual fantasy and the reality of the camp brothels, as well as the moral aspects of visiting the brothel, were other topics of conversation among the prisoners. See Kupfer-Koberwitz, *Tagebücher*, 293, 315–16.

4. See the testimony of Beulig, AUSHMM, RG-06.005.05M Reel 1, 2.

5. Nansen, *Tag*, 188.

6. See the testimony of Dekeyser, Interv. Sommer 2003-07-19 Dekeyser, 10.

7. See the testimony of Löwenberg, Interv. Sommer 2004-04-06 Löwenberg, 01.12.00.

8. On the meaning and function of rumors, see Antje Michel, "Gerüchte im KZ Sachsenhausen: Ein Paradigma für die Kommunikationsstruktur einer Zwangsgesellschaft von Konzentrationslagerhäftlingen," in *Abgeschlossene Kapitel? Zur Geschichte der Konzentrationslager und der NS Prozesse*, ed. Sabine Moller, Miriam Rürup, and Christel Trouvé (Kimmerle G, 2002), 59–68; and Betlen, *Leben*, 254.

9. Federn, *Psychologie*, 59–60. One example is the testimony by the Jewish survivor Schmuel Lubochinski: "Buna had its own brothel, most of them were supposed to have been French women. I don't know anything else about it" (testimony of Schmuel Lubochinski, WL, Section II, Reel 53). A particularly sensational description of the camp brothel can be found in Pierre d'Harcourt, *The Real Enemy* (Scribner, 1967), 124–25.

10. Testimony of Dekeyser, Interv. Sommer 2003-07-19 Dekeyser, 10.

11. See the testimony of Gibillini, Interv. Sommer 2003-07-20 Mariconti Gibillini. On Neuengamme, see Louis Martin-Chauffier, *L'homme et la bête* (Gallimard, 1948).

12. See the testimony of Bibel, Interv. Sommer 2004-06-21 Bibel, 1 (Buchenwald); and the testimony of Szymanski, Interv. Sommer 2004-02-05 S., pt. 1, 00.41.00 (Auschwitz).

13. See the testimony of Terry, Interv. Sommer 2003-07-19 Terry, 5.

14. The archives of the Auschwitz-Birkenau State Museum contain around fifty statements in which the camp brothel is mentioned. Most of these statements come from former Polish prisoners. See APMO, holdings Ośw.

15. Interv. Sommer 2004-03-19 2x Maschkowski, 15. Another example: "Everyone knew that this existed and that this was the barracks" (testimony of König, Interv. Sommer 2004-02-05 König, 4).

16. See the testimony of Długoborski, Interv. Sommer 2003-04-30 Długoborski, 4.

17. Testimony of Lykianow, Interv. Sommer 2003-04-12 Lykianow, 2. Other prisoners found out about the camp brothel only after particular incidents. The Italian survivor Teo Ducci knew nothing about the brothel in the Auschwitz main camp until one day he saw a gathering of people in front of it and noticed the women at the window. See Ducci, *Tallèt*, 83–84.

18. Testimony of Frohwein, Interv. Sommer 2003-05-07 Frohwein, pt. 3, 00.02.03.

19. Testimony of Frohwein, pt. 4, 00.28.44.

20. See the testimony of Stolecki, APMO, Ośw./Stolecki/1703, 9.

21. The former Monowitz prisoner Adam König reports that his friend saw the women during his work as the camp gardener. See testimony of König, Interv. Sommer 2004-02-05 König, 4.

22. See the testimony of Tauber, APMO, Ośw./Tauber/1938, 86.

23. See the testimony of Diament, Interv. Sommer 2004-06-15 Diament, 00.05.00.

24. Tadeusz Borowski, *Here in Our Auschwitz*, 13.

25. See the testimony of Raimondi, Interv. Sommer 2005-04-22 Raimondi, 1.

26. See Muggenthaler, *Häftlinge*, 146.

27. See the testimony of Dubitzki, Interv. Sommer 2004-04-06 D., pt. 2, 00.34.00.

28. See the testimony of Maršálek, IKF, H. Marsalek Video–Int. 2, 16, 26.

29. See the testimony of Bator, APMO, Ośw./68/Bator, BJBS, without signature, 27–30.

30. Testimony of Bator, 27.

31. Millu describes a room "handsomely furnished with armchairs, sofas, mirrors, and a large glowing stove." Millu, *Smoke Over Birkenau*, 167.

32. Millu, *Smoke Over Birkenau*, 167.

33. Millu, *Smoke Over Birkenau*, 168.

34. In the case of Millu, it is not clear what is truth and what is fiction, as I was unable to verify the origins and names of the women she mentions. See Appendix, "Auschwitz and Monowitz" and Table 7.

35. Ella Lingens, *Eine Frau im Konzentrationslager* (Europa Verlag, 1966), 23.

36. Lingens, *Eine Frau im Konzentrationslager*, 23.

37. Lingens, *Eine Frau im Konzentrationslager*, 23. The French survivor of Mittelbau-Dora, Yves Béon, describes the camp brothel in connection with the arrival at night of an "evacuation transport" of Jewish prisoners. Instead of taking the prisoners to the huts, the SS simply left them in the roll-call area until they died of exhaustion and cold. The women in the camp brothel closed the shutters to avoid having to watch. Yves Béon, *Planet Dora: Als Gefangener im Schatten der V2-Rakete* (Bleicher Verlag, 1999), 157–58. See also the testimony of Bernhard Natt, WL, Section II, Reel 55.

38. Barbiano di Belgiojoso, *Gusen*, 49. It is not clear if this scene is fictitious. It is possible that the man was a Ukrainian guard, as the brothel in Gusen was a combination of a brothel for prisoners and for Ukrainian guards. See Appendix, "Mauthausen and Gusen."

39. See Millu, *Smoke Over Birkenau*, 166; and the testimony of Bator, APMO, Oświ./68/Bator, BJBS, without signature, 27.

40. Testimony of Gerd Maschkowski, Interv. Sommer 2004-03-19 2x Maschkowski, 1–2. See also the testimony of Maršálek, IKF, H. Marsalek Video-Int. 2, 15; the testimony of Feuchtbaum, APMO, Oświ./Feuchtbaum/1981, 4; and the testimony of Szymanski, Interv. Sommer 2005-01-28, pt. 1, 01.01.00.

41. Kogon, *The Theory and Practice of Hell*, 135.

42. See Jorge Semprun, *Was für ein schöner Sonntag*, trans. Johannes Piron (Suhrkamp 1984), 161–63.

43. Heger, *Männer*, 141.

44. Testimony of Swiatloch, APMO, Oświ./Swiatloch/1315, 68.

45. Zywulska, *Birken*, 58–59.

46. Kupfer-Koberwitz, *Tagebücher*, 316.

47. Kupfer-Koberwitz, *Tagebücher*, 316.

48. Kupfer-Koberwitz, *Tagebücher*, 316.

49. See the testimony of J.B., BJBS, without signature, 5 (Auschwitz); Garrigoux, "Neuengamme," 18; and Muggenthaler, *Häftlinge*, 146 (Flossenbürg).

50. Dr. Paulina Trocki-Musnicki, who also stayed there with the children, stated in her account: "They were with us a lot and took great care of us, brought us lots of good food from their kitchen, and as we had no exercise, we became very fat" (testimony of Dr. Trocki, AGN, NG 2.8., account 1066, p. 4).

51. Testimony of Fürst, https://furstnaftali.com/German/NaftaliStory.html, January 3, 2024. Fürst describes the day the camp was liberated: "On the morning of April 11, 1945, we heard the roar of artillery. As the front lines drew

ever closer, resistance rose up in the camp. Buchenwald was liberated on that very day. And where was I liberated? In the pleasure house [*Freudenhaus*]! Not every twelve-year-old experienced such a special honor."

52. Millu, *Smoke Over Birkenau*, 172. See the testimony of Salus, WL, Section II, Reel 53; see also Salus, *Nichts*, 73.

53. Stephan Szymanski said in an interview: "You could say that everybody collaborated, because they worked for the German war machine. What about people in Buna-Werke, the chemists? I don't think that argument would stand. Because we were forced to collaborate" (Interv. Sommer 2005-01-28 S., pt. 2, 00.19.00).

54. Testimony of a former camp elder during the Dora trial in 1947. Quoted in Wagner, *Produktion*, 418.

55. See Appendix, "Mauthausen and Gusen," "Glossenbürg," "Auschwitz," "Sachsenhausen," and "Mittelbau-Dora."

56. Dachauer Häftlinge, *Dachau*, 24.

57. Dachauer Häftlinge, *Dachau*, 24. Another slogan was: "If we've had to put up with it for so long, we'll want to put up with it now" (24).

58. Karl Adolf Gross, *Zweitausend Tage Dachau: Erlebnisse eines Christenmenschen unter Herrenmenschen und Herdenmenschen: Berichte und Tagebücher des Häftlings Nr. 16921* (Neubau Verlag, 1946), 204. See also Kupfer-Koberwitz, *Tagebücher*, 293.

59. Zeidler, "Widerstand," AGD, 8.355.

60. Kalmar, *Zeit*, 176.

61. See Kalmar, *Zeit*, 176; and Kupfer-Koberwitz, *Tagebücher*, 293.

62. Oertel, *Gefangener*, 211.

63. See Appendix, "Dachau."

64. Ducci, *Tallèt*, 83–84.

65. He is also said to have played the "Bostin" (female boss) himself. See the testimony of Kampfert, AGN, 516, 15.

66. Testimony of Bringmann, Interv. Sommer 2004-03-29 Bringmann, 1.

67. Testimony of Bringmann, 1.

68. See Klausch, *Widerstand*, 91.

69. See Pike, *Spaniards*, 335.

70. See the testimony of M.W., 1988, WdE, Sig. 295, 14.

71. Testimony of M.W., WdE, Sig. 295, 12.

72. On the question of their motives, see Niethammer, *Antifaschismus*, 303.

73. The dilemma can be clearly seen in the person of Ernst Busse. He was one of the three leaders of the Communist Party in Buchenwald and the kapo of the infirmary. He was of central importance for the communist resistance in the camp because he was able to distribute medication, provide rooms for clandestine meetings, and facilitate communication within the resistance movement. However, Busse also had to participate in the murder of Russian prisoners of war and sick prisoners. Refusing to do so would have resulted in

his dismissal, which would have dealt a serious blow to the resistance movement. This was precisely his undoing after the war. The Soviet military administration in Germany arrested him in 1950 and sentenced him as a war criminal. He died in a Gulag camp in 1952. See Niethammer, *Antifaschismus*, 95–103. On the dilemma of the "red triangle kapos," see Karin Hartewig, "Wolf unter Wölfen? Die prekäre Macht der kommunistischen Kapos im Konzentrationslager Buchenwald," in *Abgeleitete Macht: Funktionshäftlinge zwischen Widerstand und Kollaboration. Beiträge zur Geschichte der nationalsozialistischen Verfolgung in Norddeutschland*, ed. KZ-Gedenkstätte Neuengamme (Edition Temmen, 1998), 4:117–22; and Harriet Scharnberg, "'Tätertausch'? Anfragen an die Diskussion um die kommunistischen Funktionshäftlinge im Konzentrationslager Buchenwald," in KZ-Gedenkstätte Neuengamme, *Abgeleitete Macht*, 4:123–33.

74. Niethammer, *Antifaschismus*, 152.

75. Testimony of Löwenberg, Interv. Sommer 2004-04-06 Löwenberg, 00.38.00.

76. See Federn, *Eros*, 69. A Dachau survivor reported something similar: "The political prisoners were always disciplined" (Matussek, *Konzentrationslagerhaft*, 29).

77. See Interv. Sommer 2004-04-06 Löwenberg, 00.45.00.

78. Matussek, *Konzentrationslagerhaft*, 29.

79. Schoppmann, *Homosexualität*, 247–48.

80. Federn, *Eros*, 69.

81. Testimony of Löwenberg, Interv. Sommer 2004-04-06 Löwenberg, 00.42.00. See also Federn, *Eros*, 69.

82. See the chapter "Prostitution a Necessary Social Institution of Bourgeois Society" in August Bebel, *Woman and Socialism*, trans Meta Stern Lilienthal (Socialist Literature Co., 1910), 174–82, https://www.gutenberg.org/cache/epub/47244/pg47244-images.html.

83. See Weidlich, "Sonderbau," AMGB, 31–494, 4–5.

84. Weidlich, "Sonderbau," 5.

85. Both Weidlich, "Sonderbau," AMGB, 31–494, 6.

86. Weidlich, "Sonderbau," 7.

87. Weidlich, "Sonderbau," 8. Löwenberg reported: "And the most important thing, why the comrades of the KPD and the SPD took such a position and conveyed it to us younger people, was their view that women were not a commodity, that was their political point of view. . . . Second . . . was that most of these women were comrades of ours who went into the brothels under pressure, with promises" (testimony of Löwenberg, Interv. Sommer 2004-04-06 Löwenberg, 00.08.00. See also Interv. Sommer 2004-06-21 Bibel, 1).

88. Niethammer, *Antifaschismus*, 49.

89. Testimony of Drewnitzky, in Niethammer, *Antifaschismus*, 279.

90. Weidlich, "Sonderbau," AMGB, 31–494, 5.

91. See Weidlich, "Sonderbau," 5; and the testimony of Löwenberg, Interv. Sommer 2004-04-06 Löwenberg, 00.05.00.

92. No further information is known about the author. However, the tone and style suggest a male author who wrote the poem during imprisonment in Buchenwald.

93. Author unknown, "Und Deine Mutter, Deine Braut?," AMGB, 995-70.

94. Ella Lingens also constructs a similar antagonism in a weakened form. See Lingens, *Frau*, 23.

95. Unknown author, "Weg zum Lumpen," AMGB, 995–70.

96. Weidlich, "Sonderbau," AMGB, 31–494, 8.

97. Ernst Busse made this statement while he was being investigated by the East German SED about his behavior in Buchenwald. See Niethammer, *Antifaschismus*, 280, also 49.

98. This was possible in Buchenwald because the communist inmates Willi Seifert and Herbert Weidlich worked as prisoner functionaries in the labor statistics department and compiled lists for transports to other camps in coordination with the resistance organization. See Hackett, *Buchenwald-Report*, 339–41.

99. Löwenberg considers this statement to be an exaggeration. See the testimony of Löwenberg Interv. Sommer 2004-04-06 Löwenberg, 00.34.00.

100. See statements made by Gärtig and quoted in Niethammer, *Antifaschismus*, 312; and the testimony of M.W., in Mieder and Schwarz, "Häftlingsbordell." In addition to Reschke and Busse, Heinz D., Karl G., Mr. M., and Mr. L. were well-known visitors to the camp brothel. See the testimony of Bartel, in Niethammer, *Antifaschismus*, 316.

101. According to the report, a total of thirteen reprimands were issued. Other reasons for reprimands included disobeying orders and leaking secrets. See "1. Bericht der Tätigkeit der Partei-Kontroll-Kommission," AMGB Sig. 71-2-21. Instances of communists being condemned by their comrades for visiting brothels are also known from other concentration camps. A young Czech communist who was imprisoned in Mauthausen was still blamed for the visit many years after the liberation. See the testimony of Maršálek, IKF, H. Marsalek Video-Int. 2, 16–17.

9. The Camp Brothel: An Outpost of Nazi Biopolitics

1. See Foucault, *Discipline and Punish*, 195–230; and Ehresmann, *Zellenbau im Konzentrationslager Ravensbrück*, 50–73. On the planning of a prison as panopticon, see Luigi Cajani, "Surveillance and Redemption: The Casa di Correzione of San Michele a Ripa in Rome," in Finzsch and Jütte, *Institutions*, 301–24.

2. Michel Foucault, *The History of Sexuality*, trans. Robert Hurley (Random House, 1978), 1:4.

3. See Meinen, *Wehrmacht*, 205; and Seidler, *Sanitätsführung*, 160–66.

4. See Internes Schreiben des KZ Sachsenhausen, "Die Bearbeitung der Versicherungsangelegenheiten von Häftlingen während der Schutzhaft," AUSHMM, RG- 11.001M Reel 84.

5. On the integration of concentration camps into communal structures, see Jens Schley, *Nachbar Buchenwald: Die Stadt Weimar und ihr Konzentrationslager 1937–1945* (Böhlau, 1999); and Annette Leo, *"Das ist so'n zweischneidiges Schwert hier unser KZ . . . ." Der Fürstenberger Alltag und das Frauenkonzentrationslager Ravensbrück* (Metropol, 2007).

6. See Halbmayr, "Arbeitskommando," 226.

7. Bruno Bettelheim, "Individual and Mass Behavior in Extreme Situations," *Journal of Abnormal and Social Psychology* 38, no. 4 (1943): 432.

8. Testimony of Stanisław Hantz, Interv. Sommer 2003-05-01 Hantz II, 2.

Appendix: Brief Histories and Sex Worker Statistics by Camp

1. On the history of Mauthausen, see Maršálek, *Geschichte des Konzentrationslagers Mauthausen*, 235; and Baumgartner, *Frauen von Mauthausen*, 87–92.

2. See Maršálek, "Stammlager," 51.

3. See Peter Witte et al., *Dienstkalender Heinrich Himmlers*, 165.

4. See Tätigkeitsbericht Nr. 2, started on October 1, 1941, AMM, no signature.

5. See Maršálek, *Geschichte des Konzentrationslagers Mauthausen*, 72.

6. See Bestandsskizze Baracke 1, AMM; and David Wingeate Pike, *Spaniards in the Holocaust: Mauthausen, Horror on the Danube*, corrected 11th ed. (Taylor & Francis, 2000), 72–73.

7. Maršálek states that there were eleven women in Mauthausen on June 1, 1942. See Maršálek, *Geschichte des Konzentrationslagers Mauthausen*, 115.

8. This is the first day recorded in the visitor logbook of Block 3. The brothel visits by prisoners begin one day later. See Bordellbuch Block 3, AMM, K 2/1.

9. See the testimony of Beck, Interv. Sommer 2005-02-15 Beck, 3; and Pike, *Spaniards in the Holocaust*, 72–73.

10. See Pike, *Spaniards in the Holocaust*, 335.

11. See Maršálek, *Geschichte des Konzentrationslagers Mauthausen*, 200.

12. See the testimony of Beck, Interv. Sommer 2005-02-15 Beck, 2; and the testimony of Kanthack, AMM, V 3/20, 25.

13. See the testimony of Kanthack.

14. See the testimony of Kanthack, 56. The prisoner personnel cards of former sex forced workers note that they were employed as prisoner supervisors starting on April 12, 1945. See Häftlings-Personal-Karten F.S. and B.W., NARA, Arolsen Documents, Mauthausen, Reel 7 and 8; and Häftlings-Personal-Karten M.H., C.S. and H.S., AUSHMM 1996.A.0342 Reel 120.

15. See Strebel, *KZ Ravensbrück*, 340–42.

16. See the testimony of Heinrich Kodré, AMM, V 3/24, 17.

17. On the history of Gusen, see Hans Maršálek, *Konzentrationslager Gusen: Ein Nebenlager des KZ Mauthausen* (Österreichische Lagergemeinschaft Mauthausen, 1987), 5–7; Bertrand Perz, "Gusen I und II," in Benz and Distel, *Ort IV*, 371–80; and Kaienburg, *Wirtschaft der SS*, 622–41.

18. See Perz, "Gusen I und II," 377–78.

19. See Maršálek, *Konzentrationslager Gusen*, 7; and the testimony of Maršálek, IKF, H. Marsalek Video-Int. 2, 14–19.

20. See Tätigkeitsbericht 2, entry October 12, 1942, AMM, no signature.

21. The Gusen survivor Aldo Carpi completed a charcoal sketch of the brothel titled "baracca delle 'donne' per le SS" ("barrack hut for the women of the SS"). See Aldo Carpi, *Diario di Gusen* (Einaudi, 1993), image section.

22. See also Häftlings-Personal-Karten F.S. and B.W., NARA, Arolsen Documents, Mauthausen, Reel 7 and 8, Häftlings-Personal-Karten M.H., C.S. and H.S., AUSHMM 1996.A.0342 Reel 120.

23. See Barbiano di Belgiojoso, *Diario di Gusen*, 44, 100.

24. See Pike, *Spaniards in the Holocaust*, 335. For Gusen, the total of ten women was corroborated by the number of mattresses delivered in April 1943. See the Tätigkeitsbericht 2, entry April 28, 1943, AMM, no signature.

25. See Maršálek, *Geschichte des Konzentrationslagers Mauthausen*, 133; and circular letter RSHA, June 4, 1942, GLAK, Abt. 330 Zug. 1991/34/Nr. 269.

26. See the testimony of Beck, Interv. Sommer 2005-02-15 Beck, 3; and Baumgartner, *Frauen von Mauthausen*, 93–94.

27. See Pike, *Spaniards in the Holocaust*, 72.

28. See Pike, *Spaniards in the Holocaust*, 335.

29. Prisoner records and Hollerith index cards have survived for a total of twenty women from the brothels in Mauthausen and Gusen. See WVHA-Kartei, Archiwum Państwowe we Wrocławiu (APW), Nummernkartei Polski Czerwony Krzyż; BArch D-H, NS 3/1577; and AUSHMM 1996.A.0342 Reel 120; NARA, Arolsen Documents, Mauthausen, Reel 6 and 7; and ITS, KLM/Mauthausen.

30. See Robert Sommer, Forced Sex Worker Database, last updated 11/2020, AMGR, MS Sommer. The forced sex workers from the brothel for Ukrainian guards (two of whom were also in the Mauthausen camp brothel) were probably the four "antisocial" Polish women C.P. and M.S. (Ravensbrück entry list of February 15, 1944, AMGR, AGGB, 01062702) as well as C.O. and S.C. (ITS, KLD/Mauthausen, T/D No. 1948659 and 1033117).

31. See the Zugangsbuch Mauthausen, AMGR, AGGB, 030259. L.S. came to Mauthausen-Gusen on the same transport and was probably a "cashier" in the *Sonderbau*. See Zugangsbuch Dachau, AUSHMM, RG-04.006 M Reel 5; and Zugangsbuch weibliche Häftlinge Mauthausen, AMGR, AGGB, 030259.

32. See Zugangsbuch Dachau, AUSHMM, RG-04.006 M Reel 5; Geldanforderung für Frauen des "Sonderbaus" Dachau, November 17, 1944, AGD, Document 996 (AA87/9); and Kupfer-Koberwitz, *Dachauer Tagebücher*, 316.

33. See Zugangsliste Februar 15, 1944, AMGR, AGGB, 01062702; Strebel, *KZ Ravensbrück*, 209.

34. This was L.R. (*Operationsbuch*, entry dated February 12, 1943, AMM, H 12/2). After that she was in a satellite camp in Leipzig and was brought back to Ravensbrück on July 22, 1943. See AMGR, AGGB, 011756.

35. This was E.B., Zugangsbuch Dachau, April 16, 1944, AUSHMM, RG-04.006 M Reel 5.

36. According to a list from August 24, 1942, two female guards worked at the Mauthausen concentration camp: Mrs. Boeddeker and Mrs. Fraede. Hildegard Schönfelder stated that she had been a supervisor in the brothel in Mauthausen for three months. See the Liste Arbeitseinteilung, in Füllberg-Stolberg et al., *Frauen in Konzentrationslagern*, 229; and Baumgartner, *Frauen von Mauthausen*, 99; and Vernehmungsniederschrift LKA Baden-Württemberg April 26, 1968, BArch L, B162/476, 179.

37. Operationsbuch, AMM, H 12/2.

38. L.S. was taken to Dachau on June 3, 1944 and transferred to Mauthausen on August 17 of that year. Her surname suggests a Ukrainian origin. Her age (forty-seven) differs greatly from the average age of the women in the camp brothel. See Zugangsbuch Dachau, June 3, 1944, AUSHMM, RG-04.006 M Reel 4; and the Dachau database.

39. There are contradictory statements about the reason for the imprisonment of some women who were in the Gusen concentration camp as well as later or earlier in Dachau. See the List of Prisoners of Dachau, AUSHMM, 1996 A.0342.

40. See the testimony of Maršálek, IKF, H. Marsalek Video-Int. 2, 15.

41. See the Dachau section of the Appendix.

42. At the time she was sent to the concentration camp, she was classified as an "antisocial Reich German." See entry F.K., in Zugangsliste Ravensbrück, AMGR, AGGB, 01012601; E.R., in Zugangsliste Ravensbrück, June 5, 1942, AMGR, AGGB, 01023002; and Table 1.

43. See Table 1.

44. In seventeen cases, this can be proven on the basis of SS documents. See Table 1; Zugangsbuch Mauthausen, AMGR, AGGB, 030259; and Baumgartner, *Frauen von Mauthausen*, 102.

45. See Baumgartner, *Frauen von Mauthausen*, 101; Zugangsbuch weibliche Häftlinge Mauthausen, AMGR, AGGB, 030259; and Operationsbuch, AMM, H 12/2.

46. Sommer, Forced Sex Worker Database, AMGR, MS Sommer. This number comes up when one assumes that most of the women were in Mauthausen or Gusen for the entire time the camp brothels existed and that apart from the women known by name, only two other women were brought to the brothel for Ukrainian guards. In the case of B.W. it can be proven that she came to Mauthausen only at the end of 1943 or the beginning of 1944. She may have

replaced another woman (maybe L.R.), whose name appears in the logbook of surgical procedures but later was no longer found on the list of new arrivals. See the Zugangsbuch weibliche Häftlinge Mauthausen, AMGR, AGGB, 030259; Operationsbuch, AMM, H 12/2; and Table 1.

47. This was their age at the date of the opening of the Mauthausen camp brothel on July 11, 1942.

48. See Table 1. The date of birth is unknown. The list of new arrivals from Ravensbrück on February 15, 1944, records her age ("eighteen years") instead of her date of birth. See AMGR, AGGB, 01062702.

49. See the Erbgesundheitsakte B.W., GLAK, 446 Zugang 1990-26/485; and Table 1.

50. See Table 1. One Mauthausen sex forced worker was registered in the Hamburg brothel street Herbertstraße before being sent to prison. See the Gefangenenkartei des Frauengefängnisses Fuhlsbüttel, StA-HH, 242–1 II Abt 13 JüGefKarte C.K.

51. See Table 1.

52. Prisoner deaths were usually noted in the arrivals book, and the number was often reassigned. Such entries cannot be found for the twenty forced sex workers recorded in the arrivals book. See Zugangsbuch weibliche Häftlinge Mauthausen, AMGR, AGGB, 030259; and Sommer, Forced Sex Worker Database, AMGR, MS Sommer.

53. See Table 1.

54. Testimony of Maršálek, IKF, H. Marsalek Video-Int. 2, 15.

55. The names are based on prisoner cards ("Hollerith-Vorkartei"). See APW, Nummernkartei Polski Czerwony Krzyż and BArch D-H, NS 3/1577; Häftlings-Personalkarten, AUSHMM, 1996.A.0342, Reel 120 and NARA, Arolsen Documents, Mauthausen, Reel 6; and Zugangsbuch Dachau, AUSHMM, RG-04.006 M Reel 4–6 and Zugangsbuch weibliche Häftlinge Mauthausen, AMGR, AGGB, 030259. Unknown values are marked with "–."

56. Nationality and prisoner category are based on SS documents (prisoner records and arrivals book for Dachau and Mauthausen). The prisoner category indicates the reason for imprisonment in the camp.

57. Age on July 11, 1942, the day that the Mauthausen camp brothel opened.

58. Marital status on arrival in the concentration camp.

59. Number of children on arrival in the concentration camp.

60. Occupation before arrival in concentration camp.

61. Ukr SS = Ukrainian SS.

62. See list of liberated prisoners at Bergen-Belsen, ABB, L162.

63. "Sch" is short for *Schutzhäftling*, or preventative detainee. This category was used for political prisoners.

64. These statistics are based on the "Sonderbau" list, Dachau, December 12, 1944 "Reich German-Sch" (AGD, AD 87/3, 987); and Zugangsbuch Ravensbrück, "antisocial" (AMGR, AGGB, 01149401).

65. She escaped from Ravensbrück on January 13, 1945. See Zugangsbuch Dachau, AUSHMM, RG-04.006 M Reel 5.

66. Based on the "Sonderbau" list, Dachau, December 12, 1944 "Reich German-Sch" (AGD, AD 87/3, 987); and the Zugangsbuch Ravensbrück, "antisocial" (AMGR, AGGB, 010313).

67. The Agfa Kamerawerk Munich was a women's subcamp of Dachau.

68. Based on Zugangsbuch Ravensbrück, June 5, 1942, "polit. . . . Polin rückfällig" (AMGR, AGGB, 01023002); and "Sonderbau" list, Dachau, December 12, 1944 "Reich German-Sch" (AGD, AD 87/3, 987).

69. According to the WVHA registry, her first main job was "worker" and her second was "prostitute."

70. She was registered at the Mauthausen camp until July 10, 1945, according to the Nuremberg registry. See the Einwohnermeldekartei, Stadtarchiv Nürnberg, without signature.

71. According to her prisoner card, she was a *Schutzhäftling*, but the designation was later crossed out. Most likely it was a typo. See Häftlings-Personal-Karte, KLD/Mauthausen, Umschlag T/D Nr. 779157.

72. Her prisoner card says she was domestic servant, while her personnel card indicates "composer." See NARA, Arolsen Documents, Mauthausen Reel 8 and Häftlingskarte, BArch D-H, NS 3/1577.

73. The database of the Dachau Memorial Site indicates that she was a *Schutzhäftling*. This is probably based on information she provided. According to her personnel card, she was "antisocial." See Datenbank KZ-Gedenkstätte Dachau; and Häftlings-Personal-Karte, AUSHMM, 1996.A.0342 Reel 120.

74. According to the WVHA registry, she was a housewife, but the personnel card indicates that she didn't have an occupation. See the Häftlings-Personal-Karte, AUSHMM, 1996.A.0342 Reel 120; and Häftlingskarte, BArch D-H, NS 3/1577.

75. The WVHA registry indicates that she was a *Schutzhäftling*, but the category is crossed out and replaced by "antisocial." It was probably a typo because her personnel card and the Mauthausen arrivals book say she was "antisocial" or "AZR" (*Arbeitszwang-Reich*). See Zugangsbuch Mauthausen, AMGR, AGGB, 030259; and WVHA-Kartei, BArch D-H, NS 3/1577.

76. The database of the Dachau Memorial Site says she was a *Schutzhäftling*, but this was most likely based on information she provided. The SS prisoner card classified her as "antisocial." See Datenbank KZ-Gedenkstätte Dachau; and WVHA-Kartei, BArch D-H, NS 3/1577.

77. These numbers include women from brothels for Ukrainian guards.

78. Both women later wore the red triangle in Dachau, indicating that they had been reclassified as political prisoners.

79. Based on "Sonderbau" list, Dachau, December 12,1944 "Reich German-Sch" (AGD, AD 87/3, 987); and Ravensbrück, "antisocial," AMGR, AGGB, 010313.

80. These numbers are only for those whose marital status is known. They also include women from brothels for Ukrainian guards.

81. These include all the brothels in which women from the Mauthausen brothel had to serve.

82. Frequency of visits for the period from August 1942 to December 1942. The brothel visitor log documents visits starting in July 1942, although the month is incomplete. The complete accounting begins on August 1, 1942. See the Bordellbuch Block 3, AMM, K2/1.

83. The number of regular brothel visitors accounted for 33.3% of all brothel visitors, while the total number of visits by regular brothel visitors accounted for 75.5% of all brothel visits. See the Bordellbuch Block 3, AMM, K2/1.

84. See Bordellbuch Block 3, AMM, K2/1.

85. Specifically, the category here was "Arbeitszwang Reich" (AZR), a subcategory of "antisocial."

86. On the history of Flossenbürg concentration camp, see Toni Siegert, *30 000 Tote mahnen! Die Geschichte des Konzentrationslagers Flossenbürg und seine 100 Außenlager von 1939 bis 1945* (Taubald, 1984); Skriebeleit, "Flossenbürg," 17–66; Hans Brenner, "Der 'Arbeitseinsatz' der KZ Häftlinge in den Außenlagern des Konzentrationslagers Flossenbürg: Ein Überblick," in Herbert, Orth, and Dieckmann, *Konzentrationslager*, 682–706; Kaienburg, *Wirtschaft der SS*, 609–62; and Peter Heigl, *Konzentrationslager Flossenbürg in Geschichte und Gegenwart* (Mittelbayer. Dr.-u.-Verl.-Ges, 1994).

87. See Erläuterungsbericht zum Vorentwurf für die Erstellung eines Häftlings-Sonderbaues im Konzentrationslager Flossenbürg/Opf., BArch, NS 4 Fl/183; and Figures 6, 7, and 8.

88. See Vollzugsmeldung, March 25, 1944, BArch, NS 4 Fl/185; and Abrechnung des Häftlingseinsatzes BW 18 Sonderbau, August 1942, BArch, NS 4 Fl/183. On the planning and construction history of the *Sonderbau* Flossenbürg, see Chapter 4, "The Brothel Within the Topography of the Camps."

89. As of July 16, 1943, ten women appeared on the list of work assignments under *Sonderbau*. See Arbeitseinteilung July 16, 1943, BArch, NS 4 Fl/39.

90. See Heigl, *Konzentrationslager Flossenbürg*, 34.

91. The *Häftlingsstärkemeldungen* of the *Kommandantur* from March 1, 7, 8, 9 and 11, 1945, indicate that thirteen women worked in the *Sonderbau*. The reports from March 31 to April 8, however, mention twelve women. See BArch, NS 4 Fl/392.

92. Hans-Peter Klausch, "Das Lagerbordell von Flossenbürg," *Beiträge zur Geschichte der Arbeiterbewegung*, no. 4 (December 1992), 89.

93. Ten prisoners are listed on a work schedule from July 16, 1943. It is possible that the women from the brothel for the Ukrainian guards had not yet arrived. See Arbeitseinteilung, July 16, 1943, BArch, NS 4 Fl/391.

94. A punishment report states: "During an inspection in the special prisoner building, SS-Oberscharführer Müllerschön discovered that female prisoner No. 7 . . . had cut up a bed sheet and used it to make private clothing. A

proof of debt of RM 10,– was issued by the administration." Meldung an den Lagerkommandanten, February 14, 1944, BArch, NS 4 Fl/371.

95. Her name was J.U. See Letter betr. Häftlinge für den Sonderbau SH, October 5, 1944, AMGR, AGGB, 03017001; Zugangsliste Ravensbrück, March 11, 1944, AMGR, AGGB, 01069801; and Strebel, *KZ Ravensbrück*, 209.

96. See Letter K.L. Ravensbrück betr. Übernahme von Lagern, September 1, 1944, AMGR, AGGB, 03020101; Nummernbücher Flossenbürg, AUSHMM, 1996.A.0342 Reel 4; and Überstellliste Arbeitskommando Sonderbau, September 17, 1944, AMGR, AGGB, 03006901.

97. These were possibly two of the three women that the SS brought back to Ravensbrück in the spring of 1944. They were then probably replaced by two other women.

98. See Table 3. In one case, the reason for detention was not noted in the prisoner books. Since foreigners were usually classified as *Schutzhäftlinge*—preventive detainees—it can be assumed that she was too.

99. See AMGR, AGGB, 01110401; and Gefängnisbuch J.P., Archivum Państwowe w Łodzi (APL), Więzienie dla Kobiet przy u.l. Gdanskiej, Sig. 2.

100. See Haftkarteikarten L-K., StA-HH Jüngere Gefangenen Kartei 242–1II Abl.13; StA-HH 242-1II Gefangenen Verwaltung II Abl. 2000/1; U-Haft Kartei Frauen 1930–1952; and Grit Philipp, *Kalendarium der Ereignisse im Frauen-Konzentrationslager Ravensbrück 1939–1945* (Metropol, 1999), 254.

101. See Interv. Sommer 2003-07-19 Dekeyser, 7, 14.

102. The youngest woman (S.B.) was eighteen years old on her first day in the brothel (September 1, 1944). See the Nummernbücher Flossenbürg, AUSHMM, 1996.A.0342 Reel 4; Zugangsliste Ravensbrück, AMGR, AGGB, 01012601; and Sommer, Forced Sex Worker Database, AMGR, MS Sommer.

103. Nummernbücher Flossenbürg, AUSHMM 1996.A.0342 Reel 4.

104. If one assumes that nine women, including two women from the Ukrainian brothel, were exchanged in the camp brothel before mid-September 1944 and that a total of three women were in Flossenbürg for the entire time the camp brothel existed, this results in a total of twenty-one women. See Sommer, Forced Sex Worker Database, AMGR, MS Sommer.

105. There are no deaths of forced sex workers recorded in the Flossenbürg books. See Nummernbücher Flossenbürg, AUSHMM 1996.A.0342 Reel 4; and Sommer, Forced Sex Worker Database, AMGR, MS Sommer.

106. Her name suggests a Ukrainian origin.

107. Age on day the brothel opened (July 1, 1943).

108. On the history of Buchenwald, see Kogon, *The Theory and Practice of Hell*; David A. Hackett, *The Buchenwald Report* (Westview, 1995); and Harry Stein, "Buchenwald–Stammlager," in *Der Ort des Terrors: Geschichte der nationalsozialistischen Konzentrationslager. Band III. Sachsenhausen, Buchenwald*, ed. Wolfgang Benz and Barbara Distel (C.H. Beck, 2006), 301–56.

109. See the daily report of the 4th Armored Division of the US Army, April 11, 1945, NARA, Modern Military Archives, 4. Armored Division, 604-2.2-daily reports, June 1944–May 1945.

110. See the letter of Himmler, March 5, 1943, in Heiber, *Reichsführer*, 194–96.

111. See Heiber, *Reichsführer*; and Kogon, *The Theory and Practice of Hell*, 48.

112. See Pike, *Spaniards in the Holocaust*, 73.

113. See the testimony of Beulig, AUSHMM, RG-06.005.05M, Reel 1, 8.

114. See the testimony of Beulig, 3; and the testimony of M.W., November 15, 1988, WDE, Sig. 295, 20.

115. See the Diensttagebuch, July 2 and 4, 1943, BArch D-H, ZM 1461 A3. As of July 4, 1943, the "Sonderbau" is indicated to have sixteen women. See the Küchenbücher Buchenwald, BArch, NS 4 Bu/55.

116. The brothel's accounts begin on July 11, 1943, BArch, NS 4 Bu/41.

117. See Table 6 and Abrechnungsbögen from July and August 1943, BArch, NS 4 Bu/41.

118. See the testimony of Beulig, AUSHMM, RG-06.005.05M, Reel 1, 5.

119. See the testimony of Beulig, 1–9; see also the testimony M.W., WdE, Sig. 295.

120. See the testimony of Beulig, 5–6.

121. This emerges from the ten documented days of the SS brothel, which was closed for one day during this time. See Abrechnungsbögen Buchenwald February 26 to March 6, 1944, BArch, NS 4 Bu/41.

122. See the testimony of Beulig, AUSHMM, RG-06.005.05M, Reel 1, 5.

123. See the testimony of M.W., WdE, Sig. 295, 28; Beulig, AUSHMM, RG-06.005.05M, Reel 1, 7.

124. See the testimony of Beulig, 5.

125. See Figure 18; Abrechnungsbögen, August 25 and 30, September 9, 10, 18 and 19, 1943; and March 1, 1944 and March 1, 1945, BArch, NS 4 Bu/41.

126. According to the kitchen records, there were nineteen women in the Buchenwald brothels by October 31, 1944, including the women of the brothel for Ukrainian guards. See Küchenbücher Buchenwald, October 1944, BArch, NS 4 Fl/367.

127. See Abrechnungsbögen March 1945, BArch, NS 4 Bu/41.

128. See the image series by photographer Merge from April 24, 1945, on the occasion of a visit by American congressmen to the liberated Buchenwald concentration camp, NARA, 111-SC-26 39 86.

129. E.G. was released from the camp brothel on August 14, 1943, and W.K. on September 23, 1943. See the Abrechnungsbögen Sonderbau August/September 1943, BArch, NS 4 Bu/41 and Häftlingsüberstellungen Flossenbürg, BArch, NS 4 Fl/390.

130. See Beulig, AUSHMM, RG-06.005.05M, Reel 1, 3.

131. See Abrechnungsbögen February 1944, BArch, NS 4 Bu/41; and Küchenbücher February 1944, BArch, MF5/6 Bu/77.

132. Beulig, AUSHMM, RG-06.005.05M, Reel 1, 8–9; and the Abrechnungsbögen February 1944, BArch, NS 4 Bu/41.

133. See Telex of March 29, 1944, to the Lagerkommandant of K.L. Ravensbrück, ThHStA, KZ und Haftanstalten Buchenwald Nr.10, 587; and Küchenbücher April 1944, BArch, NS 4 Fl/366.

134. See Liste Zugänge weibliche Häftlinge October 29, 1944, AMGR, AGG 030089; Neuzugänge AK Meuselwitz. October 29, 1944, AMGR, AGGB, 03008804.

135. See Neuzugänge AK Meuselwitz, October 29, 1944, AMGR, AGGB, 03008804.

136. See the Fernschreiben an Kommandantur und Arbeitseinsatz Buchenwald, September 1,1944, AMGR, AGGB, no signature; and the Küchenbuch Buchenwald, May 13, 1944, BArch NS 4 Bu/77.

137. The forced sex workers were released on the following dates: A.M. on November 30, 1944; M.R. on December 28, 1944, to the Kripo Gerlebock; M.W. on December 13, 1944, to the *Kripo Wittenburg*; W. Z. on December 11, 1944, to Hamburg; K.Z. on October 26, 1944, to the *Kripo Königsberg*; E.F. on December 7, 1944; L.B. on January 9, 1945, to the *Kripo Krefeld*; E.C. on March 10, 1945, to the Graz police; and the “cashier” H.J. on March 25, 1945, to the Karlsruhe police department. See ITS, KLD/Buchenwald, Umschläge Nr. 15661, 19352, 27238, 27724, 27977, 5371, 2863, 3092 and 10197.

138. See the Abrechnungsbogen March 23, 1945, BArch, NS 4 Bu/41; and Gedenkstätte Buchenwald, *Konzentrationslager*, 145.

139. See Table 4. The two forced sex workers from the Ukrainian brothel stayed in the brothel command for one month and the other for six months. See Häftlingsakten W.C. and B.M., ITS, KLD/Buchenwald, Umschläge Nr. 16686 and 3293.

140. See Beulig, AUSHMM, RG-06.005.05M, Reel 1, 8.

141. See Überstellliste Sonderbau-Kommando Buchenwald, September 7, 1944, AMGR, AGGB, 03005301.

142. See Table 4; and Sommer, Forced Sex Worker Database, AMGR, MS Sommer.

143. See Sommer, Forced Sex Worker Database, AMGR, MS Sommer.

144. See Table 4.

145. See Akte A.H., StA-HH, JüngGefKart 242-1II Abl.13; and 242-1II GefVerwaltung II Abl. 2000/1 and U-Haft-Kartei Frauen 1930–1952.

146. See the questionnaire of the Military Government of Germany for C.S., A.E., A.H., and M.G.: Military Government of Germany, Fragebogen für Insassen der Konzentrationslager, ITS, KLD/Buchenwald, Umschlag-Nr. 23140, 4519, 8591 and 6819.

147. Forced sex workers from brothels for Ukrainian guards are not included.

148. According to transport records issued by the Katowice police, W.K. was a Polish citizen, but she claims she was an “ethnic German.” According to the arrivals book from September 29, 1943 (“return from the camp brothel to

Ravensbrück"), she was an "antisocial" German. See Transportzettel April 23, 1942, ITS, without signature; and Zugangsliste, AMGR, AGGB, 01021102.

149. See Sommer, Forced Sex Worker Database, AMGR, MS Sommer; and Überstellliste "Sonderbau"-Kommando Buchenwald September 7, 1944, AMGR, AGGB, 03005301.

150. Forced sex workers from brothels for Ukrainian guards are not included.

151. Age at arrival at the Buchenwald camp brothel.

152. Forced sex workers from brothels for Ukrainian guards are not included.

153. Forced sex workers from brothels for Ukrainian guards are not included. See Abrechnungsbögen Buchenwald, BArch, NS 4 Bu/41; and Küchenbücher Buchenwald BArch, MF5/6 Bu/77 and NS 4 Fl/366. The two women from the Ukrainian brothel remained in the brothel detachment for one month and six months, respectively. See Häftlingsakten W.C. and B.M., ITS, KLD/Buchenwald, Umschläge Nr. 16686 and 3293.

154. Average daily number of visitors for the month. See Abrechnungsbögen "Sonderbau" Buchenwald, BArch, NS 4 Bu/41.

155. The number reflects the camp prisoner population on the first day of the month. See Stein, "Funktionswandel," 178–88.

156. Percentage of daily visitors to the camp brothel (monthly average), compared with the prisoner population size of the Buchenwald main camp.

157. On the history of Auschwitz, see van Pelt and Dwork, *Auschwitz*; Wagner, *IG Auschwitz*; Staatliches Museum Auschwitz-Birkenau, *Auschwitz*; Wolfgang Benz et al., "Auschwitz," in *Der Ort des Terrors: Geschichte der nationalsozialistischen Konzentrationslager. Band V. Hinzert, Auschwitz, Neuengamme*, ed. Wolfgang Benz and Barbara Distel (C. H. Beck, 2007), 79–173, 276–84; and Götz Aly, *"Final Solution": Nazi Population Policy and the Murder of the European Jews*, trans. Belinda Cooper and Allison Brown (Arnold, 1999).

158. See Schulte, "Wirtschaftsimperium der SS," 338; Benz et al., "Auschwitz"; and Jean-Claude Pressac, *Die Krematorien von Auschwitz: Die Technik des Massenmordes*, trans. Eliane Hagedorn (Piper, 1994).

159. See van Pelt and Dwork, *Auschwitz*, 217–57; Wagner, *IG Auschwitz*, 91–102.

160. See Wagner, *IG Auschwitz*, 91–102.

161. See Wagner, *IG Auschwitz*, 91–102; and Susanne Willems, "Monowitz (Monowice)," in *Der Ort des Terrors: Geschichte der nationalsozialistischen Konzentrationslager. Band V. Hinzert, Auschwitz, Neuengamme*, ed. Wolfgang Benz and Barbara Distel (C. H. Beck, 2007), 276–84.

162. See Wolfgang Benz et al., "Auschwitz," 79.

163. See letter, Leiter der Bauinspektion Reich-Ost, June 12, 1943, in Bauantrag zur Erstellung einer Häftlings-Sonderbaracke "B" BW 93 im K.L. Auschwitz, June 29, 1943, AUSHMM, RG-11.001M Reel 23.

164. See Erläuterungsbericht, Bauantrag zur Erstellung einer Häftlings-Sonderbaracke "B" BW 93 im K.L. Auschwitz, June 29, 1943, AUSHMM, RG-11.001M

Reel 23; and Grundriss Sonderbaracke für das KZ Auschwitz, APMO, Dp.-Z.Bau. 1016-1. See also Figure 10.

165. See the Lageskizze, Bauantrag zur Erstellung einer Häftlings-Sonderbaracke "B," BW 93 im K.L. Auschwitz June 29, 1943, AUSHMM, RG-11.001M Reel 23.

166. See Kostenvoranschlag BW 93, Bauantrag zur Erstellung einer Häftlings-Sonderbaracke "B," BW 93 im K.L. Auschwitz, June 29,1943, AUSHMM, RG-11.001M3 Reel 23.

167. See the letter from Bauleitung to Zentralbauleitung in Auschwitz, January 5, 1944, AUSHMM, RG-11.001M.03 Reel 21; and Aufstellung der genehmigten Baumittel, AUSHMM, RG-11.001M.03 Reel 26.

168. See the floorplan for Block 24, APMO, no signature; the testimony from Karl Güssow, APMO, Ośw./Wehle/2078, 2; Tadeusz Borowski, *Bei uns in Auschwitz. Erzählungen,* trans. Vera Cerny (Oświęcim: Książka I Wiedza 1963), 142; and Figures 30 and 31.

169. See the construction drawing of Block 11, in Franciszek Brol, Gerald Włoch, and Jan Pilecki, "Das Bunkerbuch des Blocks 11 im Nazi-Konzentrationslager Auschwitz," *Hefte von Auschwitz* 1 (1959): 11–13; and Bestandsplan des Gebäudes Nr. 20 B.W. 20 P./Block 24, January 12, 1942, APMO, no signature.

170. See the Begleitzettel for Blocks 24a, October 4, 1943, APMO, Akta HI Rajsko, 391/20a.

171. See the testimony of Dacko, APMO, Ośw./Dacko/1568.

172. See Interv. Sommer 2003-05-05 P. II, 18, Interv. Sommer 2003-03-30 P. I, 2.

173. See the testimony Szymanski, Interv. Sommer 2005-01-28 S., 1, 00.47.00; and Teo Ducci, *Un tallèt ad Auschwitz. 10.2.1944–5.5.1945* (Giuntina, 2000), 83–84.

174. See Begleitzettel April 3, 1944, APMO, Akta HI Rajsko, 364/6; Borowski, *Bei uns in Auschwitz,* 143.

175. See the Interv. Sommer 2003-05-01 Hantz 1, pt. 1, 00.28.00; Interv. Sommer 2004-04-06 D., pt. 2, 00.26.00.

176. See Jenny Spritzer, *Ich war 10291: Tatsachenbericht einer Schreiberin der politischen Abteilung aus dem Konzentrationslager Auschwitz* (Verlag Darmstädter Blätter, 1980), 118; and Interv. Sommer 2003-05-01 Hantz 1, pt. 1, 00.28.00.

177. See the testimony of Chladzyski, APMO, Ośw/Chladzyski/61, 51.

178. See the testimony of Gajdal, APMO, Ośw./Gajdal/61, 72.

179. See the testimony of Dubitzki, Interv. Sommer 2004-04-06 D., pt. 2, 10.00.

180. See the testimony of Szymanski, Interv. Sommer 2005-01-28 S., pt. 1, 00.42.00.

181. See Begleitzettel, APMO, Akta HI Rajsko; the testimony of Buthner, APMO, Ośw./Buthner/1936, p. 54; and the testimony of Szymanski, Interv. Sommer 2003-03-30 P. pt. 1, 5.

182. See the testimony of Szymanski, Interv. Sommer 2005-01-28 S., pt. 1, 00.43.00.

183. See Szymanski, pt. 1, 01.01.00; Jerzy Adam Brandhuber, report on the artistic work of the prisoners, June 6, 1973, BJBS; and the testimony of Rawicz, APMO, Ośw./Rawicz/1905, 2.

184. See Spritzer, *Ich war 10291*, 118; and the testimony of Przybyła, APMO, Ośw./Przybyła/2287, 18–19.

185. See Interv. Sommer 2003-05-05 P. II, 17.

186. See Sommer, Forced Sex Worker Database, AMGR, MS Sommer.

187. The last surviving record from January 10, 1945, lists twelve women by name who were examined for gonorrhea and syphilis. See Begleitzettel Block 24a, January 9 and 10, 1945, APMO, Akta HI Rajsko, 189/62 and 95/62.

188. See the Begleitzettel Block 24a, October 4, 1943, APMO, Akta HI Rajsko, 391/20a.

189. A record from October 14 shows two women. See Begleitzettel, October 14, 1943, APMO, Akta HI Rajsko,197/20b.

190. One woman was brought to the brothel in Monowitz; the other was probably taken back to Birkenau. See Begleitzettel Block 24a, November 1, 1943, APMO, Akta HI Rajsko, 702/21. The floor plan of Block 24 shows only nineteen brothel rooms. See the evacuation plan of Block 24, APMO, no signature.

191. On the Begleitzettel from March 6, ten forced sex workers plus the madam are listed. The numbering of the rooms on the note usually corresponds with the number of women. It suggests that there were fifteen women in the brothel. See Begleitzettel March 6, 1944, APMO, Akta HI Rajsko, 12/5; Begleitzettel September 5, 1944, APMO, Akta HI Rajsko, 602/11a; and the Begleitzettel January 6, 1945, APMO, Akta HI Rajsko, 74/61a.

192. These were the women L.B., I.S., and H.N. See the Begleitzettel October 4, 1943 and January 9, 1945, APMO, Akta HI Rajsko, 391/20a and 189/62.

193. The name E.N. can be found under the dates October 12 and 14 on the Begleitzettel (APMO, Akta HI Rajsko, 534/20b and 197/20b). Other women—for instance M.K. and M.M.—stayed only one to three weeks at the brothel. See the Begleitzettel October 4, 1943, APMO, Akta HI Rajsko, 391/20a. The names of the two women can then be found on records from Birkenau. For the length of stay, see Table 7.

194. See Sommer, Forced Sex Worker Database, AMGR, MS Sommer. Former prisoners have confirmed the women's assumed nationalities. Alina Brewda writes that the women selected for Block 24a were mostly German, Polish, and Russian. See Langbein, *People in Auschwitz*, 406. See also the testimony of Hantz, Interv. Summer 2003-05-01 Hantz 1, pt. 1, 00.17.00. Dubitzki stated that there were only Polish women and "Reichsdeutsche" in the brothel, although one woman was "sort of Polish-Russian" (Interv. Summer 2004-04-06 D., pt. 1, 01.06.00).

195. See Begleitzettel, January 10, 1945, APMO, Akta HI Rajsko, 95/62.

196. See the testimony of Hantz, Interv. Sommer 2003-05-01 Hantz 1, pt. 1, 00.17.00; the testimony of Piecha, Interv. Sommer 2003-05-05 P. II, 20; and the testimony of Szymanski, Interv. Sommer 2005-01-28 S., pt. 1, 00.58.00. See Table 7.

197. See Strebel, *KZ Ravensbrück*, 346–47.

198. See Sommer, Forced Sex Worker Database, AMGR, MS Sommer.

199. See Table 10. The SS transferred them first to Mittelbau-Dora, then after a few days to Bergen-Belsen, before return them to the camp brothel in Mittelbau-Dora. See Liste Neuzugänge vom KL Auschwitz, January 28, 1945, AUSHMM, RG-04.006 Reel 18; Liste Neuzugänge KL Mittelbau von Bergen-Belsen, February 18, 1945, AGMD, DMD D1b, Bd.5, 113; and Veränderungsmeldung Sachsenhausen, January 22, 1945, AUSHMM RG-11.001M Reel 85.

200. This conclusion was reached by researching the names of the women in Block 24a in the database of the Auschwitz-Birkenau State Museum.

201. See the Begleitzettel, January 10, 1945, APMO, Akta HI Rajsko 95/62.

202. These are the Auschwitz camp numbers 89251–89265. The women were probably in quarantine as was common at the time.

203. These are the camp numbers 89259, 89261, and 89264. However, these numbers appear on transfer lists for the camp brothel in Mittelbau-Dora. See Überstellliste Bergen-Belsen nach Mittelbau-Dora, February 18, 1945, AGMD, DMD, D1b, Bd.5, 113.

204. See the testimony of Dubitzki, Interv. 2004-04-06 D., pt. 2, 00.11.00, Wagner, *Produktion des Todes*, 415.

205. See the testimony of Minc, APMO, Ośw./Minc/1942, 167.

206. See the testimony of Stolecki, APMO, Ośw./Stolecki/1703, 9; the testimony of Niedojadło, APMO, Ośw./Niedojadło/997, 7; and the map of Monowitz concentration camp, in Hans Frankenthal, *Verweigerte Rückkehr: Erfahrungen nach dem Judenmord* (Fischer Taschenbuch 1999), 150–51.

207. See the testimony of Tauber, APMO, Ośw./Tauber/1938, 86.

208. The exact date is not known. The first known "regular examination" of eight women from the camp brothel is proven to have taken place on November 15, 1943. See Regelmäßige Untersuchung des Bordells, November 15, 1943, APMO, Akta HI Rajsko 1201/23.

209. See the testimony of Stolecki, APMO, Ośw./Stolecki/1703, 9.

210. Eleven rooms are noted on the "regular inspection of the brothel." Regular examination of the brothel from November 15, 1943, APMO, Akta HI Rajsko 1201/23. The number of women is usually given as ten in the reports of the former prisoners. See the testimony of Tauber, APMO, Ośw./Tauber/1938, 86; the testimony of Niedojadło, APMO, Ośw./Niedojadło/997, 7; and Interv. Sommer 2004-06-15 Diament, 00.06.00; testimony of Piłat, APMO, Ośw./Piłat/1941, 143.

211. See the testimony of Diament, Interv. Sommer 2004-06-15 Diament, 00.12.00; the testimony of Minc, APMO, Ośw./Minc/1942, 167; and the testimony of Niedojadło, APMO, Ośw./Niedojadło/997, 7.

212. See the testimony of Stefaniak, APMO, Ośw./Stefaniak/818, 59 (Janinagrube); the testimony of Tawnicki, APMO, Ośw./Tawnicki/1305, 111 (Fürstengrube); and the testimony of Gajdal, APMO, Ośw./Gajdal/61, 72 (Eintrachthütte).

213. See Interv Sommer. 2004-06-15 Diament, 00.08.00; the testimony of Szpunar, APMO, Ośw./Szpunar/1935, 13; the testimony of Halbreich, APMO, Ośw./Halbreich/1939, 108; the testimony of Makowski, APMO, Ośw./Makowski/1097, 7; Langbein, *People in Auschwitz*, 408; the testimony of Buthner, APMO, Ośw./Buthner/1936, 54; the testimony of Posener, APMO, Ośw./36/Posener, 2; and the testimony of Waitz, quoted in Langbein, *People in Auschwitz*, 408.

214. See the testimony of Minc, APMO, Ośw./Minc/1942, 167, Niedojadło, APMO, Ośw./Niedojadło/997, 7; and the testimony of Makowski, APMO, Ośw./Makowski/1097, 7.

215. See Begleitzettel, November 15, 1943, APMO, Akta HI Rajsko 1201/23. See also Table 1.

216. This is a list with the names of twelve women. Of these, eight were later transferred to Monowitz, two of them to the brothel in Block 24a. After that, two women are no longer on any lists. They were probably transferred back to the Birkenau women's camp. See Begleitzettel für Vaginalabstrich zur Untersuchung auf "Gonococcen" des Blocks 10 in Auschwitz 1, October 10, 1943 APMO, Akta HI Rajsko 906/20b.

217. See Sommer, Forced Sex Worker Database, AMGR, MS Sommer. E.B. was transferred to the Monowitz brothel on November 15, 1943. At the beginning of June 1944, the SS sent her back to the Birkenau women's camp. On January 22, 1945, E.B. was transferred to the Sachsenhausen brothel. See Liste Go-Untersuchungen Frauenlager Birkenau, APMO, Akta HI Rajsko, 720/39; and Veränderungsmeldung Sachsenhausen, January 22, 1945, AUSHMM, RG-11.001M Reel 85.

218. These were probably M.P. (Auschwitz-Nr. 89 261), L.M. (Auschwitz-Nr. 89 259), and J.H. (Auschwitz Nr. 89 264). Two of were classified as "antisocials" and the other one as "criminal." See Liste Neuzugänge vom KL Auschwitz, January 28, 1945, AUSHMM, RG-04.006 Reel 18; Liste Neuzugänge KL Mittelbau von Bergen-Belsen, February18, 1945, AGMD, DMD D1b, Bd.5, 113.

219. H.P. was in the Monowitz camp brothel from October 15, 1943, to January 31, 1944, and in the AL Graslitz from September 1, 1944, to November 4, 1944. See Mahn- und Gedenkstätte Ravensbrück, eds., *Gedenkbuch für die Opfer des Konzentrationslagers Ravensbrück 1939–1945* (Metropol, 2005), 490.

220. See the testimony of Stopka, APMO, Ośw./Stopka/951, 7; and the testimony of Tabaczyńki, APMO, Ośw./Tabaczyńki/917, 61.

221. See Table 7.

222. Sum of the women who worked in each of the camp brothels at Auschwitz (including those counted twice). This table does not include three women (Au 89 261, Au 89 259, Au 89 264) who were probably forced sex

workers in the Monowitz brothel, although this cannot be proven from surviving records. The women who were recorded at the camp brothel on January 10, 1945, are also included.

223. According to the places of birth in SS files, these women were from Ukraine, central Russia, or Belarus.

224. The names of the women suggest a Slavic origin, but other interpretations are conceivable.

225. The table includes only the fifty-one women who were sex workers in the Auschwitz camp brothel before January 9, 1945. It does not include the women whose names appear on the last record from Block 24 dated January 10, 1945. In the case of forced sex workers who were in both brothels—at the main camp and at Monowitz—I used the time in the brothel with the longer duration.

226. The table includes all sixty-seven women documented by name from both camp brothels at Auschwitz.

227. In three other cases—women with the Dora numbers F-3, F-4, and F-10—the women were also in the brothel in Monowitz. They had been transferred from Ravensbrück to Auschwitz together with other sex workers from the main camp brothel and later from Mittelbau-Dora. See Chapter 3, "The End of the War."

228. On the history of Dachau, see Wolfgang Benz and Barbara Distel, *Das Konzentrationslager Dachau 1933–1945: Geschichte und Bedeutung* (Bayerische Landeszentrale für Politische Bildungsarbeit, 1994); and Stanislav Zámečník, "Dachau-Stammlager," in *Der Ort des Terrors: Geschichte der nationalsozialistischen Konzentrationslager. Band II. Frühe Lager, Dachau, Emslandlager*, eds. Wolfgang Benz and Barbara Distel (C. H. Beck, 2005), 133–74.

229. See Rudolf Kalmar, *Zeit ohne Gnade* (Schönbrunn-Verlag, 1946), 171; and Kupfer-Koberwitz, *Dachauer Tagebücher*, 128. See also Figure 27.

230. See Kupfer-Koberwitz, *Dachauer Tagebücher*, 286, 293; and Engelhardt, "Frauen im Konzentrationslager Dachau," 223–24.

231. See Zugangsbuch Dachau, AUSHMM, RG-04.006 M Reel 5.

232. Josef Zeidler, "Solidarität und Widerstand in Dachau," AGD, 8.35; Kupfer-Koberwitz, *Dachauer Tagebücher*, 293; and Dachauer Häftlinge, *Konzentrationslager Dachau* (Stern Verlag, 1945), 24.

233. See Kalmar, *Zeit ohne Gnade*, 176; Zeidler, "Widerstand," AGD, 8.355; and Kupfer-Koberwitz, *Dachauer Tagebücher*, 293.

234. See Engelhardt, "Frauen im Konzentrationslager Dachau," 224; Kupfer-Koberwitz, *Dachauer Tagebücher*, 293; and Otto Oertel, *Als Gefangener der SS* (BIS, 1990), 211.

235. Nine forced sex workers are noted on the pay slip. The other three women were probably either sick or menstruating. See Einzahlungsbeleg Sonderbau, October 24, 1944, AGD, 20.277.

236. See Kalmar, *Zeit ohne Gnade*, 179–81; and Engelhardt, "Frauen im Konzentrationslager Dachau," 225.

237. See Kupfer-Koberwitz, *Dachauer Tagebücher*, 316.

238. See Kupfer-Koberwitz, *Dachauer Tagebücher*, 316; and Zugangsbuch Dachau, AUSHMM, RG-04.006 M Reel 5.

239. See Einzahlungsbeleg, AGD, Sig. 20.277; and Zugangsbuch Dachau, AUSHMM, RG-04.006 M Reel 5.

240. See the Schutzhaftbefehl Nr.10/44, AGD, Sig. 970.

241. See Kupfer-Koberwitz, *Dachauer Tagebücher*, 418.

242. These included, among others, Prince Xavier of Bourbon-Parma, Prince Leopold of Prussia-Hohenzollern, Pastor Niemöller, and German and foreign officials. See Johann Steinbock, *Das Ende von Dachau* (Österreichischer Kulturverlag 1948), 80–81.

243. See Protokoll der Sitzung des I.P.C. May 9, 1945, BArch D-H, K 183/11.

244. See Harold Marcuse, *Legacies of Dachau: The Uses and Abuses of a Concentration Camp, 1933– 2001* (Cambridge University Press, 2001), 165–66, map.

245. They received the camp numbers 66884–66889. See the Zugangsbuch Dachau, April 16, 1944, AUSHMM, RG-04.006 M Reel 4.

246. See Kalmar, *Zeit ohne Gnade*, 175.

247. They received the camp numbers 67572 and 67573. See the Zugangsbuch Dachau, May 4, 1944, AUSHMM, RG-04.006 M Reel 4; and Zahlungsbeleg October 24, 1944, AGD, Sig. 20.27.

248. Those women received the camp numbers 69844–69849. The Ukrainian woman was categorized as Russian, but her name suggests a Ukrainian origin. See Zugangsbuch Dachau, June 3, 1944, AUSHMM, RG-04.006 M Reel 4.

249. S.R. was transferred from Ravensbrück to the Berlin-Spandau subcamp and liberated there. See the Zugangsbuch Dachau, June 3, 1944, AUSHMM, RG-04.006 M Reel 4; Zugangsliste AMGR, MF Nr.135 Syg. 56/23–24; and Karteikarte zu Fragebögen, AMGR, AGGB, 020390.

250. Five women came from Gusen on July 15, 1944, and were given the numbers 80169 to 80173. In their place, five women were transferred to Gusen (DA 66884, 66885, 66888, 66889, 69844). See Zugangsbuch Dachau, AUSHMM, RG-04.006 M Reel 4 and 5.

251. See Liste Geldanforderung weibliche Häftlinge (Sonderbau), November 17, 1944, AGD, AA 87/9 (996); and Liste weibliche Häftlinge Sonderbau, December 12, 1944, AGD, AD 87/3 (987). The woman who was released was the "antisocial" German L.B. She was released on December 9, 1944. See Arolsen-Liste, AUSHMM 1996 A.0342 Reel 15.

252. See Liste weibliche Häftlinge Sonderbau. The "cashier" was the "antisocial" German F.E. Her age (thirty-eight) and the fact that she listed without a room indicates her being the "madame." See also Zahlungsbeleg October 24, 1944, AGD, Sig. 20.27.

253. See Table 8. These are B.R and C.K. For the former, see the Zugangsliste von Ravensbrück, AMGR, AGGB010313 ("asozial"); Zugangsliste Ravensbrück "vom Sonderbau KL Dachau zurück," January 12, 1945, AMGR, AGGB, 01149401

("asozial"); and Liste weibliche Häftlinge des Sonderbaus December 12, 1944, AGD, AD 87/3 ("Schutzhäftling"). For the latter, see C.K., Liste weibliche Häftlinge des Sonderbaus December 12, 1944, AGD, AD 87/3 ("Schutzhäftling"), Zugangsliste Ravensbrück, January 12, 1945, AMGR, AGGB, 01149401 ("asozial").

254. See Table 8.

255. See Steinbock, *Das Ende von Dachau*, 80.

256. B.R. and C.K. escaped on January 5 and L.S. on January 13, 1945. See Engelhardt, "Frauen im Konzentrationslager Dachau," 225; and Zugangsbuch Dachau, July 15, 1944, AUSHMM, RG-04.006 M Reel 5.

257. B.R. was at the camp brothel of Gusen until July 15, 1944, at Dachau until January 5, 1945, and starting on March 23, 1945, at the *Sonderbau* Mittelbau-Dora. See also Begleitzettel, March 24, 1945, ITS, KLD/Mittelbau/O. Nr. 43.

258. O.H., E.D., E.S., J.G., H.S., F.E., and M.P. were liberated at the Agfa subcamp. E.R. was freed from the Dachau main camp. See the database of Dachau and the lists of ITS Arolsen, AUSHMM 1996.A.0342 Reels 16 to 19.

259. The women in the camp brothel do not include the "cashiers" L.S. (Da 69 849) and F.E. (Da 80 159). See the Zugangsbücher Dachau, AUSHMM, RG-04.006 M Reel 4-6; Dachau Concentration Camp Memorial Database; Häftlings-Personal-Karten, AUSHMM 1996.A.0342 Reel 19 and 120; Liste weibliche Häftlinge des "Sonderbaus," December 12, 1944, AGD, AD 87/3 (987); and Geldanforderung November 17, 1944, AGD, AA 87/9 (996).

260. This includes women who were sent to the concentration camp as AZR (*Arbeitszwang Reich*) prisoners.

261. PSV stands for *Polizeiliche Sicherungsverwahrung*, or police preventive detention.

262. Age at start in the Dachau camp brothel.

263 On the history of Neuengamme concentration camp, see Kaienburg, *Vernichtung durch Arbeit*; Kaienburg, *Wirtschaft der SS*, 690–95, 925–28; and Detlef Garbe, "Neuengamme-Stammlager," in *Der Ort des Terrors. Geschichte der nationalsozialistischen Konzentrationslager. Band V. Hinzert, Auschwitz, Neuengamme*, ed. Wolfgang Benz and Barbara Distel (C. H. Beck, 2007), 315–46.

264. See Kaienburg, *Vernichtung durch Arbeit*, 411; and the testimony of Christiansen, AGN, Sig. 1273, 94–95.

265. See David Rousset, *Les jours de notre mort* (Le Pavois, 1947); drawing view of brothel from the camp hospital, AGN, 1985–5771; and photograph, AGN, 1993–180.

266. See testimony of N.N., AGN, 2.8./1391; and Heinrich Christian Meier, *So war es: Das Leben im KZ Neuengamme* (Phönix-Verlag, 1948), 52.

267. See Kaienburg, *Vernichtung durch Arbeit*, 411.

268. See the testimony of Büttig (Frau X), AGN, transcript, 21.

269. They were given the camp numbers 6302 to 6307. The "cashier" can be identified based on the age of one of the women (6305), which at thirty-seven

was significantly higher than the others. See Bericht des ehemaligen Neuengamme-Häftlings N.N. about the camp brothel, AGN, 2.8./1391.

270. See Bericht des ehemaligen Neuengamme-Häftlings N.N. about the camp brothel, AGN, 2.8./1391.

271. See Christiansen, AGN, 1273, 95; see also Meier, *So war es*, 53.

272. The date of the transfer on September 16, 1944, can be determined using the women's prisoner cards with the Neuengamme numbers 6581 and 6584. See the WVHA-Kartei, BArch D-H, NS 3/1577.

273. See N.N., AGN, 2.8./1391; and Kaienburg, *Vernichtung durch Arbeit*, 451; testimony of Büttig (Frau X), AGN, transcript, 38.

274. Such prisoner cards have been preserved for twelve women. See WVHA file, BArch D-H, NS 3/1577. The women's names are not written on the prisoner cards. In ten cases, they can be identified using other documents from SS sources such as *Effektenumschläge*, envelopes containing prisoners' personal effects. See ITS, KLD/Neuengamme T/D 268205, 1059779, and 1102298.

275. See Glaser Piotrowski, AGN, Sig. 839. According to N.N., one of them came from the Gleiwitz area and spoke Polish better than German. Another woman lived in the "Sudetengau" and spoke German and Czech. N.N., AGN, 2.8./1391.

276. See WVHA-Kartei, BArch D-H, NS 3/1577.

277. See Häftlingskarten 6302 and 6305, WVHA-Kartei, BArch D-H, NS 3/1577 and Zugangsliste Ravensbrück May 5, 1944, AUSHMM, RG-04.006 M Reel 22.

278. This is the prisoner with the number 6304. See WVHA-Kartei, BArch D-H, NS 3/1577; and Zugangsliste Ravensbrück April 19, 1944, AUSHMM, RG-04.006 M Reel 22.

279. This is the prisoner with the number 6306. See WVHA-Kartei, BArch D-H, NS 3/1577; and Zugangsliste Ravensbrück, March 24, 1944, AUSHMM, RG-04.006 M Reel 22; and the testimony N.N., AGN, 2.8./1391.

280. Women with the numbers 6582 and 6583 were cited for *Sittenübertretung* (violation of mores) and Kontrollübertr.[etung] (violation of prostitution rules). See WVHA-Kartei, BArch D-H, NS 3/1577; and Meier, *So war es*, 52.

281. Häftlingskarte 6583 in WVHA-Kartei, BArch D-H, NS 3/1577.

282. See Table 9; and WVHA-Kartei, BArch D-H, NS 3/1577. The two "cashiers" (6305 and 6580) were thirty-two and thirty-seven, older than the forced sex workers. See WVHA-Kartei, BArch D-H, NS 3/1577.

283. The name is a pseudonym.

284. Max Pauly (1907–1946) was, among other things, the camp commander of the Stutthof and Neuengamme concentration camps. Notorious for his cruelty, Pauly was sentenced to death by a British military court in Hamburg, and he was hanged in Hameln prison on October 7, 1946.

285. See N.N., AGN, 2.8./1391.

286. See N.N.

287. See N.N.

288. See Henri Garrigoux, *Prisons et transports, Neuengamme. Guerre 1939/1945. Témoignage.* (Nice: n.p., December 1986), 18.

289. This information was provided by Reimer Möller, February 22, 2008.

290. See WVHA-Kartei, BArch D-H, NS 3/1577.

291. This does not include the "cashier" G.H. (a German "political" prisoner) and the "cashier" E.T. (a German antisocial prisoner).

292. Data is based on the WVHA registry. Only the "first occupation" is recorded. The two "cashiers" are not included in the table. See WVHA-Kartei, BArch D-H, NS 3/1577.

293. This job title includes "house daughter" (*Haustochter*), "housemaid" (*Hausmädchen*), and "domestic helper" (*Hausgehilfin*). The two "cashiers" are not included in the table. See WVHA-Kartei, BArch D-H, NS 3/1577.

294. Age on May 29, 1944, the day the camp brothel opened. The two "cashiers"—one thirty-two, the other thirty-seven—are not included in the table. See WVHA-Kartei, BArch D-H, NS 3/1577. The average age of the forced sex workers was twenty-three.

295. On the history of Sachsenhausen, see Hermann Kaienburg, "Sachsenhausen-Stammlager," in *Der Ort des Terrors: Geschichte der nationalsozialistischen Konzentrationslager. Band III. Sachsenhausen, Buchenwald*, ed. Wolfgang Benz and Barbara Distel (C. H. Beck, 2006), 17–71; Hermann Kaienburg, *Der Militär- und Wirtschaftskomplex der SS im KZ-Standort Sachsenhausen-Oranienburg: Schnittpunkt von KZ-System, Waffen-SS und Judenmord* (Metropol, 2006); Günter Morsch, "Oranienburg—Sachsenhausen, Sachsenhausen—Oranienburg," in *Die nationalsozialistischen Konzentrationslager: Entwicklung und Struktur, Band 1 und 2*, ed. Ulrich Herbert, Karin Orth, and Christoph Dieckmann (Wallenstein ,1998), 111–34; and Tuchel, *Inspektion der Konzentrationslager.*

296. See Tuchel, *Inspektion der Konzentrationslager*, 50–51.

297. See Knop and Wickert, "Frauen," 7.

298. See the testimony of Walter Klose and Arnold Weiß-Rüthel, AGS, V/10; and Arnold Weiß-Rüthel, "K.L. Sachsenhausen: Aufzeichnungen aus fünf Jahren Schutzhaft," unpublished manuscript, AGS, DY 30 A Bd. 8/3, 135. On the location of the brothel, see Tuchel, *Inspektion der Konzentrationslager*, 12.

299. See the Bestandsaufnahme Sachsenhausen 1947/48, AGS, 49/59; Baupläne der neuen Pathologie, BArch, NS 3/3774; and Figure 29.

300. See Figure 29. According to the 1947/48 report, eight rooms measured six-and-a-half feet by thirty-three feet, and two measured six-and-a-half feet by thirteen feet. See the Bestandsaufnahme 1947/48, AGS, 49/59.

301. See the Bestandsaufnahme; and the construction plans of the new pathology building, BArch, NS 3/377.

302. See Nansen, *Tag*, 187.

303. See Roßmann, *Leben für Sozialismus und Demokratie*, 175.

304. See the Veränderungsmeldung April 17 and 19, 1945, AGS, D1A 1/26.

305. See the testimony of K.G., HStAD, Akte Gerichte Rep. 388 Nr. 12, 118.

306. See Bestandsaufnahme, AGS, 49/59.

307. See Jürgen Rostock's description of Sachsenhausen, in Morsch, *Von der Erinnerung zum Monument*, 245.

308. Karola Groß testified: "In August 1944, I came from Ravensbrück to Sachsenhausen together with about eight to eleven other female prisoners" (testimony of K.G., HStAD, Akte Gerichte Rep. 388 Nr. 12, 188–89). Bullerjahn speaks of ten women ("Sonderbau," 34). This is also supported by the number of brothel rooms. See the Bestandsaufnahme zum sowjetischen Speziallager von 1946/47, AGS, 49/59.

309. See Schreiben betr. Häftlinge für den Sonderbau SH October 5, 1944, AMGR, AGGB, 03017001.

310. See the Urteil of the Nuremberg-Fürth Regional Court. Quoted in Mildt and Rüter, *Justiz Bd. 17*, 121.

311. See the testimony of K.G., HStAD, Akte Gerichte Rep. 388 Nr. 12, 118.

312. Reports recording changes to the prisoner population survived for the period from December 31, 1944, to April 19, 1945. Six days are missing in January 1945 and eight days in February. The months of March and April are complete. April 19, 1945, is the last documented day. See Veränderungsmeldungen, AGS, D1A 1/26.

313. See the Veränderungsmeldungen January 23 and 25, 1945, AGS, D1A 1/26.

314. See the Begleitzettel January 13, 1944, APMO, Akta HI Rajsko, 389/26a.

315. Initially, ten women were transferred to the camp brothel in August 1944. Two of these women are known by name, as they were transported back to Ravensbrück on January 22, 1945. They were given the Sachsenhausen numbers 503 and 509. It can be assumed that the first women in the *Sonderbau* were given the numbers 500 to 509. Three women were brought to the brothel through an exchange that took place in October 1944. Four more came on January 22, 1945. See Veränderungsmeldung, January 22, 23 and 25 1945, AUSHMM RG-11.001M Reel 85; Schreiben betr. Häftlinge für den Sonderbau SH, October 5 1944, AMGR, AGGB 03017001, Rücküberstellung von Sachsenhausen nach Ravensbrück, January 18 1945, AMGR, AGGB, 011527; and the testimony of K.G., HStAD, Akte Gerichte Rep. 388 Nr. 12 Bl. 188–89.

316. See Table 10.

317. Zugangsliste Ravensbrück, March 11, 1944, AMGR, AGGB, 01069801.

318. These were Minna Möller and Karola Groß. See Eschebach, "Stigma," 69–81; and the testimony of K. (also C.) G. in the run-up to the investigations against Höhn, Landesarchiv Nordrhein-Westfalen/Hauptstaatsarchiv Düsseldorf (HstAD), Akte Gerichte Rep. 388 Nr. 12, p. 118–19.

319. See testimony of K.G., 118.

320. The name is a pseudonym.

321. See Urteil im Verfahren gegen Minna Möller vor dem Landgericht Magdeburg April 18, 1952. Quoted in Eschebach, "Stigma," 72. Möller was sentenced to three years in prison for crimes against humanity. Her "volunteering" for the Sachsenhausen camp brothel was one of the reasons for the particularly harsh sentence, although the GDR judiciary assessed it less negatively than the violence she perpetrated against women prisoners during her time in the camp police. See the Verdict, May 3, 1952, BStU, MfS-HA IX/11 AV 8/74 Bd.37 Teil 1.

322. See the meeting minutes, Titz with Lottchen Fischer, August 16, 1990, AGS, R 103/3.

323. See Sommer, Forced Sex Worker Database, AMGR, MS Sommer.

324. Names, nationality, and prisoner category are known for ten women. In total there were seventeen women.

325. One of these women was classified as a foreign civilian worker ("Ausländische Zivilarbeiterin") in a report dated January 22, 1945. She was sent to the concentration camp for "sabotage."

326. Age at start in camp brothel (August 8, 1944).

327. Only the women whose names were recorded have been included.

328. This includes all seventeen forced sex workers.

329. On the history of Mittelbau-Dora concentration camp, see Wagner, *Produktion des Todes*; Neander, *Konzentrationslager "Mittelbau."*

330. See the Liste der Neuzugänge, February 18, 1945, AGMD, DMD D1b, Bd.5, 113; Kochheim, *Bilanz*, 74.

331. See Figure 26; and the testimony of Eli and Abe Stern, Interv. Sommer 2003-04-11 Eli u Abe Stern, 1; Interv. Sommer 2003-04-12 Lykianow, 1; and the testimony of L.B., WdE, Sig. 294T, 14.

332. See the testimony of L.B., WdE, Sig. 294T, 14; and tape-recording Lehmann, AGMD, DMD-EB/HD-40.

333. See Neuzugänge KZ Mittelbau from Auschwitz, January 28, 1945, AUSHMM, RG-04.006 M, Reel 18.

334. See the testimony of L.B., WdE, Sig. 294T, 31.

335. Linda Bachmann remembered: "The prisoners came to us and dragged us out of the brothel. Yes, then we were with them in the barracks. They cooked food or something. So, we were with them in the barracks. Maybe they wanted to protect us from the SS or something" (testimony of L.B., WdE, Sig. 294T, 26–27).

336. See the testimony of L.B., 15; and the testimony of Hildegard K., October 17, 1945, AGMD, ZNW (PRO) 309/1699.

337. The guards were Magdalene K., Hannah H., Gertrud L., and Hildegard K. This last one had been in charge of brothel supervision. She had previously worked as a guard at Groß-Werther, a Mittelbau-Dora subcamp. See the testimony of Hildegard K.; and Wagner, *Produktion des Todes*, 372.

338. See the testimony of Lehmann, AGMD, DMD-EB-HD/40, 11.

339. List Neuzugänge KL Mittelbau from Bergen-Belsen February 18, 1945, AGMD, DMD D1b, Bd.5, 113; and Wagner, *Produktion des Todes*, 415.

340. According to Drung, the women were Russian and Polish (testimony of Drung at the Dachau Dora Trial 1947, NARA, Microfilm M-1079, Roll 6). Two women were, according to their places of birth, Ukrainian and Belarussian. See Wagner, *Produktion des Todes*, 415; and List Neuzugänge KL Mittelbau from Bergen-Belsen February 18, 1945, AGMD, DMD D1b, Bd.5, 113.

341. See the testimony of Drung, NARA, Microfilm M-1079, Roll 6.

342. See Begleitzettel Block 24, July 10, 1944, APMO, Akte HI 967/43.

343. See Neuzugänge KL Mittelbau from Bergen-Belsen February 18, 1945, AGMD, DMD D1b, Bd.5, 113; and Wagner, *Produktion des Todes*, 417.

344. They were assigned the numbers F 331–341. See Begleitzettel March 24, 1945, ITS, KLD/Mittelbau/O.Nr 43; and Zugangslisten HKB, March 27 and 28, 1945, AUSHMM, RG-04.006 M Reel 18.

345. See Philipp, *Kalendarium Ravensbrück*, 322; and ITS, KLD/Herzogenbusch, Umschlag W.D.

346. See the testimony of Dr. Groeneveld, AGMD, DMD-EB/HN-5, 18.

347. See Sommer, Forced Sex Worker Database, AMGR, MS Sommer.

348. See Sommer, Forced Sex Worker Database, AMGR, MS Sommer; and the table below.

349. H.J. was sent to Ravensbrück on September 24, 1942, as a *BV* (career criminal) (AMGR, AGGB, 01047901), and H.O. on February 19, 1943, as a *SV* (preventive detention prisoner) (AMGR, AGGB, 01042901). E.S. was initially transferred to Ravensbrück on December 7, 1940, as a "political prisoner" for "*verk. m. Polen*" (intercourse with Poles), and then released and committed to Ravensbrück again as a "recidivist" on August 21, 1942. AMGR, AGGB, 01014201 and 01027502.

350. M.R. was transferred to Ravensbrück on January 24, 1945, AMGR, AGGB, 01154803.

351. See Table 11.

352. L.R. Her number was F-25; she was born in 1897. See Zugangsliste HKB, März 12, 1945, AUSHMM, RG-04.006 M Reel 18; Revierkarte, ITS, KLD/Mittelbau, Umschlag Nr. 36439.

353. B.G. was born in 1914 and came from Trnava in Slovakia. See the Begleitzettel Blutproben WA.-Reaktion to Hygiene-Institut der Waffen-SS Weimar-Buchenwald, March 24, 1945, ITS/KLD/Mittelbau//O.Nr.43 and Application for Location Service, ITS, Do. ID 106560921.

354. See the testimony of L.B., WdE, Sig. 294T, 11–12.

355. See the testimony of L.B., 14. The survivors are I.P. and L.M. BStU, MfS SK 5 Blatt B 43886.

356. See the testimony of L.B., 5–16.

357. See the testimony of L.B., 16–17.

358. See Sommer, Forced Sex Worker Database, AMGR, MS Sommer; and Zugangslisten HKB, March 1945, AUSHMM, RG-04.006 M Reel 18.

359. Two "cashiers" are not included.

360. Age at start in camp brothel. See Sommer, Forced Sex Worker Database, AMGR, MS Sommer.

361. Dates of birth are known for only nineteen of the twenty women.

362. The estimates are based on statements by former prisoners and on inferences—for instance, when the number but not the names of the women who were swapped out are known. It is also possible to determine the number of women transferred to a camp brothel based on prisoner identity numbers.

363. Two Polish women worked at both the Mauthausen brothel for prisoners and the Gusen brothel for Ukrainian guards. They are counted only once each.

364. Women who worked at both types of brothels are counted only once.

365. Age at start in camp brothel.

366. Number of women identified by name, including women in brothels for Ukrainian SS men. See Sommer, Forced Sex Worker Database, AMGR, MS Sommer.

367. One woman was categorized as an "antisocial" German and a "political" Polish woman, while the other two were categorized as "political" for each nationality.

368. All women from Russia were classified as "political" prisoners.

369. Judging by their names, the women were probably from the Ukraine, Belarus, or Poland.

370. These categories indicate the reason for imprisonment of all forced sex workers regardless of nationality, including forced sex workers from brothels for Ukrainian guards. In case of doubt, the prisoner category is used as the reason for incarceration in the concentration camp.

371. There were different reasons for imprisonment: in two cases "antisocial" or "political" German, and in another case "antisocial German" or "political Pole."

372. Only the women whose names are known are included here. The prisoner category is not known for eleven women.

373. Number of women identified by name, including women in brothels for Ukrainian SS men. See Sommer, Forced Sex Worker Database, AMGR, MS Sommer.

374. Two women were classified as "preventive detainees" (*Sicherungsverwahrte*, or "SV" and "PSV") and two as "career criminals" (*Berufsverbrecher*, or BV).

375. Number of women identified by name, including those taken to brothels for Ukrainian SS men. See Sommer, Forced Sex Worker Database, AMGR, MS Sommer.

376. Only the women whose names are known are included in the analysis. The reason for imprisonment is not known for ten women.

Sources and Bibliography

Archival Sources

	Archiv der Gedenkstätte Bergen-Belsen (ABB)
	Dokumentensammlung
	Archiv der Mahn- und Gedenkstätte Buchenwald (AMGB)
BwA	Buchenwaldarchiv
F1 4059	Bestand Besançon
	Archiv der Gedenkstätte Dachau (AGD)
	Bestand KZ-Gedenkstätte Dachau
	Archiv der Gedenkstätte Flossenbürg (AGF)
	Bestand Erinnerungsberichte
	Bestand Originale
	Häftlingsdatenbank
	Archiv der Gedenkstätte Mittelbau-Dora (AGMD)
DMD-D	Zugangslisten
DMD-EB	Erlebnisberichte ehemaliger Häftlinge
DMD-FG	Forschungsgruppe Dora der Russischen Universität
	Archiv der Gedenkstätte Neuengamme (AGN)
	Bestand Erlebnisberichte
	Archiv der Humboldt-Universität zu Berlin (AHUB)
	Bestand Hygiene-Institut
	Archiv der Mahn- und Gedenkstätte Ravensbrück (AMGR)
RA Bd. 1–47	Bestand Erika Buchmann
AGGB	Bestand Arbeitsgemeinschaft Gedenkbuch
	Archiv der Gedenkstätte Sachsenhausen (AGS)
NMG	Bestand Nationale Mahn- und Gedenkstätte 1961–90
D1	Duplikate aus Archiven und KL Sachsenhausen 1936–1945
LAG	Sachsenhausensammlung "Lagerarbeitsgemeinschaft Sachsenhausen"
J	Akten von Ermittlungs- und Strafverfahren
	Archiv der KZ-Gedenkstätte Mauthausen (AMM)
	Dokumentensammlung
	Archives of the United States Holocaust Memorial Museum (AUSHMM)

1996.A.0342	Records Relating to Concentration Camps from the National Archives
RG-04	Concentration and Other Camps
RG-06	War Crimes Investigations and Prosecutions
RG-09	Liberation of the Camps and Ghettos
RG-11	Selected Records from the Former Special State Archive in the Russian State Military Archive (RGVA)
RG-14	Federal Republic of Germany
RG-18	Latvia
RG-48	Czech Republic
RG-53	Belarus
	Archives of the Wiener Library, London (WL)
	Series One, Section II Eyewitness Accounts
	Archiwum Państwowe Muzeum Auschwitz-Birkenau w Oświęcimiu/Archiv des Staatlichen Museums Auschwitz-Birkenau (APMO)
Akta_HI Rajsko	Hygiene-Institut der Waffen-SS Rajsko
D-Au III	IG Farben/Monowitz
Ośw	Berichte ehemaliger Häftlinge
	Archiwum Państwowe Muzeum Majdanek (APMM)
VII	Erinnerungen und Zeitzeugenberichte
	Archiwum Państwowe w Krakowie/Staatsarchiv Krakau (APK)
SMKr	Stadthauptmann von Krakau
	Archivum Państwowe w Łodzi/Staatsarchiv Lodz (APL)
	Więzienie dla Kobiet przy u.l. Gdanskiej
	Archiwum Państwowe we Wrocławiu/Staatsarchiv BRESLAU (APW)
	Nummernkartei Polski Czerwony Krzyż
	Bibliothek der Jugendbegegnungsstätte Auschwitz (BJBS)
	Sammlung Zeitzeugenaussagen
	Brandenburgisches Landeshauptarchiv (BLHA)
Rep. 35 H	Sachsenhausen
Rep. 45 D	Westhavelland
Rep. 75	IG Farben Premnitz
	Bundesarchiv Lichterfelde (BArch)
BY 5	Vereinigung der Verfolgten des Naziregimes 1933–1963
NS 3	SS-Wirtschafts-Verwaltungshauptamt
NS 4	Konzentrationslager
NS 6	Partei-Kanzlei
NS 17	Leibstandarte-SS Adolf Hitler
NS 19	Persönlicher Stab Reichsführer-SS
NS 31	SS-Hauptamt
NS 33	SS-Führungshauptamt

NS 43	Reichskanzlei
NS 47	Allgemeine SS: SS-Oberabschnitte
NS 51	Kanzlei des Führers der NSDAP
R 2	Reichsfinanzministerium
R 11	Reichswirtschaftskammer
R 187	Sammlung Schuhmacher
	Bundesarchiv Dahlwitz-Hoppegarten (BArch D-H)
NS 3/1577	WVHA-Kartei
ZM	SS, Waffen-SS, Polizei, Gendarmerie, SS-Polizei-Einheiten, KZ-Wachpersonal, Unterlagen über SS-Verbrechen
	Bundesarchiv-Militärarchiv Freiburg (BArch F)
RH 12–23	Heeressanitätsinspektion
RW 2	Chef OKW
RW 6	Allgemeines Wehrmachtsamt
	Bundesarchiv Ludwigsburg (BArch L)
	Unterlagen der Zentralen Stelle der Landesjustizverwaltungen zur Aufklärung nationalsozialistischer Verbrechen
	Bundesarchiv Koblenz (BArch K)
Z 42 III	Spruchgericht Bergedorf
	Bundesbeauftragte für die Unterlagen des Staatssicherheitsdienstes der ehemaligen Deutschen Demokratischen Republik (BStU)
Abt. XII	Personenregistratur und Archiv (from 1951)
MfS—ASKS	Ministerium für Staatssicherheit, Archivmaterial Strafnachweise (A)
MfS—BV Halle	Ministerium für Staatssicherheit, Bezirksverwaltung Halle
MfS—DSKS	Ministerium für Staatssicherheit, Archivmaterial Strafnachweise (D)
MfS—GH	Ministerium für Staatssicherheit, Geheime Hauptablage
MfS—HA VIII	Ministerium für Staatssicherheit, Hauptabteilung VIII
MfS—HA IX	Ministerium für Staatssicherheit, Hauptabteilung IX
MfS—HA XX	Ministerium für Staatssicherheit, Hauptabteilung XX
MfS—SK 5	Ministerium für Staatssicherheit, Strafkartei 5
MfS—SK 17	Ministerium für Staatssicherheit, Strafkartei 17
Mgbg. AST I	Bezirksverwaltung Magdeburg, Bezirksstaatsanwalt, Abteilung I
	Fortunoff Video Archive Yale (FVA)
T	Holocaust Testimonies
	Gemeindearchiv Dachau
	Bestand Umsiedlung der Familien in den Baracken Prittlbach nach Dachau
	Generallandesarchiv Karlsruhe (GLAK)
Abt. 330	Zug. 1991/34—Polizeipräsidium Karlsruhe
Abt. 446	Zug. 1990-26/485—Gesundheitsamt Heidelberg

	Institut für Zeitgeschichte München (IfZ)
F 13	Autobiografische Aufzeichnungen von Rudolf Höß
NO	Nürnberger Dokumente
	International Tracing Service of the Red Cross Bad Arolsen (ITS)
KLD	Bestand Buchenwald, Dachau, Flossenbürg, Mauthausen, Mittelbau, Ravensbrück
T/D	Ablage Suchanfragen
	Landesarchiv Nordrhein-Westfalen/Hauptstaatsarchiv Düsseldorf (HStAD)
Rep. 388	Gerichte
RW 0058	Geheime Staatspolizei—Staatspolizei(leit)stelle Düsseldorf
	Staatsarchiv Bremen (StA-B)
4,13/1	Senator für Inneres, Allgemeine Registratur (1940-1956)
4,130/1	Hauptgesundheitsamt, Allgemeine Registratur (1928-1957)
4,130/2	Hauptgesundheitsamt, Unfruchtbarmachungen
4.54	Landesamt für Wiedergutmachung
	Staatsarchiv Hamburg (StA-HH)
213-11	Staatsanwaltschaft Landgericht Strafsachen
242–1 II	Gefängnisverwaltung II
351–14	Arbeits- und Sozialfürsorge—Sonderakten
352–3	Medizinalkollegium
352–12	Gesundheitsbehörde—Sonderakten
	Staatsarchiv München (StAM)
8001	Bestand Polizeidirektion
	Staatsarchiv Nürnberg (StAN)
Rep. 501	IG Farben Prozess (KV-Prozesse Fall 6)
	Stadtarchiv Linz (SdtAL)
	Bestand Neubau Städte, Bauvorgang Tschechenbordell
	Stadtarchiv Nürnberg (SdtAN)
	Einwohnermeldeamt-Karteien
	Stadtarchiv OŚwięcim (SdtA-Os)
	Zespot Bürgermeister
	Stadtarchiv Oldenburg (SdtAO)
	FD Bauordnung und Denkmalschutz
	Thüringisches Hauptstaatsarchiv Weimar (ThHStA)
	Konzentrationslager und Haftanstalten Buchenwald
	Thüringisches Landesamt für Rassewesen
	Bestand Ministerium des Innern Thüringen (MDI)
	US National Archives and Records Administration (NARA)
	Arolsen Documents
	Modern Military Records

Interviews

Beck, Walter	Interv. Sommer 2005-02-15 Beck
Bibel, Benno	Interv. Sommer 2004-06-21 Bibel
Bringmann, Fritz	Interv. Sommer 2004-03-29 Bringmann
Dekeyser, Charles	Interv. Sommer 2003-07-19 Dekeyser
Diament, Fredi	Interv. Sommer 2004-06-15 Diament
Długoborski, Vacłav	Interv. Sommer 2003-04-30 Dlugoborski
Dubitzki, Romek (pseudonym)	Interv. Sommer 2004-04-06 D.
Frohwein, Willi	Interv. Sommer 2003-05-07 Frohwein
Gibillini, Vernanzio	Interv. Sommer 2003-07-20 Mariconti Gibillini
Hájková, Anna	Interv. Sommer 2006-02-13 Hájková
Hantz, Stanisław	Interv. Sommer 2003-02-01 Hantz; II; III
König, Adam	Interv. Sommer 2004-02-05 König
Löwenberg, Fred	Interv. Sommer 2004-04-06 Löwenberg
Lykianow, Wassili	Interv. Sommer 2003-04-12 Lykianow
Mariconti, Gianfranco	Interv. Sommer 2004-05-12 Mariconti II
Maschkowski, Gerhard, and Ursula	Interv. Sommer 2004-03-19 2x Maschkowski
Obidzinska, Henryka	Interv. Sommer 2002-03-16 Obidzinska
Ostermann, Dagmar	Interv. Sommer 2003-05-22 Ostermann
Piecha, Jakub (pseudonym)	Interv. Sommer 2003-03-30 P. I; P. II
Raimondi, Mario	Interv. Sommer 2005-04-22 Raimondi
Stenzel, Karl	Interv. Sommer 2004-02-05 Stenzel
Stern, Eli and Abe	Interv. Sommer 2003-04-11 Stern Eli u Abe
Szymanski, Stephan (pseudonym)	Interv. Sommer 2005-01-28 S.
Terry, Jack	Interv. Sommer 2003-07-19 Terry
Bruha, Antonia	IKF Wie, Rav-Int.20_3 (administered by IFK)
Górski, Adolf	Interv. Kuwalek 2003-03-19—Gorski (administered by Robert Kuwalek)
Jablonski, Tomasz (pseudonym)	Paul private collection (Herr J.) (administered by Christa Paul)
L.B.	WdE, Sig. 294T (administered by Paul/Kassing)
Maršálek, Hans	IKF Wien, Marsalek Video-Int. 2 (administered by IFK)
M.W. (November 15, 1988)	WdE, Sig. 295 (administered by Hans Jürgen Plaumannn)
M.W.	WdE, Sig. 295 (administered by Paul/Kassing)

Bibliography

LITERATURE BEFORE 1945

Bebel, August. *Woman and Socialism.* Translated by Meta Stern Lilienthal. Socialist Literature Co., 1910. https://www.gutenberg.org/cache/epub/47244/pg47244-images.html.

Bettelheim, Bruno. "Individual and Mass Behavior in Extreme Situations." *Journal of Abnormal and Social Psychology* 38, no. 4 (1943): 417–52.

Bludau, Hans, and Herta Burger. *Ausführung und Beurteilung serologischer Untersuchungsverfahren: Arbeitsanweisungen für Laboratorium und Klinik der Waffen-SS, Berlin. Heft* 2. Edited by Joachim Mrugowsky. Urban & Schwarzenberg, 1942.

Breger, Johannes. *Die Geschlechtskrankheiten und ihre Gefahren für das Volk.* R. v. Decker's Verlag and G. Schenk, 1937.

Dwinger, Edwin Erich. *Die Armee hinter Stacheldraht: Das sibirische Tagebuch.* E. Diederichs Verlag, 1941.

Fuchs, Eduard. *Illustrierte Sittengeschichte: Renaissance.* Albert Langen Verlag, 1909.

Haag, Friedrich Erhard. *Lagerhygiene.* J. F. Lehmanns Verlag, 1943.

Hitler, Adolf. *Mein Kampf.* Translated by Ralph Mannheim. Houghton Mifflin, 1943.

———. "Zum Kampf gegen Prostitution und Geschlechtskrankheiten." *Mitteilungen der Deutschen Gesellschaft zur Bekämpfung der Geschlechtskrankheiten* 5/6 (May/June 1933): 74–82.

Gorky, Maxim. *Belomor: An Account of the Construction of the New Canal Between the White Sea and the Baltic Sea.* Translated by Amabel Williams-Ellis. Harrison Smith and Robert Haas, 1935.

Nigmann, Joachim. "Prostitution und Nachwuchs im Hinblick auf das Ehegesundheitsgesetz." Inaugural-Dissertation. Ludwig-Maximilians-Universität, Munich, 1943.

Pfeiffer, Hans. "Über Lagerhygiene: Erfahrungen aus den Strafgefangenenlagern bei Papenburg-Ems." Inaugural-Dissertation. Rheinischen Friedrich-Wilhelms-Universität, Bonn, 1935.

Plättner, Karl. *Eros im Zuchthaus: Sehnsuchtsschrei gequälter Menschen nach Liebe. Eine Beleuchtung der Geschlechtsnot der Gefangenen, bearbeitet auf der Grundlage von Eigenerlebnissen, Beobachtungen und Mitteilungen in achtjähriger Haft.* Verlag Paul Witte, 1931.

Seger, Gerhart. *Oranienburg: Erster authentischer Bericht eines aus dem Konzentrationslager Geflüchteten.* Verlagsanstalt Graphia, 1934.

Spiethoff, Bodo. "Leitartikel." *Mitteilungen der Deutschen Gesellschaft zur Bekämpfung der Geschlechtskrankheiten* 5/6 (May/June 1933): 1.

LITERATURE AFTER 1945

Abramowitch, Maja *To Forgive . . . but Not to Forget: Maja's Story.* Vallentine Mitchell, 2002.

Adelsberger, Lucie. *Auschwitz: Ein Tatsachenbericht.* Lettner Verlag, 1956.

Agamben, Giorgio. *Homo Sacer: Sovereign Power and Bare Life.* Translated by Daniel Heller-Roazen. Stanford University Press, 1998.

Alakus, Baris, Katharina Kniefacz, and Robert Vorberg, eds. *Sex-Zwangsarbeit in nationalsozialistischen Konzentrationslagern.* Mandelbaum Verlag, 2007.

Aldebert, Bernard. *Gusen II—Leidensweg in 50 Stationen | Gusen II—Chemin de Croix en 50 Stations. Von Compiègne nach Gusen II über Buchenwald—Mauthausen—Gusen I | De Compiègne à Gusen II en passant par Buchenwald—Mauthausen—Gusen I .* Translated by Elisabeth Hölzl. Bibliothek der Provinz Verlag für Literatur, Kunst, 2022.

Applebaum, Anne. *Gulag: A History of the Soviet Camps.* Penguin, 2004.

Aly, Götz. *"Final Solution": Nazi Population Policy and the Murder of the European Jews.* Translated by Belinda Cooper and Allison Brown. Arnold, 1999.

Aly, Götz, and Karl Heinz Roth. *Die restlose Erfassung: Volkszählen, Identifizieren, Aussondern im Nationalsozialismus.* S. Fischer, 2000.

Amesberger, Helga, and Brigitte Halbmayr. *Vom Leben und Überleben—Wege nach Ravensbrück: Das Frauenkonzentrationslager in der Erinnerung.* Band 1: *Dokumentation und Analyse.* Promedia, 2001.

———. *Vom Leben und Überleben—Wege nach Ravensbrück: Das Frauenkonzentrationslager in der Erinnerung.* Band 2: *Lebensgeschichten.* Promedia, 2001.

Amesberger, Helga, Katrin Auer, and Brigitte Halbmayr. *Sexualisierte Gewalt: Weibliche Erfahrungen in NS-Konzentrationslagern.* Mandelbaum Verlag, 2004.

Anschütz, Janet, Kerstin Meier, Sanja Obajdin. "' . . . dieses leere Gefühl, und die Blicke der anderen . . .': Sexuelle Gewalt gegen Frauen." In *Frauen in Konzentrationslagern: Bergen-Belsen. Ravensbrück,* edited by Claus Füllberg-Stolberg, Martina Jung, Renate Riebe, and Martina Scheitenberger, 123–34. Edition Temmen, 1994.

Aoláin, Fionnuala D. Ní. "Rethinking the Concept of Harm and Legal Categorizations of Sexual Violence During War." *Theoretical Inquiries in Law* 1, no. 2 (2000): 307–40.

Auschwitz-Birkenau State Museum, ed. *Auschwitz: A History in Photographs.* Auschwitz-Birkenau State Museum, 1999.

Aussteller, Die, ed. *Sex-Zwangsarbeit in NS-Konzentrationslagern: Katalog zur Ausstellung.* Die Aussteller—Verein zur Förderung von historischen und kunsthistorischen Ausstellungen, 2005.

Austrian, Geoffrey D. *Herman Hollerith: Forgotten Giant of Information Processing.* Columbia University Press, 1982.

Autorenkollektiv. "Der *Sonderbau* in Sachsenhausen." *Der Appell* 119 (1990): 2.

Ayaß, Wolfgang. *"Asoziale" im Nationalsozialismus.* Klett-Cotta,1995.

———, ed. *"Gemeinschaftsfremde": Quellen zur Verfolgung von "Asozialen" 1933–1945.* Bundesarchiv, 1998.

Barbiano di Belgiojoso, Ludovico. *Notte, Nebbia: Racconto di Gusen.* Guanda, 1996.

Barkow, Ben. *Alfred Wiener and the Making of the Holocaust Library*. Vallentine Mitchell & Co., 1997.

Bauer, Fritz, Irene Sagel-Grande, H. H. Fuchs, C. F. Rüter, and Adelheid L. Rüter-Ehlermann, eds. *Justiz und NS-Verbrechen: Sammlung deutscher Strafurteile wegen nationalsozialistischer Tötungsverbrechen 1945–1966*. Vol. 17. APA-Holland University Press, 1977.

Baumgartner, Andreas. *Die vergessenen Frauen von Mauthausen: Die weiblichen Häftlinge des Konzentrationslagers Mauthausen und ihre Geschichte*. Edition Mauthausen, 1997.

Beccaria Rolfi, Lidia. *Zurückkehren als Fremde: Von Ravensbrück nach Italien: 1945–1948*. Edited by Johanna Kootz. Metropol, 2008.

Beck, Birgit. "Vergewaltigungen: Sexualdelikte von Soldaten vor Militärgerichten der deutschen Wehrmacht 1939–1944." In *Heimat-Front: Militär und Geschlechterverhältnisse im Zeitalter der Weltkriege*, edited by Karen Hagemann, 258–74. Campus, 2002.

Begov, Lucie. *Mit meinen Augen: Botschaft einer Auschwitzüberlebenden*. Bleicher, 1983.

Beischl, Konrad. *Dr. med. Eduard Wirths und seine Tätigkeit als SS-Standortarzt im KL Auschwitz*. Königshausen u. Neumann, 2005.

Benz, Wolfgang. "Dr. med. Sigmund Rascher: Eine Karriere." *Dachauer Hefte* 4 (1988): 190–214.

Benz, Wolfgang, and Barbara Distel. *Das Konzentrationslager Dachau 1933–1945: Geschichte und Bedeutung*. Bayerische Landeszentrale für Politische Bildungsarbeit, 1994.

———, eds. *Der Ort des Terrors: Geschichte der nationalsozialistischen Konzentrationslager*. Band I: *Die Organisation des Terrors*. C. H. Beck, 2005.

———. *Der Ort des Terrors: Geschichte der nationalsozialistischen Konzentrationslager*. Band II: *Frühe Lager, Dachau, Emslandlager*. C. H. Beck, 2005.

———, eds. *Der Ort des Terrors: Geschichte der nationalsozialistischen Konzentrationslager*. Band III: *Sachsenhausen, Buchenwald*. C. H. Beck, 2006.

———, eds. *Der Ort des Terrors: Geschichte der nationalsozialistischen Konzentrationslager*. Band IV: *Flossenbürg, Mauthaushausen, Ravensbrück*. C. H. Beck, 2006.

———, eds. *Der Ort des Terrors: Geschichte der nationalsozialistischen Konzentrationslager*. Band V: *Hinzert, Auschwitz, Neuengamme*. C. H. Beck, 2007.

———, eds. *Der Ort des Terrors: Geschichte der nationalsozialistischen Konzentrationslager*. Band VI: *Natzweiler, Groß-Rosen, Stutthof*. C. H. Beck, 2007.

———, eds. *Der Ort des Terrors: Geschichte der nationalsozialistischen Konzentrationslager*. Band VII: *Niederhagen/Wewelsburg, Lublin-Majdanek, Arbeitsdorf, Herzogenbusch (Vught), Bergen-Belsen, Mittelbau-Dora*. C. H. Beck, 2008.

———, eds. *Der Ort des Terrors: Geschichte der nationalsozialistischen Konzentrationslager.* Band VIII: *Riga, Warschau, Vaivara, Kaunas, Plaszów, Kulmhof/Chełmno, Bełżec, Sobibór, Treblinka.* C. H. Beck, 2008.

Benz, Wolfgang, Miriam Bistrović, Claudia Curio, Barbara Distel, Franziska Jahn, Angelika Königseder, Brigitte Mihok, and Verena Walter. "Auschwitz." In *Der Ort des Terrors: Geschichte der nationalsozialistischen Konzentrationslager,* Band V: *Hinzert, Auschwitz, Neuengamme,* edited by Wolfgang Benz and Barbara Distel, 79–312. C. H. Beck, 2007.

Béon, Yves. *Planet Dora: Als Gefangener im Schatten der V2-Rakete.* Bleicher Verlag, 1999.

Bergen, Doris L. "Sexual Violence in the Holocaust: Unique and Typical?" In *The Holocaust in International Perspective: Lessons and Legacies,* edited by Dagmar Herzog, 7:179–200. Northwestern University Press, 2006.

Bergen, Doris L., Sara E. Brown, Stephanie Corazza, Paula David, Henry Greenspan, and Sara R. Horowitz. "Buried Words: A Forum on Sexuality, Violence, and Holocaust Testimonies." *Holocaust Studies: A Journal of Culture and History* 27, no. 4: (2021), 501–20.

Berger, Karin, and Elisabeth Holzinger, eds. *"Ich geb Dir einen Mantel, dass Du ihn noch in Freiheit tragen kannst": Widerstehen im KZ: Österreichische Frauen erzählen.* Promedia, 1987.

Betlen, Oszkár. *Leben auf dem Acker des Todes.* Dietz Verlag, 1962.

Bezwinska, Jadwiga, Danuta Czech, Ingeborg Goslinowska, and Anneliese Nowak. *KL Auschwitz in den Augen der SS: Höss Broad Kremer.* Krajnowa Agencja Wydawnicza, 1981.

Birn, Ruth Bettina. *Die höheren SS- und Polizeiführer: Himmlers Vertreter im Reich und in den besetzten Gebieten.* Droste Verlag, 1986.

Black, Edwin. *IBM and the Holocaust: The Strategic Alliance Between Nazi Germany and America's Most Powerful Corporation.* Dialog, 2012.

Black, Peter R. *Ernst Kaltenbrunner: Ideological Soldier of the Third Reich.* Princeton University Press, 1984.

Blüher, Hans. *Studien zur Inversion und Perversion: Das uralte Phänomen der geschlechtlichen Inversion in natürlicher Sicht.* Franz Decker Verlag, 1965.

Boberach, Heinz, ed. *Meldungen aus dem Reich 1938–1945.* Pawlak Verlag, 1984.

Bock, Gisela, ed. *Genozid und Geschlecht: Jüdische Frauen im nationalsozialistischen Lagersystem.* Campus, 2005.

———. "Einführung." In *Genozid und Geschlecht: Jüdische Frauen im nationalsozialistischen Lagersystem,* edited by Gisela Bock, 7–21. Campus, 2005.

———. *Zwangssterilisation im Nationalsozialismus: Studien zur Rassenpolitik und Frauenpolitik.* Westdeutscher Verlag, 1986.

Böhme, Hartmut. "Gewalt im 20. Jahrhundert: Genozide in der Sicht von Erinnerungsliteratur, Statistik und qualitativer Sozialforschung." *figurationen gender literatur kultur* 0 (1999): 139–57.

Bolaritsch, Friedrich. *Wege des Schicksals.* Elfriede Wild, 1998.

Borkin, Joseph. *Die unheilige Allianz der IG Farben: Eine Interessengemeinschaft im Dritten Reich.* Campus Verlag, 1990.

Borowski, Tadeusz. *Bei uns in Auschwitz: Erzählungen.* Translated by Vera Cerny. Książka I Wiedza, 1963.

———. *Here in Our Auschwitz and Other Stories.* Translated by Madeline G. Levine. Yale University Press, 2021.

Boulanger, Jakob, and Michael Tschesno-Hell. *24073: Eine Ziffer über dem Herzen: Erlebnisbericht aus zwölf Jahren Haft.* Verlag des Ministeriums für Nationale Verteidigung, 1960.

Bourdieu, Pierre. "The Forms of Capital." In *Handbook of Theory and Research for the Sociology of Education,* edited by J. G. Richardson, 241–58. Greenwood, 1986.

Bravo, Anna, and Daniele Jalla, eds. *La vita offesa.* Franco Angeli, 2001.

Brenner, Hans. "Der 'Arbeitseinsatz' der KZ-Häftlinge in den Außenlagern des Konzentrationslagers Flossenbürg: Ein Überblick." In *Die nationalsozialistischen Konzentrationslager: Entwicklung und Struktur,* vols. 1–2, edited by Ulrich Herbert, Karin Orth, and Christoph Dieckmann, 682–706. Wallenstein, 1998.

———. *Frauen in den Außenlagern des KZ Flossenbürg.* Arbeitsgemeinschaft ehem. KZ Flossenbürg e.V., 1999.

Bringmann, Fritz. *KZ Neuengamme: Berichte, Erinnerungen, Dokumente.* Röderberg, 1982.

Brink, Cornelia. *Ikonen der Vernichtung: Öffentlicher Gebrauch von Fotografien aus nationalsozialistischen Konzentrationslagern nach 1945.* Akademie Verlag, 1998.

Brodersen, Uwe, ed. *Gesetze des NS-Staates: Dokumente eines Unrechtssystems.* Schöningh, 1982.

Brömmer, Gabriele. *Die Bedeutung Alfred Blaschkos bei der Bekämpfung von Geschlechtskrankheiten in Deutschland.* Dissertation. Medizinische Fakultät der Humboldt-Universität zu Berlin, 1986.

Brunnegger, Herbert. *Die Saat in den Sturm: Ein Soldat der Waffen-SS berichtet.* Stocker, 2000.

Buber-Neumann, Margarete. *Als Gefangene bei Stalin und Hitler: Eine Welt im Dunkel.* Ullstein Taschenbuch, 2002.

Bullerjahn, Günther. "Der Sonderbau im KZ-Sachsenhausen." In *KZ Sachsenhausen,* edited by Lucie Großer, 33–35. Lucie Großer, 1946.

Bussmann, Georg, ed. *Kunst im 3. Reich: Dokumente der Unterwerfung.* Zweitausendeins, 1980.

Cajani, Luigi. "Surveillance and Redemption: The Casa di Correzione of San Michele a Ripa in Rome." In *Institutions of Confinement: Hospitals, Asylums, and Prisons in Western Europe and North America, 1500–1950,* edited by Norbert Finzsch and Robert Jütte, 301–24. Cambridge University Press, 1996.

Campagna, Norbert. *Prostitution: Eine philosophische Untersuchung.* Parerga Verlag, 2005.

Cantaluppi, Gaetano. *Flossenbürg: Ricordi di un generale deportato*. Ugo Mursia Editore, 1995.

Carlebach, Emil, Willy Schmidt, and Ulrich Schneider. *Buchenwald ein Konzentrationslager: Berichte—Bilder—Dokumente*. Pahl-Rugenstein Nachfolger, 2000.

Carpi, Aldo. *Diario di Gusen*. Einaudi, 1993.

Català, Neus. *"In Ravensbrück ging meine Jugend zu Ende": Vierzehn spanische Frauen berichten über ihre Deportation in deutsche Konzentrationslager*. Translated by Dorothee von Keitz and Andreas Ruppert. Walter Frey, 1994.

Collins, Max Allan, George Hagenauer, Richard Oberg, and Steven Heller, eds. *Men's Adventure Magazines in Postwar America*. Taschen, 2004.

Comité International de Dachau. *Konzentrationslager Dachau 1933–1945*. Comité International de Dachau, 1978.

Czajka, Maya. "Huren in Bewegung." In *Sexarbeit: Prostitution—Lebenswelten und Mythen*, edited by Elisabeth von Dücker and Museum der Arbeit, 206–7. Edition Temmen, 2005.

Czech, Danuta. "Entstehungsgeschichte des KL Auschwitz: Aufbau- und Ausbauperiode." In *Auschwitz. Nationalsozialistisches Konzentrationslager*, edited by Staatliches Museum Auschwitz-Birkenau, 43–45. Verlag Staatliches Museum Auschwitz-Birkenau, 1997.

———. *Kalendarium der Ereignisse im Konzentrationslager Auschwitz–Birkenau 1939–1945*. Translated by Jochen August, Nina Kozlowska, Silke Lent, and Jan Parcer. Rowohlt, 1989.

Dachauer Häftlinge. *Konzentrationslager Dachau*. Stern Verlag, 1945.

Davidsen-Nielsen, Hans. *Carl Vaernet: Der dänische SS-Arzt im KZ Buchenwald*. Edition Regenbogen, 2004.

Deselaers, Manfred. *"Und Sie hatten nie Gewissensbisse?" Die Biografie von Rudolf Höß, Kommandant von Auschwitz, und die Frage nach seiner Verantwortung vor Gott und den Menschen*. St. Benno Verlag, 1997.

D'Harcourt, Pierre. *The Real Enemy*. Longmans, Green, 1967.

Distel, Barbara. "Das Zeugnis der Zurückgekehrten." In *Die nationalsozialistischen Konzentrationslager: Entwicklung und Struktur*, Band 1–2, edited by Ulrich Herbert, Karin Orth, and Christoph Dieckmann, 11–16. Wallenstein, 1998.

Donat, Alexander, ed., *The Death Camp Treblinka: A Documentary*. Holocaust Library, 1979.

Drinck, Barbara and Chung-noh Gross, eds. *Forced Prostitution in Times of War and Peace: Sexual Violence Against Women and Girls*. Kleine Verlag, 2007.

Ducci, Teo. *Un tallèt ad Auschwitz: 10.2.1944–5.5.1945*. Giuntina, 2000.

Dücker, Elisabeth, and Museum der Arbeit Hamburg, ed. *Sexarbeit: Prostitution—Lebenswelten und Mythen*, edited by Elisabeth von Dücker and Museum der Arbeit. Edition Temmen, 2005.

Ebbinghaus, Angelika, and Klaus Dörner, eds. *Vernichten und Heilen: Der Nürnberger Ärzteprozeß und seine Folgen*. Aufbau Taschenbuch, 2001.

Eberle, Annette. "Häftlingskategorien und Kennzeichnungen." In *Der Ort des Terrors: Geschichte der nationalsozialistischen Konzentrationslager*, Band 1: *Die Organisation des Terrors*, edited by Wolfgang Benz and Barbara Distel, 91–109. C. H. Beck, 2005.

Edwards, David. "Joy Divisions." *Daily Mirror*, January 27, 2007.

Ehresmann, Andreas. "Der Zellenbau im Konzentrationslager Ravensbrück: Eine bautypologische Annäherung." In *Ravensbrück: Der Zellenbau. Geschichte und Gedenken: Begleitband zur Ausstellung*, edited by Insa Eschebach, 50–73. Metropol, 2008.

Eisner, Jack. *The Survivor.* William Morrow, 1980.

Endlich, Stefanie. "Die äußere Gestalt des Terrors: Zu Städtebau und Architektur des Konzentrationslagers." In *Der Ort des Terrors: Geschichte der nationalsozialistischen Konzentrationslager*, Band 1: *Die Organisation des Terrors*, edited by Wolfgang Benz and Barbara Distel, 210–29. C. H. Beck, 2005.

Engelhardt, Kerstin. "*Frauen* im Konzentrationslager Dachau." *Dachauer Hefte* 14 (1998): 218–44.

Eschebach, Insa. "Das Stigma des Asozialen: Drei Urteile der DDR-Justiz gegen ehemalige Funktionshäftlinge des Frauenkonzentrationslagers Ravensbrück." In *Abgeleitete Macht: Funktionshäftlinge zwischen Widerstand und Kollaboration*, edited by KZ-Gedenkstätte Neuengamme, Beiträge zur Geschichte der nationalsozialistischen Verfolgung in Norddeutschland, no. 4, 69–81. Edition Temmen, 1998.

Eschebach, Insa, and Katja Jedermann, "Sex-Zwangsarbeit in NS-Konzentrationslagern: Anmerkungen zu einer Werkstatt-Ausstellung der Gedenkstätte Ravensbrück." *Feministische Studien* 1 (May/2007): 122–28.

Eschebach, Insa, and Regina Mühlhäuser, eds. *Krieg und Geschlecht: Sexuelle Gewalt im Krieg und Sex-Zwangsarbeit in NS-Konzentrationslagern.* Metropol, 2008.

Eschebach, Insa, Sigrid Jacobeit, and Silke Wenk, eds. *Gedächtnis und Geschlecht: Deutungsmuster in Darstellungen des nationalsozialistischen Genozids.* Campus, 2002.

Federn, Ernst. "Eros hinter Stacheldraht: Interview-Auszug." In *Stimmen aus Buchenwald: Ein Lesebuch*, edited by Holm und Ulf Kirsten, 69–72. Wallstein, 2002.

———. "Versuch einer Psychologie des Terrors (1946/1989)." In *Ernst Federn: Versuche zur Psychologie des Terrors*, edited by Roland Kaufbold, 51–91. Edition Psychosozial, 1998.

Fénelon, Fania. *Playing for Time.* Translated by Judith Landry. Atheneum, 1977.

Fings, Karola. *Krieg, Gesellschaft und KZ: Himmlers SS-Baubrigaden.* Schöningh, 2005.

Finzsch, Norbert. "Comparing Apples and Oranges? The History of Early Prisons in Germany and the United States, 1800–1860." In *Institutions of*

Confinement: Hospitals, Asylums, and Prisons in Western Europe and North America, 1500–1950, edited by Norbert Finzsch and Robert Jütte, 213–33. Cambridge University Press, 1996.

Finzsch, Norbert, and Robert Jütte, eds. *Institutions of Confinement: Hospitals, Asylums, and Prisons in Western Europe and North America, 1500–1950.* Cambridge University Press, 1996.

Foucault, Michel. *Discipline and Punish: The Birth of the Prison.* Translated by Alan Sheridan. Pantheon, 1977.

———. *The History of Sexuality.* Vol. 1: *An Introduction.* Translated by Robert Hurley. Pantheon, 1978.

Fraenkel, Heinrich, and Roger Manvell. *Himmler: Kleinbürger und Massenmörder.* Ullstein, 1965.

Frankenthal, Hans. *Verweigerte Rückkehr: Erfahrungen nach dem Judenmord.* Fischer Taschenbuch, 1999.

Frankl, Viktor E. *Ein Psycholog erlebt das Konzentrationslager.* Verlag Jugend und Volk, 1947.

Frei, Norbert. *1945 und wir: Das Dritte Reich im Bewußtsein der Deutschen.* Deutscher Taschenbuch Verlag, 2005.

Frei, Norbert, Sybille Steinbacher, and Bernd C. Wagner, eds. *Ausbeutung, Vernichtung, Öffentlichkeit: Neue Studien zur nationalsozialistischen Lagerpolitik.* K. G. Saur, 2000.

Frei, Norbert, Thomas Grotum, Jan Parcer, Sybille Steinbacher, and Bernd C. Wagner, eds. *Standort- und Kommandanturbefehle des Konzentrationslagers Auschwitz: 1940–1945.* De Gruyter, 2000.

Freund, Florian. *"Arbeitslager Zement:" Das Konzentrationslager Ebensee und die Raketenrüstung.* Verlag für Gesellschaftskritik, 1989.

Freund, Florian, and Bertrand Perz. "Mauthausen-Stammlager." In *Der Ort des Terrors: Geschichte der nationalsozialistischen Konzentrationslager*, Band IV: *Flossenbürg, Mauthausen, Ravensbrück*, edited by Wolfgang Benz and Barbara Distel, 293–346. C. H. Beck, 2005.

Freund-Widder, Michaela. *Frauen unter Kontrolle: Prostitution und ihre staatliche Bekämpfung in Hamburg vom Ende des Kaiserreiches bis zu den Anfängen der Bundesrepublik.* LIT, 2003.

Friedman, Paul. "Aspekte einer Konzentrationslager-Psychologie." *PSYCHE. Zeitschrift für Psychoanalyse und ihre Anwendung* 44. Jg. (2/1990): 165–72.

Frister, Roman. *The Cap: The Price of a Life.* Grove/Atlantic, 2001.

Fritz, Mali. *Essig gegen den Durst: 565 Tage in Auschwitz-Birkenau.* Verlag für Gesellschaftskritik, 1986.

Fröbe, Rainer. "KZ-Häftlinge als Reserve qualifizierter Arbeitskraft: Eine späte Entdeckung der deutschen Industrie und ihre Folgen," In *Die nationalsozialistischen Konzentrationslager: Entwicklung und Struktur*, Band 1–2, edited by Ulrich Herbert, Karin Orth, and Christoph Dieckmann, 636–81. Wallenstein, 1998.

Füllberg-Stolberg, Claus, Martina Jung, Renate Riebe, and Martina Scheitenberger, eds. *Frauen in Konzentrationslagern: Bergen-Belsen – Ravensbrück.* Edition Temmen, 1994.

Gabriel, Ralph, "Von Normvorstellungen und totaler Macht: Baugeschichtliche Monographie des Krankenreviers im Konzentrationslager Sachsenhausen." In *Abgeschlossene Kapitel? Zur Geschichte der Konzentrationslager und der NS Prozesse*, edited by Sabine Moller, Miriam Rürup, and Christel Trouvé, 46–58. Kimmerle G, 2002.

Garbe, Detlef. "Neuengamme-Stammlager." In *Der Ort des Terrors: Geschichte der nationalsozialistischen Konzentrationslager*, Band V: *Hinzert, Auschwitz, Neuengamme*, edited by Wolfgang Benz and Barbara Distel, 315–46. C. H. Beck, 2007.

———. *Zwischen Widerstand und Martyrium: Die Zeugen Jehovas im "Dritten Reich."* Oldenbourg, 1997.

Garrigoux, Dr. Henri, *Prisons et transports. Neuengamme. Guerre 1939/1945. Témoignage.* Nice: n.p., 1986.

Gedenkstätte Buchenwald, eds. *Konzentrationslager Buchenwald 1937–1945: Begleitband zur ständigen historischen Ausstellung.* Wallstein, 1999.

Gertjejanssen, Wendy Jo. "Victims, Heroes, Survivors: Sexual Violence on the Eastern Front During World War II." PhD diss., University of Minnesota, 2004. http://www.victimsheroessurvivors.info/VictimsHeroesSurvivors.pdf.

Giza, Jerzy St., and Wiesław Morasiewicz. "Poobozowe zaburzenia seksualne u kobiet jako elemet tzw. KZ-syndromu." *Przegląd Lekarski* 1 (1974): 68–75.

———. "Z zagadnień popędów w obozach koncentracyjnych: Przyczynek do analiz tzw. KZ-syndromu." *Przegląd Lekarski* 1 (1973): 29–41.

Graf, Karin. *Zitronen aus Kanada: Das Leben mit Auschwitz des Stanisław Hantz. Bibliografische Erzählungen.* Verlag des Staatlichen Museums Auschwitz-Birkenau, n.d.

Grau, Günter, ed., *Homosexualität in der NS-Zeit: Dokumente einer Diskriminierung und Verfolgung.* Fischer Taschenbuch, 1993.

Greif, Gideon. *We Wept Without Tears: Testimonies of the Jewish Sonderkommando from Auschwitz.* Yale University Press, 2014.

Grele, Ronald J. "Ziellose Bewegung: Methodologische und theoretische Probleme der Oral History." In *Lebenserfahrung und kollektives Gedächtnis: Die Praxis der "Oral History,"* edited by Lutz Niethammer, 195–220. Syndikat, 1980.

Grenz, Sabine. *(Un)heimliche Lust: Über den Konsum sexueller Dienstleistungen.* Verlag für Sozialwissenschaften, 2005.

Gross, Karl Adolf. *Zweitausend Tage Dachau: Erlebnisse eines Christenmenschen unter Herrenmenschen und Herdenmenschen: Berichte und Tagebücher des Häftlings Nr. 16921.* Neubau Verlag, 1946.

Großer, Lucie, ed. *KZ Sachsenhausen.* Lucie Großer, 1946.

Grossmann, Wassilij. *Die Hölle von Treblinka.* Verlag für fremdsprachige Literatur, 1946.

Grotum, Thomas. *Das digitale Archiv: Aufbau und Auswertung einer Datenbank zur Geschichte des Konzentrationslagers Auschwitz.* Campus, 2004.

Gutman, Israel, ed., *The Encyclopedia of the Holocaust.* Vol. 3. Macmillan, 1990.

Hackett, David A. *The Buchenwald Report.* Westview, 1995.

Hájková, Anna. "Strukturen weiblichen Verhaltens in Theresienstadt." In *Genozid und Geschlecht: Jüdische Frauen im nationalsozialistischen Lagersystem,* edited by Gisela Bock, 202–19. Campus, 2005.

Hájková, Anna, Elissa Mailaender, Doris Bergen, Patrick Farges, and Atina Grossmann. "Forum: Holocaust and History of Gender and Sexuality." *German History* 36, no. 1 (2018): 78–100.

Halbmayr, Brigitte. "Arbeitskommando 'Sonderbau': Zur Bedeutung und Funktion von Bordellen im KZ." *Dachauer Hefte 21* (2005): 217–36.

———. "Sexzwangsarbeit in NS-Konzentrationslagern." In *Frauen in Widerstand und Verfolgung: Jahrbuch 2005,* edited by Dokumentationsarchiv des österreichischen Widerstandes, 96–115. Münster: Lit Verlag, 2005.

Hamburger Institut für Sozialforschung, ed., *Die Auschwitz-Hefte: Texte der polnischen Zeitschrift "Przegląd Lekarski" über historische, psychische und medizinische Aspekte des Lebens und Sterbens in Auschwitz.* Vol. 1–2. Rogner und Bernhard, 1995.

Hamburger Stiftung zur Förderung von Wissenschaft und Kultur, eds. *"Deutsche Wirtschaft": Zwangsarbeit von KZ-Häftlingen für Industrie und Behörden.* VSA-Verlag,1991.

Hartewig, Karin. "Wolf unter Wölfen? Die prekäre Macht der kommunistischen Kapos im Konzentrationslager Buchenwald." In *Abgeleitete Macht: Funktionshäftlinge zwischen Widerstand und Kollaboration,* Beiträge zur Geschichte der nationalsozialistischen Verfolgung in Norddeutschland, vol. 4, edited by KZ-Gedenkstätte Neuengamme, 117–22. Edition Temmen, 1998.

Haustein, Sabine. "Weibliche Prostituierte und Prostitution in Leipzig in den Jahren 1933 bis 1945." In *Frauenforscherinnen stellen sich vor,* edited by Ilse Nagelschmidt, 130–51. Leipzig: Leipziger Universitätsverlag, 1995.

———. "Zur Geschichte von Prostituierten in Leipzig in der NS-Zeit." In *Frauenalltag in Leipzig: Weibliche Lebenszusammenhänge im 19. und 20. Jahrhundert,* edited by Susanne Schötz, 237–70. Böhlau, 1997.

Havryshko, Marta. "Listening to Women's Voices: Jewish Rape Survivors' Testimonies in Soviet War Crimes Trials." In *If This Is a Woman: Studies on Women and Gender in the Holocaust,* edited by Denisa Nešťáková, Katja Grosse-Sommer, Borbála Klacsmann, and Jakub Drábik, 221–42. Academic Studies Press, 2021.

Hedeler, Wladislaw. "Das Beispiel KARLag: Die Verwaltung eines Besserungsarbeitslagers." In *Stalinistischer Terror 1934–1941: Eine Forschungsbilanz,* edited by Wladislaw Hedeler, 109–32. Basis Druck Verlag, 2002.

———, ed. *Stalinscher Terror 1934–1941: Eine Forschungsbilanz.* Basis Druck Verlag, 2002.

Hedgepeth, Sonja M., and Rochelle G. Saidel, eds. *Sexual Violence Against Jewish Women During the Holocaust.* Brandeis University Press, 2010.

Heger, Heinz. *Wir Männer mit dem rosa Winkel.* Merlin Verlag, 2001.

Heiber, Helmut, ed., *Reichsführer! . . . Briefe an und von Himmler.* Deutsche Verlags-Anstalt, 1968.

Heigl, Peter. *Konzentrationslager Flossenbürg in Geschichte und Gegenwart.* Mittelbayerische Druckerei- und Verlags-Gesellschaft, 1994.

———. "Zwangsprostitution im KZ-Lagerbordell Flossenbürg." *Geschichte Quer* 6 (1998): 44–45.

Heinemann, Isabel, and Patrick Wagner, eds. *Wissenschaft—Planung—Vertreibung: Neuordnungskonzepte und Umsiedlungspolitik im 20. Jahrhundert.* Franz Steiner Verlag, 2006.

Heller, Michel. *Stacheldraht der Revolution: Die Welt der Konzentrationslager in der sowjetischen Literatur.* Seewald, 1975.

Heller, Steven. "Sweat, Nazis, and SS Sex Slaves: A Social History." In *Men's Adventure Magazines in Postwar America*, edited by Max Allan Collins, George Hagenauer, Richard Oberg, and Steven Heller, 285–90. Taschen, 2004.

Herbermann, Nanda. *The Blessed Abyss: Inmate #6582 in Ravensbrück Concentration Camp for Women.* Translated by Hester Baer. Wayne State University Press, 2000.

Herbert, Ulrich. *Fremdarbeiter: Politik und Praxis des "Ausländer-Einsatzes" in der Kriegswirtschaft des Dritten Reiches.* J. H. W. Dietz Nachfolger, 1999.

Herbert, Ulrich, Karin Orth, and Christoph Dieckmann. "Die nationalsozialistischen Konzentrationslager: Geschichte, Erinnerung, Forschung." In *Die nationalsozialistischen Konzentrationslager: Entwicklung und Struktur*, edited by Ulrich Herbert, Karin Orth, and Christoph Dieckmann, 17–40. Wallenstein, 1998.

———, eds. *Die nationalsozialistischen Konzentrationslager: Entwicklung und Struktur.* Vols. 1–2. Wallenstein, 1998.

Herzog, Dagmar, ed. *Brutality and Desire: War and Sexuality in Europe's Twentieth Century.* Palgrave Macmillan, 2009.

———. "Hubris and Hypocrisy, Incitement and Disavowal: Sexuality and German Fascism." *Journal of the History of Sexuality* 11, no. 1/2, Special Issue: Sexuality and German Fascism (January–April 2002): 3–21.

———. *Sexuality in Europe: A Twentieth-Century History.* Cambridge University Press, 2011.

Hesse, Hans, ed. *"Am mutigsten waren immer wieder die Zeugen Jehovas": Verfolgung und Widerstand der Zeugen Jehovas im Nationalsozialismus.* Edition Temmen, 1998.

Hilberg, Raul. *The Destruction of the European Jews.* Holmes & Meier, 1985.

———. *Sources of Holocaust Research: An Analysis.* Ivan R. Dee, 2001.

Himmler, Heinrich. *Geheimreden 1933 bis 1945 und andere Ansprachen.* Edited by Bradley F. Smith and Agnes F. Peterson. Propyläen, 1974.

Hoess, Rudolf. *Commandant of Auschwitz.* Translated by Constantino Fitz Gibbon. Popular Library, 1961.

Hoffmann, Detlef. "Dachau." In *Das Gedächtnis der Dinge: KZ-Relikte und KZ-Denkmäler 1945–1995*, edited by Detlef Hoffmann, 36–91. Campus, 1998.

———, ed. *Das Gedächtnis der Dinge: KZ-Relikte und KZ-Denkmäler 1945–1995.* Campus Verlag, 1998.

Hoffmann, Katharina, and Andreas Lembeck, eds. *Nationalsozialismus und Zwangsarbeit in der Region Oldenburg.* Bibliotheks- und Informationssystem der Carl von Ossietzky Universität Oldenburg, 1999.

Holzhaider, Hans. "'Schwester Pia': Nutznießerin zwischen Opfern und Tätern." *Dachauer Hefte* 10 (1994): 101–14.

Höß, Rudolf. *Kommandant in Auschwitz.* Edited by Martin Broszat. dtv dokumente, 1958.

Hrdlicka, Manuela R. *Alltag im KZ: Das Lager Sachsenhausen bei Berlin.* Leske und Budrich Verlag, 1991.

Internationaler Militärgerichtshof Nürnberg. *Der Nürnberger Prozess gegen die Hauptkriegsverbrecher vom 14. November 1945–1. Oktober 1946.* Reichenbach Verlag, 1947.

Internationales Lager Komitee Buchenwald, ed. *Bericht des Internationalen Lagerkomitees Buchenwald.* Vol. 1. Thüringer Volksverlag GmbH, 1949.

Jäger, Gudrun. "'Was für ein schönes Seidenhemd ich hatte!' Liana Millu über die 'Umwertung der Werte' in Auschwitz-Birkenau und die weibliche Lebenswelt im Konzentrationslager." *Werkstatt Geschichte* 20 (1998): 95–104.

Jah, Akim, Christoph Kopke, Alexander Korb, and Alexa Stiller, eds. *Nationalsozialistische Lager: Neue Beiträge zur Geschichte der Verfolgungs- und Vernichtungspolitik und zur Theorie und Praxis von Gedenkstättenarbeit.* Klemm und Oelschläger, 2006.

Jaiser, Constanze. "Repräsentation von Sexualität und Gewalt in Zeugnissen jüdischer und nichtjüdischer Überlebender." In *Genozid und Geschlecht: Jüdische Frauen im nationalsozialistischen Lagersystem*, edited by Gisela Bock, 123–48. Campus, 2005.

Jellonnek, Burkhard. *Homosexuelle unter dem Hakenkreuz: Die Verfolgung von Homosexuellen im Dritten Reich.* Schöningh Verlag, 1990.

Joos, Joseph. *Leben auf Widerruf: Begegnungen und Beobachtungen im K.Z. Dachau 1941–1945.* Paulinus-Verlag, 1948.

Jureit, Ulrike, and Beate Meyer. "Einleitung." In *Verletzungen: Lebensgeschichtliche Verarbeitung von Kriegserfahrungen*, edited by Ulrike Jureit and Beate Meyer, 6–25. Dölling & Galitz, 1994.

———, eds. *Verletzungen: Lebensgeschichtliche Verarbeitung von Kriegserfahrungen.* Dölling & Galitz, 1994.

Jureit, Ulrike, and Karin Orth. *Überlebensgeschichten: Gespräche mit Überlebenden des KZ-Neuengamme.* Dölling & Galitz, 1994.

Kaienburg, Hermann. *Der Militär- und Wirtschaftskomplex der SS im KZ-Standort Sachsenhausen-Oranienburg: Schnittpunkt von KZ-System, Waffen-SS und Judenmord.* Metropol, 2006.

———. *Die Wirtschaft der SS.* Metropol, 2003.

———, ed. *Konzentrationslager und deutsche Wirtschaft 1939–1945.* Leske und Budrich, 1996.

———. "KZ-Haft und Wirtschaftsinteresse: Das Wirtschaftsverwaltungshauptamt der SS als Leitungszentrale der Konzentrationslager und der SS-Wirtschaft der SS." In *Konzentrationslager und deutsche Wirtschaft 1939–1945,* edited by Hermann Kaienburg, 29–60. Leske und Budrich, 1996.

———. "*Sachsenhausen-Stammlager.*" In *Der Ort des Terrors: Geschichte der nationalsozialistischen Konzentrationslager,* Band III: *Sachsenhausen, Buchenwald,* edited by Wolfgang Benz and Barbara Distel, 17–71. C. H. Beck, 2006.

———. "*Vernichtung durch Arbeit:" Der Fall Neuengamme. Die Wirtschaftsbestrebungen der SS und ihre Auswirkungen auf die Existenzbedingungen der KZ-Gefangenen.* J. H. W. Dietz, 1991.

Kalmar, Rudolf. *Zeit ohne Gnade.* Schönbrunn-Verlag, 1946.

Kaminski, Andrzej J. *Konzentrationslager 1896 bis heute.* Piper, 1990.

Kárný, Miroslav. "Das Theresienstädter Familienlager (BIIb) in Birkenau: September 1943–Juli 1944." *Hefte von Auschwitz* 20 (1997): 133–237.

Kassing, Reinhild, and Christa Paul. "Bordelle in deutschen Konzentrationslagern." *K(r)ampfader* 6, no. 1 (1991): 26–31.

Katz, Steven T. "Thoughts on the Intersection of Rape and Rassenchande During the Holocaust." *Modern Judaism—a Journal of Jewish Ideas and Experience* 32, no. 3 (October 2012): 293–322.

Ka-tzetnik 135633 [Yehiel De-Nur]. *House of Dolls.* Translated by Moshe Kohn. Frederick Mueller, 1955.

Kaufbold, Roland, ed. *Ernst Federn: Versuche zur Psychologie des Terrors.* Edition Psychosozial, 1998.

Keller, Rolf, ed. *Konzentrationslager Bergen-Belsen: Berichte und Dokumente.* Vandenhoeck und Ruprecht, 1995.

Kempowski, Walter. "'Das Wichtigste: Unser Führer lebt.' Der 20. Juli 1944. Echo eines Attentats: Ein Zeitbild aus Tagebüchern, Briefen und Erinnerungen." *Die Zeit,* July 8, 2004.

Kępinski, Antoni. "Das sogenannte KZ-Syndrom: Der Versuch einer Synthese." In *Die Auschwitz-Hefte: Texte der polnischen Zeitschrift "Przegląd Lekarski" über historische, psychische und medizinische Aspekte des Lebens und Sterbens in Auschwitz,* edited by the Hamburger Institut für Sozialforschung, 2:7–14. Rogner und Bernhard, 1995.

Kershner, Isabel. "Israel's Unexpected Spinoff from a Holocaust Trial." *New York Times*, September 6, 2007.

Kießling, Regine, Gisela Kraut, and Ulrich Wanitzek. "Großbauten des Staates und der Partei (München, Nürnberg, Berlin)." In *Kunst im 3. Reich: Dokumente der Unterwerfung*, edited by Georg Bussmann. Zweitausendeins, 1974.

Kielar, Wieslaw. *Anus Mundi: 1500 Days in Auschwitz/Birkenau.* Translated by Susanne Flatauer. Times Books, 1980.

———. *Anus Mundi: Fünf Jahre Auschwitz.* Translated by Wera Kapkajew. Fischer Taschenbuch, 2002.

Kieta, Mieczysław. "Das Hygiene-Institut der Waffen-SS und Polizei in Auschwitz." In *Die Auschwitz-Hefte: Texte der polnischen Zeitschrift "Przegląd Lekarski" über historische, psychische und medizinische Aspekte des Lebens und Sterbens in Auschwitz*, edited by Hamburger Institut für Sozialforschung, 1:213–17. Rogner und Bernhard, 1995.

Klausch, Hans-Peter. "Das *Lagerbordell* von Flossenbürg"*: Beiträge zur Geschichte der Arbeiterbewegung* 4 (December 1992): 86–94.

———. *Widerstand in Flossenbürg: Zum antifaschistischen Widerstandskampf der deutschen, österreichischen und sowjetischen Kommunisten im Konzentrationslager Flossenbürg 1940–1945*. BIS, 1990.

Kleiber, Dieter, and Doris Velten. *Prostitutionskunden: Eine Untersuchung über soziale und psychologische Charakteristika von Besuchern weiblicher Prostituierter in Zeiten von Aids.* Nomos-Verlagsgesellschaft, 1994.

Klemperer, Viktor. *LTI: Notizbuch eines Philologen.* Reclam, 2007.

Klier, Freya. *Die Kaninchen von Ravensbrück: Medizinische Versuche an Frauen in der NS-Zeit.* Knaur, 1994.

Knigge, Volkhard, and Norbert Frei, eds. *Verbrechen erinnern: Die Auseinandersetzung mit Holocaust und Völkermord.* C. H. Beck, 2002.

Knoch, Habbo. "Die Emslandlager 1933–1945." In *Der Ort des Terrors: Geschichte der nationalsozialistischen Konzentrationslager*, Band II: *Frühe Lager, Dachau, Emslandlager*, edited by Wolfgang Benz and Barbara Distel, 533–70. C. H. Beck, 2005.

Kochheim, Friedrich. *Bilanz: Erlebnisse und Gedanken.* Westkreuz-Verlag, 2003.

Kogon, Eugen. *Der SS-Staat: Das System der deutschen Konzentrationslager.* Wilhelm Heyne Verlag, 1974.

———. *The Theory and Practice of Hell: The Classic Account of the Nazi Concentration Camps Used as a Basis for the Nuremberg Investigations.* Translated by Heinz Norden. 1950; Berkley Books, 1998.

Kollektiv Buchenwald Berlin. "Zur Gestaltung der Gedenkstätte Sachsenhausen." In *Von der Erinnerung zum Monument: Die Entstehungsgeschichte der Nationalen Mahn- und Gedenkstätte Sachsenhausen*, edited by Günter Morsch, 164–216. Edition Hentrich, 1996.

Komitee der Antifaschistischen Widerstandskämpfer der DDR, ed. *Aktenvermerk R.U.* Militärverlag der DDR, 1981.

———, ed. *Die Frauen von Ravensbrück*. Kongress-Verlag, 1961.

———, ed. *Sachsenhausen: Dokumente, Aussagen, Forschungsergebnisse und Überlebensberichte über das ehemalige Konzentrationslager Sachsenhausen*. Deutscher Verlag der Wissenschaften, 1977.

Königseder, Angelika. "Die Entwicklung des KZ-Systems." In *Der Ort des Terrors: Geschichte der nationalsozialistischen Konzentrationslager*, Band 1: *Die Organisation des Terrors*, edited by Wolfgang Benz and Barbara Distel, 30–42. C. H. Beck, 2005.

Konieczny, Alfred. "Das KZ *Groß-Rosen* in Niederschlesien." In *Die nationalsozialistischen Konzentrationslager: Entwicklung und Struktur*, vols. 1–2, edited by Ulrich Herbert, Karin Orth, and Christoph Dieckmann, 309–26. Wallenstein, 1998.

Korzilius, Sven. *"Asoziale" und "Parasiten" im Recht der SBZ/DDR: Randgruppen im Sozialismus zwischen Repression und Ausgrenzung*. Böhlau, 2004.

Kreis, Michael. "Die Deutsche Gesellschaft zur Bekämpfung der Geschlechtskrankheiten (DGBG/GBGK) 1902 bis 1987: Ein historischer Abriß." Dissertation, Medizinische Fakultät der Technischen Universität München, 1988.

Kudryashov, Sergei. "Ordinary Collaborators: The Case of the Travniki Guards." In *Russia: War, Peace, and Diplomacy: Essays in Honour of John Erickson*, edited by Mark Erickson and Ljubica Erickson, 226–39. Weidenfeld & Nicolson, 2004.

Kühnrich, Heinz. *Der KZ-Staat: Die faschistischen Konzentrationslager 1933–1945*. Dietz Verlag, 1980.

Kulisiewicz, Aleksander. *Adresse Sachsenhausen: Literarische Momentaufnahmen aus dem KZ*. Bleicher Verlag, 1997.

Kundrus, Birte. "Forbidden Company: Romantic Relationships Between Germans and Foreigners, 1939 to 1945." *Journal of the History of Sexuality* 11 (2002): 201–22.

Kupfer-Koberwitz, Edgar. *Dachauer Tagebücher: Die Aufzeichnungen des Häftlings 24814*. Kindler Verlag, 1997.

KZ-Gedenkstätte Neuengamme, ed. *Abgeleitete Macht: Funktionshäftlinge zwischen Widerstand und Kollaboration*. Beiträge zur Geschichte der nationalsozialistischen Verfolgung in Norddeutschland, Heft 4. Edition Temmen, 1998.

———, ed. *Zeitspuren: Die Ausstellungen. Dreisprachige Ausgabe: Deutsch—English—Français*. Edition Temmen, 2005.

Land Oberösterreich, ed. *Oberösterreichische Gedenkstätten für KZ-Opfer*. Oberösterreichisches Landesarchiv, 2001.

Langbein, Hermann. *Menschen in Auschwitz*. Europaverlag, 1995.

———. *People in Auschwitz*. Translated by Harry Zohn. University of North Carolina Press, 2004.

Lanzmann, Claude: *Shoah*. Deutscher Taschenbuch-Verlag, 1988.

Lazarus, Richard S. *Emotion and Adaptation.* Oxford University Press, 1991.

Lemke, Jürgen. *Ganz normal anders.* Aufbau Verlag, 1989.

Lenarczyk, Wojciech, Andreas Mix, Johannes Schwartz, and Veronika Springmann, eds. *KZ-Verbrechen: Beiträge zur Geschichte der nationalsozialistischen Konzentrationslager und ihrer Erinnerung.* Metropol, 2007.

Leo, Annette. *"Das ist so'n zweischneidiges Schwert hier unser KZ . . .": Der Fürstenberger Alltag und das Frauenkonzentrationslager Ravensbrück.* Metropol, 2007.

Lesniak, Roman, Jan Mitarski, Maria Orwid, Adam Szymusik, and Alexander Treutsch. "Einige psychiatrische Probleme des KZ-Lagers Auschwitz im Lichte eigener Untersuchungen." *Przegląd Lekarski* 1 (1962): 42–52.

Levi, Primo. *If This Is A Man/The Truce.* Translated by Stuart Woolf. Abacus, 1988.

Levine, Philippa. *Prostitution, Race, and Politics: Policing Venereal Disease in the British Empire.* Routledge, 2003.

Ley, Astrid, and Günter Morsch. *Medizin und Verbrechen: Das Krankenrevier des KZ Sachsenhausen 1936–1945.* Metropol, 2007.

Liblau, Charles. *Die Kapos von Auschwitz.* Verlag Auschwitz-Birkenau Staatliches Museum, 1998.

Lingens, Ella. *Eine Frau im Konzentrationslager.* Europa Verlag, 1966.

Lohner, Margret. "Die Prostitution und ihre Bedeutung in der venerologischen Sicht." Disseration. Medizinische Fakultät der Technischen Universität München, 1991.

Longerich, Peter. *Heinrich Himmler: A Life.* Oxford University Press, 2011.

Loos, Karina. "*Planen* und Bauen im Nationalsozialismus: Ein Überblick zu Weimar." In *Klassikerstadt und Nationalsozialismus: Kultur und Politik in Weimar 1933 bis 1945,* edited by Justus H. Ulbricht, 128–44. Glaux, 2002.

Lundholm, Anja. *Das Höllentor: Bericht einer Überlebenden.* Rowohlt Buchverlag, 1988.

Mac, Juno, and Molly Smith, *Revolting Prostitutes: The Fight for Sex Workers' Rights.* Verso, 2018.

Maciejewski, Zdziłsaw Maciej. "*Wyniki badań ginekologicznych* byłych więźniarek mieszkających w Koszalinie," *Przegląd Lekarski* 1 (1975): 67–70.

Mahn- und Gedenkstätte Ravensbrück, ed. *Gedenkbuch für die Opfer des Konzentrationslagers Ravensbrück.* Metropol, 2005.

Majer, Dietmut. *"Fremdvölkische" im Dritten Reich: Ein Beitrag zur nationalsozialistischen Rechtssetzung und Rechtspraxis in Verwaltung und Justiz unter besonderer Berücksichtigung der eingegliederten Ostgebiete und des Generalgouvernements.* Boldt, 1981.

———. *Grundlagen des nationalsozialistischen Rechtssystems: Führerprinzip, Sonderrecht, Einheitspartei.* Kohlhammer, 1987.

Makowski, Antoni. "Organisation, Entwicklung und Tätigkeit des Häftlingskrankenbaus in Monowitz (KL Auschwitz III)." *Hefte von Auschwitz* 15 (1975): 113–81.

Marcuse, Harold. "Die museale Darstellung des Holocaust an Orten ehemaliger Konzentrationslager in der Bundesrepublik." In *Erinnerung: Zur Gegenwart des Holocaust in Deutschland-West und Deutschland-Ost*, edited by Bernhard Moltmann, Doron Kiesel, Cilly Kugelmann, Hanno Loewy, and Dietrich Neuhaus, 79–98. Haag and Herchen, 1993.

———. *Legacies of Dachau: The Uses and Abuses of a Concentration Camp, 1933–2001*. Cambridge University Press, 2001.

Maršálek, Hans. "Das KZ Mauthausen (Stammlager) 1938–1945." In *Oberösterreichische Gedenkstätten für KZ-Opfer*, edited by Land Oberösterreich, 43–51. Oberösterreichisches Landesarchiv, 2001.

———. *Die Geschichte des Konzentrationslagers Mauthausen: Dokumentation*. Mauthausen-Komitee Österreich, 1980.

———. *Konzentrationslager Gusen: Ein Nebenlager des KZ Mauthausen*. Österreichische Lagergemeinschaft Mauthausen, 1987.

———. *Vergasungsaktionen im Konzentrationslager Mauthausen*. Österreichische Lagergemeinschaft Mauthausen, 1998.

Marszałek, Józef. *Majdanek: The Concentration Camp in Lublin*. Interpress, 1984.

Martin-Chauffier, Louis. *L'homme et la bête*. Paris: Gallimard, 1948.

Matussek, Paul. *Die Konzentrationslagerhaft und ihre Folgen*. Springer Verlag, 1971.

Mayer, Arno. *Der Krieg als Kreuzzug: Das Deutsche Reich, Hitlers Wehrmacht und die Endlösung*. Rowohlt, 1989.

Mayrhofer, Fritz, and Walter Schuster, eds. *Nationalsozialismus in Linz*. 2 vols. Archiv der Stadt Linz, 2001.

Meier, Heinrich Christian. *So war es: Das Leben im KZ Neuengamme*. Phönix-Verlag, 1948.

Meinen, Insa. *Wehrmacht und Prostitution während des Zweiten Weltkrieges in Frankreich*. Edition Temmen, 2002.

Melodia, Giovanni. *Non dimenticare Dachau: I giorni del massacro e della speranza in un Lager nazista*. Mursia, 1993.

Michel, Antje. "Gerüchte im KZ Sachsenhausen: Ein Paradigma für die Kommunikationsstruktur einer Zwangsgesellschaft von Konzentrationslagerhäftlingen." In *Abgeschlossene Kapitel? Zur Geschichte der Konzentrationslager und der NS Prozesse*, edited by Sabine Moller, Miriam Rürup, and Christel Trouvé, 58–69. Kimmerle G, 2002.

Michel, Jean. *Dora: The Nazi Concentration Camp Where Modern Space Technology Was Born and 30,000 Prisoners Died*. Holt Rinehart & Winston, 1980.

Mielke, Fred, and Alexander Mitscherlich. *Das Diktat der Menschenverachtung: Der Nürnberger Ärzteprozess und seine Quellen*. Schneider, 1947.

Mildt, Dirk Welmoed de, and Christiaan F. Rüter, eds. *Justiz und NS-Verbrechen: Sammlung deutscher Strafurteile wegen nationalsozialistischer Tötungsverbrechen 1945–1966*. Amsterdam University Press, 1998.

Millu, Liana. *Die Brücke von Schwerin.* Fischer Taschenbuch, 2001.

———. *Il fumo di Birkenau.* Giuntina, 2001.

———. *Smoke Over Birkenau.* Translated by Lynne Sharon Schwartz. Varda, 2001.

Minney, R. J. *I Shall Fear no Evil: The Story of Dr. Alina Brewda.* Kimber, 1966.

Moller, Sabine, Miriam Rürup, and Christel Trouvé. *Abgeschlossene Kapitel? Zur Geschichte der Konzentrationslager und der NS Prozesse.* Kimmerle G, 2002.

Moltmann, Bernhard, Kiesel Doron, Cilly Kugelmann, Hanno Loewy, and Dietrich Neuhaus, eds. *Erinnerung: Zur Gegenwart des Holocaust in Deutschland-West und Deutschland-Ost.* Haag & Herchen, 1993.

Morsch, Günter. *Mord und Massenmord im Konzentrationslager Sachsenhausen.* Metropol, 2005.

———. "Oranienburg—Sachsenhausen, Sachsenhausen—Oranienburg." In *Die nationalsozialistischen Konzentrationslager: Entwicklung und Struktur,* vols. 1–2, edited by Ulrich Herbert, Karin Orth, and Christoph Dieckmann, 111–34. Wallenstein, 1998.

———. *Von der Erinnerung zum Monument: Die Entstehungsgeschichte der Nationalen Mahn- und Gedenkstätte Sachsenhausen.* Edition Hentrich, 1996.

Morsey, Rudolf. *Die Bundesrepublik Deutschland: Entstehung und Entwicklung bis 1969.* Oldenbourg Wissenschaftsverlag, 1990.

Muggenthaler, Thomas. *"Ich lege mich hin und sterbe!" Ehemalige Häftlinge des KZ Flossenbürg berichten.* E. Vögel, 2005.

Mühlhäuser, Regina. "Rasse, Blut und Männlichkeit: Politiken sexueller Regulierung in den besetzten Gebieten der Sowjetunion (1941–1945)." *Feministische Studien* 1 (2007): 55–69.

Mühlhäuser, Regina, Gaby Zipfel, and Kirsten Campbell, eds. *In Plain Sight: Sexual Violence in Armed Conflict.* Zubaan, 2019.

Mühlhäuser, Regina, and Insa Eschebach. "Sexuelle Gewalt im Krieg und Sex-Zwangsarbeit in NS-Konzentrationslagern." In *Krieg und Geschlecht: Sexuelle Gewalt im Krieg und Sex-Zwangsarbeit in NS-Konzentrationslagern,* edited by Insa Eschebach and Regina Mühlhäuser, 11–32. Metropol, 2008.

Müller, Charlotte. *Die Klempnerkolonne in Ravensbrück: Erinnerungen des Häftlings Nr. 10787.* Diez, 1990.

Nagelschmidt, Ilse, ed. *Frauenforscherinnen stellen sich vor: Ringvorlesung Teil VI. Wintersemester 1997/98.* Leipziger Uni-Verlag, 1995.

Nansen, Odd. *Fra dag til dag.* Dreyers Forlag, 1946.

———. *Von Tag zu Tag: Ein Tagebuch.* Translated by Ingeborg Goebel. Dulk, 1949.

Naor, Simha. *Krankengymnastin in Auschwitz: Aufzeichnungen des Häftlings Nr. 80574.* Herder, 1989.

Naujoks, Harry. *Mein Leben im KZ Sachsenhausen 1936–1942: Erinnerungen des ehemaligen Lagerältesten.* Dietz, 1989.

Neander, Joachim. *Das Konzentrationslager "Mittelbau" in der Endphase der national-sozialistischen Diktatur: Zur Geschichte des letzten im "Dritten Reich" gegründeten selbständigen Konzentrationslagers unter besonderer Berücksichtigung seiner Auflösungsphase.* Papierflieger, 1998.

Neuhäuslers, Johannes. *Wie war das im KZ Dachau? Ein Versuch, der Wahrheit näherzukommen.* Kuratorium für Sühnemal KZ Dachau, 1996.

Niedojadło, Eugeiusz. "Der Lager-,Krankenbau' in Buna." In *Przegląd Lekarski. Anthologie,* vol. II, pt. 2, edited by the Internationales Auschwitz Komitee, 43–53. International Auschwitz Committee, 1970.

Niethammer, Lutz, ed. *Der "gesäuberte" Antifaschismus: Die SED und die roten Kapos von Buchenwald.* Akademie Verlag, 1994.

———, ed. *"Die Jahre weiß man nicht, wo man die heute hinsetzen soll": Faschismuserfahrungen im Ruhrgebiet.* Verlag J. H. W. Dietz Nachfolger, 1983.

———. *Lebenserfahrung und kollektives Gedächtnis: Die Praxis der "Oral History."* Suhrkamp, 1985.

Nomberg-Przytyk, Sara. *Auschwitz: True Tales form a Grotesque Land.* Translated by Roslyn Hirsch. University of North Carolina Press, 1985.

Northeast Asian History Foundation. *The Truth of the Japanese Military "Comfort Women."* Northeast Asian History Foundation, 2007.

Oertel, Otto. *Als Gefangener der SS.* BIS, 1990.

Ogan, Bernd, and Wolfgang Weiß, eds. *Faszination und Gewalt: Zur politischen Ästhetik des Nationalsozialismus.* Tümmel Verlag, 1992.

Orth, Karin. *Die Konzentrationslager-SS: Sozialstrukturelle Analysen und biografische Studien einer nationalsozialistischen Führungselite.* Wallstein, 2001.

———. "Gab es eine Lagergesellschaft? 'Kriminelle' und politische Häftlinge im Konzentrationslager." In *Ausbeutung, Vernichtung, Öffentlichkeit: Neue Studien zur nationalsozialistischen Lagerpolitik,* edited by Norbert Frei, Sybille Steinbacher, and Bernd C. Wagner, 109–33. K. G. Saur, 2000.

Ostrowska, Joanna. *Przemilczane: Seksualna praca przymusowa w czasie II wojny światowej.* Maginesy, 2018.

Pachaly, Erhard, and Kurt Pelny. *KZ Mittelbau-Dora: Zum antifaschistischen Widerstandskampf im KZ Dora 1943 bis 1945.* Dietz Verlag, 1990.

Pappalettera, Vincenzo. *Tu passerai per il camino: Vita e morte a Mauthausen.* Mursia, 1997.

Pätzold, Kurt. "Häftlingsgesellschaft." In *Der Ort des Terrors: Geschichte der nationalsozialistischen Konzentrationslager,* Band I: *Die Organisation des Terrors,* edited by Wolfgang Benz and Barbara Distel, 110–25. C. H. Beck, 2005.

Paul, Christa. "Frühe Weichenstellungen: Zum Ausschluss 'asozialer' Häftlinge von Ansprüchen auf besondere Unterstützungsleistungen und auf Entschädigung." In *Opfer als Akteure: Interventionen ehemaliger NS-Verfolgter in der Nachkriegszeit,* edited by Fritz Bauer Institut and Katharina Stengel, 67–86. Campus Verlag, 2008.

———. "Prostitution, Krieg und sexuelle Sklaverei." In *Sexarbeit: Prostitution—Lebenswelten und Mythen,* edited by Elisabeth von Dücker and Museum der Arbeit, 302–4. Edition Temmen, 2005.

———. *Zwangsprostitution: Staatlich errichtete Bordelle im Nationalsozialismus.* Edition Hentrich, 1994.

Paul, Christa, and Robert Sommer. "SS-Bordelle und Oral History: Problematische Quellen und die Existenz von Bordellen für die SS in Konzentrationslagern." *BIOS* 19, no. 1 (2006): 124–42.

Pawełczyńska, Anna. *Werte gegen Gewalt: Betrachtungen einer Soziologin über Auschwitz.* Verlag des Staatlichen Museums Auschwitz-Birkenau, 2001.

Pelt, Robert-Jan van, and Debórah Dwork. *Auschwitz von 1270 bis heute.* Translated by Klaus Rupprecht. Büchergilde Gutenberg, 1999.

Person, Katarzyna. "Sexual Violence During the Holocaust: The Case of Forced Prostitution in the Warsaw Ghetto." *Shofar* 33, no. 2 (Winter 2015): 103–21.

Perz, Bertrand. "Der Arbeitseinsatz im KZ Mauthausen." In *Die nationalsozialistischen Konzentrationslager: Entwicklung und Struktur,* vols. 1–2, edited by Ulrich Herbert, Karin Orth, and Christoph Dieckmann, 533–57. Wallenstein, 1998.

———. "Gusen I und II." In *Der Ort des Terrors: Geschichte der nationalsozialistischen Konzentrationslager,* Band IV: *Flossenbürg, Mauthausen, Ravensbrück,* edited by Wolfgang Benz and Barbara Distel, 371–80. C. H. Beck, 2005.

———. *Projekt Quarz: Steyr-Daimler-Puch und das Konzentrationslager Melk.* Verlag für Gesellschaftskritik, 1991.

Pflock, Andreas. "'Bitteschön, und jetzt können Sie mich verhaften:' Ilse Stephan." In *Frauen in Konzentrationslagern: Bergen-Belsen. Ravensbrück,* edited by Claus Füllberg-Stolberg, Martina Jung, Renate Riebe, and Martina Scheitenberger, 291–98. Edition Temmen, 1994.

Philipp, Grit. *Kalendarium der Ereignisse im Frauen-Konzentrationslager Ravensbrück 1939–1945.* Metropol, 1999.

Pike, David Wingate. *Spaniards in the Holocaust: Mauthausen, Horror on the Danube.* Corrected 11th ed. Taylor & Francis, 2000.

Pingel, Falk. *Häftlinge unter SS-Herrschaft: Widerstand, Selbstbehauptung und Vernichtung im Konzentrationslager.* Hoffmann und Campe, 1978.

Piper, Franciszek. *Arbeitseinsatz der Häftlinge aus dem KL Auschwitz.* Verlag Staatliches Museum in Oświęcim, 1995.

———. "Die Rolle des Lagers Auschwitz bei der Verwirklichung der nationalsozialistischen Ausrottungspolitik: Die doppelte Funktion von Auschwitz als Konzentrationslager und als Zentrum der Judenvernichtung." In *Die nationalsozialistischen Konzentrationslager: Entwicklung und Struktur,* vols. 1–2, edited by Ulrich Herbert, Karin Orth, and Christoph Dieckmann, 390–414. Wallenstein, 1998.

———. "Die Zahl der Opfer von Auschwitz." In *Auschwitz: Nationalsozialistisches Konzentrationslager,* edited by the Staatliches Museum Auschwitz-Birkenau, 271–92. Verlag Staatliches Museum Auschwitz-Birkenau, 1997.

———. "Industrieunternehmen als Initiatoren des Einsatzes von KZ-Häftlingen: Das Beispiel Auschwitz." In *"Deutsche Wirtschaft": Zwangsarbeit von KZ-Häftlingen für Industrie und Behörden*, edited by Hamburger Stiftung zur Förderung von Wissenschaft und Kultur, 97–139. VSA-Verlag, 1991.

———. "Massenvernichtung von Juden in Gaskammern des KL Auschwitz." In *Auschwitz: Nationalsozialistisches Konzentrationslager*, edited by the Staatliches Museum Auschwitz-Birkenau, 243–58. Verlag Staatliches Museum Auschwitz-Birkenau, 1997.

Pisar, Samuel. *Das Blut der Hoffnung*. Translated by Jürgen Abel. Rowohlt, 1983.

———. *Of Blood and Hope*. Cassell, 1980.

Plewe, Reinhard, and Jan Thomas Köhler. *Baugeschichte Frauen-Konzentrationslager Ravensbrück*. Edition Hentrich, 2000.

Plöckinger, Othmar. *Geschichte eines Buches: Adolf Hitlers 'Mein Kampf' 1922–1945*. Oldenbourg Wissenschaftsverlag, 2006.

Południak, Jan. *Sonder: An Interview with Sonderkommando Member Henryk Mandelbaum*. Frap-Books, 2008.

Press, Bernhard. *Judenmord in Lettland: 1941–1945*. Metropol Verlag, 1992.

Pressac, Jean-Claude. *Die Krematorien von Auschwitz: Die Technik des Massenmordes*. Translated by Eliane Hagedorn. Piper, 1994.

Pucher, Siegfried. *" . . . in der Bewegung führend tätig": Odilo Globočnik—Kämpfer für den "Anschluß," Vollstrecker des Holocaust*. Drava, 1997.

Rabinovici, Schoschana. *Dank meiner Mutter*. Translated by Mirjam Pressler. Fischer, 2002.

Rafetseder, Hermann. "Der 'Ausländereinsatz' zur Zeit des NS-Regimes am Beispiel der Stadt Linz." In *Nationalsozialismus in Linz*, edited by Fritz Mayrhofer and Walter Schuster, 2:1163–67. Archiv der Stadt Linz, 2001.

Rahe, Thomas. "Zeugen Jehovas im Konzentrationslager Bergen-Belsen." In *"Am mutigsten waren immer wieder die Zeugen Jehovas": Verfolgung und Widerstand der Zeugen Jehovas im Nationalsozialismus*, edited by Hans Hesse, 121–34. Edition Temmen, 1998.

Raßloff, Steffen. *Fritz Sauckel: Hitlers "Muster-Gauleiter" und "Sklavenhalter."* Schriften der Landeszentrale für politische Bildung Thüringen. Bd. 29. Landeszentrale für politische Bildung Thüringen, 2007.

Reese, Laurence. *Auschwitz: The Nazis and the "Final Solution."* BBC Books, 2005.

Richardi, Hans-Günter. *Schule der Gewalt: Das Konzentrationslager Dachau 1933–1934*. C. H. Beck, 1983.

Röder, Karl. *Nachtwache: 10 Jahre KZ Dachau und Flossenbürg*. Böhlau, 1985.

Röll, Wolfgang. *Homosexuelle Häftlinge im Konzentrationslager Buchenwald*. Nationale Mahn- und Gedenkstätte 1991.

Roos, Julia. "Backlash Against Prostitutes' Rights: Origins and Dynamics of Nazi Prostitution Policies." *Journal of the History of Sexuality* 11, nos. 1–2 (January/April 2002): 67–94.

Roos, Peter. "Gepäppelt und verbraucht: In Mauthausen ist die erste Ausstellung über Bordelle in den Konzentrationslagern zu sehen." *Die Zeit*, June 20, 2006.

Roseman, Mark. "Surviving Memory: Truth and Inaccuracy in Holocaust Memory." *Journal of Holocaust Education* 8, no. 1 (1999): 1–20.

Roßmann, Erich. *Ein Leben für Sozialismus und Demokratie*. Wunderlich, 1946.

Rost, Nico. *Goethe in Dachau*. Ullstein Taschenbuch, 2001.

Rostock, Jürgen. "Kurzbeschreibung der auf dem Gelände der künftigen Gedenkstätte Sachsenhausen noch vorhandenen Gebäude und Reste des ehemaligen Konzentrationslagers sowie der Bauten der DDR in den Jahren 1958 bis 1961." In *Von der Erinnerung zum Monument: Die Entstehungsgeschichte der Nationalen Mahn- und Gedenkstätte Sachsenhausen*, edited by Günter Morsch, 244–46. Edition Hentrich, 1996.

Rousset, David. *A World Apart*. Translated by Yvonne Moyse and Roger Senhouse. Secker and Warburg, 1951.

Salus, Grete. *Niemand, nichts—ein Jude: Theresienstadt, Auschwitz, Oederan*. Verlag Darmstädter Blätter, 1958.

Schäfer, Annette. *Zwangsarbeiter und NS-Rassenpolitik: Russische und polnische Arbeitskräfte in Württemberg 1939–1945*. Kohlhammer, 2000.

Schäfer, Silke. "Zum Selbstverständnis von Frauen im Konzentrationslager: Das Lager Ravensbrück." PhD diss., Fakultät I Geisteswissenschaften Technische Universität Berlin, 2002.

Schalm, Sabine. "München (Agfakamerawerke)." In *Der Ort des Terrors: Geschichte der nationalsozialistischen Konzentrationslager*, Band II: *Frühe Lager, Dachau, Emslandlager*, edited by Wolfgang Benz and Barbara Distel, 396–98. C. H. Beck, 2005.

Scharnberg, Harriet. "'Tätertausch'? Anfragen an die Diskussion um die kommunistischen Funktionshäftlinge im Konzentrationslager Buchenwald." In *Abgeleitete Macht: Funktionshäftlinge zwischen Widerstand und Kollaboration*, edited by KZ-Gedenkstätte Neuengamme, Beiträge zur Geschichte der nationalsozialistischen Verfolgung in Norddeutschland, no. 4, 123–33. Edition Temmen, 1998.

Schikorra, Christa. *Kontinuitäten der Ausgrenzung: "Asoziale" Häftlinge im Frauen-Konzentrationslager Ravensbrück*. Metropol, 2001.

———. "Prostitution weiblicher Häftlinge als Zwangsarbeit: Zur Situation 'asozialer' Häftlinge im Frauen-KZ Ravensbrück." *Dachauer Hefte* 16 (2000): 112–24.

Schley, Jens. *Nachbar Buchenwald: Die Stadt Weimar und ihr Konzentrationslager 1937–1945*. Böhlau,1999.

Schoppmann, Claudia. *Nationalsozialistische Sexualpolitik und weibliche Homosexualität*. Centaurus Verlag & Media UG, 1997.

Schötz, Susanne, ed. *Frauenalltag in Leipzig: Weibliche Lebenszusammenhänge im 19. und 20. Jahrhundert*. Böhlau, 1997.

Schulte, Jan Erik. *Zwangsarbeit und Vernichtung: Das Wirtschaftsimperium der SS. Oswald Pohl und das SS-Wirtschafts-Verwaltungshauptamt 1933–1945.* Schöningh, 2001.

Schulz, Christa. "Weibliche Häftlinge aus Ravensbrück in den Bordellen der Männerkonzentrationslager." In *Frauen in Konzentrationslagern: Bergen-Belsen – Ravensbrück*, edited by Claus Füllberg-Stolberg, Martina Jung, Renate Riebe, and Martina Scheitenberger, 135–46. Edition Temmen, 1994.

Seidel, Irmgard. "*Meuselwitz* (Frauen)." In *Der Ort des Terrors: Geschichte der nationalsozialistischen Konzentrationslager*, Band III: *Sachsenhausen, Buchenwald*, edited by Wolfgang Benz and Barbara Distel, 523–26. C. H. Beck, 2006.

Seidler, Franz. *Prostitution Homosexualität Selbstverstümmelung: Probleme der deutschen Sanitätsführung 1939–1945.* Kurt Vowinkel, 1977.

Sereny, Gitta. *Into That Darkness: An Examination of Conscience.* Knopf, 1995.

Setkiewicz, Piotr. "Häftlingsarbeit im KZ Auschwitz III-Monowitz: Die Frage nach der Wirtschaftlichkeit der Arbeit," In *Die nationalsozialistischen Konzentrationslager: Entwicklung und Struktur*, vols. 1–2, edited by Ulrich Herbert, Karin Orth, and Christoph Dieckmann, 584–605. Wallenstein, 1998.

Shik, Na'ama. "Sexual Abuse of Jewish Women in Auschwitz-Birkenau." In *Brutality and Desire: War and Sexuality in Europe's Twentieth Century*, 221–47. Palgrave Macmillan, 2009.

———. "Weibliche *Erfahrungen* in Auschwitz-Birkenau," In *Genozid und Geschlecht: Jüdische Frauen im nationalsozialistischen Lagersystem*, edited by Gisela Bock, 103–22. Campus, 2005.

Siegert, Toni. *30,000 Tote mahnen! Die Geschichte des Konzentrationslagers Flossenbürg und seine 100 Außenlager von 1939 bis 1945.* Taubald, 1984.

Skriebeleit, Jörg. "Flossenbürg–Stammlager." In *Der Ort des Terrors: Geschichte der nationalsozialistischen Konzentrationslager*, Band IV: *Flossenbürg, Mauthausen, Ravensbrück*, edited by Wolfgang Benz and Barbara Distel, 17–66. C. H. Beck, 2006.

———. "KZ Gedenkstätte Flossenbürg: *Retrospektiven* und Ausblicke." *Gedenkstättenrundbrief* 83, no. 6 (1998): 11–18.

———. "Neue Perspektiven für die KZ-Gedenkstätte Flossenbürg." In *Informationen für Mitglieder, Freunde und Förderer des Vereins "Gegen das Vergessen—für Demokratie" e.V.* Flossenbürg: n.p., 1998.

Sofsky, Wolfgang. *The Order of Terror: The Concentration Camp.* Translated by William Templer. Princeton University Press, 1999.

———. *Traktat über die Gewalt.* S. Fischer, 2003.

———. *Zeiten des Schreckens: Amok, Terror, Krieg.* S. Fischer, 2002.

Sommer, Robert. *Der Sonderbau: Die Errichtung von Bordellen in nationalsozialistischen Konzentrationslagern.* Lulu, 2006.

———. "Die Häftlingsbordelle im KZ-Komplex Auschwitz-Birkenau: Sexzwangsarbeit im Spannungsfeld von NS-'Rassenpolitik' und der

Bekämpfung von Geschlechtskrankheiten." In *Nationalsozialistische Lager: Neue Beiträge zur Geschichte der Verfolgungs- und Vernichtungspolitik und zur Theorie und Praxis von Gedenkstättenarbeit*, edited by Akim Jah, Christoph Kopke, Alexander Korb, and Alexa Stiller, 81–103. Klemm und Oelschläger, 2006.

———. "'Sonderbau' und Lagergesellschaft: Die Bedeutung von Bordellen in den KZ," in *Theresienstädter Studien und Dokumente 2006*, edited by Jaroslava Milotová, Michael Wögerbauer, and Anna Hájková, 288–339. Sefer, 2007.

———. "Warum das Schweigen? Berichte von ehemaligen Häftlingen über Sex-Zwangsarbeit in nationalsozialistischen Konzentrationslagern." In: *Krieg und Geschlecht: Sexuelle Gewalt im Krieg und Sex-Zwangsarbeit in NS-Konzentrationslagern*, edited by Insa Eschebach and Regina Mühlhäuser, 147–65. Metropol, 2008.

Spierenburg, Pieter. "Four Centuries of Prison History: Punishment, Suffering, the Body, and Power." In *Institutions of Confinement: Hospitals, Asylums, and Prisons in Western Europe and North America, 1500–1950*, edited by Norbert Finzsch and Robert Jütte, 17–96. Cambridge University Press, 1996.

Springmann, Veronika. "'*Sport* machen:' Eine Praxis der Gewalt im Konzentrationslager." In *KZ-Verbrechen: Beiträge zur Geschichte der nationalsozialistischen Konzentrationslager und ihrer Erinnerung*, edited by Wojciech Lenarczyk, Andreas Mix, Johannes Schwartz, and Veronika Springmann, 89–109. Metropol, 2007.

Spritzer, Jenny. *Ich war 10291: Tatsachenbericht einer Schreiberin der politischen Abteilung aus dem Konzentrationslager Auschwitz.* Verlag Darmstädter Blätter, 1980.

Staatliches Museum Auschwitz-Birkenau, ed. *Architektur des Verbrechens: Das Gebäude der "Zentralen Sauna" im Konzentrationslager Auschwitz II-Birkenau.* Verlag Staatliches Museum Auschwitz-Birkenau, 2001.

———, ed. *Auschwitz: Nationalsozialistisches Konzentrationslager.* Verlag Staatliches Museum Auschwitz-Birkenau, 1997.

———, ed. *Inmitten des grauenvollen Verbrechens: Handschriften von Mitgliedern des Sonderkommandos.* Verlag Staatliches Museum Auschwitz-Birkenau, 1996.

Stark, Meinhard. *Frauen im Gulag: Alltag und Überleben 1936 bis 1956.* Weltbild, 2006.

Stein, Harry. "Buchenwald–Stammlager." In *Der Ort des Terrors: Geschichte der nationalsozialistischen Konzentrationslager*, Band III: *Sachsenhausen, Buchenwald*, edited by Wolfgang Benz and Barbara Distel, 301–56. C. H. Beck, 2006.

———. "Funktionswandel des Konzentrationslagers Buchenwald im Spiegel der Lagerstatistiken." In *Die nationalsozialistischen Konzentrationslager: Entwicklung und Struktur*, vols. 1–2, edited by Ulrich Herbert, Karin Orth, and Christoph Dieckmann, 167–92. Wallenstein, 1998.

Steinbacher, Sybille: *Dachau: Die Stadt und das Konzentrationslager in der NS-Zeit. Die Untersuchung einer Nachbarschaft.* Peter Lang GmbH, 1994.

Steinbock, Johann. *Das Ende von Dachau.* Österreichischer Kulturverlag, 1948.

Stettner, Ralf. *"Archipel GULag:" Stalins Zwangslager—Terrorinstrument und Wirtschaftsgigant. Entstehung, Organisation und Funktion des sowjetischen Lagersystems 1928–1956.* Schöningh, 1996.

Stiglegger, Marcus. *Sadiconazista: Faschismus und Sexualität im Film.* Gardez! Verlag, 1999.

Strebel, Bernhard. *Das KZ Ravensbrück: Geschichte eines Lagerkomplexes.* Schöningh, 2003.

———. "Ravensbrück—das zentrale Frauenkonzentrationslager." In *Die nationalsozialistischen Konzentrationslager: Entwicklung und Struktur,* vols. 1 and 2, edited by Ulrich Herbert, Karin Orth, and Christoph Dieckmann, 215–58. Wallenstein, 1998.

Strzelecka, Irena. "Die Frauenabteilung im Stammlager." *Hefte von Auschwitz* 20 (1997): 7–67.

Tanenbaum, Roy D. *Prisoner 88: The Man in Stripes.* University of Calgary Press, 1998.

Terry, Jack, and Alicia Nitecki. *Jakub's World: A Boy's Story of Loss and Survival in the Holocaust.* State University of New York Press, 2005.

Thamer, Hans-Ulrich. "Von der 'Ästhetisierung der Politik'. Die Nürnberger Reichsparteitage der NSDAP." In *Faszination und Gewalt: Zur politischen Ästhetik des Nationalsozialismus,* edited by Bernd Ogan and Wolfgang Weiß, 95–105. Tümmel Verlag, 1992.

Thygesen, Paul. "*Arzt* im Konzentrationslager." *Nordfriesland* 63/64 (November 1982): 96–97.

Timm, Annette F. "The Challenges of Including Sexual Violence and Transgressive Love in Historical Writing on World War II and the Holocaust." *Journal of the History of Sexuality* 26, no. 3 (September 2017): 351–65.

———, ed. *Holocaust History and the Readings of Ka-Tzetnik.* Bloomsbury, 2018.

———. "Introduction: The Dilemmas of Ka-Tzetnik's International Fame." In *Holocaust History and the Readings of Ka-Tzetnik,* edited by Annette F. Timm, 1–12. Bloomsbury, 2018.

———. "Sex with a Purpose: Prostitution, Venereal Disease, and Militarized Masculinity in the Third Reich." *Journal of the History of Sexuality* 11, nos. 1/2, (January/April 2002): 223–55.

———. "Testimony in Holocaust Historiography." In *Holocaust History and the Readings of Ka-Tzetnik,* edited by Annette F. Timm, 37–66. Bloomsbury, 2018.

Tuchel, Johannes. *Die Inspektion der Konzentrationslager 1938–1945: Das System des Terrors.* Edition Hentrich, 1994.

Ulbricht, Justus H., ed. *Klassikerstadt und Nationalsozialismus: Kultur und Politik in Weimar 1933 bis 1945.* Glaux, 2002.

Vossler, Frank. *Propaganda in die eigene Truppe: Die Truppenbetreuung in der Wehrmacht 1939–1945*. Ferdinand Schöningh, 2006.

Wachsmann, Nikolaus. *KL: A History of the Nazi Concentration Camps*. Abacus, 2015.

Wagner, Bernd C. *IG Auschwitz: Zwangsarbeit und Vernichtung von Häftlingen des Lagers Monowitz 1941–1945*. K. G. Saur, 2000.

Wagner, Jens-Christian. "Das Außenlagersystem des KL Mittelbau-Dora." In *Die nationalsozialistischen Konzentrationslager: Entwicklung und Struktur*, vols. 1–2, edited by Ulrich Herbert, Karin Orth, and Christoph Dieckmann, 707–29. Wallenstein, 1998.

———. "Noch einmal: Arbeit und Vernichtung. Häftlingseinsatz im KL Mittelbau-Dora 1943–1945." In *Ausbeutung, Vernichtung, Öffentlichkeit: Neue Studien zur nationalsozialistischen Lagerpolitik*, edited by Norbert Frei, Sybille Steinbacher, and Bernd C. Wagner, 11–41. K.G. Saur, 2000.

———. *Produktion des Todes: Das KZ-Mittelbau-Dora*. Wallenstein, 2001.

Walleitner, Hugo. *Zebra: Ein Tatsachenbericht aus dem Konzentrationslager Flossenbürg*. Self-published, 1946.

Walter, Verena. *"Raub."* In *Der Ort des Terrors: Geschichte der nationalsozialistischen Konzentrationslager*, Band V: *Hinzert, Auschwitz, Neuengamme*, edited by Wolfgang Benz and Barbara Distel, 128–30. C. H. Beck, 2007.

Wegner, Bernd. *Hitlers politische Soldaten: Die Waffen-SS 1933–1945. Leitbild, Struktur und Funktion einer nationalsozialistischen Elite*. Schöningh, 1990.

Wenck, Alexandra-Eileen. *Zwischen Menschenhandel und "Endlösung:" Das Konzentrationslager Bergen-Belsen*. Schöningh Verlag, 2000.

Wenk, Silke. "Rhetoriken der Pornografisierung: Rahmen des Blicks auf die NS-Verbrechen." In *Gedächtnis und Geschlecht: Deutungsmuster in Darstellungen des nationalsozialistischen Genozids*, edited by Insa Eschebach, Sigrid Jacobeit, and Silke Wenk, 269–94. Campus, 2002.

Wesołowska, Danuta. *Wörter aus der Hölle: Die "lagerszpracha" der Häftlinge von Auschwitz*. Translated by Jochen August. Impuls, 1998.

Wickert, Christl. "Tabu Lagerbordell: Vom Umgang mit der Zwangsprostitution nach 1945." In *Gedächtnis und Geschlecht: Deutungsmuster in Darstellungen des nationalsozialistischen Genozids*, edited by Insa Eschebach, Sigrid Jacobeit, and Silke Wenk, 41–58. Campus, 2002.

Willems, Susanne. "Monowitz (Monowice)," In *Der Ort des Terrors: Geschichte der nationalsozialistischen Konzentrationslager*, Band V: *Hinzert, Auschwitz, Neuengamme*, edited by Wolfgang Benz and Barbara Distel, 276–84. C. H. Beck, 2007.

Witte, Peter, Michael Wildt, Martina Voigt, Dieter Pohl, Peter Klein, Christian Gerlach, Christoph Dieckmann, and Andrej Angrick, eds. *Der Dienstkalender Heinrich Himmlers 1941/1942*. Christians Verlag, 1999.

Witusik, W., and R. Witusik. "The Auschwitz Environment." In *It Did Not End in Forty-Five: Przegląd Lekarski. Anthology*, vol. III, pt. 1, edited by the International Auschwitz Committee, 105–51. International Auschwitz Committee, 1971.

Wolf, Christine. "'Zentralpunkt nationalsozialistischen Lebens'. Der 'Platz Adolf Hitlers' in Weimar." In *Klassikerstadt und Nationalsozialismus: Kultur und Politik in Weimar 1933 bis 1945*, edited by Justus H. Ulbricht, 157–67. Glaux, 2002.

Wolff, Jeanette. *Mit Bibel und Bebel*. Verlag Neue Gesellschaft, 1991.

Wolfrum, Edgar. "Die beiden Deutschland," in *Verbrechen erinnern: Die Auseinandersetzung mit Holocaust und Völkermord*, edited by Volkhard Knigge and Norbert Frei, 133–49. C. H.Beck, 2002.

Working Group of Former Prisoners of the Auschwitz Concentration Camp of the Committee of Anti-Fascist Resistance Fighters in the German Democratic Republic, eds. *IG-Farben Auschwitz—Mass Murder: On the Guilt of IG-Farben; from the Documents on the Auschwitz-Trial*. Halle: self-published, 1964.

Wrocklage, Ute. "Neuengamme." In *Das Gedächtnis der Dinge: KZ-Relikte und KZ-Denkmäler 1945–1995*, edited by Hoffmann, Detlef, 174–205. Campus Verlag, 1998.

Zabierowski, Stanislaw. *Pustków: Hitlerowskie obozy wyniszczenia w służbie poligonu SS*. Krajowa Agencja Wydawnicza, 1981.

Zámečník, Stanislav. "Dachau–Stammlager." In *Der Ort des Terrors: Geschichte der nationalsozialistischen Konzentrationslager*, Band II: *Frühe Lager, Dachau, Emslandlager*, edited by Wolfgang Benz and Barbara Distel, 133–74. C. H. Beck, 2005.

Zimmer, Hasko. *Der Buchenwaldkonflikt: Zum Streit um Geschichte und Erinnerung im Kontext der deutschen Vereinigung*. Agenda-Verlag, 1999.

Zimmermann, Michael. "Die nationalsozialistische Zigeunerverfolgung, das System der Konzentrationslager und das Zigeunerlager in Auschwitz-Birkenau." In *Die nationalsozialistischen Konzentrationslager: Entwicklung und Struktur*, vols. 1–2, edited by Ulrich Herbert, Karin Orth, and Christoph Dieckmann, 887–910. Wallenstein, 1998.

Zipfel, Gabi. "'Blood, Sperm, and Tears': *Sexuelle Gewalt* in Kriegen," *Mittelweg* 36, no. 15 (2001): 3–20.

Zürn, Gabi. "Prostitution in Hamburg im 'Dritten Reich' 1933–1945." Magisterarbeit. Universität Hamburg, 1989.

Zywulska, Krystina. *Wo vorher Birken waren: Überlebensbericht einer jungen Frau aus Auschwitz-Birkenau*. Verlag Darmstädter Blätter, 1980.

Unpublished Manuscripts

Hájková, Anna. "Rational Relationships in Theresienstadt Nazi Ghetto." Prague, 2009.

Ibel, Johannes. *Vorläufige Dokumentation der bekannten Teile der WVHA-Häftlingskartei: 148.247 Häftlingskarten in deutschen und polnischen Archiven.* Flossenbürg: Unpublished report, 2004.

Peer, Yvonne. "Gewalt gegen Männer in heterosexuellen Beziehungen: Ein gesellschaftliches Tabu. Diplomarbeit am Fachbereich Sozialwesen." Diplomarbeit, Fachbereich Sozialwesen an der Hochschule Zittau/Görlitz, 2001. http://www.frauengewalt.fall.vn/Frauengewalt/Wissenschaft/2008-04-17_Yvonne_Peer_Diplomarbeit_Gewalt_gg_Maenner.pdf.

Sommer, Robert. "Das Häftlingsbordell im Kontext der Wirtschaftsinteressen der SS: Das Beispiel Mittelbau-Dora." Manuscript of lecture held on November 10, 2003, Fachhochschule Nordhausen, Germany.

Film, TV, and Radio Broadcasts

Alles für zwei Mark: Das Häftlingsbordell von Buchenwald. Radio feature directed by Rosemarie Mieder and Gislinde Schwarz, MDR 2002, broadcast on RBB Kulturradio, April 22, 2018.

Auschwitz: The Nazis and "The Final Solution." Documentary directed by Laurence Reese. BBC, London, 2005.

Das große Schweigen. Directed by Maren Niemeyer and Caroline von der Tann. ARD, first broadcast on November 9, 1995.

SS als Zuhälter: Zwangsprostitution im Dritten Reich. Directed by Eva Schmitz-Gümbel and Karsten Deventer. Documentary, Frontal 21, ZDF, broadcast on October 28, 2003.

Pseudonyms

Female eyewitnesses: Linda Bachmann, Laura Büttig, Elenora Franke, Erna Geißler, Karola Groß, Anna Harder, Anni Kramer, Angelika Leuchter, Antonia Michaelis, Izabela Michalek, Minna Möller, Anna Rudolf, Betty Schreiber, Elisabeth Stein, Magdalena Walter.

Male eyewitnesses: Keith Random, Joris Brouwer, Romek Dubitzki, Jakub Piecha, Stephan Szymanski, Tomasz Jablonski

Abbreviations

ABB	Archiv der Gedenkstätte Bergen-Belsen
AGD	Archiv der Gedenkstätte Dachau
AGF	Archiv der Gedenkstätte Flossenbürg
AGMD	Archiv der Gedenkstätte Mittelbau-Dora
AGN	Archiv der Gedenkstätte Neuengamme
AGS	Archiv der Gedenkstätte Sachsenhausen
AHUB	Archiv der Humboldt-Universität zu Berlin
AK	Außenkommando (external work camp of a concentration camp)
AL	Außenlager (subcamp of a concentration camp)
AMGB	Archiv der Gedenkstätte Buchenwald

AMGR	Archiv der Mahn- und Gedenkstätte Ravensbrück
AMM	Archiv des Museums Mauthausen
APK	Archiwum Państwowe w Krakowie
APL	Archivum Państwowe w Łodzi
APMM	Archiwum Państwowe Muzeum Majdanek
APMO	Archiwum Państwowe Muzeum Auschwitz-Birkenau w Oświęcimiu
APW	Archiwum Państwowe we Wrocławiu
Au	Auschwitz
AUSHMM	Archive of the United States Holocaust Memorial Museum (Washington)
AZ	Aktenzeichen (record number)
AZA	Ausländische Zivilarbeiter (prisoner category)
AZR	Arbeitszwang Reich (prisoner category)
BArch	Bundesarchiv Lichterfelde
BArch D-H	Bundesarchiv Dahlwitz-Hoppegarten
BArch F	Bundesarchiv-Militärarchiv Freiburg
BArch L	Bundesarchiv Ludwigsburg
B-B	Bergen-Belsen
BEG	Bundesentschädigungsgesetz (German Restitution Laws)
BJBS	Bibliothek der Jugendbegegnungsstätte Auschwitz
BLHA	Brandenburgisches Landeshauptarchiv (Potsdam)
BStU	Bundesbeauftragte für die Unterlagen des Staatssicherheitsdienstes der ehemaligen Deutschen Demokratischen Republik
Bu	Buchenwald
BVer	Berufsverbrecher (career criminal)
Da	Dachau
DAF	Deutsche Arbeitsfront (German Labor Front)
DAW	Deutsche Ausrüstungswerke GmbH (SS-owned enterprise)
DEHOMAG	Deutsche Hollerith-Maschinen Gesellschaft mbH
DEST	Deutsche Erd- und Steinwerke (SS-owned enterprise)
DGBG	Deutsche Gesellschaft zur Bekämpfung von Geschlechtskrankheiten
DLG	Deutsche Lebensmittel GmbH (SS-owned enterprise)
DP	Displaced person
DR	Deutsches Reich
DuLag	Durchgangslager (transit camp)
FKL/FL	Frauenkonzentrationslager/Frauenlager (women's concentration camp, women's camp)
Fl	Flossenbürg
FVA	Fortunoff Video Archive for Holocaust Testimonies (Yale University Library)

GBA	Generalbevollmächtigter für den Arbeitseinsatz (General Plenipotentiary for Labor Deployment)
GBI	Generalbauinspektor für die Reichshauptstadt (General Building Inspector for the Reich Capital)
gesch.	geschieden (divorced)
GLAK	Generallandesarchiv Karlsruhe
GPU	Glawnoje Polititscheskoje Uprawlenije—Staatspolizei in der Sowjetunion
Gu	Gusen
GULag	Glavnoe Upravlenije Lagerej—Sowjetisches Straflager
GV	Geschlechtsverkehr (sexual intercourse)
HASAG	Hugo Schneider AG (arms manufacturer)
HAHuB	Hauptamt Haushalt und Bauten (budgets and building department of the SS central command)
HAVuW	Hauptamt Verwaltung und Wirtschaft (administration and economy department of the SS central command)
HKB	Häftlingskrankenbau (prisoner infirmary)
hwG	häufig wechselnder Geschlechtsverkehr (sex with frequently changing partners)
HSchF	SS-Hauptscharführer (SS rank)
HstAD	Hauptstaatsarchiv Düsseldorf/Landesarchiv Nordrhein-Westfalen
IKF	Institut für Konfliktforschung (Vienna)
IfZ	Institut für Zeitgeschichte (Munich)
IG	Interessen-Gemeinschaft (joint venture)
IHK	Industrie- und Handelskammer (chamber of industry and commerce)
IKL	Inspektion der Konzentrationslager (Concentration Camps Inspectorate)
IPC	International Prisoners Committee
ITS	International Tracing Service of the Red Cross (Bad Arolsen)
KARLag	Karagandinskij-Sonderlager (Soviet penal camp)
KGL	Kriegsgefangenenlager (prisoners of war camp)
KL	Konzentrationslager (concentration camp)
KLM	Konzentrationslager Mauthausen (Mauthausen concentration camp)
KP	Kommunistische Partei (Communist Party)
LA/LÄ	Lagerältester (camp elder)
LAG	Lagerarbeitsgemeinschaft (camp working group)
LG	Landgericht (district court)
Ma	Mauthausen
MDGBG	Mitteilungen der Deutschen Gesellschaft zur Bekämpfung der Geschlechtskrankheiten (journal on venereal disease)
Mo	Monowitz

MWD	Ministerium für Innere Angelegenheiten (Ministry for the Interior, USSR)
NARA	National Archives (USA)
Ng	Neuengamme
NKWD	Narodny Kommissariat Wnutrennich Djel (People's Commissariat for Internal Affairs, NKVD)
NMG	Nationale Mahn- und Gedenkstätte (Sachsenhausen)
NN	"Nacht und Nebel" (category for resistance fighters rounded up in the occupied territories)
NSDAP	Nationalsozialistische Arbeiterpartei (National Socialist Workers' Party)
OKW	Oberkommando der Wehrmacht (high command of the German armed forces)
Oscha	Oberscharführer (SS rank)
OSTI	Ostindustrie GmbH
PKK	Partei-Kontroll-Kommission (Central Party Control Commission of the Socialist Unity Party of Germany)
PSV	Polizeiliche Sicherungsverwahrung (police preventive custody—category of imprisonment)
Rav	Ravensbrück
RAD	Reichsarbeitsdienst (Reich Labour Service)
RD	Reichsdeutsch (Reich German)
RF-SS	Reichsführer-SS
RGBG	Reichsgesetz zur Bekämpfung der Geschlechtskrankheiten (Law to Combat Venereal Disease)
RJM	Reichsjustizministerium (Federal Ministry of Justice)
RKF	Reichskommissar für die Festigung deutschen Volkstums (Reich Commissioner for the Consolidation of German Nationhood)
RM(d)I	Reichsminister des Innern (Ministry of the Interior)
RML	Reichsminister der Luftfahrt (Ministry of Aviation)
RSHA	Reichssicherheitshauptamt (Reich Security Main Office)
R.U.	Rückkehr unerwünscht ("return undesirable," file note at the Mauthausen camp to indicate that a prisoner had been slated for death)
RuSHA	Rasse- und Siedlungshauptamt-SS (race and settlement department of the SS central command
RWK	Reichswirtschaftskammer (Reich chamber of commerce)
RZA	Russische(r) Zivilarbeiter(in) (Russian civilian worker)
SA	Sturmabteilung (storm troopers)
S.B.	Sonderbehandlung (special treatment)
Sch	Schutzhäftling (a political prisoner arrested preventively after being deemed a danger to the population at large)
SD	Sicherheitsdienst (security service of the SS)

SDG	Sanitätsdienstgrad (medical orderly)
SED	Sozialistische Einheitspartei Deutschlands (Socialist Unity Party of Germany)
Sh	Sachsenhausen
SIPO	Sicherheitspolizei (security police)
SMAD	Sowjetische Militäradministration Deutschlands (Soviet Military Administration in Germany)
SS	Schutzstaffel
SS-WVHA	SS-Wirtschafts-Verwaltungshauptamt (SS Main Economic and Administrative Office)
SdtAL	Stadtarchiv Linz
SdtAO	Stadtarchiv Oldenburg
SdtAN	Stadtarchiv Nürnberg
StA-B	Staatsarchiv Bremen
StA-HH	Staatsarchiv Hamburg
StAM	Staatsarchiv München
StAN	Staatsarchiv Nürnberg
Stapo	Staatspolizei (state police)
StGB	Strafgesetzbuch (German criminal code)
StuBaF	Sturmbahnführer (SS rank)
SV	Sicherungsverwahrung (preventive custody—category of imprisonment)
Texled	Gesellschaft für Textil-und Lederverwertung (SS-owned enterprise)
ThHStA	Thüringisches Hauptstaatsarchiv Weimar
ukr	Ukrainian
Uscha	Unterscharführer (SS rank)
USHMM	United States Holocaust Memorial Archives (Washington)
UWZ-Lager	Lager der Umwandererzentralstelle
verh.	verheiratet (married)
WdE	Werkstatt der Erinnerung (Hamburg)
WEHOBA	Weilheimer Holzhaus- und Barackenbau GmbH
WIFO	Wirtschaftliche Forschungsgesellschaft
WL	Archives of the Wiener Library (London)
WVHA	(see SS-WVHA)
ZA/ZivA	Zivilarbeiter(in) (civilian worker)
ZGF	Zivilgefangenenlager (civilian detention center)

Robert Sommer is a distinguished historian specializing in the intersections of violence, sexuality, and human rights, with a focus on the Holocaust. He teaches at the University of Cooperative Education, Berlin, Germany. Sommer has served as a historical consultant for museums and film productions, including the BBC documentary *Auschwitz: The Nazis and the Final Solution* (2005).

Dominic Bonfiglio is a translator with a background in Germanic studies and philosophy. His translations are known for their precision and clarity, making German scholarship accessible to a global audience.

World War II: The Global, Human, and Ethical Dimension

G. Kurt Piehler, *series editor*

Lawrence Cane, David E. Cane, Judy Barrett Litoff, and David C. Smith, eds., *Fighting Fascism in Europe: The World War II Letters of an American Veteran of the Spanish Civil War*

Angelo M. Spinelli and Lewis H. Carlson, *Life behind Barbed Wire: The Secret World War II Photographs of Prisoner of War Angelo M. Spinelli*

Don Whitehead and John B. Romeiser, *"Beachhead Don": Reporting the War from the European Theater, 1942–1945*

Scott H. Bennett, ed., *Army GI, Pacifist CO: The World War II Letters of Frank and Albert Dietrich*

Alexander Jefferson with Lewis H. Carlson, *Red Tail Captured, Red Tail Free: Memoirs of a Tuskegee Airman and POW*

Jonathan G. Utley, *Going to War with Japan, 1937–1941*

Grant K. Goodman, *America's Japan: The First Year, 1945–1946*

Patricia Kollander with John O'Sullivan, *"I Must Be a Part of This War": One Man's Fight against Hitler and Nazism*

Judy Barrett Litoff, *An American Heroine in the French Resistance: The Diary and Memoir of Virginia d'Albert-Lake*

Thomas R. Christofferson and Michael S. Christofferson, *France during World War II: From Defeat to Liberation*

Don Whitehead, *Combat Reporter: Don Whitehead's World War II Diary and Memoirs*, edited by John B. Romeiser

James M. Gavin, *The General and His Daughter: The Wartime Letters of General James M. Gavin to His Daughter Barbara*, edited by Barbara Gavin Fauntleroy et al.

Carol Adele Kelly, ed., *Voices of My Comrades: America's Reserve Officers Remember World War II*, foreword by Senators Ted Stevens and Daniel K. Inouye

John J. Toffey IV, *Jack Toffey's War: A Son's Memoir*

Lt. General James V. Edmundson, *Letters to Lee: From Pearl Harbor to the War's Final Mission*, edited by Dr. Celia Edmundson

John K. Stutterheim, *The Diary of Prisoner 17326: A Boy's Life in a Japanese Labor Camp*, foreword by Mark Parillo

G. Kurt Piehler and Sidney Pash, eds., *The United States and the Second World War: New Perspectives on Diplomacy, War, and the Home Front*

Susan E. Wiant, *Between the Bylines: A Father's Legacy*, foreword by Walter Cronkite

Deborah S. Cornelius, *Hungary in World War II: Caught in the Cauldron*

Gilya Gerda Schmidt, *Süssen Is Now Free of Jews: World War II, The Holocaust, and Rural Judaism*

Emanuel Rota, *A Pact with Vichy: Angelo Tasca from Italian Socialism to French Collaboration*

Panteleymon Anastasakis, *The Church of Greece under Axis Occupation*

Louise DeSalvo, *Chasing Ghosts: A Memoir of a Father, Gone to War*

Alexander Jefferson with Lewis H. Carlson, *Red Tail Captured, Red Tail Free: Memoirs of a Tuskegee Airman and POW*, Revised Edition

Kent Puckett, *War Pictures: Cinema, Violence, and Style in Britain, 1939–1945*

Marisa Escolar, *Allied Encounters: The Gendered Redemption of World War II Italy*

Courtney A. Short, *The Most Vital Question: Race and Identity in the U.S. Occupation of Okinawa, 1945–1946*

James Cassidy, *NBC Goes to War: The Diary of Radio Correspondent James Cassidy from London to the Bulge*, edited by Michael S. Sweeney

Rebecca Schwartz Greene, *Breaking Point: The Ironic Evolution of Psychiatry in World War II*

Franco Baldasso, *Against Redemption: Democracy, Memory, and Literature in Post-Fascist Italy*

G. Kurt Piehler and Ingo Trauschweizer, eds., *Reporting World War II*

Kevin T Hall, *Forgotten Casualties: Downed American Airmen and Axis Violence in World War II*

Chad R. Diehl, ed., *Shadows of Nagasaki: Trauma, Religion, and Memory after the Atomic Bombing*

Raffaella Perin, *The Popes on Air: The History of Vatican Radio from Its Origins to World War II*

Daniel McKay, *Beyond Hostile Islands: The Pacific War in American and New Zealand Fiction Writing*, foreword by Patrick Porter

Robert Sommer, *The Concentration Camp Brothel: Forced Sexual Labor under Nazi Rule*, translated by Dominic Bonfiglio, foreword by Annette F. Timm

www.ingramcontent.com/pod-product-compliance
Lightning Source LLC
LaVergne TN
LVHW041627060925
820435LV00016B/114

* 9 7 8 1 5 3 1 5 0 9 9 1 0 *